The Computer Glossary

The Computer Glossary

The Complete Illustrated Dictionary

Seventh Edition

Alan Freedman

American Management Association

New York • Atlanta • Boston • Chicago • Kansas City • San Francisco • Washington, D.C.
Brussels • Toronto • Mexico City

This book is available at a special discount when ordered in bulk quantities. For information, contact Special Sales Department, AMACOM, a division of American Management Association, 135 West 50th Street, New York, NY 10020.

This publication is designed to provide accurate and authoritative information in regard to the subject matter covered. It is sold with the understanding that the publisher is not engaged in rendering legal, accounting, or other professional service. If legal advice or other expert assistance is required, the services of a competent professional person should be sought.

Library of Congress Cataloging-in-Publication Data

Freedman, Alan, 1942–
    The computer glossary : the complete illustrated desk reference /
Alan Freedman. — 7th ed.
        p.   cm.
        ISBN 0-8144-0268-2 (hardcover). — ISBN 0-8144-7872-7 (pbk.). —
ISBN 0-8144-0127-9 (pbk.-diskette)
        1. Computers—Dictionaries.   2. Electronic data processing—
Dictionaries.   I. Title.
QA76.15.F734   1994
004'.03—dc20   94-37624
                                                                CIP

Previous editions were published by Prentice-Hall and
The Computer Language Company, Inc.

Printing number

10 9 8 7 6 5 4 3

To my Mother,
Who had the vision to send me to
Automation School
in 1960.

ILLUSTRATIONS: Peter Felperin, Alan Freedman, Irma Lee Morrison,
            Eric Jon Nones and Joseph D. Russo
EDITORIAL/PRODUCTION: Irma Lee Morrison
COPY EDITING: Mary McCann
TYPESET BY: The Computer Language Company Inc., Point Pleasant, PA 18950
PUBLISHING SOFTWARE: Corel VENTURA 4.2
PRINTER: LaserJet 4 with LaserMaster WinJet board
FONTS: Garamond, Cooper Black, Arial

A Note from the Author

The purpose of *The Computer Glossary* is to provide a meaningful definition of every important computer term, be it a concept or a hardware or software product, old or new, for personal computers, minicomputers or mainframes. The degree of technical explanation chosen for each term is based on the term. General terms are explained for the lay person. Specific technical terms are explained with other technical terms. But, all the terms used in the definitions are defined in the book.

The Computer Glossary includes history about the major hardware vendors; the companies that truly drive this industry, as well as some historical photos of the first computers and electronic devices. The old photos should remind us of the extraordinary acceleration of technology in our era. Virtually all of this has come about in little over a hundred years, since the harnessing of electricity. It's a good idea to stop and smell the roses while we race towards the newest and the fastest.

It is also the purpose of this book to make sense out of this industry in general. As impossible a task as that may be, I keep on trying with each edition. What started out over fourteen years ago as a 300-term compendium for my seminars has now become my life's work. Lucky for me I like computers, because some of this is mind-boggingly difficult to figure out. I've rewritten some of the same definitions countless times in an effort to clarify them.

I hope you find the Glossary helpful. If there are terms and products you feel should be included in the next book, please let me know. In addition, if you can add facts and perspective to anything in the book, I would appreciate hearing from you.

Alan Freedman

The Computer Language Company Inc.
5521 State Park Road
Point Pleasant, PA 18950
(215) 297-5999
FAX (215) 297-8424

Table of Contents

Acknowledgments

It would be impossible to put this book together without the help of hundreds of technical engineers and public relations people who work for the hardware and software companies. In addition, many readers have contributed terms, suggestions and comments. To all of you, thank you for your assistance.

There are some people that have made important contributions throughout the history of this book, and I would like to acknowledge each of them. Many thanks to Joel Orr, Orr Associates, Stephen C. Diascro, Jr., Tandy Corporation, Margaret A. Herrick, Margann Associates, Leonard Mikolajczak, DACOM, Paul T. Bergevin, IBM, Garry Dawson, Hewlett-Packard, Jagdish Dalal, Unisys, , Pamela J. Brannan, Hayes Microcomputer Products, Walter A. Levy, Edgewood Computer Associates, Joan Zachary, Cuttalossa Training Partners, Stephen Slade, Yale University, Robert F. Williams, Cohasset Associates and the staff at Black Box Corporation, including Pat Flanigan, Mark Bennett, Mike Ramos, Larry Clark, Randy Morse and Bill Ihrig.

There are some people, however, who have made significant contributions, but more than that, they just keep on helping. Thank you all. Your help is really appreciated.

Thom Drewke, *Technical Directions*
James J.Farrell, III, *VLSI Technology*
Max B. Fetzer, *Envirotronics*
Lynn S. Frankel, *Byrd Press*
Steve Gibson, *Gibson Research*
Peter Hermsen, *Apple Computer*
Terry O'Donnell, *Adobe Systems*
Gary Saxer, *Quarterdeck Office Systems*
Mark J. E. Shapiro, *Network in a Box*
Jim Stroh, *LXD, Inc.*
Skip Vaccarello, *The Saratoga Group*
David Wallace, *Dun & Bradstreet Software*
Irving L. Wieselman, *Computer Printer Corporation*
Paul and Jan Witte, *Originetics*

I want to thank the staff at AMACOM for all their help. Special thanks to Weldon Rackley, director, who has faithfully supported this book since the 4th edition. Thanks for believing in me. Also many thanks to Tony Vlamis, my editor, who has spent considerable time on this and related projects, and to Steve Arkin, marketing director, for his assistance and inspiration.

In addition, I would like to thank Joseph Russo for his help with the design of the 4th edition of this book, much of which is still carried over to the 7th edition, and Mary McCann for copy editing.

Last and most important, I would like to thank Irma Lee Morrison, my wife and partner, for the countless hours of devotion she has made to this book and, especially, for putting up with me each time I create it. Thank you Irmalee. I love you dearly.

Introduction

THE COMPUTER GLOSSARY is not just a glossary... It's a guide to Computer Literacy

Reading *The Computer Glossary* on a regular basis will help you keep up with the terminology, concepts and perspective necessary to interact with computer professionals effectively and get the most out of computers.

If you hear a term that is not in this book, it may be the trade name of a hardware product or software package. Find out what category it falls into, and then look it up.

On the following pages are lists of terms that will guide you through the Glossary like a textbook. They contain the fundamental terms in each subset of the industry. Use the lists as a springboard to all the other terms in the book.

The Perspective

The following chart depicts the interrelationships of systems within the computer industry from a managers point of view. Understanding this relationship will help you put the various pieces of this industry into perspective.

The management system is the set of goals, objectives, strategies, tactics, plans and controls within an organization.

The information system is the database and application programs that turn the raw data into information required by management.

The computer system is the machinery that automates the process.

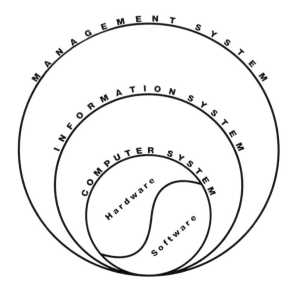

Topics

BASICS
hardware
software
data
computer
computer system

information system
program
analog
digital
bit

binary
byte
peripheral
floppy disk
hard disk

laser printer
scanner
monitor
modem
VGA

font
operating sytem
bus
space/time
chip

PC
Macintosh
PowerPC
LAN
x86
how to select a personal computer

NETWORKING
communications protocol
LAN
OSI
client/server
baseband
Ethernet

Token Ring
FDDI
ATM
NetWare
Appletalk

SNA
TCP/IP
X Window
routable protocol
repeater

bridge
router
brouter
gateway
hub

BBS
online services
modem
emoticon
RS-232

V.32
V.32bis
V.34
V.42
V.42bis

SLANG
flame
frob
droupie
trashware
shelfware

kludge
RTFM
dribbleware
phone hawk
Big Blue

dweeb
buffer flush
sneakernet

INTERNET
Internet
USENET
TCP/IP
PDIAL

Telnet
FTP
Archie
Gopher
Veronica

Worldwide Web
Mosaic
Cello
WAIS
Mbone

GRAPHICS & MULTIMEDIA

graphics
paint program
drawing program
CAD
CAD/CAM

bit depth
wireframe modeling
solid modeling
surface modeling
ray tracing

digitizer tablet
Renderman interface
artifact
JPEG
AutoCAD

Bezier
spline
GKS
PHIGS
bitblt

PCX
GIF
TIFF
PIC
HSV

multimedia
MPC
CD
CD-ROM
sound card

Video for Windows
QuickTime
MIDI
Video CD
virtual reality

JOB CATEGORIES

user
systems analyst
business analyst
programmer
programmer analyst

data administrator
database administrator
network administrator
system administrator
operator

MAINFRAMES

mainframe
channel
front end processor
communications controller
TP monitor

DASD
IBM mainframes
VAX
dumb terminal
intelligent terminal

frontware
ES/9000
System/360
System/370
ESA/370

ESA/390
3270
IRMAboard
ESCON
Sysplex

SNA
MVS
VM
VSE
CICS

IMS
TSO
SQL
DB2

PERSONAL COMPUTERS
how to select a personal computer
PC
Macintosh
PowerMac
Amiga

laptop
palmtop
computer
memory
floppy disk

hard disk
keyboard
modem
optical disk
laser printer

serial port
parallel port
game port
mouse
tape backup

x86
68000
PowerPC
ISA
EISA
Micro Channel

NuBus
local bus
VL-bus
PCI
operating system

DOS
Windows
Windows NT
OS/2
UNIX
Plug and Play

DMI
PowerOpen
word processing
DBMS
spreadsheet
business graphics
communications program

integrated software package
paint program
drawing program

PROGRAMMING
programming
assembly language
high-level language
machine language
microcode

reentrant code
function
object-oriented programming
COBOL
BASIC

FORTRAN
Pascal
C
C++
LISP

Prolog
LOGO
MUMPS
REXX
ASCII chart

UNIX
TCP/IP
NFS
NIS
SMTP

SNMP
Motif
Open Look
USL
OSF

X Window
X terminal
BSD UNIX
STREAMS
emacs

vi
awk
sed
grep
DESQview/X

SCO Open Desktop
Solaris 2.0
Lan Workplace
UnixWare
NetWare NFS

SYSTEMS DESIGN

Overview
  information system
  system development cycle
  enterprise networking
  Systemantics

People
  systems analyst
  application programmer
  programmer analyst
  systems programmer
  operator

Development
  data administration
  prototyping
  functional specification
  documentation
  CASE

Software
  query language
  report writer
  spreadsheet
  DBMS
  financial planning system

  DSS
  EIS
  EPSS
  expert system
  case-based reasoning

STANDARDS BODIES
ANSI   (U.S. standards)
NIST   (U.S. standards)
CCIA   (Communications)
ITU-TSS (International standards)
IEC   (International standards)

ISO   (International standards)
EIA   (Interface standards; RS-232)
IEEE   (Electronics standards)
JEDEC   (IC standards)
JEIDA   (Japanese electronics)

PCMCIA (PC card standards)
XAPIA   (X.400 standards)UNIX

ASSOCIATIONS
ACM   (Information processing)
BCS   (Personal computers)
CBEMA   (Equipment vendors)
CPA   (Computer press)
DPMA   (DP management)

EMA   (Electronic Mail)
ICCP   (Industry certification)
IMA   (Interactive multimedia)
ITAA   (Information technology)

MMA   (Microcomputer managers)
MUG   (Mac users)
NASI   (Systems integrators)
NCF   (Donating old equipment)
NCGA   (Computer graphics)

NOMDA (Office equipment dealers)
SPA   (Software publishers)
WUGNET (Windows users)

Use Acronyms...

Most of the terms in this book are defined by their acronymns, not their formal names. If you cannot find a multi-word term in the book, TRY ITS ACRONYM!

A

A: The designation for the first floppy disk drive in a PC.

AA (Auto Answer) See *modem*.

AAUI (Apple AUI) Apple's version of the Ethernet AUI connector.

abend (ABnormal END) Also called a *crash* or *bomb*, it occurs when the computer is presented with instructions or data it cannot recognize or the program is reaching beyond its protective boundary. It is the result of erroneous software logic or hardware failure.

ABI (Application Binary Interface) A specification for a particular hardware platform and operating system. It details the machine language of the CPU family as well as the calls between the application and the operating system.

abort (1) To exit a function or application without saving any data that has been changed.

(2) To stop a transmission.

ABR (AutoBaud Rate detect) The analysis of the first characters of a message to determine its transmission speed and number of start and stop bits.

absolute In programming, a mathematical function that always returns a positive number. For example, ABS(25-100) yields 75, not -75.

absolute address An explicit identification of a memory location, peripheral device, or location within a device. For example, memory byte 107,443, disk drive 2 and sector 238 are absolute addresses. The computer uses absolute addresses to reference memory and peripherals. See *base address* and *relative address*.

absolute path Same as *full path*.

absolute vector In computer graphics, a vector with end points designated in absolute coordinates. Contrast with *relative vector*.

absolute zero The theoretical temperature at which molecular activity ceases (-273.15 C, -459.67 F).

abstract data type A user-defined data type used in object-oriented programming that contains its own data and processing.

AC (Alternating Current) The common form of electricity from power plant to home/office. Its direction is reversed 60 times per second in the U.S.; 50 times in Europe. Contrast with *DC*.

accelerator A key combination used to activate a task. See *accelerator board* and *graphics accelerator*.

accelerator board An add-in board that replaces the existing CPU with a higher performance CPU. See *graphics accelerator*.

acceptance test A test performed by the end user to determine if the system is working according to the specifications in the contract.

access To store data on and retrieve data from a disk or other peripheral device. See *access arm, access method* and *Microsoft Access.*

access arm The mechanical arm that moves the read/write head across the surface of a disk similar to a tone arm on a phonograph. The access arm is directed by instructions in the operating system to move the read/write head to a specific track on the disk. The rotation of the disk positions the read/write head over the required sector.

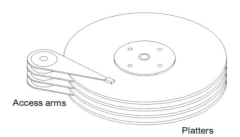

Access arms

Platters

ACCESS.bus A serial bus that is expected to become popular in the 1995 timeframe. It allows multiple devices to be daisy chained together using a four-wire cable and connector similar to a phone jack.

access charge The charge imposed by a communications service or telephone company for the use of its network.

access code (1) An identification number and/or password used to gain access into a computer system.

(2) The number used as a prefix to a calling number in order to gain access to a particular telephone service.

access denied The system is unable to retrieve the file you are requesting. In DOS, this error message usually means that the file you are deleting is protected.

access line The line from a customer site to a telephone company's central office.

access method A software routine that is part of the operating system or network control program which performs the storing/retrieving or transmitting/receiving of data. It is also responsible for detecting a bad transfer of data caused by hardware or network malfunction and correcting it if possible.

access server See *communications server.*

access time (1) Memory access time is how long it takes for a character in memory to be transferred to or from the CPU. In a personal computer, fast RAM chips have an access time of 70 nanoseconds or less.

(2) Disk access time is an average of the time it takes to position the read/write head over the requested track. Fast personal computer hard disks have access times of 18 milliseconds or less. Mainframe disks can be less than one millisecond.

accumulator A hardware register used to hold the results or partial results of arithmetic and logical operations.

ACD (Automatic Call Distribution) The routing of an incoming telephone call to the next available operator.

ACE (Advanced Computing Environment) An open standard based on UNIX and Windows NT introduced in 1991 by MIPS Computer Systems and others. It was later disbanded.

ACF (Advanced Communications Function) An official product line name for IBM SNA programs, such as VTAM (ACF/VTAM), NCP (ACF/NCP), etc.

ACK (ACKnowledgment code) The communications code sent from a receiving station to a transmitting station to indicate that it is ready to accept data. It is also used to acknowlege the error-free receipt of transmitted data. Contrast with *NAK.*

ACM (Association for Computing Machinery) A membership organization founded in 1947 dedicated to advancing the arts and sciences of information processing. In addition to awards and publications, ACM also maintains special interest groups (SIGs) in the computer field. Address: 1515 Broadway, New York, NY 10036, 212/869-7440.

acoustic coupler A device that connects a terminal or computer to the handset of a telephone. It contains a shaped foam bed that the handset is placed in, and it may also contain the modem.

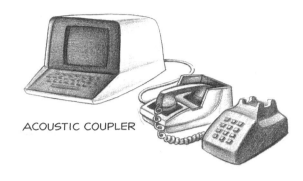

ACOUSTIC COUPLER

Acrobat Document exchange software from Adobe Systems, Inc., Mountain View, CA, that runs on DOS, Windows, UNIX and Macintosh computers. It allows documents created on one platform to be displayed and printed exactly the same on another. Documents are converted into the Acrobat PDF (Portable Data Format), which contains all the information about the appearance of the document.

ACS (Asynchronous Communications Server) A communications server that manages a pool of modems. It directs outgoing messages to the next available modem and directs incoming messages to the appropriate workstation.

active addressing A technology that improves passive matrix LCD screens. Rather than having a transistor attached to each pixel on the back of the screen, the transistors are on chips on the motherboard. The resulting display looks almost as good as active matrix without the high cost. This emerging technology is expected in 1994. See *LCD*.

active hub The central connecting device in a network that regenerates signals. Contrast with *passive hub* and *intelligent hub*. See *hub*.

active matrix An LCD technology used in flat panel computer displays. Using a transistor for each pixel, it produces a high quality display and eliminates the submarining associated with passive matrix screens.

active star See *active hub*.

ACTOR An object-oriented programming language for PCs from The Whitewater Group Inc., Evanston, IL. It runs under Windows and has a Pascal-like syntax to ease the transition to object-oriented languages.

actuator A mechanism that causes a device to be turned on or off, adjusted or moved. The component that moves the head assembly on a disk drive or an arm of a robot is called an actuator.

A/D converter (Analog to Digital Converter) A device that converts continuously varying analog signals from instruments that monitor such conditions as movement, temperature, sound, etc., into binary code for the computer. It may be contained on a single chip or can be one circuit within a chip. See *modem* and *codec*. Contrast with *D/A converter*.

AD/Cycle (Application Development/Cycle) SAA-compliant software from IBM that provides a system for managing systems development. It provides a structure for storing information about all phases of an information system including systems analysis and design, database design and programming.

Ada A high-level programming language developed by the U.S. Department of Defense along with the European Economic Community and many other organizations. It was designed for embedded applications and process control but is also used for logistics applications. Ada is a Pascal-based language that is very comprehensive.

Ada was named after Augusta Ada Byron (1815-1852), Countess of Lovelace and daughter of Lord Byron. She was a mathematician and colleague of Charles Babbage, who was developing his Analytical Engine. Some of her programming notes for the machine have survived, giving her the distinction of being the first documented programmer in the world.

The following Ada program converts Fahrenheit to Celsius:

```
with Text_IO;
procedure Convert is
 package Int_IO is new Text_IO.Integer_IO(Integer);
 Fahrenheit : Integer;
begin
 Text_IO.Put_Line("Enter Fahrenheit");
 Int_IO.Get(Fahrenheit);
 Text_IO.Put("Celsius is ");
 Int_IO.Put((Fahrenheit-32) * 5 / 9);
 Text_IO.New_Line;
end Convert;
```

ADABAS A DBMS from Software AG, Reston, VA, for IBM mainframes, VAXes, various UNIX platforms and OS/2 PCs. It is an inverted list DBMS with relational capabilities. A 4GL called NATURAL, text retrieval, GIS processing, SQL and distributed database functions are also available. Introduced in 1969, it was one of the first DBMSs.

ADAPSO See *ITAA*.

adapter A device that allows one system to connect to and work with another. Display adapters and network adapters are really controllers, not adapters. See *host adapter* and *expansion bus*.

adaptive compression A data compression technique that dynamically adjusts the algorithm used based on the content of the data being compressed.

adaptive equalization A transmission technique that dynamically adjusts its modulation method based on the quality of the line.

adaptive routing The ability to select a new communications path to get around heavy traffic or a node or circuit failure.

ADB (Apple Desktop Bus) The Macintosh communications port for keyboards, mice, trackballs, graphics tablets and other input devices.

ADC See *A/D converter*.

ADCCP (Advanced Data Communications Control Procedure) An ANSI communications protocol that is similar to the SDLC and HDLC protocols.

adder An elementary electronic circuit that adds the bits of two numbers together.

add-in, add-on Refers to hardware modules, such as printed circuit boards, that are designed to be plugged into a socket within the computer.

address (1) The number of a particular memory or peripheral storage location. Like post office boxes, each byte of memory and each disk sector has its own unique address. Programs are compiled into machine language, which references actual addresses in the computer.

(2) As a verb, to manage or work with. For example, "the computer can address 2MB of memory."

address bus An internal channel from the CPU to memory across which the addresses of data (not the data) are transmitted. The number of lines (wires) in the address bus determines the amount of memory that can be directly addressed as each line carries one bit of the address.

address mode The method by which an instruction references memory. An *indexed address* is modified by the contents of an index register before execution. An *indirect address* points to another address. Ultimately, in order to do any actual processing, the instruction must derive *real*, or *absolute addresses*, where the required data is located.

address register A high-speed circuit that holds the addresses of data to be processed or of the next instruction to be executed.

address resolution Obtaining a physical address that is ultimately needed to perform an operation. All instructions executing at the machine level require a physical memory, storage or network node address when referencing the actual hardware. Machine addresses are derived using table lookups and/or algorithms.

address space The total amount of memory that can be used by a program. It may also refer to virtual memory, which includes memory and disk. For example, the 386 can address 4GB of physical memory and 64TB of virtual memory.

address translation Transforming one address into another. For example, assemblers and compilers translate symbolic addresses into machine addresses. Virtual memory systems translate a virtual address into a real address.

addressable cursor A screen cursor that can be programmed to move to any row or column on the screen.

ADF (Application Development Facility) An IBM programmer-oriented mainframe application generator that runs under IMS.

ad hoc query A non-standardized inquiry. An ad hoc query is composed to answer a question when the need arises.

Adobe fonts See *PostScript*.

Adobe Type Manager A PostScript font utility for the Macintosh and Windows from Adobe Systems. It scales Type 1 fonts into screen fonts and prints them on non-PostScript dot matrix and HP laser printers. Rather than downloading the font to the printer, it sends a bitmap of the entire page of text to the printer.

ATM technology is built into OS/2 and NeXTstep, and was originally developed to provide WYSIWYG screen fonts for the Mac. See *PostScript*.

ADP (1) (Automatic Data Processing) Synonymous with data processing (DP), electronic data processing (EDP) and information processing.

(2) (Automatic Data Processing, Inc., Roseland, NJ) A nationwide computer services organization that specializes in payroll processing.

ADPCM (Adaptive Differential PCM) An advanced PCM technique that converts speech to 32 or 16 Kbits/sec. Instead of coding an absolute measurement at each sample point, it codes the difference between samples and can dynamically switch the coding scale to compensate for variations in amplitude and frequency.

ADRS (A Departmental Reporting System) An IBM mainframe report writer.

ADS (AutoCAD Development System) A facility that allows C routines to be run from within AutoCAD.

ADT (Asynchronous Data Transfer) A transmission technique used in ISDN PBXs that dynamically allocates bandwidth. See also *abstract data type*.

AFE (Apple File Exchange) A Macintosh utility that converts data files between Mac and PC formats. It also includes a file translator between IBM's DCA format and MacWrite; however, MacLink Plus Translators can be used for additional capability.

AFIPS (American Federation of Information Processing Societies Inc.) An organization founded in 1961 dedicated to advancing information processing in the U.S. It was the U.S. representative of IFIP and umbrella for 11 membership societies. Dissolved in 1990 and superseded by FOCUS.

AFP (AppleTalk Filing Protocol) A client/server protocol used in AppleTalk communications networks. In order for non-Apple networks to access data in an AppleShare server, their protocols must translate into the AFT language.

AFS A distributed file system for large, widely-dispersed UNIX networks from Transarc Corporation, Pittsburgh, PA. It is noted for its ease of administration and expandability and stems from Carnegie-Mellon's Andrew File System.

After Dark A popular screen saver program for Macs and PCs from Berkeley Systems, Inc., that allows the user to develop custom animations. After Dark popularized the "flying toaster" display in 1989.

agent A software routine that waits in the background and performs an action when a specified event occurs. For example, agents could transmit a summary file on the first day of the month or monitor incoming data and alert the user when a certain transaction has arrived. See *workflow automation*.

AI (Artificial Intelligence) Devices and applications that exhibit human intelligence and behavior including robots, expert systems, voice recognition, natural and foreign language processing. It also implies the ability to learn or adapt through experience.

AIX (Advanced Interactive eXecutive) IBM's version of UNIX, which runs on PCs (386 and up), RS/6000 workstations and 390 mainframes. It is based on AT&T's UNIX System V with Berkeley extensions. A Workplace-enabled version of AIX is being developed for the PowerPC and is expected in 1995.

alarm filtering In network management, the ability to pinpoint the device that has failed. If one device in a network fails, others may fail as a result and cause alarms. Without alarm filtering, the management console reports all deteriorating devices with equal attention.

Aldus Persuasion A desktop presentation program for the Mac from Aldus Corporation, Seattle, WA. It is used to create output for overheads, handouts, speaker notes and film recorders and provides sophisticated transition features (fades, gravel, swipes, etc.).

algebraic expression One or more characters or symbols associated with algebra; for example, A+B=C or A/B.

ALGOL (ALGOrithmic Language) A high-level compiler language that was developed as an international language for the expression of algorithms between people and between people and machines. ALGOL-60 (1960) was simple and widely used in Europe. ALGOL-68 (1968) was more complicated and scarcely used, but was the inspiration for Pascal.

The following example changes Fahrenheit to Celsius:

```
fahrenheit
begin
  real fahr;
  print ("Enter Fahrenheit ");
  read (fahr);
  print ("Celsius is ", (fahr-32.0) * 5.0/9.0);
end
finish
```

The Computer Glossary

algorithm A set of ordered steps for solving a problem, such as a mathematical formula or the instructions in a program.

alias (1) An alternate name used for a field, file or other item.

(2) A phony signal created under certain conditions when digitizing voice.

aliasing In computer graphics, the stair-stepped appearance of diagonal lines. See *anti-aliasing*.

ALL-IN-1 Office systems software from Digital for the VAX series. It provides a menu to all of Digital's office systems programs, including word processing, appointment calendars and e-mail systems.

allocate To reserve a resource such as memory or disk. See *memory allocation*.

ALM (Application Loadable Module) A software module that provides services under Novell's AppWare architecture. See *AppWare*.

Alpha A family of advanced RISC-based, 64-bit CPUs from Digital. The first model introduced in early 1992 was the 150MHz 21064-AA, considered equivalent to a Cray-1 on a single chip. Alpha AXP computer systems use the Alpha CPU and run under Windows NT, OpenVMS and OpenOSF operating systems.

alpha channel The high-order eight bits in a 32-bit graphics pixel used as a separate layer to mask an area for editing or creating special effects (textures, montages, etc.).

alpha test The first test of newly developed hardware or software in a laboratory setting. The next step is *beta testing* with actual users.

alphageometric See *alphamosaic*.

alphamosaic A very-low-resolution display technique that uses elementary graphics characters as part of its character set.

alphanumeric The use of alphabetic letters mixed with numbers and special characters as in name, address, city and state. The text you're reading is alphanumeric.

Altair 8800 A microcomputer kit introduced in 1974 from Micro Instrumentation and Telemetry Systems. It sold for $400 and used an 8080 microprocessor. In 1975, it was packaged with Microsoft's MBASIC. Although computer kits were advertised earlier by others, an estimated 10,000 Altairs were sold, making it the first commercially successful microcomputer.

alternate routing The ability to use another transmission line if the regular line is busy.

alt key A keyboard key that is pressed with a letter or digit key to command the computer.

ALU (Arithmetic Logic Unit) The high-speed CPU circuit that does calculating and comparing. Numbers are transferred from memory into the ALU for calculation, and the results are sent back into memory.

ALTAIR 8800
(Courtesy The Computer Museum, Boston)

Alphanumeric data is sent from memory into the ALU for comparing. The results are tested by GOTOs; for example, IF ITEMA EQUALS ITEMB GOTO UPDATE ROUTINE.

AM (Amplitude Modulation) A transmission technique that blends the data signal into a carrier by varying (modulating) the amplitude of the carrier. See *modulate*.

ambient Surrounding. For example, ambient temperature and humidity are atmospheric conditions that exist at the moment.

Amdahl (Amdahl Corporation, Sunnyvale, CA) A computer manufacturer founded in 1970 by Gene Amdahl, chief architect of the IBM System/360. In 1975, Amdahl installed its first IBM-compatible mainframe, the 470/V6. Although not the first to make IBM-compatible mainframes, it succeeded where others failed. Amdahl offers a full range of IBM-compatible mainframes as well as application development software and midrange UNIX servers.

THE FIRST AMDAHL COMPUTER
(Courtesy Dr. Gene Amdahl)
This 1975 photo shows him next to the Wisconsin Integrally Synchronized Computer that he designed in 1950.

Dr. Amdahl left the company to form Trilogy in 1979 and later Andor Corporation, a manufacturer of products for large IBM mainframe installations.

America Online An online information service that provides conferencing, news, e-mail, education, technical support forums, more than 70,000 software files and access to a large variety of databases, including National Geographic and PC World magazine. Software for DOS, Windows, Mac and Apple II provides navigation through the system. See *online services*.

AMI BIOS A popular PC-compatible ROM BIOS from American Megatrends, Inc., Norcross, GA.

Ami Pro A windows word processing program from Lotus that includes desktop publishing features. It allows for the creation of presentation-quality charts and graphs. Ami was one of the first full-featured word processors for Windows and was originally developed by Samna Corporation.

Amiga A personal computer series from Commodore that runs under the AmigaDOS operating system. It uses the 68000 CPU family and features the Workbench graphical user interface.

amp (AMPere) A unit of electrical current in a circuit. *Volts* measure the force or pressure behind the current. *Watts* are a total measurement of power derived from multiplying amps times volts.

amplitude The strength or volume of a signal, usually measured in decibels.

amplitude modulation See *AM*.

analog A representation of an object that resembles the original. Analog devices monitor conditions, such as movement, temperature and sound, and convert them into analogous electronic or mechanical patterns. For example, an analog watch represents the planet's rotation with the rotating hands on the watch face. Telephones turn voice vibrations into electrical vibrations of the same shape. Analog implies continuous operation in contrast with digital, which is broken up into numbers.

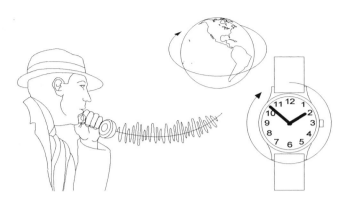

ANALOG

analog channel In communications, a channel that carries voice or video in analog form as a varying range of electrical frequencies. Contrast with *digital channel*.

analog computer A device that processes infinitely varying signals, such as voltage or frequencies. A thermometer is a simple analog computer. As the temperature varies, the mercury moves correspondingly. Although special-purpose, complex analog computers are built, almost all computers are digital. Digital methods provide programming flexibility.

analog monitor A video monitor that accepts analog signals from the computer (digital to analog conversion is performed in the video display board). It may accept only a narrow range of display resolutions; for example, only VGA or VGA and Super VGA, or it may accept a wide range of signals including TV. See *multisync monitor* and *RGB monitor*. Contrast with *digital monitor*.

analysis See *systems analysis & design*.

analyst See *systems analyst* and *business analyst*.

AND, OR & NOT The fundamental operations of Boolean logic. AND is true if both inputs are true, OR is true if any input is true, and NOT is an inverter; the output is always the opposite. See *Boolean search* and *gate*.

angstrom A unit of measurement equal to approximately 1/250 millionth of an inch (.1 nanometer). It is used to measure the tiny elements in a chip.

ANI (Automatic Number Identification) A telephone service that provides the telephone number of the incoming call. ISDN supports ANI by carrying the calling telephone number in the D channel.

animated graphics Moving diagrams or cartoons. Often found in computer-based courseware, animated graphics take up far less disk space than video images.

anisotropic Refers to properties, such as transmission speed, that vary depending on the direction of measurement. Contrast with *isotropic*.

anode In electronics, a positively charged receiver of electrons that flow from the negatively charged *cathode*.

anomaly Abnormality or deviation. It is a favorite word among computer people when complex systems produce output that is inexplicable.

ANSI (American National Standards Institute) A membership organization founded in 1918 that coordinates the development of U.S. voluntary national standards in both the private and public sectors. It is the U.S. member body to ISO and IEC. Information technology standards pertain to programming languages, EDI, telecommunications and physical properties of diskettes, cartridges and magnetic tapes. Address: 11 West 42 St., New York, NY 10036, 212/642-4900.

ANSI character set The ANSI-standard character set that defines 256 characters. The first 128 are ASCII, and the second 128 contain math and foreign language symbols, which are different than those on the PC. See *extended ASCII*.

ANSI terminal A display terminal that follows commands in the ANSI standard terminal language. Uses escape sequences to control the cursor, clear the screen and set colors, for example. Communications programs often support the ANSI terminal.

ANSI.SYS A DOS driver used for cursor movement and screen control. Some early applications require ANSI.SYS, but new applications do not.

answer only modem A modem capable of answering a call, but not initiating one.

anti-aliasing In computer graphics, a category of techniques that is used to smooth the jagged appearance of diagonal lines. For example, the pixels that surround the edges of the line are filled in with varying shades of gray or color in order to blend the sharp edge into the background. See *dithering*.

antivirus A program that detects and removes a virus.

ANVIL A family of CADD/CAM software packages from Manufacturing and Consulting Services Inc., Scottsdale, AZ. ANVIL products include 2 1/2-D and 3-D mechanical engineering systems for PCs, workstations, minis and mainframes.

any key The message "press any key" means that you must press a key on the keyboard to continue. It doesn't matter which one you press: a letter key, return key, the space bar, etc.

AOCE (Apple Open Collaboration Environment) Extensions to the Macintosh System 7 operating system from Apple that provide a technology framework for sharing services across a multiplatform enterprise. PowerTalk and PowerShare are the first AOCE products.

AOL See *America Online*.

APA (All Points Addressable) Refers to an array (bitmapped screen, matrix, etc.) in which all bits or cells can be individually manipulated.

APCUG (Association of Personal Computer User Groups) A non-profit organization dedicated to fostering communication among and between user groups and between user groups and vendors. Address: Suite 700, 1730 M St. N.W., Washington, DC 20036.

aperture card A punched card that holds a frame of microfilm.

API (Application Program Interface) A language and message format used by an application program to communicate with another program that provides services for it. APIs are usually implemented

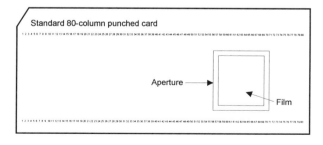

APERTURE CARD

by writing function calls. Examples of APIs are the calls made by an application program to such programs as an operating system, messaging system or database management system (DBMS). See *interface*.

APL (A Programming Language) A high-level, interactive scientific language noted for its brevity and matrix generation capabilities. Developed by Kenneth Iverson in the mid 1960s, it runs on micros to mainframes and is often used to develop mathematical models. It is primarily an interpreted language, but compilers are available.

PROGRAMS TALK TO EACH OTHER!

APL uses unique character symbols and requires special software or ROM chips to enable the computer to display and print them. APL is popular in Europe. The following example converts Fahrenheit to Celsius.

```
[0] CONVERT
[1] 'Enter fahrenheit
[2] fahr ←
[3] cels ← 5 x (fahr-32)÷9
[4] 'Celsius is ', (⍕ cels)
```

APM (Advanced Power Management) An API from Intel and Microsoft for battery-powered computers that lets programs communicate power requirements to slow down and speed up components. The 386SL takes full advantage of APM.

app See *application*.

app code (APPlication code) Instructions in a program that actually process data.

APPC (Advanced Program-to-Program Communications) A high-level communications protocol from IBM that allows a program to interact with another program. It supports client/server and distributed computing by providing a common programming interface across all IBM platforms for communications over a variety of transport protocols. It provides commands for managing a session, sending and receiving data and transaction security and integrity (two-phase commit).

append To add to the end of an existing structure.

Apple (Apple Computer, Inc., Cupertino, CA) A manufacturer of personal computers and the industry's most fabled story. Founded in a garage by Steve Wozniak and Steve Jobs in 1976 and guided by Mike Markkula, Apple blazed the trails for the personal computer industry.

From its Apple II series to the Macintosh to today's new PowerMacs, Apple has always provided a unique alternative to personal computing. The Macintosh's graphical user interface, introduced ahead of its time in 1984, has set the standard for ease of use that is unmatched.

THE FIRST APPLE COMPUTER
(Courtesy Apple Computer)
The "Apple I" was introduced in 1976.

Apple II The personal computer family from Apple that pioneered the microcomputer revolution and has been widely used in schools and home. It uses the 8-bit 6502 microprocessor running at 1MHz, an 8-bit bus and runs Apple's DOS or ProDOS operating system.

Apple key The original name of the Command key.

Apple menu The menu at the top left side of a Macintosh screen that is always available to provide access to desk accessories.

AppleScript A system-level scripting language used for automating routine tasks. It is part of the System 7 Pro operating system.

AppleShare Software from Apple that turns a Macintosh into a file server. It works in conjunction with the Mac operating system and can coexist with other Macintosh applications in a non-dedicated mode.

APPLE IIe

AppleShare PC Software for PCs from Apple that allows a PC to connect to an AppleTalk network. It requires a LocalTalk PC Card from Apple for ISA PCs, or a LocalTalk Card from DayStar Communications for Micro Channel PCs.

AppleSoft BASIC Apple's version of BASIC that comes with Apple II models. It is installed in firmware and is always available.

applet A small application, such as a utility program or a limited-function spreadsheet or word processor.

AppleTalk Apple's local area network architecture introduced in 1985. It supports Apple's proprietary LocalTalk access method as well as Ethernet and Token Ring. The AppleTalk network manager and the LocalTalk access method are built into all Macintoshes and LaserWriters.

    With other products from Apple and third parties, AppleTalk can run in PCs, VAXs and UNIX workstations. Since AppleTalk is patterned after the OSI model, it is a routable protocol that contains a network layer (OSI layer 3).

AppleWorks An integrated software package for Apple IIs from Claris Corporation. Introduced in 1983 by Apple, it combines word processing, file management, spreadsheet, business graphics and communications.

application (1) A specific use of the computer, such as for payroll, inventory and billing.

(2) Same as *application program* and *software package*.

application developer An individual that develops a business application and usually performs the duties of a systems analyst and application programmer.

application development language Same as *programming language*.

application development system A programming language and associated utility programs that allow for the creation, development and running of application programs. DBMSs are often full application development systems, which include a programming language, query language, report writer and the capability to interactively create and manage database files.

application framework (1) The building blocks of an application.

(2) A class library that provides the foundation for programming an object-oriented application.

application generator Software that generates application programs from descriptions of the problem rather than by traditional programming. It is at a higher level than a high-level programming language. One statement or descriptive line may generate a huge routine or an entire program. However, application generators always have limits as to what they can be used for.

application layer In communications, the interaction at the user or application program level. It is the highest layer within the protocol hierarchy. See *OSI model*.

application notes Instructions and recommendations from the vendor provided in addition to the normal reference manuals.

application package A software package that is created for a specific purpose or industry.

application processor A computer that processes data in contrast with one that performs control functions, such as a front end processor or database machine.

application program Any data entry, update, query or report program that processes data for the user. It includes the generic productivity software (spreadsheets, word processors, database programs, etc.) as well as custom and packaged programs for payroll, billing, inventory and other accounting purposes. Contrast with *system program*.

application program interface See *API*.

application program library Application programs used by an organization.

application programmer An individual who writes application programs in a user organization. Most programmers are application programmers. Contrast with *systems programmer*.

application server A server in a LAN that contains applications used by network clients.

application suite A set of applications designed to work together. In the Windows environment, the application suite is the successor to the integrated package, except that the individual applications are stand alone and can be purchased separately.

APPN (Advanced Peer-to-Peer Networking) Extensions to IBM's SNA communications that provide necessary enhancements for routing data in a mainframe/LAN environment. It includes improved administration, intermediate node routing and dynamic network services. APPN makes use of LU 6.2 protocols and is implemented in an SNA Node Type 2.1.

Approach A relational database from Lotus that is also part of Lotus' SmartSuite set. It provides the ability to graphically create Windows applications using industry standard database formats, such as dBASE and Paradox.

AppWare A development environment for writing client/server applications from Novell introduced in 1993. Applications are writen as Application Loadable Modules (ALMs), which are network-independent and interact via a software bus (AppWare Bus) on the server.

APT (Automatic Programmed Tools) A high-level programming language used to generate instructions for numerical control machines.

arbitration A set of rules for allocating machine resources, such as memory or peripheral devices, to more than one user or program.

ARC, ARC+Plus (1) PC compression programs from System Enhancement Associates, Inc., Clifton, NJ. ARC was one of the first compression utilities to become popular in the early 1980s. ARC+Plus provides enhanced features and speed.

(2) The ARC extension was previously used by PKWARE Inc. in its PKARC program.

Archie (ARCHIvE) An internet utility used for searching file names. Machines called "Archie servers" periodically update catalogs of local files that are available to the public. The Archie program lets users search those catalogs. If you don't have Archie, some Internet hosts let you log on via Telnet as user "archie."

architecture See *computer architecture, network architecture* and *software architecture.*

archive (1) To copy data onto a different disk or tape for backup. Archived files are often compressed to maximize storage media.

(2) To save data onto the disk.

archive attribute A file classification that indicates whether the file has been updated since the last backup.

ARCNET (Attached Resource Computer NETwork) The first local area network (LAN) introduced in 1968 by Datapoint Corporation. It connects up to 255 nodes in a star topology at 2.5 Mbits/sec over twisted pair or coax. A 20 Mbits/sec version was introduced in 1989. Although not as popular as Ethernet and Token Ring, a lot of ARCNET networks were sold due to their lower-cost adapters.

Ardis (Advanced National Radio Data Service) A joint venture of IBM and Motorola that provides wireless data transmission in the 800MHz FM band. It covers most U.S. metropolitan areas with over 1,000 base stations.

areal density The bits per square inch of disk surface (BPI x TPI).

arg See *argument.*

argument In programming, a value that is passed between programs, subroutines or functions. Arguments are independent items, or variables, that contain data or codes. When an argument is used to customize a program for a user, it is typically called a *parameter.*

arithmetic coding A statistical data compression method that converts strings of data into single floating point numbers between 0 and 1.

arithmetic expression (1) In mathematics, one or more characters or symbols associated with arithmetic, such as $1 + 2 = 3$ or $8 / 6$.

(2) In programming, a non-text expression.

arithmetic logic unit See *ALU.*

arithmetic operators Symbols for arithmetic functions: + add, − subtract, * multiply, / divide. See *precedence.*

arithmetic overflow The result from an arithmetic calculation that exceeds the space designated to hold it.

arithmetic underflow The result from an arithmetic calculation that is too small to be expressed properly. For example, in floating point, a negative exponent can be generated that is too large (too small a number) to be stored in its allotted space.

ARP (Address Resolution Protocol) A low-level TCP/IP protocol used to obtain a node's physical address when only its logical IP address is known. An ARP request with the IP address is broadcast onto the network. The node with that IP address sends back its hardware address so that packets can be transmitted.

ARPANET (Advanced Research Projects Agency NETwork) The research network funded by DARPA (originally ARPA) and built by BBN, Inc., in 1969. It pioneered packet switching technology and was the original backbone and testbed for the now-gigantic Internet. In 1983, the military communications part of it was split off into MILNET.

ARQ (Automatic Repeat Request) A method of handling communications errors in which the receiving station requests retransmission if an error occurs.

array An ordered arrangement of data elements. A vector is a one dimensional array, a matrix is a two-dimensional array. Most programming languages have the ability to store and manipulate arrays in one or more dimensions. Multi-dimensional arrays are used extensively in scientific simulation and mathematical processing; however, an array can be as simple as a pricing table held in memory for instant access by an order entry program. See *subscript*.

array element One item in an array.

Item	Amount	Item	Amount	Item	Amount	Item	Amount
0001	016.54	0002	005.44	0003	159.95	0004	249.95

Price list in one-dimensional array

array processor A computer, or extension to its arithmetic unit, that is capable of performing simultaneous computations on elements of an array of

Jan	Feb	Dec	Jan	Feb	Dec	Jan	Feb	Dec
24484	09880	77855	58254	11876	37665	24484	09843	30387

Sales figures in two-dimensional array

ARRAYS

data in some number of dimensions. Common uses include analysis of fluid dynamics and rotation of 3-D objects, as well as data retrieval, in which elements in a database are scanned simultaneously. See *vector processor* and *math coprocessor*.

artifact Some distortion of an image or sound caused by a limitation or malfunction in the graphics hardware or software.

artificial intelligence See *AI*.

artificial language A language that has been predefined before it is ever used. Contrast with *natural language*.

AS (Application System) An IBM mainframe 4GL that runs under MVS. It was originally designed for non-computer people and includes commands for planning, budgeting and graphics. However, a programmer can also produce complex applications. It also provides computer conferencing.

AS/400 (Application System/400) IBM's minicomputer series introduced in 1988 that superseded the earlier System/36 and System/38 lines. The AS/400 serves in a variety of networking configurations: as a host or intermediate node to other AS/400s and System/3x machines, as a remote system to mainframe-controlled networks and as a network server to PCs.

ascender The part of lowercase b, d, f, h, k, l, and t, that extends above the body of the letters.

ASCII (American Standard Code for Information Interchange) Pronounced "ask-ee." A binary code for text as well as communications and printer control. It is used for most communications and is in the built-in character code in most minicomputers and all personal computers.

ASCII is a 7-bit code providing 128 character combinations, the first 32 of which are control characters. Since the common storage unit is an 8-bit byte (256 combinations) and ASCII uses only 7 bits, the extra bit is used differently depending on the computer.

For example, the PC uses the additional values for foreign language and graphics symbols (see ASCII chart below). In the Macintosh, the additional values can be user-defined. In the Mac version of this Glossary, the PC symbols are designed into the font used for the definitions.

STANDARD ASCII

The first 32 characters (0-31) are control codes

0	NUL	Null
1	SOH	Start of heading
2	STX	Start of text
3	ETX	End of text
4	EOT	End of transmit
5	ENQ	Enquiry
6	ACK	Acknowledge
7	BEL	Audible bell
8	BS	Backspace
9	HT	Horizontal tab
10	LF	Line feed
11	VT	Vertical tab
12	FF	Form feed
13	CR	Carriage return
14	SO	Shift out
15	SI	Shift in
16	DLE	Data link escape
17	DC1	Device control 1
18	DC2	Device control 2
19	DC3	Device control 3
20	DC4	Device control 4
21	NAK	Neg. acknowledge
22	SYN	Synchronous idle
23	ETB	End trans. block
24	CAN	Cancel
25	EM	End of medium
26	SUB	Substitution
27	ESC	Escape
28	FS	Figures shift
29	GS	Group separator
30	RS	Record separator
31	US	Unit separator
32	SP	Blank space (Space bar)

33	!
34	"
35	#
36	$
37	%
38	&
39	'
40	(
41	)
42	*
43	+
44	,
45	–
46	.
47	/
48	0
49	1
50	2
51	3
52	4
53	5
54	6
55	7
56	8
57	9
58	:
59	;
60	<
61	=
62	>
63	?
64	@
65	A
66	B
67	C
68	D
69	E
70	F
71	G
72	H
73	I
74	J
75	K
76	L
77	M
78	N
79	O
80	P

81	Q
82	R
83	S
84	T
85	U
86	V
87	W
88	X
89	Y
90	Z
91	[
92	\
93	]
94	^
95	_
96	`
97	a
98	b
99	c
100	d
101	e
102	f
103	g
104	h
105	i
106	j
107	k
108	l
109	m
110	n
111	o
112	p
113	q
114	r
115	s
116	t
117	u
118	v
119	w
120	x
121	y
122	z
123	{
124	¦
125	}
126	~
127	※

EXTENDED ASCII
(IBM PC)

128	Ç
129	ü
130	é
131	â
132	ä
133	à
134	å
135	ç
136	ê
137	ë
138	è
139	ï
140	î
141	ì
142	Ä
143	Å
144	É
145	æ
146	Æ
147	ô
148	ö
149	ò
150	û
151	ù
152	ÿ
153	Ö
154	Ü
155	¢
156	£
157	¥
158	₧
159	ƒ
160	á
161	í
162	ó
163	ú
164	ñ
165	Ñ
166	ª
167	º
168	¿
169	⌐
170	¬
171	½
172	¼
173	¡
174	«
175	»

174	«
175	»
176	░
177	▒
178	▓
179	│
180	┤
181	╡
182	╢
183	╖
184	╕
185	╣
186	║
187	╗
188	╝
189	╜
190	╛
191	┐
192	└
193	┴
194	┬
195	├
196	─
197	┼
198	╞
199	╟
200	╚
201	╔
202	╩
203	╦
204	╠
205	═
206	╬
207	╧
208	╨
209	╤
210	╥
211	╙
212	╘
213	╒
214	╓
215	╫
216	╪
217	┘
218	┌
219	█
220	▄
221	▌

220	▄
221	▌
222	▐
223	▀
224	α
225	β
226	Γ
227	π
228	Σ
229	σ
230	μ
231	τ
232	Φ
233	Θ
234	Ω
235	δ
236	∞
237	φ
238	ε
239	∩
240	≡
241	±
242	≥
243	≤
244	⌠
245	⌡
246	÷
247	≈
248	°
249	·
250	·
251	√
252	η
253	²
254	▪
255	

ASCII CHART

This chart shows the order assigned to ASCII characters. They are numbered starting with 0. The first 128 are standard, but the second 128, known as extended ASCII, are used differently by computer manufacturers. The extended ASCII shown above are the symbols selected by IBM for use in its PC under DOS. They include common foreign language and math symbols as well as a variety of character graphics for making simple forms and graphs. These extended ASCII symbols are the not the same in every font used in today's PCs. Only fonts known as the OEM or System font, or fonts that use the PC symbol set, will reproduce these symbols.

ASCII file A file that contains data made up of ASCII characters. It is essentially raw text just like the words you're reading now. Each byte in the file contains one character that conforms to the standard ASCII code. Program source code, DOS batch files, macros and scripts are written as straight text and stored as ASCII files.

ASCII text files become a common denominator between applications that do not import each other's formats. If both applications can import and export ASCII files, you can transfer your files between them. Contrast with *graphics file* and *binary file*.

ASCII protocol The simplest communications protocol for text. It transmits only ASCII characters and uses ASCII control codes. It implies little or no error checking.

ASCII sort The sequential order of ASCII data. In ASCII code, lower case characters follow upper case. True ASCII order would put the words DATA, data and SYSTEM into the sequence: DATA, SYSTEM, data.

ASIC (Application Specific Integrated Circuit) A custom chip designed for a specific application. It is designed by integrating standard cells from a library. ASIC design is faster than designing a chip from scratch, and design changes can be made more easily.

askSam A text management system for PCs from askSam Systems, Perry FL. It holds unstructured text as well as standard data fields. The product is noted for its flexible text retrieval and hypertext capabilities.

ASM (1) (Association for Systems Management) An international membership organization founded in 1947 with over 10,000 administrative executives and specialists in information systems. It sponsors conferences in all phases of administrative systems and management and serves business, education, government and the military. Address: 24587 Bagley Rd., Cleveland, OH 44138, 216/243-6900.

(2) File extension for assembly language source programs.

ASN.1 (Abstract Syntax Notation.1) The rules for defining data structures transmitted over an OSI network.

ASP (Association of Shareware Professionals) A trade organization for shareware founded in 1987. Author members submit products to ASP, which are approved, virus checked and distributed monthly via CD to member vendors and BBSs. CDs are periodically made available to the public. Address: 545 Grover Road, Muskegon, MI 49422, 616/788-5131.

aspect ratio The ratio of width to height of an object.

ASPI (Advanced SCSI Programming Interface) An interface from Adaptec, Inc., Milpitas, CA, that provides a common language between drivers and SCSI host adapters. See *CAM* and *CorelSCSI*.

assembler Software that translates assembly language into machine language. Contrast with *compiler*, which is used to translate a high-level language, such as COBOL or C, into assembly language first and then into machine language.

assembly language A programming language that is one step away from machine language. Each assembly language statement is translated into one machine instruction by the assembler. Programmers must be well versed in the computer's architecture, and, undocumented assembly language programs are difficult to maintain. Assembly language is hardware dependent; there is a different assembly language for each CPU series.

Although often used synonymously, assembly language and machine language are not the same. Assembly language is turned into machine language. For example, the assembly instruction COMPARE A,B is translated into COMPARE the contents of memory bytes 2340-2350 with 4567-4577 (where A and B happen to be located).

The physical binary format of the machine instruction is specific to the computer it's running in.

assignment statement In programming, a compiler directive that places a value into a variable. For example, `counter = 0` creates a variable named counter and fills it with zeros. The VARIABLE NAME = VALUE syntax is common among programming languages.

associative storage Storage that is accessed by comparing the content of the data stored in it rather than by addressing predetermined locations.

ASSP (Application Specific Standard Part) An ASIC chip originally designed for one customer and then released to the general public.

asymmetric modem A full-duplex modem that transmits data in one direction at one speed and simultaneously in the other direction at another speed. For example, data flows at high-speed in one direction while acknowledgement is returned at low speed in the other. Contrast with *ping pong*.

asymmetric multiprocessing A multiprocessing design in which each CPU is dedicated to a specific function. For example, the operating system runs in one CPU and the user application in another. Contrast with *symmetric multiprocessing*.

asymmetric system (1) A system in which major components or properties are different.

(2) In video compression, a system that requires more equipment to compress the data than to decompress it.

asynchronous (1) Unsynchronized events, for example, the time interval between event A and B is not the same as B and C.

(2) Able to initiate a transmission at either end.

(3) In SNA, refers to independent events rather than concurrent events. For example, if one user sends mail to a party who is not available, the ability to forward the mail at a later time is considered asynchronous.

(4) Starting the next I/O operation before the current one is completed.

(5) In SCSI, the acknowledgment of each byte of data transferred.
   Contrast with *synchronous*.

asynchronous protocol A communications protocol that controls an asynchronous transmission, for example, ASCII, TTY, Kermit and Xmodem. Contrast with *synchronous protocol*.

asynchronous transmission The transmission of data in which each character is a self-contained unit with its own start and stop bits. Intervals between characters may be uneven. It is the common method of transmission between a computer and a modem, although the modem may switch to synchronous transmission to communicate with the other modem. Also called start/stop transmission. Contrast with *synchronous transmission*.

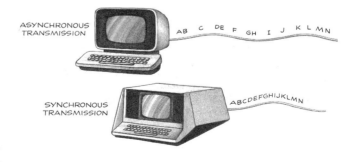

ASYNCHRONOUS TRANSMISSION — AB C DE F GH I J K L MN

SYNCHRONOUS TRANSMISSION — ABCDEFGHIJKLMN

AT (Advanced Technology) IBM's first 286-based PC, introduced in 1984. It was the most advanced machine in the PC line and featured a new keyboard, 1.2MB floppy and 16-bit data bus. AT-class machines run considerably faster than XTs (8088-based PCs).

AT&T GIS (AT&T Global Information Solutions, Dayton, OH) Formerly the NCR Corporation, AT&T GIS is a wholly owned subsidiary of AT&T. It is a major manufacturer of computers and financial terminals that was founded in 1884 when John Henry Patterson purchased National Manufacturing Company of Dayton, Ohio, and renamed it National Cash Register.

ATA The interface specification for IDE drives. ATA is often not specified on documents relating to IDE drives, but it is the formal name for the IDE interface. The ATA interface is also used for PCMCIA solid state disks.

Atari (Atari Computer, Sunnyvale, CA) A manufacturer of personal computers founded in 1972 by Nolan Bushnell and originally famous for its "Pong" video games. Atari's product lines are aimed at providing quality computing at affordable prices.

IBM AT

AT bus Refers to the 16-bit bus introduced with the IBM AT. It was the early term for what is today called the "ISA bus."

AT class Refers to second-generation PCs that use the 286 CPU and 16-bit AT (ISA) bus. In the mid 1980s, AT class machines were the high-speed PCs of the day.

AT command set A series of machine instructions used to activate features on an intelligent modem. Developed by Hayes Microcomputer Products, Inc., and formally called the Hayes Standard AT Command Set, it is used entirely or partially by most every modem manufacturer. AT is a mnemonic code for ATtention, which is the prefix that initiates each command to the modem. See *Hayes Smartmodem*.

ATE (Automatic Test Equipment) Machines that test electronic systems, primarily chips. See *EDA* and *DTA*.

AT interface See *AT bus*. See also *ATA*.

AT keyboard An 84-key keyboard provided with the PC AT. It corrected the non-standard placement of the PC's return and left shift keys. See *PC keyboard* and *Enhanced keyboard*.

ATM (1) (Asynchronous Transfer Mode) A high-speed cell-switching network technology for LANs and WANs that handles data and realtime voice and video. It combines the high efficiency of packet switching used in data networks, with the guaranteed bandwidth of circuit switching used in voice networks. ATM is defined in the Broadband ISDN (BISDN) standard. Also see *Adobe Type Manager*.

▶ *The electronic and encyclopedic versions of this book provide more detail on asynchronous transfer mode.*

(2) (**A**utomatic **T**eller **M**achine) A banking terminal that accepts deposits and

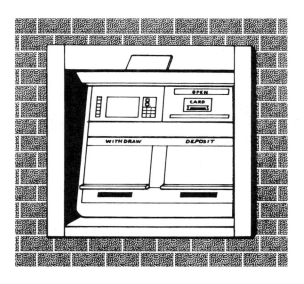

ATM

dispenses cash. Stand alone or online to a central computer, ATMs are activated by inserting a magnetic card (cash or credit card) that contains the user's account number.

atom In list processing languages, a single element in a list.

atomic Indivisible. An atomic operation, or atomicity, implies an operation that must be performed entirely or not at all. For example, if machine failure prevents a transaction to be processed to completion, the system will be rolled back to the start of the transaction. See *two-phase commit*.

attached processor An additional CPU connected to the primary CPU in a multiprocessing environment. It operates as an extension of the primary CPU and shares the system software and peripheral devices.

attenuation Loss of signal power in a transmission.

attribute (1) In relational database management, a field within a record.

(2) For printers and display screens, a characteristic that changes a font, for example, from normal to boldface or underlined, or from normal to reverse video.

(3) See *file attribute*.

At Work An operating environment from Microsoft designed for office equipment such as telephones, copiers and fax machines.

audio The range of frequencies within human hearing, approximately 20Hz at the low to a high of 20,000Hz.

audio adapter Same as *sound card*.

audio board Same as *sound card*.

audio CD The music compact disc (CD) format that has replaced the phonograph record. See *CD* and *Red Book*.

audio response See *voice response*.

audiotex A voice response application that allows users to enter and retrieve information over the telephone. In response to a voice menu, users press the keys or answer questions to select their way down a path of choices. It is used for obtaining the latest financial quotes as well as for ordering products. It is also built into interactive systems that allows databases to be changed. See *VIS*.

audiovisual Audio and/or video capability.

audit An examination of systems, programming and datacenter procedures in order to determine the efficiency of computer operations.

audit software Specialized programs that perform a variety of audit functions, such as sampling databases and generating confirmation letters to customers. It can highlight exceptions to categories of data and alert the examiner to possible error. Audit software often includes a non-procedural language that lets the auditor describe the computer and data environment without detailed programming.

audit trail A record of transactions in an information system that provides verification of the activity of the system. The simplest audit trail is the transaction itself. If a person's salary is increased, the change transaction includes the date, amount of raise and name of authorizing manager.

A more elaborate audit trail can be created when the system is being verified for accuracy; for example, samples of processing results can be recorded at various stages. Item counts and hash totals are used to verify that all input has been processed through the system.

AUI (Attachment Unit Interface) The type of connector used on a network adapter for attaching standard Ethernet cable (thick Ethernet).

authoring program Software that allows for the development of tutorials and CBT programs.

authorization code An identification number or password that is used to gain access to a local or remote computer system.

auto (AUTOmatic) Refers to a wide variety of devices that perform unattended operation.

auto answer A modem feature that accepts a telephone call and establishes the connection. See *auto dial*.

auto attendant A voice store and forward system that replaces the human operator and directs callers to the appropriate extensions or voice mailboxes.

auto baud detect A modem feature that detects the highest speed of the called modem and switches to it.

auto bypass The ability to bypass a terminal or other device in a network if it fails, allowing the remaining devices to continue functioning.

AutoCAD A full-featured CAD program from AutoDesk Inc., Sausalito, CA, that runs on PCs, VAXs, Macs and UNIX workstations. Originally developed for CP/M machines, it was one of the first major CAD programs for personal computers and became an industry standard. Many software packages import and export graphics files in DXF, AutoCAD's external file format.

autocoder An IBM assembly language for 1960s-vintage 1400 and 7000 series computers.

auto dial A modem feature that opens the line and dials the telephone number of another computer to establish connection. See *auto answer*.

AUTOEXEC.BAT (AUTOmatic EXECute BATch) A DOS batch file that executes when the computer is started. It must be stored in the root directory. It is used to load various drivers and TSRs that must reside in memory at all times and to customize DOS for the user's requirements.

autoflow Wrapping text around a graphic image or from one page to the next.

auto line feed A feature that moves the cursor or print head to the next line when a CR (carriage return) is sensed. PCs put a LF (line feed) after the CR and do not use this feature. The Mac uses only a CR for end of line and requires it.

AutoLISP An AutoCAD language used to create customized menus and routines.

auto logon Performing the complete log-on sequence necessary to gain entry into a computer system without user intervention.

automata theory An open-ended computer science discipline that concerns an abstract device called an "automaton," which performs a specific computational or recognition function. Networks of automata are designed to mimic human behavior.

automatic feature negotiation The ability of a modem to determine and adjust to the speed, error control and data compression method of the modem at the other end of the line.

automation The replacement of manual operations by computerized methods. Office automation refers to integrating clerical tasks such as typing, filing and appointment scheduling. Factory automation refers to computer-driven assembly lines.

automounting Making remote files available to a client at the time the file is accessed. Remote directories are associated with a local directory on the client ahead of time, and the mounting takes places the first time a remote file is opened by the client.

A VISION OF AUTOMATION (Circa 1890)
(Courtesy Rosemont Engineering)

auto redial A modem, fax or telephone feature that redials a busy number a fixed number of times before giving up.

auto reliable A modem feature that enables it to send to a modem with or without built-in error detection and compression.

auto resume A feature that lets you stop working on the computer and take up where you left off at a later date without having to reload applications. Memory contents are stored on disk or kept active by battery and/or AC power.

autosave Saving data to the disk at periodic intervals without user intervention.

autosizing The ability of a monitor to maintain the same rectangular image size when changing from one resolution to another.

autostart routine Instructions built into the computer and activated when it is turned on. The routine performs diagnostic tests, such as checking the computer's memory, and then loads the operating system and passes control to it.

autotrace A routine that locates outlines of raster graphics images and converts them into vector graphics.

AUX (AUXiliary) The DOS name for the first connected serial port. See *A/UX*.

A/UX Apple's version of UNIX for the Macintosh. It is based on AT&T's UNIX System V with Berkeley extensions.

auxiliary memory A high-speed memory bank used in mainframes and supercomputers. It is not directly addressable by the CPU, rather it functions like a disk. Data is transferred from auxiliary memory to main memory over a high-bandwidth channel. See *auxiliary storage*.

auxiliary storage External storage devices, such as disk and tape.

AVI (Audio Video Interleaved) Microsoft's video format for Windows.

avionics The electronic instrumentation and control equipment used in airplanes and space vehicles.

awk (Aho Weinberger Kernighan) A UNIX programming utility developed in 1977 by Aho, Weinberger and Kernighan. Due to its unique pattern-matching syntax, it is often used in data retrieval and data transformation. DOS versions are also available.

AXP A family of computer systems from Digital that use the Alpha CPU chip.

azimuth The trajectory of an angle measured in degrees going clockwise from a base point. A disk azimuth alignment test checks for the correct positioning of the read/write head to the track.

B

B1 The computer system security level required by the Department of Defence (DOD). See *NCSC*.

B: The designation for the second floppy disk drive in a PC.

backbone In communications, the part of a network that handles the major traffic. It often employs the highest-speed transmission paths in the network and may also run the longest distance. Smaller networks are attached to the backbone.

A backbone can span a large geographic area or be as small as a backplane in a single cabinet. See *collapsed backbone*.

backdoor See *trapdoor*.

back-end CASE CASE tools that generate program code. Contrast with *front-end CASE*.

back end processor Same as *database machine*.

backfilling Assigning EMS memory to conventional memory in XTs and ATs in order to let DESQview run more programs concurrently. Motherboard chips are disabled and EMS chips are assigned the low memory addresses.

background (1) Non-interactive processing in the computer. See *foreground/background*.

(2) The base, or backdrop, color on screen. For example, in the DOS version of this Glossary, the text color is white on a blue background.

background ink A highly reflective OCR ink used to print the parts of the form not recognized by a scanner.

background noise An extraneous signal that has crept into a line, channel or circuit.

background processing Processing in which the program is not visibly interacting with the user. Most personal computers use operating systems that run background tasks only when foreground tasks are idle, such as between keystrokes. Advanced multitasking operating systems let background programs be given any priority from low to high.

backing storage Same as *auxiliary storage*.

backlit An LCD screen that has its own light source from the back of the screen, making the background brighter and characters appear sharper.

backplane (1) The reverse side of a panel or board that contains interconnecting wires.

(2) A printed circuit board, or device, containing slots or sockets for plugging in boards or cables. See *bus*.

backslash key A character used in DOS commands. See *path*.

backsolver See *solver*.

backspace (1) To move the screen cursor one column to the left, deleting the character that was in that position. A backspace to the printer moves the print head one column to the left.

(2) To move to the previous block on a magnetic tape.

back up To make a copy of important data onto a different storage medium for safety.

backup Additional resources or duplicate copies of data on different storage media for emergency purposes. See *backup types*.

backup & recovery The combination of manual and machine procedures that can restore lost data in the event of hardware or software failure. Routine backup of databases and logs of computer activity are part of a backup & recovery program. See *checkpoint/restart*.

backup copy A disk, tape or other machine readable copy of a data or program file. Making backup copies is a discipline most computer users learn the hard way–after a week's work is lost.

backup disk A disk used to hold duplicate copies of important files. Floppy disks and disks cartridges are used for backup disks.

backup power An additional power source that can be used in the event of power failure. See *UPS*.

backup tape See *tape backup*.

backup types A full backup backs up all selected files. A differential backup backs up selected files that have been changed. This is used when only the latest version of a file is required.

    An incremental backup backs up selected files that have been changed, but if a file has been changed for the second or subsequent time since the last full backup, the file doesn't replace the already-backed-up file, rather it is appended to the backup medium. Incremental backups are used when each revision of a file must be maintained for backup.

Backus-Naur form Also known as Backus normal form, it was the first metalanguage to define programming languages, developed by John Backus and Peter Naur in 1959.

backward chaining In AI, a form of reasoning that starts with the conclusion and works backward. The goal is broken into many subgoals or sub-subgoals which can be solved more easily. Known as top-down approach. Contrast with *forward chaining*.

backward compatible Same as *downward compatible*.

bad sector A segment of disk storage that cannot be read or written due to a physical problem in the disk. Bad sectors on hard disks are marked by the operating system and bypassed. If data is recorded in a sector that becomes bad, file recovery software, and sometimes special hardware, must be used to restore it.

BAK file (BAcKup file) A DOS and OS/2 file extension for backup files.

ballistic gain A trackball or mouse feature that changes cursor travel relative to hand speed. The faster the ball is moved, the farther the cursor is moved.

baloon help On-screen help displayed in a cartoon-style dialogue box that appears when the pointer (cursor) is placed over the object in question.

balun (BALanced UNbalanced) A small connecting device that attaches a balanced line to an unbalanced line; for example, a twisted pair to a coaxial cable. A balanced line is one in which both wires are electrically equal. In an unbalanced line, such as a coax, one line has different properties than the other.

band (1) The range of frequencies used for transmitting a signal. A band is identified by its lower and upper limits; for example, a 10MHz band in the 100 to 110MHz range.

(2) A contiguous group of tracks that are treated as a unit.

(3) The printing element in a band printer.

band pass filter An electronic device that prohibits all but a specific range of frequencies to pass through it.

band printer A line printer that uses a metal band, or loop, of type characters as its printing mechanism. The band spins horizontally around a set of hammers. When the desired character is in front of the selected print position, the corresponding hammer hits the paper into the ribbon and onto the character in the band.

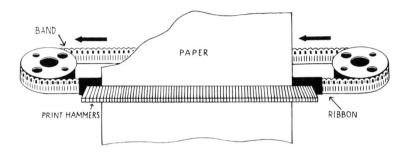

BAND PRINTER

bandwidth The transmission capacity of a computer channel, communications line or bus. It is expressed in cycles per second (Hertz), the bandwidth being the difference between the lowest and highest frequencies transmitted. The frequency is equal to or greater than the bits per second. Bandwidth is also often stated in bits or bytes per second. See *video bandwidth*.

bank An arrangement of identical hardware components.

bank switching Engaging and disengaging electronic circuits. Bank switching is used when the design of a system prohibits all circuits from being addressed or activated at the same time, requiring that one unit be turned on while the others are turned off.

bar chart A graphical representation of information in the form of bars. See *business graphics*.

bar code The printed code used for recognition by a scanner. Traditional one-dimensional bar codes use the bar's width as the code, but encode just an ID or account number. Two-dimensional systems, such as PDF 417 from Symbol Technology, hold 1,800 characters in an area the size of a postage stamp. See *UPC*.

barrel distortion A screen distortion in which the sides bow out. Contrast with *pincushioning*.

barrel printer Same as *drum printer*.

base (1) A starting or reference point.

(2) A component in a bipolar transistor that activates the switch. Same as *gate* in a MOS transistor.

ONE-DIMENSIONAL
BAR CODE

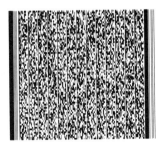

TWO-DIMENSIONAL
BAR CODE
(Courtesy Symbol Technology Inc.)
This image contains the Gettysburg address.

(3) A multiplier in a numbering system. In a decimal system, each digit position is worth 10x the position to its right. In binary, each digit position is worth 2x the position to its right.

base address The starting address (beginning point) of a program or table. See *base/displacement* and *relative address*.

base alignment The alignment of a variety of font sizes on a baseline.

base/displacement A machine architecture that runs programs no matter where they reside in memory. Addresses in a machine language program are displacement addresses, which are relative to the beginning of the program. At runtime, the hardware adds the address of the current first byte of the program (base address) to each displacement address and derives an absolute address for execution.

All modern computers use some form of base/displacement or offset mechanism in order to to run multiple programs in memory at the same time.

base font The default font used for printing if none other is specified.

baseband A communications technique in which digital signals are placed onto the transmission line without change in modulation. It is usually limited to a few miles and does not require the complex modems used in broadband transmission. Common baseband LAN techniques are token passing ring (Token Ring) and CSMA/CD (Ethernet).

In baseband, the full bandwidth of the channel is used, and simultaneous transmission of multiple sets of data is accomplished by interleaving pulses using TDM (time division multiplexing).

Contrast with *broadband* transmission, which transmits data, voice and video simultaneously by modulating each signal onto a different frequency, using FDM (frequency division multiplexing).

baseline The horizontal line to which the bottoms of lowercase characters (without descenders) are aligned. See *typeface*.

baselining tool A network monitor that analyzes communications usage in order to establish routine traffic patterns.

BASIC (Beginners All purpose Symbolic Instruction Code) A programming language developed by John Kemeny and Thomas Kurtz in the mid 1960s at Dartmouth College. Originally developed as an interactive, mainframe timesharing language, it has become widely used on small computers.

BASIC is available in both compiler and interpreter form. As an interpreter, the language is conversational and can be debugged a line at a time. BASIC is also used as a quick calculator.

The following BASIC example converts Fahrenheit to Celsius:

```
10 INPUT "Enter Fahrenheit "; FAHR
20 PRINT "Celsius is ", (FAHR-32) * 5 / 9
```

BASIC in ROM A BASIC interpreter stored in a read only memory chip that is available to the user at all times.

BAT file (BATch file) A file of DOS or OS/2 commands, which are executed one after the other. It has a .BAT extension and is created with a text editor.

batch A group, or collection, of items.

batch data entry Entering a group of source documents into the computer.

batch file (1) A file containing data that is processed or transmitted from beginning to end.

(2) A file containing instructions that are executed one after the other. See *BAT file* and *shell script*.

batch file transfer The consecutive transmission of two or more files.

batch job Same as *batch program*.

batch operation Some action performed on a group of items at one time.

batch processing Processing a group of transactions at one time. Transactions are collected and processed against the master files (master files updated) at the end of the day or some other time period. Contrast with *transaction processing*.

Batch and Transaction Processing

Information systems typically use both batch and transaction processing methods. For example, in an order processing system, transaction processing is the continuous updating of the customer and inventory files as orders are entered.

At the end of the day, batch processing programs generate picking lists for the warehouse. At the end of some period, batch programs print invoices and management reports.

batch program
A non-interactive (non-conversational) program such as a report listing or sort.

batch session
Transmitting or updating an entire file. Implies a non-interactive or non-interruptible operation from beginning to end. Contrast with *interactive session*.

batch stream
A collection of batch processing programs that are scheduled to run in the computer.

batch system
See *batch processing*.

batch terminal
A terminal that is designed for transmitting or

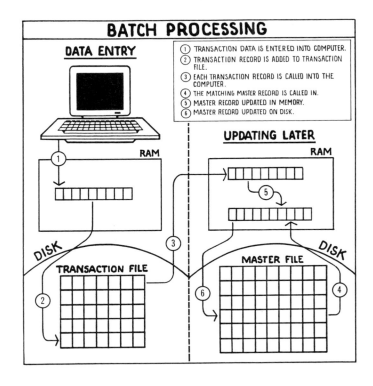

BATCH PROCESSING

DATA ENTRY

① TRANSACTION DATA IS ENTERED INTO COMPUTER.
② TRANSACTION RECORD IS ADDED TO TRANSACTION FILE.
③ EACH TRANSACTION RECORD IS CALLED INTO THE COMPUTER.
④ THE MATCHING MASTER RECORD IS CALLED IN.
⑤ MASTER RECORD UPDATED IN MEMORY.
⑥ MASTER RECORD UPDATED ON DISK.

UPDATING LATER

RAM

RAM

DISK

TRANSACTION FILE

DISK

MASTER FILE

receiving blocks of data, such as a card reader or printer.

batch total The sum of a particular field in a collection of items used as a control total to ensure that all data has been entered into the computer. For example, using account number as a batch total, all account numbers would be summed manually before entry into the computer. After entry, the total is checked with the computer's sum of the numbers. If it does not match, source documents are manually checked against the computer's listing.

batteries See *lead acid, lithium ion, nickel cadmium, nickel hydride* and *zinc air*.

baud (1) The signalling rate of a line. It's the switching speed, or number of transitions (voltage or frequency changes) that are made per second. Only at low speeds are bauds equal to bits per second; for example, 300 baud is equal to 300 bps. However, one baud can be made to represent more than one bit per second. For example, the V.22bis modem generates 1200 bps at 600 baud.

(2) Commonly (and erroneously) used to specify bits per second for modem speed; for example, 1200 baud means 1200 bps. See previous paragraph.

baud rate A redundant reference to baud. Baud is a rate.

baudot code Pronounced "baw-doh." One of the first standards for international telegraphy developed in the late 19th century by Emile Baudot. It uses five bits per character.

BBS (Bulletin Board System) A computer system used as an information source and message system for a particular interest group. Users dial into the BBS, review and leave messages for other users as well as communicate to other users on the system at the same time. BBSs are used to distribute shareware and may provide access (doors) to other application programs.
▶ *The electronic and encyclopedic versions of this book include a list of over 250 national BBSs with their modem telephone numbers.*

BCD (Binary Coded Decimal) The storage of numbers in which each decimal digit is converted into binary and is stored in a single character or byte. For example, a 12-digit number would take 12 bytes. See *numbers*.

BCS (The Boston Computer Society) A nonprofit membership organization founded in 1977 by Jonathan Rotenberg. Services include user and special interest groups, a subscription to BCS publications, access to the Resource Center, public-domain software and shareware. Address: 1 Kendall Square, Cambridge, MA 02139, 617/252-0600.

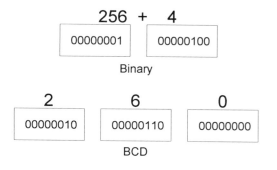

BDOS error See *read error* and *write error*.

beaconing A continuous signalling of error conditions on a LAN.

bead (1) A small programming subroutine. A sequence of beads that are strung together is called a *thread*.

(2) The insulator surrounding the inner wire of a coaxial cable.

BEL See *bell character*.

Bell 103 An AT&T standard for asynchronous 300 bps full-duplex modems using FSK modulation on dial-up lines.

Bell 113 An AT&T standard for asynchronous 300 bps full-duplex modems using FSK modulation on dial-up lines. The 113A can originate but not answer calls, while the 113D can answer but not originate.

Bell 201 An AT&T standard for synchronous 2400 bps full-duplex modems using DPSK modulation. Bell 201B was originally designed for dial-up lines and later for leased lines. Bell 201C was designed for half-duplex operation over dial-up lines.

Bell 202 An AT&T standard for asynchronous 1800 bps full-duplex modems using DPSK modulation over four-wire leased lines as well as 1200 bps half-duplex operation over dial-up lines.

Bell 208 An AT&T standard for synchronous 4800 bps modems. Bell 208A is a full-duplex modem using DPSK modulation over four-wire leased lines. Bell 208B was designed for half-duplex operation over dial-up lines.

Bell 209 An AT&T standard for synchronous 9600 bps full-duplex modems using QAM modulation over four-wire leased lines or half-duplex over dial-up lines.

Bell 212 An AT&T standard for asynchronous 1200 bps full-duplex modems using DPSK modulation on dial-up lines.

bell character The control code used to sound an audible bell or tone in order to alert the user (ASCII 7, EBCDIC 2F).

Bell compatible A modem that is compatible with modems originally introduced by the Bell Telephone System.

Bell Labs The research and development center of AT&T and one of the most renowned scientific laboratories in the world.

Bell System AT&T and the Bell Telephone Companies before divestiture. See *divestiture* and *RBOC*.

Bellcore (BELL COmmunications REsearch) The research and development organization created at divestiture and jointly owned by the regional Bell telephone companies (RBOCs). It is also involved in communications issues of the U.S. government regarding national security and emergency preparedness.

benchmark A test of performance of a computer or peripheral device. The best benchmark is the actual set of application programs and data files that the organization will use. Running benchmarks on a single user computer is reasonably effective; however, benchmarking a multiuser system is complicated. Unless the user environment can be duplicated closely, the benchmark may be inaccurate. See *Linpack, Dhrystones, Whetstones, Khornerstones* and *SPECmark*.

BER (1) (Basic Encoding Rules) One method for encoding information in the OSI environment. For example, it defines how Boolean data is coded.

(2) (Bit Error Rate) The average number of bits transmitted in error.

Berkeley extensions See *BSD UNIX*.

Bernoulli Box A removable disk system for personal computers from Iomega Corporation, Roy, UT. It uses a SCSI interface and floppy-disk-like cartridges up to 150MB. The name comes from 18th century Swiss scientist, Daniel Bernoulli, who demonstrated fluid dynamics principles. Unlike a hard disk in which the read/write head flies over a rigid disk, the Bernoulli floppy is spun at high speed and bends up close to the head. Upon power failure, a hard disk must retract the head to prevent a crash, whereas the Bernoulli floppy naturally bends down.

Beta The first home VCR format, now defunct. Developed by Sony, it used 1/2" tape cassettes.

beta test A test of hardware or software that is performed by users under normal operating conditions. See *alpha test*.

betaware Software in beta test that has been provided to a large number of users in advance of the formal release.

Bezier curve In computer graphics, a curve that is generated using a mathematical formula which assures continuity with other Bezier curves. It is mathematically simpler, but more difficult to blend than a b-spline curve. Within CAD and drawing programs, Bezier curves are typically reshaped by moving the handles that appear off of the curve.

BFT (Binary File Transfer) An extension to the fax protocol that allows transmission of raw text instead of an image of the text document. The ability to transfer actual data similar to a common data modem provides a true e-mail capability via fax boards.

BI bus A proprietary high-speed bus used in the VAX series.

bi-endian The ability to switch between big endian and little endian ordering.

bias The voltage used to control or stabilize an electronic circuit.

bidirectional The ability to move, transfer or transmit in both directions.

bidirectional printer A printer that prints alternate lines from right to left.

BIFF (Binary Interchange File Format) A spreadsheet file format that holds data and charts, introduced with Excel Version 2.2.

bifurcate To divide into two.

Big Blue Slang for IBM coined from the blue covers on most of its earlier mainframes.

big endian The order of bytes in a word in which the most significant byte is first. Little endian reverses the order. For example, the number 23,041, which is 5A01 in hex, would also be stored as 5A01 in a big endian Motorola 680x0 CPU. The Intel x86 architecture uses little endian, and 015A would be stored instead. See *bi-endian*.

bill of materials The list of components that make up a system. For example, a bill of materials for a house would include the cement block, lumber, shingles, doors, windows, plumbing, electric, heating and so on. Each subassembly also contains a bill of materials; the heating system is made up of the furnace, ducts, etc. A bill of materials "implosion" links component pieces to a major assembly, while a bill of materials "explosion" breaks apart each assembly or subassembly into its component parts.

The first hierarchical databases were developed for automating bills of materials for manufacturing organizations in the early 1960s.

billion One thousand times one million or 10^9. See gig*a* and *nanosecond*.

bin (BINary) A popular directory name for storing executable programs, device drivers, etc. (binary files).

binaries Executable programs in machine language.

binary Meaning two. The principle behind digital computers. All input to the computer is converted into binary numbers made up of the two digits 0 and 1 (bits). For example, when you press the "A" key on your personal computer, the keyboard generates and transmits the number 01000001 to the computer's memory as a series of pulses. The 1 bits are transmitted as high voltage; the 0 bits are transmitted as low.

Bits are stored as charged and uncharged cells in memory, as positively and negatively charged spots on disk and tape and as pits and no pits on optical media.

binary code A coding system made up of binary digits. See *BCD* and *data code*.

binary compatible Refers to any data, hardware or software structure (data file, machine code, instruction set, etc.) in binary form that is 100% identical to another. It most often refers to executable programs.

binary field A field that contains binary numbers. It may refer to the storage of binary numbers for calculation purposes, or to a field that is capable of holding any information, including data, text, graphics images, voice and video. See *BLOB*.

binary file (1) An executable program in machine language ready to run.

(2) A file that contains binary numbers.

binary format (1) Numbers stored in pure binary form in contrast with *BCD* form. See *binary numbers*.

(2) Information stored in a binary coded form, such as data, text, images, voice and video. See *binary file, binary field* and *BLOB*.

(3) A file transfer mode that transmits any type of file without loss of data.

binary notation The use of binary numbers to represent values.

binary numbers Numbers stored in pure binary form. Within one byte (8 bits), the values 0 to 255 can be held. Two contiguous bytes (16 bits) can hold values from 0 to 65,535. See *numbers* and *binary values*.

binary search A technique for quickly locating an item in a sequential list. The desired key is compared to the data in the middle of the list. The half that contains the data is then compared in the middle, and so on, either until the key is located or a small enough group is isolated to be sequentially searched.

binary synchronous See *bisync*.

binary tree A data structure in which each node contains one parent and no more than two children.

bind (1) To assign a machine address to a logical or symbolic reference or address.

(2) To assign a type or value to a variable or parameter. See *binding time*.

(3) Bind may be used in place of terms such as link or interface when referencing software that is made to communicate with other software or with hardware. See *linkage editor*.

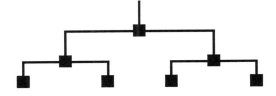

BINARY TREE

bindery A NetWare file used for security and accounting in NetWare 2.x and 3.x. A bindery pertains only to the server it resides in and contains the names and passwords of users and groups of users authorized to log in to that server.

binding time (1) In program compilation, the point in time when symbolic references to data are converted into physical machine addresses.

(2) In programming languages, when a variable is assigned its type (integer, string, etc.). Traditional compilers and assemblers provide early binding and assign types at compilation. Object-oriented languages provide late binding and assign types at runtime when the variable receives a value from the keyboard or other source.

biomechanics The study of the anatomical principles of movement. Biomechanical applications on the computer employ stick modeling to analyze the movement of athletes as well as racing horses.

bionic A machine that is patterned after principles found in humans or nature; for example, robots. It also refers to artificial devices implanted into humans replacing or extending normal human functions.

BIOS (Basic I/O System) Detailed instructions that activate peripheral devices. Although BIOS's have been around for more than 30 years, today, the term generally refers to the ROM BIOS in a PC, which holds certain parts of the operating system. See *ROM BIOS*.

bipolar A category of high-speed microelectronic circuit design, which was used to create the first transistor and the first integrated circuit. The most common variety of bipolar chip is TTL (transistor transistor logic). Emitter coupled logic (ECL) and integrated injection logic (I^2L) are also part of the bipolar family.

Bipolar and MOS are the two major categories of chip design.

bipolar transmission A digital transmission technique that alternates between positive and negative signals. The 1s and 0s are determined by varying amplitudes at both polarities while non-data is zero amplitude.

BIPS (Billion Instructions Per Second) See *MIPS*.

biquinary code Meaning two-five code. A system for storing decimal digits in a four-bit binary number.

birefringence Using a crystal to split light into two frequencies that travel at different speeds and at right angles to each other. It's used to filter out a color in an LCD display.

bis Second version. It means twice in Old Latin, or encore in French.

BISDN (Broadband IDSN) The specification for a future high-speed ISDN network.

bison The Free Software Foundation's version of yacc.

bistable circuit Same as *flip-flop*.

bisync (BInary SYNChronous) A major category of synchronous communications protocols used in mainframe networks. Bisync communications require that both sending and receiving devices are synchronized before transmission of data is started. Contrast with *asynchronous* transmission.

bisynchronous See *bisync*.

bit (BInary digiT) A single digit in a binary number (0 or 1). Within the computer, a bit is physically a transistor or capacitor in a memory cell, a magnetic spot on disk or tape or a high or low voltage pulsing through a circuit. A bit is like a light bulb: on or off.

Groups of bits make up storage units in the computer, called characters, bytes, or words, which are manipulated as a group. The most common is the byte, made up of eight bits and equivalent to one alphanumeric character. See *space/time*.

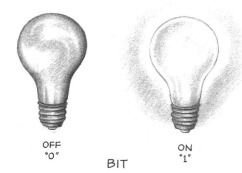

OFF
"0"

ON
"1"

BIT

bitblit See *bitblt*.

bitblt (BIT BLock Transfer) In computer graphics, a hardware feature that moves a rectangular block of bits from main memory into display memory. It speeds the display of moving objects. Contrast with *vector graphics* and *character graphics*.

bit cell A boundary in which a single bit is recorded on a tape or disk.

bit density The number of bits that can be stored within a given physical area.

bit depth The number of bits used to represent an object. It typically refers to the number of colors that can be displayed at one time, which is based on the number of bits used to hold a pixel. Digital video requires at least 16 bits, while 24 bits produces realistic TV-like colors.

Four bits provide 16 colors; 8 bits 256; 16 bits 65,536; 24-bits 16,777,216. With 32-bit color, 24 bits are used for colors, and the remainder is used for an alpha channel.

bite See *byte*.

bit flipping Same as *bit manipulation*.

bit level device A device, such as a disk drive, that inputs and outputs data bits. Contrast with *pulse level device*.

bit manipulation Processing individual bits within a byte. Bit-level manipulation is very low-level programming, often done in graphics and systems programming.

bitmap A binary representation in which a bit or set of bits corresponds to some part of an object such as an image or font. For example, in monochrome systems, one bit in the bitmap represents one pixel on screen. For gray scale or color, several bits in the bitmap represent one pixel or group of pixels. The term may also refer to the memory area that holds the bitmap.

A bitmap is usually associated with graphics objects, in which the bits are a direct representation of the picture image. However, bitmaps can be used to represent and keep track of anything, where each bit location is assigned a different value or condition.

bitmapped font A set of dot patterns for each letter and digit in a particular typeface (Times Roman, Helvetica, etc.) for a specified type size (10 points, 12 points, etc.). Bitmapped typefaces are either purchased in groups of pre-generated point sizes, or, for a wide supply of fonts, font generators allow the user to create a variety of point sizes. Bitmapped fonts take up disk space for each point size. Contrast with *scalable font*. See *font* and *font generator*.

bitmapped graphics The raster graphics method for generating images.

bit-oriented protocol A communications protocol that uses individual bits within the byte as control codes, such as IBM's SDLC. Contrast with *byte-oriented protocol*.

bit parallel The transmission of several bits at the same time, each bit travelling over a different wire in the cable.

bit pattern A specific layout of binary digits.

bit plane A segment of memory used to control an object, such as a color, cursor or sprite. Bit planes may be reserved parts of a common memory or independent memory banks each designed for one purpose.

bit rate The transmission speed of binary coded data. Same as *data rate*.

bit serial The transmission of one bit after the other on a single line or wire.

bit slice processor A logic chip that is used as an elementary building block for the computer designer. Bit slice processors usually come in 4-bit increments and are strung together to make larger processors (8 bit, 12 bit, etc.).

bit stream The transmission of binary signals.

bit stuffing Adding bits to a transmitted message in order to round out a fixed frame or to break up a pattern of data bits that could be misconstrued for control codes.

bit twiddler Same as *hacker*.

bitwise Dealing with bits rather than larger structures such as a byte. Bitwise operators are programming commands or statements that work with individual bits. See *bit manipulation*.

black box (1) A custom-made electronic device, such as a protocol converter or encryption system. Yesterday's black boxes often become today's off-the-shelf products.

(2) (Black Box Corporation, Pittsburgh, PA) An organization that specializes in communications and LAN products. It offers expert services, custom solutions and hard-to-find products.

blank character A space character that takes up one byte in the computer just like a letter or digit. When you press the space bar on a personal computer keyboard, the ASCII character with a numeric value of 32 is created.

blank squash The removal of blanks between items of data. For example, in the expression `city + ", " + state`, the data is concatenated with a blank squash resulting in DALLAS, TX rather than DALLAS   TX.

blip A mark, line or spot on a medium, such as microfilm, that is optically sensed and used for timing or counting purposes.

blit See *bitblt*.

blitting Using a bitblt to transfer data.

BLOB (Binary Large OBject) A database field that holds any digitized information. This is one method of storing multimedia objects (audio, video) in a DBMS, since it holds any binary data. However, most relational DBMSs are better suited to small fields typical of transaction data, such as name, amount, etc. The object-oriented DBMS is more efficient for managing the storage of long, linear amounts of data. See *object-oriented DBMS*.

block (1) A group of disk or tape records that is stored and transferred as a single unit.

(2) A group of bits or characters that is transmitted as a unit.

(3) A group of text characters that has been marked for moving, copying, saving or other operation.

block device A peripheral device that transfers a group of bytes (block, sector, etc.) of data at a time such as a disk. Contrast with *character device*.

block diagram A chart that contains squares and rectangles connected with arrows to depict hardware and software interconnections. For program flow charts, information system flow charts, circuit diagrams and communications networks, more elaborate graphical representations are usually used.

block move The ability to mark a contiguous segment of text or data and move it.

blocking factor The number of records in a block.

blow To write code or data into a PROM chip by blowing the fuses of the 0 bits. The 1 bits are left alone.

blow up Same as *crash*, *bomb* or *abend*.

BLOCK DIAGRAM OF A COMPUTER

BMP (Bit MaP) A Windows graphics format that may be device dependent or independent. Device independent BMP files (DIB) are coded for translation to a wide variety of displays and printers.

BNC (British Naval Connector) A commonly used connector for coaxial cable. The plug looks like a tiny tin can with the lid off and two short pins sticking out on the upper edge on opposite sides. After insertion, the plug is turned, tightening the pins in the socket.

board See *printed circuit board* and *BBS*.

board level Electronic components that are mounted on a printed circuit board instead of in a cabinet or finished housing.

BOC (Bell Operating Company) One of 22 telephone companies that was formerly part of AT&T and now part of one of the seven regional Bell telephone companies.

body type The typeface and size commonly used for text in paragraph copy. Typically 10 points.

BOF (Beginning Of File) The status of a file when it is first opened or when an instruction or command has reset the file pointer.

boilerplate A common phrase or expression used over and over. Boilerplate is stored on disk and copied into the document as needed.

boldface Characters that are heavier and darker on printed output and brighter than normal on a display screen.

boldface attribute A code that turns normal characters into boldface characters on a printer or display screen.

boldface font A set of type characters that are darker and heavier than normal type such as the characters in this sentence.

bomb Same as *abend* and *crash*.

BOMP (Bill Of Materials Processor) One of the first DBMSs used for bill of materials explosion in the early 1960s from IBM. A subsequent version, DBOMP, was used in manufacturing during the 1970s.

Boolean data Yes/no or true/false data.

Boolean expression A statement using Boolean operators that expresses a condition which is either true or false.

Boolean logic The "mathematics of logic," developed by English mathematician George Boole in the mid 19th century. Its rules govern logical functions (true/false). As add, subtract, multiply and divide are the primary arithmetic operators, AND, OR and NOT are the primary Boolean operators.
▶ *The electronic and encyclopedic versions of this book provide more detail on this subject.*

Boolean search A search for specific data. It implies that any condition can be searched for using the Boolean operators AND, OR and NOT. For example, the English language request: "Search for all Spanish and French speaking employees who have MBAs, but don't work in Sales." is expressed in the following dBASE command:

```
list for degree = "MBA" .and.
  (language = "Spanish" .or. language = "French")
    .and. .not. department = "Sales"
```

boot Causing the computer to start executing instructions. Personal computers contain built-in instructions in a ROM chip that are automatically executed on startup. These instructions search for the operating system, load it and pass control to it. Starting up a large computer may require more button pushing and keyboard input.

The term comes from "bootstrap," since bootstraps help you get your boots on, booting the computer helps it get its first instructions. See *cold boot, warm boot* and *clean boot*.

bootable disk A disk that contains the operating system in a form ready to load into the computer. It often refers to a floppy disk that contains the operating system in its boot sectors. If a hard disk personal computer does not find a bootable floppy disk in the primary floppy drive at startup (A: in a PC), it boots from the hard disk.

boot drive A disk drive that contains the operating system.

boot failure The inability to locate and/or read the operating system from the designated disk.

boot record See *boot sector*.

boot ROM A memory chip that allows a workstation to be booted from the server or other remote station.

BOOTSTRAP

boot sector The sectors on disk that are reserverd for the operating system. They are typically the first sectors in the first disk partition.

boot virus A virus written into the boot sectors of a floppy disk. If the floppy is booted, it infects the system. For example, the Michelangelo virus, which destroys data on March 6th, Michelangelo's birthday, infects a computer if the virus diskette is left in the drive and booted inadvertently when the computer is turned back on.

bootstrap See *boot*.

Borland (Borland International, Inc., Scotts Valley, CA) A personal computer software company founded in 1983 by Philippe Kahn. It specializes in programming languages and database management systems. Bortland's Turbo Pascal compiler single handedly moved Pascal out of the academic halls and into the commercial world. Its C++ compiler is a very popular programming environment for developing Windows applications, and its dBASE and Paradox database programs are industry standards.

Borland C++ An ANSI C and C++ compiler from Borland for DOS and Windows applications. It is Turbo C-compatible and its debugger supports Windows programs written in Microsoft C. It includes application frameworks for Windows (ObjectWindows) and DOS (Turbo Vision). Borland C++ for OS/2 is also available.

Bourne shell See *UNIX*.

bpi (Bits Per Inch) The measurement of the number of bits stored in a linear inch of a track on a recording surface, such as on a disk or tape.

BPR (Business Process Reengineering) See *reengineering*.

B protocol A file transfer protocol from CompuServe. Quick B is a faster version only for downloading. Later versions of B will automatically select Quick B.

bps (Bits Per Second) The measurement of the speed of data transfer in a communications system.

braces Symbols used in programming and other technical references to mark the beginning and end of a contained area. They are the { and } characters.

branch (1) Same as *GOTO*.

(2) A connection between two blocks in a flowchart or two nodes in a network.

braze To solder using metals with a very high melting point, such as with an alloy of zinc and copper.

breadboard A thin plastic board full of holes used to hold components (transistors, chips, etc.) that are wired together. It is used to develop electronic prototypes or one-of-a-kind systems.

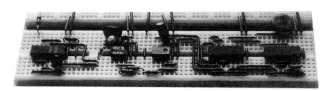

BREADBOARD
(Courtesy 3M Company)

break To temporarily or permanently stop executing, printing or transmitting.

break key A keyboard key that is pressed to stop the execution of the current program or transmission.

breakout box A device inserted into a multiple-line cable for testing purposes that provides an external connecting point to each wire. A small LED may be attached to each line, which glows when a signal is present.

breakpoint The location in a program used to temporarily halt the program for testing and debugging.

BRI See *ISDN*.

bridge (1) To cross from one circuit, channel or element over to another.

(2) A device that connects two LAN segments together, which may be of similar or dissimilar types, such as Ethernet and Token Ring. Bridges are inserted into a network to improve performance by keeping traffic contained within smaller segments. Bridges work at the data link layer (OSI layer 2), whereas routers work at the network layer

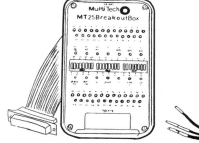

BREAKOUT BOX

(layer 3). Bridges are faster than routers because they do not have to read the protocol to glean routing information. See *transparent bridge, repeater, router, gateway* and *hub*.

bridgeware Hardware or software that converts data or translates programs from one format into another.

Brief A text editor for PC programming from Borland. It provides automatic indentation and the ability to edit different parts of a source program at the same time.

brightness The light level on a display screen. Contrast with *contrast*.

British Telecom A division of the British Post Office that manages telecommunications throughout Great Britain and Northern Ireland.

broadband (1) A technique for transmitting data, voice and video over long distances. Using high frequency transmission over coaxial cable or optical fibers, broadband transmission requires modems for connecting terminals and computers to the network. Using the same FDM (frequency division multiplexing) technique as cable TV, several streams of data can be transmitted simultaneously. Contrast with *baseband*.

(2) High-speed transmission. Used in this manner, the term generally refers to the highest-speed technologies available or to ones just emerging.

broadcast To disseminate information to several recipients simultaneously.

brouter (Bridging ROUTER) A communications device that is part bridge and router. Like a bridge, it functions at the data link level (OSI layer 2) and remains independent of higher protocols. Like a router, it manages multiple lines and routes messages. See *router, gateway* and *hub*.

browse (1) To view the contents of a file or a group of files. Browser programs generally let you view data by scrolling through the documents or databases. In a database program, the browse mode often lets you edit the data.

(2) To view and edit the class hierarchy of the objects in an object-oriented programming language.

BSC (Binary Synchronous Communications) See *bisync*.

BSD socket A communications interface in UNIX first introduced in BSD UNIX. See *UNIX socket*.

BSD UNIX (Berkeley Software Distribution UNIX) A version of UNIX developed by the Computer Systems Research Group of the University of California at Berkeley from 1979 to 1993. BSD enhancements, known as the "Berkeley Extensions," include networking, virtual memory, task switching and large file names (up to 255 chars.). BSD's UNIX was distributed free, with a charge only for the media.

b-spline In computer graphics, a curve that is generated using a mathematical formula which assures continuity with other b-splines.

BT font (BitsTream font) Refers to fonts from Bitstream Inc., Cambridge, MA. See *FaceLift* and *FontWare*.

BTAM (Basic Telecommunications Access Method) IBM communications software used in bisynch, non-SNA mainframe networks. Application programs must interface directly with the BTAM access method.

BTLZ (British Telecom Lempel Ziv) A data compression algorithm based on the Lempel-Ziv method that can achieve up to 4x the throughput of 2400 and 9600 bps modems.

B-tree (Balanced-tree) A technique for organizing indexes. In order to keep access time to a minimum, it stores the data keys in a balanced hierarchy that continually realigns itself as items are inserted and deleted. Thus, all nodes always have a similar number of keys.

B+tree is a version of B-tree that maintains a hierarchy of indexes while also linking the data sequentially, providing fast direct access and fast sequential access. IBM's VSAM uses this.

Btrieve A file manager from Novell that accompanies its NetWare operating systems. It allows for the creation of indexed files, using the b-tree organization method. Btrieve functions can be called from within many common programming languages. See *Xtrieve*.

bubble A bit in bubble memory or a symbol in a bubble chart.

bubble chart A chart that uses bubble-like symbols often used to depict data flow diagrams.

bubble memory A solid state semiconductor and magnetic storage device suited for rugged applications. It is about as fast as a slow hard disk and holds its content without power.

It is conceptually a stationary disk with spinning bits. The unit, only a couple of square inches in size, contains a thin film magnetic recording layer. Globular-shaped bubbles (bits) are electromagnetically generated in circular strings inside this layer. In order to read or write the bubbles, they are rotated past the equivalent of a read/write head.

bubble sort A multiple-pass sorting technique that starts by sequencing the first two items, then the second with the third, then the third with the fourth and so on until the end of the set has been reached. The process is repeated until all items are in the correct sequence.

bucket Another term for a variable. It's just a place to store something.

buffer A reserved segment of memory used to hold data while it is being processed. In a program, buffers are created to hold some amount of data from each of the files that will be read or written. A buffer may also be a small hardware memory bank used for special purposes.

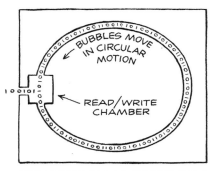

CONCEPTUAL PICTURE OF A
TRACK OF BUBBLE MEMORY

buffer flush The transfer of data from memory to disk. Whenever you command your application to save the document you're working on, the program is actually flushing its buffer (writing the contents of one or more reserved areas of memory to the hard disk).

Go Flush Your Cold Buffer!

Try this one out on your colleagues. A cold buffer is a reserved area of memory that contains data, which hasn't been updated for a while. Cold buffers are flushed at periodic intervals. More importantly, this phrase sounds as strange as they get. Better yet, try "go flush your cold buffer into your SCSI DASD" (pronounced scuzzy dazdy). Be sure to say this without cracking a smile, and expect quite a grin from a systems professional. If your friend doesn't understand this phrase, be sure to recommend a good glossary!

buffer pool An area of memory reserved for buffers.

bug A persistent error in software or hardware. If the bug is in software, it can be corrected by changing the program. If the bug is in hardware, new circuits have to be designed.

   Although the derivation of bug is generally attributed to the moth that was found squashed between the points of an electromechanical relay in a computer in the 1940s, the term was already in use in the late 1800s. See *software bug*. Contrast with *glitch*.

A Note from the Author

On October 19, 1992, I found my first "real bug." When I fired up my laser printer, it printed blotchy pages. Upon inspection, I found a bug lying belly up in the trough below the corona wire. The printer worked fine after removing it!

bug compatible A hardware device that contains the same design flaws as the original.

bulk storage Storage that is not used for high-speed execution. May refer to auxiliary memory, tape or disk.

Bull HN (Bull HN Information Systems Inc., Billerica, MA) The American subsidiary of the French company, Compagnie des Machines Bull (CMB), founded in 1932. The HN stands for Honeywell and NEC, which were partners in joint development that had varying amounts of ownership until 1991. Bull offers a full range of computer systems and services that have evolved from the acquisition of Honewell's computer division in the U.S.

bulletin board See *BBS*.

bump mapping In computer graphics, a technique for simulating rough textures by creating irregularities in shading.

bundle To sell hardware and software as a single product or to combine several software packages for sale as a single unit. Contrast with *unbundle*.

bunny suit The protective clothing worn by an individual in a clean room that keeps human bacteria from infecting the chip-making process. The outfit makes people look like oversized rabbits.

burn in To test a new electronic system by running it for some length of time. Weak components often fail within the first few hours of use.

burst mode A high-speed transmission mode in a communications or computer channel. Under certain conditions, the system sends a burst of data at higher speed. For example, a multiplexor channel may suspend transmitting several streams of data and send one high-speed transmission using the entire bandwidth.

BUNNY SUIT
(Coutesy Hewlett-Packard Company)

burster A mechanical device that separates continuous paper forms into cut sheets. A burster can be attached to the end of a collator, which separates multipart forms into single parts.

bus A common pathway, or channel, between multiple devices. A bus is always designed to attach multiple devices, whereas channels such as the serial port on a PC are used to connect only one device. Buses are generally hardware, although software can be designed and linked via a so-called "software bus."

The term was coined after a real bus, because a bus stops at all the bus stops on the route. The same goes for an electronic bus. All signals on the bus go to all stations or devices connected to it.

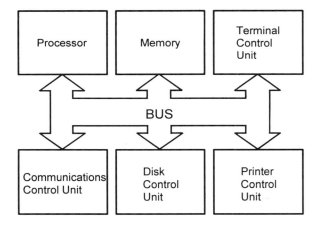

bus bridge A device that connects two similar or dissimilar busses together, such as two VMEbuses or a VMEbus and a Futurebus. This is not the same as a communications bridge, which connects network segments together. See *bridge*.

bus card An expansion board (card) that plugs into the computer's expansion bus.

bus extender (1) A board that pushes a printed circuit board out of the way of surrounding boards for testing purposes. It plugs into an expansion slot, and the expansion board plugs into the bus extender.

(2) A device that extends the physical distance of a bus. See *repeater*.

(3) A device that increases the number of expansion slots. It is either an expansion board containing multiple expansion slots, or an expansion board that cables to a separate housing that contains the slots and its own power supply.

bus mastering A bus design that allows add-in boards to process independently of the CPU and to be able to access the computer's memory and peripherals on their own.

bus mouse A mouse that plugs into an expansion board. It takes up an expansion slot whereas a serial mouse takes up a serial port. The choice depends on how many devices must be connected to each type of socket.

business analyst An individual who analyzes the operations of a department or functional unit with the purpose of developing a general systems solution to the problem that may or may not require automation. The business analyst can provide insights into an operation for an information systems analyst.

business graphics Numeric data represented in graphic form. While line graphs, bar charts and pie charts are the common forms of business graphics, there are many others. People think in pictures. By transforming numerical data into graphic form, patterns of business activity can be recognized more easily.

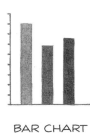
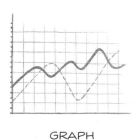

PIE CHART   BAR CHART   GRAPH

business machine Any office machine, such as a typewriter or calculator, that is used in clerical and accounting functions. The term has traditionally excluded computers and terminals.

button (1) A knob, such as on a printer or a mouse, which is pushed with the finger to activate a function.

(2) A simulated button on screen that is "pushed" by moving the cursor onto it and clicking the mouse.

bypass In communications, to avoid the local telephone company by using satellites and microwave systems.

byte The common unit of computer storage from micro to mainframe. It is made up of eight binary digits (bits). A ninth bit may be added in the circuitry as a parity bit for error checking.

A byte holds the equivalent of a single character, such as the letter A, a dollar sign or decimal point. For numbers, a byte can hold a single decimal digit (0 to 9), two numeric digits (packed decimal) or a number from 0 to 255 (binary numbers). See *ASCII chart*.

byte addressable The ability to address each byte of memory independently of the others. This is the concept behind memory. It allows individual units of data, or fields, made up of one or more bytes, to be worked on independently. Contrast with *word addressable*.

byte ordering See *big endian*.

byte-oriented protocol A communications protocol that uses control codes made up of full bytes. The bisynchronous protocols used by IBM and other vendors are examples. Contrast with *bit-oriented protocol*.

C A high-level programming language developed at Bell Labs that is able to manipulate the computer at a low level like assembly language. During the last half of the 1980s, C has become the language of choice for developing commercial software.

C can be compiled into machine languages for almost all computers. For example, UNIX is written in C and runs in a wide variety of micros, minis and mainframes.

C is programmed as a series of functions that call each other for processing. Even the body of the program is a function named "main." Functions are very flexible, allowing programmers to choose from the standard library that comes with the compiler, to use third party functions from other C suppliers, or to develop their own.

The following C example converts fahrenheit to centigrade:

```
main()    {
float fahr;
printf("Enter Fahrenheit ");
scanf("%f", &fahr);
printf("Celsius is %f\n", (fahr-32)*5/9);
         }
```

C++ An object-oriented version of C created by Bjarne Stroustrup. C++ has become popular because it combines traditional C programming with OOP capability. Smalltalk and other original OOP languages did not provide the familiar structures of conventional languages such as C and Pascal. See *Borland C++* and *Visual C++*.

C2 The minimum security level defined by the National Computer Security Center. See *NCSC*.

C: A designation for the primary hard disk in a PC.

CA (Computer Associates International, Inc., Islandia, NY) The world's largest diversified software vendor offering more than 350 applications from micro to mainframe. Founded in 1976 by Charles Wang and three associates, its first product was an IBM mainframe utility.

CA-Clipper An application development system from Computer Associates. Originally a dBASE compiler, it has become a complete stand-alone development environment with many unique features. Clipper was originally developed by Nantucket Corporation.

CA-Easytrieve An application development system for IBM mainframes, DOS and OS/2 from Computer Associates. It includes 4GL query and reporting capabilities and can access many IBM mainframe and PC database formats. Easytrieve was originally developed by Pansophic Systems.

CA-IDMS A full-featured relational DBMS from Computer Associates that runs on minis and mainframes. IDMS (Integrated Data Management System) was developed at GE in the 1960s and marketed by Cullinane, later renamed Cullinet and then acquired by CA in 1989.

CA-Librarian A version control system for IBM mainframes from Computer Associates. Librarian's master files can be simultaneously accessed on shared disks by different operating systems. Librarian was originally developed by ADR, Inc.

CA-Panvalet A version control system for IBM mainframes from Computer Associates that keeps track of source code, JCL and object modules. Panvalet was originally developed by Pansophic Systems. CA-PAN/LCM is a similar product for PCs, which also provides interfaces to mainframe systems, such as CA-Panvalet and CA-Librarian.

CA-RAMIS A fourth-generation retrieval language for IBM mainframes and PCs from Computer Associates. Originally developed by Mathematica, RAMIS was later acquired by Martin Marietta Data Systems, On-Line Software, then CA in 1991. The earliest version of RAMIS was one of the first database packages with a non-procedural language for IBM mainframes.

CA-Realizer A Windows development software from Computer Associates that uses a structured superset of BASIC, has its own forms design utilities and includes a runtime module. Realizer was originally developed by Within Technologies.

CA-Telon An application generator from Computer Associates that generates COBOL and PL/I code for IBM mainframes and COBOL code for AS/400s. Development can be performed on mainframes or PCs. Telon was originally developed by Pansophic Systems.

cable A flexible metal or glass wire or group of wires. All cables used in electronics are insulated with a material such as plastic or rubber.

cable categories The following categories are based on their transmission capacity. The majority of new wiring installations use Category 5 UTP wire in order to be able to run or upgrade to the faster network technologies that will require it. Categories 1 through 5 are based on the EIA/TIA-568 standard.

Category	Cable type	Application
1	UTP	Analog voice
2	UTP	Digital voice, 1 Mbps data
3	UTP, STP	16 Mbps data
4	UTP, STP	20 Mbps data
5	UTP, STP	100 Mbps data
6	Coax	100 Mbps+ data
7	Fiber optic	100 Mbps+ data

cable matcher Same as *gender changer*.

cable modem A modem used to connect a computer to a cable TV system that offers online services.

cable types See *cable categories*.

cabletext A videotex service that uses coaxial cable. See *videotex*.

cache Pronounced "cash." A method for improving system performance by creating a secondary memory area closer to the CPU's higher speed. A memory cache, or CPU cache, is a dedicated bank of high-speed memory used to cache data from main memory. A disk cache is a reserved section of main memory used to cache data from the disk. In both cases, a larger block of the program or database is retrieved into the cache than is immediately necessary with the supposition that the next item will be waiting in a higher-speed location when required.

caching controller A disk controller with a built-in cache. See *cache*.

CAD (Computer-Aided Design) Using computers to design products. CAD systems are high-speed workstations or personal computers using CAD software and input devices such as graphic tablets and scanners. CAD output is a printed design or electronic input to CAM systems (see *CAD/CAM*).

CAD software is available for generic design or specialized uses, such as architectural, electrical and mechanical design. CAD software may also be highly specialized for creating products such as printed circuits and integrated circuits. See *graphics, CADD*, and *CAE*.

CAD/CAM (Computer-Aided Design/Computer-Aided Manufacturing) The integration of CAD and CAM. Products designed by CAD are direct input into the CAM system. For example, a device is designed and its electronic image is translated into a numerical control programming language, which generates the instructions for the machine that makes it.

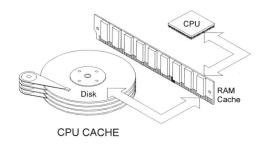

CPU CACHE

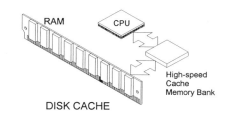

DISK CACHE

CADAM A full-featured IBM mainframe CAD application, which includes 3-D capability, solid modeling and numerical control. Originally developed by Lockheed for internal use, it was distributed by IBM starting in the late 1970s. In 1989, IBM purchased the Lockheed subsidiary, CADAM, Inc.

CADD (Computer-Aided Design and Drafting) CAD systems with additional features for drafting, such as dimensioning and text entry.

CADKEY An integrated 2-D drafting and 3-D design system for PCs from CADKEY, Inc., Manchester, CT. It offers a total design solution with solids creation and built-in DXF and IGES translators. Over 200 manufacturing systems link to CADKEY through its CADL programming language.

CAE (1) (Computer-Aided Engineering) Software that analyzes designs which have been created in the computer or that have been created elsewhere and entered into the computer. Different kinds of engineering analyses can be performed, such as structural analysis and electronic circuit analysis.

(2) (Common Application Environment) Software development platform that is specified by X/Open.

CAI (1) (Computer-Assisted Instruction) Same as *CBT*.

(2) See *CA*.

Cairo The code name for an object-oriented version of Windows NT to be released after Windows NT is established.

CAL (1) (Computer-Assisted Learning) Same as *CBT*.

(2) (Conversational Algebraic Language) A timesharing language from the University of California.

calculated field A numeric or date field that derives its data from the calculation of other fields. Data is not entered into a calculated field by the user.

calculator A machine that provides arithmetic capabilities. It accepts keypad input and displays results on a readout and/or paper tape. Unlike a computer, it cannot handle alphabetic data.

call (1) In programming, a statement that references an independent subroutine or program. The call is turned into a branch instruction by the assembler, compiler or interpreter. The routine that is called is responsible for returning to the calling program after it has finished processing.

(2) In communications, the action taken by the transmitting station to establish a connection with the receiving station in a dial-up network.

call by reference In programming, a call to a subroutine that passes addresses of the parameters used in the subroutine.

call by value In programming, a call to a subroutine that passes the actual data of the parameters used in the subroutine.

call control Also called *call processing*, it is the controlling of telephone and PBX functions. It includes connecting, disconnecting and transferring the call, but it does not affect the content of the call. Contrast with *media control*.

call distributor A PBX feature that routes incoming calls to the next available agent or operator.

called routine In programming, a program subroutine that performs a task and is accessed by a call or branch instruction in the program.

calling program In programming, a program that initiates a call to another program.

calling routine In programming, a program subroutine that initiates a call to another program routine.

CALS (Computer-Aided Acquisition and Logistics Support) A DOD initiative for electronically capturing military documentation and linking related information.

CAM (1) (Computer-Aided Manufacturing) The automation of manufacturing systems and techniques, including numerical control, process control, robotics and materials requirements planning (MRP). See *CAD/CAM*.

(2) (Common Access Method) An ANSI standard interface that provides a common language between drivers and SCSI host adapters. It is primarily supported by Future Domain and NCR. See *ASPI*.

candela A unit of measurement of the intensity of light. An ordinary wax candle generates one candela. See *lumen*.

canned program A software package that provides a fixed solution to a problem. Canned business applications should be analyzed carefully as they usually cannot be changed much, if at all.

canned routine A program subroutine that performs a specific processing task.

canonical synthesis The process of designing a model of a database without redundant data items. A canonical model, or schema, is independent of the hardware and software that will process the data.

capacitor An electronic component that holds a charge. It comes in varying sizes for use in power supplies to the tiny cells in dynamic RAM chips.

capstan On magnetic tape drives, a motorized cylinder that traps the tape against a free-wheeling roller and moves it at a regulated speed.

capture buffer A reserved memory area for holding an incoming transmission.

card See *printed circuit board, magnetic stripe, punched card* and *HyperCard*.

card cage A cabinet or metal frame that holds printed circuit cards.

card column A vertical column that is used to represent a single character of data by its pattern of punched holes. The common IBM card contains 80 card columns.

card image The representation of punched cards in which each hole in the card is represented by a bit on tape or disk.

card punch (1) An early peripheral device that punches holes into cards at 100 to 300 cards per minute.

(2) Same as *keypunch machine*.

card reader (1) A peripheral device that reads magnetic stripes on the back of a credit card.

(2) An early peripheral device that reads punched cards at 500 to 2,000 cards/minute. The code is detected by light patterns created by the holes in the card.

card services Software that manages PCMCIA cards. See *PCMCIA*.

cardinal number The number that states how much or how many. In "record 43 has 7 fields," the 7 is cardinal. Contrast with *ordinal number*.

caret An up-arrow (^) symbol used to represent a decimal point or the control key. For example, ^Y means Ctrl-Y. It is Shift-6 on the keyboard.

carpal tunnel syndrome The compression of the main nerve to the hand due to scarring or swelling of the surrounding soft tissue in the wrist (area formed by carpal bones on top and muscle tendons below). Caused by trauma, arthritis and improper positioning of the wrist, it can result in severe damage to the hands. See *RSI* and *Wrist Pro*.

carriage A printer or typewriter mechanism that holds the platen and controls paper feeding and movement.

carriage return See *return key*.

carrier An alternating current that vibrates at a fixed frequency, used to establish a boundary, or envelope, in which a signal is transmitted. Carriers are commonly used in radio transmission (AM, FM, TV, microwave, satellite, etc.) in order to differentiate transmitting stations. For example, an FM station's channel number is actually its carrier frequency. The FM station merges (modulates) its audio broadcast (data signal) onto its carrier and transmits the combined signal over the airwaves. At the receiving end, the FM tuner latches onto the carrier frequency, filters out the audio signal, amplifies it and sends it to the speaker.

Carriers can be used to transmit several signals simultaneously. For example, multiple voice, data and/or video signals can travel over the same line with each residing in its own carrier vibrating at a different frequency.

carrier based A transmission system that generates a fixed frequency (carrier) to contain the data being transmitted.

carrier detect A signal that indicates a connection has been made by sensing a carrier frequency on the line. See *RS-232* and *modem*.

carrier frequency A unique frequency used to "carry" data within its boundaries. It is measured in cycles per second, or Hertz. See *carrier* and *FDM*.

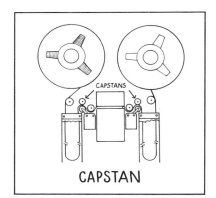

CAPSTAN

cartridge A self-contained, removable storage module that contains disks, magnetic tape or memory chips. Cartridges are inserted into slots in the drive, printer or computer. See *font cartridge*.

CAS (Communications Application Specification) Intel's fax/modem protocol that allows personal computers to exchange data with fax machines. Introduced in 1988, Intel provides both the boards and the chips.

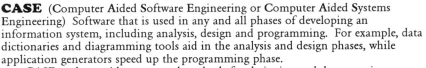

TAPE CARTRIDGE

cascade A connected series of devices or images. For example, cascading tapes in a dual-tape backup system means the second tape is written after the first one is full. In a 286 or higher PC, a second IRQ chip is cascaded to the first, doubling the number of interrupts.

CASE (Computer Aided Software Engineering or Computer Aided Systems Engineering) Software that is used in any and all phases of developing an information system, including analysis, design and programming. For example, data dictionaries and diagramming tools aid in the analysis and design phases, while application generators speed up the programming phase.

CASE tools provide automated methods for designing and documenting traditional structured programming techniques. The ultimate goal of CASE is to provide a language for describing the overall system that is sufficient to generate all the necessary programs.

case-based reasoning An AI problem solving technique that catalogs experience into "cases" and matches the current problem to the experience. Such systems are easier to maintain than rule-based expert systems, because changes require adding new cases without the complexity of adding new rules. It is used in many areas including pattern recognition, diagnosis, troubleshooting and planning.

case sensitive Distinguishing lower case from upper case. In a case sensitive language, "abc" is considered different data than "ABC."

case statement In programming, a variation of the if-then-else statement that is used when several ifs are required in a row. The following C example tests the variable KEY1 and performs functions based on the results.

```
switch (key1)    {
   case '+':  add();  break;
   case '-':  subtract();  break;
   case '*':  multiply();  break;
   case '/':  divide();  break;
      }
```

cash memory See *cache*.

cassette A removable storage module that contains a supply reel of magnetic tape and a takeup reel. Data cassettes look like audio cassettes, but are made to higher tolerances.

casting In programming, the conversion of one data type into another.

cat (conCATenate) A UNIX command that displays the contents of a file.

catalog A directory of disk files or files used in an application. Also any map, list or directory of storage space used by the computer.

Category 3, 5, etc. See *cable categories*.

cathode In electronics, a device that emits electrons, which flow from the negatively charged cathode to the positively charged *anode*.

cathode ray tube See *CRT*.

CATV (Community Antenna TV) The original name for cable TV, which used a single antenna at the highest location in the community. Now refers to cable TV.

TAPE CASSETTE

CAU (Controlled Access Unit) An intelligent hub from IBM for Token Ring networks. Failed nodes are identified by the hub and reported via IBM's LAN Network Manager software.

CAV (Constant Angular Velocity) A disk technique that spins the disk at a constant speed. The number of bits in each track is the same, but their density varies because the inner tracks have smaller circumferences than the outer tracks. Contrast with *CLV*.

CB (Citizen's Band) The frequency band for public radio transmission in the 27 MHz range.

CB simulator See *teleconferencing (3)*.

CBEMA (Computer and Business Equipment Manufacturers Association) A membership organization founded in 1916 composed of over 25 manufacturers and suppliers. It is concerned with the development of standards for data processing and business equipment in the U.S. and abroad. Address: 311 First St., N.W., Washington, DC 20001, 202/737-8888.

CBR (1) (Computer-Based Reference) Reference materials accessible by computer in order to help people do their jobs quicker. For example, this Glossary on disk!

(2) (Constant Bit Rate) A uniform transmission rate. For example, voice traffic requires a CBR.

(3) See *case-based reasoning*.

CBT (Computer-Based Training) Using the computer for training and instruction. CBT programs are called *courseware* and provide interactive training sessions for all disciplines. It uses graphics extensively, as well as CD-ROM and videodisc.
　　CBT courseware is developed with authoring languages, such as Adroit, PILOT and Demo II, which allow for the creation of interactive sessions.

CBX (Computerized Branch eXchange) Same as *PBX*.

CCA (1) (Common Cryptographic Architecture) IBM encryption software for MVS and DOS applications.

(2) (Compatible Communications Architecture) A Network Equipment Technology protocol for transmitting asynchronous data over X.25 networks.

(3) (Communications Control Architecture) The U.S. Navy network that includes an ISDN backbone called BITS (Base Information Transfer System).

CCD (Charge Coupled Device) An electronic memory made of a special type of MOS transistor that can store patterns of charges in a sequential fashion. CCDs are used in TV and scanning devices since they can be charged by light as well as by electricity.

CCFL (Cold Cathode Flurorescent Lamp) Same as *CCFT*.

CCFT (Cold Cathode Fluorescent Tube) A type of light source for a backlit screen. It weighs more and uses more power than other backlights.

CCIA (Computer and Communications Industry Association) A membership organization composed of over 60 hardware and software vendors, service bureaus, leasing and repair companies. It represents their interests in domestic and foreign trade, and, working with the NIST, keeps members advised of regulatory policy. Address: 666 11th St., N.W., Washington, DC 20001, 202/783-0070.

CCIS (Common Channel Interoffice Signaling) A telephone communications technique that transmits voice and control signals over separate channels. Control signals are transmitted over a packet-switched digital network, providing faster connects and disconnects and allowing data, such as calling number, to be included. See *CCS (2)*.

CCITT See *ITU-TSS*.

cc:Mail A widely-used messaging system from Lotus that runs on PC LANs. Originally developed by cc:Mail, Inc., Mountain View, CA, Lotus acquired the company in 1991. Mail-enabled applications that are written to the VIM programming interface can use the cc:Mail system.

CCP (Certificate in Computer Programming) The award for successful completion of an examination in computer programming offered by ICCP.

CCS (1) (Common Communications Support) SAA specifications for communications, which includes data streams (DCA, 3270), application services (DIA, DDM), session services (LU 6.2) and data links (X.25, Token Ring).

(2) (Common Channel Signaling) An integral part of ISDN known as "Signaling System 7," which advances the CCIS method for transmitting control signals. It allows call forwarding, call waiting, etc., to be provided anywhere in the network.

(3) (Common Command Set) The de facto instruction set between a SCSI-1 adapter and a hard disk.

CD (Compact Disc) A digital audio disc that contains up to 72 minutes of hi-fi stereo sound. Introduced in 1982, the disc is a plastic platter 4.75" in diameter, with binary code recorded as microscopic pits on one side. Individual selections are playable in any sequence. Other forms of CDs (CD-ROM, CD-ROM XA, CD-I and DVI) all stem from the audio CD. Also see *carrier detect*.

   For hi-fi sound, sound waves are sampled 44,056 times per second, and each sample is converted into a 16-bit number. It takes approximately 1.5 million bits of storage for one second of stereo.

The Books

Documentation for various CD formats are found in books commonly known by the color of their covers.

Red Book	-	Audio CDs
Yellow Book	-	CD-ROM
Orange Book	-	Write-once (Photo CD, etc.)
Green Book	-	CD-I
White Book	-	Video CD

CD32 A multimedia and video game technology from Commodore that is the successor to CDTV. CD32 is a 32-bit system that also plays Video CDs.

CDA (Compound Document Architecture) A compound document format from Digital that creates hot links between documents.

CD audio Same as *CD* and *DAD*.

CDC See *Control Data*.

CD caddy A plastic container that holds a CD-ROM disc. The caddy is inserted into the disc drive.

CDDI (Copper Distributed Data Interface) A version of FDDI that uses UTP (unshielded twisted pair) wires rather than optical fiber. The term is a trademark of Crescendo Communications, Sunnyvale, CA. ANSI's standard for FDDI over UTP is officially TP-PMD (Twisted Pair-Physical Media Dependent).

CDE (Common Desktop Environment) A graphical user interface for open systems. It is based on Motif with elements from HP, IBM and others. Originally developed by COSE, it is now governed by X/Open.

cdev (Control Panel DEVice) Customizable settings in the Macintosh Control Panel that pertain to a particular program or device. Cdevs for the mouse, keyboard and startup disk, among others, come with the Mac. Others are provided with software packages and utilities.

CDF (Central Distribution Frame) A connecting unit (typically a hub) that acts a central distribution point to all the nodes in a zone or domain. See *MDF*.

CD-I (Compact Disc-Interactive) A compact disc format developed by Philips and Sony that holds data, audio, still video and animated graphics. It provides up to 144 minutes of CD-quality stereo, 9.5 hours of AM-radio-quality stereo or 19 hours of monophonic audio. CD-I discs require a CD-I player and will not play in a CD-ROM player.

CDIF (CASE Data Interchange Format) An EIA standard for exchanging data between CASE tools. See *PCTE*.

CDIP (Sidebrazed Ceramic DIP) A high-qualty ceramic DIP that typically uses gold-plated leads attached by brazing.

CDMA (Code Division Multiple Access) A spread spectrum technique that converts analog signals into digital for transmission over the cellular network. It provides up to 35 times the capacity of the analog network. Qualcomm, Inc., San Diego, CA, has several patents on products using its CDMA implementation. See *FDMA, TDMA* and *CDPD*.

CDP (Certificate in Data Processing) The award for the successful completion of an examination in hardware, software, systems analysis, programming, management and accounting, offered by ICCP.

CDPD (Cellular Digital Packet Data) A type of digital transmission using the cellular network. Based on IBM's CelluPlan II, it moves data at 19.2Kbps over ever-changing unused intervals in the voice channels. It is being implemented by IBM, AT&T (through McCaw Cellular) and most major telephone companies. See *FDMA, TDMA* and *CDMA*.

CD-R (CD-Recordable) A recordable CD-ROM technology using a disc that can be written only once. The CD-R drives that write the CD-R discs are also called one-off machines. CD-R discs are used for beta versions and original masters of CD-ROM material as well as a means to distribute a large amount of data to a small number of recipients.

CDRAM (Cache DRAM) A high-speed DRAM memory chip developed by Mitsubishi that includes a small SRAM cache.

CD recorder See *CD-R*.

CD-ROM (Compact Disc Read Only Memory) A compact disc format used to hold text, graphics and hi-fi stereo sound. It's like an audio CD, but uses a different track format for data. The audio CD player cannot play CD-ROMs, but CD-ROM players usually play audio CDs and have output jacks for a headphone or amplified speakers.

CD-ROMs hold in excess of 600MB of data, which is equivalent to about 250,000 pages of text or 20,000 medium-resolution images.

Earlier CD-ROM drives transfer data at 150KB per second. Double, triple and quad-spin drives provide 2x, 3x and 4x the 150KB transfer rate. Access times run from a slow half second to under 200 milliseconds.

CD-ROM changer A CD-ROM player that houses several CD-ROMs, although only one is playable at one time. CD-ROM changers, also called CD-ROM jukeboxes, come in as many varieties just like audio CD players. They can hold from six to 200 or more discs.

CD-ROM Extensions The software required to use a CD-ROM drive on a PC running DOS. It allows the CD-ROM disc to be addressed like a hard or floppy disk and take on the next available drive letter. For example, the hard disk in the computer is C:, and if there are no additional hard disks, then the CD-ROM becomes the D: drive. The CD-ROM Extensions from Microsoft are provided in a file named MSCDEX.EXE.

CD-ROM jukebox See *CD-ROM changer*.

CD-ROM XA (CD-ROM eXtended Architecture) A CD-ROM enhancement introduced in 1988 by Philips, Sony and Microsoft that lets text and pictures be narrated by allowing concurrent audio and video. CD-ROM XA drives are required for Kodak's Photo CD discs.

CDTV (Commodore Dynamic Total Vision) A multimedia and video game technology from Commodore that has been superseded by the CD32 system. It also plays audio CDs.

CDV (1) (Compressed Digital Video) The compression of full-motion video for high-speed, economical transmission.

(2) (CD Video) A small videodisc (5" diameter) that provides five minutes of video with digital sound plus an additional 20 minutes of audio. Most videodisc players can play CDVs along with LDs.

CEbus (Consumer Electronics **bus**) An EIA standard for a control network.

cell (1) An elementary unit of storage for data (bit) or power (battery).

(2) In a spreadsheet, the intersection of a row and column.

cell relay A transmission technology that uses small fixed-length packets (cells) that can be switched at high speed. It is easier to build a switch that switches fixed-length packets than variable ones. ATM uses a type of cell relay technology.

Cello An Internet utility that lets you browse through the Worldwide Web.

centering cone A short plastic or metal cone used to align a 5.25" floppy disk to the drive spindle. It is inserted into the diskette's center hole when the drive door is closed.

centimeter A unit of measurement that is 1/100th of a meter or approximately 4/10ths of an inch (0.39 inch).

central office The telephone switching facility that interconnects subscribers' telephone lines to each other and to intra and intercity trunk lines.

central processing unit See *CPU*.

central processor Same as *CPU*.

centralized processing Processing performed in one or more computers in a single location. All terminals in the organization are connected to the central computers. Contrast with *distributed processing* and *decentralized processing*.

CENTREX PBX services provided by a local telephone company. Switching is done in the telephone company's central office. Some services do the switching at the customer's site, but control it in the central office.

Centronics A standard 36-pin parallel interface for connecting printers and other devices to a computer. It defines the plug, socket and signals used and transfers data asynchronously up to 200 Kbytes/sec. This de facto standard was developed by Centronics Corporation, maker of the first successful dot matrix printers. See *printer cable*.

CEO (Comprehensive Electronic Office) Office software from Data General introduced in 1981. It includes word processing, e-mail, spreadsheets, business graphics and desktop accessories.

CERDIP (CERamic DIP) A type of DIP that uses two ceramic layers epoxied together.

CGA (Color/Graphics Adapter) An IBM video display standard that provided low-resolution text and graphics. It was the first graphics standard for the IBM PC and has been superseded by EGA and VGA. CGA requires a digital RGB Color Display monitor. See *PC display modes*.

CGI (Computer Graphics Interface) A device independent graphics language for display screens, printers and plotters that stemmed from GKS.

CGM (Computer Graphics Metafile) A standard format for interchanging graphics images. CGM stores images primarily in vector graphics, but also provides a raster format. Earlier GDM and VDM formats have been merged into the CGM standard.

chad A piece of paper that is punched out on a punched card, paper tape or on the borders of continuous forms. A chadded form is when the holes are cut completely through. A chadless form is when the chads are still attached to one edge of the hole.

chain printer A line printer that uses character typefaces linked together in a chain as its printing mechanism. The chain spins horizontally around a set of hammers. When the desired character is in front of the selected print position, the corresponding hammer hits the paper into the ribbon and onto the character in the chain.

chained list A group of items in which

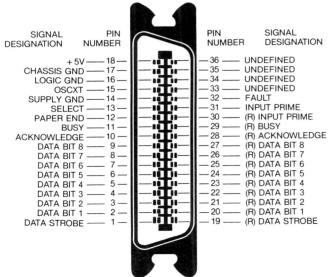

(R) INDICATES SIGNAL GROUND RETURN

SIGNAL DESIGNATION	PIN NUMBER		PIN NUMBER	SIGNAL DESIGNATION
+5V	18		36	UNDEFINED
CHASSIS GND	17		35	UNDEFINED
LOGIC GND	16		34	UNDEFINED
OSCXT	15		33	UNDEFINED
SUPPLY GND	14		32	FAULT
SELECT	13		31	INPUT PRIME
PAPER END	12		30	(R) INPUT PRIME
BUSY	11		29	(R) BUSY
ACKNOWLEDGE	10		28	(R) ACKNOWLEDGE
DATA BIT 8	9		27	(R) DATA BIT 8
DATA BIT 7	8		26	(R) DATA BIT 7
DATA BIT 6	7		25	(R) DATA BIT 6
DATA BIT 5	6		24	(R) DATA BIT 5
DATA BIT 4	5		23	(R) DATA BIT 4
DATA BIT 3	4		22	(R) DATA BIT 3
DATA BIT 2	3		21	(R) DATA BIT 2
DATA BIT 1	2		20	(R) DATA BIT 1
DATA STROBE	1		19	(R) DATA STROBE

CENTRONICS PARALLEL INTERFACE
(Courtesy Black Box Corporation)

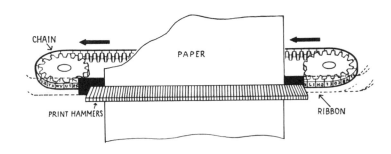

each item contains the location of the next item in sequence.

chaining Linking items or records to form a chain. Each link in the chain points to the next item.

change file A transaction file used to update a master file.

change management See *version control*.

channel (1) A high-speed metal or optical fiber pathway between the computer and the control units of the peripheral devices. Channels are used in mainframes and high-end machines. Each channel is an independent unit that can transfer data concurrently with other channels as well as the CPU. For example, in a 10-channel computer, 10 streams of data are being transmitted to and from the CPU at the same time. In contrast, the bus in a personal computer serves as a common, shared channel between all devices. Each device must wait for its turn on the bus.

(2) In communications, any pathway between two computers or terminals. It may refer to the physical medium, such as coaxial cable, or to a specific carrier frequency (subchannel) within a larger channel or wireless medium.

channel bank A multiplexor that merges several low-speed voice or data lines into one high-speed (typically T1) line and vice versa.

channel program Instructions executed by a peripheral channel. The channel executes the channel program independently of the CPU, allowing concurrent operations to take place in the computer.

chaos The science that deals with the underlying order of the seemingly random nature of the universe. See *fractals*.

character A single alphabetic letter, numeric digit, or special symbol such as a decimal point or comma. A character is equivalent to a byte; for example, 50,000 characters take up 50,000 bytes.

character based Same as *text based*.

character cell A matrix of dots used to form a single character on a display screen or printer. For example, an 8x16 cell is made up of 16 rows each containing eight dots. Character cells are displayed and printed contiguously; therefore the design of each letter, digit or symbol within the cell must include surrounding blank space.

character code Same as *data code*.

character data Alphanumeric data or text. Contrast with *numeric data*.

character device A peripheral device that transfers data one byte at a time at a time, such as a parallel or serial port. Contrast with *block device*.

character field A data field that holds alphanumeric characters. Contrast with *numeric field*.

character generator (1) Circuitry that converts data characters into dot patterns for a display screen.

(2) A device that creates text characters that are superimposed onto video frames.

character graphics A set of special symbols strung together like letters of the alphabet to create elementary graphics and forms, as in the following example:

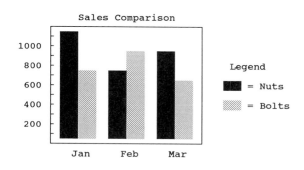

CHARACTER GRAPHICS

Character Map A Windows utility that displays all the characters in a particular font.

character mode Same as *text mode*.

character-oriented protocol See *byte-oriented protocol*.

character pitch The measurement of the number of characters per inch. See *cpi*.

character printer A printer that prints one character at a time, such as a daisy wheel or dot matrix printer. See *printer*.

character recognition The ability of a machine to recognize printed text. See *OCR* and *MICR*.

CHARACTER PRINTER

character set (1) A group of unique symbols and codes. For example, the ASCII character set contains 128 characters numbered 0 to 127. The English character set is 26 symbols (A-Z).

(2) See *symbol set*.

character string A group of alphanumeric characters. Contrast with *numeric data*.

character terminal A display screen without graphics capability.

characteristic In logarithms and floating point, the number that indicates where the decimal point is placed.

chat mode A communications option that lets users type messages back and forth to each other. Each keystroke is transmitted as it is pressed.

check bits A calculated number used for error checking. The number is derived by some formula from the binary value of one or more bytes of data. See *parity checking, checksum* and *CRC*.

check box A small box that displays an X or checkmark when the associated option is selected.

check digit A numeric digit used to ensure that account numbers are correctly entered into the computer. Using a formula, a check digit is calculated for each new account number, which then becomes part of the number, often the last digit.

When an account number is entered, the data entry program recalculates the check digit and compares it to the check digit entered. If the digits are not equal, the account number is considered invalid.

check sum See *checksum*.

checkpoint/restart A method of recovering from a system failure. A checkpoint is a copy of the computer's memory that is periodically saved on disk along with the current register settings (last instruction executed, etc.). In the event of any failure, the last checkpoint serves as a recovery point.

When the problem has been fixed, the restart program copies the last checkpoint into memory, resets all the hardware registers and starts the computer from that point. Any transactions in memory after the last checkpoint was taken until the failure occurred will be lost.

checksum A value used to ensure data is transmitted without error. It is created by adding the binary value of each alphanumeric character in a block of data and sending it with the data. At the receiving end, a new checksum is computed and matched against the transmitted checksum. A non-match indicates an error.

Just as a check digit tests the accuracy of a single number, a checksum tests a block of data. Checksums detect single bit errors and some multiple bit errors, but are not as effective as the CRC method.

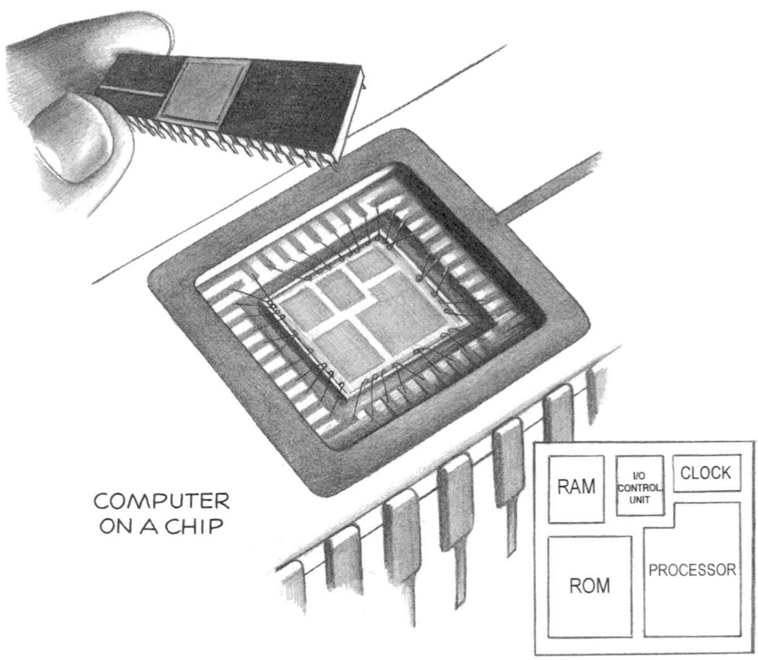

Chicago See *Windows 95.*

chicklet keyboard A keyboard with small, square keys not suitable for touch typing.

child In database management, the data that is dependent on its parent. See *parent-child.*

COMPUTER ON A CHIP

child program A secondary or subprogram called for and loaded into memory by the main program. See *parent program.*

chip An integrated circuit. Chips are squares or rectangles that measure approximately from 1/16th to 5/8th of an inch on a side. They are about 1/30th of an inch thick, although only the top 1/1000th of an inch holds the actual circuits. Chips contain from a few dozen to several million electronic components (transistors, resistors, etc.). The terms *chip, integrated circuit* and *microelectronic* are synonymous. Following are the major types of chips.

LOGIC CHIPS are single chips that perform some or all of the functions of a processor. A microprocessor is an entire processor on a single chip. Desktop and portable computers use one microprocessor for their CPU while larger computers may employ several types of microprocessors as well as hundreds or thousands of specialized logic chips.

MEMORY CHIPS are RAM chips that contains from a couple of hundred thousand to several million storage cells (bits). They are the computer's working storage and require constant power to keep their bits charged. Firmware chips, such as ROMs, PROMs, EPROMs, and EEPROMs are permanent memory chips that hold their content without power.

COMPUTERS ON A CHIP are single chips that holds the processor, RAM, ROM, I/O control unit, and a timing clock. It is used in myriads of consumer and industrial products.

A/D & D/A CONVERTERS are single chips that perform the conversion between analog and digital signals. A programmable CPU called a *DSP* (digital signal processor) is also used in many analog/digital conversions. It contains fast instructions sequences commonly used in such applications.

SPECIAL PURPOSE CHIPS made for watches, calculators and video games as well as higher-cost products, such as automobile control, may be designed from scratch to obtain economical and effective performance. Today's ASIC chips can be quickly created for any specific purpose.

LOGIC ARRAYS & GATE ARRAYS are chips that contain logic gates which have not been tied together. A final set of steps applies the top metal layer onto the chip stringing the logic gates together into the pattern required by the customer. This method eliminates much of the design and fabrication time for producing a chip.

BIT SLICE PROCESSORS are chips that contain elementary electronic circuits that serve as building blocks for the computer architect. They are used to custom-build a processor for specialized purposes.

▶ *The electronic and encyclopedic versions of this book provide details on the evolution and fabrication of the chip.*

chip carrier (1) The package that a chip is mounted in.

(2) A chip package with connectors on all sides. See *leaded chip carrier* and *leadless chip carrier*.

chipset A group of chips designed to work as a unit to perform a function. For example, a modem chipset contains all the primary circuits for transmitting and receiving. A PC chipset contains the system, memory and bus controllers. Combine the chipset on the motherboard with the clock, CPU and memory, and you have a complete computer. Today, an entire PC chipset can be made to fit on a single chip.

Chkdsk A DOS external command that reports free memory and disk space.

CHMOS (High-density CMOS) A chip with a high density of CMOS transistors.

Chooser A Macintosh desk accessory that allows the user to select a printer, file server or network device, such as a network modem.

chroma key See *color key*.

chromatic dispersion The spreading of light rays within an optical fiber, which causes decreased bandwidth.

CICS (Customer Information Control System) A TP monitor from IBM that provides transaction processing for IBM mainframes. It controls the interaction between applications and users and lets programmers develop screen displays without detailed knowledge of the terminals used. It provides terminal routing, password security, transaction logging for error recovery and activity journals for performance analysis.

CICS commands are written into assembly language, COBOL, PL/I and RPG programs. It implements SNA layers 4, 5 and 6.

CIF (Common Intermediate Format) A video format that transmits 36.45 Mbits/sec at 30 frames/sec. See *QCIF* and *H.261*.

CIM (1) (Computer-Integrated Manufacturing) Integrating office/accounting functions with automated factory systems. Point of sale, billing, machine tool scheduling and supply ordering are part of CIM.

(2) (CompuServe Information Manager) See *CompuServe*.

cine-oriented A film-image orientation like that of movie film, which runs parallel to the outer edge of the medium. Contrast with *comic-strip oriented*.

CIO (Chief Information Officer) The executive officer in charge of all information processing in an organization.

ciphertext Data that has been coded (enciphered, encrypted, encoded) for security purposes.

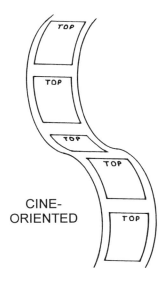

CINE-
ORIENTED

CIR (Committed Information Rate) In a frame relay network, the minimum speed maintained between nodes.

circuit (1) A set of electronic components that perform a particular function in an electronic system.

(2) Same as *communications channel*.

circuit analyzer (1) A device that tests the validity of an electronic circuit.

(2) In communications, same as *data line monitor*.

circuit board Same as *printed circuit board*.

circuit breaker A protective device that opens a circuit upon sensing a current overload. Unlike a fuse, it can be reset.

circuit card Same as *printed circuit board*.

circuit cellular The transmission of data over the cellular network using a voice channel and modem similar to using land-based modems. Contrast with *packet cellular*. See *wireless*.

circuit switching The temporary connection of two or more communications channels. Users have full use of the circuit until the connection is terminated. Contrast with *message switching*, which stores messages and forwards them later, and contrast with *packet switching*, which breaks up a message into packets and routes each packet through the most expedient path at that moment.

Circuit switching is used by the telephone company for its voice networks in order to guarantee steady, consistent service for two people engaged in a telephone conversation.

CIS (1) (CompuServe Information Service) See *CompuServe*.

(2) (Card Information Structure) A data structure on a PCMCIA card that contains information about the card's contents. It allows the card to describe its configuration requirements to its host computer.

CIS B (CompuServe Information Service B) A proprietary communications protocol from CompuServe that is used for transferring files. See *B protocol*.

CISC (Complex Instruction Set Computer) Pronounced "sisk." The traditional architecture of a computer which uses microcode to execute very comprehensive instructions. Instructions may be variable in length and use all addressing modes, requiring complex circuitry to decode them. Contrast with *RISC*.

CL/1 (Connectivity Language/1) A database language from Apple that lets a Macintosh access an SQL-based database in another computer. CL/1 applications communicate with the CL/1 client program in the Mac, and the client program communicates with the CL/1 server program in the host computer.

cladding The plastic or glass sheath that is fused to and surrounds the core of an optical fiber. It keeps the light waves inside the core and adds strength to it. The cladding is covered with a protective outer jacket.

clamping ring The part of a 5.25" floppy disk drive that presses the disk onto the spindle. It is usually part of the centering cone.

Claris (Claris Corporation, Santa Clara, CA) Software subsidiary of Apple that was separated from the corporation (although mostly owned by it) in 1988 and then bought back in 1990.

Claris CAD A full-featured 2-D CAD program for the Macintosh from Claris Corporation that is noted for its ease of use. It provides an easy-to-learn path into CAD, while offering most features found in CAD programs.

class In object-oriented programming, a user-defined data type that defines a collection of objects that share the same characteristics. A class member (object) is an "instance" of the class. Concrete classes are designed to be "instantiated." Abstract classes are designed to pass on characteristics through inheritance.

Class A, B See *FCC Class*.

class library An object-oriented programming classes suplied by third parties; for example, a GUI library.

Classic The name later given to the original Macintosh model that was housed in a high-rise cabinet.

CLCC (Ceramic Leaded Chip Carrier) See *leaded chip carrier*.

clean boot Booting the computer without loading anything but the main part of the operating system.

clean room A room in which the air is highly filtered in order to keep out impurities. See *bunny suit*.

clear memory To reset all RAM and hardware registers to a zero or blank condition. Rebooting the computer may or may not clear memory, but turning the computer off and on again guarantees that memory is cleared.

click To select an object by pressing the mouse button when the cursor is pointing to the required menu option or icon.

client (1) A workstation or personal computer in a client/server environment. See *client/server*.

(2) One end of the spectrum in a request/supply relationship between programs. See *X Window*.

client application An application running in a workstation or personal computer on a network.

client-client-server An Apple architecture that allows users with remote devices, such as laptops and PDAs, to have easy access to their desktop machines (clients) as well as to the servers.

client/server architecture An architecture in which the client (personal computer or workstation) is the requesting machine and the server is the supplying machine. Servers can be high-speed microcomputers, minicomputers or even mainframes. The client provides the user interface and performs some or all of the application processing. The server maintains the databases and processes requests from the client to extract data from or update the database.

   Client/server architecture is not using a file server as a remote disk drive to hold programs and databases. It implies that processing is done in the server. For example, in a database query, the server performs the search and returns the results to the requesting client machine. If the server were only storing the database, all the records in the database file would have to be transmitted over the network to the client machine doing the search.
▶ *The electronic and encyclopedic versions of this book provide more detail on this subject.*

client/server network A communications network that uses dedicated servers for all clients in the network. Contrast to *peer-to-peer network*, which allows any client to also be a server.

client/server protocol A communications protocol that provides a structure for requests between client and server in a network. It refers to OSI layer 7.

clip art A set of canned images used to illustrate word processing and desktop publishing documents.

clipboard Reserved memory used to hold data that has been copied from one application in order to be inserted into another.

Clipper (1) See *CA-Clipper*.

(2) A family of 32-bit RISC microprocessors from Intergraph Corporation, Huntsville, AL.

(3) An encryption chip endorsed by the U.S. government for general use that would let authorities unscramble the data if needed.

clipping Cutting off the outer edges or boundaries of a word, signal or image. See *scissoring*.

clipping level A disk's ability to maintain its magnetic properties and hold its content. A high-quality level range is 65-70%; low quality is below 55%.

clock An internal timing device. Following are the different varieties.
CPU CLOCKS use a quartz crystal to generate a uniform electrical frequency from which digital pulses are created and used. See *clock speed*.
REALTIME CLOCKS are time-of-day clocks that keeps track of hours, minutes and seconds and makes this data available to the programs.
TIMESHARING CLOCKS are timers set to interrupt the CPU at regular intervals in order to provide equal time to all the users of the computer.
COMMUNICATION CLOCKS are synchronous communications devices that maintain uniform transmission of data between the sending and receiving terminals and computers.

clock/calendar An internal time clock and month/year calendar that is kept active with a battery. Its output allows software to remind users of appointments, to determine the age of a transaction and to activate tasks at specified times.

clock doubling Doubling the internal processing speed of a CPU while maintaining the original clock speed for I/O (transfers in/out of the chip). Intel popularized the technique with its Speed Doubler chips. See *486* and *clock tripling*.

clock pulse A signal used to synchronize the operations of an electronic system. Clock pulses are continuous, precisely spaced changes in voltage. See *clock speed*.

clock speed The internal heartbeat of a computer. The clock circuit uses fixed vibrations generated from a quartz crystal to deliver a steady stream of pulses to the CPU.
A faster clock will speed up internal processing provided the computer's circuits can handle the increased speed. For example, the same processor running at 20MHz is twice as fast internally as one running at 10MHz.

clock tripling Tripling the internal processing speed of a CPU while maintaining the original clock speed for I/O (transfers in/out of the chip). See *DX4*.

clone A device that works like the original, but does not necessarily look like it. It implies 100% functional compatibility.

closed With regard to a switch, closed is "on." Open is "off."

closed architecture A system whose technical specifications are not made public. Contrast with *open architecture*.

closed shop An environment in which only data processing staff is allowed access to the computer. Contrast with *open shop*.

closed system A system in which specficiations are kept proprietary to prevent third-party hardware or software from being used. Contrast with *open system*.

cluster Some number of disk sectors (typically two to 16) treated as a unit. The entire disk is divided into clusters, each one a minimum unit of storage. Thus, a 30-byte file may use up 2,048 bytes on disk if the disk cluster is four 512-byte sectors. See *lost cluster*.

cluster controller A control unit that manages several peripheral devices, such as terminals or disk drives.

CLUT (Color Look Up Table) A hardware or software table that contains color mixing information (intensity of red, green and blue) for each color in a palette or series of palettes.

CLV (Constant Linear Velocity) A disk technique that spins a disk at different speeds. By varying the speed depending on which track is being accessed, the physical density of bits in each track can be the same, thus allowing the outer tracks to hold more data than the inner tracks.

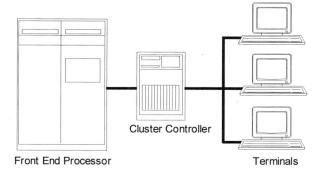

Front End Processor   Cluster Controller   Terminals

CLUSTER CONTROLLER

CLV mechanisms are used in CD-ROM players in order to store larger amounts of data. Contrast with *CAV*. See *ZBR*.

CM/2 (Communications Manager/2) A communications program for OS/2 from IBM that provides cross platform connectivity. It provides terminal emulation to IBM mainframes, AS/400s and VAXes and supports APPN and APPC protocols.

CMC (Common Messaging Calls) A programming interface specified by the XAPIA as the standard messaging API for X.400 and other messaging systems. CMC is intended to provide a common API for applications that want to become mail enabled.

CMI (Computer-Managed Instruction) Using computers to organize and manage an instructional program for students. It helps create test materials, tracks the results and monitors student progress.

CMIP (Common Management Information Protocol) Pronounced "C-mip." A network monitoring and control standard from ISO. CMOT (CMIP over TCP) is a version that runs on TCP/IP networks, and CMOL (CMIP over LLC) runs on IEEE 802 LANs (Ethernet, Token Ring, etc.).

CMIS (Common Management Information Services) Pronounced "C-miss." An OSI standard that defines the functions for network monitoring and control.

CMOL See *CMIP*.

CMOS (Complementary MOS) Pronounced "C moss." A type of integrated circuit widely used for processors and memories. It uses PMOS and NMOS transistors in a complementary fashion that results in less power to operate. The term is used loosely to refer to the CMOS RAM in a PC.

CMOS RAM (1) A small, battery-backed memory bank in a personal computer that is used to hold time, date and system information such as drive types. In a PC, if disk drives are added, removed or changed, the CMOS memory must be updated in order for the operating system to recognize the new devices. Pressing a certain key at boot time, often the DEL key, accesses the CMOS configuration program to allow for editing the data.

(2) Memory made of CMOS chips. Due to their low power requirement, they are increasingly being used for main memory in portable computers.

CMOT See *CMIP*.

CMS (1) (Conversational Monitor System) Software that provides interactive communications for IBM's VM operating system. It allows a user or programmer to launch an application from a terminal and interactively work with it. The CMS counterpart in MVS is called TSO. Contrast with *RSCS*, which provides batch communications for VM.

(2) (Call Management System) An AT&T call accounting package for its PBXs.

CMYK (Cyan Magenta Yellow blacK) A color model used for printing. In theory, cyan, magenta and yellow (CMY) can print all colors, but inks are not pure and black comes out muddy. Black ink is required for quality printing. See *colors* and *RGB*.

CNC (Computerized Numerical Control) See *numerical control*.

CO (Central Office) A local telephone company switching station that covers a geographic area such as a town or part of a city.

coaxial cable A high-capacity cable used in communications and video, commonly called co-ax. It contains an insulated solid or stranded wire surrounded by a solid or braided metallic shield, wrapped in a plastic cover. Fire-safe teflon coating is optional.

Although similar in appearance, there are several types of coaxial cable, each designed with a different width and impedance for a particular purpose (TV, baseband, broadband). Coax provides a higher bandwidth than twisted wire pair. See *cable categories*.

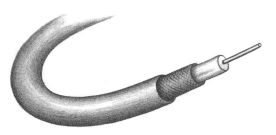

COAXIAL CABLE

COBOL (COmmon Business Oriented Language) A high-level programming language that has been the primary business application language on mainframes and minis. It is a compiled language and was one of the first high-level languages developed. Formally adopted in 1960, it stemmed from a language called Flowmatic in the mid 1950s. COBOL is a very wordy language.

Although mathematical expressions can also be written like other programming languages (see example below), its verbose mode is very readable for a novice. For example, `multiply hourly-rate by hours-worked giving gross-pay` is self-explanatory.

COBOL is structured into Identification, Environment, Data and Procedure divisions as in the following example, which converts Fahrenheit to Celsius. To keep the syntax simple, this program performs the operation on the operator's terminal rather than a user terminal.

```
IDENTIFICATION DIVISION.
PROGRAM-ID.  EXAMPLE.

ENVIRONMENT DIVISION.
CONFIGURATION SECTION.
SOURCE-COMPUTER.    IBM-370.
OBJECT-COMPUTER.    IBM-370.

DATA DIVISION.
WORKING-STORAGE SECTION.
77 FAHR   PICTURE 999.
77 CENT   PICTURE 999.

PROCEDURE DIVISION.
DISPLAY 'Enter Fahrenheit ' UPON CONSOLE.
ACCEPT FAHR FROM CONSOLE.
COMPUTE CENT = (FAHR- 32) * 5 / 9.
DISPLAY 'Celsius is ' CENT UPON CONSOLE.
GOBACK.
```

CODASYL (COnference on DAta SYstems Languages) An organization devoted to the development of computer languages. Founded in 1959, it is made up of individuals and institutions that contribute their own time and effort. COBOL is a product of CODASYL. For information, contact Jan Prokop, 29 Hartwell Avenue, Lexington, MA 02173, 617/863-5100.

code (1) A set of machine symbols that represents data or instructions. See *data code* and *machine language*.

(2) Any representation of one set of data for another. For example, a parts code is an abbreviated name of a product, product type or category. A discount code is a percentage.

(3) To write a program. See *source code* and *line of code*.

(4) To encode for security purposes. See *encryption*.

code generator See *application generator* and *macro recorder*.

code page In DOS 3.3 and higher, a table that sets up the keyboard and display characters for various foreign languages.

codec (1) (COder-DECoder) An electronic circuit that converts audio or video into digital code (and vice versa) using techniques such as pulse code modulation and delta modulation. A codec is an A/D and D/A converter.

(2) (COmpression/DECompression) A hardware circuit or software routine (software codec) used to compress and decompress digitized audio, video or images. A single codec may include the functions of A/D and D/A conversion as well as compression and decompression.

coder (1) A junior, or trainee, programmer who writes simple programs or writes the code for a larger program that has been designed by someone else.

(2) Person who assigns special codes to data.

COGO (COordinate GeOmetry) A programming language used for solving civil engineering problems.

COLD (Computer Output to LaserDisk) Replacing paper output with optical media. Instead of printing large paper reports, printed output is stored on optical disks and extracted online by users as necessary.

cold boot Starting the computer by turning power on. Turning power off and then back on again clears memory and many internal settings. Some program failures will lock up the computer and require a cold boot to use the computer again. In other cases, only a warm boot is required. See *boot*, *warm boot* and *clean boot*.

cold start Same as *cold boot*.

collapsed backbone A network configuration in which a high-speed bus within a single equipment cabinet is used as the backbone.

collating sequence The sequence, or order, of the character set built into a computer. See *ASCII chart*.

collator (1) A punched card machine that merges two decks of cards into one or more stacks.

(2) A utility program that merges records from two or more files into one file.

collector The output side of a bipolar transistor. Same as *drain* in a MOS transistor.

collision detection See *CSMA/CD*.

color bits The number of bits associated with each pixel that represent its color. For 16 colors, four bits are used; for 256 colors, eight bits. See *bit depth*.

color cycling In computer graphics, a technique that simulates animation by continuously changing colors rather than moving the objects. Also called *color lookup table animation.*

color depth See *bit depth.*

color graphics The ability to display graphic images in colors.

color key A technique for superimposing a video image onto another. For example, to float a car on the ocean, the car image is placed onto a blue background. The car and ocean images are scanned together. The ocean is made to appear in the resulting image wherever background (blue) exists in the car image. The ocean is cancelled wherever the car appears (no background).

color map See *CLUT.*

color model The method used to represent color for display and printing. See *RGB, CMYK, HSV, HLS* and *YIQ.*

color monitor A monitor that displays colors.

color printer A printer that prints in color using dot matrix, electrophotographic, Cycolor, electrostatic, ink jet or thermal-transfer techniques.

color separation Separating a picture by colors in order to make negatives and plates for color printing. Full color requires four separations: cyan, magenta, yellow and black (CMYK).

column A vertical set of data or components. Contrast with *row.*

column move Relocating a rectangular block of characters within a text document or a column in a spreadsheet.

COM (Computer Output Microfilm) Creating microfilm or microfiche from computer output. A COM machine can be online or stand-alone (transfer via tape/disk). It receives print-image output from the computer and creates a film image of each page. Additional graphics (lines, logos, etc.) may be added.

COM file (1) (COMmand file) An executable DOS or OS/2 program that takes up less than 64K and fits within one segment. It is an exact replica of how it looks in memory. See *EXE file.*

(2) A VMS file containing commands to be executed.

COM port A serial communications port on a PC. See *COM1* and *serial port.*

COM1 The logical name assigned to serial port #1 in DOS and OS/2. COM ports are usually connected to a modem or mouse and sometimes to a printer. DOS versions up to 3.2 support COM1 and COM2. Version 3.3 supports up to COM4, and OS/2 supports eight COM ports. Contrast with *LPT1.*

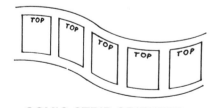

comic-strip oriented A film-image orientation like a comic strip, which runs perpendicular to the outer edge of the film. Contrast with *cine-oriented.*

COMIC-STRIP ORIENTED

comm port May refer to any serial communications port or specifically to the serial ports on a PC. See *COM1.*

comma delimited A record layout that separates data fields with a comma and usually surrounds character data with quotes, for example:

```
"Pat Smith","5 Main St.","New Hope","PA","18938"
"K. Jones","34 E. 88 Ave.","Syosset","NY","11797"
```

command Instruction for the computer. See *command-driven, menu-driven* and *function*.

COMMAND.COM The command processor for DOS and OS/2. COMMAND.COM displays the DOS prompt and executes the internal DOS commands such as Dir and Copy.

command-driven A program that accepts commands as typed-in phrases. It is usually harder to learn, but may offer more flexibility than a menu-driven program. Once learned, command-driven programs may be faster to use, because the user can state a request succinctly. Contrast with *menu-driven*.

command interpreter Same as *command processor*.

Command key On Apple keyboards, a key with the outline of an Apple, a propeller, or both. It is pressed along with another key to command the computer.

command language A special-purpose language that accepts a limited number of commands, such as a query language, job control language (JCL) or command processor. Contrast with *programming language*, which is a general purpose language.

command line In a command-driven system, the area on screen that accepts typed-in commands.

command mode An operating mode that causes the computer or modem to accept commands for execution.

command processor A system program that accepts a limited number of user commands and converts them into the machine commands required by the operating system or some other control program or application. COMMAND.COM is the command processor that accompanies DOS. See *4DOS*.

command queuing The ability to store multiple commands and execute them one at a time.

command set Same as *instruction set*.

command shell Same as *command processor*.

comment A descriptive statement in a source language program that is used for documentation.

comment out To disable lines of code in a program by surrounding them with comment-start and comment-stop characters.

commercial software Software that is designed and developed for sale to the general public.

Commodore (Commodore Business Machines, Inc., West Chester, PA) After introducing the PET in 1977, one of the first personal computers, it launched its successful line of Commodore 64 and 128 home computers. Its Amiga series introduced in 1985 became very popular for imaging and video production.

COMMODORE 128

common carrier A government-regulated organization that provides telecommunications services for public use, such as AT&T, the telephone companies, ITT, MCI and Western Union.

Common OS API A specification for a standard UNIX programming interface (API) which was defined in 1993 by all major UNIX vendors, including Sun, HP,

IBM, DEC, Novell and SCO. It led to Spec 1170, which is governed by the X/Open consortium.

communications The electronic transfer of information from one location to another. *Data communications* refers to digital transmission, and *telecommunications* refers to analog and digital transmission, including voice and video. See *communications protocol* and *OSI*.

▶ *The electronic and encyclopedic versions of this book provide more detail on this subject.*

communications channel Also called a *circuit* or *line*, it is a pathway over which data is transferred between remote devices. It may refer to the entire physical medium, such as a telephone line, optical fiber, coaxial cable or twisted wire pair, or, it may refer to one of several carrier frequencies transmitted simultaneously within the line as in broadband transmission (see *broadband*).

communications controller A peripheral control unit that connects several communications lines to a computer and performs the actual transmitting and receiving as well as various message coding and decoding activities.

Communications controllers are typically nonprogrammable units designed for specific protocols and communications tasks. Contrast with *front end processor*, which can be programmed for a variety of protocols and network conditions.

communications network The transmission channels interconnecting all client and server stations as well as all supporting hardware and software.

communications parameters The basic settings for modem transmission, which include bit rate (2400 bps, 9600 bps, etc.), parity (none, even, odd), number of data bits (7 or 8) and number of stop bits (typically 1). See *N-8-1*.

communications program Software that manages the transmission of data between computers and terminals. In personal computers, it manages transmission to and from the computer's serial port. It includes several communications protocols and can usually emulate dumb terminals for hookup to minis and mainframes.

In a file server, the communications program is called the *network operating system* (NetWare, LANtastic). In mini and mainframe networks, the programs that support communications are called *access methods, network control programs* and *TP monitors*. See *front end processor*.

communications protocol Hardware and software standards that govern transmission between two stations. On personal computers, communications programs offer a variety of protocols (Kermit, Xmodem, Zmodem, etc.) to transfer files via modem.

On LANs, data link protocols such as Ethernet, Token Ring and FDDI provide the access method (OSI layers 1 and 2) that moves packets from station to station, and higher level protocols, such as NetBIOS, IPX and TCP/IP (OSI layers 3, 4 and 5) control and route the transmission.

The following conceptual exchange is at the data link level (Zmodem, Ethernet, etc.), which ensures that a block of data is transferred between two nodes without error.

The Data Link Protocol
Are you there? **Yes, I am.** Are you ready to receive? **Yes, I am.** Here comes the message–bla, bla, bla– did you get it? **Yes, I did.** Here comes the next part–bla, bla, bla– did you get it? **No, I didn't.** Here it comes again– bla, bla, bla– did you get it? **Yes, I did.** There is no more. Goodbye. **Goodbye.**

communications satellite A radio relay station in orbit 22,300 miles above the equator. It travels at the same rate of speed as the earth (geosynchronous), so that it appears stationary. It contains many communications channels that receive analog and digital signals from earth stations. All signals are transmitted within a carrier frequency.

communications server A computer in a LAN that manages access to external networks. It controls a pool of modems allowing remote users access to the network or allowing network users access to outside lines. Sometimes gateways are called communications servers.

compact disc See *CD*.

compandor (COMpressor/exPANDOR) A device that improves the signal for AM radio transmission. On outgoing transmission, it raises the amplitude of weak signals and lowers the amplitude of strong signals. On incoming transmission, it restores the signal to its original form.

Compaq (Compaq Computer Corporation, Houston, TX) A leading PC manufacturer founded in 1982 by Rod Canion, Bill Murto and Jim Harris. In 1983, it shipped 53,000 PC-compatible COMPAQ Portables, which resulted in $111 million in revenues and an American business record. Compaq has been well respected for its computer products.

comparator A device that compares two quantities and determines their equality.

compare A fundamental computer capability. By comparing one set of data with another, the computer can locate, analyze, select, reorder and make decisions. After comparing, the computer can indicate whether the data were equal or which set was numerically greater or less than the other.

compatibility See *standards & compatibility*.

compatibility mode A feature of a computer or operating system that allows it to run programs written for a different system. Programs often run slower in compatiblity mode.

compilation Compiling a program. See *compiler*.

compile time The time it takes to translate a program from source language into machine language. Link editing time may also be included in compile time.

compiler (1) Software that translates a high-level programming language (COBOL, C, etc.) into machine language. A compiler usually generates assembly language first and then translates the assembly language into machine language.

The following example compiles program statements into machine language:

Source code	Assembly Language	Machine language
IF COUNT=10	Compare A to B	Compare 3477 2883
GOTO DONE	If equal go to C	If = go to 23883
ELSE	Go to D	Go to 23343
GOTO AGAIN		
ENDIF		

Actual machine language binary code
1001010100101000101010010010101
1010101001010100100101010100101010
1010010101000101001001010000010110

(2) Software that converts a high-level language into a lower-level representation. For example, a help compiler converts a text document embedded with appropriate commands into an online help system. A dictionary compiler converts terms and definitions into a dictionary lookup system.

compiler language See *high-level language* and *compiler*.

complement The number derived by subtracting a number from a base number. For example, the tens complement of 8 is 2. In set theory, complement refers to all the objects in one set that are not in another set. Complements are used in digital circuits, because it's faster to subtract by adding complements than by performing true subtraction.

component One element of a larger system. A hardware component can be a device as small as a transistor or as large as a disk drive as long as it is part of a larger system. Software components are routines or modules within a larger system.

composite video The video-only (no audio) part of a TV signal. Used on early personal computers for TV hookup, it mixes red, green, blue and sync signals like a standard TV and is not as crisp as separate red, green and blue cables (RGB).

compound document A single document that contains a combination of data structures such as text, graphics, spreadsheets, sound and video clips. OLE and OpenDoc are examples of compound document architectures for the desktop. They allow the user to edit each of the data objects by automatically calling in the application that created them.

compress To compact data to save space. See *data compression*.

compression See *data compression*.

compression ratio The measurement of compressed data. For example, a file compressed into 1/4th of its original size can be expressed as 4:1, 25%, 75% or 2 bits per byte.

compressor (1) A device that diminishes the range between the strongest and weakest transmission signals. See *compandor*.

(2) A routine or program that compresses data. See *data compression*.

CompuServe An online information service that provides conferencing, news, e-mail and access to a huge number of technical support forums, software files and databases. The CompuServe Information Manager (CIM) software makes it easier to navigate through the system. See *online services*.

compute To perform mathematical operations or general computer processing.

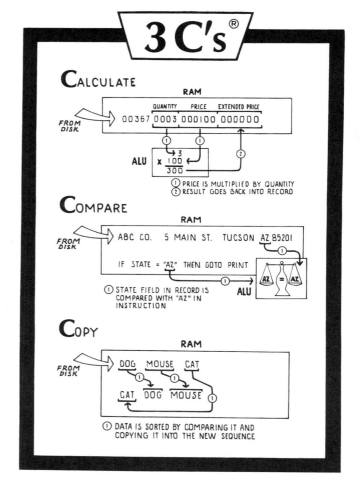

compute bound Same as *process bound*.

computer A general-purpose machine that processes data according to a set of instructions that are stored internally either temporarily or permanently. The computer and all equipment attached to it are called *hardware*. The instructions that tell it what to do are called *software*. A set of instructions that perform a particular task is called a *program*, or *software program*.

A computer processes data by retrieving it from the keyboard, disk or communications channel into memory (RAM) and calculating, comparing and copying it. It then outputs the results to the screen, saves them on disk or perhaps transmits them back over a communcations channel.

▶ *The electronic and encyclopedic versions of this book provide more detail on The 3 C's.*

computer architecture The design of a computer system. It sets the standard for all devices that connect to it and all the software that runs on it. It is based on the type of programs that will run (business, scientific) and the number of them run concurrently. It includes such components and features as the instruction set, internal bus, caching, RISC vs CISC, memory and storage capacities, virtual memory and fault tolerance.

Computer Associates See *CA*.

computer cracker A person who gains illegal entrance into a computer system.

computer designer A person who designs the electronic structure of a computer.

computer exchange A commodity exchange through which the public can buy and sell used computers. After a match, the buyer sends a check to the exchange and the seller sends the equipment to the buyer. If the buyer accepts it, the money is sent to the seller less commission. Commissions usually range from 10 to 20%.

> **American Computer Exchange (AmCoEx)**
> 800/786-0717   FAX 404/250-1399
>
> **Boston Computer Exchange (BoCoEx)**
> 617/542-4414   FAX 617/542-8849
>
> **National Computer Exchange (NaComEx)**
> 212/614-0700   FAX 212/777-1290
>
> **The Newman Group**
> 313/426-3200   FAX 313/426-0777

computer graphics See *graphics*.

computer language A programming language, machine language or the language of the computer industry.

computer literacy Understanding computers and related systems. It includes a working vocabulary of computer and information system components, the fundamental principles of computer processing and a perspective for how non-technical people interact with technical people.

computer on a chip A single chip that contains the processor, RAM, ROM, clock and I/O control unit. It is used for myriads of applications from automobiles to toys.

computer power The effective performance of a computer. It can be expressed in MIPS (millions of instructions per second), clock speed (33Mhz, 66MHz) and in word or bus size, (16-bit, 32-bit). However, as with automobile horsepower, valves and cylinders, such specifications are only guidelines. Real power is whether it gets your job done quickly.

A software package is "powerful" if it has a large number of features.

computer readable Same as *machine readable*.

computer science The field of computer hardware and software. It includes systems analysis & design, application and system software design and programming and datacenter operations. For young students, the emphasis in typically on learning a programming language or running a personal computer with little attention to information science, the study of information and its uses.

   If students were introduced to data administration, DBMS concepts and transaction and master files, they would have a better grasp of an organization's typical information requirements.

computer services Data processing (timesharing, batch processing), software development and consulting services. See *service bureau.*

computer system The complete computer made up of the CPU, memory and related electronics (main cabinet), all the peripheral devices connected to it and its operating system. Computer systems fall into ranges called *microcomputers* (personal computers), *minicomputers* and *mainframes*, roughly small, medium and large. See illustration on opposite page.

COMSAT (COMmunications SATellite Corporation) A private communications satellite company created by Congress in 1962 that provides communications capacity to carriers such as AT&T and MCI. In 1965, it launched Early Bird, the first commercial satellite to transmit signals from a geosynchronous orbit.

CON (CONsole) The DOS name for the keyboard and screen.

concatenate To link structures together. Concatenating files appends one file to another. In speech synthesis, units of speech called phonemes (k, sh, ch, etc.) are concatenated to produce meaningful sounds.

concentrator A device that joins several communications channels together. It is similar to a multiplexor except that it does not spread the signals back out again on the other end. The receiving computer performs that function.

concurrency control In a DBMS, managing the simultaneous access to a database. It prevents two users from editing the same record at the same time and is also concerned with serializing transactions for backup and recovery.

concurrent operation See *multitasking, multiprocessing* and *parallel processing.*

concurrent processing See *multiprocessing.*

conditional branch In programming, an instruction that directs the computer to another part of the program based on the results of a compare. In the following (simulated) assembly language example, the second line is the conditional branch.

```
COMPARE FIELDA with FIELDB
GOTO MATCHROUTINE if EQUAL.
```

   High-level language statements, such as IF THEN ELSE and CASE, are used to express the compare and conditional branch.

conditioning Extra cost options in a private telephone line that improve performance by reducing distortion and amplifying weak signals.

conductor A material that can carry electrical current. Contrast with *insulator.*

conferencing Conducting a communications session with three or more users. See *teleconferencing.*

CONFIG.SYS A DOS and OS/2 configuration file. It resides in the root directory and is used to load drivers and change settings at startup. Install programs often modify CONFIG.SYS in order to customize the computer for their particular use.

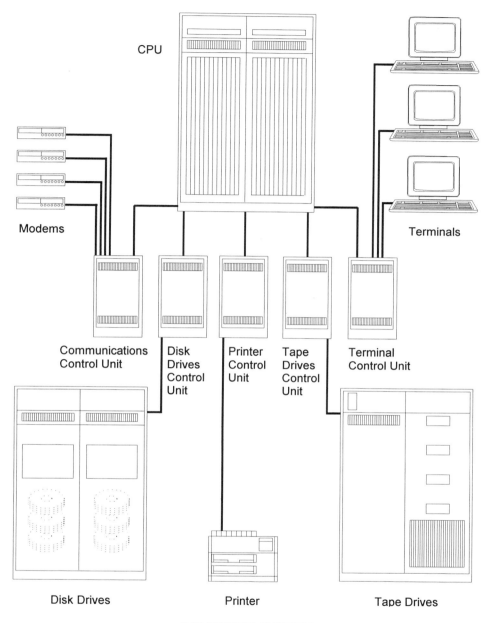

CPU

Modems

Terminals

Communications Control Unit

Disk Drives Control Unit

Printer Control Unit

Tape Drives Control Unit

Terminal Control Unit

Disk Drives

Printer

Tape Drives

COMPUTER SYSTEM

configuration The makeup of a system. To "configure" is to choose options in order to create a custom system. "Configurability" is a system's ability to be changed or customized.

configuration file A file that contains information about a specific user, program, computer or file.

configuration management (1) A system for gathering current configuration information from all nodes in a LAN.

(2) Same as *version control*.

configure See *configuration*.

connect time The amount of time a user at a terminal is logged on to a computer system. See *online services* and *service bureau*.

Connection Machine A family of parallel processing computers from Thinking Machines Corporation, Cambridge, MA, that contain from 4K to 64K processors. They can be set up as hypercubes or other topologies and require another computer as a front end. Used for such applications as signal processing, simulation and database retrieval.

connection oriented In communications, requiring a direct connection or established session or circuit between two nodes for transmission. Transmission within a wide area network (WAN) is typically connection oriented. Once established, the circuit, whether physical or virtual, is dedicated to that single transmission until the session is completed. Contrast with *connectionless*.

connectionless In communications, the inclusion of source and destination addresses within each packet so that a direct connection or established session between nodes is not required. Transmission within a local area network (LAN) is typically connectionless. Each data packet sent contains the address of where it is going. Contrast with *connection oriented*.

connectivity (1) Generally, the term refers to communications networks or the act of communicating between computers and terminals.

(2) Specifically, the term refers to devices such as bridges, routers and gateways that link networks together.

connector (1) Any plug, socket or wire that links two devices together.

(2) In database management, a link or pointer between two data structures.

(3) In flowcharting, a symbol used to break a sequence and resume the sequence elsewhere. It is often a small circle with a number in it.

console (1) A terminal used to monitor and control a computer or network.

(2) Any display terminal.

constant In programming, a fixed value in a program. Minimum and maximum amounts, dates, prices, headlines and error messages are examples.

constant ratio code A code that always contains the same ratio of 0s to 1s.

consultant An independent specialist that may act as an advisor or perform detailed systems analysis and design. They often help users create functional specifications from which hardware or software vendors can respond.

contact A metal strip in a switch or socket that touches a corresponding strip in order to make a connection for current to pass. Contacts may be made of precious metals to avoid corrosion.

contention A condition that arises when two devices attempt to use a single resource at the same time. See *CSMA/CD*.

contention resolution Deciding which device gains access to a resource first when more than one wants it at the same time.

context sensitive help Help screens that provide specific information about the condition or mode the program is in at the time help is sought.

context switching Switching between active applications. It often refers to a user jumping back and forth between several programs in contrast with repeated task switching performed by the operating system. However, the terms context switching and task switching are used synonymously.

contextual search To search for records or documents based upon the text contained in any part of the file as opposed to searching on a pre-defined key field.

contiguous Adjacent or touching. Contrast with *fragmentation*.

continuity check A test of a line, channel or circuit to determine if the pathway exists from beginning to end and can transmit signals.

continuous carrier In communications, a carrier frequency that is transmitted even when data is not being sent over the line.

continuous forms A roll of paper forms with perforations for separation into individual sheets after printing. See *pin feed* and *burster*.

contrast The difference between the lightest and darkest areas on a display screen. Contrast with *brightness*.

control ball Same as *trackball*.

control block A segment of disk or memory that contains a group of codes used for identification and control purposes.

control break (1) A change of category used to trigger a subtotal. For example, if data is subtotalled by state, a control break occurs when NJ changes to NM.

(2) See *Ctrl-Break*.

control character See *control code*.

control code One or more characters used as a command to control a device. The first 32 characters in the ASCII character set are control codes for communications and printers. There are countless codes used to control electronic devices. See *escape character*.

Control Data (Control Data Systems, Inc., Arden Hills, MN) One of the first computer companies. Founded in 1957, Bill Norris was its first president and guiding force. For more than 30 years, the company has been widely respected for its high-speed computers used for government and science. Today, it no longer manufactures hardware, but is involved in systems integration using a variety of computers from other companies.

control field Same as *key field*.

control key Abbreviated "ctrl" or "ctl." A key that is pressed with a letter or digit key to command the computer; for example, holding down control and pressing U, turns on underline in some word processors. The caret (shift-6) symbol represents the control key: ^Y means control-Y.

control network A network of sensors and actuators used for home automation and industrial control.

Control Panel A routine that changes the computer's environment settings, such as keyboard and mouse sensitivity, sounds, colors and communications and printer access. It is a desk accessory in the Macintosh and a utility program in Windows.

control parallel Same as *MIMD*.

control program Software that controls the operation of and has highest priority in a computer. Operating systems, network operating systems and network control programs are examples. Contrast with *application program*.

control total Same as *hash total*.

control unit (1) Within the processor, the circuitry that locates, analyzes and executes each instruction in the program.

(2) Within the computer, a *control unit*, or *controller*, is hardware that performs the physical data transfers between memory and a peripheral device, such as a disk or screen, or a network.

Personal computer control units are contained on a single plug-in expansion board, called a controller or adapter (disk controller, display adapter, network adapter, etc.). In large computers, they may be contained on one or more boards or in a stand-alone cabinet.

In single chip computers, a built-in control unit accepts keyboard input and provides serial output to a display.

control variable In programming, a variable that keeps track of the number of iterations of a process. Its value is incremented or decremented with each iteration, and it is compared to a constant or other variable to test the end of the process or loop.

controller An electronic circuit board or system that controls a peripheral device. See *control unit (2)*.

conventional memory In a PC, the first 640K of memory. The next 384K is called the UMA (upper memory area). The term may also refer to the entire first megabyte (1024K) of RAM, which is the memory that DOS can directly manage without the use of additional memory managers.

conventional programming Writing a program in a traditional procedural language, such as assembly language or a high-level compiler language (C, Pascal, COBOL, FORTRAN, etc.).

convergence (1) The intersection of red, green and blue electron beams on one CRT pixel. Poor convergence decreases resolution and muddies white pixels.

(2) See *digital convergence*.

conversational An interactive dialogue between the user and the computer.

conversion (1) Data conversion is changing data from one file or database format to another. It may also require code conversion between ASCII and EBCDIC.

(2) Media conversion is changing storage media such as from tape to disk.

(3) Program conversion is changing the programming source language from one dialect to another, or changing application programs to link to a new operating system or DBMS.

(4) Computer system conversion is changing the computer model and peripheral devices.

(5) Information system conversion requires data conversion and either program conversion or the installation of newly purchased or created application programs.

converter (1) A device that changes one set of codes, modes, sequences or frequencies to a different set. See *A/D converter*.

(2) A device that changes current from 60Hz to 50Hz, and vice versa.

cooperative multitasking Same as *non-preemtive multitasking*.

cooperative processing Sharing a job among two or more computers such as a mainframe and a personal computer. It implies splitting the workload for the most efficiency.

coordinate Belonging to a system of indexing by two or more terms. For example, points on a plane, cells in a spreadsheet and bits in dynamic RAM chips are identified by a pair of coordinates. Points in space are identified by sets of three coordinates.

copper (Cu) A reddish-brown metal that is highly conductive and widely used for electrical wire. When a signal "runs over copper," it means that a metal wire is used rather than a glass wire (optical fiber).

coprocessor A secondary processor used to speed up operations by handling some of the workload of the main CPU. See *math coprocessor* and *graphics coprocessor*.

copy To make a duplicate of the original. In digital electronics, all copies are identical.

copy buster A program that bypasses the copy protection scheme in a software program and allows normal, unprotected copies to be made.

copy protection Resistance to unauthorized copying of software. Copy protection was never a serious issue with mainframes and minicomputers, since vendor support has always been vital in those environments.

The only copy protection system that works is the hardware key, which is used for high-end software, because it is too costly for low-priced products.

CORBA (Common ORB Architecture) An ORB standard endorsed by the OMG (Object Management Group). An ORB is software that handles the communication of messages between objects in a distributed, multi-platform environment.

core A round magnetic doughnut that represents one bit in a core storage system. A computer's main memory used to be referred to as core.

co-resident A program or module that resides in memory along with other programs.

core storage A non-volatile memory that holds magnetic charges in ferrite cores about 1/16th" diameter. The direction of the flux determines the 0 or 1. Developed in the late 1940s by Jay W. Forrester and Dr. An Wang, it was used extensively in the 1950s and 1960s. Since it holds its content without power, it is still used in specialized applications in the military and in space vehicles.

CORE STORAGE
(Courtesy The MITRE Corporation Archives)
In 1952, this core plane held 256 bits for the Whirlwind I compute Today, a single RAM chip can hold millions of bits.

Corel VENTURA Formerly Ventura Publisher, a Windows desktop publishing program from Corel Corporation, Ottawa, Ontario. It is a high-end DTP program that is noted for its sophisticated full-scale pagination capabilities for long documents. It is designed to import data from other graphics and word processing programs and includes several graphics functions from CorelDRAW.

CorelDRAW A suite of Windows graphics applications from Corel Corporation, Ottawa, Ontario. CorelDRAW was originally a drawing program introduced in 1989, which became popular due to its speed and ease of use. As of CorelDRAW 5, it is a complete suite of applications for image editing, charting and presentations as well as desktop publishing, with the inclusion of Corel VENTURA.

corona wire A charged wire in a laser printer that draws the toner off the drum onto the paper. It must be cleaned when the toner cartridge is replaced.

corrupted file A data or program file that has been altered accidentally by hardware or software failure, causing the bits to be rearranged and rendering it unreadable.

corruption Altering of data or programs due to viruses, hardware or software failure or power failure. See *data recovery*.

COS (Corporation for Open Systems International) A not for profit R&D consortium founded in 1986, dedicated to assuring acceptance of a worldwide open network architecture. It is made up of manufacturers and user organizations that provide development, service, and support of systems that conform to international standards, including OSI and ISDN. Address: 1750 Old Meadow Road, Suite 400, McLean, VA 22102, 703/883-2700.

COSE (Common Open Software Environment) Pronounced "cozy." An alliance of major UNIX vendors (IBM, HP, Sun, Univel, USL and SCO) dedicated to standardizing open systems. In 1993, COSE's first specification was the CDE (Common Desktop Environment), a user interface based on Motif.

COSE is expected to disband as soon as CDE Version 1.0 is completed. All future work will be done by OSF.

cost/benefits analysis The study that projects the costs and benefits of a new information system. Costs include people and machine resources for development as well as running the system.

Tangible benefits are derived by estimating the cost savings of both human and machine resources to run the new system versus the old one. Intangible benefits, such as improved customer service and employee relations, may ultimately provide the largest payback, but are harder to quantify.

counter (1) In programming, a variable that is used to keep track of anything that must be counted. The programming language determines the number of counters (variables) that are available to a programmer.

(2) In electronics, a circuit that counts pulses and generates an output at a specified time.

Courier A monospaced typeface originating from the typewriter that is commonly used for letters. It is still considered by many to be the "appropriate" typeface for business correspondence.

courseware Educational software. See *CBT*.

covert channel A transfer of information that violates a computer's built-in security systems. A covert storage channel refers to depositing information in a memory or storage location that can be accessed by different security clearances. A covert timing channel is the manipulation of a system resource in such a way that it can be detected by another process.

cow See *CAU*.

CP (1) (Copy Protected) See *copy protection*.

(2) (Central Processor) See *processor* and *CPU*.

(3) See *control program*.

CPA (Computer Press Association) An organization founded in 1983 that promotes excellence in computer journalism. Comprised of approximately 300 members (1992), its annual awards honor outstanding journalism in print, broadcast and electronic media. Address is 529 18th Ave., San Francisco, CA 94121, 415/750-9281.

CPE (Customer Premises Equipment) Communications equipment that resides on the customer's premises.

CPF (Control Program Facility) The IBM System/38 operating system that included an integrated relational DBMS.

CPGA (Ceramic PGA) See *PGA*.

cpi (1) (Characters Per Inch) The measurement of the density of characters per inch on tape or paper. A printer's CPI button switches character pitch.

(2) (Counts Per Inch) The measurement of the resolution of a mouse/trackball as flywheel notches per inch (horizontal and vertical flywheels rotate as the ball is moved). Notches are converted to cursor movement.

(3) (CPI) (Common Programming Interface) See *SAA* and *CPI-C*.

CPI-C (Common Programming Interface for Communications) A general-purpose communications interface under IBM's SAA. Using APPC verbs as its foundation, it provides a common programming interface across IBM platforms. See *APPC*.

CP/M (Control Program for Microprocessors) A single user operating system for the 8080 and Z80 microprocessors from Digital Research. Created by Gary Kildall, CP/M had its heyday in the early 1980s.

CPM (Critical Path Method) A project management planning and control technique implemented on computers. The critical path is the series of activities and tasks in the project that have no built-in slack time. Any task in the critical path that takes longer than expected will lengthen the total time of the project.

cps (Characters Per Second) The measurement of the speed of a serial printer or the speed of a data transfer between hardware devices or over a communications channel. CPS is equivalent to bytes per second.

CPU (Central Processing Unit) The computing part of the computer. Also called the processor, it is made up of the control unit and ALU. A personal computer CPU is a single microprocessor chip. A minicomputer CPU is contained on one or more printed circuit boards. A mainframe CPU is made up of several boards.

CPU bound Same as *process bound*.

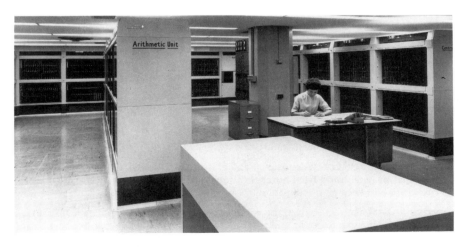

THE CPU OF THE DATAMATIC 1000 (1957)
(Courtesy Honeywell Inc.)
The two large structures that the woman is sitting between were the arithmetic unit (ALU) and control unit of Honeywell's DATAMATIC 1000 in 1957. This circuitry today takes up a quarter of a square inch!

CPU cache See *cache.*

CPU chip Same as *microprocessor.*

CPU time The amount of time it takes for the CPU to execute a set of instructions and explicitly excludes the waiting time for input and output.

CR (Carriage Return) The return key or the actual code that is generated when the key is pressed (decimal 13, hex 0D). See *return key.*

CR/LF (Carriage Return/Line Feed) The end of line characters used in standard PC text files (ASCII 13 10). In the Mac, only the CR is used; in UNIX, the LF.

crash See *abend* and *head crash.*

crash recovery The ability to automatically correct a hardware, software or line failure.

Cray (Cray Research, Inc., Eagan, MN) A supercomputer manufacturer founded in 1972 by Seymour Cray. The CRAY-1 shipped in 1976 and could perform 160 million floating point operations per second. Today, Cray's fastest computer can perform 16 billion floating point operations per second.

CRC (Cyclical Redundancy Checking) An error checking technique used to ensure the accuracy of transmitting digital data. The transmitted messages are divided into predetermined lengths which, used as dividends, are divided by a fixed divisor. The remainder of the calculation is appended onto and sent with the message. At the receiving end, the computer recalculates the remainder. If it does not match the transmitted remainder, an error is detected.

crippleware Demonstration software with built-in limitations; for example, a database package that lets only 50 records be entered.

criteria range Conditions for selecting records; for example, "Illinois customers with balances over $10,000."

crop marks Printed lines on paper used to cut the form into its intended size.

cross assembler An assembler that generates machine language for a foreign computer. It is used to develop programs for computers on a chip or microprocessors used in specialized applications, which are either too small or are incapable of handling the development software.

crossbar switch See *crosspoint switch.*

cross compiler A compiler that generates machine language for a foreign computer. See *cross assembler.*

crossfoot A numerical error checking technique that compares the sum of the columns with the sum of the rows.

crosshatch A criss-crossed pattern used to fill in sections of a drawing to distinguish them from each other.

crossover cable Same as *null modem cable.*

crosspoint switch Also known as a crossbar or NxN switch, it is a switching device that provides for a fixed number of inputs and outputs. For example, a 32x32 switch is able to keep 32 nodes communicating at full speed to 32 other nodes.

cross tabulate To analyze and summarize data. Summarizing data from the detail records in a database file and entering them as totals for a spreadsheet is a common example. The following example places the details of order records into summary form.

Transactions being cross tabbed				Results of cross tab				
Date	Customer	Quantity		Customer	Jan	Feb	Mar	Total
1-07-93	Smith	7		Smith	7		12	19
1-13-93	Jones	12		Jones	12			12
2-05-93	Gonzales	4		Gonzales		4	15	19
2-11-93	Fetzer	6		Fetzer		6		6
3-10-93	Smith	12		Total	19	10	27	56
3-22-93	Gonzales	15						

crosstalk (1) In communications, interference from an adjacent channel.

(2) (Crosstalk) Communications programs for DOS and Windows from DCA, Inc., Alpharetta, GA. Crosstalk products were originally developed by Microstuf, Inc., which was later merged with DCA. Crosstalk was one of the first personal computer communications programs, originating in the CP/M days.

CRT (Cathode Ray Tube) A vacuum tube used as a display screen in a video terminal or TV. The term often refers to the entire terminal.

crunch (1) To process data. See *number crunching*.

(2) To compress data. See *data compression*.

cryogenics Using materials that operate at very cold temperatures. See *superconductor*.

cryptography Conversion of data into a secret code for security purposes. Same as *encryption*.

crystal A solid material containing a uniform arrangement of molecules. See *quartz crystal*.

crystalline The solid state of a crystal. Contrast with *nematic*.

CSA (1) (Canadian Standards Association) The Canadian counterpart of U.S. Underwriters Laboratory.

(2) (Client Server Architecture) See *client/server*.

(3) (CallPath Services Architecture) An IBM standard that integrates applications with the telephone system, designed for use with AT&T, Northern Telecom and other PBX vendors.

CSMA/CD (Carrier Sense Multiple Access/Collision Detection) A baseband communications access method. When a device wants to gain access to the network, it checks to see if the network is free. If it is not, it waits a random amount of time before retrying. If the network is free and two devices attempt access at exactly the same time, they both back off to avoid a collision and each wait a random amount of time before retrying.

CSP (1) (Cross System Product) An IBM application generator that runs in all SAA environments. CSP/AD (CSP/Application Development) programs provide the interactive development environment and generate a pseudo code that is interpreted by CSP/AE (CSP/Application Execution) software in the running computer.

(2) (Certified Systems Professional) The award for successful completion of an ICCP examination in systems development.

CSTA (Computer Supported Telephony Application) An international standard interface between a network server and a telephone switch (PBX) established by the European Computer Manufacturers Association (ECMA).

CSU See *DSU/CSU*.

CSV (Comma Separated Value) Same as *comma delimited*.

CTI (Computer Telephone Integration) Combining data with voice systems in order to enhance telephone services. For example, automatic number identification (ANI) allows a caller's records to be retrieved from the database while the call is routed to the appropriate party. Automatic telephone dialing from an address list is an outbound example.

Ctl See *control key*.

CTO (Chief Technical Officer) The executive responsible for the technical direction of an organization.

CTOS An operating system that runs on Unisys' x86-based SuperGen series (formerly the B-series). It was originally developed by Convergent Technologies, which was acquired by Unisys. Designed for network use, its message-based approach allows program requests to be directed to any station in the network.

Ctrl See *control key*.

Ctrl-Alt-Del In a PC, holding down the CTRL and ALT keys and pressing the DEL key reboots the system.

Ctrl-Break In a PC, holding down the CTRL key and pressing the BREAK key cancels the running program or batch file. Same as *Ctrl-C*.

Ctrl-C In a PC, holding down the CTRL key and pressing the C key cancels the running program or batch file. Same as *Ctrl-Break*.

CTS (1) (Clear To Send) The RS-232 signal sent from the receiving station to the transmitting station that indicates it is ready to accept data. Contrast with *RTS*.

(2) See *carpal tunnel syndrome*.

CUA (Common User Access) SAA specifications for user interfaces, which includes OS/2 PM and character-based formats of 3270 terminals. It is intended to provide a consistent look and feel across platforms and between applications.

CUI (Character-based User Interface) A user interface that uses the character, or text, mode of the computer and typically refers to typing in commands. Contrast with *GUI*.

Curie point The temperature (150 C) at which certain elements are susceptible to magnetism. See *magneto-optic*.

current The flow of electrons within a wire or circuit, measured in amps.

current directory The disk directory the system is presently working in. Unless otherwise specified, commands that deal with disk files refer to the current directory.

current loop A serial transmission method originating with teletype machines that transmits 20 milliAmperes of current for a 1 bit and no current for a 0 bit. Today's circuit boards can't handle 20mA current and use optical isolators at the receiving end to detect lower current. Contrast with *RS-232*.

cursive writing Handwriting.

cursor (1) A movable symbol on screen that is the contact point between the user and the data. In text systems, it is a blinking rectangle or underline. On graphic systems, it is also called a pointer, and it usually changes shape (arrow, square, paintbrush, etc.) when it moves into a different part of the screen.

(2) A pen-like or puck-like device used with a digitizer tablet. As the tablet cursor is moved across the tablet, the screen cursor moves correspondingly. See *digitizer tablet*.

cursor keys The keys that move the cursor on screen, which include the up, down, left and right arrow, home, end, PgUp and PgDn keys. In addition to cursor keys, a mouse or tablet cursor also moves the cursor.

custom control The functionality in an application that differs from the stock objects provided in the development system. For example, a custom control is the creation of an animated cursor or a unique style of dialog box or menu, which is not part of the standard system.

customized software Software designed for an individual customer.

customized toolbar A toolbar that can be custom configured by the user. Buttons can be added and deleted as required.

cut & paste To move or copy a block of text or graphics from one document to another.

CUT mode (Control Unit Terminal mode) A mode that allows a 3270 terminal to have a single session with the mainframe. Micro to mainframe software emulates this mode to communicate with the mainframe. Contrast with *DFT mode*.

cybernetics The comparative study of human and machine processes in order to understand their similarities and differences. It often refers to machines that imitate human behavior. See *AI* and *robot*.

cyberpunk Relating to futuristic delinquency: hackers breaking into computer banks, survival based on high-tech wits. Stems from science fiction novels such as "Neuromancer" and "Shockwave Rider."

cyberspace The term coined by William Gibson in his novel "Neuromancer," to refer to a futuristic computer network that people use by plugging their minds into it! See *virtual reality*.

cycle (1) A single event that is repeated. For example, in a carrier frequency, one cycle is one complete wave.

(2) A set of events that is repeated. For example, in a polling system, all of the attached terminals are tested in one cycle. See *machine cycle* and *memory cycle*.

cycle stealing A CPU design technique that periodically "grabs" machine cycles from the main processor usually by some peripheral control unit, such as a DMA (direct memory access) device. In this way, processing and peripheral operations can be performed concurrently or with some degree of overlap.

cycle time The time interval between the start of one cycle and the start of the next cycle.

cycles per second The number of times an event or set of events is repeated in a second. See *Hertz*.

cylinder The aggregate of all tracks that reside in the same location on every disk surface. On multiple-platter disks, the cylinder is the sum total of every track with the same track number

Multi-platter hard disk

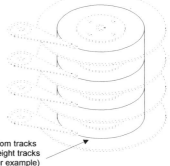

The top and bottom tracks of each platter (eight tracks in this four-platter example) make up one cylinder.

CYLINDER

on every surface. On a floppy disk, a cylinder comprises the top and corresponding bottom track.

When storing data, the operating system fills an entire cylinder before moving to the next one. The access arm remains stationary until all the tracks in the cylinder have been read or written.

cylinder skew The offset distance from the start of the last track of the previous cylinder so that the head has time to seek from cylinder to cylinder and be at the start of the first track of the new cylinder. See *head skew*.

D

D4 A framing format for T1 transmission that places 12 T1 frames into a superframe. See *ESF*.

DA See *desk accessory* and *data administrator*.

DAC (1) See *D/A converter*.

(2) (Discretionary Access Control) A security control that does not require clearance levels. See *NCSC*.

D/A converter (Digital to Analog Converter) A device that converts digital pulses into analog signals. Contrast with *A/D converter*. See *DSP*.

DAD (1) (Database Action Diagram) Documentation that describes the processing performed on data in a database.

(2) (Digital Audio Disc) Same as *CD*.

daemon Pronounced "demon." A UNIX program that executes in the background ready to perform an operation when required. It is usually an unattended process initiated at startup. Typical daemons are print spoolers and e-mail handlers or a scheduler that starts up another process at a designated time. The term comes from Greek mythology meaning "guardian spirit." Same as *agent*.

daisy chain Connected in series, one after the other. Transmitted signals go to the first device, then to the second and so on.

DAISY WHEEL

daisy wheel An earlier print mechanism that used a plastic or metal hub with spokes like an old-fashioned wagon wheel minus the outer rim. At the end of each spoke is the carved image of a type character.

DAL (Data Access Language) A database interface from Apple that allows the Mac to access DAL-supported databases on Macs or non-Apple computers. It is a superset of SQL. Database vendors license the specs and translate DAL calls to their database engines.

damping A technique for stabilizing an electronic or mechanical device by eliminating unwanted or excessive oscillations.

Darlington circuit An amplification circuit that uses two transistors coupled together.

DARPA (Defense Advanced Research Projects Agency) See *ARPANET*.

DASD (Direct Access Storage Device) Pronounced "dazdee." A peripheral device that is directly addressable, such as a disk or drum. The term is used in the mainframe world.

DAT (1) (Digital Audio Tape) A CD-quality, digital recording technology for magnetic tape. A 4mm helical-scan DAT drive holds several gigabytes with extended-length tapes when adapted for data storage use. See *tape backup*.

(2) (Dynamic Address Translator) A hardware circuit that converts a virtual memory address into a real address.

data (1) Technically, raw facts and figures, such as orders and payments, which are processed into information, such as balance due and quantity on hand. However, in common usage, the terms data and information are used synonymously.

The amount of data versus information kept in the computer is a tradeoff. Data can be processed into different forms of information, but it takes time to sort and sum transactions. Up-to-date information can provide instant answers.

A common misconception is that software is also data. Software is executed, or run, by the computer. Data is "processed." Software is "run."

(2) Any form of information whether in paper or electronic form. In electronic form, data refers to files and databases, text documents, images and digitally-encoded voice and video.

(3) The plural form of datum.

data abstraction In object-oriented programming, creating user-defined data types that contain their own data and processing. These data structures, or objects, are unaware of each other's physical details and know only what services each other performs. This is the basis for polymorphism and information hiding.

data acquisition (1) The automatic collection of data from sensors and readers in a factory, laboratory, medical or scientific environment.

(2) The gathering of source data for data entry into the computer.

data administration The analysis, classification and maintenance of an organization's data and data relationships. It includes the development of data models and data dictionaries, which, combined with transaction volume, are the raw materials for database design.

Database administration often falls within the jurisdiction of data administration; however, data administration functions provide the overall management of data as an organizational resource. Database administration is the technical design and management of the database.

data administrator A person who coordinates activities within the data administration department. Contrast with *database administrator*.

data bank Any electronic depository of data.

database (1) A set of interrelated files that is created and managed by a DBMS.

(2) Any electronically-stored collection of data.

DATABASE 2 See *DB2*.

database administrator A person responsible for the physical design and management of the database and for the evaluation, selection and implementation of the DBMS.

In small organizations, the database administrator and data administrator are one in the same; however, when the two responsibilities are managed separately, the database administrator's function is more technical.

database analyst See *data administrator* and *database administrator*.

database driver A software routine that accesses a database. It allows an application or compiler to access a particular database format.

database engine Same as *database manager*.

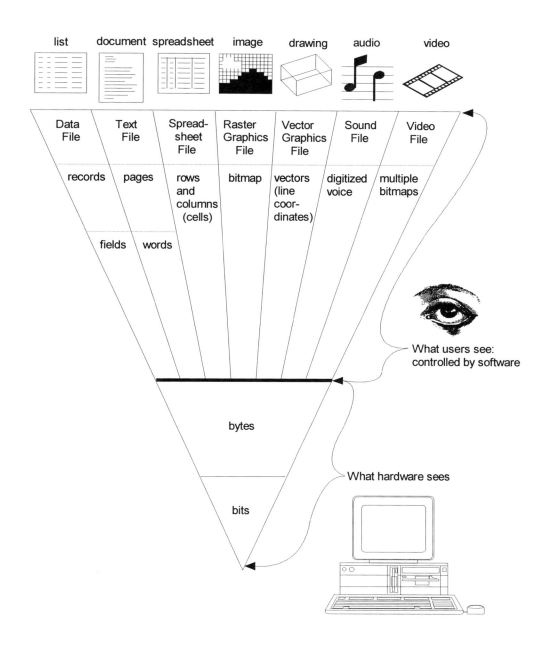

THE DATABASE

database machine A specially-designed computer for database access. This technology never caught on. Today, a massively parallel computer can provide ultra fast searches, but it is very expensive.

database management system See *DBMS*.

database manager (1) With personal computers, software that allows a user to manage multiple data files (same as *DBMS*). Contrast with *file manager*, which works with one file at a time.

(2) Software that provides database management capability for traditional programming languages, such as COBOL, BASIC and C, but without the interactive capabilities.

(3) The part of the DBMS that stores and retrieves the data.

database program A software application that allows for the storage and retrieval of information, which is structured as fields, records and files. Database programs provide a way of creating and manipulating the electronic equivalent of a name and address card that can hold large amounts of information.

database publishing Using desktop publishing to produce reports of database contents.

database server A computer in a LAN dedicated to database storage and retrieval. Contrast with *file server*, which stores many kinds of files and programs for shared use.

data bits The number of bits used to represent one character of data. When transmitting ASCII text via modem, either seven or eight bits may be used. Most other forms of data require eight bits.

data bus See *bus*.

data carrier (1) Any medium such as a disk or tape that can hold machine readable data.

(2) A carrier frequency into which data is modulated for transmission in a network.

data cartridge A removable magnetic tape module driven by a wheel inside the drive that presses against a passive roller in the cartridge. A tension belt is attached to the roller that presses against the supply and takeup reel.

data cassette An audio cassette made to higher tolerances for data storage.

DATA CARTRIDGE

DATACENTER

datacenter The department that houses the computer systems and related equipment, including the data library. Data entry and systems programming may also come under its jurisdiction. A control section is usually provided that accepts work from and releases output to user departments.

data code (1) A digital coding system in a computer such as *ASCII* and *EBCDIC*.

(2) A coding system used to abbreviate data; for example, codes for regions, classes, products and status.

data collection Acquiring source documents for the data entry department. It comes under the jurisdiction of the data control or data entry department. See *data acquisition*.

datacom (DATA COMmunications) See *communications*.

data compression Encoding data to take up less storage space. Data compression searches for redundant strings of 0s and 1s and stores pointers to them using a variety of methods. Text files compress better than graphics files and executable programs.

data control department The function responsible for collecting data for input into a computer's batch processing operations as well as the dissemination of the finished reports. The data entry department may be under the jursidiction of the data control department or vice versa.

DATA/DAT (DATA/Digital Audio Tape) A DAT format for data backup that can be divided into as many as 254 partitions allowing for updating in place.

data definition (1) In a source language program, the definitions of data structures (variables, arrays, fields, records, etc.).

(2) A description of the record layout in a file system or DBMS.

data dictionary A database about data and databases. It holds the name, type, range of values, source, and authorization for access for each data element in the organization's files and databases. It also indicates which application programs use that data so that when a change in a data structure is contemplated, a list of affected programs can be generated.
  The data dictionary may be a stand-alone system or an integral part of the DBMS. Data integrity and accuracy is better ensured in the latter case.

data dipper Software in a personal computer that queries a mainframe database.

data division The part of a COBOL program that defines the data files and record layouts.

DataEase A relational DBMS for PCs from DataEase International, Inc., Trumbull, CT. It provides a menu-driven interface for developing applications without programming and is noted for its ease of use.

data element The fundamental data structure in a data processing system. Any unit of data defined for processing is a data element; for example, ACCOUNT NUMBER, NAME, ADDRESS and CITY. A data element is defined by size (in characters) and type (alphanumeric, numeric only, true/false, date, etc.). A specific set of values or range of values may also be part of the definition.
  Technically, a data element is a logical definition of data, whereas a field is the physical unit of storage in a record. For example, the data element ACCOUNT NUMBER, which exists only once, is stored in the ACCOUNT NUMBER field in the customer record and in the ACCOUNT NUMBER field in the order records.
  Data element, data item, field and *variable* all describe the same unit of data and are used interchangeably.

data encryption See *encryption*, *DES* and *RSA*.

data entry Entering data into the computer, which includes keyboard entry, scanning and voice recognition. When transactions are entered after the fact (batch data entry), they are just stacks of source documents to the keyboard operator. Deciphering poor handwriting from a source document is a judgment call that is often error prone. In online data entry operations, in which the operator takes information in person or by phone, there's interaction and involvement with the transaction and less chance for error.

data entry department The part of the datacenter where the data entry terminals and operators are located.

data entry operator A person who enters data into the computer via keyboard or other reading or scanning device.

data entry program An application program that accepts data from the keyboard or other input device and stores it in the computer. It may be part of an application that also provides updating, querying and reporting.

The data entry program establishes the data in the database and should test for all possible input errors. See *validity checking, table lookup, check digit* and *intelligent database.*

data error A condition in which data on a digital medium has been corrupted. The error can be as little as one bit.

data file A collection of data records. This term may refer specifically to a database file that contains records and fields in contrast to other files such as a word processing document or spreadsheet. Or, it may refer to a file that contains any type of information structure including documents and spreadsheets in contrast to a program file.

data flow (1) In computers, the path of data from source document to data entry to processing to final reports. Data changes format and sequence (within a file) as it moves from program to program.

(2) In communications, the path taken by a message from origination to destination and includes all nodes through which the data travels.

data flow diagram A description of data and the manual and machine processing performed on the data.

data fork The part of a Macintosh file that contains data. For example, in a HyperCard stack, text, graphics and HyperTalk scripts reside in the data fork, while fonts, sounds, control information and external functions reside in the resource fork.

data format Same as *file format.*

Data General (Data General Corporation, Westboro, MA) One of the first minicomputer companies, founded in 1968 by Edson de Castro. It has introduced a variety of computer series over the years and specializes in UNIX-based servers.

data glove A glove used to report the position of a user's hand and fingers to a computer. See *virtual reality.*

datagram A TCP/IP message unit that contains internet source and destination addresses and data.

data independence A DBMS technique that separates data from the processing and allows the database to be structurally changed without affecting most existing programs. Programs access data in a DBMS by field and are concerned with only the data fields they use, not the format of the complete record. Thus, when the record layout is updated (fields added, deleted or changed in size), the only programs that must be changed are those that use those new fields.

▶ *The electronic and encyclopedic versions of this book provide more detail on this subject.*

data integrity The process of preventing accidental erasure or adulteration in a database.

data item A unit of data stored in a field. See *field*.

data library The section of the datacenter that houses offline disks and tapes. Data library personnel are responsible for cataloging and maintaining the media.

data line An individual circuit, or line, that carries data within a computer or communications channel.

data line monitor In communications, a test instrument that analyzes the signals and timing of a communications line. It either visually displays the patterns or stores the activity for further analysis.

DATA LIBRARY

data link In communications, the physical interconnection between two points (OSI layers 1 and 2). It may also refer to the modems, protocols and all required hardware and software to perform the transmission.

data link escape A communications control character which indicates that the following character is not data, but a control code.

data link protocol In communications, the transmission of a unit of data from one node to another (OSI layer 2). It is responsible for ensuring that the bits received are the same as the bits sent. All transmission of data requires a data link function, which may be all that is necessary. For example, Xmodem and Zmodem provide data link services when transmitting between two personal computers via modem. Ethernet and Token Ring provide data link services over a network.

data management (1) The part of the operating system that manages the physical storage and retrieval of data on a disk or other device. See *access method*.

(2) Software that allows for the creation, storage, retrieval and manipulation of files interactively at a terminal or personal computer. See *file manager* and *DBMS*.

(3) The function that manages data as an organizational resource. See *data administration*.

(4) The management of all data/information in an organization. It includes data administration, the standards for defining data and the way in which people perceive and use it.

data management system See *DBMS*.

data manipulation language A language that requests data from a DBMS. It is coded within the application program such as COBOL or C.

data model A description of the principles of organization of a database.

data modeling The identification of the design principles for a data model.

data modem A modem used for sending data and not faxes. See *modem* and *fax/modem*.

data module A sealed, removable storage module containing magnetic disks and their associated access arms and read/write heads.

data name The name assigned to a field or variable.

data network A communications network that transmits data. See *communications*.

data packet One frame in a packet-switched message. Most data communications is based on dividing the transmitted message into packets. For example, an Ethernet packet can be from 64 to 1518 bytes in length.

data processing The capturing, storing, updating and retrieving data and information. It may refer to the industry or to data processing tasks in contrast with other operations, such as word processing.

data processor (1) A person who works in data processing.

(2) A computer that is processing data, in contrast with a computer performing another task, such as controlling a network.

data projector A video machine that projects output from a computer onto a remote screen. It is bulkier than a flat LCD panel, but is faster for displaying high-speed animation.

data pump A circuit that transmits pulses in a digital device. It typically refers to the chipset in a modem that generates the bits based on the modem's modulation techniques.

data rate (1) The data transfer speed within the computer or between a peripheral and computer.

(2) The data transmission speed in a network.

data recovery Restoring data that has been physically damaged or corrupted on a disk or tape. Disks and tapes can become corrupted due to viruses, bad software, hardware failure as well as from power failures that occur while the magnetic media is being written.

data representation How data types are structured; for example, how signs are represented in numerical values or how strings are formatted (enclosed in quotes, terminated with a null, etc.).

data resource management Same as *data administration*.

data set (1) A data file or collection of interrelated data.

(2) The AT&T name for modem.

data sheet A page or two of detailed information about a product.

data signal Physical data as it travels over a line or channel (pulses or vibrations of electricity or light).

data sink A device or part of the computer that receives data.

data source A device or part of the computer in which data is originated.

data stream The continuous flow of data from one place to another.

data striping See *disk striping*.

data structure The physical layout of data. Data fields, memo fields, fixed length fields, variable length fields, records, word processing documents, spreadsheets, data files, database files and indexes are all examples of data structures.

data switch A switch box that routes one line to another; for example, to connect two computers to one printer. Manual switches have dials or buttons. Automatic switches test for signals and provide first-come, first-served switching.

DATA SWITCH

data system Same as *information system*.

data tablet Same as *digitizer tablet*.

data transfer The movement of data within the computer system. Typically, data is said to be transferred within the computer, but it is "transmitted" over a communications network. A transfer is actually a copy function since the data is not automatically erased at the source. See *data rate*.

data transmission Sending data over a communications network.

data transparency The ability to easily access and work with data no matter where it is located or what application created it.

data type A category of data. Typical data types are numeric, alphanumeric (character), dates and logical (true/false). Programming languages allow for the creation of different data types.
   When data is assigned a type, it cannot be treated like another type. For example, alphanumeric data cannot be calculated, and digits within numeric data cannot be isolated. Date types can only contain valid dates.

date math Calculations made upon dates. For example, March 30 + 5 yields April 4.

datum The singular form of data; for example, one datum. It is rarely used, and data, its plural form, is commonly used for both singular and plural.

daughter board A small printed circuit board that is attached to or plugs into a removable printed circuit board.

dazdee See *DASD*.

DB See *database* and *decibel*.

DB-9, DB-15, DB-25... A category of plugs and sockets with 9, 15, 25, 37 and 50 pins respectively, used to hook up communications and computer devices. The DB refers to the physical structure of the connector, not the purpose of each line.
   DB-9 and DB-25 connectors are commonly used for RS-232 interfaces.
   A high-density DB-15 connector is used for the VGA port on a PC, which has 15 pins in the same shell as the DB-9 connector. See *printer cable*.

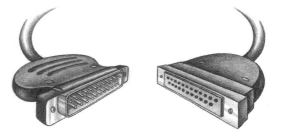

DB-25 PLUG AND SOCKET

DB/DC (DataBase/Data Communications) Refers to software that performs database and data communications functions.

DB2 (DATABASE 2) A relational DBMS from IBM that was originally developed for its mainframes. It is a full-featured SQL language DBMS that has become IBM's major database product. Known for its industrial strength reliability, IBM is making DB/2 available for all of its own platforms as well as non-IBM platforms, including the HP 9000, Sun Solaris and Windows NT.

DB2/2 The OS/2 version of DB2 from IBM. It is a 32-bit DBMS that is compatible with the mainframe DB2. It replaces OS/2's 16-bit Database Manager. DB2/400 is the AS/400 version, and DB2/6000 is the RS/6000 version.

DBA See *database administrator*.

dBASE A database program for DOS and Windows from Borland. dBASE was the first comprehensive relational DBMS for personal computers and was originally developed for CP/M machines. It was originally marketed by Ashton-Tate, which was later acquired by Borland. The dBASE DBF file format has become a de facto standard used by many applications.

▶ *The electronic and encyclopedic versions of this book provide more detail on this subject.*

dBASE compiler Software that converts dBASE source language into machine language. The resulting programs execute on their own like COBOL or C programs and do not run under dBASE.

DBF file The dBASE data file extension. dBASE II and dBASE III files both use DBF, but are not compatible.

DBMS (DataBase Management System) Software that controls the organization, storage, retrieval, security and integrity of data in a database. It accepts requests from the application and instructs the operating system to transfer the appropriate data.

DBMSs may work with traditional programming languages (COBOL, C, etc.) or they may include their own programming language. For example, dBASE and Paradox are database programs with a DBMS, a full programming language and a fourth-generation (4GL) language, making them complete application development systems. 4GL commands let users interactively create database files, edit them, ask questions and print reports without programming. Thousands of applications have been developed in environments such as these.

The following diagram shows the interaction of the DBMS with other system and application software running in the computer.

▶ *The electronic and encyclopedic versions of this book provide more detail on this subject.*

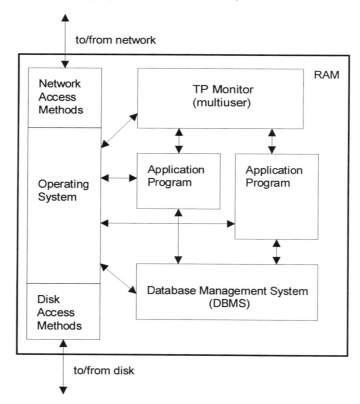

DBMS INTERACTION

This chart shows the interaction between the DBMS and other system and application software in the computer.

DBS (Direct Broadcast Satellite) A one-way TV broadcast service direct from a satellite to a small 18" dish antenna. Although DBS service exists in other countries, the first DBS satellite for the United States was launched in December 1993 by Hughes Communications and Hubbard Broadcasting with a combined investment of $1 billion.

dBXL A dBASE III PLUS-compatible DBMS from WordTech Systems, Inc., Orinda, CA, that features a menu-driven option for interactive use.

DC (1) (Direct Current) An electrical current that travels in one direction and used within the computer's electronic circuits. Contrast with AC.

(2) (Data Communications) See *DB/DC*.

DCA (1) (Document Content Architecture) IBM file formats for text documents. DCA/RFT (Revisable-Form Text) is the primary format and can be edited. DCA/FFT (Final-Form Text) has been formatted for a particular output device and cannot be changed. For example, page numbers, headers and footers are placed on every page.

(2) (Distributed Communications Architecture) A network architecture from Unisys.

(3) (Digital Communications Associates, Inc., Alpharetta, GA) Manufacturer of communications products. See *IRMAboard*.

D/CAS (Data/CASsette) A tape backup technology that uses an upgraded version of the common audio tape cassette. It can hold as much as 600MB of data.

DCC (Digital Compact Cassette) A digital tape format that uses a variation of the common analog audio cassette. DCC tape players also play analog tape cassettes.

DCE (1) (Data Communications Equipment or Data Circuit-terminating Equipment) A device that establishes, maintains and terminates a session on a network. It may also convert signals for transmission. It is typically the modem. Contrast with *DTE*.

(2) (Distributed Computing Environment) A set of programs from OSF used for developing and maintaining client/server applications across heterogeneous platforms in a network.

DCI (Display Control Interface) An Intel and Microsoft standard for full-motion video in Windows. It improves performance by bypassing the Windows GDI interface and addressing the display adapter directly. It requires updated drivers from the adapter vendor and the DCI DLL from Microsoft.

DCS (1) (Distributed Communications System) A telephone system that puts small switches close to subscribers making local loops shorter and maximizing long lines to the central office.

(2) (Distributed Control System) A process control system that uses disbursed computers throughout the manufacturing line for control.

(3) (Digital Cross-connect System) A high-speed data channel switch that accepts separate instructions for switching independently of the data travelling through it.

(4) (Document Control Software) A menu-driven query system from Workgroup Technologies for Oracle databases on PCs and Sun stations.

(5) (Desktop Color Separation) The QuarkXpress format for defining color separated output from a personal computer.

DCT (Discrete Cosine Transform) An algorithm, similar to Fast Fourier Transform, that converts data (pixels, waveforms, etc.) into sets of frequencies. The first frequencies in the set are the most meaningful; the latter, the least. For compression, latter frequencies are stripped away based on allowable resolution loss. The DCT method is used in the JPEG and MPEG compression.

DD (Double Density) The designation for low-density diskettes, typically the 5.25" 360K and 3.5" 720K floppies. See *double density*. Contrast with *HD*.

DDBMS (Distributed Database Management System) See *distributed database.*

DDCMP (Digital Data Communications Message Protocol) Digital's proprietary, synchronous data link protocol used in DECnet.

DDE (Dynamic Data Exchange) A message protocol in Windows that allows application programs to request and exchange data between them automatically.

DDL (1) (Data Description Language) A language used to define data and their relationships to other data. It is used to create files, databases and data dictionaries.

(2) (Document Description Language) A printer control language from Imagen that runs on the HP LaserJet series.

(3) (Direct Data Link) The ability of a supplier to directly interrogate a customer's inventory database in order to manage scheduling and shipping more efficiently. Pioneered by Ford Motor Co. in 1988, Ford lets suppliers check stock levels in assembly plants throughout North America.

DDM (Distributed Data Management) Software in an IBM SNA environment that allows users to access data in remote files within the network. DDM works with IBM's LU 6.2 session to provide peer-to-peer communications and file sharing.

DDP (Distributed Data Processing) See *distributed processing.*

DDS (1) (Dataphone Digital Service) An AT&T private line digital service with data rates from 2400 bps to 56Kbps. Private analog lines can be connected to DDS lines.

(2) (Digital Data Service) A private line digital service from a non-AT&T carrier.

(3) (Digital Data Storage) A DAT format for data backup. It is a sequential recording method; data must be appended at the end of previous data. See *tape backup.*

de facto standard A widely-used format or language not endorsed by a standards organization.

de jure standard A format or language endorsed by a standards organization.

deadlock See *deadly embrace.*

deadly embrace A stalemate that occurs when two elements in a process are each waiting for the other to respond. For example, in a network, if one user is working on file A and needs file B to continue, but another user is working on file B and needs file A to continue, each one waits for the other. Both are temporarily locked out. The software must be able to deal with this.

deallocate To release a computer resource that is currently assigned to a program or user, such as memory or a peripheral device.

deblock To separate records from a block.

debug To correct a problem in hardware or software. Debugging software is finding the errors in the program logic. Debugging hardware is finding the errors in circuit design.

debugger Software that helps a programmer debug a program by stopping at certain breakpoints and displaying various programming elements. The programmer can step through source code statements one at a time while the corresponding machine instructions are being executed.

DEC (Digital Equipment Corporation) The trade name for Digital's products (DECmate, DECnet, etc.). Many people refer to the company as DEC.

decay The reduction of strength of a signal or charge.

decentralized processing Computer systems in different locations. Although data may be transmitted between the computers periodically, it implies limited daily communications. Contrast with *distributed processing* and *centralized processing*.

decibel (dB) The unit that measures loudness or strength of a signal. dBs are a relative measurement derived from an initial reference level and a final observed level. A whisper is about 10 dB, a noisy factory 90 dB, loud thunder 110 dB. 120 dB is painful.

decimal Meaning 10. The universal numbering system that uses 10 digits. Computers use binary numbers because it is easier to design electronic systems that can maintain two states rather than 10.

decision box A diamond-shaped symbol that is used to document a decision point in a flowchart. The decision is written in the decision box, and the results of the decision branch off from the points in the box.

decision instruction In programming, an instruction that compares one set of data with another and branches to a different part of the program depending on the results.

decision support system See *DSS* and *EIS*.

decision table A list of decisions and their criteria. Designed as a matrix, it lists criteria (inputs) and the results (outputs) of all possible combinations of the criteria. It can be placed into a program to direct its processing. By changing the decision table, the program is changed accordingly.

decision tree A graphical representation of all alternatives in a decision making process.

OUTPUTS

INPUTS	APPROVE LOAN	DENY LOAN	SEE LOAN OFFICER	SEE LOAN OFFICER
SAME JOB OVER 5 YRS	YES	NO	NO	YES
OWNS CAR	YES	NO	YES	NO
OWNS HOME	YES	NO	YES	NO
IN DEBT	NO	YES	NO	NO

DECISION TABLE

deck The part of a magnetic tape unit that holds and moves the tape reels. See also *DEC*.

declaration In programming, an instruction or statement that defines data (fields, variables, arrays, etc.) and resources, but does not create executable code.

DECnet Digital's communications network, which supports Ethernet-style LANs and baseband and broadband WANs over private and public lines. It interconnects PDPs, VAXs, PCs, Macs and workstations. In DECnet philosophy, a node must be an intelligent machine and not simply a terminal as in other systems. See *DNA*.

decoder A hardware device or software program that converts a coded signal back into its original form.

decollator A device that separates multiple-part paper forms while removing the carbon paper.

decompiler A program that converts machine language back into a high-level source language. The resulting code may be very difficult to maintain as variables and routines are named generically: A0001, A0002, etc.

decompress To restore compressed data back to its original size.

decrement To subtract a number from another number. Decrementing a counter means to subtract 1 or some other number from its current value.

dedicated channel A computer channel or communications line that is used for one purpose.

dedicated service A service that is not shared by other users or organizations.

default The current setting or action taken by hardware or software if the user has not specified otherwise.

default directory Same as *current directory*.

default drive The disk drive used if no other drive is specified.

default font The typeface and type size used if none other is specified.

defragment To reorganize the disk by putting files into contiguous order. Because the operating system stores new data in whatever free space is available, data files become spread out across the disk if they are updated often. This causes extra read/write head movement to read them back. Periodically, the hard disk should be defragmented to put files back into order.

degausser A device that removes unwanted magnetism from a monitor or the read/write head in a disk or tape drive.

DEL key (DELete key) The keyboard key used to delete the character under the screen cursor or some other currently-highlighted object.

delay line A communications or electronic circuit that has a built-in delay. Acoustic delay lines were used to create the earliest computer memories. For example, the UNIVAC I used tubes of liquid mercury that would slow down the digital pulses long enough (a fraction of a second) to serve as storage.

delete To remove an item of data from a file or to remove a file from the disk. See *undelete*.

delimiter A character or combination of characters used to separate one item or set of data from another. For example, in comma delimited records, a comma is used to separate each field of data.

deliverable The measurable result or output of a process.

Dell (Dell Computer Corporation, Austin, TX) A PC manufacturer founded in 1984 by Michael Dell. Originally selling under the "PCs Limited" brand, Dell was the first to legitimize mail-order PCs by providing quality telephone support. Dell made the Fortune 500 in 1991, and its fiscal 1993 revenues exceeded two billion dollars.

delta modulation A technique that is used to sample voice waves and convert them into digital code. Delta modulation typically samples the wave 32,000 times per second, but generates only one bit per sample. See *PCM*.

DEMA (Association for Input Technology and Management) An organization devoted to the advancement of managers in data entry technologies. Founded in 1976 as the Data Entry Management Association, it sponsors educational courses and conferences. Address: 101 Merritt 7, Norwalk, CT 06851, 203/846-3777.

demand paging Copying a program page from disk into memory when required by the program.

demand processing Same as *transaction processing*.

demodulate To filter out the data signal from the carrier. See *modulate*.

demon See *daemon*.

demultiplex To reconvert a transmission that contains several intermixed signals back into its original separate signals.

density See *packing density* and *bit density*.

departmental computing Processing a department's data with its own computer system. See *distributed processing*.

dependent segment In database management, data that depends on data in a higher level for its full meaning.

dequeue Pronounced "d-q." To remove items from a queue in order to process or transmit them.

DES (Data Encryption Standard) A NIST-standard encryption technique that scrambles data into an unbreakable code for public transmission. It uses a binary number as an encryption key with 72 quadrillion possible combinations. The key, randomly chosen for each session, is used to create the encryption pattern for transmission. See *RSA*.

descenders The parts of the lower case characters g, j, p, q and y that fall below the line. Sometimes these characters are displayed and printed with shortened descenders in order to fit into a smaller character cell, making them difficult to read.

descending sort Arranging data from high to low sequence (Z to A, 9 to 0).

descriptor (1) A word or phrase that identifies a document in an indexed information retrieval system.

(2) A category name used to identify data.

deserialize To convert a serial stream of bits into parallel streams of bits.

Designer A full-featured Windows drawing program from Micrografx, Inc., Richardson, TX. It was the first PC program to provide almost all the design tools found in Macintosh drawing programs. It creates its own DRW (2.x and 3.x) and DS3 (4.x) file formats and supports PIC files compatible with other Micrografx products.

desk accessory In the Macintosh, a program that is always available from the Apple menu no matter what application is running. With System 7, all applications can be turned into desk accessories.

desk checking Manually testing the logic of a program.

DeskJet A family of popular desktop ink-jet printers for PCs from HP.

DESKPRO A Compaq trade name for its PCs.

desktop (1) An on-screen representation of a desktop. The windowing capabilities built into graphical user interfaces (GUIs) provide a "virtual desktop," in which the user views an infinite desktop full of documents. Both the Macintosh and Windows use this metaphor, but the Mac more closely simulates a real desktop.

(2) A buzzword attached to applications traditionally performed on more expensive machines that are now on a personal computer (desktop publishing, desktop mapping, etc.).

desktop accessory Software that simulates an object normally found on an office desktop, such as a calculator, notepad and appointment calendar. See *TSR*.

desktop application See *desktop accessory*.

desktop computer A computer that is small enough to reside on a desktop. It either refers to personal computers (PCs, Macs, Amigas, PowerPCs, etc.) or to workstations from Sun, IBM, HP, Digital and others.

desktop manager The part of a GUI that displays the desktop and icons, allows programs to be launched from the icon and files to be visually dragged & dropped (copied, deleted, etc.). The desktop manager combined with the window manager make up the GUI. The desktop manager is included with the Mac and

Windows. In OSF/Motif and Open Look, products such as IXI's X.desktop and Visix Software's Looking Glass add this capability.

desktop mapping Using a desktop computer to perform digital mapping functions.

desktop media The integration of desktop presentations, desktop publishing and multimedia (coined by Apple).

desktop organizer See *desktop accessory*.

desktop presentations The creation of presentation materials on a personal computer, which includes charts, graphs and other graphics-oriented information. It implies a wide variety of special effects for both text and graphics that will produce output for use as handouts, overheads and slides as well as sequences that can be viewed on screen. Advanced systems generate animation and control multimedia devices.

desktop publishing Abbreviated "DTP." Using a personal computer to produce high-quality printed output or camera-ready output for commercial printing. It requires a desktop publishing program, high-speed personal computer, large monitor and a laser printer.

Since DTP has dramatically brought down the cost of high-end page makeup, it is often thought of as "the" way to produce inhouse newsletters and brochures. However, creating quality material takes experience. Desktop publishing is no substitute for a graphics designer who knows which fonts to use and how to lay out the page artistically.

DESQview A multitasking, windows environment for DOS from Quarterdeck Office Systems, Santa Monica, CA. It runs multiple DOS text and graphics programs in resizable windows. DESQview was very popular when DOS was the rage.

DESQview/X A version of DESQview that allows DOS and Windows applications to run in an X Window network under UNIX or any other X-based environment.

destructive memory Memory that loses its content when it is read, requiring that the circuitry regenerate the bits after the read operation.

detail file Same as *transaction file*.

developer's toolkit A set of software routines and utilities used to help programmers write an application. In graphical interfaces, it provides the tools for creating resources, such as menus, dialog boxes, fonts and icons. It provides the means to link the new application to its operating environment (OS, DBMS, protocol, etc.). See *development system*.

development cycle See *system development cycle*.

development system (1) A programming language and related components. It includes the compiler, text editor, debugger, function library and any other supporting programs that enable a programmer to write a program. See *developer's toolkit*.

(2) A computer and related software for developing applications.

development tool Any hardware or software that assists in the creation of electronic machines or software. See *developer's toolkit*.

device (1) Any electronic or electromechanical machine or component from a transistor to a disk drive. Device always refers to hardware.

(2) In semiconductor design, it is an active component, such as a transistor or diode, in contrast to a passive component, such as a resistor or capacitor.

device adapter Same as *interface adapter*.

device address See *address, I/O address* and *port address*.

device control character A communications code that activates a function on a terminal. See *ASCII chart (17-20)*.

device dependent Refers to programs that address specific hardware features and work with only one type of peripheral device. Contrast with *device independent*. See *machine dependent*.

device driver See *driver*.

device independent Refers to programs that work with a variety of peripheral devices. The hardware-specific instructions are in some other program (OS, DBMS, etc.). Contrast with *device dependent*. See *machine independent*.

device level (1) In circuit design, refers to working with individual transistors rather than complete circuits.

(2) Refers to communicating directly with the hardware at a machine language level.

device name A name assigned to a hardware device that represents its physical address. For example, LPT1 is a DOS device name for the parallel port.

DFT mode (Distributed Function Terminal mode) A mode that allows a 3270 terminal to have five concurrent sessions with the mainframe. Contrast with *CUT mode*.

DG See *Data General*.

Dhrystones A benchmark program that tests a general mix of instructions. The results in Dhrystones per second are the number of times the program can be executed in one second. See *Whetstones*.

DIA (Document Interchange Architecture) An IBM SNA format used to exchange documents from dissimilar machines within an LU 6.2 session. It acts as an envelope to hold the document and does not set any standards for the content of the document, such as layout settings or graphics standards.

Diablo emulation A printer that accepts the same commands as the Diablo printer.

diacritical A small mark added to a letter that changes its pronunciation, such as the French cedilla (Ç).

diagnostic board An expansion board with built-in diagnostic tests that reports results via its own readout. Boards for PCs, such as Landmark's KickStart and UNICORE's POSTcard, have their own POST system and can test a malfunctioning computer that doesn't boot.

diagnostic tracks The spare tracks on a disk used by the drive or controller for testing purposes.

diagnostics (1) Software routines that test hardware components (memory, keyboard, disks, etc.). In personal computers, they are often stored in ROM and activated on startup.

(2) Error messages in a programmer's source code that refer to statements or syntax that the compiler or assembler cannot understand.

diagramming program Software that allows the user to create flow charts, organization charts and other interconnected diagrams. It is similar to a drawing program, but keeps the lines connected to the blocks when the blocks are moved. It may also provide text annotation of the graphic items, allowing an equipment list to be maintained with a network diagram, for example.

DIALOG An online information service that contains the world's largest collection of databases. Address: 3460 Hillview Ave., Palo Alto CA 94304, 415/858-2700.

dialog box A small, on-screen window displayed in response to some request. It provides the options currently available to the user.

dial-up line A two-wire line as used in the dial-up telephone network. Contrast with *leased line*.

dial-up network The switched telephone network regulated by government and administered by common carriers.

diazo film A film used to make microfilm or microfiche copies. It is exposed to the original film under ultraviolet light and is developed into identical copies. Copy color is typically blue, blue-black or purple.

DIB (Device Independent Bit map) See *BMP*.

dibit Any one of four patterns from two consecutive bits: 00, 01, 10 and 11. Using phase modulation, a dibit can be modulated onto a carrier as a different shift in the phase of the wave.

DIBOL (DIgital coBOL) A version of COBOL from Digital that runs on the PDP and VAX series.

DID (Direct Inward Dialing) The ability to make a telephone call directly into an internal extension within an organization, without having to go through the operator.

die The formal term for the square of silicon containing an integrated circuit. The popular term is chip.

dielectric An insulator (glass, rubber, plastic, etc.). Dielectric materials can be made to hold an electrostatic charge, but current cannot flow through them.

DIF (1) (Data Interchange Format) A standard file format for spreadsheet and other data structured in row and column form. Originally developed for VisiCalc, DIF is now under Lotus' jurisdiction.

(2) (Display Information Facility) An IBM System/38 program that lets users build custom programs for online access to data.

(3) (Document Interchange Format) A file standard developed by the U.S. Navy in 1982.

(4) (Dual In-line Flatpack) A type of surface mount DIP with pins extending horizontally outward.

differential backup See *backup types*.

differential configuration The use of individual wire pairs for each electrical signal for high immunity to noise and crosstalk. Contrast with *single-ended configuration*.

diffusion A semiconductor manufacturing process that infuses tiny quantities of impurities into a base material, such as silicon, to change its electrical characteristics.

digit A single character in a numbering system. In decimal, digits are 0 through 9. In binary, digits are 0 and 1.

digital Traditionally, the use of numbers and comes from digit, or finger. Today, digital is synonymous with computer. See also *Digital Equipment*.

digital camera A video camera that records its images in digital form. Unlike traditional analog cameras that convert light intensities into infinitely variable signals, digital cameras convert light intensities into discrete numbers.
    It breaks down the picture image into a fixed number of pixels (dots), tests each pixel for light intensity and converts the intensity into a number. In a color digital

camera, three numbers are created, representing the amount of red, green and blue in each pixel.

digital channel A communications path that handles only digital signals. All voice and video signals have to be converted from analog to digital in order to be carried over a digital channel. Contrast with *analog channel*.

digital circuit An electronic circuit that accepts and processes binary data (on/off) according to the rules of Boolean logic.

digital computer A computer that accepts and processes data that has been converted into binary numbers. All common computers are digital. Contrast with *analog computer*.

digital convergence The integration of computers, communications and consumer electronics.

digital data Data in digital form. All data in the computer is in digital form.

digital domain The world of digital. When something is done in the digital domain, it implies that the original data (images, sounds, video, etc.) has been converted into a digital format and is manipulated inside the computer's memory.

digital effects Special sounds and animations that have been created in the digital domain. Synthetic sounds and reverberation, morphing and transitions between video frames (fades, wipes, dissolves, etc.) are examples.

Digital Equipment (Digital Equipment Corporation, Maynard, MA) A major computer manufacturer, commonly known as DEC or Digital. It was founded in 1957 by Kenneth Olsen, who headed the company until he retired in 1992. Digital pioneered the minicomputer industry with its PDP series and became very successful with its VAX line in the 1980s. Its new Alpha architecture is designed to take Digital into the 21st century.

digital mapping Digitizing geographic information for a geographic information system (GIS).

digital monitor A video monitor that accepts a digital signal from the computer and converts it into analog signals to illuminate the screen. Common examples are MDA, CGA and EGA monitors. Contrast with *analog monitor*.

THE PDP-1, DIGITAL'S FIRST COMPUTER
(Courtesy Digital Equipment Corporation)

digital nonlinear editing See *nonlinear video editing*.

Digital Paper A non-erasable storage material from ICI Electronics used for tape and disk archival storage. It uses a polyester film coated with a reflective layer on top of which is adhered a dye polymer layer that is sensitive to infrared light. A laser burns pits into the film as close as half a micron apart. Capacities are about one Gbyte on a 5.25" disk and 600 GBytes on a 2,400 foot tape reel.

digital PBX (digital Private Branch Exchange) A modern PBX that uses digital methods for switching in contrast to older PBXs that use analog methods.

digital radio The microwave transmission of digital data via line of sight transmitters.

digital recording See *digital video, digital nonlinear editing* and *magnetic recording.*

Digital Research (Digital Research, Inc., Monterey, CA) A software company founded in 1976 by Gary Kildall that spearheaded the microcomputer revolution with its CP/M operating system. In 1991, it was acquired by Novell.

digital signal processing See *DSP.*

digital signature A coded message added to data transmitted over a network that verifies to the recipient that the sender is authentic. Digital signatures ensure that senders are who they say they are. See *RSA* and *DSS (2).*

digital video Video recording in digital form. In order to edit video in the computer or to embed video clips into multimedia documents, a video source must originate as digital (digital camera) or be converted to digital. Frames from analog video cameras and VCRs are converted into digital frames (bitmaps) using frame grabbers or similar devices attached to a personal computer.

Uncompressed digital video signals consume huge amounts of storage and require large bandwidth for transmission. High-ratio realtime compression schemes are essential for effective use. See *digital nonlinear editing* and *HDTV.*

digitize To convert an image or signal into digital code by scanning, tracing on a graphics tablet or using an analog to digital conversion device. 3-D objects can be digitized by a device with a mechanical arm that is moved onto all the corners.

digitizer tablet A graphics drawing tablet used for sketching new images or tracing old ones and for selecting from menus. The user makes contact with the tablet with a pen-like or puck-like device called a cursor (mistakenly called a mouse), which is connected to the tablet by a wire. For sketching, the user draws with the tablet cursor and the screen cursor "draws" a corresponding image. When tracing an image on the tablet, a series of x-y coordinates (vector graphics) are created, either as a continuous stream of coordinates, or as end points.

Menu selection is accomplished by a tablet overlay or by a screen display. The tablet cursor selects an item by making contact with it on the overlay, or by controlling the screen cursor.

DIGITIZER TABLET

dimension One axis in an array. In programming, a dimension statement defines the array and sets up the number of elements within the dimensions.

dimensioning In CAD programs, the management and display of the measurements of an object. There are various standards that determine such things as tolerances, sizes of arrowheads and orientation on the paper.

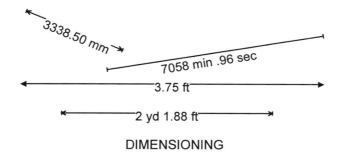

DIMENSIONING

DIN connector (Deutsches Institut für Normung - German Standards Institute) A plug and socket used to connect a variety of devices; for example, the PC keyboard uses a five-pin DIN. DIN plugs look like an open metal can about a half inch in diameter with pins inside in a circular pattern.

dingbats A group of typesetting and desktop publishing symbols from International Typeface Corporation that include arrows, pointing hands, stars and circled numbers. They are formally called ITC Zapf Dingbats.

diode An electronic component that acts primarily as a one-way valve. As a discrete component or built into a chip, it is used in a variety of functions. It is a key element in changing AC into DC. They are used as temperature and light sensors and light emitters (LEDs). In communications, they filter out analog and digital signals from carriers and modulate signals onto carriers. In digital logic, they're used as one-way valves and as switches similar to transistors.

DIP (Dual In-line Package) A common rectangular chip housing with leads (pins) on both long sides. Tiny wires bond the chip to metal leads that wind their way down into spider-like feet that are inserted into a socket or are soldered onto the board.

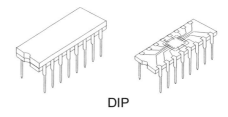

DIP

DIP switch (Dual In-line Package switch) A set of tiny toggle switches built into a DIP, which is mounted directly on a circuit board. The tip of a pen or pencil is required to flip the switch on or off.
    Remember! Open is "off." Closed is "on."

Dir (DIRectory) A CP/M, DOS and OS/2 command that lists the file names on the disk.

direct access The ability to go directly to a specific storage location without having to go through what's in front of it. Memories (RAMs, ROMs, PROMs, etc.) and disks are the major direct access devices.

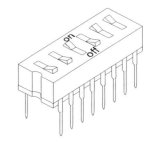

DIP SWITCH

direct access method A technique for finding data on a disk by deriving its storage address from an identifying key in the record, such as account number. Using a formula, the account number is converted into a sector address. This is faster than comparing entries in an index, but it only works well when keys are numerically close: 100, 101, 102, etc.

direct-connect modem A modem that connects to a telephone line without the use of an acoustic coupler.

directory A simulated file drawer on disk. Programs and data for each application are typically kept in a separate directory (spreadsheets, word processing, etc.). Directories create the illusion of compartments, but are actually indexes to the files which may be scattered all over the disk.

directory management The maintenance and control of directories on a hard disk. Usually refers to menuing software that is easier to use than entering commands.

directory service In a messaging system, it is a directory of names and addresses of every mail recipient on the network. When sent a user name as a query, it returns the logical mail address (mailbox) of that user. A directory service usually differs from a network naming service in that a directory service returns a logical address, whereas a naming service returns the physical address of a node. Sometimes, either term refers to either function.

directory tree A graphic representation of a hierarchical directory as in the following example.

dirty power A non-uniform AC power (voltage fluctuations, noise and spikes), which comes from the electric utility or from electronic equipment in the office.

disable To turn off a function. Disabled means turned off, not broken. Contrast with *enable*.

disassembler Software that converts machine language back into assembly language. Since there is no way to easily determine the human thinking behind the logic of the instructions, the resulting assembly language routines and variables are named and numbered generically (A001, A002, etc.). Disassembled code can be very difficult to maintain.

DIRECTORY TREE

disc An alternate spelling for disk. Compact discs and videodiscs are spelled with the "c." Most computer disks are spelled with a "k."

discrete A component or device that is separate and distinct and treated as a singular unit.

discrete component An elementary electronic device constructed as a single unit. Before integrated circuits (chips), all transistors, resistors and diodes were discrete. They are widely used in amplifiers and other devices that use large amounts of current. They are also still used on circuit boards intermingled with the chips.

discrete cosine transform See *DCT*.

discretionary hyphen A user-designated place in a word for hyphenation. If the word goes over the margin, it will split in that location.

dish A saucer-shaped antenna that receives, or transmits and receives, signals from a satellite.

disk A direct access storage device. See *floppy disk, hard disk, magnetic disk, optical disk* and *LaserDisc.*

disk array Two or more disk drives combined in a single unit for increased capacity, speed and/or fault tolerant operation. See *RAID*.

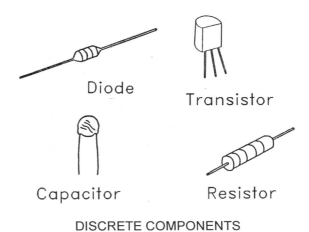

Diode   Transistor

Capacitor   Resistor

DISCRETE COMPONENTS

disk based (1) A computer system that uses disks as its storage medium.

(2) An application that retrieves data from the disk as required. Contrast with *memory based*.

disk cartridge A removable disk module that contains a single hard disk platter or a floppy disk.

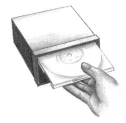

DISK CARTRIDGES

disk controller A circuit that controls transmission to and from the disk drive. In a personal computer, it is an expansion board that plugs into an expansion slot in the bus. See *hard disk*.

Diskcopy A DOS and OS/2 utility used to copy entire floppy disks track by track.

disk drive A peripheral storage device that holds, spins, reads and writes magnetic or optical disks. It may be a receptacle for disk cartridges, disk packs or floppy disks, or it may contain non-removable disk platters like most personal computer hard disks.

disk dump A printout of disk contents without report formatting.

disk duplicator A device that formats and makes identical copies of floppy disks for software distribution. Simple units contain two floppy disks and require manual loading, elaborate units have automatic loading and may also attach the labels.

disk emulator A solid state replication of a disk drive.

diskette Same as *floppy disk*.

disk file A set of instructions or data that is recorded, cataloged and treated as a single unit on a disk. Source language programs, machine language programs, spreadsheets, data files, text documents, graphics files and batch files are examples.

disk format The storage layout of a disk as determined by its physical medium and as initialized by a format program. For example, a 5.25" 360KB floppy vs a 3.5" 1.44MB floppy or a DOS disk vs a Mac disk. See *low-level format, high-level format* and *file format*.

diskless workstation A workstation without a disk. Programs and data are retrieved from the network server.

disk management The maintenance and control of a hard disk. Refers to a variety of utilities that provide format, copy, diagnostic, directory management and defragmenting functions.

disk memory Same as *disk*. In this Glossary, disks and tapes are called storage devices, not memory devices.

disk mirroring The recording of redundant data for fault tolerant operation. Data is written on two partitions of the same disk, on two separate disks within the same system or on two separate computer systems.

disk operating system See *DOS*.

disk optimizer A utility program that defragments a hard disk. See *defragment*.

disk pack A removable hard disk module used in minis and mainframes that contains two or more platters housed in a dust-free container. For mounting, the bottom of the container is removed. After insertion, the top is removed.

disk partition A subdivision of a hard disk. The maximum size of a disk partition depends on the operating system used.

disk striping The spreading of data over multiple disk drives to improve performance. Data is interleaved by bytes or by sectors across the drives. For example, with four drives and a controller designed to overlap reads and writes, four sectors could be read in the same time it normally takes to read one. Disk striping does not inherently provide fault tolerance or error checking. It is used in conjunction with various other methods. See *RAID*.

DISOSS (DIStributed Office Support System) An IBM mainframe centralized document distribution and filing application that runs under MVS. Its counterpart under VM is PROFS. It allows for e-mail and the exchange of documents between a variety of IBM office devices, including word processors and PCs. DISOSS uses the SNADS messaging protocol.

dispatcher Same as *scheduler*.

dispersed intelligence Same as *distributed intelligence*.

displacement Same as *offset*. See *base/displacement*.

display adapter Same as *video display board*.

display attribute See *attribute*.

display board, display card Same as *video display board*.

display cycle In computer graphics, the series of operations required to display an image.

display device See *display screen* and *video display board*.

display element (1) In graphics, a basic graphic arts component, such as background, foreground, text or graphics image.

(2) In computer graphics, any component of an image.

display entity In computer graphics, a collection of display elements that can be manipulated as a unit.

display font Same as *screen font*.

display frame In computer graphics, a single frame in a series of animation frames.

display list In computer graphics, a collection of vectors that make up an image stored in vector graphics format.

display list processor In computer graphics, an engine that generates graphic geometry (draws lines, circles, etc.) directly from the display list and independently of the CPU.

Display PostScript The screen counterpart of the PostScript printer language that translates elementary commands in an application to graphics and text elements on screen. It is designed for inclusion in an operating system to provide a standard, device-independent display language.

display screen A surface area upon which text and graphics are temporarily made to appear for human viewing. It is typically a CRT or flat panel technology.

display terminal See *video terminal*.

DisplayWrite A full-featured IBM word processing program for PCs that stems from the typewriter-oriented DisplayWriter word processing system first introduced in 1980.

distributed computing Same as *distributed processing*. See *parallel computing*.

distributed data processing See *distributed processing*.

distributed database A database physically stored in two or more computer systems. Although geographically dispersed, a distributed database system manages and controls the entire database as a single collection of data. If redundant data is stored in separate databases due to performance requirements, updates to one set of data will automatically update the additional sets in a timely manner.

distributed file system Software that keeps track of files stored across multiple networks. It converts file names into physical locations.

distributed function The distribution of processing functions throughout the organization.

distributed intelligence The placing processing capability in terminals and other peripheral devices. Intelligent terminals handle screen layouts, data entry validation and other pre-processing steps. Intelligence placed into disk drives and other peripherals relieves the central computer from routine tasks.

distributed logic See *distributed intelligence*.

distributed processing Also called *distributed computing*, it is a system of computers connected by a communications network. The term is used loosely to refer to any computers with communications between them. However, in true distributed processing, each computer system is sized to handle its local workload, and the network has been designed to support the system as a whole. Contrast with *centralized processing* and *decentralized processing*.

dithering In computer graphics, the creation of additional colors and shades from an existing palette. In monochrome displays, shades of grays are created by varying the density and patterns of the dots. In color displays, colors and patterns are created by mixing and varying the dots of existing colors.

Dithering is used to create a wide variety of patterns for use as backgrounds, fills and shading, as well as for creating halftones for printing. It is also used in anti-aliasing.

divide overflow A program error in which a number is accidentally divided by zero or by a number that creates a result too large for the computer to handle.

DL/1 (Data Language 1) The database language in IMS.

DLC (1) (Data Link Control) See *data link* and *OSI*.

(2) (Data Link Control) The protocol used in IBM's Token Ring networks.

(3) (Digital Loop Carrier) See *loop carrier*.

DLC chip Any one of several Intel-compatible CPUs from Cyrix Corporation. See *486DLC*.

DLL (Dynamic Link Library) Executable routines available to applications at runtime. They are typically written in reentrant code so they can serve more than one application at the same time.

Under DOS, TSRs have been used as a way of adding functionality at runtime. They remain in memory, intercept upon certain conditions, then perform their function. TSRs have never been formally sanctioned and are prone to conflict. Windows, however, has adopted the dynamic link library, or DLL, method as a standard way of creating new functionality that can be shared in the system.

DMA (Direct Memory Access) Specialized circuitry or a dedicated microprocessor that transfers data from memory to memory without using the CPU. On PCs, there are eight DMA channels. Most sound cards are set to use DMA channel 1.

DME (Distributed Managment Environment) A set of programs from OSF that provides coherent management of networks and systems.

DMI (Desktop Managment Interface) A management system for PCs that provides a bi-directional path to interrogate all the hardware and software components within a

PC. When PCs are DMI-enabled, their hardware and software configurations can be monitored from a central station in the network.

DMPL (Digital Microprocessor Plotter Language) A vector graphics file format from Houston Instruments that was developed for plotters. Most plotters support the DMPL or HPGL standards.

DMTF (Desktop Management Task Force) Initiated by Intel in 1992, it created the DMI interface. See *DMI*.

DNA (Digital Network Architecture) Introduced in 1978, DNA defines Digital's protocols, formats and control of message exchange over a network. DECnet is the implementation of this architecture.

DNS (Domain Naming System) An e-mail addressing system used in networks such as the Internet and BITNET. It converts an e-mail address, such as joe@clc.com to the internet address (IP) for transmission.

do loop A high-level programming language structure that repeats instructions based on the results of a comparison. In a DO WHILE loop, the instructions within the loop are performed if the comparison is true. In a DO UNTIL loop, the instructions are bypassed if the comparison is true. The following DO WHILE loop prints 1 through 10 and stops.

```
COUNTER = 0
DO WHILE COUNTER < 10
  COUNTER = COUNTER + 1
  ? COUNTER
ENDDO
```

do nothing instruction Same as *no-op*.

docking station A base station for a laptop that includes a power supply and expansion slots as well as monitor and keyboard connectors. See *port replicator*.

docs Short for documents or documentation.

document (1) Any paper form that has been filled in.

(2) A word processing text file.

(3) In the Macintosh, any text, data or graphics file created in the computer.

document handling A procedure for transporting and handling paper documents for data entry and scanning.

document image management See *document imaging*.

document image processing See *document imaging*.

document imaging The online storage, retrieval and management of electronic images of documents. The main method of capturing images is by scanning paper documents.

Document imaging systems replace large paper-intensive operations. Documents can be shared by all users on a network and document routing can be controlled by the computer (workflow automation). The systems are often simpler to develop and implement than traditional data processing systems, because users are already familiar with the paper documents that appear on screen.

document management Keeping track of stored documents that have been scanned into the computer or created via word processing, spreadsheet or other applications. A document management system may be an integral part of a document imaging system.

document mark In micrographics, a small optical blip on each frame on a roll of microfilm that is used to automatically count the frames.

document processing Processing text documents, which includes indexing methods for text retrieval based on content. See *document imaging*.

documentation The narrative and graphical description of a system. Documentation for an information system includes:

Operating Procedures

1. Instructions for turning the system on and getting the programs initiated (loaded).
2. Instructions for obtaining source documents for data entry.
3. Instructions for entering data at the terminal, which includes a picture of each screen layout the user will encounter.
4. A description of error messages that can occur and the alternative methods for handling them.
5. A description of the defaults taken in the programs and the instructions for changing them.
6. Instructions for distributing the computer's output, which includes sample pages for each type of report.

System Documentation

1. Data dictionary - the description of the files and databases.
2. System flow chart - the description of the data as it flows from source document to final reports.
3. Application program documentation - the description of the inputs, processing and outputs for each data entry, query, update and report program in the system.

Technical Documentation

1. File structures and access methods
2. Program flow charts
3. Program source code listings
4. Machine procedures (JCL)

docuterm A word or phrase in a text document that is used to identify the contents of the document.

domain (1) In database management, all possible values contained in a particular field for every record in the file.

(2) In communications, all resources under control of a single computer system. In a LAN, a domain is a subnetwork comprised of a group of clients and servers under the control of one security database. Dividing LANs into domains improves performance and security.

(3) In magnetic storage devices, a group of molecules that makes up one bit.

(4) In a hierarchy, a named group that has control over the groups under it, which may be domains themselves.

dominant carrier A telecommunications services provider that has control over a large segment of a particular market.

dongle Same as *hardware key*.

door (1) In a BBS system, a programming interface that lets an online user run an application program in the BBS.

(2) See *drive door*.

doorway mode In a communications program, a mode that passes function, cursor, ctrl and alt keystrokes to the BBS computer in order to use the remote application as if it were on the local machine.

dopant An element diffused into pure silicon in order to alter its electrical characteristics.

doping Altering the electrical conductivity of a semiconductor material, such as silicon, by chemically combining it with foreign elements. It results in an excess of electrons (n-type) or a lack of electrons (p-type) in the silicon.

DOS (1) (Disk Operating System) Pronounced "dahss." A generic term for operating system.

(2) (Disk Operating System) A single-user operating system for the PC. It is the most widely used operating system in the world. The version provided by IBM is called PC-DOS to distinguish it from MS-DOS, the version for non-IBM PCs. All versions of DOS and MS-DOS have been developed by Microsoft with IBM participating in varying degrees. The more recent versions of DOS are developed independently.

Except for DOS 6, both versions are almost identical. Microsoft's MS-DOS 6 and IBM's PC-DOS 6 provide different versions of the utilities, although all commands and primary functions are the same. In this Glossary, DOS refers to both PC-DOS and MS-DOS.

▶ *The electronic versions of this book provide more detail on this subject, including a DOS tutorial and command examples for more than 150 DOS commands.*

DOS box The DOS compatibility mode. When a DOS application is running under Windows or OS/2, it is running in a DOS box. The "box" is actually one instance of the Intel x86 Virtual 8086 Mode, which simulates an independent, fully functional PC environment.

DOS device names Reserved names for common input and output devices.

Reserved name	Device
AUX	First connected serial port
PRN	First connected parallel port
COM1 thru COM4	Serial ports (modem, mouse, etc.)
LPT1 thru LPT3	Parallel ports (printer)
CON	Keyboard and screen
NUL	Dummy (testing purposes)

DOS environment A reserved area in DOS for holding values used by DOS and other applications. The values stored in this area are called "environment variables" and are created with the Set command.

DOS extender Software that is combined with a DOS application to allow it to run in extended memory (beyond 1MB). To gain access to extended memory, it runs the application in Protected Mode.

DOS external command A separate utility program that comes with DOS, such as Format, Diskcopy, XCopy, Tree, Backup and Restore, but is not resident within DOS, such as Copy and Dir. Contrast with *DOS internal command*.

DOS file (1) Any computer file created under DOS.

(2) An ASCII text file.

DOS format The disk file structure required by DOS. All floppy disks and hard disks must be initialized with this format before use. The format process creates the sectors on the disk (low-level format) that are later filled with data and also generates the tables that DOS uses (high-level format) to keep track of the data.

Hard disks are regularly formatted at the factory, but floppies may or may not be.

DOS internal command A command capability within DOS at all times, such as Dir, Copy, Del, Ren, Type and Cls. The internal commands are part of DOS' COMMAND.COM file. If you delete COMMAND.COM, you can no longer command DOS to do anything at the command line. Contrast with *DOS external command*.

DOSmark A unit of performance based on Ziff-Davis' PC Labs tests. It rates a PC's ability to run DOS applications, which is a composite of CPU, memory, disk and video tests. See *Winmark*.

DOS memory manager Software that expands DOS' ability to manage more than one megabyte of memory or to manage its first megabyte more effectively. Since the early days of DOS, third party memory managers, such as QEMM and 386MAX, have used every trick in the book to move TSRs and drivers out of the lower 640K and into the 384K upper memory area (UMA).

Starting with DOS 5, DOS includes its own memory managers. HIMEM.SYS manages extended memory, and EMM386.EXE manages expanded memory.

DOS Memory Areas

Conventional memory	0-640K
Upper memory area (UMA)	640-1024K
High memory area (HMA)	1024-1088K
Extended memory	1024 and up
Expanded memory	Bank switched memory

DOS prompt The message DOS displays when ready to accept user input. The DOS prompt usually looks like `c:\>` when the computer boots up.

DOS shell The user interface in DOS. COMMAND.COM is the program that provides the command-driven user interface. Other shells can be substituted for COMMAND.COM in order to provide a more friendly interface or to add more features.

DOS switch A parameter that modifies a DOS command. DOS switches use a forward slash (not a backslash) followed by a letter, digit or code. For example, in the command `dir /w`, the /w changes the Dir command to list "wide" across the screen instead of in a column.

DOS text file A file that does not contain any proprietary coding schemes. Batch files and source language programs are examples. It contains only ASCII characters and has a CR/LF (carriage return/line feed) code at the end of each line. Text files are read by text editors as well as word processors with "ASCII" or "text" input options.

DOS/V A Japanese version of DOS that supports two-byte-long characters for handling the Kanji character set. It can switch between English and Japanese and is geared for 286s and up with VGA graphics. Backed by IBM Japan and the OADG. In Japan, NEC is the major personal computer vendor with its PC-9801 series.

DOS/VSE See *VSE*.

dot (1) A tiny round, rectangular or square spot that is one element in a matrix, which is used to display or print a graphics or text image. See *dot matrix*.

(2) A period; for example, V dot 22 is the same as V.22.

dot addressable The ability to program each individual dot on a video display, dot matrix printer or laser printer.

dot chart Same as *scatter diagram*.

dot gain An increase in size of each dot of ink when printed due to temperature, ink and paper type.

dot matrix The pattern of dots that form character and graphic images on video screens and printers. Display screens use a matrix (rows and columns) of dots just like TVs. Serial printers use one or two columns of dot hammers that are moved across the paper. Laser printers "paint" dots of light a line at a time onto a light-sensitive photographic drum.

The more dots per square inch, the higher the resolution of the characters and graphics.

dot matrix printer A printer that forms images out of dots. The common desktop dot matrix printer uses one or two columns of dot hammers that are moved serially across the paper. The more dot hammers used, the higher the resolution of the printed image. 24-pin dot matrix printers produce typewriter-like output.

dot pitch The distance between a red (or green or blue) dot and the closest red (or green or blue) dot on a color monitor (typically from .28 to .51mm; large presentation monitors may go up to 1.0mm). The smaller the dot pitch, the crisper the image. A .28 dot pitch means dots are 28/100ths of a millimeter apart. A dot pitch of .31 or less provides a sharp image, especially on text.

Dot pitch measurements between conventional tubes and Sony's Trinitron tubes are roughly, but not exactly equivalent. Sony's CRTs use vertical stripes, not dots, and its measurement is the distance between stripes, not the diagonal distance between dots.

7–pin 9–pin 18–pin 24–pin

SERIAL DOT MATRIX PIN CONFIGURATIONS

double buffering A programming technique that uses two buffers to speed up a computer that can overlap I/O with processing. For example, data in one buffer is being processed while the next set of data is read into the second buffer.

double click To press the mouse button twice in rapid succession.

double density Twice the capacity of the prior format. Yesterday's double density can be today's low density (see *DD*).

double precision Using two computer words instead of one to hold a number used for calculations, thus allowing twice as large a number for more arithmetic precision. Contrast with *single precision*.

double scan CGA A hardware circuit that improves CGA resolution.

double sided disk A floppy disk that is recorded on both of its sides.

DoubleSpace A realtime compression technique built into DOS 6 and removed in DOS 6.21.

double strike Printing a character twice in order to darken the image.

double twist Same as *supertwist*.

double word Twice the length of a single computer word. A double word is typically 32 bits long. See *word*.

down Refers to a computer that fails to operate due to hardware or software failure. A communications line is down when it is unable to transfer data.

downlink A communications channel from a satellite to an earth station. Contrast with *uplink*.

download To transmit a file from one computer to another. When conducting the session, download means receive, upload means transmit. It implies sending a file rather than interacting in a conversational mode.

downloadable font Same as *soft font*.

downsizing Converting mainframe and mini-based systems to personal computer LANs.

downtime The time during which a computer is not functioning due to hardware or system software failure. That's when you truly understand how important it is to have reliable hardware.

downward compatible Also called backward compatible. Refers to hardware or software that is compatible with earlier versions. Contrast with *upward compatible*.

DP See *data processing* and *dot pitch*.

DPCM (Differential PCM) An audio digitization technique that codes the difference between samples rather than coding an absolute measurement at each sample point. See *ADPCM*.

dpi (Dots Per Inch) The measurement of printer resolution. A 300 dpi printer means 90,000 dots are printable in one square inch (300x300). 400 dpi generates 160,000 dots; 500 dpi yields 250,000 dots.

DPMA (Data Processing Management Association) A membership organization founded in 1951 with over 40,000 managers of DP installations, programmers, systems analysts and research specialists. It founded the CDP examinations, now administrated by ICCP. Offers many educational programs and seminars, in addition to sponsoring student organizations around the country interested in DP. Address: 505 Busse Highway, Park Ridge, IL 60068, 312/825-8124.

DPMI (DOS Protected Mode Interface) A DOS extender specification for 286s and up that allows DOS extended programs to cooperatively run under Windows 3.x. Developed by Microsoft, it keeps a DOS-extended application from crashing the computer and usurping Windows' control. It is not compatible with VCPI, the first DOS extender standard, but Windows 3.1 is more tolerant of VCPI applications than Windows 3.0.

XMS Versus VCPI/DPMI

XMS, VCPI and DPMI all deal with extended memory. However, XMS allows data and programs to be stored in and retrieved from extended memory, whereas the VCPI and DPMI interfaces allow programs to "run" in extended memory.

DPPX (Distributed Processing Programming EXecutive) An operating system for the 8100, now defunct. DPPX/370 is a version allowing users to migrate to 9370s.

DPS Minicomputer series from Bull HN.

DPSK (Differential Phase Shift Keying) A common form of phase modulation used in modems. It does not require complex demodulation circuitry and is not susceptible to random phase changes in the transmitted waveform. Contrast with *FSK*.

DQDB (Distributed Queue Dual Bus) An IEEE 802.6 packet switching network technology for MANs. The first SMDS services offered by the local telephone companies use DQDB.

DR DOS (Digital Research DOS) A DOS-compatible operating system noted for its many features. It was originally developed by Digital Research, which was later acquired by Novell. See *Novell DOS*.

Drafix A family of 2-D and 3-D CAD packages for PCs and Atari STs from Foresight Resources Corporation, Kansas City, MO. It features professional functions and provides constant on-screen information during drawing.

draft mode The highest-speed, lowest-quality printing mode.

drag To move an object on screen in which its complete movement is visible from starting location to destination. The movement may be activated with a stylus, mouse or keyboard keys.

To drag an object with the mouse, point to it. Press the mouse button and hold the button down while moving the mouse. When the object is at its new location, release the mouse button.

drag & drop The ability to execute a function graphically without typing in a command. For example, in the Macintosh, selecting a floppy disk icon and dragging it onto the trashcan icon causes the floppy to be ejected.

drag lock The ability to lock onto a screen object so that it can be dragged with the mouse without continuously holding down the mouse (or trackball) button.

drain The output (receiving) side of the bridge in a field effect transistor. When the *gate* is charged, current flows from the *source* to the drain. Same as *collector* in a bipolar transistor.

DRAM See *dynamic RAM*.

DRAW (Direct Read After Write) Reading data immediately after it has been written to check for recording errors.

drawing program A graphics program used for creating illustrations. It maintains an image in vector graphics format, which allows all elements of the graphic object to be isolated and manipulated individually.

Drawing programs and CAD programs are similar; however, drawing programs usually provide a large number of special effects for fancy illustrations, while CAD programs provide precise dimensioning and positioning of each graphic element in order that the objects can be transferred to other systems for engineering analysis and manufacturing. Contrast with *paint program*. See *diagramming program*.

DRDA (Distributed Relational Database Architecture) An SAA-compliant enhancement that allows data to be distributed among DB2 and SQL/DS databases. Users or programs can access data from SAA or non-SAA systems that implement DRDA.

DRDBMS (Distributed Relational DBMS) A relational DBMS that manages distributed databases. See *distributed database*.

DRI See *Digital Research*.

dribbleware Software that is publicly displayed and previewed well in advance of its actual release. Dribbleware is one stage beyond vaporware.

drift Change in frequency or time synchronization of a signal that occurs slowly.

drill down To move from summary information to the detailed data that created it.

drive (1) An electromechanical device that spins disks and tapes at a specified speed. Also refers to the entire peripheral unit such as *disk drive* or *tape drive*.

(2) To provide power and signals to a device. For example, "this control unit can drive up to 15 terminals."

drive bay A cavity for a disk drive in a computer cabinet.

drive door A panel, gate or lever used to lock a disk in a disk drive. In a 5.25" floppy drive, the drive door is the lever that is turned down over the slot after inserting the disk.

drive type See *hard disk*.

driver (1) Also called a *device driver*, a program routine that links a peripheral device to the operating system. It contains the precise machine language necessary to activate the device and uses detailed knowledge of the device's characteristics, such as sectors per track and screen resolution, to perform the functions that are requested by the application.

Basic drivers come with the operating system, and drivers are added when new peripheral devices are installed. For example, if you add a mouse or CD-ROM player to your computer, you have to install the appropriate driver so that the operating system knows how to handle it. Drivers are also installed to manage memory and other internal functions.

(2) A device that provides signals or electrical current to activate a transmission line or display screen. See *line driver*.

DriveSpace Microsoft's disk compression that replaces the DoubleSpace technology previously used. It is included starting with MS-DOS 6.22.

drop cap In typography, a large capital letter at the beginning of a sentence that drops below the first line.

drop in An extraneous bit on a magnetic medium that was not intentionally written, due to a surface defect or recording malfunction.

drop out (1) On magnetic media, a bit that has lost its strength due to a surface defect or recording malfunction.

(2) In data transmission, a momentary loss of signal that is due to system malfunction or excessive noise.

droupie (Data gROUPIE) A person who likes to spend time in the company of programmers and data processing professionals.

drum See *magnetic drum*.

drum plotter A graphics plotter that wraps the paper around a drum. The drum turns to produce one direction of the plot; the pen moves to provide the other.

drum printer A line printer that uses formed character images around a cylindrical drum as its printing mechanism. There is a band of characters for each print position. When the desired character for the selected print position has rotated around to the hammer line, the hammer hits the paper from behind and pushes it into the ribbon and onto the character.

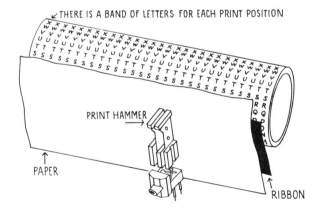

DRUM PRINTER

dry plasma etching A method for inscribing a pattern on a wafer by shooting hot ions through a mask to evaporate the silicon dioxide insulation layer. Dry plasma etching replaces the wet processing method that uses film and acid for developing the pattern.

drystone See *Dhrystones*.

DS (Digital Signal) A classification of digital circuits. The DS technically refers to the rate and format of the signal, while the T designation refers to the equipment providing the signals. In practice, "DS" and "T" are used synonymously; for example, DS1 and T1, DS3 and T3.

North America, Japan, Korea, etc.			Europe (ITU-TSS)		
Service	Voice Channels	Speed	Service	Voice Channels	Speed (Mbps)
DS0	1	64 Kbps	E1	30	2.048
DS1	24	1.544 Mbps (T1)	E2	120	8.448
DS3	672	44.736 Mbps (T3)	E3	480	34.368
			E4	1920	139.264
			E5	7680	565.148

DSA (Directory Systems Agent) An X.500 routine that looks up the location of a message recipient. It accepts requests from the Directory User Agent counterpart in the workstation.

DS/DD (Double Sided/Double Density) Refers to floppy disks, such as the 5.25" 360KB PC format and 3.5" 720KB PC and 800KB Mac formats.

DS/HD (Double Sided/High Density) Refers to floppy disks, such as the 5.25" 1.2MB PC format and 3.5" 1.44MB PC and Mac formats.

DSOM See *SOM*.

DSP (1) (Digital Signal Processor) A special-purpose CPU used for digital signal processing (see below). It provides extra fast instruction sequences, such as shift and add and multiply and add, commonly used in math-intensive signal processing applications.

(2) (Digital Signal Processing) A category of techniques that analyze signals from sources such as sound, weather satellites and earthquake monitors. Signals are converted into digital data and analyzed using various algorithms such as Fast Fourier Transform.
   In sound cards, DSP chips are used to compress and decompress audio formats as well as to assist with recording and playback and speech synthesis. Other audio uses are the DSP chips in stereo amplifiers, which are programmed to simulate concert hall and cinema effects for home theater and music listening.

DSR (Data Set Ready) An RS-232 signal sent from the modem to the computer or terminal indicating that it is able to accept data. Contrast with *DTR*.

DSS (1) (Decision Support System) An information and planning system that provides the ability to interrogate computers on an ad hoc basis, analyze information and predict the impact of decisions before they are made.
   DBMSs let you select data and derive information for reporting and analysis. Spreadsheets and modeling programs provide both analysis and "what if?" planning. However, any single application that supports decision making is not a DSS. A DSS is a cohesive and integrated set of programs that share data and information. A DSS might also retrieve industry data from external sources that can be compared and used for historical and statistical purposes.
   An integrated DSS directly impacts management's decision-making process and can be a very cost-beneficial computer application. See *EIS*.

(2) (Digital Signature Standard) A National Security Administration standard for authenticating an electronic message. See *RSA* and *digital signature*.

DSTN (Double SuperTwisted Nematic) An LCD display that uses an extra display layer (compensating layer) between the main display and the rear polarizer, resulting in an almost-pure black and white display with little color tinge.

DSU/CSU (Digital (or Data) Service Unit/Channel Service Unit) A pair of communications devices that connect an inhouse line to an external digital circuit (T1, DDS, etc.). It is similar to a modem, but connects a digital circuit rather than an analog one.

DSX-1 (Digital Signal Cross-connect Level 1) A standard that defines the voltage, pulse width and plug and socket for connecting DS-1 (T1) signals.

DTA (Design and Test Alliance) A group of ATE and EDA vendors, chip makers and systems houses dedicated to improving testing of complicated electronic systems.

DTD See *SGML*.

DTE (Data Terminating Equipment) A communications device that is the source or destination of signals on a network. It is typically a terminal or computer. Contrast with *DCE*.

DTMF (Dual Tone Multi Frequency) The formal name of touch tone (pushbutton) technology found on telephone keypads.

DTP See *desktop publishing*.

DTR (Data Terminal Ready) An RS-232 signal sent from the computer or terminal to the modem indicating that it is able to accept data. Contrast with *DSR*.

DTS (1) (Digital Termination Service) A microwave-based, line-of-sight communications provided directly to the end user.

(2) (DeskTop Server) A motorola 68000-based network server from Banyan.

(3) (Developer Technical Support) The tech-support group for developers at Apple.

DUA (Directory User Agent) An X.500 routine that sends a request to the Directory Systems Agent to look up the location of a user on the network.

dual boot A computer configuration that allows it to be started with either one of two different operating systems. The dual boot feature is contained in one of the operating systems.

dual in-line package See *DIP*.

dual-scan LCD A technique used to improve passive matrix color screens. It provides a sharper appearance, but still does not approach the richness of active matrix.

dumb terminal A display terminal without processing capability. It is entirely dependent on the main computer for processing. Contrast with *smart terminal* and *intelligent terminal*.

dump To print the contents of memory, disk or tape without any report formatting. See *memory dump*.

Dun & Bradstreet Software (Dun & Bradstreet Software, Atlanta, GA; The Dun & Bradstreet Corporation) A software and consulting organization formed in 1990 as a merger of Management Science America (MSA) and McCormack & Dodge. It specializes in mainframe and client/server software.

duplex channel See *full-duplex*.

duplexed system Two systems that are functionally identical. They both may perform the same functions, or one may be standby, ready to take over if the other fails.

duplicate keys Identical key data in a file. Primary keys, such as account number cannot be duplicated, since no two customers or employees should be assigned the same number. Secondary keys, such as date, product and city, may be duplicated in the file or database.

DVE (Digital Video Effects) Video effects such as fades, wipes, dissolves, page flips, and iris and funnel effects performed by computer.

DVI (Digital Video Interactive) An Intel compression technique for images, audio and full-motion video. It provides up to 72 minutes of full-screen video on a CD-ROM and compresses as high as 100 to 1.

Dvorak keyboard A keyboard layout designed in the 1930s by August Dvorak, University of Washington, and his brother-in-law, William Dealey. 70% of words are typed on the home row compared to 32% with qwerty, and, more words are typed using both hands. In eight hours, fingers of a qwerty typist travel 16 miles, but only one for the Dvorak typist.

DVORAK KEYBOARD LAYOUT

DVST (Direct View Storage Tube) An early graphics screen that maintained an image without refreshing. The entire screen had to be redrawn for any change.

dweeb Slang for a very technical person. Dweebs sometimes call sales people "slime," anybody interested in technology for profit rather than the art of it.

DX In an Intel 386 CPU, DX, or 386DX, refers to the full 386, which contains a 32-bit data path, in contrast to the slower 386SX, which uses a 16-bit data path. In an Intel 486 CPU, DX, or 486DX, refers to the full 486, which contains the math coprocessor, in contrast to the 486SX, which does not have the coprocessor.

This is a prime example of the careless naming so common in this industry. People have been thoroughly confused by the DX and SX designations, because they have different meanings depending on whether they refer to a 386 or a 486. See *386* and *486*.

DX2 A 486 with a clock-doubled CPU. Clock doubling doubles the internal speed of the CPU without requiring any changes in the chip's external connections. For example, the 486DX2/66 has an internal speed of 66MHz, while its external bus from the CPU to RAM runs at 33MHz.

DX4 A 486 with a clock-tripled CPU. Clock tripling triples the internal speed of the CPU without requiring any changes in the chip's external connections. DX4s come in 75MHz and 100MHz versions that access RAM at 25MHz and 33MHz respectively.

DXF An AutoCAD 2-D graphics file format. Many CAD systems import and export the DXF format for graphics interchange.

dyadic Two. Refers to two components being used.

dye diffusion See *thermal dye diffusion*.

dye polymer recording An optical recording technique that uses dyed plastic layers as the recording medium. WORM disks typically use a single layer, and erasable disks use two layers: a top retention layer and a bottom expansion layer. A bit is written by shining a laser through the retention layer onto the expansion layer, which heats the area and forms a bump that expands into the retention layer. The retention layer bumps are the actual bits read by the unit. To erase a bit, another laser (different wavelength) strikes the retention layer and the bump subsides.

dye sublimation See *thermal dye transfer*.

dynamic Refers to operations performed while the program is running. The expression, "buffers are dynamically created," means that space was created when actually needed, not reserved beforehand.

dynamic address translation In a virtual memory system, the ability to determine what the real address is at the time of execution.

dynamic binding Linking a routine or object at runtime based on the conditions at that moment. See *polymorphism*.

dynamic compression The ability to compress and decompress data in realtime; for example, as it's being written to or read from the disk.

dynamic link The connection established at runtime from one program to another.

dynamic link library See *DLL*.

dynamic network services Realtime networking capabilities, such as adaptive routing, automatically reconfiguring the network when a node is added or deleted and the ability to locate any user on the network.

dynamic RAM The most common type of computer memory, also called D-RAM ("dee-RAM") and DRAM. It usually uses one transistor and a capacitor to represent a bit. The capacitors must be energized hundreds of times per second in order to maintain the charges. Unlike firmware chips (ROMs, PROMs, etc.) both major varieties of RAM (dynamic and static) lose their content when the power is turned off. Contrast with *static RAM*.

In memory advertising, dynamic RAM is often erroneously stated as a package type; for example, "DRAMs, SIMMs and SIPs on sale." It should be "DIPs, SIMMs and SIPs," as all three packages typically hold dynamic RAM chips.

dynamic range A range of signals from the weakest to the strongest.

dynamic SQL SQL statements interpreted by the SQL database at runtime. Dynamic SQL may be generated by programs or entered interactively by the user. Contrast with *embedded SQL*.

DYNIX A UNIX-based operating system from Sequent Computer Systems.

dynlink See *dynamic link*.

E See *exponent*.

E1 The European counterpart to T1, which transmits at 2.048 Mbits/sec. See *DS* for chart.

EAM (Electronic Accounting Machine) Same as *tabulating equipment*.

early binding Assigning types in the compilation phase. See *binding time*.

EAROM (Electrically Alterable ROM) Same as *EEPROM*.

earth station A transmitting/receiving station for satellite communications. It uses a dish-shaped antenna for microwave transmission.

EasyCAD 2 A full-featured PC CAD program from Evolution Computing, Tempe, AZ, that is known for its ease of use. EasyCAD users can migrate to FastCAD, which looks almost identical on screen, but provides multiple windows and is designed for high-speed operations.

Easytrieve See *CA-Easytrieve*.

EBCDIC (Extended Binary Coded Decimal Interchange Code) Pronounced "eb-suh-dick." The binary code for text as well as communications and printer control from IBM. This code originated with the System/360 and is still used in IBM mainframes and most IBM midrange computers. It is an 8-bit code (256 combinations) that stores one alphanumeric character or two decimal digits in a byte.
EBCDIC and ASCII are the two codes most widely used to represent data.

e-beam See *electron beam*.

ECC memory (Error-Correcting Code memory) A memory system that tests for and corrects errors on the fly. It uses circuitry that generates checksums to correct errors greater than one bit.

ECCO A Windows PIM from Arabesque Software, Bellevue, WA. ECCO provides a phone book, calendar, to-do list, outlining and notetaking. It is noted for its tightly integrated and sophisticated functions.

ECF (Enhanced Connectivity Facilities) IBM software that allows DOS PCs to query and download data from mainframes as well as issue mainframe commands. It also allows printer output to be directed from the PC to the mainframe. It uses the SRPI interface and resides in the PC (client) and mainframe (server). Applications issue SRPI commands to request services.

echo (1) Same as *echoplex*.

(2) A DOS and OS/2 screen command that displays messages and turns off/on screen responses.

echo cancellation A high-speed modem technique that isolates and filters out unwanted signals caused by echoes from the main transmitted signal. This permits full-duplex modems to send and receive on the same frequency.
Telephone networks often use echo cancellers in addition to or in place of echo suppressors. Network-based echo cancellation can interfere with modems that do

their own, such as V.32, so a method is provided for those modems to disable network echo cancellers.

echo check In communications, an error checking method that retransmits the data back to the sending device for comparison with the original.

echo suppressor A communications technique that turns off reverse transmission in a telephone line, thus effectively making the circuit one way. It is used to reduce the annoying effects of echoes in telephone connections, especially in satellite circuits.

echoplex A communications protocol that transmits the received data back to the sending station allowing the user to visually inspect what was received.

ECL (Emitter-Coupled Logic) A variety of bipolar transistor that is noted for its extremely fast switching speeds.

ECLIPSE An earlier series of 32-bit minicomputers from Data General. The development of the initial 32-bit ECLIPSE MV/8000 was the subject of Tracy Kidders' best-selling book, "Soul of a New Machine" published in 1981 by Little, Brown and Company.

ECMA (European Computer Manufacturers Association) An organization devoted to international standards. Address: Rue du Rhone 114, CH-1204 Geneva, Switzerland.

ECP (Enhanced Capabilities Port) See *IEEE 1284*.

ED (1) (Extra High Density) Refers to 2.88M floppy disks.

(2) (EDitor) An early UNIX line editor that contained functionality later incorporated into vi.

EDA (1) (Electronic Design Automation) Using the computer to design and simulate the performance of electronic circuits on a chip. See *ATE*.

(2) (EDA/SQL) (Enterprise Data Access/SQL) Software from Information Builders, Inc., New York, that provides a common interface between a wide variety of SQL programs and SQL databases. It also allows queries on data from different types of databases at the same time.

(3) (Electronic Document Authorization) Authorizing certificates used to identify public keys for encrypting data under the RSA method.

edge connector The protruding part of an expansion board that is inserted into an expansion slot. It contains a series of printed lines that go to and come from the circuits on the board. The number of lines (pins) and the width and depth of the lines are different on the various interfaces (ISA, EISA, PCI, Micro Channel, etc.).

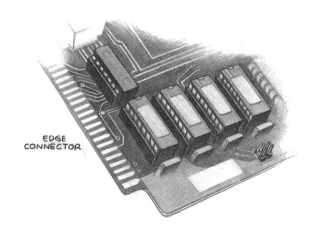

EDGE CONNECTOR

EDI (Electronic Data Interchange) The electronic communication of business transactions, such as orders, confirmations and invoices, between organizations. Third parties provide EDI services that enable organizations with different equipment to connect. See *X12, Tradacoms* and *EDIFACT*.

EDIFACT (Electronic Data Interchange For Administration Commerce and Transport) An ISO standard for EDI that is proposed to supersede both X12 and Tradacoms standards to become the worldwide standard.

e-disk (Emulated-disk) Same as *RAM disk.*

edit To make a change to existing data. See *update.*

editable PostScript A file of PostScript commands that can be edited by a word processor or other program. This allows PostScript documents to be changed without requiring the use of the application that originally created it.

edit checking Same as *validity checking.*

edit instruction A computer instruction that formats a field for display or printing. Using an edit mask, it inserts decimal points, commas and dollar signs into the data.

edit key A key combination or function key that changes the program into edit mode when pressed.

edit mask A pattern of characters that represent formatting codes through which data is filtered for display or printing. See *picture.*

edit mode An operational state in a program that allows existing data to be changed.

editor See *text editor* and *linkage editor.*

edit program (1) A data entry program that validates user input and stores the newly created records in the file.

(2) A program that allows users to change data that already exists in a file. See *update.*

edit routine A routine in a program that tests for valid data. See *validity checking.*

EDL See *nonlinear video editing.*

Edlin An archaic text editor used in DOS. The OS/2 counterpart is SSE.

EDP (Electronic Data Processing) The first name used for the computer field.

EDRAM (Enhanced DRAM) A high-speed DRAM chip developed by Ramtron International Corporation, Colorado Springs, CO. It allows overlap of a read at the trailing end of a write operation to obtain its speed.

education Teaching concepts and perspectives. Computer education includes computer systems and information systems. Contrast with *training.*

edutainment Educational material that is also entertaining.

EEMS Earlier standard for EMS memory. See *EMS.*

EEPROM (Electrically Erasable Programmable Read Only Memory) A memory chip that holds its content without power. It can be erased, either within the computer or externally. It usually requires more voltage for erasure than the common +5 volts used in logic circuits. It functions like non-volatile RAM, but writing to EEPROM is slower than writing to RAM.

eesa See *EISA* and *ESA/370.*

EFF (Electronic Frontier Foundation) An organization founded in 1990 by Mitchell Kapor and John Perry Barlow dedicated to raising public awareness of the opportunities and challenges posed by computing and telecommunications. Address: 155 Second St., Cambridge, MA 02141, 617/864-0665.

EFT (Electronic Funds Transfer) The transfer of money from one account to another by computer.

EGA (Enhanced Graphics Adapter) An IBM video display standard that provides medium-resolution text and graphics. It supports previous display modes and requires a digital RGB Enhanced Color Display or equivalent monitor. EGA was superseded by VGA. See *PC display modes*.

EGP (Exterior Gateway Protocol) A protocol that broadcasts TCP/IP addresses to the gateway in another network.

EHLLAPI See *HLLAPI*.

EIA (Electronic Industries Association) A membership organization founded in 1924 as the Radio Manufacturing Association. It sets standards for consumer products and electronic components. In 1988, it spun off its Information & Telecommunications Technology Group into a separate organization called the TIA. Address: 2001 Pennsylvania Ave., N.W., Washington, DC 20006, 202/457-4900.

EIA-232, 422, 423, 449, 485 See *RS-232, 422, 423, 449, 485*.

EIA-568 An EIA standard for telecommunications wiring in a commercial building. See *cable categories*.

Eiffel An object-oriented programming language developed by Bertrand Meyer, Interactive Software Engineering Inc., Goleta, CA. It runs on DOS, OS/2 and most UNIX platforms. The Eiffel compiler generates C code, which can be modified and recompiled with a C compiler.

EIS (Executive Information System) An information system that consolidates and summarizes ongoing transactions within the organization. It should provide management with all the information it requires at all times from internal as well as external sources. Increasingly, EISs are providing some of the "what if?" manipulation features of a DSS (decision support system); however, a DSS provides true modeling capabilities. See *DSS*.

EISA (Extended ISA) Pronounced "e-suh." A PC bus standard that extends the AT bus (ISA bus) to 32 bits and provides bus mastering. ISA cards can plug into EISA slots. It was announced in 1988 as a 32-bit alternative to the Micro Channel that would preserve investment in existing boards. EISA is also used in various workstations.

EISA still runs at the slow 8MHz speed of the ISA bus in order to accomodate all the ISA cards that may be plugged into it. PCI and VL-bus local buses provide higher speeds than EISA.

EL See *electroluminescent*.

electricity The flow of electrons in a circuit. The speed of electricity is the speed of light (approximately 186,000 miles per second). In a wire, it is slowed due to the resistance in the material.

Its pressure, or force, is measured in *volts* and its flow, or current, is measured in *amperes*. The amount of work it produces is measured in *watts* (amps X volts).

electrode A device that emits or controls the flow of electricity.

electroluminescent A flat panel display that provides a sharp, clear image and wide viewing angle. It contains a powdered or thin film phosphor layer sandwiched between an x-axis and a y-axis panel. When an x-y coordinate is charged, the phosphor in that vicinity emits visible light. Phosphors are typically amber, but green is also used.

electrolyte In a rechargeable battery, the material that allows electricity to flow from one plate to another by conducting ions.

electromagnet A magnet that is energized by electricity. A coil of wire is wrapped around an iron core. When current flows in the wire, the core generates an energy called magnetic *flux*.

electromagnetic radiation The energy that exists in all things, including humans, which incorporates cosmic rays, gamma rays, x-rays, ultraviolet light, visible light, infrared light and radar.

electromagnetic spectrum The range of electromagnetic radiation in our known universe, which includes radio waves with large wavelengths to cosmic rays with small wavelengths.

electromechanical The use of electricity to run moving parts. Disk drives, printers and motors are examples. Electromechanical systems must be designed for the eventual deterioration of moving parts.

electromotive force The pressure in an electric circuit measured in volts.

electron An elementary particle that circles the nucleus of an atom. Electrons are considered to be negatively charged.

electron beam A stream of electrons, or electricity, that is directed towards a receiving object.

electron gun A device which creates a fine beam of electrons that is focused on a phosphor screen in a CRT.

electronic The use of electricity in intelligence-bearing devices, such as radios, TVs, instruments, computers and telecommunications. Electricity used as raw power for heat, light and motors is considered electrical, not electronic.

Although coined earlier, "Electronics" magazine (1930) popularized the term. The magazine subheading read "Electron Tubes - Their Radio, Audio, Visio and Industrial Applications." The term was derived from the electron (vacuum) tube.

electronic circuit See *circuit* and *digital circuit*.

electronic mail Also called *e-mail*, it is the transmission of memos and messages over a network. An electronic mail system requires a messaging system, which provides the store and forward capability, and a mail program that provides the user interface with its send and receive functions.

Today, the fax machine has become the most universal kind of electronic mail. However, since fax documents are not raw text and cannot be readily edited at the receiving end, fax is not technically e-mail. Fax documents have to be scanned and processed with optical character recognition (OCR) software in order to turn them into editable text. See *messaging system* and *EDI*.

Electronic Mail Association See *EMA*. Remember... use the acronymn first!

electronic messaging See *electronic mail* and *messaging system*.

electronic printer A printer that uses electronics to control the printing mechanism, such as a laser printer and certain line printers.

electronic publishing Providing information in electronic form to readers or subscribers of the service. See *information utility*.

electronic switch An on/off switch activated by electrical current.

electronic typewriter See *memory typewriter* and *word processing*.

electron tube Same as *vacuum tube*.

electrophotographic The printing technique used in copy machines and laser printers. A negative image made of dots of light is painted onto a photosensitive drum or belt that has been electrically charged. The light comes from a laser, LEDs or liquid crystals that shutter a light source.

Wherever light is applied, the drum becomes uncharged. A toner (dry ink) is applied and adheres to the charged areas of the drum. The drum transfers the toner to the paper, and pressure and heat fuse the toner and paper permanently.

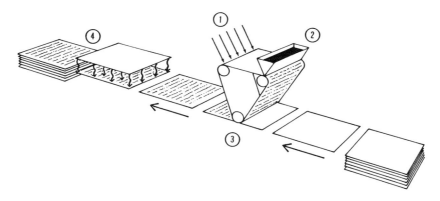

ELECTROPHOTOGRAPHIC PROCESS

(1) Belt or drum is charged. (2) Dry ink (toner) is adhered to the charged areas. (3) Toner is transferred onto the paper. (4) Toner is fused to the paper.

Some electrophotographic systems use a positive approach in which the toner is attracted to the laser-produced latent image.

electrosensitive printer A dot matrix printer that burns away dots on the outer silver coating of a special black paper.

electrostatic Stationary electrical charges in which no current flows.

electrostatic plotter A plotter that uses a special paper that is charged as it passes by a line of electrodes. Toner is then applied to the charged paper. Models print in in black and white or color, and some handle paper up to six feet wide.

electrostatic printer Same as *electrostatic plotter*.

elegant program A program that is simple in design and uses the least amount of computer resources (memory, disk, etc.).

elevator Also called a *thumb*, it is a square box that slides within a scroll bar. The elevator is dragged up and down to position the text or image on screen.

elevator seeking A disk access technique that processes multiple requests in a priority based upon which ones are closest to the current position of the read/write head.

ELF (Extemely Low Frequency) See *low radiation*.

elite A typeface that prints 12 cpi.

em In typography, a unit of measure equal to the width of the capital letter M in a particular font.

EMA (1) (Enterprise Management Architecture) Digital's stategic plan for integrating network, system and application management. It provides the operating environment for managing a multi-vendor network.

(2) (Electronic Mail Association) A membership organization founded in 1983 with over 250 vendor and user companies involved in electronic messaging and information exchange. Concerns include marketing e-mail within the corporation, privacy, security, interconnection and standards. Address: 1555 Wilson Blvd., Suite 300, Arlington, VA 22209, 703/875-8620.

EMACS (Editor MACroS) A UNIX text editor developed at MIT that is used for writing programs. It provides a wide variety of editing features including multiple windows.

e-mail See *electronic mail*.

EMBARC (EMBARC Communications Service, Boyton Beach, FL) A Motorola subsidiary that provides wireless broadcasting of mail and news to mobile computers that have a Motorola NewStream, SkyTel SkyStream, PCMCIA NewsCard or similar receiver. EMBARC stands for Electronic Mail Broadcast to a Roaming Computer. It uses a 930-931MHz channel licensed to Motorola and can handle long messages of 30,000 characters and more.

embedded command (1) A command inserted within text or other codes.

(2) In word processing, a command within the text that directs the printer to change fonts, print underline, boldface, etc. The command is inserted when the user selects a layout change. Commands are often invisible on screen, but can be revealed if required.

embedded controller Controller circuitry built into a device or on the main system board in contrast with a removable card or module.

embedded SQL SQL statements written into a high-level language source program, such as C or Pascal. In a separate compiling phase, the SQL may be optimized and converted into special function calls. Contrast with *dynamic SQL*.

embedded system A specialized computer used to control a device such as an automobile, appliance or space vehicle. Operating system and application functions are often combined in the same program.

EMI (ElectroMagnetic Interference) Electromagnetic waves that eminate from an electrical device. It often refers to both low-frequency waves from electromechanical devices and high-frequency waves (RFI) from chips and other electronic devices. Allowable limits are governed by the FCC.

emitter The supply of current in a bipolar transistor. Same as source in a MOS transistor.

emitter-coupled logic See *ECL*.

EMM (Expanded Memory Manager) Software that manages expanded memory (EMS). In XTs and ATs, expanded memory boards must also be used. In 386s and up, the EMM converts extended memory into EMS.

EMM386 An expanded memory (EMS) manager that accompanies DOS and Windows. It also allows drivers and TSRs to be stored in the upper memory area (UMA).

emoticon (EMOTional ICON) An expression of emotion in a typed message using character combinations. The following examples are viewed sideways.

:)	original smiley face
: -)	smile
: - (	frown
; -)	wink
: -D	big smile
: -O	mouth open in amazement
: -Q	tounge hanging out in nausea
: - {)	smile (user has moustache)
: - {) }	moustache and beard
8 -)	smile (user wears glasses)
(-:	smile (user left handed or Australian)
: *)	red nosed smile, suggesting inebriation
*< : {) }	Santa Claus!
@ : {) ===	sikh with turban and long beard

For an extensive list of more than 650 emoticons, read "Smileys" by David Sanderson, published by O'Reilly & Associates, Inc., ISBN 1-56592-041-4.

EMS (Expanded Memory Specification) A technique for increasing memory in DOS PCs. It allows DOS to work with up to 32MB of extra memory by bank switching segments of EMS memory into conventional memory. A 64KB chunk of upper memory (UMA) must be reserved for the EMS page frame, the tunnel through which the CPU accesses the EMS memory.

In 386s and up, extended memory is turned into EMS memory by a software memory manager. All modern memory managers, such as EMM386 (DOS 5 and up), QEMM and 386MAX, can dynamically allocate expanded memory as needed, but the 64KB page frame must be reserved at startup if EMS is to be used at any time during the session.

In order to use EMS, the application is either written to use it directly (Lotus 1-2-3 Ver. 2.x, AutoCAD, etc.) or the application is run in an environment that uses it, such as DESQview. Windows does not use EMS, but supports it for DOS applications that require it.

Expanded versus Extended

Expanded memory (EMS) and extended memory are not the same. EMS can be installed in XT-class machines and up, whereas extended memory requires at least a 286. EMS broke the 1MB memory barrier in the early days, but since Windows and DOS-extended applications also break the 1MB barrier and use regular contiguous memory beyond 1MB (extended memory), EMS is only used for older DOS applications.

EMS emulator As of the 386, EMS emulator refers to a memory manager (EMM) that runs in 386s and up and creates EMS out of extended memory. Technically, the 386 is really not emulating anything. The 386 can map any memory to any other memory, thus it is merely mapping memory according to the EMS specification.

emulation mode An operational state of a computer when it is running a foreign program under emulation.

emulator A device that is built to work like another. A computer can be designed to emulate another model and execute software that was written to run in the other machine. A terminal can be designed to emulate various communications protocols and connect to different networks. The emulator can be hardware, software or both.

en In typography, a unit of measure equal to one half the width of an em. An en is typically the width of one numeric digit.

enable To turn on. Contrast with *disable*.

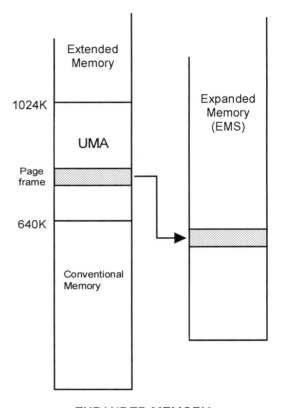

EXPANDED MEMORY

DOS can only reach the first megabyte of memory. When expanded memory is used, a 64K chunk of the UMA (upper memory area) is reserved for the EMS page frame, which serves as a window into the EMS memory bank.

Enable/OA An integrated software package for PCs from Enable Software, Inc., Ballston Lake, NY. It is noted for being a very comprehensive package rivaling many stand-alone programs. Version 4.0 also runs under UNIX.

Encapsulated PostScript A PostScript file format that contains PostScript code for the document as well as optional preview images in TIFF, Windows Metafile or Macintosh PICT formats. The PostScript code drives a PostScript printer directly, and the preview formats allow the image to be manipulated on screen. DOS and OS/2 files use an EPS extension.

encapsulation (1) In object-oriented programming, making the data and processing private within an object, which allows it to be modified without causing problems elsewhere in the program.

(2) In communications, inserting the frame header and data from a higher level protocol into the data frame of a lower level protocol.

encipher To encode data for security purposes. See *encryption*.

encode (1) To assign a code to represent data, such as a parts code.

(2) Same as *encipher* or *encrypt*. See *encryption*.

encryption Using cryptography to encode data for security purposes for transmission over a public network. The original text, or plaintext, is converted into a coded equivalent called ciphertext via an encryption algorithm. The ciphertext is decoded (decrypted) at the receiving end with the use of a decryption key.

Secret versus Public Key

There are two methods of encrypting data. The traditional method uses a secret key, such as DES, where both sender and receiver use the same key. This is the fastest method, but transmitting the secret key to the recipient is not secure. The second method is public-key cryptography, such as RSA, which uses both a private and a public key. Each recipient has a private key that is kept secret and a public key that is published for everyone. The sender looks up the recipient's public key and uses it to encrypt the message. The recipient uses the private key to decrypt the message.

If speed is an issue, the public-key method can be used to send the secret key followed by the message encrypted with the secret key. See *DES* and *RSA*.

end key A keyboard key commonly used to move the cursor to the bottom of the screen or file or to the next word or end of line.

end points In vector graphics, the two ends of a line (vector). In 2-D graphics, each end point is typically two numbers representing coordinates on x and y axes. In 3-D, each end point is made up of three numbers representing coordinates on x, y and z axes. See *x-y matrix* and *x-y-x matrix*.

end user Same as *user*.

endless loop A series of instructions that are constantly repeated. It can be caused by an error in the program or it can be intentional; for example, a screen demo on continuous replay.

endnote See *footnote*.

Energy Star Conservation requirements set forth by the Environmental Protection Agency of the U.S. Government. In its initial requirements, devices (PCs, monitors, printers, etc.) must draw less than 30 watts of power when inactive.

engine (1) A specialized processor, such as a graphics processor. Like any engine, the faster it runs, the quicker the job gets done. See *graphics engine* and *printer engine*.

(2) Software that performs a primary and highly repetitive function such as a database engine, graphics engine or dictionary engine.

(3) Slang for processor.

engineering cylinder See *diagnostic tracks*.

engineering drawing sizes Following are the standard sizes of engineering drawings.

A - 8 1/2 x 11
B - 11 x 17
C - 17 x 22
D - 22 x 34
E - 34 x 44

Enhanced IDE A hard disk and CD-ROM interface that provides data transfer up to 13 MBytes/sec. An Enhanced IDE controller can also handle four hard disks rather than two. It is expected that Enhanced IDE drives will become popular by 1995.

Enhanced keyboard An IBM 101-key keyboard that superseded the PC and AT keyboards. It has a separate cursor key cluster located between the original numeric/cursor keypad and the letter keys.

enhancement Any improvement made to a software package or hardware device.

ENIAC (Electronic Numerical Integrator And Calculator) The first operational electronic digital computer developed for the U.S. Army by John Eckert and John Mauchly at the University of Pennsylvania. Completed in 1946, it was decimal-based, used 18,000 vacuum tubes, took up 1,800 square feet and performed 5,000 additions/second. Today, the equivalent technology is used in a watch.

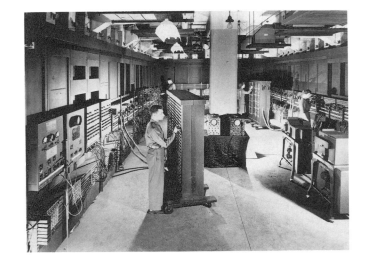

ENIAC
(Courtesy The Moore School of Electrical Engineering, University of Pennsylvania)

enquiry character In communications, a control character that requests a response from the receiving station.

enter key See *return key*.

enterprise The entire organization. See *enterprise networking*.

enterprise data Centralized data that is shared by many users throughout the organization.

enterprise model A model of how an organization does business. Information systems are designed from this model.

enterprise network A geographically-dispersed network under the jurisdiction of one organization. It often includes several different types of networks and computer systems from different vendors.

enterprise networking Managing the network infrastructure in a large enterprise. Much of what goes on has little to do with application development and real data processing of the payroll and orders. Enormous effort is spent planning the integration of disparate networks and systems and managing them, and, planning again for yet more interfaces as marketing pressures force vendors to develop new techniques that routinely change the ground rules.

▶ *The electronic and encyclopedic versions of this book provide more detail on this subject.*

entity In a database, anything about which information can be stored; for example, a person, concept, physical object or event. Typically refers to a record structure.

entity relationship model In a database, a data model that describes attributes of entities and the relationships among them.

entity type In a database, a particular kind of file; for example, a customer or product file.

entropy In data compression, a measure of the amount of non-redundant, non-compressible information in an object.

entry The input of an item or set of items at a terminal. See *data entry*.

entry point In programming, the starting point of the instructions in a subroutine.

enumerate To count or list one by one. For example, an enumerated data type defines a list of all possible values for a variable, and no other value can then be placed into it.

envelope (1) A range of frequencies for a particular operation.

(2) A group of bits or items that is packaged and treated as a single unit.

environment A computer configuration that includes the CPU model and system software (operating system, data communications and database systems). It may also include the programming language used. It sets the standards for the applications that run in it. The term often refers only to the operating system; for example, "This program is running in a UNIX environment." The terms environment and platform are used synonymously.

environment variable In DOS, a value that is set at startup which is used by the operating system as well as applications for a variety of purposes. The values are initialized using the DOS Set command in the AUTOEXEC.BAT file.

EOF (End Of File) The status of a file when its end has been reached or when an instruction or command resets the file pointer to the end.

EOL, EOM, EOT (End Of Line, End Of Message, End Of Transmission)

epitaxial layer In chip making, a semiconductor layer that is created on top of the silicon base rather than below it. See *molecular beam epitaxy*.

epoch date The starting point from which time is measured as the number of days, minutes, etc., from that time.

EPP (1) (Enhanced Parallel Port) See *IEEE 1284*.

(2) (Ethernet Packet Processor) A chip from Kalpana, Inc., Santa, Clara, CA, that doubles speed of Ethernet transmission to 20Mbits/sec.

EPROM (Erasable Programmable ROM) A programmable and reusable chip that holds its content until erased under ultraviolet light. EPROMS have a lifespan of a few hundred write cycles. EPROMS are expected to eventually give way to flash memory.

EPROM programmer A device that writes instructions and data into EPROM chips. Some earlier units were capable of programming both PROMs and EPROMs.

EPS See *Encapsulated PostScript*.

Epson emulation Compatible with Epson dot matrix printers. The command set in the Epson MX, RX and FX printers has become an industry standard.

EPSS (Electronic Performance Support System) A computer system that provides quick assistance and information without requiring prior training to use it. It may incorporate all forms of multimedia delivery as well as AI techniques such as expert systems and natural language recognition.

EQ (EQual to) See *relational operator*.

equalization In communications, techniques used to reduce distortion and compensate for signal loss (attenuation) over long distances.

equation An arithmetic expression that equates one set of conditions to another; for example, $A = B + C$. In a programming language, assignment statements take the form of an equation. The above example would assign the sum of B and C to the variable A.

ER model See *entity relationship model*.

ERA (Electrically Reconfigurable Array) A programmable logic chip (PLD) technology from Plessey Semiconductor that allows the chip to be reprogrammed electrically.

erase See *delete*.

erase head In a magnetic tape drive, the device that erases the tape before a new block of data is recorded.

ergonomics The science of people-machine relationships. An ergonomically-designed product implies that the device blends smoothly with a person's body or actions.

Erlang A unit of traffic use that specifies the total capacity or average use of a telephone system. One Erlang is equivalent to the continuous usage of a telephone line. Traffic in Erlangs is the sum of the holding times of all lines divided by the period of measurement.

error checking (1) Testing for accurate transmission of data over a communications network or internally within the computer system. See *parity checking* and *CRC*.

(2) Same as *validity checking*.

ERGONOMICS
(Courtesy Hewlett-Packard)

error control Same as *error checking*.

error detection & correction See *error checking* and *validity checking*.

error-free channel An interface (wire, cable, etc.) between devices that is not subject to external interference; specifically not the dial-up telephone system.

error handling Routines in a program that respond to errors. The measurement of quality in error handling is based on how the system informs the user of such conditions and what alternatives it provides for dealing with them.

error rate The measurement of the effectiveness of a communications channel. It is the ratio of the number of erroneous units of data to the total number of units of data transmitted.

ES See *expert system*.

ES/3090 A high-end IBM mainframe that incorporates the ESA/370 enhancements.

ES/9000 The IBM System/390 computer line introduced in late 1990 that uses 31-bit addressing with maximum memory capacities from 256MB to 9GB. It's 18 models (Model 120 to Model 960) offered the widest range of power in a single introduction at one time with prices ranging from $70K to $23M. Vector processing is optional on high-end water-cooled and certain air-cooled models. See *System/390*.

ESA/370 (Enterprise System Architecture/370) IBM enhancements that increase the performance of high-end 4381 and 3090 mainframes. Introduced in 1988, it increases virtual memory from 2GB to 16TB and adds techniques for managing it more effectively. This architecture is built into System/390 ES/9000 computers.

ESA/390 (Enterprise System Architecture/390) Extensions to ESA/370 for the System/390 series. It includes MVS/ESA, VM/ESA and VSE/ESA operating systems.

Esc See *escape character* and *escape key*.

escape character A control character often used to precede other characters to control a printer or other device. For example, escape, followed by &l1O, sets the LaserJet to landscape mode. In ASCII, escape is decimal 27, hex 1B; in EBCDIC, it is hex 27.

escape key A keyboard key commonly used to exit a mode or routine, or cancel some function.

escape sequence (1) A machine command that starts with an escape character. Printers are often commanded by escape sequences. See *escape character*.

(2) In a modem, a unique sequence of characters that precedes a command. It allows modem commands (dial, hang up, etc.) to be transmitted with the data. See *TIES* and *Hayes Smartmodem*.

ESCON (Enterprise Systems CONnection) An IBM System/390 fiber optic channel that transfers 10 Mbytes/sec up to 5.6 miles. An ESCON Director is the coupling device that provides 8-16 ports (Model 1) or 28-60 ports (Model 2).

ESD (1) (Electronic Software Distribution) Distributing new software and upgrades via the network rather than individual installations on each machine. See *ESL*.

(2) (ElectroStatic Discharge) Sparks (electrons) that jump from an electrically-charged object to an approaching conductive object.

(3) (Entry Systems Division) The IBM division that conceived and developed the original IBM PC.

ESDI (Enhanced Small Device Interface) A hard disk interface that transfers data in the one to three MByte/sec range. ESDI was the high-speed interface for small computers for a while, but has been superseded by IDE and SCSI drives.

ESDL (Electronic Software Distribution and Licensing) The combination of ESD and ESL.

ESDS (Entry Sequence DataSet) A VSAM structure that stores records one after the other without regard to content. Records are retrieved by address. Contrast with *KSDS*.

ESF (1) (Extended SuperFrame) An enhanced T1 format that allows a line to be monitored during normal operation. It uses 24 frames grouped together (instead of the 12-frame D4 superframe) and provides room for CRC bits and other diagnostic commands.

(2) (External Source Format) A specification language for defining an application in IBM's CSP/AD application generator.

ESL (Electronic Software Licensing) Software that keeps track of the number of active users per application in order to comply with the multiuser licensing contracts that have been purchased.

ESP (1) (Enhanced-Service Provider) An organization that adds value to basic telephone service by offering such features as call-forwarding, call-detailing and protocol conversion.

(2) (Electronic Still Photography) Digitizing and transmitting images over a telephone line.

ESS (1) (Electronic Switching System) A large-scale computer used to switch telephone conversations in a central office.

(2) (Executive Support System) See *EIS*.

(3) (Electronic SpreadSheet) See *spreadsheet*.

Ethernet A local area network (LAN) developed by Xerox, Digital and Intel. It is the most widely used LAN access method (Token Ring is next). Ethernet is a shared media LAN. All messages are broadcast to all nodes on the network segment. Ethernet connects up to 1,024 nodes at 10 Mbits per second over twisted pair, coax and optical fiber.

The three major types are (1) 10Base5 Standard Ethernet, which uses a thick coaxial cable in a bus topology between nodes with a maximum segment length of up to 1,640 feet, (2) 10Base2 Thin Ethernet, also called *ThinNet* and *Cheapernet*, which uses a thinner coax cable up to 607 feet per segment, and (3) 10BaseT, which uses twisted pairs connected in a star configuration through a hub with a maximum

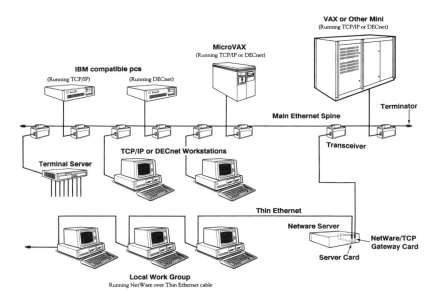

ETHERNET
(Courtesy Black Box Corporation)
This sample installation uses TCP/IP, DECnet and NetWare protocols.

segment length of 328 feet. Faster Ethernets are emerging: switched Ethernet gives each user a dedicated 10 Mbps channel. Fast Ethernet runs at 100 Mbps shared.

▶ *The electronic and encyclopedic versions of this book provide more detail on this subject.*

EtherTalk Macintosh software from Apple that accompanies its Ethernet Interface NB Card and adapts the Mac to Ethernet networks.

E-time See *execution time*.

Eurocard A family of European-designed printed circuit boards that uses a 96-pin plug rather than edge connectors. The 3U is a 4x6" board with one plug; the 6U is a 6x12" board with two plugs; the 9U is a 14x18" board with three plugs.

even parity See *parity checking*.

event driven An application that responds to input from the user or other application at unregulated times. It's driven by choices that the user makes (select menu, press button, etc.). Contrast with *procedure oriented*.

eWorld Online service from Apple aimed at the consumer market. Introduced in 1994 initially for Macintoshes, Windows capability is expected in 1995.

Exabyte (Exabyte Corporation, Boulder, CO) A maker of high-capacity, proprietary 8mm tape backup systems. Single-tape units are in the 2 to 25GB range, and multi-tape library units can hold terabytes.

Excel A full-featured spreadsheet for PCs and the Macintosh from Microsoft. It can link many spreadsheets for consolidation and provides a wide variety of business graphics and charts for creating presentation materials.

exception report A listing of abnormal items or items that fall outside of a specified range.

Exchange Server An enterprise-wide messaging and mail system from Microsoft that runs under Windows NT. It is expected in late 1994 or early 1995.

exclusive NOR, exclusive OR See *NOR* and *OR*.

executable A program in machine language that is ready to run in a particular computer environment.

execute To follow instructions in a program. Same as *run*.

execution time The time in which a single instruction is executed. It makes up the last half of the instruction cycle.

executive Refers to an operating system or only to the operating system's kernel.

EXE file (EXEcutable file) A runnable program in DOS, OS/2 and VMS. In DOS, if a program fits within 64K, it may be a COM file.

exit (1) To get out of the current mode or quit the program.

(2) In programming, to get out of the loop, routine or function that the computer is currently in.

expanded memory See *EMS*, *EMM* and *expanded storage*.

expanded memory emulator A memory manager for 386s and up that converts extended memory into EMS memory. See *EMM*.

expanded storage Auxiliary memory in IBM mainframes. Data is usually transferred in 4K chunks from expanded storage to central storage (main memory).

expansion board (1) A printed circuit board that plugs into an expansion slot. All the boards (cards) that plug into a personal computer's bus are expansion boards, such as display adapters, disk controllers and sound cards.

(2) See *bus extender*.

expansion bus (1) The computer's bus comprised of a series of receptacles or slots into which expansion boards (video display, disk controller, etc.) are plugged.

(2) Sometimes refers to *bus extender (3)*.

expansion card Same as *expansion board*.

expansion slot A receptacle inside a computer or other electronic system that accepts printed circuit boards. The number of slots determines future expansion. In personal computers, expansion slots are connected to the bus.

expert system An AI application that uses a knowledge base of human expertise for problem solving. Its success is based on the quality of the data and rules obtained from the human expert. In practice, expert systems perform both below and above that of a human. An expert system contains a knowledge base of if-then-else rules that are processed through an inference engine (software) that uses a variety of techniques to obtain the result.

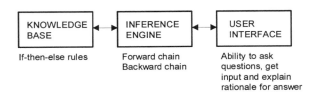

EXPERT SYSTEM

expireware Software with a built-in expiration date, either by date or number of uses.

explode (1) To break down an assembly into its component pieces. Contrast with *implode*.

(2) To decompress data back to its original form.

exponent The number written above the line and to the right of a number that indicates the power of a number, or how many zeros there are in it. For example 10^3 (10 to the 3rd power) indicates three zeros. The number 467,000 can be stated as 467 x 10^3. On a screen or printout, the number is expressed as 467E3. See *floating point*.

exponential growth Extremely fast growth. On a chart, the line curves up rather than being straight. Contrast with *linear*.

exponential smoothing A widely-used technique in forecasting trends, seasonality and level change. Works well with data that has a lot of randomness.

export To convert a data file in the current application program into the format required by another application program.

expression In programming, a statement that describes data and processing. For example, `value=2*cost` and `product="HAT" and color="GRAY"`.

extended application A DOS application that runs in extended memory under the control of a DOS extender.

extended ASCII The second half of the ASCII character set (128 through 255). The symbols are defined by ANSI, by IBM for the PC (see *ASCII chart*) and by other vendors for proprietary uses. It is non-standard ASCII.

Extended Edition The IBM version of OS/2 that includes communications and database management. The Communications Manager has built-in LU 6.2 and X.25 protocols. The Database Manager uses IBM's SQL.

extended maintenance On-call service that is ordered for periods in addition to the primary period of maintenance.

extended memory In Intel 286s and up, it is standard memory above one megabyte. Extended memory is used directly by Windows and OS/2 as well as DOS applications that run with DOS extenders.

extender See *bus extender*.

extensible Capable of being expanded or customized. For example, with extensible programming languages, programmers can add new control structures, statements or data types.

extension (1) A file type that is added to the end of DOS and OS/2 file names. The extension is separated from the file name with a dot such as LETTER.DOC. Following are some of the common extensions. Also see *Macintosh extension*.

BAK	Backup
BAT	DOS, OS/2 batch file
BIN	Driver, overlay
CFG	Configuration
CHK	DOS Chkdsk chained file
COM	Executable program
DBF	dBASE database
DCA	IBM text
DLL	Dynamic link library
DOC	Document (Multimate, Word...)
DRV	Driver
EPS	Encapsulated PostScript
EXE	Executable program
FON	Font or telephone number
GIF	CompuServe raster graphics
HLP	Help text
OVL	Overlay module
OVR	Overlay module
PCX	PC Paintbrush raster graphics
PIC	Various vector formats:
	Lotus 1-2-3,
	Micrografx Draw,
	Mac PICT format,
	IBM Storyboard raster graphics
PIF	Windows info. for DOS programs,
TIF	TIFF raster graphics
TMP	Temporary
TXT	ASCII text
WAV	Windows sound
WK*	Various Lotus spreadsheet formats (WKS, WK1, etc.)
WMF	Windows Metafile
ZIP	PKZIP compressed
$$$	Temporary

▶ *The electronic and encyclopedic versions of this book provide a long list of file extensions.*

extent Contiguous space on a disk reserved for a file or application.

external command (1) In DOS and OS/2, a function performed by a separate utility program that accompanies the operating system. Contrast with *internal command*.

(2) A user-developed HyperCard command. See *XCMD*.

external interrupt An interrupt caused by an external source such as the computer operator, external sensor or monitoring device, or another computer.

external modem A self-contained modem that is connected via cable to the serial port of a computer. It draws power from a wall outlet. The advantage of an external modem over an internal one is that a series of status lights on the outside of the case may be more helpful if a problem occurs. Contrast with *internal modem*.

external reference In programming, a call to a program or function that resides in a separate, independent library.

external sort A sort program that uses disk or tape as temporary workspace. Contrast with *internal sort*.

external storage Storage outside of the CPU, such as disk and tape.

f See *farad*.

F1 key Function key number one. There are 12 function keys on a PC keyboard. F1 is used for retrieving help in Windows and in most DOS applications.

FaceLift A font scaler for Windows and WordPerfect from Bitstream Inc., Cambridge, MA, that provides on-the-fly font scaling for Bitstream's own Speedo fonts. FaceLift for Windows also supports Type 1 fonts. FaceLift for WordPerfect lets users create a wide variety of custom fonts, including outlines, shadows and fill scaling, for the DOS version of WordPerfect.

facilities management The management of a user's computer installation by an outside organization. All operations including systems, programming and the datacenter can be performed by the facilities management organization on the user's premises.

facsimile See *fax*.

factorial The number of sequences that can exist with a set of items, derived by multiplying the number of items by the next lowest number until 1 is reached. For example, three items have six sequences (3x2x1=6): 123, 132, 231, 213, 312 and 321.

fail safe Same as *fault tolerant*.

fail soft The ability to fail with minimum destruction. For example, a disk drive can be built to automatically park the heads when power fails. Although it doesn't correct the problem, it minimizes destruction.

FAMOS (Floating gate Avalanche-injection Metal Oxide Semiconductor) A type of EPROM.

fan A device that uses motor-driven blades to circulate the air in a computer or other electronic system. Today's CPUs run extremely hot, and large computer cabinets use two and three fans to reduce temperature.

fan-fold paper Same as *continous forms*.

fan in To direct multiple signals into one receiver.

fan out To direct one signal into multiple receivers.

far pointer In an Intel x86 segmented address, a memory address that includes both segment and offset. Contrast with *near pointer*.

farad A unit of electrical charge that is used to measure the storage capacity of a capacitor. In microelectronics, measurements are usually in microfarads or picofarads.

Fast An asynchronous communications protocol used to quickly transmit files over high-quality lines. Error checking is done after the entire file has been transmitted.

Fast Ethernet High-speed Ethernet at 100 Mbps (regular Ethernet is 10 Mbps). There are two competing technologies emerging from the IEEE. The first method is the IEEE 802.3 100BaseT, which uses the CSMA/CD access method with some modification. Standards are expected in late 1994 or early 1995.

The second is IEEE 802.12 100BaseVG, adapted from HP's 100VG-AnyLAN. It uses a demand-priority method instead of CSMA/CD. For example, realtime voice and video could be given higher priority than other data.

Fast Fourier Transform See *FFT*.

FastCAD A full-featured PC CAD program from Evolution Computing, Tempe, AZ, known for its well-designed user interface. It requires a math coprocessor. Users with less sophisticated requirements can start out with FastCAD's baby brother, EasyCAD.

FastDisk A Windows 3.1 driver in 386 Enhanced Mode that speeds up disk accesses by bypassing DOS and the BIOS and communicating with the disk controller directly. Some disk controllers do not operate properly with this function, and it must be turned off. See *WinDisk*.

FAT (File Allocation Table) The part of the DOS and OS/2 file system that keeps track of where data is stored on disk. When the disk is high-level formatted, the FAT is recorded twice and contains a table with an entry for each disk cluster.

The directory list, which contains file name, extension, date, etc., points to the FAT entry where the file starts. If a file is larger than one cluster, the first FAT entry points to the next FAT entry where the second cluster of the file is stored and so on to the end of the file. If a cluster becomes damaged, its FAT entry is marked as such and that cluster is not used again.

fat binary A Macintosh executable program that contains machine language in one file for both the Macintosh and PowerMac machines (680x0 and PowerPC CPUs). Software distributed in this format will run native on whichever Mac architecture it is loaded on.

fatal error A condition that halts processing due to read errors, program bugs or anomalies.

FatBits A MacPaint option in the "Goodies" menu that lets a user edit an image a pixel at a time.

father file See *grandfather, father, son*.

fault tolerant Continous operation in case of failure. A fault tolerant system can be created using two or more computers that duplicate all processing, or having one system stand by if the other fails. It can also be built with redundant processors, control units and peripherals architecturally integrated from the ground up (Tandem, Stratus, etc.).

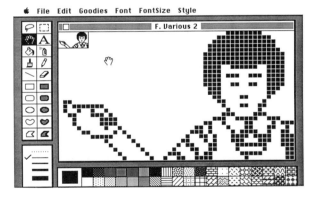

FATBITS MODE
Note the picture in the upper left hand side of the screen.

Fault tolerant operation requires backup power in the event of power failure. It may also imply duplication of systems in disparate locations in the event of natural catastrophe or vandalism.

fax (FACSimile) Originally called telecopying, it is the communication of a printed page between remote locations. Fax machines scan a paper form and transmit a coded image over the telephone system. The receiving machine prints a facsimile of the original. A fax machine is made up of a scanner, printer and modem with fax signalling.

Group 3 transmits up to 9,600 baud using data compression at less than one minute per page. Resolution is 203x98 dpi in standard mode and 203x196 dpi in fine mode. Higher-speed Group 4 machines are expected to rely on all-digital networks.

fax board Fax transmission on an expansion board. It uses software that generates fax signals directly from disk files or the screen and transmits a sharper image than a fax machine, which gets its image by scanning. Incoming faxes are printed on the computer's printer.

fax/modem A combination fax board and data modem available as an external unit or expansion board. It includes a fax switch that routes the call to the fax or the data modem.

fax switch A device that tests a phone line for a fax signal and routes the call to the fax machine. When a fax machine dials a number and the line answers, it emits an 1,100Hz tone to identify itself. Some devices handle voice, fax and data modem switching and may require keying in an extension number to switch to the modem.

FCB (File Control Block) The internal method for managing files in DOS Version 1.0. Very early applications may still use this.

FCC (Federal Communications Commission) The regulatory body for U.S. interstate telecommunications services as well as international service originating in the U.S. It was created under the U.S. Communications Act of 1934, and its board of commissioners is appointed by the President.

FCC Class An FCC certification of radiation limits on digital devices. Class A certification is for business use. Class B, for residential use, is more stringent in order to avoid interference with TV and other home reception. See Part 15, Subpart B, of the Federal Register (CFR 47, Parts 0-19).

FCFS First come, first served.

fci (Flux Changes per Inch) The measurement of polarity reversals on a magnetic surface. In MFM, each flux change is equal to one bit. In RLL, a flux change generates more than one bit.

F connector A coaxial cable connector used to connect antennas, TVs and VCRs. It is easily recognized: the plug's inner wire is stripped bare and sticks out of the connector looking very unfinished.

FD (Floppy Disk) For example, FD/HD refers to a floppy disk/hard disk device.

FDDI (Fiber Distributed Data Interface) An ANSI standard token passing network that uses optical fiber cabling and transmits at 100 Mbits/sec up to two kilometers. FDDI is used

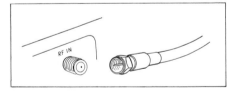

F CONNECTOR

for MANs and LANs and includes its own network management standard called STM (Station Management). The CDDI version (TP-PMD) runs over copper (UTP), although limited to distances of typically 50 to 100 meters.

FDDI provides network services at the same level as Ethernet and Token Ring (OSI layers 1 and 2).

Fdisk An external DOS command that partitions the hard disk. This is done after low-level formatting and before high-level formatting.

FDM (Frequency Division Multiplexing) A method used to transmit multiple signals over a single channel. Each signal (data, voice, etc.) modulates a carrier with a different frequency and all signals travel simultaneously over the channel. Contrast with *TDM*. See *baseband*.

FDMA (Frequency Division Multiple Access) The technology used in the analog cellular telephone network that divides the spectrum into 30KHz channels. See *TDMA, CDMA* and *CDPD.*

FD:OCA (Formatted Data:Object Content Architecture) An SAA-compliant (CCS) specification for formatting data in fields.

FDSE (Full-Duplex Switched Ethernet) A type of switched Ethenet that uses full-duplexed network adapters and provides a 20 Mbps bi-directional transmission between nodes. It is expected that by 1995, most network adapters will have built-in full duplex capability and can be used in a switched environment.

FDSE improves network throughput from server to server as well as in video conferencing, both of which benefit from full-duplexed, bi-directional transmission.

FDX See *full-duplex.*

FEA (Finite Element Analysis) A mathematical technique for analyzing stress, which breaks down a physical structure into substructures, called finite elements. The finite elements and their interrelationships are converted into equation form and solved mathematically.

Graphics-based FEA software can display the model on screen as it is being built and, after analysis, display the object's reactions under load conditions. Models created in popular CAD packages can often be accepted by FEA software.

feasibility study The analysis of a problem to determine if it can be solved effectively. The operational (will it work?), economical (costs and benefits) and technical (can it be built?) aspects are part of the study. Results of the study determine whether the solution should be implemented.

feature connector See *VGA feature connector.*

FEC See *forward error correction.*

femtosecond One quadrillionth of a second. See *space/time.*

FEP See *front end processor.*

ferric oxide (Fe^2O^3) An oxidation of iron used in the coating of magnetic disks and tapes.

ferromagnetic The capability of a material, such as iron and nickel, to be highly magnetized.

FET (Field Effect Transistor) A type of transistor used in MOS integrated circuits.

fetch To locate the next instruction in memory for execution by the CPU.

FF See *form feed.*

FFT (Fast Fourier Transform) A class of algorithms used in digital signal processing that break down complex signals into elementary components.

fiber bundle A set of adjacent optical fibers running in parallel and adhered together. It is used for transmitting light to brighten an area as well as transmitting whole images, but is not used for modern digital communications.

Fiber Channel A type of transmission path used as an internal computer channel as well as a network medium. It works with existing interfaces, such as IPI, SCSI and HiPPI. In a LAN, it can be used as a high-speed backbone. Speeds range up to 100 MBytes/sec using optical fiber.

fiber loss The amount of attenuation of signal in an optical fiber transmission.

fiber optic Communications systems that use optical fibers for transmission. Fiber-optic transmission became widely used in the 1980s when the long-distance carriers created nationwide systems for carrying voice conversations digitally over optical fibers.

Eventually, all transmission systems may become fiber optic-based. Also, in time, the internals of computers may be partially or even fully made of light circuits rather than electrical circuits. See *FDDI, Fiber Channel* and *optical fiber.*

Fibonacci numbers A series of whole numbers in which each number is the sum of the two preceding ones: 1, 1, 2, 3, 5, 8, 13, etc. It is used to speed up binary searches by dividing the search into the two lower numbers; for example, 13 items would be divided into 5 and 8 items; 8 items would be divided into 5 and 3.

fiche Same as *microfiche.*

FidoNet An E-mail protocol that originated from the Fido BBS created by Tom Jennings in 1984. Over 10,000 FidoNet nodes are in use. Users must have their networks active for one universal hour in the early morning, and the software must adhere to the FTSC-001 specification. The FidoNet address format is zone:local net/node; for example, Boardwatch Magazine's address is 1:104/555.

field A physical unit of data that is one or more bytes in size. A collection of fields make up a record. A field also defines a unit of data on a source document, screen or report. Examples of fields are NAME, ADDRESS, QUANTITY and AMOUNT DUE.

The field is the common denominator between the user and the computer. When you interactively query and update your database, you reference your data by field name.

There are several terms that refer to the same unit of storage as a field. A *data element* is the logical definition of the field, and a *data item* is the actual data stored in the field. For each data element, there are many fields in the

DATA ELEMENTS

PRODUCT DESCRIPTION   PRODUCT NO.

MANILLA FOLDER
PENCIL
RUBBER BAND   **FIELDS**
COPY PAPER
PAPER CLIP
ENVELOPE

DATA ITEMS

FIELDS IN A RECORD

database that hold the data items. For example, for the data element CITY, there are fields in the database that hold the data items CHICAGO, TOKYO and MADRID.

field engineer A person who is responsible for hardware installation, maintentance and repair. Formal training is in electronics, although many people have learned on the job.

field name An assigned name for a field (NAME, ADDRESS, CITY, STATE, etc.) that will be the same in every record.

field separator A character used to mark the separation of fields in a record. See *comma delimited* and *tab delimited.*

field service See *field engineer.*

field squeeze In a mail merge, a function that eliminates extra blank spaces between words when fixed-length fields are inserted into the document text. See *line squeeze.*

field template See *picture.*

FIF (Fractal Image Format) A graphics file format from Iterated Systems, Inc., Norcross, GA, that stores fractal images with compression ratios as high as 2,500:1.

FIFO (First In-First Out) A storage method that retrieves the item stored for the longest time. Contrast with *LIFO.*

fifth-generation computer A computer designed for AI applications. Appearing in the late 1990s, these systems will represent the next technology leap.

file A collection of bytes stored as an individual entity. All data on disk is stored as a file with an assigned file name that is unique within the directory it resides in.

To the computer, a file is nothing more than a series of bytes. The structure of a file is known to the software that manipulates it. For example, database files are made up of a series of records. Word processing files, also called documents, contain a continuous flow of text.

Following are the major types of files stored in a computer system. Except for ASCII text files, all files contain proprietary information contained in a header or interspersed throughout the file.

Type	Contents
data file	data records
document	text
spreadsheet	rows and columns of cells
image	rows and columns of bits
drawing	list of vectors
audio	digitized sound waves
MIDI	MIDI instructions
video	digital video frames
batch file	text
source program	text
object program	machine language

file and record locking A first-come, first-served technique for managing data in a multiuser environment. The first user to access the file or record prevents, or locks out, other users from accessing it. After the file or record is updated, it is unlocked and available.

file attribute A file access classification that allows a file to be retrieved or erased. Typical attributes are read/write, read only, archive and hidden.

file compression See *data compression*.

file extension See *extension*.

file format The structure of a file. There are hundreds of proprietary formats for database, word processing and graphics files. See *record layout*.

file layout Same as *record layout*.

file maintenance (1) The periodic updating of master files. For example, adding/deleting employees and customers, making address changes and changing product prices. It does not refer to daily transaction processing and batch processing (order processing, billing, etc.).

(2) The periodic reorganization of the disk drives. Data that is continuously updated becomes physically fragmented over the disk space and requires regrouping. An optimizing program is run (daily, weekly, etc.) that rewrites all files contiguously.

FileMaker II A Macintosh file manager from Claris. It is a popular program for general data management and provides a variety of statistical functions, fast search capabilities and extensive reporting features.

FileMan (1) Public-domain MUMPS software that provides a stand-alone, interactive DBMS as well as a set of utilities for the MUMPS programmer.

(2) Slang for Windows' file manager, which is precisely named "File Manager."

file manager (1) Software that manages data files. Often erroneously called database managers, file managers provide the ability to create, enter, change, query and produce reports on one file at a time. They have no relational capabilty and usually don't include a programming language.

(2) Software used to manage files on a disk. It provides functions to delete, copy, move, rename and view files as well as create and manage directories. The file manager in Windows is aptly named "File Manager."

file name A name assigned by the user or programmer that is used to identify a file.

FileNet A document imaging system from FileNet Corporation, Costa Mesa, CA. Introduced in 1985, FileNet is the most widely-used, high-end workflow automation system. It runs on PCs, Sun and Digital workstations and also offers an RS/6000 document server running UNIX and ORACLE.

file protect ring A plastic ring inserted into a reel of magnetic tape for file protection.

file protection Preventing accidental erasing of data. Physical file protection is provided on the storage medium by turning a switch, moving a lever or covering a notch.

file recovery program Software that recovers disk files that have been accidentally deleted or damaged.

file server A high-speed computer in a LAN that stores the programs and data files shared by users on the network. Also called a network server, it acts like a remote disk drive. See *database server*.

file sharing protocol A communications protocol that provides a structure for file requests (open, read, write, close, etc.) between stations in a network. If file sharing is strictly between workstation and server, it is also called a client/server protocol. It refers to layer 7 of the OSI model.

file size The length of a file in bytes.

file spec (file SPECification) A reference to the location of a file on a disk, which includes disk drive, directory name and file name. For example, in DOS and OS/2, `c:\wordstar\books\chapter` is a file spec for the file CHAPTER in the BOOKS subdirectory in the WORDSTAR directory on drive C.

file system (1) A method for cataloging files in a computer system. See *hierarchical file system*.

(2) A data processing application that manages individual files. Files are related by customized programming. Contrast with *relational database*.

file transfer program A program that transmits files from one computer to another. Such programs; for example, Travelling Software's LapLink and the Interlink utility that comes with DOS 6, allow the user to control both computers from one machine. See *FTP*.

file transfer protocol A communications protocol used to transmit files without loss of data. A file transfer protocol can handle all types of files including binary files and ASCII text files. Common examples are Xmodem, Ymodem, Zmodem and Kermit.

file viewer Software that displays the contents of a file as it would be normally displayed by the application that created it. It is usually capable of displaying a variety of common formats.

fill (1) In a paint program, to change the color of a bordered area.

(2) In a spreadsheet, to enter common or repetitive values into a group of cells.

fill pattern (1) A color, shade or pattern used to fill an area of an image.

(2) Signals transmitted by a LAN station when not receiving or transmitting data in order to maintain synchronization.

fill scaling The ability to change a fill pattern from light to dense. For example, if polka dots were used, the fill pattern could range from thick dots widely separated to very thin dots tightly packed together.

film recorder A device that takes a 35mm slide picture from a graphics file, which has been created in a CAD, paint or business graphics package. It generates very high resolution, generally from 2,000 to 4,000 lines.

It typically works by recreating the image on a built-in CRT that shines through a color wheel onto the film in a standard 35mm camera. Some units provide optional Polaroid camera backs for instant previewing. Film recorders can be connected to personal computers by plugging in a controller board cabled to the recorder.

filter (1) A process that changes data, such as a sort routine that changes the sequence of items or a conversion routine (import or export filter) that changes one data, text or graphics format into another.

(2) A pattern or mask through which only selected data is passed. For example, certain e-mail systems can be programmed to filter out important messages and alert the user. In dBASE, `set filter to file overdue`, compares all data to the matching conditions stored in OVERDUE.

financial planning language A language used to create data models and command a financial planning system.

financial planning system Software that helps the user evaluate alternatives. It allows for the creation of a data model, which is a series of data elements in equation form; for example, **gross profit = gross sales - cost of goods sold**. Different values can be plugged into the elements, and the impact of various options can be assessed (what if?).

A financial planning system is a step above a spreadsheet by providing additional analysis tools; however, increasingly, these capabilities are being built into spreadsheets. See *goal seeking*.

Finder The part of early Macintosh operating systems that keeps track of icons, controls the Clipboard and Scrapbook and allows files to be copied. Finder manages one application at a time. MultiFinder, the successor to Finder, manages multiple applications and is now an inherent part of the Mac operating system.

fingerprint reader A scanner used to identify a person's fingerprint for security purposes. After a sample is taken, access to a computer or other system is granted if the fingerprint matches the stored sample. A PIN may also be used with the fingerprint sample.

finite element See *FEA*.

firewall A network node set up as a boundary to prevent traffic from one segment to cross over into another. See *router* and *bridge*.

FireWire A serial bus developed by Apple and Texas Instruments that allows for the connection of 63 devices at speeds ranging from 100 to 400 Mbits/sec. Up to 1022 FireWire buses can be bridged together providing enormous capacity. It is envisioned as a replacement for serial, parallel and SCSI ports.

firmware A category of memory chips that hold their content without electrical power and include ROM, PROM, EPROM and EEPROM technologies. Firmware becomes "hard software" when holding program code.

first-generation computer A computer that used vacuum tubes as switching elements; for example, the UNIVAC I.

fixed disk A non-removable hard disk such as is found in most personal computers. Programs and data are copied to and from the fixed disk.

fixed-frequency monitor A monitor that accepts one type of video signal, such as VGA only. Contrast with *multiscan monitor*.

fixed head disk A direct access storage device, such as a disk or drum, that has a read/write head for each track. Since there is no access arm movement, access times are significantly improved.

fixed length field A constant field size; for example, a 25-byte name field takes up 25 bytes in each record. It is easier to program, but wastes disk space and restricts file design. Description and comment fields are always a dilemma. Short fields allow only abbreviated remarks, while long fields waste space if lengthy comments are not required in every record. Contrast with *variable length field*.

fixed length record A data record that contains fixed length fields.

fixed point A method for storing and calculating numbers in which the decimal point is always in the same location. Contrast with *floating point*.

Fkey (Function **key**) A Macintosh command sequence using command, shift and option key combinations. For example, Fkey 1 (command-shift 1) ejects the internal floppy. See also *function keys*.

flag (1) In communications, a code in the transmitted message which indicates that the following characters are a control code and not data.

(2) In programming, a "yes/no" indicator built into certain hardware or created and controlled by the programmer.

(3) A UNIX command line argument. The symbol is a dash. For example, in the command `head -15 filex`, which prints the first 15 lines of the file FILEX, the -15 flag modifies the Head command.

flame Slang for communicating emotionally and/or excessively via electronic mail. See *netiquette*.

flash BIOS A PC BIOS that is stored in flash memory rather than in a ROM. Flash BIOSs can be upgraded in place, whereas ROM BIOSs must be replaced with a newer chip.

flash disk A solid state disk made of flash memory. It emulates a standard disk drive in contrast with flash memory cards, which require proprietary software to make them function.

flash memory A memory chip that holds its content without power, but must be erased in fixed blocks rather than single bytes. Block sizes typically range from 512 bytes up to 256KB. The term was coined by Toshiba for its ability to be erased "in a flash." Derived from EEPROMs, flash chips are less expensive and provide higher bit densities. Flash is also becoming an alternative to EPROMS, because it can be easily updated.

flat address space A memory that is addressed starting with 0. Each subsequent byte is referenced by the next sequential number (0, 1, 2, 3, 4, etc.) all the way to the end of memory. This is normal addressing in contrast with segmented addressing, which addresses memory in blocks. Contrast with *segmented address space*.

flat file A stand-alone data file that does not have any pre-defined linkages or pointers to locations of data in other files. This is the type of file used in a relational database; however, the term is often used to refer to a type of file that has no relational capability, exactly the opposite. This business can drive you nuts!

flat panel display A thin display screen that uses any of a number of technologies, such as LCD, electroluminscent or plasma. Used today in laptops to reduce size and weight, they will eventually supersede CRTs.

flat screen A display screen in which the CRT viewing surface is flatter than most CRTs, which are slightly rounded. It provides less distortion at the edges.

flat shading In computer graphics, a technique for computing a one-tone shaded surface to simulate simple lighting.

flatbed plotter A graphics plotter that draws on sheets of paper that have been placed in a bed. The size of the bed determines the maximum size sheet that can be drawn.

flexible disk Same as *floppy disk* and *diskette*.

flick file A file format for animation from AutoDesk, Inc. It uses the .FLI file extension.

flicker A fluctuating image on a video screen. See *interlaced*.

flip-flop An electronic circuit that alternates between two states. When current is applied, it changes to its opposite state (0 to 1 or 1 to 0). Made of several transistors, it is used in the design of static memories and hardware registers.

flippy board A PC expansion board that connects to both ISA/EISA and Micro Channel buses. ISA/EISA connectors are on one edge of the board, MCA on the other.

float In programming, a declaration of a floating point number.

floating point A method for storing and calculating numbers in which the decimal points do not line up as in fixed point numbers. The significant digits are stored as a unit called the mantissa, and the location of the radix point (decimal point in base 10) is stored in a separate unit called the exponent. Floating point methods are used for calculating a large range of numbers quickly.

Floating point operations can be implemented in hardware (math coprocessor), or they can be done in software. They can also be performed in a separate floating point processor that is connected to the main processor via a channel.

Mantissa	Exponent		Actual value
6508	0	=	6508
6508	1	=	65080
6508	-1	=	650.8

FLOATING POINT

floating point processor An arithmetic unit designed to perform floating point operations. It may be a coprocessor chip in a personal computer, a CPU designed with built-in floating point capabilities or a separate machine, often called an *array processor*, which is connected to the main computer.

floppy disk A reusable magnetic storage medium. It is the primary method for distributing personal computer software. It is also used to transfer data between users,

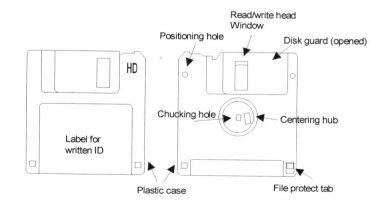

3.5" FLOPPY DISK

although local area networks can eliminate much of this "sneakernet."

FLOPS (FLoating point Operations Per Second) A unit of measurement of floating point calculations. For example, 100 megaflops is 100 million floating point operations per second.

Floptical A type of floppy disk from Insite Peripherals, Inc., San Jose, CA, that records data magnetically, but uses grooves in the disk to optically align the head over the tracks. The first 3.5" Floptical drive uses 21MB diskettes and can also read and write 720KB and 1.44MB diskettes.

flow chart A graphical representation of the sequence of operations in an information system or program. Information system flow charts show how data flows from source documents through the computer to final distribution to users. Program flow charts show the sequence of instructions in a single program or subroutine. Different symbols are used to draw each type of flow chart.

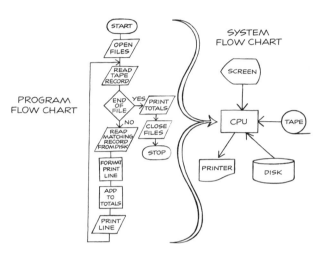

flow control (1) In communications, the management of transmission between two devices. It is concerned with the timing of signals and enables slower-speed devices to communicate with higher-speed ones. There are various techniques, but all are designed to ensure that the receiving station is able to accept the next block of data before the sending station sends it. See *xon-xoff*.

(2) In programming, the if-then and loop statements that make up the program's logic.

flush To empty the contents of a memory buffer onto disk.

flush center
The centering,
of text uniformly
between the left and right margins.

flush left The alignment of all text uniformly to the left margin. All text is typically set flush left as is the text in this book.

flush right
The alignment of all text
uniformly to the right margin
while the left margin is set
ragged left.

flux The energy field generated by a magnet.

FM (1) (Frequency Modulation) A transmission technique that blends the data signal into a carrier by varying (modulating) the frequency of the carrier. See *modulate*.

(2) (Frequency Modulation) An earlier magnetic disk encoding method that places clock bits onto the medium along with the data bits. It has been superseded by MFM and RLL.

FM synthesis A MIDI technique that simulates the sound of musical instruments. It uses operators, typically four of them, which create wave forms or modulate the wave forms. FM synthesis does not create sound as faithfully as wave table synthesis, which uses actual samples of the instruments.

Fn key (FuNction key) A keyboard key that works like a shift key to activate the second function on a dual-purpose key, typically found on laptops to reduce keyboard size. It is different than the function keys F1, F2, etc.

FOCA (Font Object Content Architecture) See *MO:DCA*.

FOCUS (1) A DBMS from Information Builders, Inc., New York, that runs on PCs, mainframes and minis. It allows relational, hierarchical and network data structures and can access a variety of databases, including standard IBM mainframe files, DB2, IMS, IDMS and others. It includes a fourth-generation language and a variety of decision support facilities.

(2) (Federation On Computing in the U.S.) The U.S. representative of IFIP. Address: IEEE Computer Society, 1730 Mass. Ave. N.W., Washington, DC 20036, 202/371-0101.

FOIA (Freedom Of Information Act) A U.S. Government rule that states that public information shall be delivered within 10 days of request.

FOIRL (Fiber Optic Inter Repeater Link) An IEEE standard for fiber optic Ethernet.

folder In the Macintosh, a simulated file folder that holds documents (text, data or graphics), applications and other folders. A folder is like a DOS directory. A folder within a folder is like a DOS subdirectory.

    Foldering is implemented in various Windows and UNIX shells in order to simplify file management.

foldering Using folders to store and manipulate documents on screen.

Folio (1) Text management software for PCs from Folio Corporation, Provo, UT, that provides storage, retrieval and hypertext capability for text databases. It can import text from over 40 file formats. Folio files are called "Infobases."

System Folder   Mac Paint   Rolodex

HyperCard   Games   Glossary

Graphics   MacTerm v2.0   Full Paint

MACINTOSH FOLDERS

In the Macintosh desktop, folders are represented by tiny pictures (icons) with captions. The Glossary folder is currently selected.

(2) (folio) In typography, a printed page number. For example, folio 3 could be the 27th physical page in a book.

font A set of type characters of a particular typeface design and size. Usually, each typeface (Times Roman, Helvetica, Arial, etc.) is made available in four variations: normal weight, bold, italic and bold italic. Thus, for bitmapped fonts, which are fully generated ahead of time, four fonts would be required for each point size used in each typeface. For scalable fonts, which are generated in any point size on the fly, only four fonts would be required for each typeface.

    Fonts come built into the printer, as plug-in cartridges or as soft fonts, which reside on the computer's hard disk or a hard disk built into the printer. See *bitmapped font* and *scalable font*.

▶ *The electronic and encyclopedic versions of this book provide more detail on this subject.*

font cartridge A set of bitmapped or outline fonts for one or more typefaces contained in a plug-in

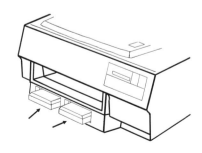

FONT CARTRIDGE

module for the printer. The fonts are stored in a ROM chip within the cartridge. Contrast with *soft font* and *internal font*.

font compiler Same as *font generator*.

font editor Software that allows fonts to be designed and modified.

font family A set of fonts of the same typeface in assorted sizes, including bold, italic and bold italic variations.

font generator Software that converts an outline font into a bitmap (dot pattern required for a particular font size). Font generation is not linear, simply expanding a letter to any size. As fonts get bigger, their characteristics must change in order to make them attractive. Font generation is used to create bitmapped fonts, which are fully generated and stored on disk before use. Contrast with *font scaler*, which generates the font in any point size the instant it is needed for display or printing.

font manager See *font scaler*.

font metric Typographic information (width, height, kerning) for each character in a font.

font number An identification number assigned to a font. A program references the font by this number.

font rasterizer See *font scaler*.

font scaler Software that converts scalable fonts into bitmaps on the fly as required for display or printing. Examples are TrueType, Adobe Type Manager and Bitstream's Facelift. See *scalable font* and *font generator*.

font style A typeface variation (normal, bold, italic, bold italic).

font utility Software that provides functions for managing fonts, including the ability to download, install, design and modify fonts.

font weight The thickness of characters (light, medium or bold).

Fontware A font generator for various DOS applications from Bitstream Inc., Cambridge, MA, which includes a library of typeface outlines in normal, italic, bold and bold italic weights. FontWare has been discontinued in favor of newer scalable font technogies. See *font scaler*.

footer In a document or report, common text that appears at the bottom of every page. It usually contains the page number.

footnote Text that appears at the bottom of a page, which adds explanation. It is often used to give credit to the source of information. When accumulated and printed at the end of a document, they are called *endnotes*.

footprint The amount of geographic space covered by an object. A computer footprint is the desk or floor surface it occupies. A satellite's footprint is the earth area covered by its downlink.

for statement A high-level programming language structure that repeats a series of instructions a specified number of times. It creates a loop that includes its own control information. The following examples in BASIC and C print "Hello" 10 times:

```
    BASIC                    C
for x = 1 to 10      for (x = 0;  x  10;  x++)
  print "hello"        printf ("hello\n");
next x
```

foreground/background The priority assigned to programs running in a multitasking environment. In a multiuser environment, foreground programs have highest priority, and background programs have lowest. Online users are given the foreground, and batch processing activities (sorts, updates, etc.) are given the background. If batch activities are given a higher priority, terminal response times may slow down considerably.

In a personal computer, the foreground program is the one the user is currently working with, and the background program might be a print spooler or communications program.

Forest & Trees A data analysis program for PCs from Trinzic Corporation, Portsmouth, NH, that integrates data from a variety of applications. It provides a control room interface that lets users monitor important business information.

fork (1) In UNIX, to make a copy of a process for execution.

(2) In the Macintosh, a part of a file. See *data fork* and *resource fork*.

form (1) A paper form used for printing.

(2) A screen display designed for a particular application.

form factor The physical size of a device.

form feed Advancing a printer form to the top of the next page. It is done by pressing the printer's form feed (FF) button or by sending the form feed code (ASCII 12) to the printer from the computer.

form view A screen display showing one item or record arranged like a preprinted form. Contrast with *table view*.

format The structure, or layout, of an item. Screen formats are fields on the screen. Report formats are columns, headers and footers on a page. Record formats are the fields within a record. File formats are the structure of data and program files, word processing documents and graphics files (display lists and bitmaps) with all their proprietary headers and codes. See *format program, disk format, DOS format* and *style sheet*.

format program Software that initializes a disk. There are two formatting levels. The low-level initializes the disk surface by creating the physical tracks and storing sector identification in them. Low-level format programs lay out the sectors as required by the particular drive technology used (IDE, SCSI, etc.).

The high-level format creates the indexes used by the operating system (Mac, DOS, etc.) to keep track of data stored in the sectors.

Floppy disk format programs perform both levels on a diskette.

forms software Workflow automation software used to create on-screen data entry forms and provide e-mail routing and tracking of the resulting electronic documents.

formula (1) An arithmetic expression that solves a problem. For example, `(fahrenheit-32)*5/9` is the formula for converting Fahrenheit to Celsius.

(2) In spreadsheets, an algorithm that identifies how the data in a specific number of cells is to be calculated. For example, `+C3*D8` means that the contents of cell C3 are to be multiplied by the contents of cell D8 and the results are to be placed where the formula is located.

FORTH (FOuRTH-generation language) A high-level programming language created by Charles Moore in the late 1960s as a way of providing direct control of the computer. Using a syntax that resembles LISP, it is used to write process control, video game and AI applications. The following polyFORTH example converts Fahrenheit to Celsius:

```
: CONV ( n) 32 - 5 9 * / . ." Celsius
: USER_INPUT  ." Enter Fahrenheit " CONV ;
```

FORTRAN (FORmula TRANslator) The first high-level programming language and compiler, developed in 1954 by IBM. It was originally designed to express mathematical formulas, and although it is used occasionally for business applications, it is still the most widely used language for scientific, engineering and mathematical problems.

FORTRAN IV is an ANSI standard, but FORTRAN V has various proprietary versions. The following example converts Fahrenheit to Celsius:

```
WRITE(6,*) 'Enter Fahrenheit '
READ(5,*) XFAHR
XCENT = (XFAHR - 32) * 5 / 9
WRITE(6,*) 'Celsius is ',XCENT
STOP
END
```

forum An information interchange regarding a specific topic or product that is hosted on an online service or BBS. It can include the latest news on the subject, a conferencing capability for questions and answers by participants as well as files for downloading fixes, demos and other related material.

forward chaining In AI, a form of reasoning that starts with what is known and works toward a solution. Known as bottom-up approach. Contrast with *backward chaining*.

forward compatible Same as *upward compatible*.

forward error correction A communications technique that can correct bad data on the receiving end. Before transmission, the data is processed through an algorithm that adds extra bits for error correction. If the transmitted message is received in error, the correction bits are used to repair it.

fountain fill In computer graphics, a painted area that smoothly changes its color or pattern density. A radial fountain fill starts at the center of an area and radiates outward.

fourth-generation computer A computer made up almost entirely of chips with limited amounts of discrete components. We are currently in the fourth generation.

fourth-generation language A computer language that is more advanced than traditional high-level programming languages. For example, in dBASE, the command List displays all the records in a data file. In second- and third-generation languages, instructions would have to be written to read each record, test for end of file, place each item of data on screen and go back and repeat the operation until there are no more records to process.

First-generation languages are machine languages; second-generation are machine dependent assembly languages; third-generation are high-level programming languages, such as FORTRAN, COBOL, BASIC, Pascal, and C. Although many languages, such as dBASE, are called fourth-generation languages, they are actually a mix of third and fourth. The dBASE List command is a fourth-generation command, but applications programmed in dBASE are third-generation.

Query language and report writers are also fourth-generation languages. Any computer language with English-like commands that doesn't require traditional input-process-output logic falls into this category.

FoxBASE+ A dBASE III PLUS-compatible DBMS for the Macintosh from Microsoft. Originally developed by Fox Software for the PC, FoxBASE gained a reputation for its speed and compatibility.

FoxPro A dBASE IV-compatible DBMS from Microsoft for PCs. An enhanced version of FoxBASE, FoxPro includes windowing, SQL and QBE interfaces and "Rushmore" technology for fast queries on large databases.

FPGA (Field Programmable Gate Array) A programmable logic chip with a high density of gates.

fps (1) (Frames Per Second) See *frame*.

(2) (FPS) (Floating Point Systems, Inc., Beaverton, OR) A supercomputer manufacturer.

FPU (Floating Point Unit) A computer circuit that handles floating point operations.

fractals A technique for describing and greatly compressing images, especially natural objects, such as trees, clouds and rivers. It turns an image into a set of data and an algorithm for expanding it back to the original.

The term comes from "fractus," which is Latin for broken or fragmented. It was coined by IBM Fellow and doctor of mathematics Benoit Mandelbrot, who expanded on ideas from earlier mathematicians and discovered similarities in chaotic and random events and shapes.

fractional T1 A service that provides less than full T1 capacity. One or more 64 Kbits/sec channels are provided.

FRAD (Frame Relay Assembler/Dissassembler) A communications device that formats outgoing data into the format required by a frame relay network. It strips the data back out at the other end. It is the frame relay counterpart to the X.25 PAD.

fragmentation The non-contiguous storage of data on disk. As files are updated, new data is stored in available free space, which may not be contiguous. Fragmented files cause extra head movement, slowing disk accesses. A disk maintenance, or optimizer, program is used to rewrite and reorder all the files.

FRAM (1) (Ferroelectronic RAM) A non-volatile semiconductor memory that retains its content without power for up to 10 years.

(2) (Ferromagnetic RAM) A non-volatile memory that records microscopic bits on a magnetic surface.

frame (1) In computer graphics, one screenful of data or its equivalent storage space.

(2) In communications, a fixed block of data transmitted as a single entity. Also called a *packet*.

(3) In desktop publishing, a movable, resizable box that holds a graphic image.

(4) In AI, a data structure that holds a general description of an object, which is derived from basic concepts and experience.

frame buffer A separate memory bank used to hold a graphic image. It can be built with one plane of memory for each bit in the pixel. For example, if eight bits are used per pixel, eight memory planes are used.

frame grabber A device that accepts standard TV signals and digitizes the current video frame into a bitmap image.

frame relay A high-speed packet switching protocol used for wide area networks (WANs). It is faster than traditional X.25 networks, because it was designed for today's reliable circuits and performs less rigorous error detection. It provides for a granular service up to DS1 rates of 1.544 Mbps and is suited for data and image transfer. Because of its variable-length packet architecture, it is not the most efficient technology for realtime voice and video.

FrameMaker A desktop publishing program from Frame Technology Corporation, San Jose, CA, that runs on UNIX platforms, Macintosh and Windows. It is noted for its large number of advanced features, including full text and graphics editing capabilities. Optional viewers let documents run on machines without FrameMaker, providing a way to distribute hypertext-based help systems.

framework (1) In object-oriented programming, a generalized subsystem design for building applications. It consists of abstract classes and their object collaboration as well as concrete classes. While object-oriented programming supports software reuse, frameworks support design reuse.

(2) (FrameWork) One of the first integrated software packages for PCs that included a programming language. It was developed by Ashton-Tate, later acquired by Borland.

framing bit Same as *start bit* and *stop bit*.

free-form database A database system that allows entry of text without regard to length or order. Although it accepts data as does a word processor, it differs by providing better methods for searching, retrieving and organizing the data.

free-form language A language in which statements can reside anywhere on a line or even cross over lines. It does not imply less syntax structure, just more freedom in placing statements. For example, any number of blank spaces are allowed between symbols. Most high-level programming languages are free-form.

Free Software Foundation A non-profit organization founded in 1985 by Richard Stallman, dedicated to eliminating restrictions on copying and modifying programs by promoting the development and use of freely redistributable software. Its GNU computing environment, X Windows and other programs are available for a transaction charge. Address: 675 Mass. Ave., Cambridge, MA 02139, 617/876-3296, Internet: gnu@prep.ai.mit.edu.

FreeHand A full-featured Macintosh drawing program from Aldus Corporation, Seattle, WA, that combines a wide range of drawing tools with special effects.

Freelance Graphics A presentation graphics program for Windows from Lotus that is also part of Lotus' SmartSuite set of applications.

freeware Software distributed without charge. Ownership is retained by the developer who has control over its redistribution, including the ability to change the next release of the freeware to payware. See *shareware* and *public domain software*.

freeze-frame video Video transmission in which the image is changed once every couple of seconds rather than 30 times per second as is required in full-motion video.

frequency The number of oscillations (vibrations) in an alternating current within one second. See *carrier*.

frequency division multiplexing See *FDM*.

frequency modulation See *FM*.

frequency shift See *FSK*.

friction feed A mechanism that allows cut paper forms to be used in a printer. The paper is passed between the platen and a roller that presses tightly against it. Contrast with *tractor feed*.

frob Slang for manipulating and adjusting dials and buttons for fun. From "frobnicate."

front-end CASE CASE tools that aid in systems analysis and design. Contrast with *back-end CASE*.

front end processor A computer that handles communications processing for a mainframe. It connects to the communications lines on one end and the mainframe on the other. It transmits and receives messages, assembles and disassembles packets and detects and corrects errors. It is sometimes synonymous with a communications controller, although the latter is usually not as flexible.

frontware Also called *screen scrapers*, frontware is software that adds a graphical user interface to mainframe applications. The frontware application is processed in the personal computer which is used as a terminal to the mainframe.

FSK (Frequency Shift Keying) A simple modulation technique that merges binary data into a carrier. It creates only two changes in frequency: one for 0, another for 1.

FSR (Free System Resource) In Windows, the amount of unused memory in a 64K block (128K for Version 3.1) reserved for managing current applications. Every open window takes some space in this area.

FT-1 See *fractional T1*.

FTAM (File Transfer Access and Management) A communications protocol for the transfer of files between systems of different vendors.

FTP (File Transfer Program & File Transfer Protocol) A set of TCP/IP commands used to log onto a network, list directories and copy files. It can also translate between ASCII and EBCDIC. See *TFTP*.

FTS 2000 (Federal Telecommunications System 2000) A digital fiber-optic network providing voice, video, e-mail and high-speed data communications for the U.S. government. AT&T and Sprint are the major equipment providers.

FUD factor (Fear Uncertainty Doubt factor) A marketing strategy used by a dominant or privileged organization that restrains competition by not revealing future plans.

full backup See *backup types*.

full-duplex Transmitting and receiving simultaneously. In pure digital networks, this is achieved with two pairs of wires. In analog networks or in digital networks using carriers, it is achieved by dividing the bandwidth of the line into two frequencies, one for sending, the other for receiving.

full-duplex Ethernet See *FDSE*.

full featured Hardware or software that provides capabilities and functions comparable to the most advanced models or programs of that category.

full-motion video Video transmission that changes the image 30 frames per second (30 fps). Motion pictures are run at 24 fps. Contrast with *freeze-frame video*.

full path A path name that includes the drive (if required), starting or root directory, all attached subdirectories and ending with the file or object name. Contrast with *relative path*. See *path*.

full project life cycle A project from inception to completion.

full-screen mode Programming capability that allows data to be displayed in any row, column or pixel location on screen. Contrast with *teletype mode*.

fully populated A circuit board whose sockets are completely filled with chips.

function In programming, a self-contained software routine that peforms a job for the program it is written in or for some other program. The function performs the operation and returns control to the instruction following the calling instruction or to the calling program. Programming languages provide a set of standard functions and may allow programmers to define others. For example, the C language is built entirely of functions.

function call A request by a program to use a function within the program itself or within another program. The request is made by stating the name of the function followed by any values (parameters, arguments) that may have to be passed to it. Values which are results from the operation performed by the function may be returned back to the calling program.

The function may be written within the program, be part of an external library that is combined with the program when it is compiled or be contained in another program, such as the operating system or DBMS.

function keys A set of keyboard keys used to command the computer (F1, F2, etc.). F1 is often the help key, but the purpose of any function key is determined by the software currently running.

function library A collection of program routines. See *function*.

function overloading In programming, using the same name for two or more functions. The compiler determines which function to use based on the type of function, arguments passed to it and type of values returned.

function prototyping In programming, formally defining each function in the program with the number and types of parameters passed to it and its return values. The compiler can then report an error if a function is not written to conform to the prototype.

functional decomposition Breaking down a process into non-redundant operations.

functional specification The blueprint for the design of an information system. It provides documentation for the database, human and machine procedures, and all the input, processing and output detail for each data entry, query, update and report program in the system.

fuse (1) A protective device that is designed to melt, or blow, when a specified amount of current is passed through it. PROM chips are created as a series of fuses that are selectively blown in order to create the binary patterns of the data or machine language.

(2) To bond together.

fusible link A circuit line in a PROM chip or similar device that is designed to be blown apart. See *PROM programmer*.

Futurebus+ An IEEE standard multisegment bus that can transfer data at 32, 64, 128 and 256-bits and can address up to 64 bits. Clock speeeds range from 25 to 100MHz. At 100MHz and 256 bits, it transfers 3.2 Gbytes/sec.

fuzzy computer A specially-designed computer that employs fuzzy logic. Using such architectural components as analog circuits and parallel processing, fuzzy computers are designed for AI applications.

fuzzy logic A mathematical technique for dealing with imprecise data and problems that have many solutions rather than one. Although it is implemented in digital computers which ultimately make only yes-no decisions, fuzzy logic works with ranges of values, solving problems in a way that more resembles human logic.

fuzzy logician An individual who is involved in developing fuzzy logic algorithms.

fuzzy search An inexact search for data that finds answers that come close to the desired data. It can get results when the exact spelling is not known or help users obtain information that is loosely related to a topic.

G See *giga*.

gain The amount of increase that an amplifier provides on the output side of the circuit.

GAL (Generic Array Logic) A programmable logic chip (PLD) technology from Lattice Semiconductor.

gallium arsenide An alloy of gallium and arsenic compound (GaAs) that is used as the base material for chips. It is several times faster than silicon.

game port An I/O connector used to attach a joy stick. It is typically a 15-pin socket on the back of a PC. See *serial port*.

gamma correction In computer graphics, using a formula to provide a range of intensities that appear uniform to the human eye.

gang punch To punch an identical set of holes into a deck of punched cards.

Gantt chart A form of floating bar chart usually used in project management to show resources or tasks over time.

gap (1) The space between blocks of data on magnetic tape.

(2) The space in a read/write head over which magnetic flux (energy) flows causing the underlying magnetic tape or disk surface to become magnetized in the corresponding direction.

gapless A magnetic tape that is recorded in a continuous stream without interblock gaps.

garbage collection A routine that searches memory for program segments or data that are no longer active in order to reclaim that space.

garbage in... See *GIGO*.

GAS See *gallium arsenide*.

gas discharge display See *plasma display*.

gas plasma See *plasma display*.

gate (1) An open/closed switch.

(2) A pattern of transistors that makes up an AND, OR or NOT Boolean logic gate. See *gate array*.

(3) In a MOS transistor, the line that triggers the switch.

gate array A type of chip that contains unconnected logic elements, typically two-input NAND gates. NAND gates can be interconnected to provide all the Boolean operations necessary for digital logic. The chip is completed by designing and adhering the top metal layer that provides the pathways between them. This final masking stage is less costly than designing the chip from scratch.

gated Switched "on" or capable of being switched on and off.

gateway (1) A computer that performs protocol conversion between different types of networks or applications. For example, a gateway can connect a personal computer LAN to a mainframe network. An electronic mail, or messaging, gateway converts messages between two different messaging protocols. See *bridge*.

(2) (Gateway) (Gateway 2000, N. Sioux City, SD) A PC manufacturer founded in 1985 by Ted Waitt and Mike Hammond. It is one of the largest direct marketers of PCs in the U.S.

gather write To output data from two or more noncontiguous memory locations with one write operation. See *scatter read*.

GatorBox A gateway from Cayman Systems, Inc., Cambridge, MA, that interconnects LocalTalk and Ethernet networks and supports TCP/IP and NFS protocols. It also functions as a router to connect AppleTalk-based computers on a LAN with remote AppleTalk devices.

gauss A unit of measurement of magnetic energy.

Gaussian distribution A random distribution of events that is often graphed as a bell-shaped curve. It is used to represent a normal or statistically probable outcome.

Gaussian noise In communications, a random interference generated by the movement of electricity in the line. Also called white noise.

GB, Gb See *gigabyte* and *gigabit*.

Gbits/sec (GigaBITS per SECond) Billion bits per second.

GBps, Gbps (GigaBytes Per Second, GigaBits Per Second) Billion bytes per second. Billion bits per second.

Gbytes/sec (GigaBYTES per SECond) Billion bytes per second.

GCOS A Bull HN operating system used in its minis and mainframes (formerly Honeywell's product).

GCR (1) (Group Code Recording) An encoding method used on magnetic tapes and Apple II and Mac 400K and 800K floppy disks.

(2) (Gray Component Replacement) A method for reducing the amount of printing ink used. It substitutes black for the amount of gray contained in a color, thus black ink is used instead of the three CMY inks. See *UCR* and *dot gain*.

GDDM (Graphical Data Display Manager) Software that generates graphics images in the IBM mainframe environment. It contains routines to generate graphics on terminals, printers and plotters as well as accepting input from scanners. Programmers use it for creating graphics, but users can employ its Interactive Chart Utility (ICU) to create business graphics without programming.

GDI (Graphics Device Interface) The Windows graphics language used to provide output to the screen and printer. Applications call the GDI functions in Windows to display and print.

GDM See *CGM*.

GE (Greater than or Equal to) See *relational operators*.

GEM (Graphics Environment Manager) A graphical user interface from Digital Research similar to the Mac/Windows environment. It is built into ROM in several Atari computers. The DOS version of Ventura Publisher came with a runtime version.

gender changer A coupler that reverses the gender of one of the connectors in order that two male connectors or two female connectors can be joined together.

General Magic (General Magic, Inc., Cupertino, CA) A spin off of Apple Computer in 1990. It is creating personal intelligent communications products and services by developing and licensing technology to a wide variety of manufacturers and service providers. See *Telescript* and *Magic Cap*.

General MIDI A standard set of 128 sounds for MIDI sound cards and devices (synthesizers, sound modules, etc.). By assigning instruments to specific MIDI patch locations, General MIDI provides a standard way of communicating MIDI sound.

MIDI's small storage requirement makes it very desirable as a musical sound source for multimedia applications compared to digitizing actual music. For example, a three-minute MIDI file may take only 20 to 30K, whereas a WAV file (digital audio) could consume up to several megabytes depending on sound quality.

general-purpose computer Refers to computers that follow instructions, thus virtually all computers from micro to mainframe are general purpose. Even computers in toys, games and single-function devices follow instructions in their built-in program. In contrast, computational devices can be designed from scratch for special purposes (see *ASIC*).

general-purpose controller A peripheral control unit that can service more than one type of peripheral device; for example, a printer and a communications line.

general-purpose language A programming language used to solve a wide variety of problems. All common programming languages (FORTRAN, COBOL, BASIC, C, Pascal, etc.) are examples. Contrast with *special-purpose language*.

generalized program Software that serves a changing environment. By allowing variable data to be introduced, the program can solve the same problem for different users or situations. For example, the electronic versions of this Glossary could be programmed to read in a different title and thus be used for any type of dictionary.

generator (1) Software that creates software. See *application generator* and *macro generator*.

(2) A device that creates electrical power or synchonization signals.

Generic CADD A full-featured PC CADD package from Generic Software, Inc., Bothell, WA, that offers levels for beginner, intermediate and advanced users.

GEnie (General Electric Network for Information Exchange) An online information service from GE Information Services that provides business information, news and access to special interest groups. See *online services*.

Genifer A dBASE application generator from Bytel Corporation, Berkeley, CA, that creates dBASE source code.

genlock (generator **lock**) Circuitry that synchronizes video signals for mixing. In personal computers, a genlock display adapter converts screen output into an NTSC video signal, which it synchronizes with an external video source.

geostationary Same as *geosynchronous*.

geosynchronous Earth aligned. Refers to communications satellites that are placed 22,300 miles above the equator and travel at the same speed as the earth's rotation, thus appearing stationary.

GeoWorks Ensemble A graphical operating environment for DOS from GeoWorks, Inc., Berkeley, CA, that includes word processing, drawing, communications, card file and calendar applications. It provides complete DOS file management and simulates file folders like the Macintosh. Users can launch all applications from within Ensemble. GeoWorks Pro includes the Quattro Pro spreadsheet.

germanium (Ge) The material used in making the first transistors. Although still used in very limited applications, germanium was replaced by silicon years ago.

gesture recognition The ability to interpret simple hand-written symbols such as check marks and slashes.

get In programming, a request for the next record in an input file. Contrast with *put*.

Gflops See *gigaflops*.

ghost (1) A faint second image that appears close to the primary image on a display or printout. In transmission, it is a result of secondary signals that arrive ahead of or later than the primary signal. On a printout, it is caused by bouncing print elements as the paper passes by.

(2) To display a menu option in a dimmed, fuzzy typeface, indicating it is not selectable at this time.

GHz (GigaHertZ) One billion cycles per second.

GIF (Graphics Interchange Format) A popular raster graphics file format developed by CompuServe that handles 8-bit color (256 colors) and uses the LZW method to achieve compression ratios of approximately 1.5:1 to 2:1.

giga Billion. Abreviated "G." It often refers to the precise value 1,073,741,824 since computer specifications are usually binary numbers. See *binary values* and *space/time*.

gigabit One billion bits. Also Gb, Gbit and G-bit. See *giga* and *space/time*.

gigabyte One billion bytes. Also GB, Gbyte and G-byte. See *giga* and *space/time*.

gigaflops (GIGA FLoating point OPerations per Second) One billion floating point operations per second.

GIGO (Garbage In Garbage Out) "Bad input produces bad output." Data entry is critical. All possible tests should be made on data entered into a computer.
  GIGO also means "Garbage In, Gospel Out." People put too much faith in computer output!

GIS (1) (Geographic Information System) A digital mapping system used for exploration, demographics, dispatching and tracking.

(2) (Generalized Information System) An early IBM mainframe query and data manipulation language.

GKS (Graphical Kernel System) A device-independent graphics language for 2-D, 3-D and raster graphics images. It allows graphics applications to be developed on one system and easily moved to another with minimal or no change. It was the first true standard for graphics applications programmers and has been adopted by both ANSI and ISO.

glare filter A fine mesh screen that is placed over a CRT screen to reduce glare from overhead and ambient light.

glitch A temporary or random hardware malfunction. It is possible that a bug in a program may cause the hardware to appear as if it had a glitch in it and vice versa. At times it can be extremely difficult to determine whether a problem lies within the hardware or the software.

global Pertaining to an entire file, database, volume, program or system.

global variable In programming, a variable that is used by all modules in a program.

glossary A term used by Microsoft Word and adopted by other word processors for the list of shorthand, keyboard macros created by a particular user.

glue chip A support chip that adds functionality to a microprocessor, for example, an I/O processor or extra memory.

GM See *General MIDI*.

GNU (Gnu's Not UNIX) A project sponsored by the Free Software Foundation that is developing a complete software environment including operating system kernel and utilities, editor, compiler and debugger. Many consultants and organizations provide support for GNU software.

goal seeking The ability to calculate a formula backward to obtain a desired input. For example, given the goal `gross margin = 50%` as well as the range of possible inputs, goal seeking attempts to obtain the optimum input.

GOCA (Graphics Object Content Architecture) See *MO:DCA*.

gooey See *GUI*.

Gopher A program that searches for file names and resources on the Internet and presents hierarchical menus to the user. As users select options, they are moved to different Gopher servers on the Internet. Where links have been established, USENET news and other information can be read directly from Gopher. See *Veronica, Archie* and *WAIS*.

GOSIP (Government Open Systems Interconnection Profile) A U.S. government mandate that after August 15, 1990, all new network procurements must comply with OSI. Testing is performed at the NIST, which maintains a database of OSI-compliant commercial products. (TCP/IP protocols can also still be used.)

GOTO (1) In a high-level programming language, a statement that directs the computer to go to some other part of the program. Low-level language equivalents are *branch* and *jump*.

(2) In dBASE, a command that directs the user to a specific record in the file.

(3) In word processing, a command that directs the user to a specific page number.

GOTO-less programming Writing a program without using GOTO instructions, an important rule in structured programming. A GOTO instruction points to a different part of the program without a guarantee of returning. Instead of using GOTOs, structures called subroutines or functions are used, which automatically return to the next instruction after the calling instruction when completed.

Gouraud shading In computer graphics, a technique developed by Henri Gouraud that computes a shaded surface based on the color and illumination at the corners of polygonal facets.

GPCmark See *PLB*.

GPF (1) (General Protection Fault) An application program abend in Windows 3.1. See *UAE*.

(2) (GUI Programming Facility) An OS/2 application generator from GPF Systems, Inc., Moodus, CT.

GPI (Graphical Programming Interface) A graphics language in OS/2 Presentation Manager. It is a derivative of the GDDM mainframe interface and includes Bezier curves.

GPIB (General Purpose Interface Bus) An IEEE 488 standard parallel interface used for attaching sensors and programmable instruments to a computer. It uses a 24-pin connector. HP's version is the HPIB.

GPS (Global Positioning System) A series of continuously-transmitting satellites used for identifying earth locations. By triangulation from three satellites, a hand-held receiving unit can pinpoint wherever you are on earth.

GPSS (General Purpose Simulation System) A programming language for discrete event simulation, which is used to build models of operations such as manufacturing environments, communications systems and traffic patterns. Originally developed by IBM for mainframes, PC versions are available, such as GPSS/PC by Minuteman Software and GPSS/H by Wolverine Software.

grabber hand A pointer in the shape of a hand that is moved by a mouse to "grab" and relocate objects on screen.

graceful degradation A system that continues to perform at some reduced level of performance after one of its components fails.

graceful exit The ability to get out of a problem situation in a program without having to turn the computer off.

grade The transmission capacity of a line. It refers to a range or class of frequencies that it can handle; for example, telegraph grade, voice grade and broadband.

gradient A color spread from light to dark to shade an object or give it a sense of depth. It is also used to create a colorful background.

GRAFCET (GRAPHe de Commande Etape-Transition - stage transition command graph) A PLC specification and programming language.

grammar checker Software that checks the grammar of a sentence. It can check for and highlight incomplete sentences, awkward phrases, wordiness and poor grammar.

Grammatik A popular grammar checking program for DOS, Windows, Macintosh and UNIX from WordPerfect Corporation.

grandfather, father, son A method for storing previous generations of master file data that are continuously updated. The son is the current file, the father is a copy of the file from the previous cycle, and the grandfather is a copy of the file from the cycle before that one.

granularity The degree of modularity of a system. The more granularity (grains or granules), the more customizable or flexible the system.

graph A pictorial representation of information. See *business graphics*.

graphic character A printable symbol that includes digits and letters.

graphical interface See *GUI*.

graphics Called *computer graphics*, it is the creation and manipulation of picture images in the computer. It is defined here as *graphics* to keep it next to the other entries that begin with "graphics."

A graphics computer system requires a graphics display screen, a graphics input device (tablet, mouse, scanner, camera, etc.), a graphics output device (dot matrix printer, laser printer, plotter, etc.) and a graphics software package; for example, a CAD, drawing or paint program.

Vector Graphics and Raster Graphics
Two methods are used for storing and maintaining pictures in a computer. The first method, called vector graphics (also known as object-oriented graphics), maintains the image as a series of points, lines, arcs and other geometric shapes. This method is

used for CAD and technical illustrations where the components of a drawing must be separable and individually scalable.

The second method, called raster graphics, resembles television, where the picture image is made up of dots. This method is used when pictures are scanned or photographed into the computer. It is also the format used by paint programs that turn the screen into an electronic canvas.

▶ *The electronic and encyclopedic versions of this book provide more detail on this subject.*

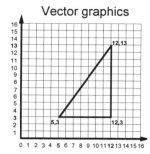

Vector graphics

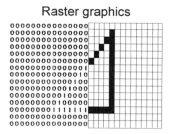

Raster graphics

HOW PICTURES ARE STORED IN A COMPUTER

graphics accelerator A high-performance video display board for graphical user interfaces that has line drawing and pixel block move functions (bitblt) built into hardware. For example, in Windows, such boards speed up the display of fonts and images and provide faster scrolling.

graphics adapter Same as *video display board*.

graphics based The display of text and pictures as graphics images; typically bitmapped images. Contrast with *text based*.

graphics card Same as *video display board*.

graphics coprocessor A programmable chip that performs much of the processing required to display graphics on a video screen. It frees the computer from such tasks as drawing dots, circles, lines and rectangles by accepting commands to perform these operations and executing them on the video adapter's coprocessor rather than the computer's CPU.

Coprocessor vs Accelerator

A graphics coprocessor is good for CAD work, especially if not running under Windows. On the other hand, a graphics accelerator is good for Windows and other GUIs, which require a lot of blitting and text drawing.

An advantage of a graphics coprocessor is that it is programmable and can be updated as required with new graphics operations, whereas the graphics accelerator is fixed and cannot be changed. This is not a disadvantage in Windows, since Windows requires limited functions to draw the screen.

graphics engine (1) Hardware that performs graphics processing tasks independently of the computer's CPU. See *graphics accelerator* and *graphics coprocessor*.
(2) Software that accepts commands from an application and builds images and text that are directed to the graphics driver and hardware. Macintosh's QuickDraw and Windows' GDI are examples.

graphics file A file that contains only graphics data. Contrast with *text file* and *binary file*.

graphics format The file format used to store a picture as vector graphics or raster graphics. There are over 100 graphics formats in use worldwide.
▶ *The electronic and encyclopedic versions of this book provide a list of nearly all the formats in use.*

graphics interface See *graphics language* and *GUI*.

graphics language A high-level language used to create graphics images. The language is translated into images by software or specialized hardware. See *graphics engine*.

graphics mode A screen display mode that displays graphics. Contrast with *text mode* and *character mode*.

graphics port (1) A socket on the computer for connecting a graphics monitor.

(2) Also called a *GrafPort*, it is a Macintosh graphics structure that defines all the characteristics of a graphics window.

graphics primitive An elementary graphics building block, such as a point, line or arc. In a solid modeling system, a cylinder, cube and sphere are examples.

graphics processor Same as *graphics engine*.

graphics tablet Same as *digitizer tablet*.

graphics terminal A terminal or personal computer that displays graphics.

graPHIGS See *GDDM*.

gray scale A series of shades from white to black. The more shades, or levels, the more realistic an image can be recorded and displayed, especially a scanned photo. Scanners differentiate typically from 16 to 256 gray levels.

Although compression techiques help reduce the size of graphics files, high-resolution gray scale requires huge amounts of storage. At a printer resolution of 300 dpi, each square inch is made up of 90,000 pixels. At 256 levels, it takes one byte per pixel, or 90,000 bytes per square inch of image. See *halftone*.

greek To display text in a representative form in which the actual letters are not discernible, because the screen resolution isn't high enough to display them properly. Desktop publishing programs let you set which font sizes should be greeked.

green PC An energy-saving personal computer or peripheral device. Green computers, printers and monitors go into a low-voltage "suspend mode" if not used after a certain period of time. Many contemporary CPUs can run at variable clock rates and can idle at very low speeds, to save current. When input is detected, they revert to full-power.

The green concept includes using less packaging materials, recycling toner cartridges, providing a return location for used batteries, distributing multi-disk software on a CD-ROM and sending e-mail rather than paper mail.

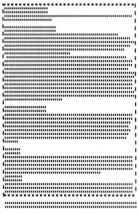

GREEKED PAGE OF TEXT

grep (Global Regular Expression and Print) A UNIX pattern matching utility that searches for a string of text and outputs any line that contains the pattern.

ground An electrically conductive body, such as the earth, which maintains a zero potential (not positively or negatively charged) for connecting to an electrical circuit.

ground current The current found in a ground line. It may be caused by imbalanced electrical sources; for example, the ground line in a communications channel between two computers deriving power separately.

ground fault The temporary current in the ground line, caused by a failing electrical component or interference from an external electrical source such as a thunderstorm.

ground loop An unwanted ground current flowing back and forth between two devices that are grounded at two or more points.

ground noise injection An intentional insertion of unwanted noise by a power supply into the ground line.

groupware Software designed for use in a network that serves a group of users working on a related project.

GSOS (GS Operating System) A graphical operating system for the Apple IIGS that also accepts ProDOS applications.

GT (Greater Than) See *relational operator*.

guard band A frequency that insulates one signal from another. In an analog telephone line, the low band is 0-300; the high band is 3300-4000Hz.

GUI (Graphical User Interface) A graphics-based user interface that incorporates icons, pull-down menus and a mouse. Macintosh, Windows and Motif are examples. See *desktop manager* and *window manager*. Contrast with *CUI*.

GUI accelerator See *graphics accelerator*.

gulp Some number of bytes!

gutter In typography, the space between two columns.

GVPN (Global Virtual Private Network) A service from cooperating carriers that provides international digital communications for multinational companies.

GW-BASIC (Gee Whiz-BASIC) A BASIC interpreter that accompanied MS-DOS in versions prior to 5.0. See *QBasic*.

h (Hexadecimal) A symbol that refers to a hex number. For example, 09h has a numeric value of 9, whereas 0Ah has a value of 10.

H&J (Hyphenation and Justification) The alignment of the right margin in a document. Hyphenation breaks up words that exceed the margin. Justification aligns text uniformly at the right margin while spacing text evenly between both margins.

H.261 An ITU-TSS standard for a video codec that uses intraframe and interframe compression and transmits over Px64 ISDN lines.

H.320 An ITU-TSS standard for video teleconferencing. It uses the H.261 compression method.

hack Program source code. You might hear a phrase like "nobody has a package to do that, so it must be done through some sort of hack." This means someone has to write some code to solve the problem. There's no pre-written package to do it.

The purist would say that doing a hack means writing in languages such as assembly language and C, which are low level and highly detailed. The more liberal person would say that writing any programming language counts as hacking.

hacker A person who writes programs in assembly language or in system-level languages, such as C. Although it may refer to any programmer, it implies very tedious "hacking away" at the bits and bytes.

The term has become widely used for people that gain illegal entrance into a computer system. This use of the term is not appreciated by the vast majority of honest hackers. See *hack* and *computer cracker*.

HAL (1) (Hardware Abstraction Layer) The translation layer in Windows NT that resides between the NT kernel and I/O system and the hardware itself.

(2) (Heuristic/Algorithmic) The computer in the film, "2001," which takes over command of the spaceship. Each of the letters in H-A-L coincidentally precede the letters I-B-M.

half-adder An elementary electronic circuit in the ALU that adds one bit to another, deriving a result bit and a carry bit.

half-duplex The transmission of data in both directions, but only one direction at a time. Two-way radio was the first to use half-duplex, for example, while one party spoke, the other party listened. Contrast with *full-duplex*.

half height drive A 5.25" disk drive that takes up half the vertical space of first-generation drives. Measuring 1 5/8" in height, it is the common 5.25" drive in use today.

halftone In printing, the simulation of a continuous-tone image (shaded drawing, photograph) with dots. In photographically-generated halftones, a camera shoots the image through a halftone screen, creating smaller dots for lighter areas and larger dots for darker areas.

In order to simulate varying size halftone dots in computer printers, which print only one size of dot, dithering is used, which creates clusters of dots in a "halftone cell." The more dots printed in the cell, the darker the gray. As the screen frequency gets higher (more lines per inch), there is less room for dots in the cell, reducing the number of gray levels that can be generated.

This tradeoff is a compromise in a 300 dpi printer, since realistic gray-scale printing reduces the resolution; for example, the 8x8 halftone cell required to create 64 grays results in a coarse 38 lpi resolution (300 dpi / 8). In high-resolution imagesetters, the highest screen frequencies can be used with ample gray scale.

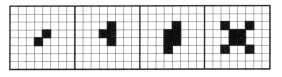

DITHERING CREATES HALFTONE DOTS

hammer In a printer, the mechanism that pushes the typeface onto the ribbon and paper or pushes the paper into the ribbon and typeface.

Hamming code A communications error correction method that intersperses three check bits at the end of each four data bits. At the receiving station, the check bits are used to detect and correct one-bit errors automatically.

handle (1) In computer graphics, a location on an image that can be grabbed for reshaping. It is usually a tiny square.

(2) A temporary name or number assigned to a file, font or other object. For example, an operating system may assign a sequential number to each file that it opens as a way of identifying and keeping track of it.

(3) A nickname used when teleconferencing on a bulletin board, like a "CB handle" used between truck drivers.

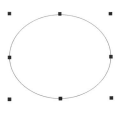

IMAGE HANDLES

handler A software routine that performs a particular task. For example, upon detection of an error, an error handler is called to recover from the error condition.

handoff Switching a cellular phone transmission from one cell to another as a mobile user moves into a new cellular area. The switch takes place in about a quarter of a second so that the caller is generally unaware of it.

handset The part of the telephone that contains the speaker and the microphone.

handshaking Signals transmitted back and forth over a communications network that establish a valid connection between two stations.

hang To have the computer freeze or lock up. When a personal computer hangs, there is often no indication of what is causing the problem. The computer could have crashed, or it could be something simple such as the printer running out of paper.

hanging paragraph A paragraph in which the first line starts at the
left margin, but subsequent lines are indented
as is this paragraph.

hard boot Same as *cold boot*.

Hardcard A family of hard disks from Plus Development Corporation, Milpitas, CA, that house the disk drive and the controller electronics on an expansion board that plugs into a PC. It uses an expansion slot, but not a drive bay.

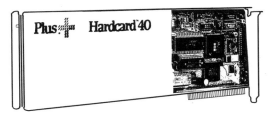

hard coded Software that performs a fixed number of tasks or works with only a fixed number of devices. For example, a program could be written to work with only two types of printers. Hard coded solutions to problems are usually the fastest to program and often run the fastest, but are not as easy to change.

hard copy Printed output. Contrast with *soft copy*.

hard disk The primary computer storage medium, which is made of one or more aluminum or glass platters. Each side of the platter is coated with a ferromagnetic material. Desktop computers use disks from 1.5" to 5" in diameter. Minicomputer and mainframe disks range up to 12" in diameter, but are increasingly becoming as compact as the desktop drives.

TYPES OF HARD DISKS

Interface Type	Typical Encoding Method*	Transfer Rate (Bytes/sec)	Storage Capacities
ST506	MFM	625K	5M - 100M
ST506 RLL	RLL	937K	30M - 200M
IDE	RLL	.625-2M	40M - 1G
Enhanced IDE	RLL	10-13M	100M - 8G
ESDI	RLL	1-3M	80M - 2G
SCSI-1	RLL	1-5M	20M - 1.5G
SCSI-2	RLL	1-40M	40M - 9G
SMD	RLL	1-4M	200M - 2G
IPI	RLL	10-25M	200M - 3G

*(Most disks use the RLL encoding method, but the encoding method is not necessarily prescribed by all interfaces.)

Hard Disk Measurements

Capacity is measured in bytes, and speed is measured in bytes per second (transfer rate) and in milliseconds (access time). Fast personal computer hard disk access times range from 9 to 14ms; in larger computers as fast as 1ms.

▶ *The electronic and encyclopedic versions of this book provide more detail on this subject.*

hard error (1) A permanent, unrecoverable error such as a disk read error. Contrast with *soft error*.

(2) A group of errors that requires user intervention and includes disk read errors, disk not ready (no disk in drive) and printer not ready (out of paper).

hard hyphen A hyphen that always prints. Contrast with *soft hyphen*.

hard return A code entered into a text document by pressing the return (enter) key. DOS and OS/2 text files use a CR/LF (carriage return/line feed) pair, but this is not standard (WordPerfect uses only an LF). The Macintosh uses a CR and UNIX uses an LF.

A hard return is sometimes represented by a symbol on screen, such as the < in WordStar, but it usually remains invisible until revealed in an expanded screen mode. Contrast with *soft return*.

hard sectored A sector identification technique that uses a physical mark. For example, hard sectored floppy disks have a hole in the disk that marks the beginning of each sector. Contrast with *soft sectored*.

hard space A special space character that acts like a letter or digit, used to prevent multiple-word, proper names from breaking between lines.

hardware Machinery and equipment (CPU, disks, tapes, modem, cables, etc.). In operation, a computer is both hardware and software. One is useless without the other. The hardware design specifies the commands it can follow, and the instructions tell it what to do. See *instruction set*.

Hardware Is "Storage and Transmission"
The more memory and disk storage a computer has, the more work it can do. The faster the memory and disks transmit data and instructions to the CPU, the faster it gets done. A hardware requirement is based on the size of the databases that will be created and the number of users or applications that will be served at the same time. How much? How fast?

Software Is "Logic and Language"
Software deals with the details of an ever-changing business and must process transactions in a logical fashion. Languages are used to program the software. The "logic and language" involved in analysis and programming is generally far more complicated than specifying a storage and transmission requirement.

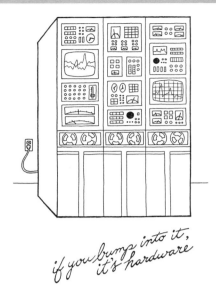

if you bump into it, it's hardware

hardware failure A malfunction within the electronic circuits or electromechanical components (disks, tapes) of a computer system. Contrast with *software failure*.

hardware interrupt An interrupt caused by some action of a hardware device, such as the depression of a key or mouse movement. See *interrupt*.

hardware key A copy protection device supplied with software that plugs into a computer port. The software interrogates the key's serial number during execution to verify its presence. The hardware key acts as a pass-through, but tests for a special code that reads the serial number.

hardware monitor A device attached to the hardware circuits of a computer that reads electronic signals directly in order to analyze system performance.

hardware vendors The hardware vendors in the computer and electronics industry are a huge force in the U.S. economy. Total revenues for calendar 1993 exceed 300 billion dollars.
▶ *The electronic and encyclopedic versions of this book includes a list of the major hardware, disk drive and semiconductor manufacturers.*

hardwired (1) Electronic circuitry that is designed to perform a specific task. See *hard coded*.

(2) Devices that are closely or tightly coupled. For example, a hardwired terminal is directly connected to a computer without going through a switched network.

harmonic distortion In communications, frequencies that are generated as multiples of the original frequency due to irregularities in the transmission line.

Harvard Graphics A popular PC presentation graphics program from Software Publishing Corporation, Mountain View, CA. It was one of the first business graphics packages and provides the ability to create columnar and free form text charts.

hash total A method for ensuring the accuracy of processed data. It is a total of several fields of data in a file, including fields not normally used in calculations, such as account number. At various stages in the processing, the hash total is recalculated and compared with the original. If any data has been lost or changed, a mismatch signals an error.

HASP (Houston Automatic Spooling Program) A mainframe spooling program that provides task, job and data management functions.

Hayes compatible Refers to modems controlled by the Hayes command language. See *AT command set.*

Hayes Smartmodem A family of intelligent modems for personal computers from Hayes Microcomputer Products, Inc., Atlanta, GA. Hayes developed the intelligent modem for first-generation personal computers in 1978, and its command language (Hayes Standard AT Command Set) for modem control has become an industry-standard.

HC See *high color.*

HD (1) (High Density) The designation for high-density diskettes; for example, the 5.25" 1.2MB and 3.5" 1.44MB floppies. Contrast with *DD.*

(2) (Hard Disk) For example, FD/HD refers to a floppy disk/hard disk.

HDA (Head Disk Assembly) The mechanical components of a disk drive (minus the electronics), which includes the actuators, access arms, read/write heads and platters.

HDLC (High-level Data Link Control) An ISO communications protocol used in X.25 packet switching networks. It provides error correction at the data link layer. SDLC, LAP and LAPB are subsets of HDLC.

HDTV (High Definition TV) A high-resolution TV standard. Japan was the first to develop HDTV and currently broadcasts an 1125-line analog signal picked up on 36" to 50" TV sets that cost about $10,000. Both Japan and Europe's HDTV use traditional analog TV signalling.

The U.S. is currently developing a single standard from specifications by various HDTV proponents. The goal is to have HDTV working for the 1996 Olympics. The result will be an all-digital HDTV standard with a resolution between 787 and 1050 lines. The current TV standard (NTSC) is a 525-line analog signal. HDTV will be transmitted on separate channels concurrently with the NTSC signals.

HDX See *half-duplex.*

head See *read/write head.*

head crash The physical destruction of a hard disk. Misalignment or contamination with dust can cause the read/write head to collide with the disk's recording surface. The data is destroyed, and both the disk platter and head have to be replaced.

Distance between read/write head and disk surface · Read/write Head · Smoke particle · Fingerprint · Dust particle · Human hair · Oxide coating · Aluminum platter

NOT MUCH ROOM FOR RECKLESS DRIVING

The read/write head touches the surface of a floppy disk, but on a hard disk, it hovers above its surface at a distance that is less than the diameter of a human hair. It has been said that the read/write head flying over the disk surface is like trying to fly a jet plane six inches above the earth's surface.

head end The originating point in a communications system. In cable TV, the head end is where the cable company has its satellite dish and TV antenna for receiving incoming programming. In online services, the head end is the service company's computer system and databases.

head-per-track disk Same as *fixed head disk.*

head skew The offset distance from the start of the previous track so that the head has time to switch from top of platter to bottom of platter and be at the start of the new track. See *cylinder skew*.

header (1) The first record in a disk or tape file. It may be used for identification only (name, date of last update, etc.), or it may describe the structural layout of the file's contents, as is common with many documents and database formats.

(2) In a document or report, common text printed at the top of every page.

(3) In communications, the first part of the message, which contains controlling data, such as originating and destination stations, message type and priority level.

(4) Any caption or description used as a headline.

header label A record used for file identification that is recorded at the beginning of the file.

heap In programming, the common pool of free memory available to the program.

heat sink A material that absorbs heat.

helical scan A recording method used on videotape and digital audio tape (DAT) that runs the tracks diagonally from top to bottom in order to increase storage capacity.

help On-screen instruction regarding the use of a program. On PCs, pressing F1 is the de facto standard for getting help. With graphics-based interfaces (Mac, Windows, etc.), clicking a "?" or HELP button gets help. See *context sensitive help*.

help compiler Software that translates text and compiler instructions into an online help system.

Hercules Graphics A video display standard for PCs from Hercules Computer Technology Inc., Berkeley, CA, that provides monochrome graphics and text with a resolution of 720x348 pixels. IBM's first PC monochrome display did not provide graphics, and Hercules introduced its display adapter to fill the void in 1982. It quickly became a de facto standard incorporated into all monochrome display boards.

Hertz The frequency of electrical vibrations (cycles) per second. Abbreviated "Hz," one Hz is equal to one cycle per second. In 1883, Heinrich Hertz detected electromagnetic waves.

heterogeneous environment Equipment from a variety of manufacturers.

heuristic A method of problem solving using exploration and trial and error methods. Heuristic program design provides a framework for solving the problem in contrast with a fixed set of rules (algorithmic) that cannot vary.

Hewlett-Packard See *HP*.

hex (HEXadecimal) Hexadecimal means 16. The base 16 numbering system is used as a shorthand for representing binary numbers. Each half byte (four bits) is assigned a hex digit as follows:

Dec	Hex	Binary	Dec	Hex	Binary	Dec	Hex	Binary
0	0	0000	6	6	0110	10	A	1010
1	1	0001	7	7	0111	11	B	1011
2	2	0010	8	8	1000	12	C	1100
3	3	0011	9	9	1001	13	D	1101
4	4	0100				14	E	1110
5	5	0101				15	F	1111

In a hex number, each digit position has a value 16 times greater than the one to its right. Two hex digits make up one byte; for example, A7h (h means hex) is equivalent to decimal 167 (10x16 + 7x1).

		A	7
4096	256	16	1

Sometimes a $ is used to represent hex values as well as upper and lower-case H; for example, $3E0, 3E0h and 3E0H are the same hex number.

▶ *The electronic and encyclopedic versions of this book provide more detail on this subject.*

HFS (Hierarchical File System) The Macintosh file system that allows files to be placed into folders, and folders to be placed within other folders.

HGC See *Hercules Graphics*.

hidden file A file classification that prevents a file from being accessed. It is usually an operating system file; however, utility programs let users hide files to prevent unauthorized access.

hierarchical A structure made up of different levels like a company organization chart. The higher levels have control or precedence over the lower levels. Hierarchical structures are a one to many relationship; each item having one or more items below it.

hierarchical communications A network controlled by a host computer that is responsible for managing all connections. Contrast with *peer-to-peer communications*.

hierarchical file system A file organization method that stores data in a top-to-bottom organization structure. All access to the data starts at the top and proceeds throughout the levels of the hierarchy.

In DOS and OS/2, the root directory is the starting point. Files can be stored in the root directory, or directories can be created off the root that hold files and subdirectories.

In the Macintosh, the disk window is the starting point. Files can be stored in the disk window, or folders can be created that can hold files and additional folders.

high color The ability to generate 32,768 colors (15 bits) or 65,536 colors (16-bit). 15-bit color uses five bits for each red, green and blue pixel. The 16th bit may be a color, such as XGA with 5-red, 6-green and 5-blue, or be an overlay bit that selects pixels to display over video input. See *true color*.

high definition TV See *HDTV*.

high density Refers to increased storage capacity of bits and/or tracks per square inch. See *HD*.

high DOS memory Same as *UMA*.

high-level format A set of indexes on the disk that the operating system uses to keep track of the data stored on the disk. See *format program*.

high-level language A machine-independent programming language, such as FORTRAN, COBOL, BASIC, Pascal and C. It lets the programmer concentrate on the logic of the problem to be solved rather than the intricacies of the machine architecture such as is required with low-level assembly languages.

There are dramatic differences between high-level languages. Look at the sample code in this Glossary under C, BASIC and COBOL as an example. What is considered high level depends on the era. There were assembly languages thirty years ago that were easier to understand than C.

high memory (1) The uppermost end of memory.

(2) In PCs, the area between 640K and 1M, or the 64K high memory area (HMA) between 1024 and 1088K.

high resolution A high-quality image on a display screen or printed form. The more dots used per square inch, the higher the quality. To display totally realistic images including the shades of human skin requires about 1,000x1,000 pixels on a 12" diagonal screen. Desktop laser printers print respectable text and graphics at 300 dpi, but typesetting machines print 1,270 and 2,540 dpi.

High Sierra The first CD-ROM standard named for an area near Lake Tahoe where it was conceived in 1985. Later evolved into the ISO 9660 standard.

high tech Refers to the latest advancements in computers and electronics as well as to the social and political environment and consequences created by such machines.

highlight To identify an area on screen in order to select, move, delete or change it in some manner.

highlight bar The currently-highlighted menu item. Choice is made by moving the bar to the desired item and pressing enter or clicking the mouse. The bar is a different color on color screens or reverse video on monochrome screens.

HiJaak A graphics file conversion and screen capture program for PCs from Inset Systems Inc., Brookfield, CT. It supports a wide variety of raster and vector formats as well as fax boards. It also handles conversion between PC and Mac formats.

HIMEM.SYS An extended memory manager that is included with DOS and Windows, starting with DOS 5 and Windows 3.0. It allows programs to cooperatively allocate extended memory in 286 and higher PCs. HIMEM.SYS is an XMS driver.

hints Font instructions that alter space and other features to improve the typeface image at low resolutions. Hints help to make a character uniform and legible especially at small point sizes; for example, they ensure that serifs and accents appear in proper proportion. Hints will have less meaning for printing as common desktop resolutions approach 600 and 800 dpi and more, but rendering typefaces on screens, which have less resolution than printers, will still benefit from hints.

HIPO (Hierarchy plus Input-Process-Output) Pronounced "hy-po." An IBM flow-charting technique that provides a graphical method for designing and documenting programs.

HiPPI (HIgh Performance Parallel Interface channel) An ANSI-standard high-speed communications channel that uses a 32-bit or 64-bit cable and transmits at 100 or 200 Mbytes/sec. It is used as a point-to-point supercomputer channel or, with a crosspoint switch, as a high-speed LAN.

hi res Same as *high resolution*.

histogram A chart displaying horizontal or vertical bars. The length of the bars are in proportion to the values of the data items they represent.

history A user's input and keystrokes entered within the current session. A history feature keeps track of user commands and/or retrieved items so that they can be quickly reused or reviewed.

HLLAPI (High Level Language Application Program Interface) An IBM programming interface that allows a PC application to communicate with a mainframe application. The hardware hookup is handled via normal micro to mainframe 3270 emulation. An extended version of the interface (EHLLAPI) has also been defined.

HLS (Hue Lightness Saturation) A variation of the HSV color model. The H and L in HLS correspond to the H and V in the HSV model. However, the saturation component is measured differently; for example, pure green in HLS is 120,1,0.5 compared to an HSV of 120,1,1. See *HSV*.

HMA (High Memory Area) In PCs, the first 64K of extended memory from 1024K to 1088K, which can be accessed by DOS. It is managed by the HIMEM.SYS driver.

It was discovered by accident that this area of memory could be used by DOS, even though it was beyond the traditional one-megabyte barrier.

HMOS (High-density **MOS**) A chip with a high density of NMOS transistors.

Hobbit A microprocessor from AT&T used in a variety of portable devices.

hog A program that uses an excessive amount of computer resources, such as memory or disk, or takes a long time to execute.

Hollerith machine The first automatic data processing system. It was used to count the 1890 U.S. census. Developed by Herman Hollerith, a statistician who had worked for the Census Bureau, the system used a hand punch to record the data in dollar-bill-sized punched cards and a tabulating machine to count them.

home brew Products that are developed at home by hobbyists.

home button An icon that represents the beginning of a file or a set of basic or starting functions.

home computer In the 1980s, a home computer was the lowest-priced computer of the time, such as an Apple II, Commodore 64 or 128, Tandy Color Computer or Atari ST. Today, the term generally refers to a PC or Mac.

home key A keyboard key used to move the cursor to the top of the screen or file or to the previous word or beginning of line. See *home button*.

home run A single wire that begins at a central distribution point (hub, PBX, etc.) and runs to its destination (workstation, telephone, etc.) without connecting to anything else.

hook In programming, instructions that provide breakpoints for future expansion. Hooks may be changed to call some outside routine or function or may be places where additional processing is added.

hop The number of gateways and routers in a transmission path. Each hop slows down transmission since the gateway or router must analyze or convert the packet of data before forwarding it to its destination.

hopper A tray, or chute, that accepts input to a mechanical device, such as a disk duplicator.

horizontal resolution The number of elements, or dots, on a horizontal line (columns in a matrix). Contrast with *vertical resolution*.

horizontal scan frequency The number of lines illuminated on a video screen in one second. For example, a resolution of 400 lines refreshed 60 times per second requires a scan rate of 24KHz plus overhead (time to bring the beam back to the beginning of the next line). Same as horizontal sync frequency in TV. Contrast with *vertical scan frequency*.

host The main computer in a distributed processing environment. It typically refers to a large timesharing computer or a central computer that controls a network.

host adapter Also called a *controller*, it is a device that connects one or more peripheral units to a computer. It is typically an expansion card that plugs into the bus. IDE drives and SCSI peripherals are examples of peripheral interfaces that call their controllers host adapters.

host based A communications system that is controlled by a large, central computer system.

host mode A communications mode that allows a computer to answer an incoming telephone call and receive data without human assistance.

hot fix The capability of being repaired while in operation. For example, many SCSI drives can move the data in sectors that are becoming hard to read to spare sectors on the fly without even the SCSI host adapter being aware of it. In some fault tolerant systems, circuit boards and components can be removed and replaced without turning the system off (also called hot swapping).

hotkey The key or key combination that causes some function to occur in the computer, no matter what else is currently running. It is commonly used to activate a memory resident (TSR) program.

hot link A predefined connection between programs so that when information in one database or file is changed, related information in other databases and files are also updated. See *hypertext, compound document* and *OLE.*

hot potato routing In communications, rerouting a message as soon as it arrives.

hot spot The exact location of the screen cursor that points to and affects the screen object when the mouse is clicked. It is typically the tip of an arrow or finger pointer or the crosspoint of an X-shaped pointer, but can be elsewhere with other cursor designs.

hot swap See *hot fix.*

housekeeping A set of instructions that are executed at the beginning of a program. It sets all counters and flags to their starting values and generally readies the program for execution.

how to select a personal computer The most important thing in selecting a personal computer is that you obtain the performance and storage capacity from your system that you need as well as the technical support from your dealer that you require. The primary decision criteria are:

1. PC versus Mac
2. DOS versus Windows
3. Desktop versus Laptop
4. Where to buy

PC versus Mac

The first decision is whether to purchase a PC or a Macintosh. It is, afterall, a PC and Mac personal computer world. Although Apple has only about 12% of the business, it is also only one company. The rest of the personal computer market is made up of countless PC vendors from thousands of mom and pop shops to the big companies such as Compaq, IBM, Dell and Gateway. Thus, Apple continues to hold its own in a largely PC world.

The advantage of the Mac is that it is easier to use compared to Windows and DOS machines. The Macintosh infrastructure is much more solid. Applications for both the PC and the Mac are increasingly becoming more feature laden and more complicated as a result. With the Mac, you can spend more time learning your application and less time configuring your computer.

It is also considerably easier to upgrade a Mac than a PC. The Mac has always been plug and play. Adding the second or third additional peripheral to a PC can be a nightmare. PCs will become easier to upgrade when the Intel/Microsoft Plug and Play standard becomes widely used; however, universal adoption of that standard plus ironing out all the bugs in it may not occur until 1996 or 1997. To implement it, you will need to run Windows 95 and have an entirely new machine with all hardware Plug and Play enabled.

The disadvantage of the Mac is compatibility. If your organization supports PCs and Macs, support personnel have most likely determined the appropriate applications and utilities that make file transfer between both platforms straightforward. There may always be some effort required to transfer your DOS/Windows file to the Mac and vice versa, but experienced personnel will show you the best ways to make the transition. If this support is not available, switching between PCs and Macs can be bothersome and in some cases not feasible.

There are also decidedly more applications for Windows than the Mac. If an application will be developed for both platforms, chances are it will be developed for Windows first, unless it's from a Mac-oriented developer. However, with the Power Macintoshes, users can run Mac, DOS and Windows applications on the same machine. The PowerMac models that are expected in 1995 and 1996 should run Windows applications as fast as a 486/66 or Pentium.

DOS versus Windows

If you've settled on a PC, then the type of applications you will run determines the system size. If you are going to run only a vertical market application (doctor, dentist, retailer, etc.) that is DOS based, you can get by with a very minimal PC configuration (see requirements below).

On the other hand, if you are running Windows, you need a fast and large machine. Windows applications can take enormous amounts of disk space, as much as 20 and 30 or more megabytes per application. You may not be entering a lot of data, but you could use up 100 megabytes of disk just by installing four or five Windows applications. In addition, if you want to keep a half dozen or more applications open at the same time, you need gobs of memory (RAM).

Future Windows applications will be even more demanding than current ones. Purchase the fastest machine you can afford.

Minimum Requirements for DOS

CPU:	386
Memory:	1MB
Disk:	100MB
Bus:	ISA
Display:	VGA
Multimedia:	Sound board, CD-ROM and speakers

Minimum Requirements for Windows

	Word processing, database, spreadsheets	CAD, imaging, desktop publishing
CPU:	486/25	Pentium/90
Memory:	4MB	16MB
Disk:	300MB	500MB
Bus:	ISA + VESA or PCI bus	
Display:	Accelerated VGA	
Multimedia:	Sound board, CD-ROM and speakers	

Regarding Windows requirements, you can always get by with a slower machine. It's all a matter of your frustration waiting for something to happen. Your experience level has nothing to do with the power of the machine you should use. You will get used to the fastest PC on the market in about 10 minutes. Then, if you go to a slower machine, you will really notice the difference.

Desktop versus Laptop

If you have a requirement for a computer in more than one location, a laptop can be an economical alternative. It can function as a desktop computer by attaching a full-size monitor and keyboard.

The caveat with laptops is that they are not as expandable as desktop machines. On desktop PCs, peripherals are mostly interchangeable. If you need more hard disk, add another or swap your current one for a larger one. On laptops, the hard disk may not be upgradable at all. If it is, there may be a limited number of options, and it will usually cost at least twice that of a desktop drive, so plan ahead.

A docking station may provide one or two expansion slots for expandability, but you will have to duplicate docking stations and peripherals if you need them in both locations. Laptops with PCMCIA slots also offer flexibility for expansion.

In addition, the display resolution on a laptop is built into the motherboard. Even if you attach a large monitor, you cannot upgrade to a higher resolution unless you have a docking station with another VGA adapter in it and the laptop is built to switch to an external adapter.

Where to Buy

The best price to pay for a personal computer and the best place to buy it often has more to do with the support you need than the equipment you purchase. If you don't need support, shop for the best price from local dealers, superstores and the mail-order houses.

Most components in PCs are highly reliable, but there are always exceptions. Hard and floppy drives come from a handful of vendors, but there are dozens of motherboard manufacturers. Look for OS/2 and Novell NetWare certification, a good sign of compatibility. Get customer referrals if possible.

One component that ought to be better in brand-name machines than in no-name clones is the power supply. If you use your computer all day, or if you keep it on 24 hours as some do, opt for the brand name. The power supply in the no-name clone might give way in a year or so. An option. Buy the no-name and put in a better power supply, such as one from PC Power and Cooling, Carlsbad, CA.

If you're new to computers, look for local dealers that specialize in hand holding for the novice. There is usually a dealer nearby that caters to the beginner. You may pay a few hundred dollars more for your system, but it may be well worth it, saving you time and frustration later.

The superstores are also a good source for computers, but the amount of support you get will vary from store to store. Remember, you can always pay a consultant by the hour to help you if you don't know any sympathetic hackers.

The mail-order houses are another good source with quality machines, but you will have to rely on technical support by phone. Ironically, the more successful the direct sales organization, the worse its phone support becomes, if only temporarily. A disadvantage of mail order is that you will have to ship back your unit if you can't fix it by phone. Look for mail-order firms with on-site support administered by a national repair organization.

Caution #1 - The Small Business

The small business looking to automate its accounting is going to need more help. Don't be fooled by the prices of hardware and off-the-shelf software. The small company often has information requirements as complicated as a much larger one. There are countless custom-designed applications that have cost $5,000 to $25,000, running on $1,500 PCs, because no off-the-shelf software package could fit the bill.

Even if a software package is viable, there are hundreds of them. Learning which ones truly meet your needs is not something most PC vendors can help you with, because that can take hours, days or weeks of analysis depending on your business and what you want to computerize. You may have to use the services of a software consulting firm or an independent consultant.

Caution #2 - The Bleeding Edge

Even if you can easily afford the newest technology, it's not always a good idea to be the first on the block to have it. Wait a bit. Ask around. When the bugs are finally fixed, and that can take several months, you may be a lot better off.

Good luck and happy computing.

HP (Hewlett-Packard Company, Palo Alto, CA) The second largest computer and electronic equipment manufacturer in the U.S. HP was founded in 1939 by William Hewlett and David Packard in a garage behind Packard's California home. First involved with instrumentation and data collection devices, HP branched into business computing in 1972.

HP sells over 10,000 different products in the electronics and computer field and has gained a worldwide reputation for its engineering.

HP 1000 A family of realtime computers from HP introduced in 1966. They are sensor-based computers used extensively in laboratory and manufacturing environments for collecting and analyzing data.

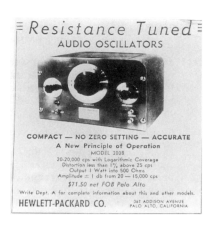

HP'S FIRST PRODUCT
(Courtesy Hewlett-Packard Co.)

HP 3000 A family of business-oriented computers from HP. Introduced in 1972, these midrange computers set a standard for reliability. It evolved into a complete line from micros to medium-scale mainframes and has been HP's major computer line. New models are RISC machines that are compatible with the original 3000s.

HP 9000 A family of high-performance UNIX workstations and business servers from HP. Introduced in 1982, it is used extensively in CAD and engineering applications. Business servers provide commercial functionality. New models use HP's RISC architecture.

HPFS (High Performance File System) The file system, introduced with OS/2 Version 1.2, that handles larger disks (2TB volumes; 2GB files), long file names (256 bytes) and can launch the program by referencing the data as in the Macintosh. It coexists with the existing FAT system.

HPGL (Hewlett-Packard Graphics Language) A vector graphics file format from HP that was developed as a standard plotter language. Most plotters support the HPGL and DMPL standards.

HPIB (Hewlett-Packard Interface Bus) HP's version of the IEEE 488 standard GPIB.

HP Precision Architecture (HP-PA) A proprietary RISC architecture from HP introduced in 1986 that is incorporated into new models of its 3000 and 9000 computer families.

HP-UX HP's version of UNIX that runs on its 9000 family. It is based on SVID and incorporates features from BSD UNIX along with several HP innovations.

HP-VUE A Motif-based graphical user interface used in HP workstations. Parts of HP-VUE are used in COSE's CDE (Common Desktop Environment).

HSB (Hue Saturation Brightness) See *HSV*.

HSL (Hue Saturation Lightness) See *HLS*.

HSM (Hierarchical Storage Management) Moving data to slower storage media when the data is no longer needed for daily use. Since magnetic disks are the most expensive storage medium, data is automatically moved based on age and other criteria. The typical hierarchy is from magnetic disk to optical disk to offline tape. Data on a hard disk is accessed in a fraction of a second. On an optical jukebox, it takes several seconds.

HSSI (High-Speed Serial Interface) A standard for a serial connection with transmission rates up to 52 Mbps. It is often used to connect to T3 lines.

HST (1) An asymmetrical modem protocol from U.S. Robotics that includes error control and compression and transmits from 4800 to 14400 bps in one direction and from 300 to 400 bps in the other. HST was the first reliable, high-speed modem protocol before the V.32bis and V.42 standards became widely used.

(2) (Hubble Space Telescope) Launched in April 1990, it views star material some 10 to 12 billion light years from earth.

HSV (Hue Saturation Value) A color model that uses a cylindrical coordinate system structured as an inverted hexcone (six-sided pyramid). The hue, or H, is measured by the angle around the vertical axis in degrees with red at 0, yellow 60, green 120, cyan 180, blue 240 and magenta 300. The saturation, or S, is the amount of color from 0 to 1 or 0 to 100%. The value, or V, is the amount of light from black to white (0 to 1 or 0 to 100%). For example, pure green would be H=120, S=1 and V=1. See *HLS*.

HTML (HyperText Markup Language) A standard for defining hypertext links between documents. It is a subset of SGML (Standard Generalized Markup Language).

HTTP (HyperText Transport Protocol) A client/server protocol used for information sharing on the Internet. It is the basis of the Worldwide Web (WWW).

hub A central connecting device in a network that joins communications lines together in a star configuration. Passive hubs are connecting units that add nothing to the data passing through them. Active hubs, also sometimes called *multiport repeaters*, regenerate the data bits in order to maintain a strong signal, and intelligent hubs provide added functionality.

hub ring A flat ring pressed around the hole in a 5.25" floppy disk for rigidity. The drive's clamping ring presses the hub ring onto the spindle.

hue In computer graphics, a particular shade or tint of a given color.

Huffman coding A statistical compression method that converts characters into variable length bit strings. Most-frequently-ocurring characters are converted to shortest bit strings; least frequent, the longest. Compression takes two passes. The first pass analyzes a block of data and creates a tree model based on its contents. The second pass compresses the data via the model. Decompression decodes the variable length strings via the tree. See *LZW*.

hybrid circuit See *hybrid microcircuit*.

hybrid computer A digital computer that accepts analog signals, converts them to digital and processes them in digital form. It is used in process control and robotics.

hybrid microcircuit An electronic circuit composed of different types of integrated circuits and discrete components, mounted on a ceramic base. Used in military and communications applications, it is especially suited for building custom analog circuits including A/D and D/A converters, amplifiers and modulators. See *MCM*.

hybrid network In communications, a network made up of equipment from multiple vendors.

Hydra (1) (Hybrid Document Reproduction Apparatus) A printer, photocopier, scanner and fax built into one machine.

(2) A device that converts analog signals to ISDN Basic Rate Interface (BRI).

(3) A utility from the Austin Mac Developer's Association that tests Macintosh graphics card performance.

Hyperaccess A PC communications program from Hilgraeve, Inc., Monroe, MI, that provides data compression, has its own script language and supports a variety of terminals and protocols.

HyperCard An application development system from Apple that runs on the Macintosh and Apple IIGS. Using visual tools, users build "stacks" of "cards" that hold data, text, graphics, sound and video with hypertext links between them. The HyperTalk programming language allows complex applications to be developed.

hypercube A parallel processing architecture made up of binary multiples of computers (4, 8, 16, etc.). The computers are interconnected so that data travel is kept to a minimum. For example, in two eight-node cubes, each node in one cube would be connected to the counterpart node in the other.

hyperlink A predefined linkage between one object and another. See *hypertext*.

hypermedia The use of data, text, graphics, video and voice as elements in a hypertext system. All the various forms of information are linked together so that a user can easily move from one to another.

HyperPAD An application development system for PCs from Brightbill-Roberts & Company, Ltd., Syracuse, NY. It is a HyperCard-like program that works in text mode and includes the PADtalk scripting language.

HyperScript An advanced macro (scripting) language that is provided with the WINGZ spreadsheet.

HyperTalk The programming language used in HyperCard.

hypertext Linking related information. For example, by selecting a word in a sentence, information about that word is retrieved if it exists, or the next occurrence of the word is found. The concept was coined by Ted Nelson as a method for making the computer respond to the way humans think and require information.

In the electronic versions of this Glossary, you can hypertext to the definition of any term used within the definitions by clicking on it or highlighting it with the mouse.

hyphen ladder
Hyphens on two or more consecutive lines, which causes distraction to the reader.

hyphenation
Breaking words that extend beyond the right margin. Software hyphenates words by matching them against a hyphenation dictionary or by using a built-in set of rules, or both. See *discretionary hyphen*.

hyphenation dictionary A word file with

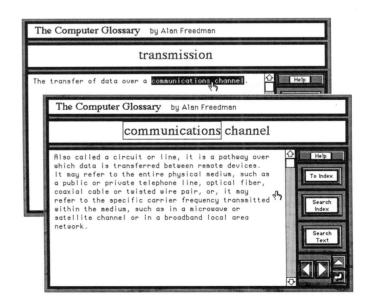

HYPERTEXT

Highlighting a term in the HyperCard version of the Glossary jumps you to the card that contains that definition.

predefined hyphen locations.

hyphenation zone The distance from the right margin within which a word may be hyphenated.

hysteresis The lag between making a change, such as increasing or decreasing power, and the response or effect of that change.

Hz (HertZ) See *Hertz*.

I

i486 See *486*.

i750 A programmable compression chip from Intel that supports a variety of techniques including DVI, MPEG and JPEG.

i860 A RISC-based, 64-bit processor from Intel that uses a 64-bit data bus, has built-in floating point and 3-D graphics capability and contains over one million transistors. It can be used as a stand-alone CPU or to accelerate performance in existing systems.

IAB See *Internet*.

IAC (InterApplication Communications) The IPC capability in Macintosh System 7.0.

IBM (International Business Machines Corporation, Armonk, NY) The world's largest computer company. It started in New York in 1911 when the Computing-Tabulating-Recording Company was created by a merger of four companies. In 1914, Thomas J. Watson, Sr., became general manager, and during the next 10 years, turned it into an international enterprise, renamed IBM in 1924.

Over the years, IBM has gained a worldwide reputation for its technology and service. It was the first to develop the floppy disk and the hard disk and has made many contributions to the computer industry.

As the world's leader in mainframes, it has also been very successful in minicomputers and workstations with its AS/400 and RS/6000 lines.

In 1981, it set the standard for the personal computer and launched the PC industry. It continues to be one of the major manufacturers of PCs.

▶ *The electronic and encyclopedic versions of this book provide more detail on the history of IBM and IBM product lines.*

IBM OFFICE, LONDON (1935)
(Courtesy IBM)
The "money making machines" sign on the truck meant that IBM's customers would become more profitable using IBM's equipment.

IBM-compatible PC A personal computer that is compatible with the IBM PC and PS/2 standards. Although this term is still used, it had more validity in the early days when PC makers were trying to copy the IBM PC, and many PCs were not compatible. Today, PCs conform to standards that, although originally set by IBM, have been modified over time by the PC industry at large.

IBM mainframe A large computer system made by IBM. IBM mainframes have evolved from the System/360 series, introduced in 1964, to today's System/390 line. IBM mainframes use SNA networking to link thousands of terminals to a centralized processing system.

IBM minicomputer See *AS/400*.

IBM PC A PC made by IBM. First generation IBM PCs had names: XT, AT, etc. The second generation, the PS/2, uses model numbers: 55, 65, etc. Subsequent introductions conform to common numbering systems used by the PC industry; for example, 486/33 and 486/66.

IBM workstation See *RS/6000*.

IC See *integrated circuit* and *information center*.

I-CASE (Integrated CASE) CASE systems that generate applications code directly from design specifications. Features include support for rapid prototyping, modeling the data and processing and drawing logic diagrams.

IC card See *PC card* and *memory card*.

ICCP (Institute for Certification of Computer Professionals) An organization founded in 1973 that offers industry certification and provides worldwide test centers. The Associate Computer Professional exam is open to all. The Certified Computer Programmer (CCP), Certified Data Processor (CDP) and Certified Systems Professional (CSP) require job experience (academic credit may substitute). Address: 2200 E. Devon Ave., Des Plaines, IL 60018, 708/299-4227.

ICE (1) (In-Circuit Emulator) A chip used for testing and debugging logic circuits typically in embedded systems. The chip emulates a particular microprocessor and contains breakpoints and other debugging functions. See *ROM emulator*.

(2) (Ice) A Lotus 1-2-3 add-on program from Baler Software Corporation, Rolling Meadows, IL, that adds extensions to Lotus macros. It is used for developing customized macro-driven 1-2-3 programs.

iCOMP (Intel COmparative Microprocessor Performance) An index of CPU performance from Intel. It tests a mix of 16-bit and 32-bit integer, floating point, graphics and video operations. iCOMP ratings range from 22 on a 386SX/16 to 815 on a 100MHz Pentium.

icon A small, pictorial, on-screen representation of an object (file, program, disk, etc.) used in graphical interfaces. For example, to delete a file in the Macintosh, the file icon is moved onto the wastebasket icon.

ICR (Intelligent Character Recognition) The ability to recognize hand printing.

IDA (Intelligent Drive Array) A high-performance hard disk interface from Compaq that controls a disk array via the EISA bus.

IDAPI (Idependent Database API) A programming interface that provides a common language for applications to access databases on a network. It includes support for non-SQL and non-relational databases. See *ODAPI* and *ODBC*.

IDC (International Data Corporation, Framingham, MA) The largest market research, analysis and consulting firm in the information field. Founded in 1964, it provides annual briefings and in-depth reports on all aspects of the industry.

IDE (1) (Integrated Drive Electronics) A hard disk that contains a built-in controller. IDE drives are widely used in PCs and range in capacity from 40MB up to 1GB. The drive connects via a 40-line flat ribbon cable to an IDE host adapter (often called an IDE controller) that plugs into an expansion slot in the PC. The host adapter controls up to two IDE drives, but advanced host adapters and Enhanced IDE adapters control up to four.

Some motherboards are built with a 40-pin IDE connector directly on the board thus freeing up an expansion slot for use by another device. The IDE drive uses the ATA interface (AT Attachment), although ATA is often only referenced in technical manuals. See *hard disk* and *Enhanced IDE*.

(2) (Integrated Development Environment) A set of programs run from a single user interface. For example, programming languages often include a text editor, compiler and debugger, which are all activated and function from a common menu.

IDE controller A common name for an IDE host adapter, which is the plug-in card used to attach IDE drives. The card very often includes floppy disk control as well as serial and parallel ports.

idle character In data communications, a character transmitted to keep the line synchronized when there is no data being sent.

idle interrupt An interrupt generated when a device changes from an operational state to an idle state.

idle time The duration of time a device is in an idle state, which means that it is operational, but not being used.

IDMS See *CA-IDMS*.

IE See *information engineering*.

I/E time See *instruction cycle*.

IEC (International Electrotechnical Commission) An organization that sets international electrical and electronics standards founded in 1906 and headquartered in Geneva. It is made up of national committees from over 40 countries. Contact is via ANSI in New York.

IEEE (Institute of Electrical and Electronic Engineers) A membership organization that includes engineers, scientists and students in electronics and allied fields. Founded in 1963, it has over 300,000 members and is involved with setting standards for computers and communications. Address: 345 E. 47th St., New York, NY 10017, 212/705-7900.

IEEE 488 See *GPIB*.

IEEE 802 IEEE standards for networking.

802.1	Covers network management, etc.
802.2	Specifies data link layer for the following access methods:
802.3	CSMA/CD, popularized by Ethernet.
802.4	Token passing bus, popularized by MAP.
802.5	Token passing ring, popularized by Token Ring.
802.6	DQDB technology used in MANs.
802.12	Demand priority technology.

IEEE 802.12 See *Fast Ethernet*.

IEEE 1284 An IEEE standard for an enhanced parallel port that is compatible with the Centronics parallel port commonly used on PCs. The standard also defines a specific type of cable that must be used in order to increase distances up to 30 feet and sustain the higher transfer rates.

IEF (Information Engineering Facility) A fully-integrated set of CASE tools from TI that runs on PCs and MVS mainframes. It generates COBOL code for PCs, MVS mainframes, VMS, Tandem, AIX, HP-UX and other UNIX platforms.

IETF See *Internet*.

IEW (Information Engineering Workbench) CASE software from Knowledgeware, Inc., Atlanta, GA, that runs on DOS PCs and generates COBOL, CICS and IMS code for MVS mainframes.

if-then-else A high-level programming language statement that compares two or more sets of data and tests the results. If the results are true, the THEN instructions are taken; if not, the ELSE instructions are taken. The following is a BASIC example:

```
10   IF ANSWER = "Y"   THEN PRINT "Yes"
20   ELSE PRINT "No"
```

In certain languages, THEN is implied. All statements between IF and ELSE are carried out if the condition is true. All instructions between ELSE and ENDIF are carried out if not true. The following dBASE example produces the same results as above:

```
IF ANSWER = "Y"
    ? "Yes"
  ELSE
    ? "No"
ENDIF
```

IFIP (International Federation of Information Processing) A multinational affiliation of professional groups concerned with information processing, founded in 1960. There is one voting representative from each country (U.S. representative is FOCUS). Address: 16 Place Longemalle, CH-1204 Geneva, Switzerland, 41 22 28 2649.

IFS (Installable File System) An OS/2 feature that supports multiple file systems. Different systems can be installed (UNIX, CD-ROM, etc.) just like drivers are installed for new peripherals.

IGES (Initial Graphics Exchange Specification) An ANSI graphics file format that is system independent and also intended for human interpretation. It evolved out of the Air Force's Integrated Computer Automated Manufacturing (ICAM) program in 1979. For more on IGES and PDES, contact: IGES Organization, National Institute of Standards & Technology, Building 220, Room A-353, Gaithersburg, MD 20899, 301/921-3691.

IIA (1) (Information Industry Association) A trade organization that includes members from all aspects of the information field. Its purpose is to conduct active government relations that safeguard the interests of a healthy, competitive information industry. IIA sponsors seminars and conferences and provides newsletters, newspapers and books. Address: 555 New Jersey Ave. N.W., Washington, DC 20001, 201/639-8262.

(2) (Information Interchange Architecture) IBM formats for exchanging documents between different systems.

illustration program Same as *drawing program*.

Illustrator 88 A Macintosh drawing program from Adobe Systems, Inc., that enhanced the original Illustrator program in 1988. It provides sophisticated tracing and text manipulation capabilities, as well as colors and color separations.

IM See *information management*.

IMA (Interactive Multimedia Association) A trade association founded in 1988 originally as the Interactive Video Industry Association. The IMA provides an open process for adopting existing technologies and is involved in subjects such as networked services, scripting languages, data formats and intellectual property rights. Address: 3 Church Circle, Annapolis, MD 21401, 410/626-1380.

image (1) A picture (graphic).

(2) See *system image*.

image editing Changing or improving graphics images either interactively using a paint program or by using software routines that alter contrast, smooth lines or filter out unwanted data. See *anti-aliasing*.

image enhancement See *image editing*.

image processing (1) The analysis of a picture using techniques that can identify shades, colors and relationships that cannot be perceived by the human eye. It is used to solve identification problems, such as in forensic medicine or in creating weather maps from satellite pictures and deals with images in raster graphics format that have been scanned in or captured with digital cameras.

(2) Any image improvement, such as refining a picture in a paint program that has been scanned or entered from a video source.

(3) Same as *imaging*.

imagesetter A typesetting machine that handles text and graphics and typically accepts PostScript input. See *phototypesetter*.

imaging Creating a film or electronic image of any picture or paper form. It is accomplished by scanning or photographing an object and turning it into a matrix of dots (raster graphics), the meaning of which is unknown to the computer, only to the human viewer. Scanned images of text may be encoded into computer data (ASCII or EBCDIC) with page recognition software (OCR). See *micrographics, image processing* and *document imaging*.

imaging model A set of rules for representing images.

imaging system See *document imaging, image processing* and *image enhancement*.

immediate access Same as *direct access*.

impact printer A printer that uses a printing mechanism that bangs the character image into the ribbon and onto the paper. See *printer* for examples.

impedance The resistance to the flow of alternating current in a circuit.

implementation (1) Computer system *implementation* is the installation of new hardware and system software.

(2) Information system *implementation* is the installation of new databases and application programs and the adoption of new manual procedures.

implode To link component pieces to a major assembly. It may also refer to compressing data using a particular technique. Contrast with *explode*.

import To convert a file in a foreign format to the format of the program being used.

Improv A multidimensional Windows spreadsheet from Lotus that allows for easy switching to different views of the data. Data is referenced by name as in a database rather than the typical spreadsheet row and column coordinates. Improv was originally developed for the NeXt computer.

IMS (Information Management System) An IBM hierarchical DBMS for mainframes under MVS. It was widely implemented throughout the 1970s and continues to be used. IMS/DC is its transaction processing component (like CICS) that handles the details of communications and SNA networking. IMS/DC is also used to access DB2 databases.

incident light In computer graphics, light that strikes an object. The color of the object is based on how the light is absorbed or reflected by the object.

increment To add a number to another number. Incrementing a counter means adding 1 to its current value.

incremental backup See *backup types*.

incremental spacing See *microspacing*.

IND$FILE An IBM mainframe program that transfers files between the mainframe and a PC functioning as a 3270 terminal.

indent To align text some number of spaces to the right of the left margin. See *hanging paragraph*.

index (1) In data management, the most common method for keeping track of data on a disk. Indexes are directory listings maintained by the OS, DBMS or the application.

An index of files contains an entry for each file name and the location of the file. An index of records has an entry for each key field (account no., name, etc.) and the location of the record.

(2) In programming, a method for keeping track of data in a table. See *indexed addressing*.

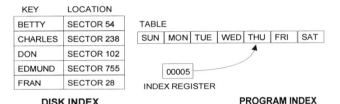

DISK INDEX

PROGRAM INDEX

indexed addressing A technique for referencing memory that automatically increments the address with the value stored in an index register. See *subscript (2)*.

indexed sequential See *ISAM*.

index hole A small hole punched into a hard sectored floppy disk that serves to mark the start of the sectors on each track.

indexing (1) Creating indexes based on key data fields or key words.

(2) Creating timing signals based on detecting a mark, slot or hole in a moving medium.

index mark A physical hole or notch, or a recorded code or mark, that is used to identify a starting point for each track on a disk.

index register A high-speed circuit used to hold the current, relative position of an item in a table (array). At execution time, its stored value is added to the instructions that reference it.

indirect addressing An address mode that points to another pointer rather than the actual data. This mode is prohibited in RISC architecture.

inductance The opposition to the changing flow of current in a circuit, measured in Henrys.

induction The process of generating an electric current in a circuit from the magnetic influence of an adjacent circuit as in a transformer or capacitor.

industrial strength Refers to software that is designed for high-volume, multiuser operation. It implies that the software is robust and that there are built-in safeguards against system failures.

inference engine The processing program in an expert system. It derives a conclusion from the facts and rules contained in the knowledge base using various artificial intelligence techniques.

infix notation The common way arithmetic operators are used to reference numeric values. For example, A+B/C is infix notation. Contrast with *Polish notation* and *reverse Polish notation*.

infopreneur A person who is in business to gather and disseminate electronic information.

informate To dispense information, as coined by Harvard Professor Shoshana Zuboff.

information The summarization of data. Technically, data are raw facts and figures that are processed into information, such as summaries and totals. But since information can also be raw data for the next job or person, the two terms cannot be precisely defined. Both terms are used synonymously and interchangeably.

As office automation and data processing merge, it may be more helpful to view information the way data is defined and used, namely: data, text, spreadsheets, pictures, voice and video. Data are discretely defined fields. Text is a collection of words. Spreadsheets are data in matrix (row and column) form. Pictures are lists of vectors or frames of bits. Voice is a continuous stream of sound waves. Video is a sequence of frames.

Future databases will routinely integrate all these forms of information.

information appliance A type of future home or office device that can transmit to or plug into common public or private networks. Envisioned is a "digital highway," like telephone and electrical power networks.

information center The division within the IS department that supports end-user computing. Responsible for training users in applications and solving related personal computer problems.

information engineering An integrated set of methodologies and products used to guide and develop information processing within an organization. It starts with enterprise-wide stategic planning and ends with running applications.

information hiding Keeping details of a routine private. Programmers only know what input is required and what outputs are expected. See *encapsulation* and *data abstraction*.

information highway See *information superhighway*.

information industry (1) Organizations that publish information via online services or through distribution by diskette or CD-ROM.

(2) All computer, communications and electronics-related organizations, including hardware, software and services.

information management The discipline that analyzes information as an organizational resource. It covers the definitions, uses, value and distribution of all data and information within an organization whether processed by computer or not. It evaluates the kinds of data/information an organization requires in order to function and progress effectively.

Information is complex because business transactions are complex. It must be analyzed and understood before effective computer solutions can be developed. See *data administration*.

information processing Same as *data processing*.

information resource management See *Information Systems* and *information management.*

information science See *information management.*

information service See *online services.*

information superhighway The telecommunications infrastructure within the U.S. that will allow access to government, industry and educational data banks for all people. While many envision a single high-speed link to and from every house in America, this is not feasible for many years. More likely is an interlinking of existing capabilities via local telephone, cable TV, satellite and online service providers.

The Internet has become synonymous with the information superhighway, because it provides an enormous source of information available to the public, but access to it is no without charge.

information system A business application of the computer. It is made up of the database, application programs, manual and machine procedures and encompasses the computer systems that do the processing.

The database stores the subjects of the business (master files) and its activities (transaction files). The application programs provide the data entry, updating, query and report processing. The manual procedures document how data is obtained for input and how the system's output is distributed. Machine procedures instruct the computer how to perform the batch processing activities, in which the output of one program is automaticaly fed into another program.

The daily processing is the interactive, realtime processing of the transactions. At the end of the day or other period, the batch processing programs update the master files that have not been updated since the last cycle. Reports are printed for the cycle's activities.

The periodic processing of an information system is the updating of the master files, which adds, deletes and changes the information about customers, employees, vendors and products.

STRUCTURE (is)	FUNCTION (does)
MANAGEMENT SYSTEM	
1. PEOPLE & MACHINES	Set organization's goals and objectives, strategies and tactics, plans, schedules and controls.
INFORMATION SYSTEM	
1. DATABASE	Defines data structures
2. APPLICATION PROGRAMS	Data entry, updating, queries and reporting
3. PROCEDURES	Defines data flow
COMPUTER SYSTEM	
1. CPU	Processes (The 3 C's)
2. PERIPHERALS	Store and retrieve
3. OPERATING SYSTEM	Manages computer system

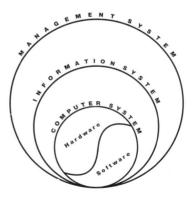

HOW SYSTEMS RELATE

Information Systems The formal title for a data processing, MIS, or IS department. Other titles are Data Processing, Information Processing, Information Services, Management Information Systems, Management Information Services and Information Technology.

information theory The study of encoding and transmitting information. From Claude Shannon's 1938 paper, "A Mathematical Theory of Communication," which proposed the use of binary digits for coding information.

information utility (1) A service bureau that maintains up-to-date databases for public access.

(2) A central source of information for an organization or group.

information warehouse The collection of all databases in an enterprise across all platforms and departments.

INFORMIX A family of DBMSs from Informix Software, Inc., Menlo Park, CA, that includes an SQL-based relational DBMS, fourth-generation language and toolkits for embedding SQL in application programs.

Info Select A personal information manager (PIM) for PCs from Micro Logic Corporation, Hackensack, NJ, that includes automatic phone dialing via modem. It is noted for its ease of use and ability to store random information and instantly retrieve it.

infoware Information sold electronically, such as the electronic versions of this Glossary.

InfoWindow The trade name for IBM display screens.

infrared An invisible band of radiation at the lower end of the electromagnetic spectrum. It starts at the middle of the microwave spectrum and goes up to the beginning of visible light. Infrared transmission requires an unobstructed line of sight between transmitter and receiver. It is used for wireless transmission between computer devices as well as most all hand-held remotes for TVs, video and stereo equipment. Contrast with *ultraviolet*. See *SIR*.

infrastructure The fundamental structure of a system or organization. The basic, fundamental architecture of any system (electronic, mechanical, social, political, etc.) determines how it functions and how flexible it is to meet future requirements.

INGRES (INteractive Graphics and REtrieval System) A relational DBMS from Ingres Corporation, Alameda, CA, that runs on VAXs and UNIX workstations. It includes a 4GL, QBE and lets users create and manage a database as a series of forms. Its Knowledge Management extension allows rules to be programmed into the database.

inheritance In object-oriented programming, the ability of one class of objects to inherit properties from a higher class.

inhouse An operation that takes place on the user's premises.

INIT (INITiate) A Macintosh routine that is run when the computer is started or restarted. It is used to load and activate drivers and system routines. Many INITs are memory resident and may conflict with each other like TSRs in the PC environment.

initial program load See *IPL*.

initialization string Same as *setup string*.

initialize To start anew, which typically involves clearing all or some part of memory or disk.

ink jet A printer mechanism that sprays one or more colors of ink onto paper and produces high-quality printing like that of a laser printer.

The continuous stream method produces droplets that are aimed onto the paper by electric field deflectors.

The drop-on-demand method uses a set of independently controlled injection chambers, the newest of which use solid ink developed by Exxon in 1983. Solid ink liquefies quickly when heated and solidifies instantly when it reaches the paper.

INMARSAT (INternational MARitime SATellite) An international organization involved in providing satellite communications to and from ships and offshore rigs. It is represented in the U.S. and partially owned by COMSAT.

innoculate To store characteristics of an executable program in order to detect a possible unknown virus if the file is changed.

i-node (Identification NODE) An individual entry in a directory system that contains the name of and pointer to a file or other object.

input (1) Data that is ready for entry into the computer.

(2) To enter data into the computer.

input area A reserved segment of memory that is used to accept data from a peripheral device. Same as *buffer*.

input device A peripheral device that generates input for the computer such as a keyboard, scanner, mouse or digitizer tablet.

input/output See *I/O*.

input program Same as *data entry program*.

input queue A reserved segment of disk or memory that holds messages that have been received or job control statements describing work to be done.

input stream A collection of job control statements entered in the computer that describe the work to be done.

inquiry program Same as *query program*.

Ins key (INSert key) A keyboard key that is used to switch between insert and overwrite mode or to insert an object at the current cursor location.

insert mode A data entry mode that causes new data typed on the keyboard to be inserted at the current cursor location on screen. Contrast with *overwrite mode*.

install program Software that prepares a software package to run in the computer. It copies the files from the distribution diskettes to the hard disk and decompresses them, if required. It may ask you to identify your computer environment in order to link in the drivers for the display, printer and other devices that you have.

installation spec Documentation from an equipment manufacturer that describes how a product should be properly installed within a physical environment.

instance In object-oriented programming, a member of a class; for example, "Lassie" is an instance of the class "dog." When an instance is created, the initial values of its instance variables are assigned."

instance variable In object-oriented programming, the data in an object.

instant print The ability to use the computer as a typewriter. Each keystroke is transferred to the printer.

instantiate In object-oriented programming, to create an object of a specific class. See *instance*.

instruction (1) A statement in a programming language.

(2) A machine instruction.

instruction cycle The time in which a single instruction is fetched from memory, decoded and executed. The first half of the cycle transfers the instruction from memory to the instruction register and decodes it. The second half executes the instruction.

instruction mix The blend of instruction types in a program. It often refers to writing generalized benchmarks, which requires that the amount of I/O versus processing versus math instructions, etc., reflects the type of application the benchmark is written for.

instruction register A high-speed circuit that holds an instruction for decoding and execution.

instruction repertoire Same as *instruction set*.

instruction set The repertoire of machine language instructions that a computer can follow (from a handful to several hundred). It is a major architectural component and is either built into the CPU or into microcode. Instructions are generally from one to four bytes long.

instruction time The time in which an instruction is fetched from memory and stored in the instruction register. It is the first half of the instruction cycle.

insulator A material that does not conduct electricity. Contrast with *conductor*.

int A programming statement that specifies an interrupt or that declares an integer variable. See *interrupt* and *integer*.

integer A whole number. In programming, the integer function would yield 123 from 123.898.

Integer BASIC Apple's version of BASIC for the Apple II that handles only fixed point numbers (non-floating point). Due to its speed, many games are written in it.

integrated A collection of distinct elements or components that have been built into one unit.

integrated CASE See *I-CASE*.

integrated circuit The formal name for chip.

integrated injection logic A type of bipolar transistor design known for its fast switching speeds.

integrated software package Software that combines several applications in one program, typically database management, word processing, spreadsheet, business graphics and communications. Such programs (Microsoft Works, AppleWorks, etc.) provide a common user interface for their applications plus the ability to cut and paste data from one to the other.

User interfaces, such as found on the Macintosh and Windows, provide this capability with all applications written for their environments.

integrator In electronics, a device that combines an input with a variable, such as time, and provides an analog output; for example, a watt-hour meter.

integrity See *data integrity*.

Intel (Intel Corporation, Santa Clara, CA) A leading manufacturer of semiconductor devices founded in 1968 by Bob Noyce and Gorden Moore in Mountain View, CA. Intel is known for its x86 microprocessor family, but it also developed the first microprocessor in 1971. Currently, Intel is the most profitable company in the computer industry. In 1993, it made over two billion dollars in profit from revenues of nearly nine billion.
▶ *The electronic and encyclopedic versions of this book provide more detail on this subject.*

Intellect A natural language query program from Trinzic Corporation, Palo Alto, CA, that runs on IBM mainframes and other computers. It was originally developed by Artificial Intelligence Corporation, which merged into Trinzic.

Intellifont A scalable font technology from Agfa CompuGraphic. Intellifont typefaces are built into LaserJet IIIs and 4s.

intelligence Processing capability. Every computer is intelligent!

intelligent cable Same as *smart cable.*

intelligent controller A peripheral control unit that uses a built-in microprocessor for controlling its operation.

intelligent database A database that contains knowledge about the content of its data. A set of validation criteria are stored with each field of data, such as the minimum and maximum values that can be entered or a list of all possible entries.

intelligent form A data entry application that provides help screens and low levels of AI in aiding the user to enter the correct data.

intelligent hub A central connecting device in a network that performs a variety of processing functions such as network management, bridging, routing and switching. Contrast with *passive hub* and *active hub.* See *hub.*

intelligent modem A modem that responds to commands and can accept new instructions during online transmission. It was originally developed by Hayes.

intelligent paper Same as *intelligent form.*

intelligent terminal A terminal with built-in processing capability, but no local disk or tape storage. It may use a general-purpose CPU or may have specialized circuitry as part of a distributed intelligence system. Contrast with *dumb terminal.*

IntelliSense Features in Microsoft applications that help the user by making decisions automatically. By analyzing activity patterns, the software can derive the next step without the user having to explicitly state it.

INTELSAT (INternational TELecommunications SATellite) An international organization involved in launching and operating commercial satellites. It was created in 1964 with only 11 countries participating. Today, over 100 nations have ownership. It is represented in the U.S. and partially owned by COMSAT.

inter To cross over boundaries; for example, internetwork means from one network to another. Contrast with *intra.*

interactive Back-and-forth dialog between the user and a computer.

interactive cable TV See *interactive TV.*

interactive fiction An adventure game that has been created or modified for the computer. It has multiple story lines, environments and endings, all of which are determined by choices the player makes at various times.

interactive session Back-and-forth dialogue between user and computer. Contrast with *batch session.*

interactive TV Two-way communications between the TV viewer and service providers. Using phone lines, cable, optical fiber or satellite, services include home shopping, movies on demand, interactive participation in live broadcasts as well as access to news, databases and other networks.

Current analog TV sets can be connected to boxes that add dial out capability via modem and phone line as well as handle digital signals interleaved with the incoming analog signals. As cable systems become more digital, more interactive programming will be provided. See *digital convergence.*

interactive video The use of CD-ROM and videodisc controlled by computer for an interactive education or entertainment program.

InterBase A relational DBMS from Borland that runs on UNIX workstations and VAXes, designed to handle online complex processing (OLCP). It can be a peer-to-peer or client/server system and uses SQL plus its own data manipulation language.

interblock gap Same as *interrecord gap.*

interface The connection and interaction between hardware, software and the user. Interfacing is a major part of what engineers, programmers and consultants do. Users "talk to" the software. The software "talks to" the hardware and other software. Hardware "talks to" other hardware. All this is interfacing. It has to be designed, developed, tested and redesigned, and with each incarnation, a new specification is born that may become yet one more de facto or regulated standard.
▶ *The electronic and encyclopedic versions of this book provide more detail on this subject.*

interface adapter In communications, a device that connects the computer or terminal to a network.

interframe coding In video compression, coding only the differences between frames. See *intraframe coding.*

interlaced Illuminating a CRT by displaying odd lines and then even lines (every other line first; then filling in the gaps). TV signals are interlaced and generate 60 half frames (30 full frames) per second. Computer display systems may also be interlaced, but usually only at the highest resolution.

Interlaced   Non-interlaced

Interleaf Desktop publishing software for DOS, Windows and a variety of UNIX-based computers from Interleaf, Inc., Waltham, MA. It is a full-featured program that supports a large number of document and image types. It is used for creating compound documents as well as extremely long documents with hundreds of thousands of pages.

interleave See *sector interleave* and *memory interleaving.*

interlock A device that prohibits an action from taking place.

intermediate language Same as *pseudo language.*

intermediate node routing Routing a message to non-adjacent nodes; for example, if three computers are connected in series A–B–C, data transmitted from A to C can be routed through B.

intermittent error An error that occurs sporadically, not consistently. It is the most difficult type of problem to diagnose and repair.

internal bus A data pathway between closely-connected components, such as between the CPU and memory. See *local bus.*

internal command In DOS and OS/2, a command, such as Copy, Dir and Rename, which may be used at all times. Internal commands are executed by the command processor programs COMMAND.COM in DOS and CMD.EXE in OS/2. The command processor is always loaded when the operating system is loaded. Contrast with *external command.*

internal font A set of characters for a particular typeface that is built into a printer. Contrast with *font cartridge* and *soft font.*

internal interrupt An interrupt that is caused by processing, for example, a request for input or output or an arithmetic overflow error. Contrast with *external interrupt.*

internal modem A modem that plugs into an expansion slot within the computer. Unlike an external modem, an internal modem does not provide a series of display lights that inform the user of the changing modem states. The user must rely entirely on the communications program. Contrast with *external modem*.

internal sort Sorting that is accomplished entirely in memory without using disks or tapes for temporary files.

internal storage Same as *memory*.

internet (1) A large network made up of a number of smaller networks.

(2) (Internet) "The" Internet is made up of thousands of interconnected networks in over 70 countries. In 1994, there was an estimated 30,000 networks on the Internet. This number is expected to double each year. Internet computers use the TCP/IP communications protocol.

Originally developed for the military, much of the Internet today is used for academic and commercial research. Users have access to unpublished data, journals and BBSs. It is also widely used as a worldwide electronic mail network. E-mail connection to the Internet is available through many online services such as CompuServe, BIX and America Online.

Internet access See *Internet address* and *PDIAL*.

Internet address The format for addressing a message to an Internet user is `recipient@location.domain`. For example, the address of the Free Software Foundation is `gnu@prep.ai.mit.edu`, which means transmitting to the GNU mailbox via nodes PREP, AI and MIT. The suffix at the end is the domain, or host classification, in this case EDU (see below).

com	business (commercial)
edu	educational and research
gov	government
mil	military agency
net	gateway or host
org	other organization

Via CompuServe

If you are a CompuServe subscriber, you can access the Internet by adding the `>internet:` prefix to the Internet address. For example, to send mail from CompuServe to the Free Software Foundation address mentioned above, you would address the message to `>internet:gnu@prep.ai.mit.edu`

Internet Protocol See *Internet* and *TCP/IP*.

InterNet Router Macintosh software from Apple that internetworks different access methods (LocalTalk, EtherTalk, TokenTalk, etc.) and can reside in any network station. Each Router can connect up to eight networks with a maximum of 1,024 networks and 16 million nodes.

Internet utility Software used to search the Internet for specific information. See *Archie, Gopher, Veronica, WAIS* and *WWW*.

internetwork To go between one network and another.

interoperable The ability for one system to communicate or work with another.

interpolate To estimate values that lie between known values.

Interpress A page description language from Xerox used on the 2700 and 9700 page printers (medium to large-scale laser printers). Ventura Publisher provides output in Interpress.

interpret To run a program one line at a time. Each line of source language is translated into machine language and then executed.

interpreter A high-level programming language translator that translate and runs the program at the same time. It translates one program statement into machine language, executes it, then proceeds to the next statement.

Interpreted programs run slower than their compiler counterparts, because the compiler translates the entire program before it is run. However, it's convenient to write an interpreted program, since a single line of code can be tested interactively.

Interpreted programs must always be run with the interpreter. For example, in order to run a BASIC or dBASE program, the BASIC or dBASE interpreter must be in the computer.

If a language can be both interpreted and compiled, a program may be developed with the interpreter and compiled for production.

interpretive language A programming language that requires an interpreter to run it.

interprocess communication See *IPC*.

interrecord gap The space generated between blocks of data on tape, created by the starting and stopping of the reel.

interrogate (1) To search, sum or count records in a file. See *query*.

(2) To test the condition or status of a terminal or computer system.

interrupt A signal that gets the attention of the CPU and is usually generated when I/O is required. For example, hardware interrupts are generated when a key is pressed or when the mouse is moved. Software interrupts are generated by a program requiring disk input or output.

An internal timer may continually interrupt the computer several times per second to keep the time of day current or for timesharing purposes.

INTERRECORD GAPS

When an interrupt occurs, control is transferred to the operating system, which determines the action to be taken. Interrupts are prioritized; the higher the priority, the faster the interrupt will be serviced.

interrupt-driven A computer or communications network that uses interrupts.

interrupt latency The time it take to service an interrupt. It becomes a critical factor when servicing realtime functions such as a communications line. See *UART overrrun*.

interrupt mask An internal switch setting that controls whether an interrupt can be processed or not. The mask is a bit that is turned on and off by the program.

interrupt priorities The sequence of importance assigned to interrupts. If two interrupts occur simultaneously, the interrupt with the highest priority is serviced first. In some systems, a higher-priority interrupt can gain control of the computer while it's processing a lower-priority interrupt.

interrupt vector In the PC, one of 256 pointers that reside in the first 1KB of memory. Each vector points to a routine in the ROM BIOS or elsewhere in memory, which handles the interrupt.

intersect In a relational database, to match two files and produce a third file with records that are common in both. For example, intersecting an American file and a programmer file would yield American programmers.

intra Within a boundary; for example, intraoffice refers to operations that take place within the office. Contrast with *inter*.

intraframe coding Compressing redundant areas within a video frame. See *interframe coding*.

inverse multiplexing Splitting a high-speed channel into several low-speed channels in order to be able to use available transmission facilities. For example, an inverse multiplexor is used to transmit high-speed LAN traffic over leased digital lines (T-carrier), which are made up of several lower-speed channels. See *DS*.

inverse video Same as *reverse video*.

inverted file In data management, a file that is indexed on many of the attributes of the data itself. For example, in an employee file, an index could be maintained for all secretaries, another for managers. It's faster to search the indexes than every record. Inverted file indexes use lots of disk space; searching is fast, updating is slower.

inverted list Same as *inverted file*.

inverter (1) A logic gate that converts the input to the opposite state for output. If the input is true, the output is false, and vice versa. An inverter performs the Boolean logic NOT operation.

(2) A circuit that converts DC current into AC current. Contrast with *rectifier*.

invoke To activate a program, routine, function or process.

I/O (Input/Output) Transferring data between the CPU and a peripheral device. Every transfer is an output from one device and an input into another.

I/O address (1) On PCs, a three-digit hexadecimal number (2AB, 2A0, etc.) used to identify and signal a peripheral device (serial port, parallel port, sound card, etc.). Address assignments must be unique, otherwise conflicts will occur. There are usually a small number of selectable addresses on each controller card.
▶ *The electronic and encyclopedic versions of this book provide more detail on this subject.*

(2) The identifying address of a peripheral device.

I/O area A reserved segment of memory used to accept data from an input device or to accumulate data for transfer to an output device. See *buffer*.

I/O bound Refers to an excessive amount of time getting data in and out of the computer in relation to the time it takes for processing it. Faster channels and disk drives improve the performance of I/O bound computers.

IOCA (Image Object Content Architecture) See *MO:DCA*.

I/O card See *expansion board* and *PC card*.

I/O channel See *channel*.

I/O device Same as *peripheral device*.

ion deposition A printing technology used in high-speed page printers. It is similar to laser printing, except instead of using light to create a charged image on a drum, it uses a printhead that deposits ions. After toner is attracted to the ions on the drum, the paper is pressed directly against the drum fusing toner to paper.
    Quality approaches that of a laser printer; however, the ink has not been embedded as deeply, and the paper can smear more easily.

I/O interface See *port* and *expansion slot*.

I/O processor Circuitry specialized for I/O operations. See *front end processor*.

I/O statement A programming instruction that requests I/O.

IP (1) (Internet Protocol) The IP part of the TCP/IP protocol, which routes a message across networks. See *TCP/IP* and *datagram*.

(2) See *image processing*.

IPC (InterProcess Communication) The exchange of data between one program and another either within the same computer or over a network. It implies a protocol that guarantees a response to a request. Examples are OS/2's Named Pipes, Windows' DDE, Novell's SPX and Macintosh's IAC.

IPCs are performed automatically by the programs. For example, a spreadsheet program could query a database program and retrieve data from one of its databases. A manual example of an IPC function is performed when users cut and paste data from one file to another using the clipboard.

IPDS (Intelligent Printer Data Stream) An IBM format for sending full pages of text and graphics from a mainframe or mini to a laser printer.

IPI (Intelligent Peripheral Interface) A high-speed hard disk interface used with minis and mainframes that transfers data in the 10 to 25 MBytes/sec range. IPI-2 and IPI-3 refer to differences in the command set that they execute. See *hard disk*.

IPL (Initial Program Load) Same as *boot*.

ips (Inches Per Second) The measurement of the speed of tape passing by a read/write head or paper passing through a pen plotter.

IPX (Internet Packet EXchange) A NetWare communications protocol used to route messages from one node to another. IPX packets include network addresses and can be routed from one network to another. An IPX packet can occasionally get lost when crossing networks, thus IPX does not guarantee delivery of a complete message. Either the application has to provide that control or NetWare's SPX protocol must be used.

IPX provides services at layers 3 and 4 of the OSI model (network and transport layers). See *SPX*.

IR (Industry Remarketer) Same as *VAR* or *VAD*. See also *infrared*.

IRG (InterRecord Gap) See *interrecord gap*.

IRIX See *Silicon Graphics*.

IRM (Information Resource Management) See *Information Systems* and *information management*.

IRMAboard A micro to mainframe board for PCs from DCA, Inc., Alpharetta, GA. It emulates the common IBM 3270 mainframe terminal allowing a PC access to centralized mainframe applications. IRMA is DCA's trade name for a variety of communications products. It is the lady's name, not an acronym.

IRMALAN A family of gateway products from DCA, Inc., Alpharetta, GA, that allow PC users connected to NetBIOS-compatible LANs to access an SNA host. It includes gateways for IEEE 802.2, SDLC and DFT environments.

iron oxide The material used to coat the surfaces of magnetic tapes and lower-capacity disks.

IRQ (Interrupt ReQuest) A hardware interrupt on a PC. Eight lines (0-7 on 8086/88s) and 16 lines (0-15 on 286s and up) accept interrupts from devices such as a scanner and network adapter. Unless specifically programmed to interact together, two devices cannot use the same line. If a new expansion board is preset to the IRQ used by an existing board, one of them must be changed.

▶ *The electronic and encyclopedic versions of this book provide more detail on this subject.*

IS See *Information Systems*.

IS-IS (Intermediate System to Intermediate System) An ISO protocol that provides dynamic routing between routers.

ISA (Industry Standard Architecture) Pronounced "eye-suh." An expansion bus commonly used in PCs. It accepts the plug-in boards that control the video display, disks and other peripherals. Most PC expansion boards on the market are ISA boards.

ISA was originally called the *AT bus*, because it was first used in the IBM AT, extending the original bus from eight to 16 bits. Most ISA PCs provides a mix of 8-bit and 16-bit expansion slots. Contrast with *EISA* and *Micro Channel*. See *local bus*.

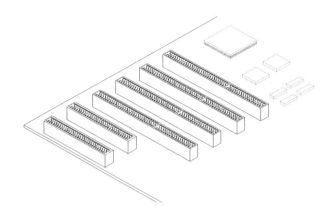

ISA BUS
This illustration shows two 8-bit slots and four 16-bit slots.

ISAM (Indexed Sequential Access Method) A common disk access method that stores data sequentially, while maintaining an index of key fields to all the records in the file for direct access. The sequential order would be the one most commonly used for batch processing and printing (account number, name, etc.).

ISDN (Integrated Services Digital Network) An international telecommunications standard for transmitting voice, video and data over digital lines running at 64 Kbits/sec. ISDN service is increasing in the U.S. ISDN uses circuit-switched bearer channels (B channels) to carry voice and data and uses a separate data channel (D channel) for control signals via a packet-switched network. This out-of-band D channel allows for features such as call forwarding, call waiting and advice of charge.

Basic Rate Service (BRI) provides two B channels and one 16 Kbps D channel. Primary Rate Service (PRI) in North America provides 23 B channels and one 64 Kbps D channel, equivalent to T1. Europe uses 30 B channels and one D channel, equivalent to the European E1 service.

ISO (International Standards Organization) An organization that sets international standards, founded in 1946 and headquartered in Geneva. It deals with all fields except electrical and electronics, which is governed by the older International Electrotechnical Commission (IEC), also in Geneva. With regard to information processing, ISO and IEC created JTC1, the Joint Technical Committee for information technology.

It carries out its work through more than 160 technical committees and 2,300 subcommittees and working groups and is made up of standards organizations from more than 75 countries, some of them serving as secretariats for these technical bodies. ANSI is the U.S. member body. Address: ANSI, 1430 Broadway, New York, NY 10018.

ISO 9660 The logical format for a CD-ROM which evolved from the High Sierra format. The physical format for a CD-ROM is defined in the Yellow Book.

isochronous Time dependent. Realtime voice, video and telemetry are examples of isochronous data.

isochronous Ethernet See *IsoENET*.

IsoENET (ISOchronous EtherNET)
National Semiconductor's enhancement to
Ethernet for handling realtime voice and video.
IsoENET adds a 6Mbps synchronous channel,
made up of 96 64Kbps ISDN subchannels, to
the 10Mbps Ethernet standard.

isometric view In computer graphics, a
rendering of a 3-D object that eliminates the
distortion of shape created by true perspective.
In isometric views, all lines on each axis are
parallel to each other, and the lines do not
converge. Such drawings are commonly used in
technical illustrations because of their clarity,
simplicity and speed of creation.

ISOMETRIC VIEW
(Courtesy Robo Systems Corporation)

isotropic Refers to properties, such as transmission speed, that are the same
regardless of the direction that is measured. Contrast with *anisotropic*.

ISPF (Interactive System Productivity Facility) IBM mainframe software that
executes interactive user interfaces on 3270 terminals. It is created with ISPF's PDF
(Program Development Facility) software.

ISR (Interrupt Service Routine) Software routine that is executed in response to an
interrupt.

ISV (Independent Software Vendor) A person or company that develops software.

IT (Information Technology) Same as *Information Systems*.

ITAA (Information Technology Association of America) Formerly Association of
Data Processing Service Organizations (ADAPSO). A membership organization
founded in 1960 that defines performance standards, improves management methods
and monitors government regulations in the computer services field. Address: 1616
N. Fort Myer Dr., Arlington, VA 22209, 703/522-5055.

item One unit or member of a group. See *data item*.

iteration One repetition of a sequence of instructions or events. For example, in
a program loop, one iteration is once through the instructions in the loop.

iterative operation An operation that requires successive executions of
instructions or processes.

I-time See *instruction time*.

ITSEC See *NCSC*.

ITU-TSS (International Telecommunications Union-Telecommunications
Standards Section) Formerly the CCITT (Consultative Committee for International
Telephony and Telegraphy), it is an international organization that sets
communications standards. TSS is one of four organs of the ITU, founded in 1865,
headquartered in Geneva and comprised of over 150 member countries.

IV See *interactive video*.

Iverson notation A set of symbols developed by Kenneth Iverson for writing
statements in APL.

IVR (Interactive Voice Response) See *voice response*.

IXC (IntereXchange Carrier) An organization that provides interstate
communications services, such as AT&T, MCI and Sprint.

jack A receptacle into which a plug is inserted.

jacket A plastic housing that contains a floppy disk. The 5.25" disk is built into a flexible jacket; the 3.25" disk uses a rigid jacket.

JAD (Joint Application Development) An approach to systems analysis and design introduced by IBM in 1977 that emphasizes teamwork between user and technician. Small groups meet to determine system objectives and the business transactions to be supported. They are run by a neutral facilitator who can move the group toward well-defined goals. Results include a prototype of the proposed system.

jaggies The stairstepped appearance of diagonal lines on a low-resolution graphics screen.

JCL (Job Control Language) A command language for mini and mainframe operating systems that launches applications. It specifies priority, program size and running sequence, as well as the files and databases used.

LOW RESOLUTION GRAPHICS

HIGH RESOLUTION GRAPHICS

JEDEC (Joint Electronic Device Engineering Council) An international body that sets integrated circuit standards.

JEIDA (Japanese Electronic Industry Development Association) A Japanese trade and standards organization. JEIDA joined with PCMCIA to standardize the PC card. In 1991, the PC card specifications JEIDA 4.1 and PCMCIA 2.0 are the same.

JES (Job Entry Subsystem) Software that provides batch communications for IBM's MVS operating system. It accepts data from remote batch terminals, executes them on a priority basis and transmits the results back to the terminals. The JES counterpart in VM is called RSCS.

jewel box A plastic container used to package an audio CD or CD-ROM disc.

JFIF See *JPEG*.

jiff See *GIF*.

jitter A flickering transmission signal or display image.

job A unit of work running in the computer. A job may be a single program or a group of programs that work together.

job class The descriptive category of a job that is based on the computer resources it requires when running.

job control language See *JCL*.

job management language Same as *JCL*.

job processing Handling and processing jobs in the computer.

job queue The lineup of programs ready to be executed.

job scheduling In a large computer, establishing a job queue to run a sequence of programs over any period of time such as a single shift, a full day, etc.

job stream A series of related programs that are run in a prescribed order. The output of one program is the input to the next program and so on.

join In relational database management, to match one file against another based on some condition creating a third file with data from the matching files. For example, a customer file can be joined with an order file creating a file of records for all customers who purchased a particular product.

Josephson junction An ultra-fast switching technology that uses superconductor materials, originally conceived by Brian Josephson. Circuits are immersed in liquid helium to obtain near-absolute zero degrees required for operation. A Josephson junction has been observed to switch in as little as 50 femtoseconds.

journal Same as *log*.

JOVIAL (Jules' Own Version of the International Algebraic Language) An ALGOL-like programming language developed by Systems Development Corp. in the early 1960s and widely used in the military. Its key architect was Jules Schwartz.

joy stick A pointing device used to move an object on screen in any direction. It employs a vertical rod mounted on a base with one or two buttons. Joy sticks are used extensively in video games and in some CAD systems.

JPEG (Joint Photographic Experts Group) An ISO/ITU-TSS standard for compressing images using discrete cosine transform. It provides lossy compression (you lose sharpness from the original) and can provide ratios of 100:1 and higher. It depends entirely on the image, but ratios of 10:1 and 20:1 may provide little noticeable loss. The more the loss can be tolerated, the more the image can be compressed. Compression is achieved by dividing the picture into tiny pixel blocks, which are halved over and over until the ratio is achieved.

jukebox A storage device for multiple sets of CD-ROMs, tape cartridges or disk modules.

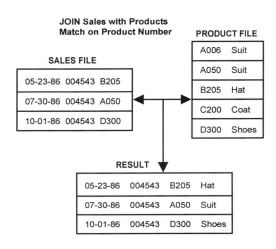

JOIN Sales with Products
Match on Product Number

PRODUCT FILE

A006	Suit
A050	Suit
B205	Hat
C200	Coat
D300	Shoes

SALES FILE

05-23-86	004543	B205
07-30-86	004543	A050
10-01-86	004543	D300

RESULT

05-23-86	004543	B205	Hat
07-30-86	004543	A050	Suit
10-01-86	004543	D300	Shoes

JOIN

JOY STICK

Julian date The representation of month and day by a consecutive number starting with Jan. 1. For example, Feb. 1 is Julian 32. Dates are converted into Julian dates for calculation.

jump Same as *GOTO*.

jumper The simplest form of an on/off switch. It is just a tiny, plastic-covered metal block, which is pushed onto two pins to close the circuit.

junction The point at which two elements make contact. In a transistor, a junction is the point where an N-type material makes contact with a P-type material.

justification In typography, the alignment of text evenly between left and right margins. Contrast with *ragged right*.

justify (1) To shift the contents of a field or register to the right or left.

(2) To align text evenly between left and right margins.

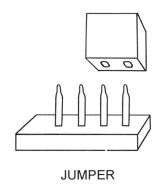

JUMPER

K

K See *kilo*.

Kaleida (Kaleida Labs, Inc., Mountain View, CA) A joint venture of IBM and Apple that is developing multimedia software. See *ScriptX*.

KB, Kb See *kilobyte* and *kilobit*.

Kbits/sec (KiloBITS per SECond) Thousand bits per second.

KBps, Kbps (KiloBytes Per Second, KiloBits Per Second) Thousand bytes per second. Thousand bits per second.

Kbytes/sec (KiloBYTES per SECond) Thousand bytes per second.

Kerberos A security system developed at MIT that authenticates users. It does not provide authorization to services or databases; it establishes identity at logon, which is used throughout the session.

Kermit An asynchronous file transfer protocol developed at Columbia University, noted for its accuracy over noisy lines.

kernel The fundamental part of a program, typically an operating system, that resides in memory at all times and provides the basic services. It is the part of the operating system that is closest to the machine and may activate the hardware directly or interface to another software layer that drives the hardware. See *microkernel*.

kerning In typography, the spacing of letter combinations, such as WA, MW and TA, where each character overlaps into some of the space of the other for improved appearance.

Fixed Spacing

Proportional Spacing

Kerned Letters

Kerr effect A change in rotation of light reflected off a magnetic field. The polarity of a magneto-optic bit causes the laser to shift one degree clockwise or counterclockwise.

key (1) A keyboard button.

(2) Data that identifies a record. Account number, product code and customer name are typical key fields used to identify a record in a file or database. As an identifier, each key value must be unique in each record. See *sort key*.

(3) A numeric code used by an algorithm to create a code for encrypting data for security purposes.

keyboard A set of input keys. On terminals and personal computers, it includes the standard typewriter keys and several specialized keys such as the control, alt and esc keys as well as a set of function keys.

keyboard buffer A memory bank or reserved memory area that stores keystrokes until the program can accept them. It lets fast typists continue typing while the program catches up.

keyboard controller A circuit that monitors keystrokes and generates the required data bits when pressed.

keyboard interrupt A signal that gets the attention of the CPU each time a key is pressed. See *interrupt*.

keyboard macro processor See *macro processor*.

keyboard processor See *keyboard controller* and *keyboard enhancer*.

keyboard template
A plastic card that fits over the function keys to identify each key's purpose in a particular software program.

key cap A replaceable, top part of a keyboard key. To identify commonly-used codes, it can be replaced with a custom-printed key cap.

key click An audible feedback provided when a key is pressed. It may be adjustable by the user.

key command A key combination (Alt-G, Ctrl-B, Command-M, etc.) used as a command to the computer.

key driven Any device that is activated by pressing keys.

key entry Data entry using a keyboard.

key field See *key (2)*.

keyframe In computer graphics animation, a frame that indicates the beginning or end of an object in motion.

key in To enter data by typing on a keyboard.

keypad A small keyboard or supplementary keyboard keys; for example, the keys on a calculator or the number/cursor cluster on a computer keyboard.

keypunch To punch holes in a punched card. Although punched cards are obsolete, some people still say "keys are punched" on a keyboard.

keypunch department
Same as *data entry department*.

keypunch machine A punched-card data entry machine. A deck of blank cards is placed into a hopper, and, upon operator command, the machine feeds one card to a punch station. As characters are typed, a series of dies at the punch station punch the

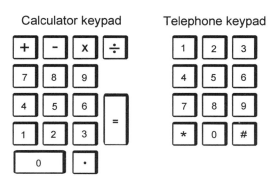

Calculator keypad   Telephone keypad

SO MUCH FOR COMPATIBILITY!

DATA PROCESSING
THE OLD FASHIONED WAY
(Courtesy Smithsonian Institution
The data for each American counted in the U.S. census of 1890 census was punched into a card with this machine. The cards were summarized on a Hollerith tabulating machine.

appropriate holes in the selected card column.

key rollover See *n-key rollover*.

key system See *key telephone system*.

key telephone system An inhouse telephone system that is not centrally connected to a PBX. Each telephone has buttons for outside lines that can be dialed directly without having to "dial 9."

key-to-disk machine A stand-alone data entry machine that stores data on magnetic disk for computer entry.

key-to-tape machine A stand-alone data entry machine that stores data on magnetic tape for computer entry.

key word (1) A word used in a text search.

(2) A word in a text document that is used in an index to best describe the contents of the document.

(3) A reserved word in a programming or command language.

Khornerstones A benchmark program that tests CPU, I/O and floating point performance.

KHz (KiloHertZ) One thousand cycles per second. See *horizontal scan frequency*.

kicks See *CICS*.

kilo Thousand. Abbreviated "K." It often refers to the precise value 1,024 since computer specifications are usually binary numbers. For example, 64K means 65,536 bytes when referring to memory or storage (64x1024), but a 64K salary means $64,000. The IEEE uses "K" for 1,024, and "k" for 1,000. See *space/time*.

kilobit One thousand bits. Also Kb, Kbit and K-bit. See *kilo* and *space/time*.

kilobyte One thousand bytes. Also KB, Kbyte and K-byte. See *kilo* and *space/time*.

Kinetics FastPath A gateway from the Kinetics division of Excelan, Inc., that connects LocalTalk and PhoneNet systems and LaserWriters to VAXs, UNIX-based computers, PCs and other Ethernet-based hosts. It supports AppleTalk, TCP/IP and DECnet protocols.

kiosk A small, self-standing structure such as a newstand or ticket booth. Unattended multimedia kiosks dispense public information via computer screens. Either a keyboard, touch screen or both are used for input.

Kittyhawk A hard disk used in laptops and portable applications from HP. It was the world's first 1.3" hard disk, introduced in 1992.

kludge Also spelled "kluge" and pronounced "klooj." A crude, inelegant system, component or program. It may refer to a makeshift, temporary solution to a problem as well as to any product that is poorly designed or that becomes unwieldy over time.

knowledge acquisition The process of acquiring knowledge from a human expert for an expert system, which must be carefully organized into IF-THEN rules or some other form of knowledge representation.

knowledge base A database of rules about a subject used in AI applications. See *expert system*.

knowledge based system An AI application that uses a database of knowledge about a subject. See *expert system*.

knowledge domain A specific area of expertise of an expert system.

knowledge engineer A person who translates the knowledge of an expert into the knowledge base of an expert system.

KnowledgeMan An application development system for DOS, OS/2, VMS and UNIX environments from Micro Data Base Systems, Inc., Lafayette, IN. It includes an RDBMS, object-based 4GL programming and integrated functions, allowing, for example, database queries to update spreadsheets or results to be embedded in text documents.

knowledge representation A method used to code knowledge in an expert system, typically a series of IF-THEN rules (IF this condition occurs, THEN take this action).

Korn shell See *UNIX*.

KSDS (Keyed Sequence DataSet) A VSAM structure that uses an index to store records in available free space. Retrieval is by key field or by address. Contrast with *ESDS*.

KSR terminal (Keyboard Send Receive terminal) Same as *teleprinter*. Contrast with *RO terminal*.

label (1) In data management, a made-up name that is assigned to a file, field or other data structure.

(2) In spreadsheets, descriptive text that is entered into a cell.

(3) In programming, a made-up name used to identify a variable or a subroutine.

(4) In computer operations, a self-sticking form attached to the outside of a disk or tape in order to identify it.

(5) In magnetic tape files, a record used for identification at the beginning or end of the file.

label prefix In a spreadsheet, a character typed at the beginning of a cell entry. For example, in 1-2-3, a single quote (') identifies what follows as a descriptive label even if it's a number.

LAN (Local Area Network) A communications network that serves users within a confined geographical area. It is made up of servers, workstations, a network operating system and a communications link.

Servers are high-speed machines that hold programs and data shared by all network users. The workstations, or clients, are the users' personal computers, which perform stand-alone processing and access the network servers as required.

The controlling software in a LAN is the network operating system, such as NetWare, UNIX and Appletalk, which resides in the server. A component part of the software resides in each client and allows the application to read and write data from the server as if it were on the local machine.

The message transfer is managed by a transport protocol such as IPX, SPX and TCP/IP. The physical transmission of data is performed by the access method (Ethernet, Token Ring, etc.) which is implemented in the network adapters that plug into the machines. The actual communications path is the cable (twisted pair, coax, optical fiber) that interconnects each network adapter. See *MAN, WAN, bridge, router, gateway* and *hub*.

▶ *The electronic and encyclopedic versions of this book provide more detail on this subject.*

LAN administrator See *network administrator*.

LAN analyzer See *network analyzer*.

LANDA (LAN Dealers Association) See *NOMDA*.

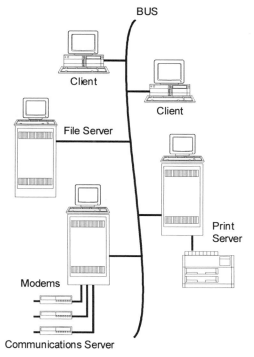

LOCAL AREA NETWORK

landing zone A safe non-data area on a hard disk used for parking the read/write head.

Landmark rating A widely-used PC performance test from Landmark Research International, Clearwater, FL, that measures CPU, video and coprocessor speed. CPU speed is rated as the clock speed required in an AT-class machine that would provide equivalent performance.

landscape A printing orientation that prints data across the wider side of the form. Contrast with *portrait*.

landscape monitor A monitor that is used to display facing text pages. It is wider than it is high.

LAN emulation The processing required to support protocols used in legacy LANs connected to an ATM network. Traditional communications protocols were designed for shared media (Ethernet, Token Ring, etc.). Broadcasting reached all nodes automatically. ATM's topology does not lend itself to broadcasting, thus LAN emulation performs lookup functions in software that provide the address resolutions required by protocols such as IP and IPX.

language A set of symbols and rules used to convey information. See *machine language, programming language, graphics language, page description language* and *fourth-generation language*.

LanguageAccess An SAA-compliant query language from IBM that translates a user's English-language request into SQL language for QMF. QMF retrieves the data.

language processor Language translation software. Programming languages, command languages, query languages, natural languages and foreign languages are all translated by software.

LAN Manager (1) A network operating system from Microsoft that runs as a server application under OS/2 and supports both DOS, Windows and OS/2 clients. It uses the Microsoft File Sharing protocol (SMB) for file sharing, the NetBEUI protocol for its transport mechanism and uses Named Pipes for interprocess communication (IPC). See *LAN Server*.

LAN Manager for Windows NT is a different product. It adds network management and services to Windows NT, which includes peer-to-peer networking.

(2) Same as *network administrator*.

LAN Network Manager IBM Token Ring network management software. LAN Station Manager is the workstation counterpart that collects data for LAN Network Manager.

LAN Requester LAN Server software that resides in the workstation.

LAN Server (1) A network operating system from IBM that runs as a server application under OS/2 and supports both DOS, Windows and OS/2 clients. Originally based on LAN Manager when OS/2 was jointly developed by IBM and Microsoft, Version 3.0 runs under IBM's own OS/2 Version 2.0.

(2) (LAN server) Generically, a file server in a network.

LAN station (1) A workstation in a local area network.

(2) See *LAN Network Manager*.

LANtastic A popular peer-to-peer LAN operating system for PCs from Artisoft, Inc., Tucson, AZ. It supports Ethernet, ARCNET and Token Ring adapaters as well as its own twisted-pair adapater at two Mbits/sec.

LAN Workplace A family of software products from Novell that allows DOS, Windows, Macintosh and OS/2 clients in a NetWare environment to access resources on a TCP/IP network. LAN Workplace for DOS can also encapsulate NetWare protocols and run NetWare-dependent applications entirely within a TCP/IP network.

LAP (Link Access Procedure) An ITU-TSS family of error correction protocols originally derived from the HDLC standard and used on X.25 packet networks. LAP-B, LAP-D, LAP-M and LAP-X are variants.

LapLink A PC file transfer program from Traveling Software, Inc., Bothell, WA, that transfers data between laptops and desktop computers. LapLink Mac transfers files between PCs and Macs.

laptop computer A portable computer that has a flat screen and usually weighs less than a dozen pounds. It uses AC power and/or batteries. Most have connectors for an external monitor and keyboard transforming them into desktop computers. See *notebook computer* and *pocket computer*.
▶ *The electronic and encyclopedic versions of this book provide more detail on this subject.*

laser (Light Amplification from the Stimulated Emission of Radiation) A device that creates a very uniform light that can be precisely focused. It generates a single wavelength or narrow band of wavelengths and is used in applications such as communications, printing and disk storage. Unlike the transmission of electricity, transmission of light pulses over optical fibers is not affected by nearby electrical interferences. See *LED*.

LaserDisc An optical disk used for full-motion video that uses the LaserVision technology developed by Philips. LaserDisc players can read the CLV format for two hours of recording (one hour per side) as well as the CAV format for a total of one hour. CAV provides direct access capability for interactive material.

LaserJet A family of desktop laser printers from HP. Introduced in 1984 at $3,495, the first LaserJet revolutionized the desktop laser printer market. LaserJets print at 300 dpi and starting with the LaserJet 4, at 600 dpi. PCL is the printer command language.
▶ *The electronic and encyclopedic versions of this book provide detail on all the LaserJet models.*

laser printer A printer that uses the electrophotographic method used in copy machines to print a page at a time. A laser "paints" the dots of light onto a photographic drum or belt. The toner is applied to the drum or belt and then transferred onto the paper. Desktop printers use cut sheets like a copy machine. Large printers may use rolls of paper.

LaserWriter A family of 300 dpi desktop laser printers from Apple introduced in 1985. All models handle bitmapped fonts, and, except for the SC models, include PostScript, built-in AppleTalk connections, as well as RS-232 ports for connecting PCs via Diablo emulation.

LAT (Local Area Transport) A communications protocol from Digital for controlling terminal traffic in a DECnet environment.

LATA (Local Access and Transport Area) The geographic region set up to differentiate local and long distance telephone calls. Any telephone call between parties within a LATA is handled by the local telephone company.

latch An electronic circuit that maintains one of two states. See *flip-flop*.

late binding Linking routines at runtime.

latency The time between initiating a request for data and the beginning of the actual data transfer. On a disk, latency is the time it takes for the selected sector to come around and be positioned under the read/write head. Channel latency is the time it takes for a computer channel to become unoccupied in order to transfer data.

latent image An invisible image typically of electrical charges. For example, in a copy machine, a latent image of the page to be copied is created on a plate or drum as an electrical charge.

launch To cause a program to load and run.

LAWN (Local Area Wireless Network) A transmitter/receiver that connects devices using radio transmission.

layer (1) In computer graphics, one of several on-screen "drawing boards" for creating elements within a picture. Layers can be manipulated independently, and the sum of all layers make up the total image.

(2) In communications, a protocol that interacts with other protocols to provide all the necessary transmission services. See *OSI*.

layout setting A value used to format a printed page. Margins, tabs, indents, headers, footers and column widths are examples.

LBRV (Low Bit Rate Voice) A voice sampling technique that analyzes each 15-30 millisecond speech segment independently and converts it into a 30-byte frame.

LCC See *leaded chip carrier*.

LCD (Liquid Crystal Display) A display technology that uses rod-shaped molecules (liquid crystals) that flow like liquid and bend light. Unenergized, the crystals direct light through two polarizing filters, allowing a natural background color to show. When energized, they redirect the light to be absorbed in one of the polarizers, causing the dark appearance of crossed polarizers to show. The more the molecules are twisted, the better the contrast and viewing angle.

LCD panel Also called a projection panel, it is a data projector that accepts computer output and displays it on a see-through liquid crystal screen that is placed on top of an overhead projector. Some laptops are built with an LCD screen that you can remove from the computer, take the back off and use as a projection panel.

LCD printer An electrophotographic printer that uses a single light source directed by liquid crystal shutters.

LD See *LaserDisc*.

LE (Less than or Equal to) See *relational operator*.

lead acid A rechargeable battery technology widely used in portable gardening tools, but has been used in some portable computers. It uses lead plates and an acid electrolyte. It provides the least amount of charge per pound of the rechargeable technologies. See *nickel cadmium, nickel hydride* and *zinc air*.

leaded chip carrier A square chip housing with pin connectors on all four sides (provides more I/O paths than a DIP). Contrast with *leadless chip carrier*.

leader (1) A length of unrecorded tape used to thread the tape onto the tape drive.

(2) A dot or dash used to draw the eye across the printed page, such as in a table of contents.

leading In typography, the vertical spacing between lines of type (between baselines). The name comes from the early days of typesetting when the space was achieved with thin bars of lead.

leading edge (1) The edge of a punched card or document that enters the reading station first.

(2) In digital electronics, a pulse as it changes from a 0 to a 1.

(3) In programming, a loop that tests a condition before the loop is entered.

(4) (Leading Edge Products, Inc., Westborough, MA) A PC manufacturer founded in 1980. Its Model M (for Mitsubishi) in 1982 was the first PC-compatible from overseas. Korean Daewoo Corporation supplied it with products since 1984 and acquired it in 1989.

leading zeros Zeros used to fill a field that do not increase the numerical value of the data. For example, all the zeros in 0000006588 are leading zeros.

leadless chip carrier A square chip housing with flat contact connectors on all four sides (provides more I/O paths than a DIP). Contrast with *leaded chip carrier*.

leaf In database management, the last node of a tree.

leapfrog test A storage diagnostic routine that replicates itself throughout the storage medium.

leased line A private communications channel leased from a common carrier. It can be ordered in pairs, providing a four-wire channel for full-duplex transmission (dial-up system provides only two-wire lines). To improve line quality, it can also be conditioned.

leased line modem A high-speed modem used in private lines. It may have built-in lower speeds for alternate use in dial-up lines.

least significant digit The rightmost digit in a number.

LEC (Local Exchange Carrier) An organization that provides local telephone services (RBOCs, GTE, etc.).

LED (Light Emitting Diode) A display technology that uses a semiconductor diode that emits light when charged. It usually gives off a red glow, although other colors can be generated. It is used in readouts and on/off lights in myriads of electronic appliances. It was the first digital watch display, but was superseded by LCD, which uses less power.

LED printer An electrophotographic printer that uses a matrix of LEDs as its light source rather than a laser.

left justify Same as *flush left*.

legacy LAN A LAN topology, such as Ethernet or Token Ring, which has a large installed base or has been in existence for a long time.

legacy system A mainframe or minicomputer information system that has been in existence for a long time.

Lempel Ziv A data compression algorithm that uses an adaptive compression technique.

LEN (Low Entry Networking) In SNA, peer-to-peer connectivity between adjacent Type 2.1 nodes, such as PCs, workstations and minicomputers. LU 6.2 sessions are supported across LEN connections.

letter quality The print quality of an electric typewriter. Laser printers, ink jet printers and daisy wheel printers provide letter quality printing. 24-pin dot matrix printers provide near letter quality (NLQ), but the characters are not as dark and crisp.

level 1 cache, level 2 cache A level 1 cache is an internal cache built into the CPU chip. A level 2 cache is an external cache of memory chips plugged into the motherboard. Both are CPU caches, and both are routinely used together. See *cache*.

lexicographic sort Arranging items in alphabetic order like a dictionary. Numbers are located by their alphabetic spelling.

LF See *line feed*.

LHARC A popular freeware compression program developed by Haruyasu Yoshizaki that uses a variant of the LZW (LZ77) dictionary method followed by a Huffman coding stage. It runs on PCs, UNIX and other platforms as its source code is also free..

librarian (1) A person who works in the data library.

(2) See *CA-Librarian*.

library (1) A collection of programs or data files.

(2) A collection of functions (subroutines) that are linked into the main program when it is compiled.

(3) See *data library*.

library function A subroutine that is part of a function library. Same as *library routine*.

library management See *version control*.

library routine A subroutine that is part of a macro or function library.

LIFO (Last In First Out) A queueing method in which the next item to be retrieved is the item most recently placed in the queue. Contrast with *FIFO*.

ligature Two or more typeface characters that are designed as a single unit (physically touch). Fi, ffi, ae and oe are common ligatures.

light bar Same as *highlight bar*.

light guide A transmission channel that contains a number of optical fibers packaged together.

light pen A light-sensitive stylus wired to a video terminal used to draw pictures or select menu options. The user brings the pen to the desired point on screen and presses the pen button to make contact.

Screen pixels are constantly being refreshed. When the user presses the button, allowing the pen to sense light, the pixel being illuminated at that instant identifies the screen location.

light source In computer graphics, the implied location of a light source in order to simulate the visual effect of a light on a 3-D object. Some programs can compute multiple light sources.

lightwave Light in the infrared, visible and ultraviolet ranges, which falls between x-rays and microwaves. Wavelengths are between 10 nanometers and one millimeter.

lightwave system A device that transmits light pulses over optical fibers at extremely high speeds (Gbits/sec range). Many intercity telephone trunks have been converted to lightwave systems.

lightweight protocol A communications protocol designed with less complexity in order to reduce overhead. For example, it uses fixed-length headers because they are faster to parse than variable-length headers. To ensure compatibility, it eliminates optional subsets of the standard so that both sides are always equipped to deal with each other.

li-ion See *lithium ion*

LIM EMS (Lotus Intel Microsoft EMS) Refers to the first versions of EMS memory.

limited distance modem Same as *short-haul modem*.

limulator See *EMS emulator*.

Linda A set of parallel processing functions added to languages, such as C and C++, that allows data to be created and transferred between processes. It was developed by Yale professor David Gelernter, when he was a 23-year old graduate student.

line (1) In text-based systems, a row of characters.

(2) In graphics-based systems, a row of pixels.

(3) Any communications channel.

line adapter In communications, a device similar to a modem, that converts a digital signal into a form suitable for transmission over a communications line and vice versa. It provides parallel/serial and serial/parallel conversion, modulation and demodulation.

line analyzer A device that monitors the transmission of a communications line.

linear Sequential or having a graph that is a straight line.

linear address space See *flat address space*.

linear editing See *linear video editing*.

linear programming A mathematical technique used to obtain an optimum solution in resource allocation problems, such as production planning.

linear video Continuous playback of videotape or videodisc. It typically refers to analog video technology.

linear video editing Editing analog videotape. Before digital editing (nonlinear video editing), video sequences were edited by inserting new frames and reconstructing the balance of the tape by adding the remainder of the frames. Contrast with *nonlinear video editing*.

line concentration See *concentrator*.

line conditioning See *conditioning*.

line dot matrix printer A line printer that uses the dot matrix method. See *printer*.

line drawing A graphic image outlined by solid lines. The mass of the drawing is imagined by the viewer. See *wire frame*.

line driver In communications, a device that is used to extend the transmission distance between terminals and computers that are connected via private lines. It is used for digital transmission and is required at each end of the line.

line editor An outmoded editing program that allows text to be created and changed one line at a time. The Edlin editor included with DOS is an example.

line feed (1) A character code that advances the screen cursor or printer to the next line. The line feed is used as an end of line code in UNIX. In DOS and OS/2 text files, the return/line feed pair (ASCII 13 10) is the standard end of line code.

(2) A printer button that advances paper one line when depressed.

line frequency The number of times each second that a wave or some repeatable set of signals is transmitted over a line. See *horizontal scan frequency*.

line level In communications, the signal strength within a transmission channel, measured in decibels or nepers.

line load (1) In communications, the percentage of time a communications channel is used.

(2) In electronics, the amount of current that is carried in a circuit.

line number (1) A specific line of programming language source code.

(2) On display screens, a specific row of text or row of dots.

(3) In communications, a specific communications channel.

line of code A statement in a source program. In assembly language, it usually generates one machine instruction, but in a high-level language, it may generate a series of instructions. Lines of code are used to measure the complexity of a program. However, comparisons are misleading if the programs are not in the same language or category. For example, 20 lines of code in COBOL might require 200 lines of code in assembly language.

line of sight An unobstructed view from transmitter to receiver.

line printer A printer that prints one line at a time. Line printers are usually connected to mainframes and minicomputers.

line segment In vector graphics, same as *vector*.

line speed See *data rate*.

line squeeze In a mail merge, the elimination of blank lines when printing names and addresses that contain no data in certain fields, such as title, company and second address line. See *field squeeze*.

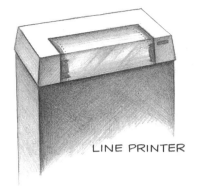

LINE PRINTER

Without line squeeze	With line squeeze
Pat Smith	Pat Smith
	10 South Main
10 South Main	Bearcat, OR 80901
Bearcat, OR 80901	

link (1) In communications, a line, channel or circuit over which data is transmitted.

(2) In data management, a pointer embedded within a record that refers to data or the location of data in another record.

(3) In programming, a call to another program or subroutine.

link edit To use a linkage editor to prepare a program for running.

linkage editor A utility program that unites a compiled or assembled program to a particular environment by linking references between program modules and libraries of subroutines. Its output is a load module.

linked list In data management, a group of items, each of which points to the next item. It allows for the organization of a sequential set of data in noncontiguous storage locations.

Linpack A package of FORTRAN programs for numerical linear algebra that is commonly used to create benchmark programs for testing a computer's floating point performance.

Linux A freeware version of a clone of the UNIX System V Release 3.0 kernel that runs on x86 machines. It is available on programming BBSs and on the Internet.

LIPS (Logical Inferences Per Second) The unit of measurement of the thinking speed of an AI application. Humans do about 2 LIPS. In the computer, one LIPS equals from 100 to 1,000 instructions.

liquid crystal shutters A method of directing light onto the drum in an electrophotographic printer. A matrix of liquid crystal dots function as shutters that are opened and closed. See *LCD*.

Lisa The first personal computer to include integrated software and use a graphical interface. Modeled after the Xerox Star and introduced in 1983 by Apple, it was

LISA

ahead of its time, but never caught on due to its $10,000 price and slow speed.

LISP (LISt Processing) A high-level programming language used in non-numeric programming. Developed in 1960 by John McCarthy, its syntax and structure is very different than traditional programming languages. For example, there is no syntactic difference between data and instructions.

LISP, available in both interpreter and compiler versions, is used extensively in AI applications as well as in compiler creation. The language can be modified and expanded by the programmer. Many varieties of LISP have been developed, including versions that perform calculations efficiently. The following Common LISP example converts Fahrenheit to Celsius:

```
(defun convert ()
  (format t "Enter Fahrenheit ")
  (let ((fahr (read)))
   (format t "Celsius is ~D"
     (truncate (* (-fahr 32)
        (/ 5 9))))))
```

list (1) An arranged set of data, often in row and column format.

(2) In fourth-generation languages, a command that displays/prints selected records. For example, in dBASE, `list name address` displays all names and addresses in the current file.

list processing Processing non-numeric data.

list processing language A programming language, such as LISP, Prolog and Logo, used to process lists of data (names, words, objects). Although operations such as selecting the next to first, or next to last element, or reversing all elements in a list, can be programmed in any language, list processing languages provide commands to do them. Recursion is also provided, allowing a subroutine to call itself over again in order to repetitively analyze a group of elements.

listing Any printed output.

literal In programming, any part of an instruction that remains unchanged when translated into machine language, such as an output message.

lithium ion A rechargeable battery technology that provides more than twice the charge per pound as nickel hydride. Although used in camcorders and other devices, Toshiba introduced the first lithium ion notebook in the U.S. with its Portégé 3400 series in late 1993.

Lithium polymer technology may provide twice as much power as lithium ion.

little endian See *big endian*.

liveware People.

LLC (Logical Link Control) The top part of the data link layer in an IEEE 802 protocol. It provides a common interface to the lower MAC (media access control) layer, which specifies the access method (CSMA/CD, token bus, token ring, etc.).

LLCC See *leadless chip carrier*.

lo-res See *low resolution*.

load (1) To copy a program from some source, such as a disk or tape, into memory for execution.

(2) To fill up a disk with data or programs.

(3) To insert a disk or tape into a drive.

(4) In programming, to store data in a register.

(5) In performance measurement, the current use of a system as a percentage of total capacity.

(6) In electronics, the flow of current through a circuit.

load high To load programs into high memory.

load module A program in machine language form ready to run in the computer. It is the output of a link editor.

load sharing Sharing the workload in two or more computers.

loaded line A telephone line from customer to central office that uses loading coils to reduce distortion.

loader A program routine that copies a program into memory for execution.

loader routine Same as *loader*.

loading coil A device used in local telephone loops (exceeding 18,000 ft.) that boosts voice-grade transmission. It often adds noise to high-speed data transmission and must be removed for such traffic.

local area network See *LAN*.

local bus A bus between the CPU, memory and peripheral devices that runs at the speed of the CPU. In a PC, the VL-bus and PCI bus provide faster data transfer than the traditional ISA bus.

Starting with the 386, when CPU speeds began to greatly accelerate, PCs have been built with two buses. The CPU accesses its memory chips via a 32-bit internal path (64 bits with the Pentium), known as the local bus, at the full clock speed of the CPU (25MHz, 33MHz, etc.). However, it has traditionally accessed its peripheral devices more slowly; over a 16-bit ISA bus at only 8MHz. Even the inherently-faster 32-bit EISA bus runs slow in order to accomodate ISA boards, which plug into it.

VESA's VL-bus and Intel's PCI local bus standards were created to tap directly into the higher CPU speeds. PCI runs at 33MHz; VL-bus up to 40MHz. Faster speeds are also expected. ISA and EISA motherboards are now built with extra slots for VL-bus or PCI cards or both.

▶ *The electronic and encyclopedic versions of this book provide more detail on this subject.*

local bypass An interconnection between two facilities without the use of the local telephone company.

local console A terminal or workstation directly connected to the computer or other device that it is monitoring and controlling.

local loop A communications line between a customer and the telephone company's central office. See *loop carrier*.

local memory The memory used by a single CPU or allocated to a single program or function.

local storage The disk storage used by a single CPU.

local variable In programming, a variable used

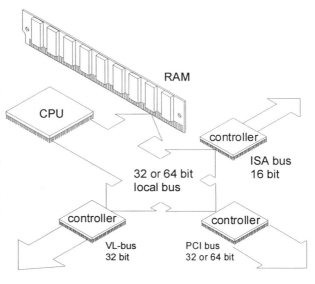

RAM

CPU

controller

ISA bus
16 bit

32 or 64 bit
local bus

controller

VL-bus
32 bit

controller

PCI bus
32 or 64 bit

only within the routine or function it is defined in.

LocalTalk A LAN access method from Apple that uses twisted pair wires and transmits at 230,400 bps. It runs under AppleTalk and uses a daisy chain topology that can connect up to 32 devices within a distance of 1,000 feet. Third party products allow it to hook up with bus, passive star and active star topologies.

Apple's LocalTalk PC Card lets a PC gain access to an AppleTalk network.

lockup Refers to a computer's inability to respond to user input. See *abend*.

log A record of computer activity used for statistical purposes as well as backup and recovery.

logic The sequence of operations performed by hardware or software. Hardware logic is made up of circuits that perform an operations. Software logic (program logic) is the sequence of instructions in a program. Note: Logic is not the same as logical. See *logical vs physical* and *logical expression*.

logical (1) A reasonable solution to a problem.

(2) A higher level view of an object; for example, the user's view versus the computer's view. See *logical vs physical*.

logical data group Data derived from several sources. Same as *view*.

logical drive An allocated part of a physical drive that is designated and managed as an independent unit.

logical expression An expression that results in true or false. Same as *Boolean expression*.

logical field A data field that contains a yes/no, true/false condition.

logical lock The prevention of user access to data that is provided by marking the file or record through the use of software. Contrast with *physical lock*.

logical operator One of the Boolean logical operators (AND, OR and NOT).

logical record A reference to a data record that is independent of its physical location. It may be physically stored in two or more locations.

logical vs physical High-level versus low-level. Logical implies a higher view than the physical. A message transmitted from Phoenix to Boston logically goes between two cities; however, the physical circuit could be Phoenix to Chicago to Philadelphia to Boston.

logic analyzer (1) A device that monitors computer performance by timing various segments of the running programs. The total running time and the time spent in selected progam modules is displayed in order to isolate the the least efficient code.

(2) A device used to test and diagnose an electronic system, which includes an oscilloscope for displaying various digital states.

logic array Same as *gate array* or *PLA*.

logic bomb A program routine that destroys data; for example, it may reformat the hard disk or insert random bits into data files. It may be brought into a personal computer by downloading a corrupt public-domain program. Once executed, it does its damage right away, whereas a virus keeps on destroying.

logic chip A processor or controller chip. Contrast with *memory chip*.

logic circuit A circuit that performs some processing or controlling function. Contrast with *memory*.

logic controller See *PLC*.

logic diagram A flow chart of hardware circuits or program logic.

logic error A program bug due to an incorrect sequence of instructions.

logic gate A collection of transistors and electronic components that make up a Boolean logical operation, such as AND, NAND, OR and NOR. Transistors make up logic gates. Logic gates make up circuits. Circuits make up electronic systems.

logic operation An operation that analyzes one or more inputs and generates a particular output based on a set of rules. See *AND, OR and NOT* and *Boolean logic*.

logic-seeking printer A printer that analyzes line content and skips over blank spaces at high speeds.

login Same as *logon*.

Logo A high-level programming language noted for its ease of use and graphics capabilities. It is a recursive language that contains many list processing functions that are in LISP, although Logo's syntax is more understandable for novices.
  The following Object Logo example converts Fahrenheit to Celsius:

```
convert
local [fahr]
print "|Enter Fahrenheit |
make "fahr ReadWord
print "|Celsius is |
print (:fahr - 32) * 5 / 9
end
```

logoff To quit, or sign off, a computer system.

logon To gain access, or sign in, to a computer system. If restricted, it requires users to identify themselves by entering an ID number and/or password. Service bureaus base their charges for the time between logon and logoff.

logout Same as *logoff*.

long In programming, an integer variable. In C, a long is four bytes and can be signed (-2G to +2G) or unsigned (4G). Contrast with *short*.

long card In PCs, a full-length controller board that plugs into an expansion slot. Contrast with *short card*.

long-haul In communications, modems or communications devices that are capable of transmitting over long distances.

long lines In communications, circuits that are capable of handling transmissions over long distances.

longitudinal redundancy check See *LRC*.

look and feel Refers to the design of a program's user interface. Some programs look and function like others, and the original developer sometimes gets rather upset about it. This issue has been and will continue to be contested in the courts.

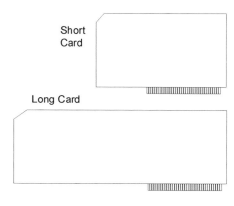

Short Card

Long Card

CARD TYPES

lookup A data search performed within a predefined table of values (array, matrix, etc.) or within a data file.

loop In programming, a repetition within a program. Whenever a process must be repeated, a loop is set up to handle it. A program has a main loop and a series of minor loops, which are nested within the main loop. Learning how to set up loops is what programming technique is all about.

The example loop at the bottom right prints an invoice. The main loop reads the order record and prints the invoice until there are no more orders to read. After printing date and name and addresses, the program prints a variable number of line items. The code that prints the line items is contained in a loop and repeated as many times as required.

Loops are accomplished by various programming structures that have a beginning, body and end. The beginning generally tests the condition that keeps the loop going. The body comprises the repeating statements, and the end is a GOTO that points back to the beginning. In assembly language, the programmer writes the GOTO, as in the following example that counts to 10.

```
        MOVE      "0" TO COUNTER
LOOP    ADD       "1" TO COUNTER
        COMPARE   COUNTER TO "10"
        GOTO      LOOP IF UNEQUAL
        STOP
```

In high-level languages, the GOTO is generated by the interpreter or compiler; for example, the same routine as above using a WHILE loop.

```
        COUNTER = 0
        DO WHILE COUNTER <> 10
            COUNTER = COUNTER + 1
        ENDDO
        STOP
```

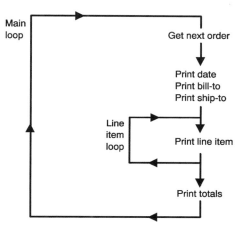

loop carrier In telephone communications, a system that concentrates a number of analog or digital lines from a remote termination station into the central office. It normally converts analog voice into digital at the remote station; however, it can be adapted to provide ISDN service to a customer.

loopback plug A diagnostic connector that directs the sending line back into the receiving line for test purposes.

loosely coupled Refers to stand-alone computers connected via a network. Loosely coupled computers process on their own and exchange data on demand. Contrast with *tightly coupled*.

lossless compression Compression techniques that decompress data 100% back to original. Contrast with *lossy compression*.

lossy compression Compression techniques that do not decompress data 100% back to original. Images and audio samples may be able to afford small losses of resolution in order to increase compression. Contrast with *lossless compression*.

lost cluster Disk records that have lost their identification with a file name. This can happen if a file is not closed properly, which can sometimes occur if the computer is turned off without formally quitting an application.

Lotus (Lotus Development Corporation, Cambridge, MA) A major software company founded in 1981 by Mitch Kapor. It achieved outstanding success by introducing Lotus 1-2-3, the first spreadsheet for the IBM PC. Over the years, it has developed a variety of applications and has helped set industry standards.

Lotus 1-2-3 The most widely-used spreadsheet application with over 20 million copies installed worldwide. It runs on DOS, Windows, Macintosh, Sun, VAX, OS/2, UNIX and IBM mainframe platforms. Major development effort centers on Windows, OS/2 and DOS. Starting with Version 3.0, it provides 3-D and dynamic linking capabilities.

The first 1-2-3 (DOS) shipped in January 1983 under a well-organized marketing campaign. It was the first innovative spreadsheet for the IBM PC. The 1-2-3 stood for the integration of spreadsheet, database and graphics. Its ability to function like a simple database was unique, and turning data into a chart with a single keystroke was dazzling for its time. The program's user interface was also easier to use than other programs (see *Lotus menu*).

Lotus menu The menu introduced with Lotus 1-2-3 that became a de facto standard. It is a row of words, each of which is an option that can be selected by highlighting it and pressing Enter or by pressing the first letter of the word. When the word is highlighted, an explanation line is displayed above or below it. Contrast with *pull-down menu*.

Lotus Notes A document database system from Lotus that runs in a client/server environment under Windows, OS/2 and various UNIX platforms. Notes is designed for workgroups that have to continually update and exchange documents and information. It provides electronic mail and outbound fax capability and allows for the attachment of all types of files to a Notes document.

Notes keeps documents in sync. When a change is made to a document, those changes are replicated throughout the organization where necessary. As of Release 3, it allows a Windows PC to act as a Notes server and will run with any VIM-compliant e-mail system such as cc:Mail.

low density Refers to an earlier version of a storage device with less bits per inch than today's version. See *DD* and *double density*.

low entry networking See *LEN*.

lower CASE See *back-end CASE*.

low frequency An electromagnetic wave that vibrates in the range from 30 to 300,000 Hertz.

low-level format The sector identification on a disk that the drive uses to locate sectors for reading and writing. See *format program*.

low-level language A programming language that is very close to machine language. All assembly languages are low-level languages. Contrast with *high-level language*.

low radiation Refers to video terminals that emit less VLF (Very Low Frequency) and ELF (Extremely Low Frequency) radiation. This level of radiation cannot be shielded by office partitions. It must be cancelled out from the CRT. Health studies on this are not conclusive and are very controversial. See *MPR II*.

low resolution A low-grade display or printing quality due to a lower number of dots or lines per inch.

lpi (Lines Per Inch) The number of lines printed in a vertical inch.

lpm (Lines Per Minute) The number of lines a printer can print or a scanner can scan in a minute.

LPT1 The logical name assigned to parallel port #1 in DOS and OS/2 (usually connected to a printer). A second parallel device is assigned LPT2. Contrast with *COM1*.

LQ See *letter quality*.

LRC (Longitudinal Redundancy Check) An error checking method that generates a parity bit from a specified string of bits on a longitudinal track. In a row and column format, such as on magnetic tape, LRC is often used with VRC, which creates a parity bit for each character.

LSAPI (Licensing Service API) A programming interface from Microsoft that allows a licensing server to track applications in use for managing multiuser software licenses.

LSI (Large Scale Integration) Between 3,000 and 100,000 transistors on a chip. See *SSI, MSI, VLSI* and *ULSI*.

LSI-11 A family of board-level computers from Digital that uses the micro version of the PDP-11. Introduced in 1974, it was the first to use the Q-bus.

LSL (Link Support Layer) A common interface for network drivers. It provides a common language between the transport layer and the data link layer and allows different transport protocols to run over one network adapter or one transport protocol to run on different network adapters.

LT (Less Than) See *relational operator*.

LU (Logical Unit) In SNA, one end of a communications session. The complete LU to LU session is defined by session type. Common types are:

1	Host to 3770 RJE terminal
2	Host to 3270 mainframe terminal
3	Host to 3270 printer
6.2	Program-to-program
7	Host to 5250 midrange terminal

LU 6.2 An SNA protocol that establishes a session between two programs. It allows peer-to-peer communications as well as interaction between programs running in the host with PCs, Macs and midrange computers.

Before LU 6.2, processing was done only in the mainframe. LU 6.2 allows processing to take place at both ends of the communications, necessary for today's distributed computing and client/server environment. See *APPC* and *CPI-C*.

lumen A unit of measurement of the flow (rate of emission) of light. A wax candle generates 13 lumens; a 100 watt bulb generates 1,200. See *candela*.

Lumena A PC paint program from Time Arts, Inc., Santa Rosa, CA, that provides sophisticated, special effects. It accepts and generates NTSC video output and requires a video graphics board.

luminance The amount of brightness, measured in lumens, that is given off by a pixel or area on a screen. It is the black/gray/white information in a video signal.

LUN (Logical Unit Number) The physical number of a device in a daisy change of drives. See *SCSI*.

LZW (Lempel-Ziv-Welch) A widely-used dictionary compression method that stems from two techniques introduced by Jacob Ziv and Abraham Lempel. LZ77 scans a fixed length block of data and creates pointers back to data when it repeats. LZ78 scans the data and creates a dictionary of repeating phrases. Pointers are created to those phrases.

M See *mega*.

Mac (1) See *Macintosh*.

(2) (MAC) (Mandatory Access Control) A security control that requires clearance levels. See *NCSC*.

MAC layer (Media Access Control layer) The protocol sublayer that controls access to the physical transmission medium on a LAN. The MAC layer is implemented in the network adapter (NIC). Common MAC standards are the CSMA/CD architecture used in Ethernet and various token passing methods such as those used in Token Ring, FDDI and MAP.

MacAPPC LU 6.2-compliant software from Apple Computer that allows a Macintosh to be a peer to an IBM APPC application.

MacDFT Software that provides 3270 emulation for the Macintosh from Apple. It accompanies Apple's TwinAx/Coax board and supports CUT and DFT modes and DFT multiple sessions under SNA.

MacDraw Pro A Macintosh drawing program from Claris Corporation that is an enhanced version of the original MacDraw from Apple and includes full on-screen slide presentation capability. It is used for illustrations and elementary CAD work. MacDraw files are a subset of the Claris CAD file format.

Mach A UNIX-like operating system developed at Carnegie-Mellon University. It is designed with a microkernel architecture that makes it easily portable to different platforms. IBM has based its future operating systems on Mach. See *Workplace*.

machine Any electronic or electromechanical unit of equipment. A machine is always hardware; however, "engine" refers to hardware or software.

machine address Same as *absolute address*.

machine code Same as *machine language*.

machine cycle The shortest interval in which an elementary operation can take place within the processor. It is made up of some number of clock cycles.

machine dependent Refers to software that accesses specific hardware features and runs in only one kind of computer. Contrast with *machine independent*. See *device dependent*.

machine independent Refers to software that runs in a variety of computers. The hardware-specific instructions are in some other program (operating system, DBMS, etc.). Contrast with *machine dependent*. See *device independent*.

machine instruction An instruction in machine language. Its anatomy is a verb followed by one or more nouns:

OP CODE   OPERANDS (one or more)
  (verb)   (nouns)

The op code is the operation to be performed (add, copy, etc.), while the operands are the data to be acted upon (add a to b). There are always machine instructions to INPUT and OUTPUT, to process data by CALCULATING, COMPARING and COPYING it, and to go to some other part of the program with a GOTO instruction.

machine language The native language of the computer. In order for a program to run, it must be in the machine language of the computer that is executing it. Although programmers are sometimes able to modify machine language in order to fix a running program, they do not create it. It is created by programs called *assemblers, compilers* and *interpreters*, which convert programming language into machine language.

Machine language tells the computer what to do and where to do it. When a programmer writes `total = total + subtotal`, that statement is converted into a machine instruction that tells the computer to add the contents of two areas of memory (where TOTAL and SUBTOTAL are stored).

A programmer deals with data logically, "add this, subtract that," but the computer must be told precisely where this and that are located.

Machine languages differ substantially. What may take one instruction in one machine can take 10 instructions in another. See *assembly language*.

machine readable Data in a form that can be read by the computer, which includes disks, tapes and punched cards. Printed fonts that can be scanned and recognized by the computer are also machine readable.

Macintosh A series of personal computers from Apple. The original Mac with its vertical cabinet was introduced in 1984. The Mac operating system with its graphics-based user interface has provided a measure of consistency and ease of use that is unmatched. The Macintosh family is the largest non-IBM compatible personal computer series in use.

Until 1994, Macs were powered exclusively by Motorola's 680x0 family of CPUs. In 1994, Apple introduced the Power Macintoshes (PowerMacs), which use the PowerPC CPUs and provide increased performance. PowerMacs use a PowerPC version of the Mac OS, which runs native PowerMac applications and emulates 680x0 Mac applications. It also runs DOS and Windows applications via emulation from Insignia Solutions.

► *The electronic and encyclopedic versions of this book provide more detail on this subject.*

POWER MACINTOSH

Macintosh extension Additional software functions for the Macintosh, which include drivers and other enhancements to the operating system. In System 7, system extensions reside in the Extensions folder. Mac extensions are the counterpart to the CONFIG.SYS file for DOS.

Macintosh Toolbox Software routines that perform the graphical user interface functions in the Macintosh. Apple is licensing the Mac Toolbox to vendors developing a version of PowerOpen for the PowerPC. This is the first time Apple has licensed the Toolbox. See *MAS*.

MacIRMA A micro to mainframe communications board for the Macintosh from DCA, Inc., Alpharetta, GA. It a 3270 terminal.

MacLink Plus A Macintosh file transfer program from DataViz Corporation, Trumbull, CT, that provides document conversion for over 45 Mac and PC formats. Versions are available for NeXt and Sun workstations and Wang OIS and VS systems.

MacPaint II A full-featured Macintosh paint program from Claris that was originally developed by Apple and bundled with every Mac up until the Mac Plus.

MacPaint's PICT file format is used for printing the screen. By pressing Command-shift-3, the current screen is stored in a PICT file for printing either in MacPaint or other program.

macro (1) A series of menu selections, keystrokes and commands that have been recorded and assigned a name or key combination. When the macro is called or the key combination is pressed, the steps in the macro are executed from beginning to end.

Macros are used to shorten long menu sequences as well as to create miniature programs within an application. Macro languages often include programming controls (IF THEN, GOTO, WHILE, etc.) that automate sequences like any programming language. See *macro recorder*, *batch file* and *shell script*.

(2) In assembly language, a prewritten subroutine that is called for throughout the program. At assembly time, the macro calls are substituted with the actual subroutine or instructions that branch to it. The high-level language equivalent is a function.

macro assembler An assembler program that lets the programmer create and use macros.

macro call Same as *macro instruction*.

macro instruction An instruction that defines a macro. In assembly language, MACRO and ENDM are examples that define the beginning and end of a macro. In C, the #DEFINE statement is used.

macro language (1) Commands used by a macro processor. Same as *script*.

(2) An assembly language that uses macros.

macro processor (1) Software that creates and executes macros from the keyboard.

(2) The part of an assembler that substitutes the macro subroutines for the macro calls.

macro recorder A program routine that converts menu selections and keystrokes into a macro. A user turns on the recorder, calls up a menu, selects a variety of options, turns the recorder off and assigns a key command to the macro. When the key command is pressed, the selections are executed.

MacTerminal Macintosh terminal emulation software from Apple that allows a Mac to function as an IBM 3278 Model 2 (when used with an AppleLine Protocol Converter) or Digital VT 52 or VT 100 terminal.

MacTwin Mac to IBM midrange connectivity from Andrew/KMW, which includes a card for the Mac that connects to the twinax cabling from the S/3x or AS/400. Software for the Mac provides 5250, 3196 and 3197 emulation.

MacWrite II A full-featured Macintosh word processing program from Claris Corporation, that was originally packaged with every Mac 128 and 512.

mag Abbreviation for "magnetic."

Magic Cap (Magic Communicating Applications Platform) An object-oriented control program from General Magic for personal intelligent communicating devices (PDAs, hand-held units, etc.) that includes the Telescript language.

magnetic card (1) See *magnetic stripe*.

(2) Magnetic tape strips used in early data storage devices and word processors.

magnetic coercivity The amount of energy required to alter the state of a magnet. The higher a magnetic disk's coercivity index, the more data it can store.

magnetic disk The primary computer storage device. Like tape, it is magnetically recorded and can be reused over and over. Disks are rotating platters with a mechanical arm that moves a read/write head between the outer and inner edges of the platter's surface. It can take as long as one second to find a location on a floppy disk to as short as one millisecond on an ultra-fast hard disk. See *hard disk, floppy disk, sector* and *track*.

magnetic drum An early high-speed, direct access storage device that used a magnetic-coated cylinder with tracks around its circumference. Each track had its own read/write head.

magnetic field An invisible energy emitted by a magnet. Same as *flux*.

magnetic ink A magnetically detectable ink used to print the MICR characters that encode account numbers on bank checks.

magnetic oxide See *ferric oxide*.

magnetic recording With regard to computers, the technique used to record, or write, digital data in the form of tiny spots (bits) of negative or positive polarity on tapes and disks. A read/write head discharges electrical impulses onto the moving ferromagnetic surface. Reading is accomplished by sensing the polarity of the bit with the read/write head.

magnetic stripe A small length of magnetic tape adhered to ledger cards, badges and credit cards. It is read by specialized readers that may be incorporated into accounting machines and terminals. Due to heavy wear, the data on the stripe is in a low-density format that may be duplicated several times.

magnetic tape A sequential storage medium used for data collection, backup and historical purposes. Like videotape, computer tape is made of flexible plastic with one side coated with a ferromagnetic material. Tapes come in reels, cartridges and cassettes of many sizes and shapes. See *track*.

magneto-optic A high-density, erasable recording method. Data is recorded magnetically like disks and tapes, but the bits are much smaller, because a laser is used to pinpoint the bit. The laser heats the bit to 150 Celsius, at which temperature the bit is realigned when subjected to a magnetic field. In order to record new data, existing bits must first be set to zero. See *Curie point, Kerr effect* and *optical disk*.

magneto-resistance A high-density magnetic recording method that uses two technologies for the read/write head. The write head is the standard inductive type, but the magneto-resistance read head can read a fainter signal on the disk, thus allowing the bits to be packed more tightly together.

magnetographic A non-impact printer technology from Groupe Bull that prints up to 90 ppm. A magnetic image is created by a set of recording heads across a magnetic drum. Monocomponent toner is applied to the drum to develop the image, which is transferred to paper by light pressure and an electrostatic field. The toner is then fused by heat. The print quality is not as good as a laser printer, but the machines require less maintenance.

mailbox A simulated mailbox on disk that holds incoming electronic mail.

mail enabled Refers to an application that has built-in, although typically very limited, mail capabilities. For example, it can send or send and receive a file that it has created over one or more messaging systems. See *messaging API*.

mail merge Printing customized form letters. A common feature of a word processor, it uses a letter and a name and address list. In the letter, Dear A: Thank you for ordering B from our C store..., A, B and C are merge points into which data is inserted from the list. See *field squeeze* and *line squeeze*.

mail protocol See *messaging protocol* and *messaging system*.

mail system See *electronic mail* and *messaging system*.

main line See *main loop*.

main loop The primary logic in a program. It contains the instructions that are repeated after each event or transaction has been processed. See *loop*.

main memory, main storage Same as *memory*.

mainframe A large computer. In the "ancient" mid 1960s, all computers were called mainframes, since the term referred to the main CPU cabinet. Today, it refers to a large computer system.

There are small, medium and large-scale mainframes, handling from a handful to several thousand online terminals. Large-scale mainframes can have hundreds of megabytes of main memory and terabytes of disk storage. Large mainframes use smaller computers as front end processors that connect to the communications networks.

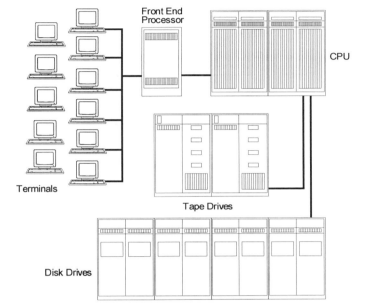

MAINFRAME

maintenance (1) Hardware maintenance is the testing and cleaning of equipment.

(2) Information system maintenance is the routine updating of master files, such as adding and deleting employees and customers and changing credit limits and product prices.

(3) Software, or program, maintenance is the updating of application programs in order to meet changing information requirements, such as adding new functions and changing data formats. It also includes fixing bugs and adapting the software to new hardware devices.

(4) Disk or file maintenance is the periodic reorganizing of disk files that have become fragmented due to continuous updating.

maintenance credits Monetary credits issued to a customer by the vendor for qualified periods during which the vendor's products are not functioning properly.

maintenance service A service provided to keep a product in good operating condition.

major key The primary key used to identify a record, such as account number or name.

make To compile a multi-module program. The make utility recompiles only those modules that have been updated since the last compilation.

MAN (Metropolitan Area Network) A communications network that covers a geographic area such as a city or suburb. See *LAN* and *WAN*.

management console A terminal or workstation used to monitor and control a network.

management science The study of statistical methods, such as linear programming and simulation, in order to analyze and solve organizational problems. Same as *operations research*.

management support See *DSS* and *EIS*.

management system The leadership and control within an organization. It is made up of people interacting with other people and machines that, together, set the goals and objectives, outline the strategies and tactics, and develop the plans, schedules and necessary controls to run an organization.

Manchester Code A self-clocking data encoding method that divides the time required to define the bit into two cycles. The first cycle is the data value (0 or 1) and the second cylce provides the timing by shifting to the opposite state.

MANTIS An application development language from Cincom Systems, Inc., Cincinnati, OH, that runs on IBM mainframes, VAXs and other mainframes. It provides procedural and non-procedural languages for developing prototypes and applications and works with Cincom's SUPRA database, DB2 and IMS.

mantissa The numeric value in a floating point number. See *floating point*.

MAP (Manufacturing Automation Protocol) A communications protocol introduced by General Motors in 1982. MAP provides common standards for interconnecting computers and programmable machine tools used in factory automation. At the lowest physical level, it uses the IEEE 802.4 token bus protocol.

MAP is often used in conjunction with *TOP*, an office protocol developed by Boeing Computer Services. TOP is used in the front office and MAP is used on the factory floor.

map (1) A set of data that has a corresponding relationship to another set of data.

(2) A list of data or objects as they are currently stored in memory or disk.

(3) To transfer a set of objects from one place to another. For example, program modules on disk are mapped into memory. A graphic image in memory is mapped onto the video screen. An address is mapped to another address.

(4) To relate one set of objects with another. For example, a logical database structure is mapped to the physical database. A vendor's protocol stack is mapped to the OSI model.

MAPI (Mail API) A programming interface that enables an application to send and receive mail over the Microsoft Mail messaging system. Simple MAPI is a subset of MAPI that includes a dozen functions for sending and retrieving mail.

MAPPER (MAintaining, Preparing and Processing Executive Reports) A Unisys mainframe fourth-generation language. In 1980, it was introduced as a high-level report writer and was later turned into a full-featured development system used successfully by non-technical users.

mapping See *map* and *digital mapping*.

marginal test A system test that introduces values far above and far below the expected values.

mark (1) A small blip printed on or notched into various storage media used for timing or counting purposes.

(2) To identify a block of text in order to perform some task on it such as deletion, copying and moving.

(3) To identify an item for future reference.

(4) In digital electronics, a 1 bit. Contrast with *space*.

(5) On magnetic disk, a recorded character used to identify the beginning of a track.

(6) In optical recognition and mark sensing, a pencil line in a preprinted box.

(7) On magnetic tape, a *tape mark* is a special character that is recorded after the last character of data.

MARK IX An application generator from Sterling Software's Answer Systems Division, Woodland Hills, CA, that runs on IBM mainframes and personal computers. It stems from MARK IV, the first report writer to use fill-in-the-blanks forms. MARK V was a subsequent online version.

mark sensing Detecting pencil lines in predefined boxes on paper forms. The form is designed with boundaries for each pencil stroke that represents a yes, no, single digit or letter, providing all possible answers to each question. A mark sense reader detects the marks and converts them into digital code.

MAS (1) (Multiple Address System) A radio service in the 932-932.5 and 941-941.5Mhz frequency that covers a 25-mile radius from the antenna. It is used for sensor-based and transaction systems (ATMs, reservations, alarms, traffic control, etc.).

(2) (Multiple Award Schedule) A list of approved products available for purchase by U.S. government agencies.

(3) (Macintosh Application System) Software that allows a Macintosh to run in a PowerPC. It includes a 68000 emulator and the Macintosh Toolbox, which contains the Mac's graphical functions. The Macintosh graphical interface runs native in the PowerPC while the Motorola 68000 instructions are emulated.

mask (1) A pattern used to transfer a design onto an object. See *photomask*.

(2) A pattern of bits used to accept or reject bit patterns in another set of data. For example, the Boolean AND operation can be used to match a mask of 0s and 1s with a string of data bits. When a 1 occurs in both the mask and the data, the resulting bit will contain a 1 in that position.

Hardware interrupts are often enabled and disabled in this manner with each interrupt assigned a bit position in a mask register.

mask bit A 1 bit in a mask used to control the corresponding bit found in data.

maskable interrupts Hardware interrupts that can be enabled and disabled by software.

masked A state of being disabled or cut off.

MASM (Macro ASeMbler) An assembly language that allows macros to be defined and used.

mass storage A high-capacity, external storage such as disk or tape.

massage To process data.

massively parallel A parallel processing architecture that uses hundreds or thousands of processors.

master Primary, controlling. See *master-slave communications* and *master file*.

master card A master record in punched card format.

master clock A clock that provides the primary source of internal timing for a processor or stand-alone control unit.

master console The main terminal used by the computer operator or systems programmer to command the computer.

master control program See *operating system*.

master file A collection of records pertaining to one of the main subjects of an information system, such as customers, employees, products and vendors. Master files contain descriptive data, such as name and address, as well as summary information, such as amount due and year-to-date sales. Contrast with *transaction file*.

Following are the kinds of fields that make up a typical master record in a business information system. There can be many more fields depending on the organization. The "key" fields below are the ones that are generally indexed for matching against the transaction records as well as fast retrieval for queries. The account number is usually the primary key, but name may also be primary. There can be secondary indexes; for example, in an inverted file structure, almost all the fields could be indexed. See *transaction file* for examples of typical transaction records.

Employee Number	Name	Address	Date of hire	Date of birth	Title	Job Class	Pay Rate	YTD Gross	
Customer Number	Name	Bill to	Ship to		Credit Limit	Date 1st Order	Sales to date	YTD Sales	Balance Due
Vendor Number	Name	Address	Terms	Quality Rating	Shipping History				
Product Number	Description	Quantity On hand	Location	Primary Vendor	Secondary Vendor				

TYPICAL MASTER RECORDS

master record A set of data for an individual subject, such as a customer, employee or vendor. See *master file*.

master-slave communications Communications in which one side, called the master, initiates and controls the session. The other side (slave) responds to the master's commands.

math coprocessor A mathematical circuit that performs high-speed floating point operations. It may be built into the CPU chip, as in the 486DX, or it may be a separate chip, such as the 387 and 487, which work with the 386 and 486SX respectively.

The math coprocessor is used primarily in CAD and spreadsheet applications to improve performance. It is so important to computation-intensive CAD work, that some CAD programs will not operate without one. Spreadsheet programs may test for its existence and then use it, but it is not mandatory. See *array processor* and *vector processor*.

Mathcad Mathematical software from Mathsoft, Inc., Cambridge, MA, for PCs and Macs. It allows complicated mathematical equations to be expressed, performed and displayed.

Mathematica Mathematical software for PCs and Macs from Wolfram Research, Inc., Champaign, IL. It includes numerical, graphical and symbolic computation capabilities, all linked to the Mathematica programming language. Its use requires a math coprocessor.

mathematical expression A group of characters or symbols representing a quantity or an operation. See *arithmetic expression*.

mathematical function A rule for creating a set of new values from an existing set; for example, the function $f(x) = 2x$ creates a set of even numbers (if x is a whole number).

matrix An array of elements in row and column form. See *x-y matrix*.

matrix printer A printer that uses the dot matrix technology.

MAU (Multi-station Access Unit) A central hub in a token ring local area network. See *hub*.

maximize In a graphical environment, to enlarge a window to full size. Contrast with *minimize*.

MB, Mb (1) (MB, upper case "B") (MegaByte or MotherBoard) MB mostly stands for megabyte, but on ads for raw components, it may refer to motherboard.

(2) (Mb, lower case "b") (MegaBit) Adherence to "b" and "B" for bit and byte is not always followed. See *space/time* for common usage.

Mbits/sec (MegaBITS per SECond) One million bits per second. See *space/time*.

Mbone (Multicast backBONE) A collection of sites on the Internet that support the IP multicasting protocol (one-to-many) and allow for live audio and videoconferencing.

MBps, Mbps (MegaBytes Per Second, MegaBits Per Second) One million bytes per second, one million bits per second. Adherence to "b" and "B" for bit and byte is not always followed. See *space/time* for common usage.

Mbytes/sec (MegaBYTES per SECond) One million bytes per second. See *space/time*.

MCA See *Micro Channel*.

MCB (Memory Control Block) An identifier (16-bytes) that DOS places in front of each block of memory it allocates.

MCGA (Multi Color Graphics Array) An IBM video display standard built into low-end PS/2 models. It is not well supported by software vendors.

MCI (Media Control Interface) A high-level programming interface from IBM/Microsoft for controlling multimedia devices. It includes text commands such as open, play and close for languages such as Visual Basic, as well as functions for languages such as C. See *RIFF* and *AVI*.

MCI decision An FCC decree in 1969 that granted MCI the right to compete with the Bell System by providing private, intercity telecommunications services.

MCM (MultiChip Module or MicroChip Module) A chip housing that uses a ceramic base and contains two or more raw chips closely connected with high-density lines. This packaging method saves space and speeds processing due to short leads between chips.

MCMs were originally called microcircuits or hybrid microcircuits, since this technique is well suited for mixing analog and digital components together.

MCMs are a more workable solution to wafer scale integration, in essence, building the "superchip," which has been very difficult to implement.

MCU (1) (MicroController Unit) A control unit on a single chip.

(2) (Multipoint Control Unit) A device that connects multiple sites for audio and video conferencing.

MD See *minidisc*.

MDA (Monochrome Display Adapter) The first IBM PC monochrome video display standard for text only. Due to its lack of graphics, MDA cards were often replaced with Hercules cards, which provided both text and graphics. See *PC display modes*.

MDBS IV A DBMS from Micro Data Base Systems, Inc., Lafayette, IN, that runs on DOS, OS/2, UNIX, MPE and VMS servers. Noted for its performance and maturity (in 1984, MDBS III was the first client/server DBMS), it provides a superset of hierarchical, network and relational storage concepts. M/4 for Windows is a single-user Windows version.

MDF (Main Distribution Frame) A connecting unit between external and internal lines. It allows for public or private lines coming into the building to connect to internal networks. See *CDF*.

MDI (1) (Multiple Document Interface) A Windows function that allows an application to display and lets the user work with more than one document at the same time. If the application is not programmed for MDI and you want to work with multiple documents of the same type concurrently, you must load the application again for each subsequent document. Contrast with *SDI*.

(2) (Medium Dependent Interface) Refers to an Ethernet port connection. The MDI-X port on an Ethernet hub is used to connect to a workstation (the X stands for crossing the transmit and recieve lines). An MDI port (not crossed) is used to connect to the MDI-X port of another hub.

mechanical mouse A mouse that uses a rubber ball that rolls against wheels inside the unit. Contrast with *optical mouse*.

media A material that stores or transmits data, for example, floppy disks, magnetic tape, coaxial cable and twisted pair.

media access method A LAN access method such as Ethernet and Token Ring.

media control Also called *media processing*, in computer telephony it refers to some processing or altering of the call; for example, digitizing the content. Contrast with *call control*.

media conversion Converting data from one storage medium to another, such as from disk to tape or from one type of disk pack to another.

media failure A condition of not being able to read from or write to a storage device, such as a disk or tape, due to a defect in the recording surface.

medium frequency An electromagnetic wave that oscillates in the range from 300,000 to 3,000,000 Hz.

meg Same as *mega*.

mega (1) Million. Abreviated "M." It often refers to the precise value 1,048,576 since computer specifications are usually binary numbers. See *space/time*.

(2) (MEGA) A personal computer series from Atari that is Motorola 68000 based, runs under GEM and the TOS operating system and includes a MIDI interface. It is ST compatible.

megabit One million bits. Also Mb, Mbit and M-bit. See *mega* and *space/time*.

megabyte One million bytes. Also MB, Mbyte and M-byte. See *mega* and *space/time*.

megaflops (mega FLoating point OPerations per Second) One million floating point operations per second.

megahertz One million cycles per second. See *MHz*.

megapel display In computer graphics, a display system that handles a million or more pixels. A resolution of 1,000 lines by 1,000 dots requires a million pixels for the full screen image.

membrane keyboard A dust and dirtproof keyboard constructed of two thin plastic sheets (membranes) that contain flexible printed circuits made of electrically conductive ink. The top membrane is the printed keyboard and a spacer sheet with holes is in the middle. When a user presses a simulated key, the top membrane is pushed through the spacer hole and makes contact with the bottom membrane, completing the circuit.

memo field A data field that holds a variable amount of text. The text may be stored in a companion file, but it is treated as if it were part of the data record. For example, in the dBASE command `list name, biography`, name is in the data file (DBF file) and biography could be a memo field in the text file (DBT file).

memory The computer's workspace (physically, a collection of RAM chips). It is an important resource, since it determines the size and number of programs that can be run at the same time, as well as the amount of data that can be processed instantly.

Memory is like an electronic checkerboard, with each square holding one byte of data or instruction. Each square has a separate address like a post office box and can be manipulated independently. As a result, the computer can break apart programs into instructions for execution and data records into fields for processing.

Oddly enough, the computer's memory doesn't remember anything when the power is turned off. That's why you have to save your files before you quit your program. Although there are memory chips that do hold their content permanently (ROMs, PROMs, EPROMs, etc.), they're used for internal control purposes and not for the user's data.

Other terms for memory are *RAM, main memory, main storage, primary storage, read/write memory, core* and *core storage.*

memory allocation

Reserving memory for specific purposes. Operating systems generally reserve all the memory they need at startup. Application programs use memory when loaded and may allocate more after being loaded. If there is not enough free memory, they cannot run.

memory bank

(1) A physical section of memory. See *memory interleaving.*

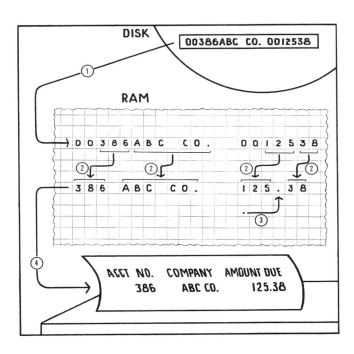

MEMORY LETS DATA BE BROKEN APART
(1) A complete data record is read from the disk and written into memory.
(2) The individual characters are copied from the input buffer to the output buffer. A format instruction strips preceding zeros out of the numeric field.
(3) The decimal point also comes from the format instruction.
(4) The formatted line is read from memory and transmitted to the printer.

(2) Refers generically to a computer system that holds data.

memory based Programs that hold all data in memory for processing. Almost all spreadsheets are memory based so that a change in data at one end of the spreadsheet can be instantly reflected at the other end.

memory card A credit-card-sized memory module used as an additional disk or disk alternative in laptops and palmtops. Called IC cards, ROM cards and RAM cards, they use a variety of chip types, including RAM, ROM, EEPROM and flash memory. RAM cards used in this manner contain a battery to keep the cells charged.

Note that when you add more memory in a laptop, the plug-in cards may also be called memory cards or RAM cards, but these are not substitutes for disk. They extend the computer's normal RAM memory and are typically contained on proprietary plug-in cards or modules. The memory card that functions as a disk typically uses the PCMCIA architecture and requires special software that accompanies the computer. See *solid state disk* and *flash memory*.

memory cell One bit of memory. In dynamic RAM memory, a cell is made up of one transistor and one capacitor. In static RAM memory, a cell is made up of about five transistors.

memory chip A chip that holds programs and data either temporarily (RAM), permanently (ROM, PROM) or permanently until changed (EPROM, EEPROM).

memory cycle A series of operations that take place to read or write a byte of memory. For destructive memories, it includes the regeneration of the bits.

memory cycle time The time it takes to perform one memory cycle.

memory dump A display or printout of the contents of memory. When a program abends, a memory dump can be taken in order to examine the status of the program at the time of the crash. The programmer looks into the buffers to see which data items were being worked on when it failed. Counters, variables, switches and flags are also inspected.

memory effect See *nickel cadmium* and *nickel hydride*.

memory interleaving A category of techniques for increasing memory speed. For example, with separate memory banks for odd and even addresses, the next byte of memory can be accessed while the current byte is being refreshed.

memory management Refers to a variety of methods used to store data and programs in memory, keep track of them and reclaim the memory space when they are no longer needed. In traditional minicomputers and mainframes, it comprises virtual memory, bank switching and memory protection techniques. See *virtual memory, memory protection* and *garbage collection*.

Memory management has become a major issue with PCs, because the PC has more different types of memory regions than any computer in history. In a PC, it refers to managing conventional memory, the upper memory area (UMA), the high memory area (HMA), extended memory and expanded memory.

By reserving fixed areas in upper memory (UMA) for use by the operating system, expanding the PC has been a memory management nightmare. Countless books have been written on a problem that never should have existed in the first place. There are even two-day courses on the subject.

memory manager Software that manages memory in a computer. See *memory management*.

memory map The location of instructions and data in memory.

memory mapped I/O A peripheral device that assigns specific memory locations to input and output. For example, in a memory mapped display, each pixel or text character derives its data from a specific memory byte or bytes. The instant this memory is updated by software, the screen is displaying the new data.

memory protection A technique that prohibits one program from accidentally clobbering another active program. Using various different techniques, a protective boundary is created around the program, and instructions within the program are prohibited from referencing data outside of that boundary.

memory resident A program that remains in memory at all times. See *TSR*.

memory sniffing Coined by Data General, a diagnostic routine that tests memory during normal processing. The processor uses cycle stealing techniques that allow it to test memory during unused machine cycles. A memory bank can be "sniffed" every few minutes.

memory typewriter A typewriter that holds a few pages of text in its memory and provides limited word processing functions. With a display screen of only one or two lines, editing is tedious.

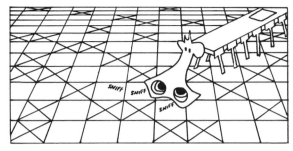

MEMORY SNIFFING

menu An on-screen list of available functions, or operations, that can be performed currently. Depending on the type of menu, selection is accomplished by (1) highlighting the menu option with a mouse and releasing the mouse, (2) pointing to the option name with the mouse and clicking on it, (3) highlighting the option with the cursor keys and pressing Enter, or (4) pressing the first letter of the option name or some designated letter within the name. See *Lotus menu* and *pull-down menu*.

menu bar A row of on-screen menu options.

menu-driven Using menus to command the computer. Contrast with *command-driven*.

menuing software Software that provides a menu for launching applications and running operating system commands.

merge See *mail merge* and *concatenate*.

merge purge To merge two or more lists together and eliminate unwanted items. For example, a new name and address list can be added to an old list while deleting duplicate names or names that meet certain criteria.

mesa A semiconductor process used in the 1960s for creating the sublayers in a transistor. Its deep etching gave way to the planar process.

mesh network A net-like communications network in which there are at least two pathways to each node. Since the term network means net-like as well as communications network, the term mesh is used to avoid saying network communications network.

message (1) In communications, a set of data that is transmitted over a communications line. Just as a program becomes a job when it's running in the computer, data becomes a message when it's transmitted over a network.

(2) In object-oriented programming, communicating between objects, similar to a function call in traditional programming.

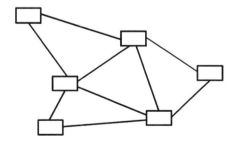

MESH NETWORK

message based An interface that is based on a set of commands. A message-based system is a type of client/server relationship, in which requests are made by a client component, and the results are provided by a server component. It implies greater flexibility and interoperability in contrast with a hard coded operation, which would have to be modified by reprogramming the source code.

message handling (1) An electronic mail system. See *messaging system*.

(2) In communications, the lower level protocols that transfer data over a network, which assemble and disassemble the data into the appropriate codes for transmission.

message handling system Same as *messaging system*.

message queue A storage space in memory or on disk that holds incoming transmissions until the computer can process them.

message switch A computer system used to switch data between various points. Computers have always been ideal switches due to their input/output and compare capabilities. It inputs the data, compares its destination with a set of stored destinations and routes it accordingly. Note: A message switch is a generic term for a data routing device, but a messaging switch converts mail and messaging protocols.

message transfer agent Store and forward capability in a messaging system. See *messaging system*.

MessagePad The first PDA from Apple to use the Newton technology. Introduced in the summer of 1993, it is a hand-held personal organizer that recognizes hand printing. It can add an appointment to a calendar and dial a phone or send a fax.

messaging API A programming interface that enables an application to send and receive messages and attached files over a messaging system. VIM, MAPI and CMC are examples. Novell's SMF-71, although also called an API, is actually the message format that mail must be placed into for submission to Novell's MHS. There are no functions associated with it.

messaging gateway A computer system that converts one messaging protocol to another. It provides an interface between two store and forward nodes, or message transfer agents (MTAs).

messaging protocol The rules, formats and functions for exchanging messages between the components of a messaging system. The major industry messaging protocols are the international X.400, SMTP (Internet), IBM's SNADS and Novell's MHS. Widely-used messaging products such as cc:Mail and Microsoft Mail use proprietary messaging protocols.

messaging switch A messaging hub that provides protocol conversion between several messaging systems. Examples of switches include Soft-Switch's EMX, HP's OpenMail and Digital's MAILbus. A messaging switch differs from a messaging gateway in that it supports more than two protocols and connections as well as providing management and directory integration.

messaging system Software that provides an electronic mail delivery system. It is comprised of three functional areas, which are either packaged together or are modularized as independent components. (1) The user agent, or UA, submits and receives the message. (2) The message transfer agent, or MTA, stores and forwards the message. (3) The message store, or MS, holds the mail and allows it to be selectively retrieved and deleted. It also provides a list of its contents.

Messaging products such as cc:Mail, Microsoft Mail, PROFS, DISOSS and ALL-IN-1 implement the entire messaging system. Other products must use components of other systems; for example, DaVinci Mail uses Novell's MHS.

metafile A data file that can store more than one type of information. For example, a Windows Metafile (WMF) can hold pictures in vector graphics and raster graphics formats as well as text. A Computer Graphics Metafile (CGM) allows for both types of graphics.

metalanguage A language used to describe another language.

metamail A public-domain UNIX utility that composes and decomposes a MIME message on the Internet.

metaphor The derivation of metaphor means "to carry over." Thus the "desktop metaphor" as so often described means that the office desktop has been brought over and simulated on computers.

meter The basic unit of the metric system (39.37 inches). A yard is about 9/10ths of a meter (0.9144 meter).

method In object-oriented programming, a method is the processing that an object performs. When a message is sent to an object, the method is implemented.

methodology The specific way of performing an operation that implies precise deliverables at the end of each stage.

metric Measurement. Although metric generally refers to the decimal-based metric system of weights and measures, software engineers often use the term as simply "measurement." For example, "is there a metric for this process?" See *software metrics*.

Mflops See *megaflops*.

MFM (Modified Frequency Modulation) A magnetic disk encoding method used on most floppy disks and most hard disks under 40MB. It has twice the capacity of the earlier FM method, transfers data at 625 Kbytes per second and uses the ST506 interface. See *hard disk*.

MGA (Monochrome Graphics Adapter) A display adapter that employs Hercules Graphics, combining graphics and text on a monochrome monitor.

MGP (Monochrome Graphics Printer port) A display adapter that employs Hercules Graphics and a parallel printer port on the same expansion board.

MHS (1) (Message Handling Service) A messaging system from Novell that supports multiple operating systems and other messaging protocols. Optional modules support SMTP, SNADS and X.400. It uses the SMF-71 messaging format. Standard MHS runs on a DOS machine attached to the server. Global MHS runs as a NetWare NLM. Under NetWare, MHS runs on top of IPX.

(2) See *messaging system*.

MHz (MegaHertZ) One million cycles per second. It often references a computer's clock rate, the raw measure of internal speed. For example, a 50MHz 486 computer processes data internally (calculates, compares, etc.) twice as fast as a 25MHz 486.

A quartz crystal in the computer's clock circuit generates the heartbeat of the computer, a steady frequency that is converted into digital pulses. See *MIPS*.

MIB (Management Information Base) An SNMP structure that describes the particular device being monitored. See *SNMP*.

mickey A unit of mouse movement typically set at 1/200th of an inch.

MICR (Magnetic Ink Character Recognition) The machine recognition of magnetically-charged characters typically found on bank checks and deposit slips. MICR readers detect the characters and convert them into digital data.

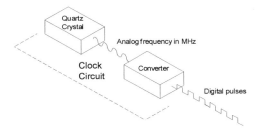

MICR CHARACTERS

micro (1) A microcomputer or personal computer.

(2) One millionth. See *space/time*.

(3) Microscopic or tiny.

Micro Channel Also known as MCA (Micro Channel Architecture), it is an IBM 32-bit bus used in most PS/2s, the RS/6000 series and certain ES/9370 models. MCA boards are not interchangeable with ISA and EISA boards. Installing an MCA board is generally easier than installing an ISA board. MCA boards contain unique ID and are configurable by software, which assists users in avoiding conflicts.

Micro Channel transfers data at 20 MBytes/sec and has modes for increasing speeds to 40 and 80MB. It also has specifications for 64 bits and 160MB transfer. Micro Channel supports up to 15 levels of bus mastering.

micro manager A person who manages personal computer operations within an organization and is responsible for the analysis, selection, installation, training and maintenance of personal computer hardware and software. See *information center* and *MMA*.

micro to mainframe An interconnection of personal computers to mainframes. See *3270 emulator*.

microchip Same as *chip*.

microchip module See *MCM*.

microcircuit A miniaturized, electronic circuit, such as is found on an integrated circuit. See *chip* and *MCM*.

microcode A permanent memory that holds the elementary circuit operations a computer must perform for each instruction in its instruction set. It acts as a translation layer between the instruction and the electronic level of the computer and enables the computer architect to more easily add new types of machine instructions without having to design electronic circuits. See *microprogramming*.

Microcom Protocol See *MNP*.

microcomputer Same as *personal computer*.

microcontroller See *MCU*.

microelectronics The miniaturization of electronic circuits. See *chip*.

microfiche Pronounced "micro-feesh." A 4x6" sheet of film that holds several hundred miniaturized document pages. See *micrographics*.

microfilm A continuous film strip that holds several thousand miniaturized document pages. See *micrographics*.

microfloppy disk A floppy disk encased in a 3.5" wide, rigid plastic shell. Developed by Sony, it has become the medium of choice as it holds more data and is easier to handle than its 5.25" counterpart.

microform In micrographics, a medium that contains microminiaturized images such as microfiche and microfilm.

micrographics The production, handling and use of microfilm and

FICHE   ROLL FILM

microfiche. Images are created by cameras or by COM units that accept computer output directly. The documents are magnified for human viewing by readers, some of which can automatically locate a page using indexing techniques.

Microfiche and microfilm have always been an economical alternative for high-volume data and picture storage. However, optical disks are competing with film-based systems and may become the preferred storage medium.

microimage In micrographics, any photographic image of information that is too small to be read without magnification.

microinstruction A microcode instruction. It is the most elementary computer operation that can take place; for example, moving a bit from one register to another. It takes several microinstructions to carry out one machine instruction.

microjacket In micrographics, two sheets of transparent plastic that are bonded together to create channels into which strips of microfilm are inserted and stored.

microkernel The hardware-dependent component of an operating system that is designed to be more easily portable to multiple platforms. The rest of the operating system interacts with the microkernel in a message-based relationship and does not have to be rewritten. Only the microkernel has to be reprogrammed to the architecture of the new hardware. See *kernel*.

micromainframe A personal computer with mainframe or near mainframe speed.

micromechanics The microminiaturization of mechanical devices (gears, motors, rotors, etc.) using similar photomasking techniques as in chip making.

micromini A personal computer with minicomputer or near minicomputer speed.

micron One millionth of a meter. Approximately 1/25,000 of an inch. The tiny elements that make up a transistor on a chip are measured in microns. For example, the 486 uses 1.0 micron technology, the Pentium .8 micron.

microprocessor A CPU on a single chip. In order to function as a computer, it requires a power supply, clock and memory. First-generation microprocessors were Intel's 8080, Zilog's Z80, Motorola's 6800 and Rockwell's 6502. The first microprocessor was created by Intel.

microprogram Same as *microcode*.

microprogramming Programming microcode.

micropublishing In micrographics, the issuing of new or reformatted information on microfilm for sale or distribution.

microrepublishing In micrographics, the issuing of microfilm that has been previously or is simultaneously published in hardcopy for sale or distribution.

microsecond One millionth of a second. See *space/time*.

Microsoft (Microsoft Corporation, Redmond, WA) The world's largest software company. Microsoft was founded in 1975 by Paul Allen and Bill Gates, two college students who wrote the first BASIC interpreter for the Intel 8080 microprocessor. Although also known for its programming languages and PC applications, Microsoft's outstanding success has come from its DOS and Windows operating systems.

Microsoft Access A DBMS for Windows from Microsoft that directly reads Paradox, dBASE and Btrieve files. Using ODBC, it directly reads Microsoft and SYBASE SQL Server and Oracle data. Access BASIC is its programming language, and "Wizards" ask you questions to create forms, reports and graphs.

Microsoft C A C compiler and development system for DOS and Windows applications from Microsoft. Windows programming requires the Windows Software Development Kit (SDK), which is included.

Version 7.0 includes C++ capability and Version 1.0 of the Microsoft Foundation Class Library (MFC), which provide a base framework of object-oriented code to build an application upon. See *Visual C++*.

Microsoft Office A suite of Windows applications from Microsoft that include Mail, Access, PowerPoint, Word and Excel. The applications have been designed for tighter integration with sharing of common functions such as spell checking and graphing. Objects can be dragged and dropped between applications. It includes MOM, the Microsoft Office Manager, a toolbar utility that launches the applications.

Microsoft Word A full-featured word processing programs for DOS, Windows and Mac from Microsoft. The Windows version, Word for Windows, or WinWord, is a sophisticated program with rudimentary desktop publishing capabilities. The DOS version provides both graphics-based and text-based interfaces for working with a document.

Microsoft Works An integrated software package for PCs and the Macintosh from Microsoft. It provides file management with relational-like capabilities, word processing, spreadsheet, business graphics and communications capabilities in one package.

microspacing Positioning characters for printing by making very small horizontal and vertical movements. Many dot matrix printers and all laser printers have this ability.

MicroStation A full-featured 2-D and 3-D CADD program from Intergraph Corporation, Huntsville, AL, for PCs, Macs and Intergraph, Sun and HP workstations.

MicroVAX A series of entry-level VAXs introduced in 1983 that run under VMS or ULTRIX. Some models use the Q-bus architecture.

microwave An electromagnetic wave that vibrates at 1GHz and above. Microwaves are the transmission frequencies used in communications satellites as well as in line-of-sight systems on earth.

middleware Software that sits between the application and the control program (operating system, network control program and DBMS). It provides a single programming interface for an application to be written to, and the application will run in as many different computer environments as the middleware runs in.

MID file A MIDI sound file. DOS and Windows files use a .MID extension.

MIDI (Musical Instrument Digital Interface) A standard protocol for the interchange of musical information between musical instruments, synthesizers and computers. It defines the codes for a musical event, which includes the start of a note, its pitch, length, volume and musical attributes, such as vibrato. It also defines codes for various button, dial and pedal adjustments used on synthesizers.

MIDI makes an ideal system for storing music on digital media due to its small storage requirement compared with digitizing actual music. Since the advent of General MIDI, a standard for defining MIDI instruments, MIDI will become more widely used for musical backgrounds in multimedia applications.

See *General MIDI, MIDI sequencer, MPU-401, wave table synthesis, FM synthesis* and *sound card*.

▶ *The electronic and encyclopedic versions of this book provide more detail on this subject.*

MIDI Mapper A Windows application that converts MIDI sound sequences (MIDI messages) to conform to a particular MIDI sound card or module. The keyboard map is used to assign values to non-standard keyboard keys. The patch map assigns sounds to an instrument number (see *MIDI patch*). The channel map assigns input channels to output channels.

MIDI sequencer A hardware device or software application that allows for the composition, editing and playback of MIDI sound sequences. Media player applications can play MIDI sound files, but creating and modifying MIDI files requires a sequencer.

midrange computer Same as *minicomputer*, but excludes single-user minicomputer workstations. For example, an IBM AS/400 would be typically called a midrange computer, but a Sun SPARCstation would not.

MIF (1) (Maker Interchange Format) An alternate file format for a FrameMaker document. A MIF file is ASCII text, which can be created in another program and imported into FrameMaker.

(2) (Managment Information File) A DMI file format that describes a hardware or software component used in a PC. It can contain data, code or both. See *DMI*.

mill A very old term for processor (number crunching!).

millimeter One thousandth of a meter, or 1/25th of an inch.

million One thousand times one thousand or 10^6. See *mega* and *microsecond*.

millisecond One thousandth of a second. See *space/time*.

MIMD (Multiple Instruction stream Multiple Data stream) A computer architecture that uses multiple processors, each processing its own set of instructions simultaneously and independently of the others. Contrast with *SIMD*.

MIME (Multipurpose Internet Mail Extensions) Extensions to the SMTP format that allow it to carry multiple types of data (binary, audio, video, etc.).

mini See *minicomputer*.

minicomputer A medium-scale computer that functions as a single workstation, or as a multiuser system with up to several hundred terminals. A minicomputer system costs roughly from $20,000 to $250,000.

In 1959, Digital launched the minicomputer industry with its PDP-1. Soon after, Data General and HP introduced minis, and eventually Wang, Tandem, Datapoint and Prime joined them. IBM has introduced several minicomputer series, including the System/36, System/38 and AS/400.

Today, the term "midrange" has become popular for medium-sized computer. High-end microcomputers and low-end mainframes overlap in minicomputer price and performance.

MiniDisc An optical disk drive from Sony that uses a 2.5" platter that holds 140MB. Used as a removable disk drive in portable machines, or potentially, as a floppy disk replacement, the drive handles three types of disks. An MD-ROM is read-only like a CD-ROM. An MD-Data disk is rewritable, and a combination disk allows for permanent and updatable information.

minifloppy The formal name for the ubiquitous floppy disk that is

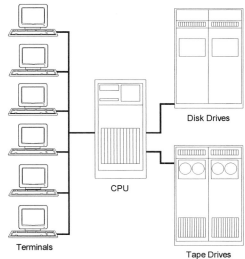

Terminals   CPU   Disk Drives   Tape Drives

MINICOMPUTER

encased in a 5.25" wide, stiff plastic jacket.

minimize In graphical environments, to reduce a window to an icon.

mini-supercomputer A computer that is 25% to 100% as fast as a supercomputer, but costs less. Note: A mini-supercomputer is not the same as a supermini.

MINIX A version of UNIX for the PC, Mac, Amiga and Atari ST developed by Andrew Tannenbaum and published by Prentice-Hall. It comes with complete source code.

minor key A secondary key used to identify a record. For example, if transactions are sorted by account number and date, account number is the major key and date is the minor key.

MIPS (1) (Million Instructions Per Second) The execution speed of a computer. High-speed personal computers and workstations perform at 100 MIPS and higher. MIPS ratings are not an exact science. Some are best-case mixes while others are averages. In addition, it takes more instructions in one machine to do the same in another (RISC vs CISC, mainframe vs micro).
▶ *The electronic and encyclopedic versions of this book provide more detail on this subject.*

(2) (MIPS Computer Systems, Inc., Sunnyvale, CA.) A microcomputer and minicomputer manufacturer that was acquired by Silicon Graphics, Inc.

mirroring See *disk mirroring.*

MIS (1) (Management Information System) An information system that integrates data from all the departments it serves and provides operations and management with the information they require.

It was "the" buzzword of the mid to late 1970s, when online systems were implemented in all large organizations. See *DSS.*

(2) (Management Information Services) See *Information Systems.*

mission critical Vital to the operation of an organization. In the past, mission critical information systems were implemented on mainframes and minicomputers. Increasingly, they are being designed for and installed on personal computer networks. See *client/server.*

mixed object Same as *compound document.*

ML A symbolic programming language developed in the 1970s at the University of Edinburgh, Scotland. Although similar to LISP, its commands and structures are like Pascal.

MM (1) See *Multiple Master.*

(2) (mm) (MilliMeter) One thousandth of a meter.

MMA (Microcomputer Manager's Association, Inc.) A membership organization with chapters throughout the U.S. devoted to educating personnel responsible for personal computers. Provides seminars, conferences, trade show events, job bank and newsletters. Address: P.O.Box 4615, Warren, NJ, 908/580-9091.

MMF See *multimode fiber.*

MMU (Memory Management Unit) A virtual memory circuit that translates logical addresses into physical addresses.

mnemonic Pronounced "nuh-monic." Means memory aid. A name assigned to a machine function. For example, in DOS, COM1 is the mnemonic assigned to serial port #1. Programming languages are almost entirely mnemonics.

MNP (Microcom Networking Protocol) A family of communications protocols from Microcom, Inc., Norwood, MA, that have become de facto standards for error correction (classes 2 though 4) and data compression (class 5).

MO See *magneto-optic*.

mod See *modulo*.

modal Mode oriented. A modal operation switches from one mode to another. Contrast with *non-modal*.

modal bandwidth The capacity of an optical fiber measured in MHz-km (megahertz over one kilometer). One MHz-km equals approximately .7 to .8 Mbps. Thus, a 100 MHz-km fiber can carry about 70 to 80 Mbps of data.

modal dispersion A signal distortion in an optical fiber in which the light pulses spread out, and the receiving device cannot detect the beginnings and ends of pulses.

MO:DCA (Mixed Object:Document Content Architecure) An IBM compound document format for text and graphics elements in a document. It supports Revisable Documents, which are editable like revisable-form DCA, Presentation Documents, which provide specific output formatting similar to DCA final-form, and Resource Documents, which hold control information such as fonts.
    Formats for specific objects are specified in OCAs (Object Content Architectures): PTOCA for Presentation and Text that has been formatted for output, GOCA for vector Graphics objects, IOCA for bitmapped Images and FOCA for Fonts.

mode An operational state that a system has been switched to. It implies at least two possible conditions. There are countless modes for hardware and software. See *Real Mode, Protected Mode, burst mode, insert mode, supervisor state* and *program state*.

model (1) A style or type of hardware device.

(2) A mathematical representation of a device or process used for analysis and planning. See *data model, data administration, financial planning system* and *scientific applications*.

model-based expert system An expert system based on fundamental knowledge of the design and function of an object. Such systems are used to diagnose equipment problems, for example. Contrast with *rule-based expert system*.

modeling Simulating a condition or activity by performing a set of equations on a set of data. See *data modeling, data administration, financial planning system* and *scientific applications*.

modem (MOdulator-DEModulator) A device that adapts a terminal or computer to a telephone line. It converts the computer's digital pulses into audio frequencies (analog) for the telephone system and converts the frequencies back into pulses at the receiving side. The modem also dials the line, answers the call and controls transmission speed, which ranges from 300 to 14,400 bps and higher.
▶ *The electronic and encyclopedic versions of this book provide more detail on this subject.*

modem eliminator A device that allows two close computers to be connected without modems. For personal computers, it is the same as a null modem cable. In synchronous systems, it provides active intelligence for synchronization.

modem server See *communications server*.

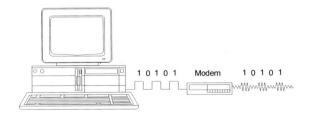

1 0 1 0 1   Modem   1 0 1 0 1

MODEM

modify structure A database command that changes a file's structure. Field lengths and field names can be changed, and fields can be added or deleted. It may convert the old data file into the new structure without data loss, unless fields have been truncated or deleted.

Modula-2 (MODUlar LAnguage-2) An enhanced version of Pascal introduced in 1979 by Swiss professor Nicklaus Wirth, creator of Pascal. It supports separate compilation of modules.

modular programming Breaking down the design of a program into individual components (modules) that can be programmed and tested independently. It is a requirement for effective development and maintenance of large programs and projects.

Modules

Main Loop

MODULAR PROGRAMMING

Modular Windows A subset of Windows for TV-based consumer electronics. It does not use Program Manager, scroll bars and overlapping windows. The application is the window.

modulate To vary a carrier wave. Modulation blends a data signal (text, voice, etc.) into a carrier for transmission over a network. Major methods are AM (amplitude modulation) - modulate the height of the carrier wave, FM (frequency modulation) - modulate the frequency of the wave, and PM (phase modulation) - modulate the polarity of the wave. Contrast with *demodulate*. See *carrier*.

module A self-contained hardware or software component that interacts with a larger system. Hardware modules are often made to plug into a main system. Program modules are designed to handle a specific task within a larger program.

modulo A mathematical operation (modulus arithmetic) in which the result is the remainder of the division. For example, 20 MOD 3 results in 2 (20/3 = 6 with a remainder of 2.

moire Pronounced "mor-ray." In computer graphics, a visible distortion. It results from a variety of conditions; for example, when scanning halftones at a resolution not consistent with the printed resolution or when superimposing curved patterns on one another. Internal monitor misalignment can also be a cause.

molecular beam epitaxy A technique that "grows" atomic-sized layers on a chip rather than creating layers by diffusion.

monadic One. A single item or operation that deals with one item or operand.

monitor (1) A display screen used to present output from a computer, camera, VCR or other video generator. A monitor's clarity is based on video bandwidth, dot pitch, refresh rate and convergence. See *analog monitor, digital monitor* and *interlaced*.

(2) Software that provides utility and control functions such as setting communications parameters. It typically resides in a ROM chip and contains startup and diagnostic routines.

(3) Software that monitors the progress of activities within a computer system.

(4) A device that gathers performance statistics of a running system via direct attachment to the CPU's circuit boards.

monochrome Also called "mono." The display of one foreground color and one background color; for example, black on white, white on black and green on black.

Non-color laptop PCs commonly use "monochrome VGA" screens, which are actually gray-scale screens. This is like black and white TV and is not the same as the monochrome screens widely used over the years on mini and mainframe terminals and PCs using the MDA adapter, which display a solid color and no shades in between.

monolithic integrated circuit The common form of chip design, in which the base material (substrate) contains the pathways as well as the active elements that take part in its operation.

monophonic Sound reproduction using a single channel. Contrast with *stereophonic.*

monospacing Uniform horizontal spacing, such as 10 characters per inch. Contrast with *proportional spacing.*

Monte Carlo method A technique that provides approximate solutions to problems expressed mathematically. Using random numbers and trial and error, it repeatedly calculates the equations to arrive at a solution.

MORE II A Macintosh desktop presentation program and outline processor from Symantec Corporation, Cupertino, CA, that includes writing, spell checking, presentation-quality text and graphics and 35mm slide output.

morphing Transforming one image into another; for example, a car into a tiger. From metamorphosis. See *tweening.*

morray See *moire.*

Morse code A character code represented by dots and dashes, developed by Samuel Morse in the mid-19th century. A dot can be a voltage, carrier wave or light beam of one duration, while a dash is a longer duration. It was used to send telegraph messages before the telephone and was used in World War II for signalling by light.

MOS (Metal Oxide Semiconductor) Pronounced "moss." One of two major categories of chip design (the other is bipolar). It derives its name from its use of metal, oxide and semiconductor layers. There are several varieties of MOS technologies, including PMOS, NMOS and CMOS.

Mosaic An Internet utility that lets you browse through the Worldwide Web.

MOSFET (Metal Oxide Semiconductor Field Effect Transistor) A common type of transistor fabricated as a discrete component or into MOS integrated circuits.

most significant digit The leftmost, non-zero digit in a number. It is the digit with the greatest value in the number.

motherboard The main printed circuit board in an electronic device, which contains sockets that accept additional boards. In a personal computer, the motherboard contains the bus, CPU and coprocessor sockets, memory sockets, keyboard controller and supporting chips.

Chips that control the video display, serial and parallel ports, mouse and disk drives may or may not be present on the motherboard. If not, they are independent controllers that are plugged into an expansion slot on the motherboard.

Motif The graphical user interface endorsed by the Open Software Foundation. It has become the standard user interface in the UNIX world. See *OSF.*

motion path In computer graphics, the path to be followed by an animated object.

Motorola (Motorola, Inc., Schaumburg, IL) A leading manufacturer of semiconductor devices founded in Chicago in 1928 by Paul V. Galvin as the Galvin Manufacturing Corporation. Its first product allowed radios to operate from household current instead of batteries. Motorola is widely known for its 680x0 and PowerPC chip families and communications products.

mount To cause a file on a remote workstation or server to be available for access locally. For example, in NFS (Network File System), a server maintains a list of its directories that are available to clients. When a client mounts a directory on the server, that directory and its subdirectories become part of the client's directory hierarchy. See *automounting*.

mouse A puck-like object used as a pointing and drawing device. As it is rolled across the desktop, the screen cursor (pointer) moves correspondingly.

mouse pad A fabric-covered rubber pad roughly 9" square that provides a smooth surface for rolling a mouse.

mouse port A socket in the computer into which a mouse is plugged.

MOV (1) (Metal Oxide Varistor) A discrete electronic component used in surge suppresssors that diverts excessive voltage to the ground and/or neutral lines.

(2) An assembly language instruction that moves (copies) data from one location to another.

move (1) In programming, to copy data from one place in memory to another. At the end of the move, source and destination data are identical.

(2) In word processing and graphics, to relocate text and images to another part of the document or drawing.

MPC (Multimedia PC) Requirements for a multimedia PC as specified by the Multimedia PC Marketing Council, a subsidiary of the Software Publishers Association. Address: 1730 M St., N.W., Washington, DC 20036, 202/331-0494. Vendors certified by the Multimedia PC Marketing Council may display the MPC logos on their products.

The minimum requirements for an MPC II system are a 25MHz 486SX, 4MB RAM, 160MB hard disk, VGA adapter that supports 64K colors at 640x480, 16-bit sound card with MIDI playback and a multisession-capable, double-spin CD-ROM drive that supports the CD-ROM XA specification (most modern CD-ROM drives meet these specs).

MPE (MultiProgramming Executive) A multitasking operating system that runs on the HP 3000 series.

MPEG (Moving Pictures Experts Group) An ISO/ITU-TSS standard for compressing full-motion video. MPEG I provides a standard image of 352x240, 30 fps, 15-bit color and CD-quality sound. MPEG II is an evolving standard for full broadcast-quality video. MPEG I is used in Video CD. See *JPEG*.

MPP (Massively Parallel Processor) See *massively parallel*.

MPR II The Swedish government standard for maximum video terminal radiation. The earlier MPR I is less stringent. See *TCO*.

MPU (MicroProcessor Unit) Same as *microprocessor*.

MPU-401 A MIDI standard from Roland Corporation that has become the de facto interface for connecting a personal computer to a MIDI device.

M-R See *magneto-resistance*.

MRCI (Microsoft Realtime Compression Interface) The programming interface for Microsoft's DoubleSpace technology used in DOS 6.

ms (1) (MilliSecond) See *space/time*.

(2) (MS) See *Microsoft*.

MSa/s
(MegaSAmples per Second) A measurement of sampling rate in millions of samples per second.

MSCDEX (MicroSoft CD-ROM EXtensions) See *CD-ROM Extensions.*

MSD (MicroSoft Diagnostics) A utility that accompanies Windows 3.1 and DOS 6 that reports on the internal configuration of the PC. A variety of information on disks, video, drivers, IRQs and port addresses is provided.

MS-DOS (MicroSoft-Disk Operating System) A single user operating system for PCs from Microsoft. It is functionaly identical to IBM's PC-DOS version, except that starting with DOS 6, MS-DOS and PC-DOS each provide different sets of auxiliary utility programs. Both MS-DOS and PC-DOS are called DOS.

MSI (Medium Scale Integration) Between 100 and 3,000 transistors on a chip. See *SSI, LSI, VLSI* and *ULSI.*

MS-Net (MicroSoft Network) Microsoft's version of PC-Network introduced in 1985.

MSP (1) A Microsoft Paint graphics file format.

(2) (Multiprocessing Server Pack) A utility that enables LAN Manager to utilize a computer's multiprocessing capabilities.

(3) An operating system used in Fujitsu IBM-compatible mainframes.

MS-Windows (MicroSoft Windows) See *Windows.*

MTA (Message Transfer Agent) The store and forward part of a messaging system. See *messaging system.*

MTBF (Mean Time Between Failure) The average time a component works without failure. It is the number of failures divided by the hours under observation.

MTS (Modular TV System) The stereo channel added to the NTSC standard, which includes the SAP audio channel for special use.

MTTR (Mean Time To Repair) The average time it takes to repair a failed component.

MUG (Macintosh User Group) There are many Mac user groups throughout the world. One organization that disseminates press releases and product ads to over 1,300 MUGs is Pawtuckaway Graphics, 53 Lakeview Dr., Raymond, NH 03077, 603/895-6227.

MULTIBUS An advanced bus architecture from Intel used in industrial, military and aerospace applications. It includes message passing, auto configuration and software interrupts. MULTIBUS I is 16-bits; MULTIBUS II is 32-bits.

multicasting The ability to transmit a message to multiple recipients at the same time. Multicasting is used in teleconferencing as well as by communications protocols that need to broadcast a request to all nodes on the network.

multichip module See *MCM.*

multicomputer A computer made up of several computers. The term generally refers to an architecture in which each processor has its own memory rather than multiple processors with a shared memory. See *parallel computing.*

multidrop line See *multipoint line.*

MultiFinder See *Finder.*

multifrequency monitor A monitor that adjusts to all frequencies within a range (multiscan) or to a set of specific frequencies, such as VGA and Super VGA.

multilaunch To open the same application based in a server simultaneously from two or more clients.

multiline A cable, channel or bus that contains two or more transmission paths (wires or optical fibers).

multimastering See *bus mastering*.

MultiMate An early PC word processing program that was similar to the Wang word processors of the 1970s.

multimedia Disseminating information in more than one form. Includes the use of text, audio, graphics, animated graphics and full-motion video. See *MPC*.

Multimedia Extensions Windows routines that support audio recording and playback, animation playback, joysticks, MIDI, the MCI interface for CD-ROM, videodiscs, videotapes, etc., and the RIFF file format. See *MPC*.

multimedia upgrade kit The hardware and software necessary to turn a standard PC into a multimedia PC (MPC). The package includes a CD-ROM drive, sound card and speakers. Some combination of bundled software and/or CD-ROMs may also be included. The advantage of the kit is that the CD-ROM controller card and sound card have been preset to avoid potential conflicts with each other, and the correct cables are included.

multimode fiber An optical fiber with a core diameter of from 50 to 100 microns. It is the most commonly used optical fiber. Light can enter the core at different angles, making it easier to connect the light source. However, light rays bounce around within the core causing some distortion and providing less bandwidth than single-mode fiber. Contrast with *single-mode fiber*.

MultiPlan An early spreadsheet for CP/M machines and PCs from Microsoft. It was one of the first spreadsheets.

Multiple Master A font technology from Adobe Systems, Mountain View, CA, that allows a typeface to be generated in different styles, from condensed to expanded and from light to heavy.

multiple zone recording See *ZBR*.

multiplexing Transmitting multiple signals over a single communications line or computer channel. The two common multiplexing techniques are FDM, which separates signals by modulating the data onto different carrier frequencies, and TDM, which separates signals by interleaving bits one after the other. See *inverse multiplexing*.

multiplexor In communications, a device that merges several low-speed transmissions into one high-speed transmission and vice versa.

multiplexor channel A computer channel that transfers data between the CPU and several low-speed peripherals (terminals, printers, etc.) simultaneously. It may have an optional burst mode that allows a high-speed transfer to only one peripheral at a time.

multiplier-accumulator A general-purpose floating point processor that multiplies and accumulates the results of the multiplication. Newer versions also perform division and square roots.

multipoint line In communications, a single line that interconnects three or more devices.

multiported memory A type of memory that provides more than one access path to its contents. It allows the same bank of memory to be read and written simultaneously. See *video RAM*.

multiprocessing Simultaneous processing with two or more processors in one computer, or two or more computers processing together. When two or more computers are used, they are tied together with a high-speed channel and share the general workload between them. If one fails, the other takes over.

It is also accomplished in special-purpose computers, such as array processors, which provide concurrent processing on sets of data. Although computers are built with various overlapping features, such as executing instructions while inputting and outputting data, multiprocessing refers specifically to concurrent instruction executions. See *parallel processing, bus mastering* and *fault tolerant.*

multiprogramming Same as *multitasking.*

multiscan monitor A monitor that adjusts to all frequencies within a range. See *multifrequency monitor.*

multisession See *Photo CD.*

MultiSync monitor A family of multiscan monitors from NEC Technologies, Inc. NEC popularized the multiscan monitor.

multitasking The running of two or more programs in one computer at the same time. It is controlled by the operating system. The number of programs that can be effectively multitasked depends on the type of multitasking performed (premtive vs cooperative), CPU speed and memory and disk capacity.

Programs can be run simultaneously in the computer because of the differences between I/O and processing speed. While one program is waiting for input, instructions in another can be executed. During the milliseconds one program waits for data to be read from a disk, millions of instructions in another program can be executed. In interactive programs, thousands of instructions can be executed between each keystroke on the keyboard.

In large computers, multiple I/O channels also allow for simultaneous I/O operations to take place. Multiple streams of data are being read and written at the exact same time.

In the days of mainframes only, multitasking was called *multiprogramming,* and multitasking meant *multithreading.*

multithreading Multitasking within a single program. It is used to process multiple transactions or messages concurrently. It is also required for creating synchronized audio and video applications. Multithreading functions are often written in *reentrant code.*

multi-timbral The ability to play multiple instrument sounds (patches) simultaneously. See *MIDI patch* and *timbre.*

multiuser A computer shared by two or more users.

multiuser DOS (1) A DOS-compatible operating system that runs multiple terminals from a single PC.

(2) (Multiuser DOS) A multiuser DOS-compatible operating system from Novell that runs multiple terminals from a single 386 or higher PC. Supersedes Concurrent DOS.

multivariate The use of multiple variables in a forecasting model.

MUMPS An advanced, high-level programming language and integrated database used for business applications. It has extensive string handling making it suitable for databases with vast amounts of free text.

MUMPS has unique features including the ability to store both data and program statements in its database. In addition, formulas written in a program can be stored and used by other programs. Developed in 1966 at Massachusetts General Hospital (Mass. Utility MultiProgramming System), it has been used extensively in health-care.

The following example converts Fahrenheit to Celsius:

```
READ "Enter Fahrenheit ",FAHR
SET CENT=(FAHR-32)*5/9
WRITE "Celsius is", CENT
```

The M Technology Association (formerly MUMPS Users Group) is an organization that supports the MUMPS community through training, meetings and distribution of publications and software. Address: 1738 Elton Rd., Suite 205, Silver Spring, MD 20903, 301/431-4070.

music CD Generally refers to an audio CD, otherwise known as "Red Book audio." However, the term could refer to a CD-ROM that contains sound files, such as WAV and MID files.

MUX (MUltipleXor) See *multiplexor*.

MVGA (Monochrome VGA) The type of display often found on a non-color laptop. It should more accurately be called "gray scale VGA," since monochrome means two colors; for example, black and white and no shades in between.

MVIP (MultiVendor Integration Protocol) A voice bus and switching protocol for PCs originated by a number of companies, including Natural Microsystems of Natick, MA, its major supporter. It provides a second communications bus within the PC that is used to multiplex up to 256 full-duplex voice channels from one voice card to another.

MVP (Multimedia Video Processor) A high-speed DSP chip from TI introduced in 1994. Formally the TMS320C80, it combines RISC technology with the functionality of four DSPs on one chip.

MVS (Multiple Virtual Storage) Introduced in 1974, the primary operating system used on IBM mainframes (the others are VM and DOS/VSE). MVS is a batch processing-oriented operating system that manages large amounts of memory and disk space. Online operations are provided with CICS, TSO and other system software.

MVS/XA (MVS/eXtended Architecture) manages the enhancements, including 2GB of virtual memory, introduced in 1981 with IBM's 370/XA architecture.

MVS/ESA (MVS/Enterprise Systems Architecture) manages the enhancements made to large scale mainframes, including 16TB of virtual memory, introduced in 1988 with IBM's ESA/370 architecture. MVS/ESA runs on all models of the System/390 ES/9000 product line introduced in 1990.

MVS/ESA See *MVS*.

MVS/XA See *MVS*.

NAK (Negative AcKnowledgement) A communications code used to indicate that a message was not received, or that a terminal does not wish to transmit. Contrast with *ACK*.

Named Pipes An IPC facility in LAN Manager that allows data to be exchanged from one application to another either over a network or running within the same computer. The use of the term pipes for interprocess communication was coined in UNIX.

naming service Software that converts a name into a physical address on a network, providing logical to physical conversion. Names can be user names, computers, printers, services or files. The transmitting station sends a name to the server containing the naming service software, which sends back the actual address of the user or resource.

It serves as a Yellow Pages for the network, which is precisely what Sun's NIS system was originally called. Novell's naming service for NetWare 4.0 is called NDS (NetWare Directory Service). In AppleTalk, the naming service is embedded within the protocol. See *directory service*.

NAND (Not AND) A Boolean logic operation that is true if any of two inputs are false. For example, 0-0, 0-1 and 1-0 all yield 1. Only 1-1 yields 0. Two-input NAND gates are often used as the sole logic element on gate array chips, because all Boolean operations can be created from NAND gates.

nanometer One billionth of a meter.

nanosecond One billionth of a second. Used to measure the speed of logic and memory chips, a nanosecond can be visualized by converting it to distance. In one nanosecond, electricity travels about six inches in a wire.

Even at 186,000 miles per second, electricity is never fast enough for the hardware designer who worries over a few inches of circuit path. The slightest delay is multiplied millions of times, since millions of pulses are sent through a wire in a single second. See *space/time*.

nanotechnology A future science that builds devices at the atomic and molecular level. For example, a bit might be represented by only one atom some time in the future. Nanotechnology could be used to build anything, not just computers and communications devices.

NAPLPS (North American Presentation-Level Protocol Syntax) An ANSI-standard protocol for videotex and teletext. It compresses data for transmission over narrow-bandwidth lines and requires decompression on the receiving end. PRODIGY uses this format for transmitting and displaying some of its graphics.

narrowband In communications, a voice grade transmission of 2,400 bps or less, or a sub-voice grade transmission from 50 to 150 bps.

NAS (Network Application Support) Digital's implementation of open systems, which provides standards-based software that allows a variety of workstations (VMS, ULTRIX, Sun, DOS, Windows, OS/2, Mac, etc.) to interface via VAX and ULTRIX servers.

NASI (1) (NetWare Asynchronous System Interface) A NetWare protocol used to interface modems onto a Novell network. It was derived from the NCSI protocol.

(2) (National Association of Systems Integrators) An organization of more than 5,000 members founded in 1991, dedicated to exchanging up-to-date information on members' products and services. Its annual Computer Suppliers & Services Directory, in print and on disk, is organized by zipcode. Address: 412 High Plain Street, Unit #1, Walpole, MA 02081, 508/668-8900.

native language Same as *machine language*. See *native mode*.

native mode (1) The normal running mode of a computer, executing programs from its built-in instruction set. Contrast with *emulation mode*.

(2) The highest performance state of a computer, such as a 486 or Pentium running in Protected Mode.

NATURAL A fourth-generation language from Software AG, Reston, VA, that runs on a variety of computers from micro to mainframe.

natural language English, Spanish, French, German, Japanese, Russian, etc.

natural language query A query expressed by typing English, French or any other spoken language in a normal manner. For example, "how many sales reps sold more than a million dollars in any eastern state in January?" In order to allow for spoken queries, both a voice recognition system and natural language query software are required.

natural language recognition Same as *voice recognition*.

NAU (1) (Network Access Unit) An interface card that adapts a computer to a local area network.

(2) (Network Addressable Unit) An SNA component that can be referenced by name and address, which includes the SSCP, LU and PU.

NB card (NuBus card) See *NuBus*.

NC See *numerical control*.

NCB (Network Control Block) A packet structure used by the NetBIOS communications protocol.

NCF (National Cristina Foundation) A not-for-profit organization, founded by Bruce McMahan and named after his daughter, that channels used and surplus computers to the disadvantaged. Address: 42 Hillcrest Dr., Pelham Manor, NY 10803, 800/CRISTINA.

NCGA (National Computer Graphics Association) An organization dedicated to developing and promoting the computer graphics industry. It maintains a clearinghouse for industry information and strives to encourage communication among computer graphics users, consultants, educators and vendors. Address: 2722 Merrilee Dr., Suite 200, Fairfax, VA 22031, 800/225-NCGA.

NCP (1) (NetWare Core Protocol) Application layer protocols in the NetWare network operating system. It is the internal NetWare language used to communicate between client and server and provides functions such as opening, closing, reading and writing files and obtaining access to the naming service databases (bindery and NDS).

(2) (Not Copy Protected) Software that can be easily copied.

NCR See *AT&T GIS*.

NCR paper (No Carbon Required paper) A multiple-part paper form that does not use carbon paper. The ink is adhered to the reverse side of the previous sheet.

NCSC (National Computer Security Center) The arm of the U.S. National Security Agency that defines criteria for trusted computer products. Following are the Trusted Computer Systems Evaluation Criteria (TCSEC), DOD Standard 5200.28, also known as the Orange Book, and the European equivalent. The Red Book is the Orange Book counterpart for networks.

Level D is a non-secure system. Level C provides discretionary access control (DAC). The owner of the data can determine who has access to it. Levels B and A provide mandatory access control (MAC). Access is based on standard DOD clearances. Each data structure contains a sensitivity level, such as top secret, secret and unclassified, and is available only to users with that level of clearance.

C1   Requires user log-on, but allows group ID.
C2   Requires individual user log-on with password and an audit mechanism.
B1   DOD clearance levels.
B2   Guarantees path between user and the security system. Provides assurances
      that system can be tested and clearances cannot be downgraded.
B3   System is characterized by a mathematical model that must be viable.
A1   System is characterized by a mathematical model that can be proven.
      Highest security. Used in military computers.

NCSI (Network Communications Services Interface) Also called "nixie," it is a protocol used to handle serial port communications on a network. NCSI applications talk to the NCSI driver rather than directly to the COM port, which allows redirection of the data to a communications server on the network. See *NASI*.

n-dimensional Some number of dimensions.

NDIS (Network Driver Interface Specification) A network driver interface from Microsoft. See *network driver interface*.

NDS (NetWare Directory Service) A global naming service in NetWare 4.0 based on X.500 for compatibility with other public directories. The NDS Directory maintains information about all the resources in the network, including users, groups, servers, volumes and printers. NDS replaces the bindery file used in previous versions of NetWare and is backward compatible with it.

NE (Not Equal to) See *relational operator*.

near pointer In an x86 segmented address, a memory address within a single segment (the offset). Contrast with *far pointer*.

negative logic The use of high voltage for a 0 bit and low voltage for a 1 bit. Contrast with *positive logic*.

nematic The stage between a crystal and a liquid that has a threadlike nature; for example, a liquid crystal.

nemonic See *mnemonic*.

neper The unit of measurement based on Napierian logarithms that represents the ratio between two values, such as current or voltage.

nerd A person typically thought of as dull socially. Nerds often like technical work and are generally introspective. Contrast with *hacker*, a technical person that may or may not be a nerd.

nesting In programming, the positioning of a loop within a loop. The number of loops that can be nested may be limited by the programming language. See *loop*.

NetBEUI (NetBIOS Extended User Interface) Pronounced "net-booey," it is an enhanced version of the NetBIOS protocol used in various network operating systems, such as LAN Manager, LAN Server, Windows for Workgroups and Windows

NT. It adds additional functions and features to NetBIOS and communicates to the network adapter via NDIS.

NetBIOS A commonly-used network protocol for PC local area networks. It provides printer and file redirection. For example, if drive J: were a hard disk on a network server, each time J: was referenced in a client PC, NetBIOS would intercept the call and redirect it to the network. NetBIOS operates at the session layer of the OSI model. There is no routing layer in NetBIOS and no inherent internetworking capability.

netbooey See *NetBEUI*.

netiquette (NETwork etIQUETTE) Proper manners when using an online service or BBS. Emily Post may not have told you to curtail your cussing via modem, but netiquette has been established to remind you that profanity is not in good form over the network. Using UPPER CASE TO MAKE A POINT all the time and interjecting emoticons throughout a message is also not good netiquette. See *flame*.

NetNews See *USENET*.

NetView IBM SNA network management software that provides centralized monitoring and control for SNA, non-SNA and non-IBM devices. NetView/PC interconnects NetView with Token Ring LANs, Rolm CBXs and non-IBM modems, while maintaining control in the host.

NetWare A family of network operating systems from Novell that support DOS, OS/2, Mac and UNIX clients and various LAN access methods including Ethernet, Token Ring and ARCNET. NetWare is the most widely-used LAN control program.

Personal NetWare is a peer-to-peer network operating system, which allows any client workstation to be a server. All other versions use stand-alone servers. NetWare 3.x, runs on 386s and higher CPUs and supports up to 250 concurrent users. NetWare 4.0 supports up to 1,000 users. See *IPX*, *SPX* and *MHS*.

▶ *The electronic and encyclopedic versions of this book provide more detail on this subject.*

NetWare NFS Software from Novell that implements the NFS distributed file system on NetWare 3.11 servers. It allows UNIX and other NFS client machines to access files on the NetWare server. See *LAN Workplace* and *UnixWare*.

NetWire Novell's BBS on CompuServe, which provides technical support for its NetWare products.

network (1) An arrangement of objects that are interconnected. See *LAN* and *network database*.

(2) In communications, the transmission channels interconnecting all client and server stations as well as all supporting hardware and software.

network accounting The reporting of network usage. It gathers details about user activity including the number of logons and resources used (disk accesses and space used, CPU time, etc.).

network adapter A printed circuit board that plugs into a client machine (personal computer or workstation) or server and controls the exchange of data over a network. It performs the electronic functions of the access method, or data link protocol, such as Ethernet, Token Ring and LocalTalk. The twisted pair, coax or fiber optic transmission medium interconnects all adapters in the network.

Network adapters are also called *NICs*, for network interface cards.

network administrator A person who manages a communications network and is responsible for its efficient operation. Responsibilities include network security, installing new applications, distributing software upgrades, monitoring daily activity, enforcing licensing agreements, developing a storage management program and providing for routine backups.

network analyzer Software only or a combination of hardware and software that monitors traffic on a network. It can also read unencrypted text transmitted over the network.

THE NETWORK ANALYZER
(Courtesy The MIT Museum)
Used for a different kind of network, this high-tech machine of the 1930s simulated electrical power grids.

network architecture (1) The design of a communications system, which includes the hardware, software, access methods and protocols used. It also defines the method of control: whether computers can act independently or are controlled by other computers monitoring the network. It determines future flexibility and connectability to foreign networks.

(2) The access method in a LAN, such as Ethernet, Token Ring and LocalTalk.

network card See *network adapter*.

network control program Software that manages the traffic between terminals and the host mini or mainframe. It resides in the communications controller or front end processor. In a personal computer LAN, it is called a *network operating system* and resides in the server and manages requests from the workstations. IBM's SNA network control program is called *NCP*.

network database (1) A database that runs in a network. It implies that the DBMS was designed with a client/server architecture.

(2) A database that holds addresses of other users in the network.

(3) A database organization method that allows for data relationships in a net-like form. A single data element can point to multiple data elements and can itself be pointed to by other data elements. Contrast with *relational database*.

network driver Software that performs the data link protocol in a network and activates the network adapter.

network driver interface A software interface between the transport protocol and the data link protocol (network driver). The interface provides a protocol manager that accepts requests from the transport layer and activates the network adapter. Network adapters with compliant network drivers can be freely interchanged. In PC LANs, the two primary network driver interfaces are Novell's ODI and Microsoft's NDIS. Novell provides an ODI interface utility that allows NDIS and ODI protocols to work in the same computer.

network layer Internetworking services provided by the network as defined by layer 3 of the OSI model. See *OSI model*.

network management Monitoring an active communications network in order to diagnose problems and gather statistics for administration and fine tuning. Examples of network management products are IBM's NetView, HP's OpenView, Sun's SunNet Manager and Novell's NMS. Examples of network management protocols are SNMP, CMIP and DME.

network manager See *network administrator*.

network modem A modem shared by all users in a network. See *ACS*.

network operating system A multiuser operating system that manages network resources. It manages multiple requests (inputs) concurrently and provides the security necessary in a multiuser environment. It may be a completely self-contained operating system, such as NetWare, or it may require an existing operating system in order to function (LAN Manager requires OS/2; LANtastic requires DOS, etc.).

A portion of the network operating system, or NOS, resides in each client machine and each server. It handles requests by clients for data and applications from the server as well as input and output to shared network devices, such as printers, faxes and modems.

▶ *The electronic and encyclopedic versions of this book provide more detail on this subject.*

network protocol A communications protocol used by the network. There are many layers of network protocols. See *OSI model*.

network ready Software designed to run in a network. It implies that multiple users can share databases without conflict.

network security The authorization of access to files and directories in a network. Users are assigned an ID number and password that allows them access to information and programs within their authority. Network security is controlled by the network administrator.

network server See *file server*.

neural network A modeling technique based on the observed behavior of biological neurons and used to mimic the performance of a system. It consists of a set of elements that start out connected in a random pattern, and, based upon operational feedback, are molded into the pattern required to generate the required results. It is used in applications such as robotics, diagnosing, forecasting, image processing and pattern recognition.

newline An end-of-line code. See *CR/LF*.

new media See *digital convergence*.

NeWS (Network Extensible Windowing Support) A networked windowing system (similar to X Windows) from SunSoft that renders PostScript fonts on screen the way they print on a PostScript printer.

news and weather See *online services*.

Newton An artificial intelligence technology from Apple for use in PDAs and other hand-held and desktop appliances. See *MessagePad*.

NewWave A PC operating environment from HP that runs between DOS and Windows. It integrates data and activates tasks within the system. Its object-management facility allows data from different applications to be merged to create a compound document. Hot links automatically update the document if data in one of the source files is updated.

NeXT (NeXT, Inc., Redwood City, CA) Founded in 1985 by Steven Jobs, co-founder of Apple, NeXT created a family of high-resolution, UNIX-based workstations running its NeXTstep environment. The first machine was introduced in 1988, but hardware was discontinued in 1993. NeXT is now a software-only company specializing in NeXTstep for the x86 platform.

NeXTstep A UNIX-based, object-oriented development environment from NeXT Computer, Redwood City, CA. It runs on NeXT computers and 386s and up providing an advanced, integrated environment for creating applications with a graphical user interface. Insiginia Solution's SoftPC allows DOS and Windows applications to run on a NeXTStep/x86 machine.

NFS (Network File System) A distributed file system from SunSoft that allows data to be shared across a network regardless of machine, operating system, network architecture or protocol. This de facto UNIX standard lets remote files appear as if they were local on a user's machine. The combination of TCP/IP, NFS and NIS comprise the primary networking components of UNIX.

NGM (NetWare Global Messaging) E-mail software from Novell for NetWare 3.x that includes directory synchronization across distributed servers and provides optional interfaces to X.400, SMTP and SNADS. See *SMF.*

nibble Half a byte (four bits).

nibble mode memory A type of dynamic RAM that outputs four consecutive bits (nibble) at one time.

NIC (Network Interface Card) Same as *network adapter.*

NICAD A trademark of SAFT America Inc., Valdosta, GA. See *nickel cadmium.*

nickel cadmium (NiCd) A rechargeable battery technology that has been widely used in portable applications, including portable computers. It provides more charge per pound than lead acid batteries, but less than nickel hydride or zinc air. Its major problem is a so-called "memory effect," in which the battery seems to remember how full it was when you last charged it, and it doesn't go past that point the next time. Nickel cadmium batteries should be completely drained periodically to maintain the longest charge. It uses a nickel and cadmium plate and potassium hydroxide as the electrolyte. See *lead acid, nickel hydride* and *zinc air.*

nickel hydride A rechargeable battery technology that provides more charge per pound than lead acid and nickel cadmium, but less than zinc air. It does not suffer from the nickel cadmium memory effect. It uses nickel and metal hydride plates with potassium hydroxide as the electrolyte. See *lead acid, nickel cadmium* and *zinc air.*

NIS (Network Information Services) A naming service from SunSoft that allows resources to be easily added, deleted or relocated. Formerly called Yellow Pages, NIS is a de facto UNIX standard. NIS+ is a redesigned NIS for Solaris 2.0 products. The combination of TCP/IP, NFS and NIS comprise the primary networking components of UNIX.

NIST (National Institute of Standards & Technology) The standards-defining agency of the U.S. government, formerly called the National Bureau of Standards.

nixie See *NCSI.*

NJE (Network Job Entry) An IBM mainframe protocol that allows two JES devices to communicate with each other.

N-key rollover A keyboard circuit built into most keyboards and vital for fast typing. To test this capability, press four adjacent keys in sequence without removing any finger from any of the keys. If all four letters appear on screen, it has this feature.

NLM (NetWare Loadable Module) Software that enhances or provides additional functions in a NetWare 3.x or higher server. Support for database engines, workstations, network protocols, fax and print servers are examples. The NetWare 2.x counterpart is a VAP.

NLQ (Near Letter Quality) The print quality that is almost as sharp as an electric typewriter. The slowest speed of a dot matrix printer often provides NLQ.

NMI (NonMaskable Interrupt) A high-priority interrupt that cannot be disabled by another interrupt. It is used to report malfunctions such as parity, bus and math coprocessor errors.

NMOS (N-Channel MOS) Pronounced "N moss." A type of microelectronic circuit used for logic and memory chips. NMOS transistors are faster than their PMOS counterpart and more of them can be put on a single chip. It is also used in CMOS design.

NMS (NetWare Management System) A SNMP-based network management software from Novell for monitoring and controlling NetWare networks.

node (1) In communications, a network junction or connection point (terminal or computer).
(2) In database management, an item of data that can be accessed by two or more routes.

(3) In computer graphics, an endpoint of a graphical element.

noise An extraneous signal that invades an electrical transmission. It can come from strong electrical or magnetic signals in nearby lines, from poorly fitting electrical contacts, and from power line spikes.

NOMAD A relational DBMS from Must Software International, Norwalk, CT, that runs on IBM mainframes, PCs and VAXs. Introduced in the mid 1970s, it was one of the first database systems to provide a non-procedural language for data manipulation.

NOMDA (National Office Machine Dealers Association) A trade organization of office equipment vendors founded in 1926. In 1993, it merged with Chicago-based LANDA (LAN Dealers Association), founded in 1986. It is currently called NOMDA/LANDA, but a new name is expected. Publications, training seminars and conferences are provided for members. Address: 12411 Wornall Rd., Kansas City, MO 64145, 816/941-3100.

non-blocking The ability of a signal to reach its destination without interference or delay.

non-breaking space See *hard space.*

non-document mode A word processing mode used for creating source language programs, batch files and other text files that contain only text and no proprietary headers and format codes. All text editors, as well as XyWrite word processors, automatically output this format.

non-impact printer A printer that prints without banging a ribbon onto paper, such as a thermal or ink jet printer. See *printer.*

non-interlaced Illuminating a CRT by displaying lines sequentially from top to bottom. Non-interlaced monitors eliminate annoying flicker found in interlaced monitors, which illuminate half the lines in the screen in the first cycle and the remaining half in the second cycle. Contrast with and see *interlaced* for a diagram.

nonlinear A system in which the output is not a uniform relationship to the input.

nonlinear video editing Storing video in the computer for editing. It is much easier to edit video in the computer than with earlier analog editing systems. Today's digital nonlinear editing systems provide high-quality post-production editing on a personal computer. However, lossy compression is used to store digital images, and some detail will be lost.

Depending on the purpose for the video presentation, output is either the final video turned back into analog or an edit decision list (EDL) that describes frame sources and time codes in order to quickly convert the original material into the final video in an editing room. For commercial production, the latter allows editing to be done offline rather than in a studio that costs several hundred dollars per hour.

Prior to digital, a system using several analog tape decks was considered a nonlinear video editing system. Contrast with *linear video editing*.

non-modal Not mode oriented. A non-modal operation moves from one situation to another without apparent mode switching.

non-numeric programming Programming that deals with objects, such as words, board game pieces and people, rather than numbers. Same as *list processing*.

non-preemptive multitasking A multitasking environment in which an application is able to give up control of the CPU to another application only at certain points, such as when it's ready to accept input from the keyboard. Under this method, one program performing a large number of calculations for example, can dominate the machine and cause other applications to have limited access to the CPU.

Non-preemtive multitasking is also called *cooperative multitasking*, because programs must be designed to cooperate with each other in order to work together effectively in this environment.

A non-preemtive multitasking operating system cannot guarantee service to a communications program running in the background. If another application has usurped the CPU, the CPU cannot process the interrupts from the communications program quickly enough to capture the incoming data, and data can be lost. Contrast with *preemptive multitasking*.

non-procedural language A computer language that does not require traditional programming logic to be stated. For example, a command, such as LIST, might display all the records in a file on screen, separating fields with a blank space. In a procedural language, such as COBOL, all the logic for inputting each record, testing for end of file and formatting the screen has to be explicitly programmed.

Query languages, report writers, interactive database programs, spreadsheets and application generators provide non-procedural languages for user operation. Contrast with and see *procedural language* for an example.

non-routable protocol A communications protocol that contains only a device address and not a network address. It does not incorporate an addressing scheme for sending data from one network to another. Examples of non-routable protocols are NetBIOS and DEC's LAT protocols. Contrast with *routable protocol*.

NonStop A family of fault tolerant computer systems from Tandem.

non trivial A favorite word used among programmers for any task that isn't simple.

non-volatile memory Memory that holds its content without power. Firmware chips (ROMs, PROMs, EPROMs, etc.) are examples. Disks and tapes may be called non-volatile memory, but they are usually considered storage devices.

no-op (NO OPeration) An instruction that does nothing but hold the place for a future machine instruction.

NOR (Not OR) A Boolean logical operation that is true if all inputs are false, and false if any input is true. For example, 0-1, 1-0 and 1-1 all yield 0. Only 0-0 yields 1. An exclusive NOR is true if both inputs are the same. For example, 0-0 and 1-1 yield 1, while 0-1 and 1-0 yield 0.

normalization In relational database management, a process which breaks down data into record groups for efficient processing. There are six stages. By the third stage (third normal form), data is identified only by the key field in the record.

For example, ordering information is identified by order number, customer information, by customer number.

normal wear Deterioration due to natural forces that act upon a product under average, everyday use.

Northgate (Northgate Computer Systems, Inc., Eden Prarie, MN) A PC systems and keyboard manufacturer founded in 1987 by Arthur Lazere. Its PCs are sold mostly through direct marketing, but its highly-praised line of OmniKey keyboards is also sold through dealers.

Norton Desktop Popular shells for DOS and Windows from Symantec. They include a comprehensive package of utilities and provide a large amount of customizability.

Norton Utilities Widely-used utility programs for the PC and Macintosh from Symantec Corporation, Cupertino, CA. It includes programs to search, edit and undelete files, to restore damaged files and to defragment the disk, plus more. Originally from Peter Norton Computing, these programs were among the first to popularize disk utilities for the PC.

NOS See *network operating system.*

NOS/VE (Network Operating System/Virtual Environment) A multitasking, virtual memory operating system from Control Data that runs on its medium to large-scale mainframes.

NOT A Boolean logic operation that reverses the input. If a 0 is input, a 1 is output, and vice versa. See *AND, OR & NOT.*

notation How a system of numbers, phrases, words or quantities is written or expressed. Positional notation is the location and value of digits in a numbering system, such as the decimal or binary system.

notebook computer A laptop computer that weighs from approximately five to seven pounds. A notebook that weighs under five pounds is usually called a *subnotebook.*

Notes See *Lotus Notes.*

NovaNET A satellite-based network for educational services created by the Education Research Lab of the University of Illinois. It includes over 10,000 hours of lesson material from third grade to post graduate work in over a hundred subject areas.

Novell (Novell Inc., Provo, UT) Novell was founded as Novell Data Systems in 1981 by Jack Davis and Geroge Canova. It initially manufactured terminals for IBM mainframes. In 1983, Ray Noorda became CEO and president of a restructured Novell, Inc., which would concentrate on the development of its NetWare operating system. NetWare has grown into the most widely used network operating system in the world.

Novell has recently become heavily involved with UNIX. First by creating Univel, a joint venture with USL, AT&T's UNIX subsidiary, and second by acquiring USL in its entirety in 1993.

Novell DOS A DOS-compatible operating system from Novell. Formerly DR DOS from Digital Research, Novell acquired the company in 1991 and revamped the product. The first release under Novell DOS 7, introduced in 1994, includes new utilities, built-in NetWare client support, peer-to-peer networking, preemptive multitasking and the ability to store drivers in extended memory.

Novell network A LAN controlled by one of Novell's NetWare operating systems. See *NetWare.*

no wait state memory Memory fast enough to meet the demands of the CPU. Idle wait states do not have to be introduced.

nroff (Nontypesetting RunOFF) A UNIX utility that formats documents for terminals and dot matrix printers. Using a text editor, troff codes are embedded into the text and the nroff command converts the document into the required output. Complex troff codes are ignored. See *troff*.

NRZ (Non-Return-To-Zero) A signalling method used in magnetic recording and communications that does not automatically return to a neutral state after each bit is transmitted.

ns (NanoSecond) See *nanosecond*.

NSTL (National Software Testing Lab, Philadelphia) An independent organization that evaluates computer hardware and software. It adheres to controlled testing methods to ensure objective results and publishes its findings in Software Digest Ratings Report and PC Digest.

NT See *Windows NT*.

NTAS (NT Advanced Server) The server version of Windows NT Version 3.1. See *Windows NT*.

NTFS (NT File System) A file system used in Windows NT which uses the Unicode character set and allows file names up to 255 characters in length. The NTFS is designed to recover on the fly from hard disk crashes. Windows NT supports multiple file systems. It can run with a DOS FAT, an OS/2 HPFS and a native NTFS, each in a different partition on the hard disk. NT's security features require that the NTFS be used.

NTSC (National TV Standards Committee) The U.S. TV standard administered by the FCC that is currently 525 lines transmitted at 60 half frames/sec (interlaced). It is a composite of red, green and blue signals for color and includes an FM frequency for audio and an MTS signal for stereo. NTSC reconvenes to change TV standards.

NuBus A bus architecture (32-bits) originally developed at MIT and defined as a Eurocard (9U). Apple has changed its electrical and physical specs for its Macintosh series. Many Macs have one or more NuBus slots for peripheral expansion.

NUI (1) (Notebook User Interface) A term coined by Go Corporation for its PenPoint pen-based interface.

(2) (NetWare Users International) A voluntary organization of more than 250 NetWare user groups worldwide. For information, call 800/228-4NUI within the U.S. or 801/429-7000 outside the U.S. and ask for NUI.

(3) (Network User Identifier) A code used to gain access into local European packed-switched networks.

null The first character in ASCII and EBCDIC. In hex, it prints as 00; in decimal, it prints as a blank. It is naturally found in binary numbers when a byte contains no 1 bits. It is also used to pad fields and act as a delimiter; for example, in C, it specifies the end of a character string.

null modem cable An RS-232 cable used to connect two personal computers in close proximity. It connects to both serial ports and crosses the sending wire on one end to the receiving wire on the other.

null pointer In programming, a reference to zero. May be the response of an unsuccessful search function.

null string In programming, a character string that contains no data.

Number 9 board A family of high-resolution display boards for PCs from Number Nine Computer Corporation, Lexington, MA, noted for its advanced features (virtual screen, built-in zoom, etc.) and speed. Products begin with #9, such as #9GXi and #9GXe.

number crunching Refers to computers running mathematical, scientific or CAD applications, which perform large amounts of calculations.

numeric data Refers to quantities and money amounts used in calculations. Contrast with *string* or *character data*.

numeric field A data field that holds only numbers to be calculated. Contrast with *character field*.

numeric keypad A four-row keyboard that is often part of a computer keyboard located to the right of the typewriter keys. See *keypad*.

numerical aperture The amount of light that can be coupled to an optical fiber. The greater the aperture, the easier it is to connect the light source to the fiber.

numerical control A category of automated machine tools, such as drills and lathes, that operate from instructions in a program. Numerical control (NC) machines are used in manufacturing tasks, such as milling, turning, punching and drilling.

First-generation machines were hardwired to perform specific tasks or programmed in a very low-level machine language. Today, they are controlled by their own microcomputers and programmed in high-level languages, such as APT and COMPACT II, which automatically generate the tool path (physical motions required to perform the operation).

The term was coined in the 1950s when the instructions to the tool were numeric codes. Just like the computer industry, symbolic languages were soon developed, but the original term remained.

Num Lock (NUMeric Lock) A keyboard key used to toggle a combination number/cursor keypad between number keys and cursor keys.

NxN switch See *crosspoint switch*.

NZ (Non Zero) A value greater or less than 0.

OA See *office automation*.

OADG (Open Architecture Development Group) An organization founded by IBM Japan in 1991 to promote PC standards in Japan. See *DOS/V*.

OAI (Open Application Interface) A computer to telephone interface that lets a computer control and customize PBX and ACD operations.

object (1) In object-oriented programming, a self-contained module of data and its associated processing. Objects are software building blocks. See *objects* and *object-oriented programming*.

(2) In a compound document, an independent block of data, text or graphics that was created by a separate application.

object code Same as *machine language*.

object computer Same as *target computer*.

object database See *object-oriented database*.

object language (1) A language defined by a metalanguage.

(2) An object-oriented programming language.

(3) Same as *machine language* or *target language*.

object module The output of an assembler or compiler, which must be linked with other modules before it can be executed.

object oriented See *objects*.

object-oriented analysis The examination of a problem by modeling it as a group of interacting objects. An object is defined by its class, data elements and behavior. For example; in an order processing system, an invoice is a class, and printing, viewing and totalling are examples of its behavior. Objects (individual invoices) inherit this behavior and combine it with their own data elements.

object-oriented database A database that holds abstract data types (objects) and is managed by an object-oriented DBMS. See *object-oriented DBMS*.

object-oriented DBMS A DBMS that manages objects (abstract data types). An object-oriented DBMS, or ODBMS, is suited for multimedia applications as well as data with complex relationships that are difficult to model and process in a relational DBMS. Because any type of data can be stored (the rules for processing the data are part of an object), an ODBMS allows for fully integrated databases that hold data, text, pictures, voice and video.
▶ *The electronic and encyclopedic versions of this book provide more detail on this subject.*

object-oriented design Transforming an object-oriented model into the specifications required to create the system. Moving from object-oriented analysis to object-oriented design is accomplished by expanding the model into more and more detail.

object-oriented graphics Same as *vector graphics*.

object-oriented interface A graphical interface that uses icons and a mouse, such as the Macintosh, Windows and GEM environments.

object-oriented programming Abbreviated "OOP," the programming technology that supports the creation and processing of objects.
▶ *The electronic and encyclopedic versions of this book provide more detail on this subject.*

object-oriented technology A variety of disciplines that support object-oriented programming, including object-oriented analysis and object-oriented design.

object program A machine language program ready to run in a particular operating environment. It has been assembled, or compiled, and link edited.

objects Software routines designed according to a set of rules that allows them to function as independent building blocks that interact with each other. This architecture is expected to be revolutionary in payback if meaningful standards become widely used across all environments and platforms.
▶ *The electronic and encyclopedic versions of this book provide more detail on this subject.*

OCR (Optical Character Recognition) Machine recognition of printed characters. OCR systems can recognize many different OCR fonts, as well as typewriter and computer-printed characters. Advanced OCR systems can recognize hand printing.

OCR-A (FULL ALPHA)

NUMERIC	0123456789
ALPHA	ABCDEFGHIJKLMNOPQRSTUVWXYZ
SYMBOLS	>$/-+-#"

OCR-A (NRMA/EURO BANKING)		OCR-B(SUBSET 1, ECMA 11 and ANSI X3.49-1975)	
NUMERIC	0123456789	NUMERIC	00123456789
ALPHA	ACDMNPRUXY	ALPHA	ACENPSTVX
SYMBOLS	>$/+#"♪♀♂	SYMBOLS	<+>-¥

OCR MULTIFONT

OCR-B	¥00123456789><++#
12L/12F	¥0123456789+#
1403-OCR	00123456789><+#
407-1	0123456789

SAMPLE OCR FONTS
(Courtesy Recognition Equipment Corporation)

octal A numbering system that uses eight digits, 0 through 7. Thus decimal 0-7 equals octal 0-7. It is used as a shorthand method for representing binary characters that use six-bits. Each three bits (half a character) is converted into a single octal digit. For example, 000 is 0, 001 is 1 and so on up to 111, which is 7.

octet An eight-bit storage unit. In the international community, octet is often used instead of byte.

ODAPI (Open Data API) A programming interface from Borland that provides a common language for applications to access databases on a network. It supports SQL. See *ODBC* and *IDAPI*.

ODBC (Open DataBase Connectivity) A programming interface from Microsoft that provides a common language for Windows applications to access databases on a network. It supports SQL and is part of WOSA. See *ODAPI* and *IDAPI*.

ODBMS See *object-oriented DBMS*.

odd parity See *parity checking*.

ODI (Open Data-Link Interface) A network driver interface from Novell. ODI is based on the LSL interface developed by AT&T for its UNIX System V operating system. See *network driver interface* and *LSL*.

ODMG (Object Database Management Group) An organization formed in 1991 to promote standards for object databases. The ODMG-93 is a standard that defines the message structure between objects. See *CORBA*.

ODT See *SCO Open Desktop*.

Oe See *Oersted*.

OEM (Original Equipment Manufacturer) A manufacturer that sells equipment to a reseller. Also refers to the reseller itself. OEM customers either add value to the product before reselling it, private label it, or bundle it with their own products. See *VAR*.

OEM font In Windows, the font used to replicate the monospaced characters of a DOS application, when DOS text has been copied to the clipboard or a DOS character mode application is running in a Windows window.

Oersted Pronounced "ers-ted," the measurement of magnetic resistance. The higher the "Oe," the more current required to magnetize it.

off-hook The state of a telephone line that allows dialing and transmission but prohibits incoming calls from being answered. The term stems from the days when a telephone handset was lifted off of a hook. Contrast with *on-hook*.

office automation The integration of office information functions, including word processing, data processing, graphics, desktop publishing and e-mail.

The backbone of office automation is a LAN, which allows users to transmit data, mail and even voice across the network. All office functions, including dictation, typing, filing, copying, fax, Telex, microfilm and records management, telephone and telephone switchboard operations, are candidates for integration.

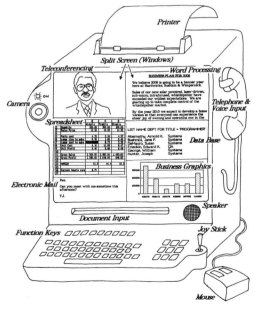

OFFICE AUTOMATION

This terminal depicts the various paper and electronic functions of a integrated office system.

Office Vision Integrated office automation applications from IBM that run in all IBM computer families. It was the first major implementation of SAA and includes e-mail, scheduling, document creation and decision support capabilities.

offline Not connected to or not installed in the computer. If a terminal, printer or other device is physically connected to the computer, but is not turned on or in ready mode, it is still considered offline.

Disks and tapes that have been demounted and stored in the data library are considered offline. Contrast with *online*.

offline browser See *offline reader*.

offline navigator See *offline reader*.

offline reader Software that downloads e-mail and selected data from an online service, allowing the user to browse the captured material after disconnecting. It automates retrieving routine data and saves online fees by shortening the connect time.

offline storage Disks and tapes that are kept in a data library.

offload To remove work from one computer and do it on another. See *cooperative processing*.

offset (1) The distance from a starting point, either the start of a file or the start of a memory address. Its value is added to a base value to derive the actual value. An offset into a file is simply the character location within that file, usually starting with 0; thus "offset 240" is actually the 241st byte of the file. See *relative address*.

(2) In word processing, the amount of space a document is printed from the left margin.

off-the-shelf Refers to products that are packaged and available for sale.

OH See *off-hook* and *modem*.

ohm A unit of measurement for electrical resistance. One ohm is the resistance in a circuit when one volt maintains a current of one amp.

OLAP database (OnLine Analytical Processing database) A database designed for fast access to summarized data. Using specialized indexing techniques, it processes queries that pertain to large amounts of data much faster than tradtional relational databases. See *EIS*.

olay See *OLE*.

OLCP (OnLine Complex Processing) Processing complex queries, long transactions and simultaneous reads and writes to the same record. Contrast with *OLTP*, in which records are updated in a more predictable manner.

OLE (Object Linking and Embedding) Windows' compound document protocol that allows one document to be embedded within or linked to another. When an object (document, drawing, sound, etc.) that is embedded is clicked, the application that created it is loaded so that you can edit it. Changes made to the embedded object affect only the document that contains it.

If an object is linked rather than embedded, it references an original file outside of the document. Thus, if you make a change to a linked object, all the documents that contain that link are automatically updated the next time you open them.

OLTP (OnLine Transaction Processing) See *transaction processing* and *OLCP*.

OME (Open Messaging Environment) An open messaging system from Novell. It is based on Microsoft's MAPI and is a superset of Novell's MHS and WordPerfect Office's messaging systems.

OMG (Object Management Group) An international organization founded in 1989 to endorse technologies as open standards for object-oriented applications. Address: 492 Old Connecticut Path, Framingham, MA 01701, 508/820-4300.

OMI (Open Messaging Interface) A messaging protocol developed by Lotus, now included in VIM.

omnidirectional In all directions. For example, an omnidirectional antenna can pick up signals in all directions.

OmniPage Character recognition software for PCs and the Macintosh from Caere Corporation, Los Gatos, CA. It was the first personal computer software that could distinguish text from graphics and convert a wide variety of fonts into text.

Omnis A development system for creating Windows and Macintosh applications from Blyth Software, Foster City, CA. It includes its own database manager for local use and supports client/server SQL databases such as ORACLE and SQL Server. Omnis includes a comprehensive programming language and set of development tools..

ONA (Open Network Architecture) An FCC plan that allows users and competing enhanced service providers (ESPs) equal access to unbundled, basic telephone services. The Open Network Provision (ONP) is the European counterpart.

ONC (Open Network Computing) A family of networking products from SunSoft for implementing distributed computing in a multivendor environment. Includes TCP/IP and OSI protocols, NFS distributed file system, NIS naming service and TI-RPC remote procedure call library. ONC+ adds Federated Services, which is an interface for third-parties to connect network services into the Solaris environment.

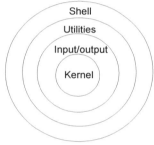

one-chip computer See *computer on a chip*.

one-off One at a time. CD-ROM recorders (CD-R drives) are commonly called one-off machines because they write one CD-ROM at a time.

ONION DIAGRAM
This shows the layers of an operating system from the innermost kernel to the outermost shell.

on-hook The state of a telephone line that can receive an incoming call. Contrast with *off-hook*.

onion diagram A graphical representation of a system that is made up of concentric circles. The innermost circle is the core, and all outer layers are dependent on the core.

online (1) A peripheral device (terminal, printer, etc.) that is ready to operate. A printer can be attached and turned on, yet still not online, if the ONLINE or SEL light is out. Pressing the ONLINE button will usually turn it back online.

(2) An online computer system refers to a system with terminals, but does not imply how the system functions. All the following are online systems. Data collection systems accept data from terminals, but do not update master files. Interactive systems imply data entry and updating. Transaction processing systems update necessary files as transactions arrive (orders, financial quotes, etc.). Realtime systems provide an immediate response to a question.

on-line means happiness!

Want to impress your friends?
Although complete overkill, it is not incorrect to say that one has an online, realtime, interactive, transaction

processing system. However, don't say this to an experienced systems analyst!

online help On-screen instruction that is immediately available.

online industry The collection of service organizations that provide dial-up access to databases, shopping, news, weather, sports, e-mail, etc. See *online services*.

online services Following are major online information service organizations, including the types of databases provided. "Wide variety" generally includes news, weather and shopping as well as information on a host of topics. Many services provide e-mail and gateways to e-mail on the Internet.

America Online, Inc.
Databases: wide variety,
    personal computer technical
8619 Westwood Center Dr.
Vienna, VA 22182
800/827-6364
703/448-8700

BIX
Databases: personal computer technical
Byte Information Exchange
General Videotex Corporation
1030 Massachusetts Ave.
Cambridge, MA 02138
800/695-4775
617/491-3393

CompuServe Information Service, Inc.
Databases: wide variety,
    personal computer technical
P.O. Box 20212
Columbus, OH 43220
800/848-8199 (Ohio)
800/848-8990
614/457-8650

DataTimes Corporation
Databases: newspapers, magazines, financial
14000 Quail Springs Pkwy., Suite 450
Oklahoma City, OK 73134
800/642-2525
405/751-6400

DELPHI
Databases: wide variety, access to DIALOG
General Videotex Corporation
1030 Massachusetts Ave.
Cambridge, MA 02138
800/544-4005
617/491-3393

DIALOG Information Services, Inc.
Databases: over 400 (largest)
3460 Hillview Avenue
Palo Alto, CA 94304
800/334-2564
415/858-2700

Dow Jones News/Retrieval Service
Databases: financial plus shopping
    airline reservations, etc.
P.O. Box 300
Princeton, NJ 08543
800/522-3567
609/520-4000

EasyLink
Services: e-mail, Telex, EDI.
Databases: access to major providers
    (DIALOG, CompuServe, etc.)
AT&T EasyLink Services
400 Interpace Pkwy.
Parsippany, NJ 07054
800/242-6005
201/331-4000

GEnie
Databases: wide variety
General Electric Information Services Co.
401 N. Washington St.
Rockville, MD 20850
800/638-9636
301/340-4000

Mead Data Central
Databases: news (NEXIS), legal (LEXIS)
P.O. Box 933
Dayton, OH 45401
800/227-4908
513/865-6800

Maxwell Online
Databases: medical (BRS),
    patent, trademark (ORBIT)
8000 Westpark Dr.
McClean, VA 22102
ORBIT 800/456-7248
BRS 800/289-4277

MEDLARS
Databases: medical
National Library of Medicine
8600 Rockville Pike
Bethesda, MD 20894
800/638-8480
301/496-6193

MCI Mail
Services: e-mail, Telex, fax
Databases: access to Dow Jones
 1133 19th St., NW
 Washington, DC 20036
 800/444-6245
 202/833-8484

National Videotex Network
Databases: wide variety
 5555 San Felipe, Suite 1200
 Houston, TX 77056
800/336-9096
 713/877-4444

NewsNet, Inc.
Databases: newsletters
 945 Haverford Rd.
 Bryn Mawr, PA 19010
 800/952-0122
 215/527-8030

PRODIGY
Databases: wide variety, shopping
 445 Hamilton Ave.
 White Plains, NY 10601
 800/776-3449
 914/993-8848

VU/TEXT Information Services, Inc.
Databases: newspapers
 325 Chestnut St., Suite 1300
 Philadelphia, PA 19106
 800/323-2940
 215/574-4400

WESTLAW
Databases: legal (plus access to
  DIALOG and Dow Jones)
 West Publishing Co.
 610 Opperman Dr.
 St. Paul, MN 55123
 800/WESTLAW
 612/687-7000

ZiffNet
Databases: personal computer
  (technical, news, shopping)
 25 First St.
 Cambridge, MA 02141
 800/666-0330
 617/252-5000

on the fly As needed. It implies little or no degradation in performance to accomplish the task. See *realtime* and *realtime compression*.

OO Object oriented.

OOA, OOD, OODB, OODBMS See *object-oriented analysis, object-oriented design, object-oriented database, object-oriented DBMS*.

OOP See *object-oriented programming*.

op amp (Operational Amplifier) A device that amplifies analog signals. It uses two inputs; one for power and one for data. It is used in myriads of applications from communications to stereo.

op code See *operation code*.

open (1) To identify a disk or tape file for reading and writing. The open procedure "locks on" to an existing file or creates a new one.

(2) With regard to a switch, open is "off."

(3) Made to operate with other products. See *open architecture* and *open systems*.

open architecture A system in which the specifications are made public in order to encourage third-party vendors to develop add-on products. Much of Apple's early success was due to the Apple II's open architecture. The PC is open architecture.

open computing See *open systems*.

Open Desktop See *SCO Open Desktop*.

OpenDoc A compound document architecture from Apple, IBM, Novell, Sun and others that allows multiple data structures (text, graphics, sound, etc.) to be stored in a single document.

open file A file, typically a disk file, that has been made available to the application by the operating system for reading and/or writing. All files must be "opened" before they can be accessed and "closed" when no longer required.

OPEN LOOK An X Window-based graphical user interface for UNIX developed by Sun. It has been widely used by Sun and was defined and distributed by AT&T when it was still involved with UNIX. OPEN LOOK is giving way to Motif, which has become the standard user interface in the UNIX world.

open pipe A continuous path from sender to receiver, such as found in a circuit-switching network or leased line. Transmitted data is not broken up into packets.

open shop A computing environment that allows users to program and run their own programs. Contrast with *closed shop*.

open system A vendor-independent system that is designed to interconnect with a variety of products. It implies that standards are determined from a consensus of interested parties rather than one or two vendors.

"Open systems" generally refers to UNIX-based computer systems, since UNIX machines are the most universal operating environment. UNIX runs on more different kinds of hardware than any other operating system. Sometimes, the PC is called an open system, but it is more an open architecture than an open system, because Intel and Microsoft have strong control over the hardware and system software. Contrast with *closed system*. See *OSI, OSF* and *X/Open*.

OpenView Network management software from HP. It supports SNMP and CMIP protocols, and third-party products that run under OpenView support SNA and DECnet network management protocols. OpenView is an enterprise-wide network management solution.

OpenVMS A version of the VMS operating system from Digital that is POSIX and XPG3-compliant and runs on VAX and Alpha systems.

operand The part of a machine instruction that references data or a peripheral device. In the instruction, **ADD A to B**, A and B are the operands (nouns), and ADD is the operation code (verb). In the instruction **READ TRACK 9, SECTOR 32**, track and sector are the operands.

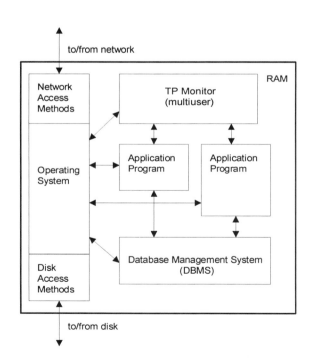

OPERATING SYSTEM INTERACTION
This chart shows how the OS interacts with other system and application software in the computer.

operating system The master control program that runs the computer. It is the first program loaded when the computer is turned on, and its main part, called the *kernel*, resides in memory at all times. It may be developed by the vendor of the computer it's running in or by a third party. The operating system sets the standards for the application programs that run in it. All programs must "talk to" the operating system.

The difference between an operating system and a network operating system is its multiuser capability. For example, DOS and Windows are single-user OSs designed for one person at a desktop computer. Windows NT and UNIX are network operating systems, because they are designed to manage multiple user requests at the same time and handle the related security.

An operating system provides the user interface and controls multitasking. It handles the input and output to the disk and all peripheral devices. In a large computer, it handles job scheduling.
▶ *The electronic and encyclopedic versions of this book provide more detail on this subject.*

operation code The part of a machine instruction that tells the computer what to do, such as input, add or branch. The operation code is the verb; the operands are the nouns.

operations See *datacenter*.

operations research See *management science*.

operator (1) A person who operates the computer and performs such activities as commanding the operating system, mounting disks and tapes and placing paper in the printer. Operators may also write the job control language (JCL), which schedules the daily work for the computer.

(2) In programming and logic, a symbol used to perform an operation on some value. See *arithmetic operator* and *Boolean operator*.

operator overloading In programming, the ability to use the same operator to perform different operations. For example, arithmetic operators such as +, −, * and / could be defined to perform differently on certain kinds of data.

OPI (Open Prepress Interface) An extension to PostScript by Aldus Corporation to provide a format for color separations.

optical disk A direct access disk written and read by light. Optical disks are generally slower than magnetic disks, but their storage capacities are greater per square inch. There are a variety of fixed and removable media on the market. See *CD, CD-ROM, videodisc, WORM* and *CD-R.*
▶ *The electronic and encyclopedic versions of this book provide more detail on this subject.*

optical fiber A thin glass wire designed for light transmission, capable of transmitting billions of bits per second. Unlike electrical pulses, light pulses are not affected by random radiation in the environment.

optical isolator A device used with current loop transmission that uses an LED and photoresistor to detect current in the line.

optical mouse A mouse that uses light to get its bearings. It is rolled over a small desktop pad that contains a reflective grid. The mouse emits a light and senses its reflection as it is moved. Contrast with *mechanical mouse.*

optical reader An input device that recognizes typewritten or printed characters and bar codes and converts them into their corresponding digital codes.

optical recognition See *OCR*.

optical scanner See *scanner*.

optimizer Hardware or software that improves performance. See *disk management*.

optoelectronics Merging light and electronics technologies, such as in optical fiber communications systems.

OR A Boolean logic operation that is true if any of the inputs is true. For example, 0-1, 1-0 and 1-1 all yield 1, while only 0-0 yields 0. An exclusive OR is true if only one of the inputs is true, but not both. For example, 0-1 and 1-0 yield 1, but 0-0 and 1-1 yield 0.

ORACLE (1) A relational DBMS from Oracle Corporation, Redwood Shores, CA, that runs on a wide variety of computers from micro to mainframe. It was the first DBMS to incorporate the SQL language. Database applications can be created on a PC and easily moved to other hardware platforms.

(2) (Oracle) A European broadcast television text-message service.

Orange Book See *NCSC* and *CD*.

ORB (Object Request Broker) Software that handles the communication of messages between objects in a distributed environment. See *CORBA*.

ordinal number The number that identifies the sequence of an item, for example, record #34. Contrast with *cardinal number*.

orientation In typography, the direction of print across a page. See *portrait*.

orphan See *widow & orphan*.

OS See *operating system*.

OS/2 A single user, multitasking operating system for PCs from IBM that runs OS/2, DOS and Windows applications. It provides both a graphical user interface known as the Workplace Shell (formerly called Presentation Manager) and a command line similar to DOS. OS/2 is highly regarded as a robust operating system and is gaining popularity.

OS/2 for Windows A special edition of OS/2 for PCs that already have DOS and Windows 3.1 installed. A new version of OS/2 is expected by the end of 1994 that will supersede OS/2 for Windows and provide increased performance.

OS/9 A UNIX-like, realtime operating system from Microware Systems Corporation for Motorola 68000 CPUs. Originally developed for the 6809 chip, a version of OS/9 was created for CD-I players.

OS/9000 A portable version of OS/9, written in C, which runs on 386s and up and 68020s and up.

oscillate To swing back and forth between the minimum and maximum values. An oscillation is one cycle, typically one complete wave in an alternating frequency.

oscillator An electronic circuit used to generate high-frequency pulses. See *clock*.

oscilloscope Test instrument that displays electronic signals (waves and pulses) on a screen. It creates its own time base against which signals can be measured, and display frames can be frozen for visual inspection.

OSF (Open Software Foundation) A non-profit organization dedicated to delivering an open computing environment based on standards. Formed in 1988, it solicits technologies from industry, invites member participation to set technical direction and licenses software to members. Address: 11 Cambridge Center, Cambridge, MA 02142, 617/621-8700.

OSF/Motif See *Motif*.

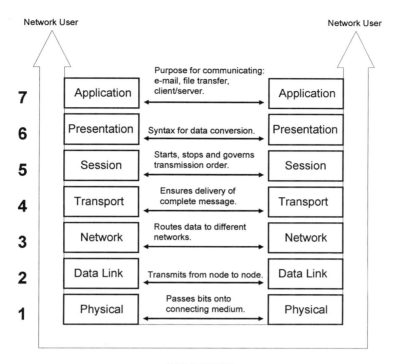

OSI MODEL

OSI (Open System Interconnection) An ISO standard for worldwide communications that defines a framework for implementing protocols in seven layers.

Control is passed from one layer to the next, starting at the application layer in one station, proceeding to the bottom layer, over the channel to the next station and back up the hierarchy.

Most of this functionality exists in all communications networks; however, non-OSI systems often incorporate two or three layers into one.

Vendors have agreed to support OSI in one form or another; however OSI serves more as a model than a universal standard. Many OSI components are too loosely defined, and proprietary standards are entrenched. One exception is the OSI-compliant X.400 e-mail protocol that is widely implemented.

Learning the OSI layers and functions is essential for understanding communications networks.

Application - Layer 7

This top layer defines the language and syntax that programs use to communicate with other programs. It represents the purpose of communicating. For example, a program in a client workstation uses commands to request data from a program in the server. Common functions at this layer are opening, closing, reading and writing files, transferring files and e-mai, executing remote jobs and obtaining directory information about network resouces.

Presentation - Layer 6

The presentation layer negotiates and manages the way data is represented and encoded between different computers. For example, it provides a common denominator between ASCII and EBCDIC machines as well as between different floating point and binary formats. Sun's XDR and OSI's ASN.1 are two protocols used for this purpose. This layer is also used for encryption and decryption.

Session - Layer 5

This layer coordinates the communications in an orderly manner. It determines one-way or two-way communications and manages the dialogue between both parties; for example, making sure that the previous request has been fulfilled before the next one is sent. It also marks significant parts of the transmitted data with checkpoints to allow for fast recovery in the event of a connection failure. Very often, services in this layer are included in the transport layer.

Transport - Layer 4

This layer ensures end to end validity and integrity. The lower data link layer (layer 2) is only responsible for delivering packets from one node to another. Thus, if a packet gets lost in a router somewhere in the enterprise internet, the transport layer will detect that. It ensures that if a 12MB file is sent, the full 12MB is received.

"OSI transport services" include layers 1 through 4, collectively responsible for delivering a complete message or file from sending to receiving station without error.

Network - Layer 3

This layer routes the messages to different networks. The node to node function of the data link layer (layer 2) is extended across the entire internetwork, because a routable protocol, such as IP, IPX, SNA and AppleTalk, contains a network address in addition to a station address. If all stations are contained within a single network segment, then the routing capability in this layer is not required.

Data Link - Layer 2

The data link is responsible for node to node validity and integrity of the transmission. The transmitted bits are divided into frames; for example, an Ethernet or Token Ring frame for local area networks (LANs). Layers 1 and 2 are required for every type of communications.

Physical - Layer 1

The physical layer is responsible for passing bits onto and receiving them from the connecting medium. This layer has no understanding of the meaning of the bits, but deals with the electrical and mechanical characteristics of the signals and signalling methods. For example, it comprises the RTS and CTS signals in an RS-232 environment, as well as TDM and FDM techniques for multiplexing data on a line.

OSPF (Open Shortest Path First) A router protocol that determines the least expensive path for routing a message. OSPF was originally developed to replace the RIP protocol.

OTPROM (One Time PROM) A PROM chip that can be programmed only once.

outdent Same as *hanging indent* and *hanging paragraph*.

outline font A type of font made from basic outlines of each character. The outlines are scaled into actual characters (bitmaps) before printing. See *scalable font*.

outline processor Software that allows the user to type in thoughts and organize them into an outline form.

out of band See *signaling in/out of band*.

output (1) Any computer-generated information displayed on screen, printed on paper or in machine readable form, such as disk and tape.

(2) To transfer or transmit from the computer to a peripheral device or communications line.

output area A reserved segment of memory used to collect data to be transferred out of the computer. Same as *buffer*.

output bound Excessive slowness due to output functions, typically slow-speed communications lines or printers. See *print buffer*.

output device Any peripheral that presents output from the computer, such as a screen or printer. Although disks and tapes receive output, they are called storage devices.

outsourcing Contracting with outside consultants, software houses or service bureaus to perform systems analysis, programming and datacenter operations. See *facilities management*.

OverDrive CPU An Intel CPU chip used to upgrade existing 486SX and 486DX PCs. The internal clock speed of the OverDrive CPU is twice that of the regular chip, thus a 486/33 becomes a 486/66 internally.

overflow error An error that occurs when calculated data cannot fit within the designated field. The result field is usually left blank or is filled with some symbol to flag the error condition.

overhead (1) The amount of processing time used by system software, such as the operating system, TP monitor or database manager.

(2) In communications, the additional codes transmitted for control and error checking, which take more time to process.

overlay (1) A preprinted, precut form placed over a screen, key or tablet for indentification purposes. See *keyboard template*.

(2) A program segment called into memory when required. When a program is larger than the memory capacity of the machine, the parts of the program that are not in constant use can be set up as overlays. When called in, the contents of the previous overlay is lost. Virtual memory is a system of automatic overlays.

overlay card A controller that digitizes NTSC signals from a video source for display in the computer.

overloading In programming, the ability to use the same name for more than one variable or procedure, requiring the compiler to differentiate them based on context.

oversampling Creating a more accurate digital representation of an analog signal. In order to work with real-world signals in the computer, analog signals are sampled some number of times per second (frequency) and converted into digital code. Using averaging and different algorithms, samples can be generated between existing samples, creating more digital information for complex signals, "smoothing out the curve" so to speak. See *sampling rate*.

overscan Outside of the normal rectangular viewing area on a display screen. Contrast with *underscan*.

overstrike (1) To type over an existing character.

(2) A character with a line through it.

overwrite (1) A data entry mode that writes over existing characters on screen when new characters are typed in. Contrast with *insert mode*.

(2) To record new data on top of existing data such as when a disk record or file is updated.

P6 The code name from Intel for the successor to the Pentium. Also called the 686 by industry analysts, since it follows the Pentium, which was originally to be named the 586. This chip is expected in 1995 with as many as six million transistors using .6 micron technology (transistor elements as small as .6 micron) and be twice as fast as the Pentium.

P7 The code name from Intel for the sucessor to the P6. It is expected in the 1996-1997 time frame with as many as 25 million transistors.

PA See *HP Precision Architecture*.

PABX (Private Automatic Branch eXchange) Same as *PBX*.

PACBASE Integrated CASE software for IBM, Bull HN and Unisys mainframes from CGI Systems, Pearl River, NY. It supports a wide variety of databases including DB2 and Oracle. PACLAN is the version for PCs running on LANs.

pack (1) To compress data in order to save space. Unpack refers to decompressing data. See *data compression*.

(2) An instruction that converts a decimal number into a packed decimal format. Unpack converts a packed decimal number into decimal.

(3) In database programs, a command that removes records that have been marked for deletion.

package See *software package*.

packaged software See *software package*.

packed decimal A storage mode that places two decimal digits into one byte, each digit occupying four bits. The sign occupies four bits in the least significant byte.

packet A frame or block of data used for transmission in packet switching and other communications methods.

packet cellular The transmission of data over the cellular network. Data is divided into packets, or frames, for error checking. Contrast with *circuit cellular*. See *CDPD* and *wireless*.

packetized voice The transmission of realtime voice in a packet switching network.

packet radio The wireless transmission of data, which is divided into packets, or frames, for error checking. See *Ardis* and *Mobiltex*.

packet switching A networking technology that breaks up a message into smaller packets for transmission. It is the most common form of data transmission technology used in LANs, MANs and WANs.

Unlike circuit switching, which requires a constant point-to-point circuit to be established, each packet in a packet switched network contains a destination address. Thus all packets in a single message do not have to travel the same path. They can be dynamically routed over the network as circuits become available or unavailable. The destination computer reassembles the packets back into their proper sequence. Contrast with *circuit* switching.

packing density The number of bits or tracks per inch of recording surface. Also refers to the number of memory bits or other electronic components on a chip.

pad (1) To fill a data structure with padding characters.

(2) (PAD) (Packet Assembler/Disassembler) A communications device that formats outgoing data into packets of the required length for transmission in an X.25 packet switching network. It also strips the data out of incoming packets.

padding Characters used to fill up unused portions of a data structure, such as a field or communications message. A field may be padded with blanks, zeros or nulls.

paddle An input device that moves the screen cursor in a back-and-forth motion. It has a dial and one or more buttons and is typically used in games to hit balls and steer objects. See *joy stick*.

page (1) In virtual memory systems, a segment of the program that is transferred into memory.

(2) In videotex systems, a transmitted frame.

(3) In word processing, a printed page.

page break In printing, a code that marks the end of a page. A "hard" page break, inserted by the user, breaks the page at that location. "Soft" page breaks are created by word processing and report programs based on the current page length setting.

page description language A device-independent, high-level language for defining printer output. If an application generates output in a page description language, such as PostScript, the output can be printed on any printer that supports it.

page fault A virtual memory interrupt that reads the required page from disk when the next instruction or item of data is not in memory.

page frame See *EMS*.

page header Common text that is printed at the top of every page. It generally includes the page number and headings above each column.

page makeup Formatting a printed page, which includes the layout of headers, footers, columns, page numbers, graphics, rules and borders.

page mode memory The common dynamic RAM chip design. Memory bits are accessed by row and column coordinates. Without page mode, each bit is accessed by pulsing the row and column select lines. With page mode, the row (page) is selected only once for all bits (columns) within the row, resulting in faster access.

page printer A type of printer that prints a page at a time. See *laser printer* and *ion deposition*.

page recognition Software that recognizes the content of a printed page which has been scanned into the computer. It uses OCR to convert the printed words into computer text and should be able to differentiate text from other elements on the page, such as pictures and captions.

PageMaker A full-featured desktop publishing program for the PC and Macintosh from Aldus Corporation, Seattle, WA. Originally introduced for the Mac in 1985, it set the standard for desktop publishing. In fact, Paul Brainerd, president of Aldus, coined the term desktop publishing. The PC version was introduced in 1987.

pagination (1) Page numbering.

(2) Laying out printed pages, which includes setting up and printing columns, rules and borders. Although pagination is used synonymously with *page makeup*, the term often refers to the printing of long manuscripts rather than ads and brochures.

paging In virtual memory, the transfer of program segments (pages) into and out of memory.

paint (1) In computer graphics, to "paint" the screen using a tablet stylus or mouse to simulate a paintbrush.

(2) To transfer a dot matrix image as in the phrase "the laser printer paints the image onto a photosensitive drum."

(3) To create a screen form by typing anywhere on screen. To "paint" the screen with text.

paint program A graphics program that allows the user to simulate painting on screen with the use of a graphics tablet or mouse. Paint programs create raster graphics images.

PAL (1) (Paradox Application Language) Paradox's programming language.

(2) (Programmable Array Logic) A programmable logic chip (PLD) technology from Advanced Micro Devices.

(3) (Phase Alternating Line) A European TV standard that uses 625 lines of resolution (100 more than NTSC).

palette (1) In computer graphics, the total range of colors that can be used for display, although typically only a subset of them can be used at one time. May also refer to the collection of painting tools available to the user.

(2) A set of functions or modes.

palmtop A computer small enough to hold in one hand and operate with the other. Palmtops may have specialized keyboards or keypads for data entry applications or have small qwerty keyboards.

pan (1) In computer graphics, to move (while viewing) to a different part of an image without changing magnification.

(2) To move (while viewing) horizontally across a text record.

Panvalet See *CA-Panvalet*.

paper tape (1) A slow, low-capacity, sequential storage medium used in the first half of the 20th century to hold data as patterns of punched holes.

(2) A paper roll printed by a calculator or cash register.

paperless office Long predicted, the paperless office is still a myth. Although paper usage has been reduced in some organizations, it has increased in others. Today's PCs make it easy to churn out documents.

paradigm Pronounced "para-dime." A model, example or pattern.

Paradise Video display boards from the Paradise subsidiary of Western Digital Corporation, Irvine, CA.

Paradox A network-ready relational DBMS for DOS and Windows from Borland known for its ease of use and query by example method for asking questions. Its PAL programming language is unique. Many PAL statements are interactive Paradox commands, so that a Paradox user can adjust to programming more easily.

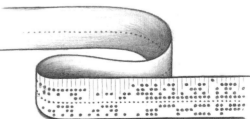

PAPER TAPE

paragraph In DOS programming, a 16 byte block. Memory addresses are generated as "segment:offset," where the segment is expressed in paragraphs. To compute an address, the segment register is shifted left four bits (multiplying it by 16). For example, the address A000:0100 = 655,616:

```
Segment   A000      655,360    (40,960 X 16)
Offset    0100          256
Result    A0100     655,616
```

This means there are 4,096 possibilities for expressing each memory byte, a situation that has helped generate confusion.

paragraph tag In desktop publishing, a style sheet assigned to a text paragraph. It defines font, tab, spacing and other settings.

parallel computing Solving a single problem with multiple computers or computers made up of multiple processors. See *array processor* and *hypercube*.

parallel interface A multiline channel that transfers one or more bytes simultaneously. Personal computers generally connect printers via a Centronics 36-wire parallel interface, which transfers one byte at a time over eight wires, the remaining ones being used for control signals. Large computer parallel interfaces transfer more than one byte at a time. It is faster than a serial interface, because it transfers several bits concurrently. Contrast with *serial interface*. See *Centronics*.

parallel port A socket on a computer used to connect a printer or other peripheral device. It may also be used to attach a portable hard disk, tape backup or CD-ROM. Transferring files between two PCs can be accomplished by cabling the parallel ports of both machines together and using a file transfer program such as LapLink.

An enhanced parallel port, or EPP, which is present on high-end PCs, dramatically improves the speed of the parallel port and is compatible with earlier devices.

parallel processing (1) An architecture within a single computer that performs more than one operation at the same time. See *pipeline processing* and *vector processor*.

(2) A multiprocessing architecture made up of multiple CPUs or computer systems. Either one operation is performed on many sets of data (SIMD), or different parts of the job are worked on simultaneously (MIMD). See *hypercube* and *multiprocessing*.

parallel transmission Transmitting data one or more bytes at a time. Contrast with *serial transmission*.

parallelizing To generate instructions for a parallel processing computer.

parameter (1) Any value passed to a program by the user or by another program in order to customize the program for a particular purpose. A parameter may be anything; for example, a file name, a coordinate, a range of values, a money amount or a code of some kind. Parameters may be required as in parameter-driven software (see below) or they may be optional. Parameters are often entered as a series of values following the program name when the program is loaded.

A DOS switch is a parameter. For example, in the DOS command dir /p the DOS switch /p (pause after every screenful) is a parameter.

(2) In programming, a value passed to a subroutine or function for processing. Programming today's graphical applications with languages such as C, C++ and Pascal requires knowledge of hundreds, if not thousands, of parameters.

parameter-driven Software that requires external values expressed at runtime. A parameter-driven program solves a problem that is partially or entirely described by the values (parameters) that are entered at the time the program is loaded. For example, typing `bio 6-20-36` might load a program that calculates biorhythms for someone born on June 20, 1936. In this case, the date is a required parameter.

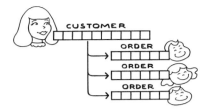

parent-child In database management, a relationship between two files. The parent file contains required data about a subject, such as employees and customers. The child is the offspring; for example, the child of a customer file may be the order file.

PARENT-CHILD

parent program The main, or primary, program or first program loaded into memory. See *child program.*

parity bit An extra bit attached to the byte, character or word used to detect errors in transmission.

parity checking An error detection technique that tests the integrity of digital data within the computer system or over a network. Parity checking uses an extra ninth bit that holds a 0 or 1 depending on the data content of the byte. Each time a byte is transferred or transmitted, the parity bit is tested.

Even parity systems make the parity bit 1 when there is an even number of 1 bits in the byte. Odd parity systems make it 1 when there is an odd number of 1 bits.

parity drive A separate disk drive that holds parity bits in a disk array. See *RAID.*

parity error An error condition that occurs when the parity bit of a character is found to be incorrect.

park To retract the read/write head on a hard disk to its home location before the unit is physically moved in order to prevent damage. Most modern drives park themselves when the power is turned off.

parse To analyze a sentence or language statement. Parsing breaks down words into functional units that can be converted into machine language. For example, to parse the dBASE expression `sum salary for title = "MANAGER"`, SUM must be identified as the primary command, FOR as a conditional search, TITLE as a field name and MANAGER as the data to be searched. Parsing breaks down a natural language request, such as "What's the total of all the managers' salaries" into the commands required by a query language, such as in the example above.

parser A routine that performs parsing operations on a computer or natural language.

partition A reserved part of disk or memory that is set aside for some purpose.

Pascal A high-level programming language developed by Swiss professor Niklaus Wirth in the early 1970s and named after the French mathematician, Blaise Pascal. It is noted for its structured programming, which caused it to achieve popularity initially in academic circles. Pascal has had strong influence on subsequent languages, such as Ada, dBASE and PAL. The following Turbo Pascal example converts Fahrenheit to Celsius:

```
program convert;
var
fahr, cent : integer;
begin
 write('Enter Fahrenheit ');
 readln(fahr);
 cent := (fahr - 32) * 5 / 9;
 writeln('Celsius is ',cent)
end.
```

passive hub A central connecting device in a network that joins wires from several stations in a star configuration. It does not provide any processing or regeneration of signals. Contrast with *active hub* and *intelligent hub*. See *hub*.

passive matrix A common LCD technology used in laptops. Using a transistor for every row and column, it provides a quality, although somewhat subdued, color display. See *active matrix*.

passive star See *passive hub*.

password A word or code used to serve as a security measure against unauthorized access to data. It is normally managed by the operating system or DBMS. However, the computer can only verify the legitimacy of the password, not the legitimacy of the user. See *NCSC*.

paste See *cut & paste*.

patch A temporary or quick fix to a program. Too many patches in a program make it difficult to maintain. It may also refer to changing the actual machine code when it is inconvenient to recompile the source program.

path (1) In communications, the route between any two nodes. Same as line, channel, link or circuit.

(2) In database management, the route from one set of data to another, for example, from customers to orders.

(3) The route to a file on a disk. In DOS and OS/2, the path for file MYLIFE located in subdirectory STORIES within directory JOSEPH on drive C: looks like:

```
c:\joseph\stories\mylife
```

The equivalent UNIX path follows. UNIX knows which drive is used:

```
/joseph/stories/mylife
```

The Macintosh also uses a path in certain command sequences; for example, with "hard disk" as the drive, the same path is:

```
hard disk:joseph:stories:mylife
```

PATHWORKS A network operating system from Digital that lets a VAX minicomputer function as a server for DOS, Windows, Windows NT, OS/2 and Macintosh clients. DECnet, TCP/IP, AppleTalk and NetWare protocols are supported.

PAX (1) (Private Automatic Exchange) An inhouse intercom system.

(2) (Parallel Architecture Extended) A parallel processing environment standard based on Intel's i860 RISC chip, UNIX System V and Alliant Computer's parallel and 3-D graphics technologies.

PBX (Private Branch eXchange) An inhouse telephone switching system that interconnects telephone extensions to each other, as well as to the outside telephone network. It may include functions such as least cost routing for outside calls, call forwarding, conference calling and call accounting.

Modern PBXs use all-digital methods for switching and can often handle digital terminals and telephones along with analog telephones.

PC (1) Also see *printed circuit board*.

(2) (Personal Computer) Although the term PC is sometimes used to refer to any kind of personal computer (Mac, Amiga, etc.), in this Glossary and in general, PC refers to computers that conform to the PC standard originally developed by IBM.

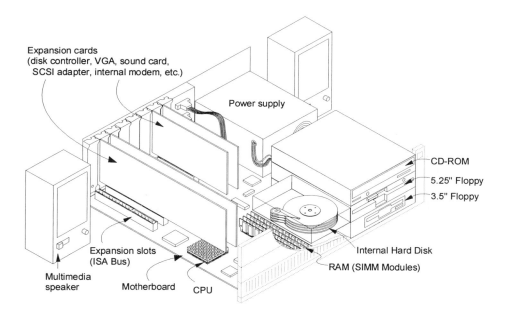

Expansion cards
(disk controller, VGA, sound card,
 SCSI adapter, internal modem, etc.)

Power supply

CD-ROM

5.25" Floppy

3.5" Floppy

Internal Hard Disk

RAM (SIMM Modules)

Expansion slots
(ISA Bus)

Multimedia
speaker

Motherboard   CPU

INTERNAL LAYOUT OF A PC

Today the PC industry is governed by Intel, Microsoft and major PC vendors collectively. The PC is the world's largest computer base; 1995 estimates are 150 to 200 million installed units. A rather wide range, one wonders who's keeping count.

▶ *The electronic and encyclopedic versions of this book provide more detail on PC models and specifications as well as tutorials and examples for DOS and Windows, zipping and unzipping files and "how to's" on a variety of related subjects.*

PC-8 A symbol set that contains the extended ASCII characters of the IBM PC.

PC-98 A personal computer series from NEC. It is the most popular PC in Japan.

PCB See *printed circuit board.*

PC board See *printed circuit board.*

PC bus The bus architecture used in first-generation IBM PCs and XTs. It refers to the original 8-bit bus, which accepted only 8-bit expansion boards. In 286s and up, it was superseded by the 16-bit AT bus, later known as the ISA bus.

PC card (1) A credit-card sized, removable module that contains memory, I/O or a hard disk. The term may refer to a variety of proprietary card-sized products; however, the term "PC Card" is PCMCIA's trademark for its PC card standard. See *PCMCIA.*

(2) An expansion board for a PC.

PC CPU models The brains of the PC is a CPU, or processor, from the Intel 8086 family (x86) of microprocessors or from a company that makes a compatible CPU. IBM also makes its own x86-compatible chips. See *x86.*

PC data buses The bus in a PC is the common pathway between the CPU and the peripheral devices. Controller boards for the video, disks and other devices plug directly into slots in the bus. See *ISA, EISA, Micro Channel* and *local bus.*

PC display modes Unlike the graphics-based Macintosh, PCs operate in two software-selectable modes: text mode (character mode) and graphics mode. Prior to Windows, business applications were text based and text scrolled quickly on screen on even the slowest PCs. DOS programs use both modes, and Windows uses only graphics mode.

Today, the PC display standard is VGA. Most VGA adapters support 640x480, 800x600 and 1024x768 resolutions. Higher-resolution adapters provide 1280x1024 and 1600x1200.

PC-DOS The DOS operating system supplied by IBM with its PCs. As of DOS 6, the utilities in PC-DOS and MS-DOS are different. Both versions are called *DOS*.

PCI (Peripheral Component Interconnect) A local bus for personal computers that provides a high-speed data path between the CPU and peripheral devices (video, disk, network, etc.). There are typically three or four PCI slots on the motherboard.

In a PC, the PCI bus coexists with the ISA or EISA bus. ISA and EISA boards still plug into an ISA or EISA slot, while high-speed PCI boards plug into a PCI slot. PCI comes in 32- and 64-bit varieties and runs at 33MHZ. Higher speeds are expected.

PCjr (PC junior) IBM's first home computer introduced in 1983. Its original keyboard was unsuitable for typing, but adequate keyboards were later added. It was discontinued in 1985.

Address			
11000:0000 1088K	High Memory Area (HMA)		Extended memory
10000:0000 1024K	PC ROM BIOS	PS/2 ROM BIOS & VGA ROM	
F000:0000 960K			
E000:0000 896K	Available for drivers and EMS page frame		Top 384K of the first megabyte of RAM is called the Upper Memory Area (UMA), comprised of Upper Memory Blocks (UMBs)
D000:0000 832K			
C800:0000 800K			
C000:0000 768K	EGA, VGA ROM BIOS		
BC00:0000 752K	Free		
	CGA graphics, CGA, EGA, VGA text	Hercules graphics	
B800:0000 736K			
B400:0000 720K	Free		
B000:0000 704K	MDA RAM		
A000:0000 640K	EGA, VGA graphics RAM		
	User programs		Lower 640K is used by DOS and user programs
0K	DOS and COMMAND.COM Interrupt vectors		

PC MEMORY MAP

This chart shows how the first megabyte of memory is used in a PC.

PC keyboard (1) The keyboard introduced with the IBM PC that provides a dual-function keypad for numeric entry and cursor movement. It was severely criticized for its non-standard shift key placement, which was corrected with the AT keyboard. Regardless of key placement, users love the feel of IBM keyboards.

(2) Any keyboard made for the PC, including the PC keyboard, AT keyboard and Enhanced keyboard.

PCL (Printer Control Language) The command language for the HP LaserJet printers. It has become a de facto standard used in many printers and typesetters. PCL Level 5, introduced with the LaserJet III in 1990, also supports Compugraphic's Intellifont scalable fonts.

PC LAN (1) A network of IBM or IBM-compatible PCs.

(2) A network of any variety of personal computers.

PCM (1) (Pulse Code Modulation) A technique for digitizing speech by sampling the sound waves and converting each sample into a binary number. It uses waveform coding that samples a 4KHz bandwidth 8,000 times a second. Each sample is an 8 bit number, resulting in 64K bits of data per second. See *ADPCM*.

(2) (Plug Compatible Manufacturer) An organization that makes a computer or electronic device that is compatible with an existing machine.

PCMCIA (Personal Computer Memory Card International Association) A non-profit trade association founded in 1989 to standardize the PC card. Address: 1030G East Duane Ave., Sunnyvale, CA 94086, 408/720-0107.

The PCMCIA card, officially called the *PC Card*, although nobody uses the name, is a credit-card sized, removable module used for attaching a modem, network adapter or hard disk to a portable computer. A Type I card is 3.3 mm thick, Type II is 5.0 mm thick, and Type III is 10.5 mm.

PC memory The original PC design was constrained to one megabyte of memory. In addition, certain parts of the operating system were placed into fixed locations in the upper part of memory without any method for cooperatively storing additional drivers and programs. This design gave rise to the most confusing platform in history. Following are the different types of memory in a PC. In other computers, there is generally just plain memory. In mainframes and supercomputers, there are also large auxiliary memory banks that function as caches between disk and RAM.

Conventional Memory	First 640K
UMA (Upper Memory Area)	Next 384K
HMA (High Memory Area)	Next 64K
Extended Memory	From 1MB up
EMS (Expanded Memory)	Additional memory beyond 1MB, which is bank-switched into the UMA

PC network (1) A network of IBM and/or IBM-compatible PCs.

(2) A network of any variety of personal computers.

(3) (PC Network) The first PC LAN from IBM introduced in 1984. It inaugurated the NetBIOS interface and uses the CSMA/CD access method. Token Ring support was added later. See *MS-Net*.

p-code See *pseudo language* and *UCSD p-System*.

PC Paintbrush A PC paint program from ZSoft Corporation, Marietta, GA, that is widely used and has set an industry standard graphics format. Its PCX raster graphics format is generated and accepted by many graphics, word processing and desktop publishing programs.

PC Tools A popular and comprehensive packages of utilities for DOS and Windows from Central Point Software, Beaverton, OR. They include a DOS or Windows shell as well as antivirus, file management, caching, backup, compression and data recovery utilities.

PCX A widely-used raster graphics file format developed by Zsoft Corporation, Marietta, GA, that handles monochrome, 2-bit, 4-bit, 8-bit and 24-bit color and uses RLE to achieve compression ratios of approximately 1.1:1 to 1.5:1. Images with large blocks of solid colors compress best under the RLE method.

PD software See *public domain software*.

PDA (Personal Digital Assistant) A handheld computer that serves an an organizer, electronic book or note taker and includes features such as pen-based entry and wireless transmission to a cellular service or desktop system.

PDES (Product Data Exchange Specification) A standard format for exchanging data between advanced CAD and CAM programs. It describes a complete product, including the geometric aspects of the images as well as manufacturing features, tolerance specifications, material properties and finish specifications. See *IGES*.

PDF See *Acrobat*.

PDIAL (Public Dialup Internet Access List) A list of Internet providers maintained by Peter Kaminsky. To get the list, send an e-mail message that says `send pdial` to Internet address `info-deli-server@netcom.com`. On CompuServe, send the message to `>internet:info-deli-server@netcom.com`.

PDIP (Plastic DIP) A common type of DIP made of plastic.

PDL See *page description language*.

PDP (Programmed Data Processor) A minicomputer family from Digital that started with the 18-bit PDP-1 in 1959. In 1965, Digital legitimized the minicomputer industry with the PDP-8, which sold for about $20,000. Other PDPs, including the PDP-11, were very successful.

PE (1) (Phase Encoding) An early magnetic encoding method used on 1600bpi tapes in which a 1 is an up transition and a 0 is a down transition in the center of the bit cell.

(2) (Processing Element) One of multiple CPUs in a parallel processing system.

(3) (Professional Engineer) An engineering degree.

peek/poke Instructions that view and alter a byte of memory by referencing a specific memory address. Peek displays the contents; poke changes it.

peer In communications, a functional unit that is on the same protocol layer as another.

peer-to-peer communications Communications in which both sides have equal responsibility for initiating, maintaining and terminating the session. Contrast with *master-slave communications*, in which the host determines which users can initiate which sessions. If the host were programmed to allow all users to initiate all sessions, it would look like a peer-to-peer system to the user.

peer-to-peer network A communications network that allows all workstations and computers in the network to act as servers to all other users on the network. Dedicated file servers may be used, but are not required as in a *client/server network*. Do not confuse this term with "peer-to-peer communications." A peer-to-peer network implies peer-to-peer communications, but peer-to-peer communications does not imply a peer-to-peer network.
▶ *Don't you love the extensive thought and analysis that goes into naming things in this business in order to make the terms perfectly clear and understandable for future generations!*

PE format (Portable Executable format) A Win32 file format for executable programs (EXEs and DLLs) supported under Windows 3.1 Enhanced Mode (Win32s) and Windows NT.

pel Same as *pixel*.

pen-based computing Using a stylus to enter hand writing and marks into a computer. See *gesture recognition*.

pen plotter See *plotter*.

Pen Windows An extension to Windows that allows pen-based computing.

PenPoint An operating system from Go Corporation, Foster City, CA, that provides a stylus (pen) interface for hand-written input. It uses a DOS-compatible file system, but does not run DOS applications. The direction, speed and order of the user's pen strokes is analyzed for recognition. See *NUI*.

Pentium Currently, the fastest CPU in the Intel x86 line. Pentium refers to the Pentium CPU chip or the PC that uses it. The Pentium is the successor to the 486 and was originally to be named the 586. Depending on the clock speed, the Pentium runs from half again to more than twice as fast as a 50MHz 486, while its floating point operations are up to four times as fast. Although its integer performance rivals major RISC-based CPUs (Alpha, HP-PA, MIPS, SPARC, etc.), its floating point performance is generally slower.

The Pentium is a 32-bit CPU with a 64-bit internal bus. Its base architecture is that of a 386 with enhancements to improve performance. See *x86*.

▶ *The electronic and encyclopedic versions of this book provide more detail on this subject.*

Pentium upgradable The ability to be upgraded to a Pentium CPU. 486 motherboards designed for Pentium upgrades contain a ZIF socket to make chip changing easy and are, in theory, designed to support the higher speeds of the Pentium chip.

People, Places and Things The code name for the user interface in Taligent's upcoming operating system. It refers to the task orientation of the interface in which a People object might refer to a name and address, a Thing could be a telephone or printer, and a Place could be a location in the network.

PEP (1) (Packet Exchange Protocol) A Xerox protocol used internally by NetWare to transport internal Netware NCP commands (NetWare Core Protocols). It uses PEP and IPX for this purpose. Application programs use SPX and IPX.

(2) A high-speed modem protocol from Telebit Corporation, Sunnyvale, CA, suited for cellular phone use.

performance ratings See *DOSmark, Winmark, SPECmark, Landmark rating, Dhrystones, Whetstones, iCOMP, PLB* and *MIPS* for the performance measurements included in this Glossary.

peripheral Any hardware device connected to a computer, such as a monitor, keyboard, printer, plotter, disk or tape drive, graphics tablet, scanner, joy stick, paddle and mouse.

peripheral controller See *control unit (2)*.

peripheral device See *peripheral*.

Perl (Practical Extraction Report Language) A UNIX programming language written by Larry Wall that combines syntax from several UNIX utilities and languages. Perl is designed to handle a variety of system administrator functions.

permanent font (1) A soft font that is kept in the printer's memory until the printer is turned off.

(2) Same as *internal font*.

permanent memory Same as *non-volatile memory*.

permutation One possible combination of items out of a larger set of items. For example, with the set of numbers 1, 2 and 3, there are six possible permutations: 12, 21, 13, 31, 23 and 32.

perpendicular recording See *vertical recording*.

persistence In a CRT, the time a phosphor dot remains illuminated after being energized. Long-persistence phosphors reduce flicker, but generate ghost-like images that linger on screen for a fraction of a second.

persistent link See *hot link*.

personal computer Synonymous with microcomputer, a computer that serves one user. PCs are the largest installed base with Macintoshes second. Amigas and Atari machines follow. Since the vast majority of computers in the world today are personal computers, the term is slowly fading to simply "computer."

▶ *The electronic and encyclopedic versions of this book provide more detail on the history of personal computers.*

personal workstation Same as *personal computer* or *workstation*.

PET computer (Personal Electronic Transaction computer) A CP/M and floppy disk-based personal computer introduced in 1977 by Commodore. It was one of the three first personal computers.

PFS:First Choice An integrated software package for PCs from SoftKey International, Inc., Cambridge, MA, that provides word processing, database, spreadsheet, graphics and communications capabilities.

PFS:Write See *Professional Write*.

PGA (1) (Pin Grid Array) A chip housing with high density of pins (200 pins can fit in 1.5" square). Used for large amounts of I/O, its underside looks like a "bed of nails."

(2) (Programmable Gate Array) A type of gate array trogrammed by the customer.

(3) (Professional Graphics Adapter) An early IBM display standard for PCs (640x480x256) with 3-D processing. It was not widely used.

PgUp/PgDn keys The Page Up and Page Down keys are typically used to move text up and down one screenful, but they can be programmed to do anything.

phase change recording An optical recording technique that uses a laser to create a bit by altering the crystalline structure of a metallic surface. The bit either reflects or absorbs light when read.

phase encoding See *PE*.

phase locked A technique for maintaining synchronization in an electronic circuit. The circuit receives its timing from input signals, but also provides a feedback circuit for synchronization.

phase modulation A transmission technique that blends a data signal into a carrier by varying (modulating) the phase of the carrier. See *modulate*.

phase-shift keying See *DPSK*.

PHIGS (Programmer's Hierarchical Interactive Graphics Standard) A graphics system and language used to create 2-D and 3-D images. Like the GKS standard, PHIGS is a device independent interface between the application program and the graphics subsystem.

It manages graphics objects in a hierarchical manner so that a complete assembly can be specified with all of its subassemblies. It is a very comprehensive standard requiring high-performance workstations and host processing.

Phoenix BIOS A PC-compatible ROM BIOS from Phoenix Technolgies, Ltd., Norwood, MA. Phoenix was the first company to successfully mass produce the ROM BIOS for the PC.

phone connector (1) A plug and socket for a two or three-wire coaxial cable used to plug microphones and headphones into amplifiers. The plug is a single, nail-like " thick prong about 1" in length. See *phono connector*.

(2) A plug and socket for a telephone line, typically the RJ-11 modular connector.

phone hawk Slang for a person who calls up a computer via modem and either copies or destroys data.

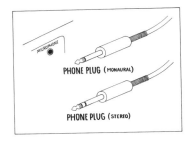

PHONE PLUG (MONAURAL)

PHONE PLUG (STEREO)

phoneme A speech utterance, such as "k," "ch," and "sh," that is used in synthetic speech systems to compose words for audio output.

Phong shading In computer graphics, a technique developed by Phong Bui Tuong that computes a shaded surface based on the color and illumination at each pixel. It is more accurate than Gouraud shading, but requires much more extensive computation.

phono connector Also called an RCA connector, a plug and socket for a two-wire coaxial cable used to connect audio and video components. The Apple II has a video out phono connector for a TV. The plug is a 1/8" thick prong that sticks out 5/16" from the middle of a cylinder. See *phone connector*.

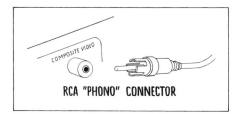

RCA "PHONO" CONNECTOR

phosphor A rare earth material used to coat the inside face of a CRT. When struck by an electron beam, the phosphor emits a visible light for a few milliseconds. In color displays, red, green and blue phosphor dots are grouped as a cluster.

Photo CD A CD imaging system from Kodak that digitizes 35mm slides or negatives onto a CD-ROM disc. The Photo CD is created by photo finishers that have a Kodak Picture Imaging Workstation. A replica of each image in the form of contact prints is also included. A multisession CD-ROM drive is required to read Photo CD images that were added after the original set. Most new drives provide this capability.

photocomposition Laying out a printed page using electrophotographic machines, such as phototypesetters and laser printers. See *page makeup* and *pagination*.

photolithography A lithographic technique used to transfer the design of the circuit paths and electronic elements on a chip onto a wafer's surface. A photomask is created with the design for each layer of the chip. The wafer is coated with a light-sensitive film (photoresist) that is hardened when exposed to light shining through the photomask. The wafer is then exposed to an acid bath (wet processing) or hot ions (dry processing), and the unhardened areas are etched away.

photomask An opaque image on a transluscent plate that is used as a light filter to transfer an image from one device to another.

photomicrography Photographing microscopic images.

photon A unit of energy. Elementary particle of electromagnetic radiation (light, radio waves, X-rays, etc.).

photonics The science of building machine circuits that use light instead of electricity.

photooptic memory A storage device that uses a laser beam to record data onto a photosensitive film.

photorealistic Having the image quality of a photograph.

photorealistic image synthesis In computer graphics, a format for describing a picture that depicts the realism of the actual image. It includes such attributes as surface texture, light sources, motion blur and reflectivity.

photoresist A film used in photolithography that temporarily holds the pattern of a circuit path or microscopic element of a chip. When exposed to light, it hardens and is resistant to the acid bath that washes away the unexposed areas.

photosensor A light-sensitive device that is used in optical scanning machinery.

Photoshop A popular image editing program for the Macintosh and Windows from Adobe Systems. The original Mac versions were the first to bring affordable image editing down to the personal computer level in the late 1980s.

phototypesetter A device that generates high-resolution text directly onto a photo-sensitive material. Input comes from the keyboard, or via disk, tape or modem. The output is a paper-like or transparent film that is processed into a camera-ready master for printing.

Phototypesetters employ various light technologies. Older machines pass light through a spinning font photomask, then through lenses that create the point size and onto film. Others create images on CRTs and expose the film. Modern imagesetters use lasers to generate the image directly onto the film.

The phototypesetter was originally the only machine that could handle multiple fonts and text composition such as kerning. Today, desktop laser printers are used for many typesetting jobs and are quickly advancing in resolution, although the 1270 and 2540 dpi resolutions of the phototypesetter combined with the high-quality of film still provide the finest printing.

Phototypesetters that handle both text and graphics are called *imagesetters*.

physical Refers to devices at the electronic, or machine, level. Contrast with *logical*. See *logical vs physical*.

physical address The actual, machine address of an item or device.

physical format See *record layout* and *low-level format*.

physical link (1) An electronic connection between two devices.

(2) In data management, a pointer in an index or record that refers to the physical location of data in another file.

physical lock A device that prevents access to data, such as a key lock switch on the computer or a file protection mechanism on a floppy disk. Contrast with *logical lock*.

PIC (1) (PICture) A file extension used for graphics formats. Lotus PIC is a vector format for 1-2-3 charts and graphs. Videoshow PIC is a vector format that is a subset of the NAPLPS standard.

(2) (Personal Intelligent Communicator) A hand-held computer from General Magic that uses 3" CD-ROMs and has a HyperCard-like interface. Cellular phone and wireless communications for networks, radio and TV are planned.

(3) (Programmable Interrupt Controller) An Intel 8259 chip that controls interrupts in PCs.

pica (1) In word processing, a monospaced font that prints 10 characters per inch.

(2) In typography, about 1/6th of an inch (0.166") or 12 points.

Pick System A multiuser operating environment from Pick Systems, Inc., Irvine, CA, that runs in a variety of computers and includes a virtual memory operating system and relational database. It is highly praised for its ease of use and flexibility.

picosecond One trillionth of a second. Pronounced "pee-co-second."

PICT (PICTure) A Macintosh graphics file format that stores images in the QuickDraw vector format. When PICT files are converted to the PC, they use the .PCT file extension.

picture In programming, a pattern that describes the type of data allowed in a field or how it will print. The pattern is made up of a character code for each character in the field; for example, 9999 is a picture for four numeric digits. A picture for a telephone number could be (999) 999-9999. XXX999 represents three alphanumerics followed by three numerics. Pictures are similar but not identical in all programming languages.

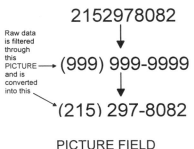

Raw data is filtered through this PICTURE and is converted into this

2152978082 → (999) 999-9999 → (215) 297-8082

PICTURE FIELD

picture element See *pixel*.

Picturephone The video telephone introduced by AT&T at the 1964 World's Fair (New York).

PID (1) (Process IDentifier) A temporary number assigned by the operating system to a process or service.

(2) (Proportional Integral Derivative) A controller used to regulate a continuous process such as grinding or cooking.

pie chart A graphical representation of information in which each unit of data is represented as a pie-shaped piece of a circle. See *business graphics*.

piezoelectric The property of certain crystals that oscillate when subjected to electrical pressure (voltage).

PIF (Program Information File) A Windows data file used to hold requirements for DOS applications running under Windows. Windows comes with a variety of PIFs, but users can edit them and new ones can be created with the PIF editor if a DOS application doesn't work properly. An application can be launched by clicking on its PIF.

piggyback board A small printed circuit board that plugs into another circuit board in order to enhance its capabilities. It does not plug into the motherboard, but would plug into the boards that plug into the motherboard.

PIL (Publishing Interchange Language) A standard for document interchange that defines the placement of text and graphics objects on the page. It does not address the content of the objects.

PILOT (Programmed Inquiry Learning Or Teaching) A high-level programming language used to generate question-and-answer courseware. A version that incorporates turtle graphics runs on Atari personal computers.

PIM (Personal Information Manager) Software that organizes random information for fast retrieval. It provides a combination of features such as a telephone list with automatic dialing, calendar, scheduler and tickler. A PIM lets you jot down text for any purpose and retrieve it based on any of the words you typed in. PIMs vary widely, but all of them attempt to provide methods for managing information the way you use it on a daily basis.

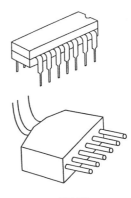

pin (1) The male lead on a connecting plug (serial port, monitor cable, keyboard connector, etc.) or the spiderlike foot on a chip. Each pin is plugged into a socket to complete the circuit.

PINS

(2) (PIN) (Personal Identification Number) A personal password used for identification purposes.

pin compatible Refers to a chip or other electronic module that can be plugged into the same socket as the chip or module it is replacing.

pin feed A method for moving continuous paper forms. Pins at both ends of a rotating platen or tractor engage the forms through pre-punched holes at both sides.

pinch roller A small, freely-turning wheel in a tape drive that pushes the tape against a motor-driven wheel in order to move it.

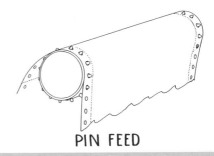

PIN FEED

pincushioning A screen distortion in which the sides bow in. Contrast with *barrel distortion*.

ping pong (1) A half-duplex communications method in which data is transmitted in one direction and acknowledgement is returned at the same speed in the other. The line is alternately switched from transmit to receive in each direction. Contrast with *asymmetric modem*.

(2) To go in one direction and then in the other.

ping-pong buffer See *double buffering*.

pinouts The description and purpose of each pin in a multiline connector.

pipe A shared space that accepts the output of one program for input into another. In DOS, OS/2 and UNIX, the pipe command is a vertical line (|). For example, in DOS and OS/2, the statement, `dir | sort` directs the output of the directory list to the sort utility.

pipeline processing A category of techniques that provide simultaneous, or parallel, processing within the computer It refers to overlapping operations by moving data or instructions into a conceptual pipe with all stages of the pipe processing simultaneously. For example, while one instruction is being executed, the computer is decoding the next instruction. In vector processors, several steps in a floating point operation can be processed simultaneously.

piracy The illegal copying of software for personal or commercial use.

pitch The number of printed characters per inch. With proportionally spaced characters, the pitch is variable and must be measured as an average. See *dot pitch*.

pixel (PIX [picture] ELement) The smallest element on a video display screen. A screen is broken up into thousands of tiny dots, and a pixel is one or more dots that are treated as a unit. A pixel can be one dot on a monochrome screen, three dots (red, green and blue) on color screens, or clusters of these dots.

pixel graphics Same as *raster graphics*.

PixelPaint A Macintosh drawing program from SuperMac Technology, Sunnyvale, CA, that is known for its extensive paint palette and color mixing schemes.

PKzip, PKunzip Popular PC shareware compression programs from PKWARE Inc., Brown Deer, WI. PKZIP compresses files into a ZIP file and PKUNZIP decompresses them.
▶ *The electronic and encyclopedic versions of this book include a tutorial on using PKZIP and PKUNZIP.*

PLA (Programmable Logic Array) A programmable logic chip (PLD) technology from Philips/Signetics.

plaintext Normal text that has not been encrypted and is readable by text editors and word processors. Contrast with *ciphertext*.

planar A technique developed by Fairchild Instruments that creates transistor sublayers by forcing chemicals under pressure into exposed areas. Planar superseded the mesa process and was a major step toward creating the chip.

planar area In computer graphics, an object that has boundaries, such as a square or polygon.

planning system See *spreadsheet* and *financial planning system*.

plasma display Also called *gas discharge*, a flat-screen technology that contains an inert ionized gas sandwiched between x- and y-axis panels. A pixel is selected by charging one x- and one y-wire, causing the gas in that vicinity to glow a bright orange.

platen A long, thin cylinder in a typewriter or printer that guides the paper through it and serves as a backstop for the printing mechanism to bang into.

platform The hardware architecture of a particular model or computer family. The term also often refers to just the operating system, which implies the particular hardware architecture that it runs on; for example, "the XYZ program runs on the Windows platform."

▶ *The electronic and encyclopedic versions of this book provide more detail on this subject.*

PLATO (Programmed Logic for Automatic Teaching Operations) Developed by Donald Bitzer and originally marketed by CDC, it was the first CBT system to combine graphics and touch-sensitive screens for interactive training.

platter One of the disks in a disk pack or hard disk drive. Each platter provides a top and bottom recording surface. See *magnetic disk*.

PLB (Picture Level Benchmark) The Graphics Performance Characterization (GPC) committee's benchmark, available through NCGA, for measuring graphics workstation performance. The Benchmark Interface Format (BIF) defines the PLB format, the Benchmark Timing Methodology (BTM) performs the test and the Benchmark Reporting Format (BRF) generates results in GPCmarks. Image quality is not rated.

PLC (Programmable Logic Controller) A computer used in process control applications. PLC microprocessors are typically RISC-based and are designed for high-speed, realtime and rugged industrial environments.

PLCC (Plastic LCC) A widely-used type of leaded chip carrier. See *LCC*.

PLD (Programmable Logic Device) A logic chip that is programmed at the customer's site. There are a wide variety of PLD techniques; however, most PLDs are compatible with the PAL method from Advanced Micro Devices.

The PLD is not a storage chip like a PROM or EPROM, although fuse-blowing techniques are used. It contains different configurations of AND, OR and NOR gates that are "blown" together. Contrast with *gate array*, which requires a manufacturing process to complete the programming.

PL/I (Programming Language 1) A high-level IBM programming language introduced in 1964 with the System/360 series. It was designed to combine features of and eventually supplant COBOL and FORTRAN, which never happened. A PL/I program is made up of procedures (modules) that can be compiled independently. There is always a main procedure and zero or more additional ones. Functions, which pass arguments back and forth, are also provided.

PL/M (Programming Language for Microprocessors) A dialect of PL/I developed by Intel as a high-level language for its microprocessors. PL/M+ is an extended version of PL/M, developed by National Semiconductor for its microprocessors.

plot To create an image by drawing a series of lines. In programming, a plot statement creates a single vector (line) or a complete circle or box that is made up of several vectors.

plotter A graphics printer that draws images with ink pens. It

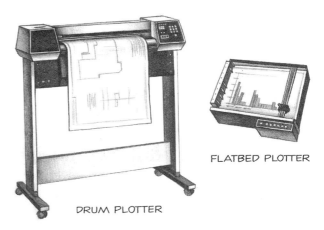

FLATBED PLOTTER

DRUM PLOTTER

requires data in vector graphics format, which makes up an image as a series of point-to-point lines. See *flatbed plotter* and *drum plotter*.

PLP (Presentation Level Protocol) A North American standard protocol for videotex.

plug and play (1) The ability to add a new component and have it work without having to perform any technical analysis or procedure.

(2) (Plug and Play) Also abbreviated PnP, it is a Microsoft/Intel standard for PCs incorporated into upcoming operating systems (Windows 95, etc.) and expansion boards. It will eliminate the frustration of configuring the system when adding new peripherals. IRQ and DMA settings and I/O and memory addresses will self configure each time the computer is turned on.

plug compatible Hardware that is designed to perform exactly like another vendor's product. A plug compatible CPU runs the same software as the machine it's compatible with. A plug compatible peripheral works the same as the device it's replacing.

plugboard A board containing a matrix of sockets used to program early tabulating machines and computers. A wire is inserted into one output and one input socket, closing a circuit and activating a function. Complicated programs looked like "mounds of spaghetti."

plugs & sockets The physical connectors used to link together all variety of electronic devices. See *DB-9*, *RS-232*, and *Centronics*.

PM See *preventive maintenance*, *Presentation Manager*, *Program Manager* and *phase modulation*.

PMOS (Positive channel MOS) Pronounced "P moss." A type of microelectronic circuit in which the base material is positively charged. PMOS transistors were used in the first microprocessors and are still used in CMOS. They are also used in low-cost products (calculators, watches, etc.).

THE AUTHOR HARD AT WORK (1962)

Plugboards and wires were the programmer's tools of the 1960s. These boards were inserted into tabulating machines (collators, reproducers, accounting machines, etc.) in order to direct their operation. In those days, "Tabulating Technicians" were the lucky ones. Instead of standing all day at their sorters and tabulators, they were allowed time to sit down while they wired their plugboards!

PMS (Pantone Matching System) A color matching system that has assigned a number to over 500 different colors.

PnP See *Plug and Play*.

pocket computer A hand-held, calculator-sized computer that runs on batteries. It can be plugged into a personal computer for data transfer.

point (1) To move the cursor onto a line or image on screen by rolling a mouse across the desk or by pressing the arrow keys.

(2) In typography, a unit equal to 1/72nd of an inch, used to measure the vertical height of a printed character.

point and shoot To select a menu option or activate a function by moving the cursor onto a line or object and pressing the return key or mouse button.

pointer (1) In database management, an address embedded within the data that specifies the location of data in another record or file.

(2) In programming, a variable that is used as a reference to the current item in a table (array) or to some other object, such as the current row or column on screen.

(3) An on-screen symbol used to identify menu selections or the current screen location. It is moved by a mouse or other pointing device.

pointing device An input device, such as a mouse or graphics tablet, used to move the cursor on screen or to draw an image.

point of sale Capturing data at the time and place of sale. Point of sale systems use personal computers or specialized terminals that are combined with cash registers, optical scanners for reading product tags, and/or magnetic stripe readers for reading credit cards.

BAR CODE

POINT OF SALE

Point of sale systems may be online to a central computer for credit checking and inventory updating, or they may be stand-alone machines that store the daily transactions until they can be delivered or transmitted to the main computer for processing.

point-to-multipoint A communications network that provides a path from one location to multiple locations (from one to many).

point-to-point A communications network that provides a path from one location to another (point A to point B).

Poisson distribution A statistical method developed by the 18th century French mathematician S. D. Poisson, which is used for predicting the probable distribution of a series of events. For example, when the average transaction volume in a communications system can be estimated, Poisson distribution is used to determine the probable minimum and maximum number of transactions that can occur within a given time period.

poke See *peek/poke*.

polarity (1) The direction of charged particles, which may determine the binary status of a bit.

(2) In micrographics, the change in the light to dark relationship of an image when copies are made. Positive polarity is dark characters on a light background; negative polarity is light characters on a dark background.

polarized A one-way direction of a signal or the molecules within a material pointing in one direction.

Polish notation A method for expressing a sequence of calculations developed by the Polish logician Jan Lukasiewicz in 1929. For example, A(B+C) would be expressed as * A + B C. In reverse Polish notation, it would be A B C + *.

polling A communications technique that determines when a terminal is ready to send data. The computer continually interrogates its connected terminals in a round robin sequence. If a terminal has data to send, it sends back an acknowledgement and the transmission begins. Contrast with *interrupt-driven*, in which the terminal generates a signal when it has data to send.

polling cycle One round in which each and every terminal connected to the computer or controller has been polled once.

polygon In computer graphics, a multi-sided object that can be filled with color or moved around as a single entity.

polyhedron A six- or more-sided object. A group of connected polygons.

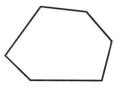

POLYGON

polyline In computer graphics, a single entity that is made up of a series of connected lines.

polymorphic tweening See *tweening*.

polymorphic virus A virus that changes its binary pattern each time it infects a new file to keep it from being identified. See *stealth virus*.

POLYLINE

polymorphism Meaning many shapes. In object-oriented programming, the ability of a generalized request (message) to produce different results based on the object that it is sent to.

polyphonic The ability to play back some number of musical notes simultaneously. For example, 16-voice polyphony means a total of 16 notes, or waveforms, can be played concurrently.

Polyvision A flat panel display from Alpine Polyvision Inc. that uses a plastic film of metal ions sandwiched between horizontal and vertical electrodes. Where current intersects, the metal ions turn black.

pop (1) See *push/pop*.

(2) (Point of Presence) The place where a line from a long distance carrier (IXC) connects to the line of the local telephone company or to the user if the local company is not involved.

POP-11 (Package for Online Programming) A general-purpose programming language with list processing and compiler writing functionality from SD-Scicon PLC.

pop-down menu See *pull-down menu*.

populate To plug in chips or components into a printed circuit board. A fully populated board is one that contains all the devices it can hold.

popup (1) A type of menu called for and displayed on top of the existing text or image. When the item is selected, the menu disappears and the screen is restored.

(2) Same as *TSR*.

port (1) A pathway into and out of the computer. The serial and parallel ports on a personal computer are external sockets for plugging in communications lines, modems and printers. On a front end processor, serial ports connect to communications lines and modems.

(2) To convert software to run in a different computer environment.

portability See *portable*.

portable Refers to software that can be easily moved from one type of machine to another. It implies a product that has a version for several hardware platforms or has built-in capabilities for switching between them. However, a program that can be easily converted from one machine type to another is also considered portable.

portable computer A personal computer that can be easily transported. Compared to desktop models, it has limited expansion slots and disk capacity.

Portable NetWare
An OEM version (C source code) of Novell's NetWare operating system that can be compiled for a specific vendor's machine.

port address A physical identification of an I/O port. See *I/O address*.

port expander A device that connects several lines to one port in the computer. A line is given access to the port either by a hardware switch or through software selection.

port replicator A device used to connect peripherals to a laptop. All the desktop devices are permanently plugged into the port replicator, which quickly connects to the laptop. It is like a docking station without expansion slots.

porting See *port*.

portrait An orientation in which the data is printed across the narrow side of the form.

POS See *point of sale*.

positive logic The use of low voltage for a 0 bit and high voltage for a 1 bit. Contrast with *negative logic*.

POSIX (Portable Operating System Interface for UNIX) An IEEE 1003.1 standard that defines the language interface between application programs and the UNIX operating system. Adherence to the standard ensures compatibility when programs are moved from one UNIX computer to another. POSIX is primarily composed of features from UNIX System V and BSD UNIX.

POST (Power On Self Test) A series of built-in diagnostics that are performed when the computer is first started. Proprietary codes are generated (POST codes) that indicate test results. See *diagnostic board*.

postfix notation See *reverse Polish notation*.

postprocessor Software that provides some final processing to data, such as formatting it for display or printing.

PostScript A page description language from Adobe Systems, Inc., Mountain View, CA, used in a wide variety of printers, imagesetters and display systems. PostScript commands do not drive the printer directly. They are language statements in ASCII text that are translated into the printer's machine language by a PostScript interpreter built into the printer. Fonts, known as *Type 1* and *Type 3* fonts, are scaled to size by the interpreter.
▶ *The electronic and encyclopedic versions of this book provide more detail on this subject.*

pot See *potentiometer*.

potentiometer A device that controls the amount of current that flows through a circuit, such as a volume switch on a radio.

POTS (Plain Old Telephone Service) The traditional analog telephone network.

power (1) See *computer power*.

(2) (POWER) (Performance Optimization With Enhanced RISC) A RISC-based CPU architecture from IBM used in its RS/6000 workstation and parallel computer line. The PowerPC, enhanced by Motorola and Apple, is a single-chip version of the POWER architecture.

power adapter A transformer that converts AC power from a wall outlet into the DC power required by an electronic device.

PowerBook A family of Macintosh portable computers from Apple that include a trackball centered in a wrist rest. PowerBooks are very popular. See *Macintosh* for specifications.

PowerBuilder A high-level application development system for Windows client/server applications from Powersoft Corporation, Concord, MA. It uses a programming language called PowerScript that is similar to BASIC. PowerBuilder supports SQL and several databases, including DB2 and Oracle.

PowerCD A consumer-oriented CD-ROM player from Apple that connects to a TV for Photo CD use, to a Macintosh for data, audio and Photo CD or to a stereo for audio CDs.

power down To turn off the computer in an orderly manner by making sure all applications have been closed normally and then shutting the power.

power good A signal transmitted from the power supply to the circuit board indicating that the power is stable. For various power supply definitions, see *power supply*.

Power Macintosh A PowerPC-based Macintosh. With the first models introduced in March 1994, Apple plans on eventually migrating all Macintoshes from the Motorola 680x0 family of CPUs to the PowerPC RISC chip. PowerMacs run the PowerPC version of the Mac System 7 operating system and also run DOS and Windows applications by way of Insignia Solutions' SoftWindows, which is an optional feature.
▶ *The electronic and encyclopedic versions of this book provide more detail on this subject.*

power management Maximizing battery power by using low-voltage CPUs and slowing down components when they are inactive. See *SMM*.

PowerOpen A UNIX-based operating system for the PowerPC. PowerOpen is considered a technology foundation, not just an operating system. Different versions of PowerOpen are being developed; for example, IBM and Apple are expected to each have a version that conforms to the PowerOpen Environment.

PowerPC A family of RISC-based CPU chips introduced in 1993 by IBM and Motorola. The PowerPC is designed to span a range from hand-held machines to supercomputers. The first model, the 601 (MPC601) runs initially at 50 and 66MHz and is as fast or faster than a Pentium, but is half the size and uses half the electricity. Upcoming models are a low-power MPC603 for notebooks, a faster MPC604 and a true 64-bit, ultra-fast MPC620 with multiple levels of parallelism.
▶ *The electronic and encyclopedic versions of this book provide more detail on this subject.*

power platform Refers to a mature, high-speed computer system.

PowerPoint A desktop presentation program from Microsoft for the Macintosh and Windows. It was the first desktop presentation program for the Mac and provides the ability to create output for overheads, handouts, speaker notes and film recorder. Color palettes for Genigraphics slides accompany the product.

PowerShare Software from Apple that resides in a Macintosh server and provides messaging store and forward, authentication of network users, encryption of messages and other workgroup/enterprise services.

power supply An electrical system that converts AC current from the wall outlet into the DC currents required by the computer circuitry. In a personal computer, +5, -5, +12 and -12 voltages are generated. The 5 volts are used for the electronic circuitry, and the 12 volts are required for the drives.
▶ *The electronic and encyclopedic versions of this book provide more detail on this subject.*

power surge An oversupply of voltage from the power company that can last up to several seconds. Power surges are the most common cause of loss to computers and electronic equipment. See *spike* and *sag*.

PowerTalk Messaging software from Apple that is included in the Macintosh System 7 Pro operating system. It provides a unified mail box that holds different types of communication including e-mail, fax, voice mail and pager. It provides for RSA digital signatures, which guarantees the authenticity of documents electronically signed by other users.

PowerTalk uses the AppleTalk transport protocol for transmission over the network. PowerTalk runs on individual Macs, while PowerShare runs on Mac servers. PowerTalk and PowerShare are part of Apple's AOCE technology framework.

power up To turn the computer on in an orderly manner.

power user A person who is very proficient with personal computers. It implies knowledge of a variety of software packages.

PPC See *PowerPC*.

PPGA (Plastic PGA) See *PGA*.

pph (Pages Per Hour) Measures printing speed.

ppi (1) (Pixels Per Inch) The measurement of the display or print elements.

(2) (Points Per Inch, Pulses Per Inch) The measurement of mouse movement.

ppm (Pages Per Minute) The measurement of printing speed.

PPP (Point-to-Point Protocol) A communications protocol that provides dial-up access to the Internet. Developed by the Internet Engineering Task Force (IETF) in 1991, PPP is more advanced than the earlier SLIP protocol, which is also commonly used for Internet access. PPP can establish and terminate a session as well as hang up and redial on a low-quality call. It can run on any full-duplex link from dial-up to high-speed DS1 and DS3 lines.

PQFP (Plastic Quad FlatPack) A surface mount chip housing with flat leads on all four sides.

PRAM (Parameter RAM) Pronounced "P RAM." A battery-backed part of the Macintosh's memory that holds Control Panel settings and the settings for the hidden desktop file. If the command and option keys are held down at startup, the desktop settings are cleared and a dialog to rebuild the desktop is initiated.

precedence The order in which an expression is processed. Mathematical precedence is normally:

> 1. unary + and - signs
> 2. exponentiation
> 3. multiplication and division
> 4. addition and subtraction

In order to properly compute the formula that converts Fahrenheit to Celsius, which is **fahrenheit-32*5/9**, the expression `(fahrenheit-32)*5/9` must be used with parentheses separating the fahrenheit-32 from the multiplication. Since multiplication is evaluated before subtraction, 32 would be multiplied by 5 first, which is not what is wanted.

Logical precedence is NOT first, then AND then OR. In the dBASE query `list for item = "TIE" .and. color = "GRAY" .or. color = "RED"` all gray ties and anything red will be selected, since ANDs are evaluated before ORs. Grouping the colors in parentheses `(color="GRAY" .or. color="RED")` yields only gray and red ties.

precision The number of digits used to express the fractional part of a number. The more digits, the more precision. See *single precision* and *double precision*.

predicate In programming, a statement that evaluates an expression and provides a true or false answer based on the condition of the data.

preemptive multitasking A multitasking method that shares processing time with all running programs. Preemtive multitasking creates a true timesharing environment in which all running programs get a recurring slice of time from the CPU. Depending on the operating system, the time slice may be the same for all programs or it may be adjustable to meet the current mix of programs and users. For example, background programs can be given more CPU time no matter how heavy the foreground load and vice versa. Contrast with *non-preemtive multitasking*.

prefix notation See *Polish notation*.

prepress In typography and printing, the preparation of camera-ready materials up to the actual printing stage, which includes typesetting and page makeup.

preprocessor Software that performs some preliminary processing on the input before it is processed by the main program.

presentation graphics Presentation materials for overheads, 35mm slide shows and computer-driven slide shows (screen shows). Presentation graphics programs provide a wide selection of predefined backgrounds and page layouts as well as the ability to create various types of business graphics for charting numerical data. They include drawing and painting tools and the ability to select from stock graphical elements to illustrate a page.

For computer-driven slide shows, the application provides a variety of special effects that can be used to fade and wipe one frame into another such as commonly found in the video world. Sound and video can also be merged into the presentation.

Presentation Manager A graphical user interface (GUI) library used to develop OS/2 applications. Character-based OS/2 applications can be developed similar to DOS applications, but OS/2 PM applications are graphics based like Macintosh, Windows and Motif applications. The term used to refer to the interface itself, which is now called *Workplace Shell*.

Prestel A commercial videotex service of British Telecom (formerly part of the British Post Office).

preventive maintenance The routine checking of hardware that is performed by a field engineer on a regularly scheduled basis. See *remedial maintenance*.

PRI See *ISDN*.

primary index The index that controls the current processing order of a file. See *secondary index*.

primary storage The computer's internal memory (RAM). Contrast with *secondary storage*.

primitive (1) In computer graphics, a graphics element that is used as a building block for creating images, such as a point, line, arc, cone or sphere.

(2) In programming, a fundamental instruction, statement or operation.

(3) In microprogramming, a microinstruction, or elementary machine operation.

print buffer See *printer buffer*.

print column A column of data on a printed report that may be subtotalled or totalled. Print columns are the heart of a report writer's description.

printed circuit board A flat board that holds chips and other electronic components. The board is made of reinforced fiberglass or plastic and interconnects components via copper pathways. The main printed circuit board in a system is called a system board or motherboard, while smaller ones that plug into the slots in the main board are called *boards* or *cards*.

The printed circuit board of the 1960s connected discrete components together. The circuit board of the 1990s interconnects chips, each containing hundreds of thousands and millions of elementary components. The "printed" circuit is really an etched circuit. A copper foil is placed over the glass or plastic base and covered with a photoresist. Light is shined through a negative image of the circuit paths onto the photoresist, hardening the areas that will remain after etching. When passed through an acid bath, the unhardened areas are washed away. A similar process creates the microminiaturized circuits on a chip.

print engine See *printer engine*.

printer A device that converts computer output into printed images. The most common types of printers are dot matrix printers and laser printers.
▶ *The electronic and encyclopedic versions of this book provide more detail on a variety of printer technologies.*

printer buffer A memory device that accepts printer output from one or more computers and transmits it to the printer. It lets the computer dispose of its printer output at full speed without waiting for each page to print. Printer buffers with automatic switching are connected to two or more computers and accept their output on a first-come, first-served basis.

printer cable A wire that connects a printer to a computer. On a PC, the cable has a 25-pin DB-25 male connector for the computer and a 36-pin Centronics male connector for the printer.

printer driver Software routine that converts an application program's printing request into the language the printer understands.

printer engine The unit within the printer that does the actual printing. For example, in a laser printer, it is the "copy machine" unit, which transfers and fuses the toner onto the paper. It is specified by its resolution and speed.

printer file (1) A document in print image format ready to be printed. See *print to disk*.

(2) Same as *printer driver*.

printer font A font used for printing. Printer and screen resolutions are not the same, thus fonts generated for the printer will not display accurately on screen. Contrast with *screen font*.

print head A mechanism that deposits ink onto paper in a character printer.

print image A text or graphics document that has been prepared for the printer. Format codes for the required printer have been embedded in the document at the appropriate places. With text files, headers, footers and page numbers have been created and inserted in every page.

print image format See *print image*.

printout (PRINTer OUTput) Same as *hard copy*.

print queue Disk space that holds output designated for the printer until the printer can receive it.

print screen The ability to print the current on-screen image. See *screen dump*.

print server A computer in a network that controls one or more printers. It stores the print-image output from all users of the system and feeds it to the printer one job at a time. This function may be part of the network operating system or an add-on utility.

print spooler Software that manages printing in the background. When an application is made to print, it quickly generates the output on disk and the spooler feeds the print images to the printer at slower printing speeds. This second step can be run in the background without appreciably interfering with user interaction in the foreground. See *spooling*.

print to disk To redirect output from the printer to the disk. The resulting file contains text and graphics with all the codes required to direct the printer to print it. The file can be printed later or at a remote location without requiring the word processor, DTP or drawing program that was originally used to create it. This is actually the first stage of a print spooling operation. See *print spooler*.

privacy The authorized distribution of information (who has a right to know?). Contrast with *security*, which deals with unauthorized access to data.

Private Eye A headband-mounted LED display system from Reflection Technology, Waltham, MA, that plugs into a PC. Its 1x1" screen gives the appearance of a 12" monitor floating in space in front of the viewer.

private file A file made available only to the user that created it. Contrast with *public file*.

private key See *encryption*.

private line (1) A dedicated line leased from a common carrier.

(2) A line owned and installed by the user.

PRMD (PRivate Management Domain) An inhouse e-mail service. See *X.400*.

PRML (Partial Response Maximum Likelihood) A technique used to differentiate a valid signal from noise by measuring the rate of change at various intervals of the rising waveform. Bits generated by a modem or hard disk platter have uniform characteristics, whereas random noise does not.

PRN (PRiNter) The DOS name for the first connected parallel port. See *DOS device names*.

problem-oriented language A computer language designed to handle a particular class of problem. For example, COBOL was designed for business, FORTRAN for scientific and GPSS for simulation.

procedural language A programming language that requires programming discipline, such as COBOL, FORTRAN, BASIC, C, Pascal and dBASE. Programmers writing in such languages must develop a proper order of actions in order to solve the problem, based on a knowledge of data processing and programming. The following dBASE example shows procedural and non-procedural language to list a file.

```
        Procedural (3GL)              Non-procedural (interactive, 4GL)

        USE FILEX                     USE FILEX
        DO WHILE .NOT. EOF            LIST NAME, AMOUNTDUE
          ? NAME, AMOUNTDUE
          SKIP
        ENDDO
```

procedure (1) Manual *procedures* are human tasks.

(2) Machine *procedures* are lists of routines or programs to be executed, such as described by the job control language (JCL) in a mini or mainframe, or the batch processing language in a personal computer.

(3) In programming, another term for a subroutine or function.

procedure oriented An application that forces the user to follow a predefined path from step A to step B. Data entry programs are typical examples. Contrast with *event driven*.

process To manipulate data in the computer. The computer is said to be processing no matter what action is taken upon the data. It may be updated or simply displayed on screen.

In order to evaluate a computer system's performance, the time it takes to process data internally is analyzed separately from the time it takes to get it in and out of the computer. I/O is usually more time consuming than processing. See *3 C's*.

process bound An excessive amount of processing causing an imbalance between I/O and processing. Process-bound applications may slow down other users in a multiuser system.

A personal computer is process bound when it is recalculating a spreadsheet, for example.

process color A color printed from four separate printing plates. Four-color process printing uses cyan, magenta, yellow and black (CMYK) inks to produce full color reproduction. Contrast with *spot color*.

process control The automated control of a process, such as a manufacturing process or assembly line. It is used extensively in industrial operations, such as oil refining, chemical processing and electrical generation. It uses analog devices to monitor real-world signals and digital computers to do the analysis and controlling. It makes extensive use of analog/digital, digital/analog conversion.

processing Manipulating data within the computer. The term is used to define a variety of computer functions and methods. See *centralized processing, distributed processing, batch processing, transaction processing* and *multiprocessing*.

processor (1) Same as *CPU*.

(2) May refer to software. See *language processor* and *word processor*.

processor unit Same as *computer*.

process printing See *process color*.

Procomm A popular PC shareware communications program from Datastorm Technologies, Inc., Columbia, MO, that supports a wide number of protocols and terminals. Procomm Plus is the commercial version with more features.

PRODIGY An online information service (partnership of IBM and Sears) that includes weather and stock market reports, airline scheduling and at-home shopping. Users receive a communications program that must be installed in their personal computer, which provides full-screen displays and simplifies the logon. See *online services*.

ProDOS (PROfessional Disk Operating System) An operating system for the Apple II family that superseded Apple's DOS 3.3. It provides a hierarchical file system with file names up to 15 characters in length.

production database A central database containing an organization's master files and daily transaction files.

production system A computer system used to process an organization's daily work. Contrast with a system used only for development and testing or for ad hoc inquiries and analysis.

productivity software Refers to word processors, spreadsheets, database management systems, PIMs, schedulers and other software packages that are designed for individual use. Contrast with custom-designed, multiuser information systems which provide the primary data processing in an organization.

Professional Write A word processing program for DOS and Windows from SoftKey International, Inc., Cambridge, MA. It is easy to use and meets the needs of many who write uncomplicated letters and memos. Originally called PFS:Write, it was one of the earliest PC word processors.

Professional YAM (Professional Yet Another Modem) A PC communications program from Omen Technology, Inc., Portland, OR, for the serious communications user. It is a flexible, full-featured program that supports a wide variety of terminals and protocols.

PROFS (PRofessional OFfice System) IBM office automation software for the VM mainframe environment. It provides an e-mail facility for text and graphics, a library service for centrally storing text, electronic calendars and appointment scheduling, and it allows document interchange with DISOSS users. PROFS uses IBM's proprietary ZIP messaging protocol.

ProgMan See *Program Manager*.

program A collection of instructions that tell the computer what to do. A program is called *software*; hence, program, software and instructions are synonymous. A program is written in a programming language and is converted into the computer's machine language by software called assemblers, compilers and interpreters.

program counter A register or variable used to keep track of the address of the current or next instruction. See *address register* and *instruction register*.

program development See *system development cycle*.

program generator See *application generator*.

program logic A sequence of instructions in a program. There are many logical solutions to a problem. If you give a specification to ten programmers, each one may create program logic that is slightly different than all the rest, but the results can be the same. The solution that runs the fastest is usually the most desired, however.

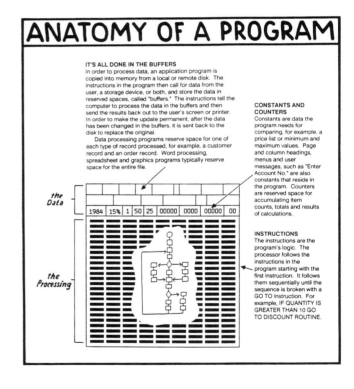

ANATOMY OF A PROGRAM

IT'S ALL DONE IN THE BUFFERS
In order to process data, an application program is copied into memory from a local or remote disk. The instructions in the program then call for data from the user, a storage device, or both, and store the data in reserved spaces, called "buffers." The instructions tell the computer to process the data in the buffers and then send the results back out to the user's screen or printer. In order to make the update permanent, after the data has been changed in the buffers, it is sent back to the disk to replace the original.

Data processing programs reserve space for one of each type of record processed, for example, a customer record and an order record. Word processing, spreadsheet and graphics programs typically reserve space for the entire file.

CONSTANTS AND COUNTERS
Constants are data the program needs for comparing, for example, a price list or minimum and maximum values. Page and column headings, menus and user messages, such as "Enter Account No." are also constants that reside in the program. Counters are reserved space for accumulating item counts, totals and results of calculations.

the Data

1984 15% 1 50 25 00000 0000 00000 00

INSTRUCTIONS
The instructions are the program's logic. The processor follows the instructions in the program starting with the first instruction. It follows them sequentially until the sequence is broken with a GO TO instruction. For example, IF QUANTITY IS GREATER THAN 10 GO TO DISCOUNT ROUTINE.

the Processing

Program logic is written using three classes of instructions: sequential processing, selection and iteration.

1. Sequential processing is the series of steps that do the actual data processing. Input, output, calculate and move (copy) instructions are used in sequential processing.

2. Selection is the decision making within the program and is performed by comparing two sets of data and branching to a different part of the program based on

the results. In assembly languages, the compare and branch instructions are used. In high-level languages, IF THEN ELSE and CASE statements are used.

3. Iteration is the repetition of a series of steps and is accomplished with DO LOOPS and FOR LOOPS in high-level languages and GOTOs in assembly languages. See *loop*.

programmable Capable of following instructions. What sets the computer apart from all other electronic devices is its programmability.

programmable calculator A limited-function computer capable of working with only numbers and not alphanumeric data.

program maintenance Updating programs to reflect changes in the organization's business or to adapt to new operating environments. Although maintaining old programs written by ex-employees is often much more difficult than writing new ones, the task is usually given to junior programmers, because the most talented professionals don't want the job.

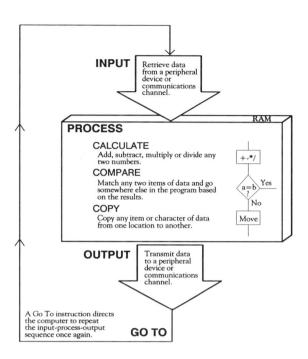

PROGRAM LOGIC

Although program logic becomes quite complicated in practice, it is all based on inputting data into memory, processing it and outputting the results. The main loop of many data processing programs performs this sequence.

YOUR BASIC HANDHELD PROGRAMMABLE CALCULATOR
(Courtesy The MIT Museum)
The Differential Analyzer in the 1930s was programmed with a screwdriver and a wrench.

Program Manager The control center for Windows 3.x operation. It provides the means to launch applications and manage the desktop. Program Manager may be replaced with another shell, such as Norton's Desktop for Windows, HP's Dashboard or Quarterdeck's SideBar, all of which provide similar functionality with a different user interface.

programmatic interface Same as *API*.

programmer A person who designs the logic for and writes the lines of codes of a computer program. See *application programmer* and *systems programmer*.

programmer analyst A person who analyzes and designs information systems and designs and writes the application programs for the system. In theory, a programmer analyst is both systems analyst and applications programmer. In practice, the title is sometimes simply a reward to a programmer for tenure. Which skill is really dominant is of concern when recruiting people with such titles.

Programmer's Switch The physical buttons included with the Macintosh (fkey on the LC) that include a System Reset button and a Debugging button that will invoke MacsBug if present or switch to the built in monitor in ROM.

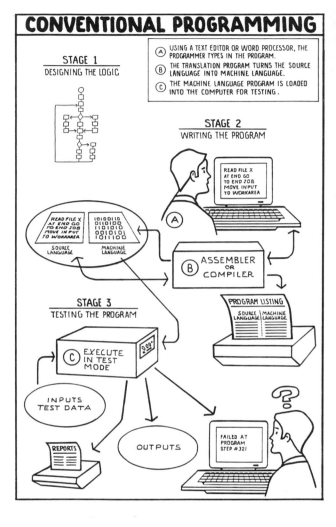

programming Creating a computer program. The steps are:
1. Developing the program logic to solve the particular problem.
2. Writing the program logic in a specific programming language (coding the program).
3. Assembling or compiling the program to turn it into machine language.
4. Testing and debugging the program.
5. Preparing the necessary documentation.

The logic is the most difficult part of programming. Writing the language statements is comparatively easy once the solution has been developed. However, regardless of how difficult the program may be, documenting it is considered the most annoying activity by most programmers.

programming interface See *API*.

programming language A language used to write instructions for the computer. It lets the programmer express data processing in a symbolic manner without regard to machine-specific details. See *ALGOL, ADA, APL, BASIC, C, C++, COBOL, dBASE, Forth, FORTRAN, Lisp, Logo, MUMPS, Pascal, Prolog, REXX* and *Visual Basic*.

program state An operating mode of the computer that executes instructions in the application program. Contrast with *supervisor state*.

program statement A phrase in a high-level programming language. One program statement may result in several machine instructions when the program is compiled.

program step An elementary instruction, such as a machine language instruction or an assembly language instruction. Contrast with *program statement*.

program-to-program communications Communications between two programs. Often confused with peer-to-peer communications, it is a set of protocols a program uses to interact with another program. Peer-to-peer establishment is the network's responsibility. You can have program-to-program communications in a master-slave environment without peer-to-peer capability.

project manager Software used to monitor the time and materials on a project. All tasks to complete the project are entered into the database, and the program computes the critical path, the series of tasks with the least amount of slack time. Any change in the critical path slows down the entire project.

progressive scan Same as *non-interlaced*.

projection panel See *LCD panel*.

Prokey A keyboard macro processor for DOS and Windows from CE Software, Inc., West Des Moines, IA, that allows users to eliminate repetitive typing by setting up an occurrence of text or a series of commands as a macro.

Prolog (PROgramming in LOGic) A programming language used for developing AI applications (natural language translation, expert systems, abstract problem solving, etc.). Developed in France in 1973, it is used throughout Europe and Japan and is gaining popularity in the U.S.

Similar to LISP, it deals with symbolic representations of objects. The following example, written in University of Edinburgh Prolog, converts Fahrenheit to Celsius:

```
convert:- write('Enter Fahrenheit'),
  read(Fahr),
  write('Celsius is '),
  Cent is (5 * (Fahr - 32)) / 9,
  write(Cent),nl.
```

PROM (Programmable Read Only Memory) A permanent memory chip that is programmed, or filled, by the customer rather than by the chip manufacturer. It differs from a ROM, which is programmed at the time of manufacture. PROMs have been mostly superseded by EPROMs, which can be reprogrammed. See *PROM programmer*.

PROM blower Same as *PROM programmer*.

PROM programmer A device that writes instructions and data into PROM chips. The bits in a new PROM are all 1s (continuous lines). The PROM programmer only creates 0s, by "blowing" the middle out of the 1s. Some earlier units were capable of programming both PROMs and EPROMs.

prompt A software message that requests action by the user; for example, "Enter employee name." Command-driven systems issue a cryptic

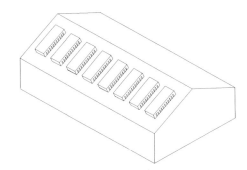

PROM PROGRAMMER

symbol when ready to accept a command; for example, the dot (.) in dBASE, the $ or % in UNIX, and the venerable C:\> in DOS. See *DOS prompt*.

propagation The transmission (spreading) from one place to another.

propagation delay The time it takes to transmit a signal from one place to another.

property list In a list processing language, an object that is assigned a descriptive attribute (property) and a value. For example, in Logo, `putprop "Karen "language "Paradox` assigns the value PARADOX to the property LANGUAGE for the person named KAREN. To find out what language Karen speaks, the Logo statement `print getprop "Karen "language` will generate PARADOX as the answer.

proportional spacing Character spacing based on the width of each character. For example, an I takes up less horizontal space than an M. In monospacing (fixed), the I and M each take up the same amount. See *kerning*.

proprietary software Software owned by an organization or individual. Contrast with *public domain software*.

Protected Mode In Intel 286s and up, an operational state that allows the computer to address all of memory. It also prevents an errant program from entering into the memory boundary of another. In a 386 and up, it provides access to 32-bit instructions and sophisticated memory management modes. See *32-bit processing, Real Mode, Virtual 8086 Mode* and *memory protection*.

protocol Rules governing transmitting and receiving of data. See *communications protocol* and *OSI*.

protocol analyzer See *network analyzer*.

protocol stack The hierarchy of protocols used in a communications network. Network architectures designed in layers, such as TCP/IP, OSI and SNA, are referred to as stacks. See *OSI model*.

protocol suite Same as *protocol stack*.

prototyping (1) Creating a demo of a new system. Prototyping is essential for clarifying information requirements. The design of a system (functional specs) must be finalized before the system can be built. While analytically-oriented people may have a clear picture of requirements, others may not.

Using fourth-generation languages, systems analysts and users can develop the new system together. Databases can be created and manipulated while the user monitors the progress.

Once users see tangible output on screen or on paper, they can figure out what's missing or what the next question might be if this were a production system. If prototyping is carefully done, the end result can be a working system.

Even if the final system must be reprogrammed in other languages for standardization or machine efficiency, prototyping has served to provide specifications for a working system rather than a theoretical one.

(2) See *function prototyping*.

PR/SM

(Processor Resource/Systems Manager) An IBM mainframe feature that allows the CPU to run as multiple logical processors, each capable of running a different operating system and set of applications. Standard on ES/9000 models, it is an upgrade to 3090 processors.

Prt Sc See *print screen*.

PS (Personal Services) IBM office automation software for PCs, minis and mainframes, which includes word processing, electronic mail and library services.

PS/1 An IBM home computer series introduced in 1990. The original models featured an integrated monitor and easy-to-open case. The first PS/1 was a 286 with an ISA bus.

PS/2 An IBM personal computer series introduced in 1987, superseding the original PC line. It introduced the 3.5" microfloppy disk, VGA graphics and Micro Channel bus. The 3.5" disks and VGA are now common in all PCs, but the Micro Channel is used primarily by IBM. Smaller PS/2 models use the ISA bus.

PS/2 bus Same as *Micro Channel*.

pseudo compiler A compiler that generates a pseudo language, or intermediate language, which must be further compiled or interpreted for execution.

pseudo-duplexing A communications technique that simulates full-duplex transmission in a half-duplex line by turning the line around very quickly.

pseudo language An intermediate language generated from a source language, but not directly executable by a CPU. It must be interpreted or compiled into machine language for execution. It facilitates the use of one source language for different types of computers. See "ANDF" in *OSF* definition.

PSK See *DPSK*.

PSN (Packet-Switched Network) A communications network that uses packet switching technology.

PSS See *EPSS*.

PSTN (Public Switched Telephone Network) The worldwide voice telephone network.

PSW (Program Status Word) A hardware register that maintains the status of the program being executed.

p-System See *UCSD p-System*.

PTOCA (Presentation Text Object Content Architecture) See *MO:DCA*.

PTT (Postal, Telegraph & Telephone) The governmental agency responsible for combined postal, telegraph and telephone services in many European countries.

PU (Physical Unit) In SNA, software responsible for managing the resources of a node, such as data links. A PU supports a connection to the host (SSCP) for gathering network management statistics.

PU 2.1 (Physical Unit 2.1) In SNA, the original term for Node Type 2.1, which is software that provides peer-to-peer communications between intelligent devices (PCs, workstations, minicomputers). Only LU 6.2 sessions are supported between Type 2.1 nodes (PU 2.1).

public domain software Software in which ownership has been relinquished to the public at large. See *freeware* and *shareware*.

public file A file made available to all other users connected to the system or network. Contrast with *private file*.

public key See *encryption*.

Publish and Subscribe A Macintosh System 7 capability that provides hot links between files. All or part of a file can be published into an "edition file," which is imported into a subscriber file. When any of the published files are updated, the subscriber file is also updated.

puck The mouse-like object used to draw on a digitizer tablet.

pull-down menu Also called a pop-down menu, a menu that is displayed from the top of the screen downward when its title is selected. The menu remains displayed while the mouse button is depressed. To select a menu option, the highlight bar is moved (with the mouse) to the appropriate line and the mouse button is let go.

The drop-down menu is a variation that keeps the menu open after its title is selected. To select a menu option, the highlight bar is moved to the line and the mouse button is clicked. Key commands may also activate drop-down menus.

pulse code modulation See *PCM*.

pulse level device A disk drive or other device that inputs and outputs raw voltages. Data coding/decoding is in the controller the device. Contrast with *bit level device*.

PUMA (Programmable Universal Micro Accelerator) A Chips and Technolgies' chipset that accelerates graphics operations for the screen and printer.

punch block Also called a quick-connect block, a device that interconnects telephone lines from remote points. The wires are pushed, or punched, down into metal teeth that strip the insulation and make a tight connection.

punched card An early storage medium made of thin cardboard stock that holds data as patterns of punched holes. Each of the 80 or 96 columns holds one character. The holes are punched by a keypunch machine or card punch peripheral and are fed into the computer by a card reader.

Although still used as turnaround documents, punched cards are practically obsolete. However, from 1890 until the 1970s, they were synonymous with data processing. Concepts were simple: the database was the file cabinet; a record was a card. Processing was performed on separate

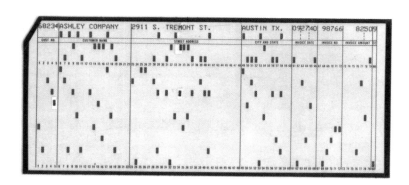

80-COLUMN PUNCHED CARD
(Courtesy IBM)

This is the common "IBM card" that evolved from Herman Hollerith's original punched card. Throughout the greater part of the 20th Century, billions of these cards were put through sorters, collators, reproducers and tabulators, each machine performing one data processing operation.

machines called sorters, collators, reproducers, calculators and accounting machines.

push/pop Instructions that store and retrieve an item on a stack. Push enters an item on the stack, and pop retrieves an item, moving the rest of the items in the stack up one level. See *stack*.

push/pull tractor A printer tractor that can be switched from pushing paper onto the platen to pulling it from the platen. Single-sheet continuous forms can be pushed, but most multipart forms and labels must be pulled to prevent jamming.

put In programming, a request to store the current record in an output file. Contrast with *get*.

PVC (Permanent Virtual Circuit) A point-to-point connection that is established ahead of time. All PVCs defined at the time of subscription to a particular service are known as a VPN (virtual private network). Contrast with *SVC.*

PVGA (Paradise **VGA**) A VGA adapter or VGA chips from the Paradise Division of Western Digital.

Px64 An ITU-TSS standard for transmitting audio and video in 64 Kbits/sec ISDN channels (P represents number of channels used). Although video conferencing can be done in only one or two channels, more channels are required for smooth motion.

Px64 uses two screen formats. The CIF (Common Intermediate Format) generates a 352x288 resolution, while QCIF (Quarter CIF) is 176x144. CIF transmits at 36.45 Mbits/sec; QCIF is 9.115 Mbits/sec. See *H.261.*

PXP (Packet eXchange Protocol) See *PEP.*

Q&A An integrated file manager and word processor for DOS and Windows from Symantec Corporation, Cupertino, CA, that includes mail merge capability as well as a programming language for customizing data entry forms and reports. Its Intelligent Assistant feature provides a query language that can learn new words from the user.

QAM (1) (Quadrature Amplitude Modulation) A modulation technique that generates four bits out of one baud. For example, a 600 baud line (600 shifts in the signal per second) can effectively transmit 2,400 bps using this method. Both phase and amplitude are shaped with each baud, resulting in four possible patterns.

(2) (Quality Assessment Measurement) A system used to measure and analyze voice transmission.

QBasic A BASIC interpreter from Microsoft that comes with DOS starting with DOS 5. It supersedes Microsoft's GW-BASIC and includes REMLINE.BAS, a program that helps convert GW-BASIC programs to QBasic.

QBE (Query By Example) A method for describing a query originally developed by IBM for mainframes. A replica of an empty record is displayed and the search conditions are typed in under their respective columns. The following query selects all Pennsylvania records that have a balance due of $5000 or more.

CUSTOMER FILE

NAME	ADDRESS	CITY	STATE	ZIP	BALANCE
			PA		>=5000

QUERY BY EXAMPLE

Q-bus A bus architecture used in Digital's PDP-11 and MicroVAX series.

QCIF (Quarter CIF) A video format that transmits 9.115 Mbits/sec at 30 frames/sec, one quarter the speed of CIF. See *H.261.*

QEMM-386 (Quarterdeck EMM-386) A popular DOS memory manager for 386s and up from Quarterdeck Office Systems, Santa Monica, CA. Its Stealth feature in Version 6.0 remaps ROM BIOS routines into EMS to free up high DOS memory. It is also part of DESQview.

QIC (Quarter Inch Cartridge.) A backup technology that uses 1/4" wide (6.35mm) magnetic tape cartridges. It uses the serpentine recording method with cartridge capacities ranging from 40MB to 20GB.

QMF (Query Management Facility) An IBM fourth-generation language for end-user interaction with DB2.

Qmodem Pro Communications programs for DOS and Windows from Mustang Software, Inc., Bakersfield, CA. The programs support a wide variety of modems as well as all the major file transfer protocols and terminal emulations. The Windows version is noted for its integrated fax facilities allowing the user to fax directly from within any Windows word processor. Mustang Software is also the publisher of the popular WILDCAT! BBS software.

QNX A multiuser, multitasking, realtime operating system for PCs from QNX Software Systems, Ltd., Kanata, Ontario, noted for its low-memory requirement and rapid response. Similar to UNIX, it has been in use since the early 1980s.

quadbit A group of four bits used in QAM modulation.

Quadra Apple's brand name for certain Macintosh computers.

quadrillion One thousand times one trillion or 10^{12}. See *femtosecond*.

quantize To assign a number to a sample. The larger the number the more the digital sample represents the analog signal. See *sampling*.

QuarkXpress A desktop publishing program for the Macintosh and Windows from Quark, Inc., Denver, CO. Originally developed for the Mac, it is noted for its precise typographic control and advanced text and graphics manipulation.

quartz crystal A slice of quartz ground to a prescribed thickness that vibrates at a steady frequency when stimulated by electricity. The tiny crystal, about 1/20th by 1/5th of an inch, creates the computer's heartbeat.

Quattro Pro A PC spreadsheet from Novell that provides advanced graphics and presentation capabilities. It has an optional interface that is keystroke, macro and file compatible with Lotus 1-2-3. Version 2.0 adds goal seeking, 3-D graphing and the ability to create multi-layered slide shows. Quattro Pro was originally developed by Borland and was purchased by Novell in 1994.

query To interrogate a database (count, sum and list selected records). Contrast with *report*, which is usually a more elaborate printout with headings and page numbers. The report may also be a selective list of items; hence, the two terms may refer to programs that produce the same results.

query by example See *QBE*.

query language A generalized language that allows a user to select records from a database. It uses a command language, menu-driven method or a query by example (QBE) format for expressing the matching condition.

Query languages are usually included in DBMSs, and stand-alone packages are available for interrogating files in non-DBMS applications. See *query program*.

query program Software that counts, sums and retrieves selected records from a database. It may be part of a large application and be limited to one or two kinds of retrieval, such as pulling up a customer account on screen, or it may refer to a query language that allows any condition to be searched and selected.

queue Pronounced "Q." A temporary holding place for data. See *message queue* and *print queue*.

Quick B CompuServe's communications protocol for downloading files.

QuickBASIC A popular BASIC compiler from Microsoft that adds advanced features to the BASIC language.

QuickC A C compiler and development system from Microsoft that is compatible with Microsoft C and used by the beginner or occasional programmer. QuickC for Windows is a version that provides a Windows-based environment for developing Windows applications. See *Visual C++*.

Quickdraw The graphics display system built into the Macintosh. It accepts commands from the application and draws the corresponding objects on the screen. It provides a consistent interface that software developers can work with.

Quicken A popular personal financial management program for PCs and Macs from Intuit, Menlo Park, CA. It writes checks, organizes investments and produces a variety of financial reports.

QuickPascal A pascal compiler from Microsoft that is compatible with Turbo Pascal and provides object oriented capabilities.

Quicksilver A family of dBASE III PLUS compilers originally developed by WordTech Systems, Inc. In 1992, the technology was acquired by Borland.

QuickTime Multimedia extensions to Macintosh's System 7 that add sound and video capabilities. A QuickTime file can contain up to 32 tracks of audio, video, MIDI or other time-based control information. Most major Macintosh DBMSs (database management systems) support QuickTime. Apple also provides a QuickTime for Windows version for Windows-based PCs.

QuickWin A library of C and FORTRAN routines from Microsoft that allows quick porting of DOS applications to the Windows environment. Character-based apps run in resizable windows.

quit To exit the current program. It's a good habit to quit a program before turning the computer off. Some programs don't close all files properly until quit is activated.

qwerty keyboard The standard English language typewriter keyboard. Q, w, e, r, t and y are the letters on the top left, alphabetic row. It was originally designed to slow typing to prevent the keys from jamming. See *Dvorak keyboard*.

QWERTY KEYBOARD

RACF (Resource Access Control Facility) IBM mainframe security software introduced in 1976 that verifies user ID and password and controls access to authorized files and resources.

rack A frame or cabinet into which components are mounted.

rack mounted Components that are built to fit in a metal frame. Electronic devices, such as testing equipment and tape drives, are often rack mounted units.

RAD (Rapid Application Development) An approach to systems development that includes automated design and development tools (CASE) and joint application development (JAD). Developed by industry guru, James Martin, it focuses on human management and user involvement as well as technology. It also emphasizes developing the system incrementally and delivering working pieces every three to four months, rather than waiting until the entire project is completed.

radio The transmission of electromagnetic energy (radiation) over the air or through a hollow tube called a waveguide. Although radio is often thought of as only AM or FM, all airborne transmission is radio, including satellite and line-of-sight microwave.

radio buttons A series of on-screen buttons that allow only one selection. If a button is currently selected, it will de-select when another button is selected.

radio frequency See *RF*.

radix The base value in a numbering system. For example, in the decimal numbering system, the radix is 10.

radix point The location in a number that separates the integral part from the fractional part. For example, in the decimal system, it is the decimal point.

ragged right In typography, non-uniform text at the right margin, such as the text you're reading now.

RAID (Redundant Arrays of Inexpensive Disks) Two or more drives working together that provide increased performance and various levels of error recovery and fault tolerance. The disk controller is designed to perform these techniques. RAID can also be implemented in software using standard drives and controllers.

Level	Configuration
0	Single disk only or multiple disks using disk striping only (essentially non-RAID).
1	Uses disk mirroring to provide 100% duplication of data.
2	Highest performance. Uses extra drives to detect 2-bit errors and correct 1-bit errors on the fly. Interleaves by bit or block.
3	Highest performance. Does parity checking but cannot guarantee on-the-fly recovery. Interleaves data by bit or block.
4	Uses dedicated drive for parity. Can be used with only two drives. Interleaves data by sector and can handle multiple I/Os from sophisticated operating systems.
5	Most popular RAID method. Works with two or more drives. Does not require dedicated parity drive. Can be made fault tolerant.

RAM (Random Access Memory) The computer's primary workspace. Also true of most memory chips (ROMs, PROMs, etc.), "random" means that the contents of each byte can be directly accessed without regard to the bytes before or after it. RAM chips require power to maintain their content. That's why you must save your files to the disk before you turn the computer off. Any running programs and all the data they currently reference, such as the spreadsheet or word processing document you're working on, are lost without power. See *dynamic RAM, static RAM* and *memory*. Contrast with *disk* and *ROM*.

RAMAC (Random Access Method of Accounting and Control) The first hard disk computer which was introduced by IBM in 1956. All 50 of its 24" platters held a total of five million characters! It was half computer, half tabulator. It had a drum memory for program storage, but its I/O was wired by plugboard. After 38 years, IBM resurrected the RAMAC name with the introduction of a high-capacity disk storage system in 1994.

RAM card (1) A printed circuit board containing memory chips that is plugged into a socket within the computer.

(2) A credit-card-sized module that contains memory chips and battery. See *memory card*.

RAM chip (Random Access Memory chip) A memory chip. See *dynamic RAM, static RAM, RAM and memory*.

RAM cram Insufficient memory to run applications, especially in DOS PCs with its 1MB memory limit.

RAMDAC (Random Access Memory Digital to Analog Converter) The VGA controller chip that maintains the color palette and converts data from memory into analog signals for the monitor.

RAM disk A disk drive simulated in memory. To use it, files are copied from magnetic disk into the RAM disk. Processing is faster, because there's no mechanical disk action, only memory transfers. Updated data files must be copied back to disk before the power is turned off, otherwise the updates are lost. Same as *E-disk* and *virtual disk*.

Ramdrive A RAM disk driver that accompanies DOS starting with DOS 4.0.

RAMIS See *CA-RAMIS*.

RAM refresh Recharging dynamic RAM chips many times per second in order to keep the bit patterns valid.

RAM resident Refers to programs that remain in memory in order to interact with other programs or to be instantly popped up when required by the user. See *TSR*.

random access Same as *direct access*.

random noise Same as *Gaussian noise*.

random number generator A program routine that produces a random number. Random numbers are created easily in a computer, since there are many random events that take place; for example, the duration between keystrokes. Only a few milliseconds' difference is enough to seed a random number generation routine with a different number each time. Once seeded, an algorithm computes different numbers throughout the session.

range (1) In data entry validation, a group of values from a minimum to a maximum.

(2) In spreadsheets, a series of cells that are worked on as a group. It may refer to a row, column or rectangular block defined by one corner and its diagonally opposite corner.

RAS (1) (Remote Access Server) A network server that provides access to remote computer users via modem.

(2) (Remote Access Service) Software in Windows for Workgroups and Windows NT that provides access to remote computer users via modem.

(3) (Reliability Availability Serviceability) Originally an IBM term, it refers to a product's quality, availability of optional features and ease of diagnosis and repair.

raster display A display terminal that generates dots line by line on the screen. TVs and almost all computer screens use the raster method. Contrast with *vector display*.

raster graphics In computer graphics, a technique for representing a picture image as a matrix of dots. It is the digital counterpart of the analog method used in TV. However, unlike TV, which uses one standard, there are many raster graphics standards. See *graphics*. Contrast with *vector graphics*.

raster image processor See *RIP*. Remember... use the acronym first!

raster scan Displaying or recording a video image line by line.

rasterize To perform the conversion of vector graphics images, vector fonts or outline fonts into bitmaps for display or printing. Unless output is printed on a plotter, which uses vectors directly, all non-bitmapped images must be rasterized into bitmaps for display or printing. See *font scaler*.

raw data Data that has not been processed.

ray tracing In computer graphics, the creation of reflections, refractions and shadows on a graphics image. It follows a series of rays from a specific light source and computes each pixel in the image to determine the effect of the light. It is a very process-intensive operation.

R:BASE A relational DBMS for PCs from Microrim, Inc., Bellevue, WA, that provides interactive data processing, a complete programming language and an application generator. It was the first DBMS to compete with dBASE II in the early 1980s.

RBHC (Regional Bell Holding Company) Same as *RBOC*.

RBOC (Regional Bell Operating Company) One of seven regional telephone companies created by divestiture: Nynex, Bell Atlantic, BellSouth, Southwestern Bell, US West, Pacific Telesis and Ameritech.

RCA connector Same as *phono connector*.

RCS (1) (Remote Computer Service) A remote timesharing service.

(2) (Revision Control System) A UNIX utility that provides version control.

Rdb (Relational DataBase/VMS) A relational DBMS from Digital for its VAX series.

RDBMS (Relational DataBase Management System) See *relational database*.

RDRAM (Rambus DRAM) A dynamic RAM chip from Rambus, Inc., that transfers data at 500MBytes/sec (3-10 times faster than DRAM and VRAM chips). It requires modified motherboards, but eliminates the need for memory caches.

read To input into the computer from a peripheral device (disk, tape, etc.). Like reading a book or playing an audio tape, reading does not destroy what is read.

A read is both an input and an output (I/O), since data is being output from the peripheral device and input into the computer. Memory is also said to be read when it is accessed to transfer data out to a peripheral device or to somewhere else in memory. Every peripheral or internal transfer of data is a read from somewhere and a write to somewhere else.

read cycle The operation of reading data from a memory or storage device.

read error A failure to read the data on a storage or memory device. Although it is not a routine phenomenon, magnetic and optical recording surfaces can become contaminated with dust or dirt or be physically damaged, and cells in memory chips can malfunction.

When a read error occurs, the program will allow you to bypass it and move on to the next set of data, or it will end, depending on the operating system. However, if the damaged part of a disk contains control information, the rest of the file may be unreadable. In such cases, a recovery program must be used to retrieve the remaining data if there is no backup.

read only (1) Refers to storage media that permanently hold their content; for example, ROM and CD-ROM.

(2) A file which can be read, but not updated or erased. See *file attribute*.

read-only attribute A file attribute that, when turned on, indicates that a file can only be read, but not updated or erased.

read/write (1) Refers to a device that can both input and output or transmit and receive.

(2) Refers to a file that can be updated and erased.

read/write channel Same as *I/O channel*.

read/write head A device that reads (senses) and writes (records) data on a magnetic disk or tape. For writing, the surface of the disk or tape is moved past the read/write head. By discharging electrical impulses at the appropriate times, bits are recorded as tiny, magnetized spots of positive or negative polarity.

For reading, the surface is moved past the read/write head, and the bits that are present induce an electrical current across the gap.read/write memory Same as *RAM*.

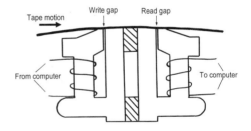

TAPE DRIVE READ/WRITE HEAD

reader A machine that captures data for the computer, such as an optical character reader, magnetic card reader and punched card reader. A microfiche or microfilm reader is a self-contained machine that reads film and displays its contents.

readme file A text file copied onto software distribution disks that contains last-minute updates or errata that have not been printed in the documentation manual.

readout (1) A small display device that typically shows only a few digits or a couple of lines of data.

(2) Any display screen or panel.

real address Same as *absolute address*.

Realizer See *CA-Realizer*.

Real Mode An operational state in Intel 286s and up in which the computer functions as an 8086/8088. It is limited to one megabyte of memory. See *Protected Mode* and *Virtual 86 Mode*.

real storage Real physical memory in a virtual memory system.

realtime An immediate response. It refers to process control and embedded systems; for example, space flight computers must respond instantly to changing conditions. It also refers to fast transaction processing systems as well as any electronic operation fast enough to keep up with its real-world counterpart (animating complex images, transmitting live video, etc.).

realtime clock An electronic circuit that maintains the time of day. It may also provide timing signals for timesharing operations.

realtime compression The ability to compress and decompress data without any noticeable loss in speed compared to non-compressed data. PC products such as Stacker and SuperStor let you create a separate compressed drive on your hard disk. All data written to that drive is compressed and decompressed when read back. Realtime compression is included in DOS starting with DOS 6. See *JPEG*.

realtime conferencing See *teleconferencing (3)*.

realtime image A graphics image that can be animated on screen at the same speed as the real-world object.

realtime information system A computer system that responds to transactions by immediately updating the appropriate master files and/or generating a response in a time frame fast enough to keep an operation moving at its required speed. See *transaction processing*.

realtime operating system A master control program that can provide immediate response to input signals and transactions.

realtime system A computer system that responds to input signals fast enough to keep an operation moving at its required speed.

realtime video The ability to transmit video live without missing any frames. It requires very high transmission capacity.

reasonable test A type of test that determines if a value falls within a range considered normal or logical. It can be made on electronic signals to detect extraneous noise as well as on data to determine possible input errors.

reboot To reload the operating system and restart the computer. See *boot*.

receiver A device that accepts signals. Contrast with *transmitter*.

record (1) A group of related fields that store data about a subject (master record) or activity (transaction record). A collection of records make up a file.

Master records contain permanent data, such as account number, and variable data, such as balance due. Transaction records contain only permanent data, such as quantity and product code. See *master file* and *transaction file* for examples of record contents.

(2) In certain disk organization methods, a record is a block of data read and written at one time without any relationship to records in a file.

record format Same as *record layout*.

record head A device that writes a signal on tape. Some tape drives and all disk drives use a combination read/write head.

record layout The format of a data record, which includes the name, type and size of each field in the record.

NAME	ADDRESS	CITY	STATE	ZIP
Conrad, James R.	809 Garibaldi Lane	Benton Falls	TN	37255-0265

RECORD LAYOUT

record locking See *file and record locking*.

record mark A symbol used to identify the end of a record.

record number The sequential number assigned to each physical record in a file. Record numbers change when the file is sorted or records are added and deleted.

records management The creation, retention and scheduled destruction of an organization's paper and film documents. Computer-generated reports and documents fall into the records management domain, but traditional data processing files do not.

recovery See *backup & recovery, checkpoint/restart* and *tape backup*.

rectifier An electrical circuit that converts AC into DC current with the use of diodes that act as one-way valves. Contrast with *inverter*.

recursion In programming, the ability of a subroutine or program module to call itself. It is helpful for writing routines that solve problems by repeatedly processing the output of the same process.

redaction The editing done to sensitive documents before release to the public.

Red Book (1) The documentation of the U.S. National Security Agency that defines criteria for secure networks. The volumes are "Trusted Network Interpretation of the Trusted Computer System Evaluation Criteria" (NCSC-TG-005) and "Trusted Network Interpetation Environments Guideline: Guidance for Applying the Trusted Network Interpretation" (NCSC-TG-011). It is the network counterpart of the Orange Book for computers. See *NCSC*.

(2) The documentation for the technical specification of audio CDs, which includes such details as sampling and transfer rates. "Red Book audio" refers to digital sound that conforms to the common standard used in music compact discs. See *CD*.

redirection Diverting data from its normal destination to another; for example, to a disk file instead of the printer, or to a server's disk instead of the local disk.

redirector In a LAN, software that routes workstation (client) requests for data to the server.

redundancy check In communications, a method for detecting transmission errors by appending a calculated number onto the end of each segment of data. See *CRC*.

reengineering Known as business process reengineering (BPR), it is the deployment of information technology to improve performance and cut costs. Its main premise, as popularized by the book "Reengineering the Corporation" by Michael Hammer and James Champy, is to examine the goals of an organization and to redesign work and business processes from the ground up rather than simply automate existing tasks and functions.

According to the authors, reengineering is driven by open markets and competition. No longer, can we enjoy the protection of our own country's borders as we could in the past. Today, we are in a global economy, and worldwide customers are more sophisticated and demanding.

reentrant code A programming routine that can be used by multiple programs simultaneously. It is used in operating systems and other system software as well as in multithreading, where concurrent events are taking place. It is written so that none of its code is modifiable (no values are changed) and it does not keep track of anything. The calling programs keep track of their own progress (variables, flags, etc.), thus one copy of the reentrant routine can be shared by an any number of users or processes.

Conceptually, it is as if several people were each baking a cake from a single copy of a recipe on the wall. Everyone looks at the master recipe, but keeps track of their own progress by jotting down the step number they are at on their own scratchpad so they can pick up where they left off. The master recipe is never disturbed.

referential integrity A database management safeguard that ensures every foreign key matches a primary key. For example, customer numbers in a customer file are the primary keys, and customer numbers in the order file are the foreign keys. If a customer record is deleted, the order records must also be deleted otherwise they are left without a primary reference. If the DBMS doesn't test for this, it must be programmed into the applications.

reflection mapping In computer graphics, a technique for simulating reflections on an object.

reflective spot A metallic foil placed on each end of a magnetic tape. It reflects light to a photosensor to signal the end of tape.

reflective VGA An LCD screen that needs bright ambient light for viewing. Backlit and sidelit screens are much easier to see.

reformat (1) To change the record layout of a file or database.

(2) To initialize a disk over again.

refraction The bending of light, heat or sound as it passes through different materials.

refresh To continuously charge a device that cannot hold its content. CRTs must be refreshed, because the phosphors hold their glow for only a few milliseconds. Dynamic RAM chips require refreshing to maintain their charged bit patterns.

refresh rate (1) The number of times per second that a device is re-energized, such as a CRT or dynamic RAM chip. See *vertical scan frequency*.

(2) In computer graphics, the time it takes to redraw or redisplay an image on screen.

regenerator (1) In communications, the same as a *repeater*.

(2) In electronics, a circuit that repeatedly supplies current to a memory or display device that continuously loses its charges or content.

ReGIS (REmote Graphics InStruction) A graphics language from Digital used on graphics terminals and first introduced on the PDP-11.

register A small, high-speed computer circuit that holds values of internal operations, such as the address of the instruction being executed and the data being processed. When a program is debugged, register contents may be analyzed to determine the computer's status at the time of failure.

In microcomputer assembly language programming, programmers reference registers routinely. Assembly languages in larger computers are often at a higher level.

register level compatibility A hardware component that is 100% compatible with another device. It implies that the same type, size and names of registers are used.

regression analysis A statistical technique for detecting relationships among multiple properties of observations in a sample.

related files Two or more data files that can be matched on some common condition, such as account number or name.

relational algebra (1) The branch of mathematics that deals with relations; for example, AND, OR, NOT, IS and CONTAINS.

(2) In relational database, a collection of rules for dealing with tables; for example, JOIN, UNION and INTERSECT.

relational calculus The rules for combining and manipulating relations; for example De Morgan's law, "the complement of a union is equal to the union of the complements."

relational database A database organization method that links files together as required. In non-relational systems (hierarchical, network), records in one file point to the locations of records in another, such as customers to orders and vendors to purchases. These are fixed links set up ahead of time to speed up daily processing.

In a relational database, relationships between files are created by comparing data, such as account numbers and names. A relational system has the flexibility to take any two or more files and generate a new file from the records that meet the matching criteria.

In relational terminology, a file is called a *table* or *relation*, a record is called a *tuple*, and a field is called an *attribute*.

relational operator A symbol that specifies a comparison between two values.

Relational Operator		Symbol
EQ	Equal to	=
NE	Not equal to	< > or # or !=
GT	Greater than	>
GE	Greater than or equal to	>=
LT	Less than	<
LE	Less than or equal to	<=

relative address A memory address that represents some distance from a starting point (base address), such as the first byte of a program or table. The absolute address is derived by adding it to the base address.

relative path An implied path. When a command is expressed that references files, the current working directory is the implied, or relative, path if the full path is not explicitly stated. Contrast with *full path*.

relative vector In computer graphics, a vector with end points designated in coordinates relative to a base address. Contrast with *absolute vector*.

relay An electrical switch that allows a low power to control a higher one. A small current energizes the relay, which closes a gate, allowing a large current to flow through.

Relay Gold A PC communications program from Microcom, Inc., Norwood, MA, that provides standard asynchronous transmission as well as mainframe file transfer and LAN support.

relocatable code Machine language that can be run from any memory location. All modern computers run relocatable code. See *base/displacement*.

REM (REMarks) A programming language statement used to document the program. Rem statements are used in DOS files as well. For example, typing the word REM in front of a line in AUTOEXEC.BAT or CONFIG.SYS turns that line into comments and prevents any executable function on that line from taking place.

rem it out To disable a command in a batch file or in programming source code by placing the letters "rem" (for remarks) in the beginning of the line. Rem is used in DOS batch files as well as in BASIC and some other languages, but it is not a universal statement.

remedial maintenance A repair service that is required due to a malfunction of the product. Contrast with *preventive maintenance*.

remote access software See *remote control software*.

remote batch See *RJE*.

remote communications (1) Communicating via long distances.

(2) See *remote control software*.

remote console A terminal or workstation in a remote location that is used to monitor and control a local computer.

remote control software Software, installed in both machines, that allows a user at a local computer to have control of a remote computer via modem. Both users run the remote computer and see the same screen. Remote control operation is used to take control of an unattended desktop personal computer from a remote location as well as to provide instruction and technical support to remote users.

Remote control is different than remote node. In remote control, only screen updates are transmitted to the remote machine as all processing takes place in the local computer. All file transfers are done locally or over a high-speed LAN. In a remote node setup, the user is logged onto the network using the phone line as an extension to the network. Thus, all traffic has to flow over a low-speed telephone line.
▶ *The electronic and encyclopedic versions of this book provide more detail on this subject.*

remote job entry See *RJE*.

remote node See *remote control software*.

removable disk A disk unit that is inserted into a disk drive for reading and writing and removed when not required; for example, floppy disks, disk cartridges and disk packs.

render To draw a real-world object as it actually appears.

rendering In computer graphics, creating a 3-D image that incorporates the simulation of lighting effects, such as shadows and reflection.

Renderman interface A graphics format from Pixar, Point Richmond, CA, that uses photorealistic image synthesis. Developer's Renderman (PCs and UNIX) and Mac Renderman (Macintosh) are Pixar programs that apply photorealistic looks and surfaces to 3-D objects.

repeater A communications device that amplifies or regenerates the data signal in order to extend the transmission distance. Available for both analog and digital signals, it is used extensively in long distance transmission. It is also used to tie two LANs of the same type together. Repeaters work at layer 1 of the OSI model. See *bridge* and *router*.

report A printed or microfilmed collection of facts and figures with page numbers and page headings. See *report writer* and *query*.

report file A file that describes how a report is printed.

report format The layout of a report showing page and column headers, page numbers and totals.

report generator Same as *report writer*.

report writer Software that prints a report based on a description of its layout. As a stand-alone program or part of a DBMS or file manager, it can sort selected records into a new sequence for printing. It may also print standard mailing labels.

A report is described by entering text for the page header and stating the position of the print columns (data fields) and which ones are totalled or subtotalled. Once created, the description is stored in a report file for future use.

Developed in the early 1970s, report writers (report generators) were the precursor to query languages and were the first programs to generate computer output without having to be programmed.

repository A database of information about applications software that includes author, data elements, inputs, processes, outputs and interrelationships. It may be the central core of a CASE system; for example, Repository Manager in IBM's AD/Cycle is designed to integrate third-party CASE products.

reproducer An early tabulating machine that duplicated punched cards.

reprographics Duplicating printed materials using various kinds of printing presses and high-speed copiers.

ResEdit (Resource Editor) A Macintosh system utility used to edit the resource fork.

reserved word A verb or noun in a programming or command language that is part of the native language.

reset button A computer button or key that reboots the computer. All current activities are stopped cold, and any data in memory is lost. On a printer, the reset button clears the printer's memory and readies it to accept new data.

resident module The part of a program that must remain in memory at all times. Instructions and data that stay in memory can be accessed instantly.

resident program A program that remains in memory at all times. See *TSR*.

resistor An electronic component that resists the flow of current in an electronic circuit.

resolution (1) The degree of sharpness of a displayed or printed character or image. On screen, resolution is expressed as a matrix of dots. VGA resolution of 640x480 means 640 dots across each of 480 lines. Sometimes the number of colors are added to the spec; for example, 640x480x16 or 640x480x256. The same resolution looks sharper on a small screen than a large one.

For printers, resolution is expressed as the number of dots per linear inch. 300 dpi means 90,000 dots per square inch (300x300). Laser printers and plotters have resolutions from 300 to 1000 dpi and more, whereas most display screens provide less than 100 dpi. That means jagged lines on screen may smooth out when they print.

(2) The number of bits used to record the value of a sample in a digitized signal. See *sampling rate*.

resolve To change, transform or solve a problem. The phrase "external references are resolved" refers to determining the addresses that link modules together; that is, solving the unknown links.

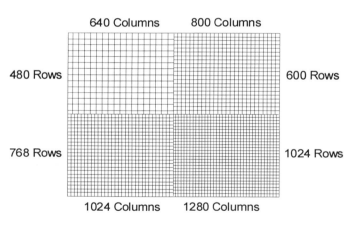

640 Columns   800 Columns

480 Rows   600 Rows

768 Rows   1024 Rows

1024 Columns   1280 Columns

resource compiler In a graphical interface (GUI), software that converts and links a resource (menu, dialog box, icon, font, etc.) into the executable program.

resource fork The resource part of a Macintosh file. For example, in a text document, it contains format codes with offsets into the text in the data fork. In a program, it contains executable code, menus, windows, dialog boxes, buttons, fonts and icons.

response time The time it takes for the computer to comply with a user's request, such as looking up a customer record.

restart To resume computer opertion after a planned or unplanned termination. See *boot, warm boot* and *checkpoint/restart*.

restricted function A computer or operating system function that cannot be used by an application program.

retrieve To call up data that has been stored in a computer system. When a user queries a database, the data is retrieved into the computer first and then transmitted to the screen.

return key Also called the *enter key*, the keyboard key used to signal the end of a line of data or the end of a command. In word processing, return is pressed at the end of a paragraph, and a return code is inserted into the text at that point. See *CR*.

reusability The ability to use all or the greater part of the same programming code or system design in another application.

reverse engineer To isolate the components of a completed system. When a chip is reverse engineered, all the individual circuits that make up the chip are identified. Source code can be reverse engineered into design models or specifications. Machine language can be reversed into assembly langauge (see *disassembler*).

reverse polish notation A mathematical expression in which the numbers precede the operation. For example, 2 + 2 would be expressed as 2 2 +, and 10 − 3 * 4 would be 10 3 4 * −.

reverse video A display mode used to highlight characters on screen. For example, if the normal display mode is black on white, reverse video would be white on black.

revision level See *version number*.

REXX (REstructured EXtended eXecutor) An IBM mainframe structured programming language that runs under VM/CMS and MVS/TSO. It can be used as a general-purpose macro language that sends commands to application programs and to the operating systems. REXX is also included in OS/2 Version 2.0.

The following REXX example converts Fahrenheit to Celsius:

```
Say "Enter Fahrenheit "
Pull FAHR
Say "Celsius is " (FAHR - 32) * (5 / 9)
```

RF (Radio Frequency) The range of electromagnetic frequencies above the audio range and below visible light. All broadcast transmission, from AM radio to satellites, falls into this range, which is between 30KHz and 300GHz.

RF/ID (Radio Frequency/IDentification) An identification system that uses tags that transmit a wireless message. The tag gets its power from a hand-held gun/reading unit.

RF modulation The transmission of a signal through a carrier frequency. In order to connect to a TV's antenna input, some home computers and all VCRs provide RF modulation of a TV channel, usually Channel 3 or 4. See *FCC class*.

RF shielding A material that prohibits electromagnetic radiation from penetrating it. Personal computers and electronic devices used in the home must meet U.S. government standards for electromagnetic interference.

RFI (Radio Frequency Interference) High-frequency electromagnetic waves that eminate from electronic devices such as chips.

RFP (Request For Proposal) A document that invites a vendor to submit a bid for hardware, software and/or services. It may provide a general or very detailed specification of the system.

RFS (Remote File System) A distributed file system for UNIX computers introduced by AT&T in 1986 with UNIX System V Release 3.0. It is similar to Sun's NFS, but only for UNIX systems.

RFT See *DCA*.

RGB (Red Green Blue) A video color generation method that displays colors as varying intensities of red, green and blue dots. When all three are turned on high, white is produced. As intensities are equally lowered, shades of gray are derived. The base color of the screen appears when all dots are off. See *colors*.

RGB monitor (1) A video display screen that requires separate red, green and blue signals from the computer. It generates a better image than composite signals (TV) which merge the three colors together. It comes in both analog and digital varieties.

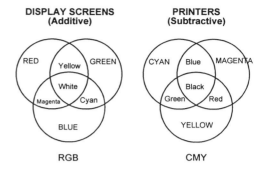

RGB AND CMY COLOR MIXING

(2) Sometimes refers to a CGA monitor that accepts digital RGB signals.

ribbon cable A thin, flat, multiconductor cable that is widely used in electronic systems; for example, to interconnect peripheral devices to the computer internally.

rich e-mail E-mail annotated with voice messages.

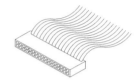

RIBBON CABLE

rich text (1) Text that includes formatting commands for bold, italic, etc. It may also refer to the mixing of graphics with text.

(2) Text in Microsoft's RTF format. See *RTF*.

RIFF (Resource Interchange File Format) A multimedia data format jointly introduced by IBM and Microsoft. See *MCI*.

right justify Same as *flush right*.

rightsizing Selecting a computer system, whether micro, mini or mainframe, that best meets the needs of the application.

rigid disk Same as *hard disk*.

ring One stage or level in a set of prioritized stages or levels, typically involved with security and password protection.

ring network A communications network that connects terminals and computers in a continuous loop.

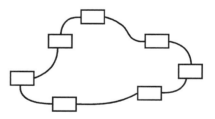

RING

RIP (1) (Raster Image Processor) In computer graphics, the component (hardware, software or both) that prepares data for a raster output device (screen or printer). RIPs are designed for a specific type of input, such as vectors, PostScript as well as different raster data.

(2) (Routing Information Protocol) A routing protocol in TCP/IP and NetWare used to identify all attached networks as well as the number of router hops required to reach them. The responses are used to update a router's routing table.

(3) (Remote Imaging Protocol) A graphics format from TeleGrafix Communications, Inc., designed for transmitting graphics over low-speed lines. Using a communications program that supports RIP enables graphical interfaces to be used on a BBS with respectable performance via modem.

RISC (Reduced Instruction Set Computer) A computer architecture that reduces chip complexity by using simpler instructions. RISC compilers have to generate software routines to perform complex instructions that were previously done in hardware by CISC computers. In RISC, the microcode layer and associated overhead is eliminated.

RISC keeps instruction size constant, bans the indirect addressing mode and retains only those instructions that can be overlapped and made to execute in one machine cycle or less. The RISC chip is faster than its CISC counterpart and is designed and built more economically.

RISC System/6000 See *RS/6000*.

RJ-11 A four or six-wire telephone connector. The four-wire plug and socket is the common connector between the handset and the telephone and for plugging telephones and modems into wall outlets.

RJ-45 An eight-wire telephone connector.

RJE (Remote Job Entry) Transmitting batches of transactions from a remote terminal or computer. The receiving computer processes the data and may transmit the results back to the RJE site for printing. RJE hardware at remote sites can employ teleprinters with disk or tape storage or complete computer systems.

RLE See *run length encoding*.

RLL (Run Length Limited) A magnetic disk encoding method that packs 50% more bits into the same space than the earlier MFM method. It is used with RLL, IDE, ESDI, SCSI, SMD and IPI interfaces.

The "run length" is the number of consecutive 0s before a 1 bit is recorded. MFM is actually a run length of 1,3; not less than one or more than three "no pulses" separating adjacent pulses. RLL increases the run length over MFM; for example, RLL 2,7 means not less than two or more than seven 0s before a 1 is recorded. ARLL (Advanced RLL) is RLL 3,9. See *hard disk*.

RLL interface See *ST506 RLL*.

RMON See *SNMP*.

RMS (1) (Record Management Services) A file management system used in VAXs.

(2) (Root Mean Square) A method used to measure electrical output in volts and watts.

RoboCAD A PC CAD program from Robo Systems International, Inc., Newtown, PA, that includes a wide variety of features and text functions. It provides up to 256 colors and layers, has two drawing pages and a scratch pad, and can transfer data to its solid modeling program.

robot A stand-alone hybrid computer system that performs physical and computational activities. It is a multiple-motion device with one or more arms and joints that is capable of performing many different tasks like a human. It can be designed similar to human form, although most industrial robots don't resemble people at all.

It is used extensively in manufacturing for welding, riveting, scraping and painting. Office and consumer applications are also being developed. Robots, designed with AI, can respond to unstructured situations. For example, specialized robots can identify objects in a pile, select the objects in the appropriate sequence and assemble them into a unit.

Robots use analog sensors for recognizing real-world objects and digital computers for their direction. Analog to digital converters convert temperature, motion, pressure, sound and images into binary code for the robot's computer. The computer directs the physical actions of the arms and joints by pulsing their motors.

robotics The art and science of the creation and use of robots.

robust Refers to software without bugs that handles abnormal conditions well. It is often said that there is no software package totally bug free. Any program can exhibit odd behavior under certain conditions, but a robust program will not lock up the computer, cause damage to data or send the user through an endless chain of dialog boxes without purpose. Whether or not a program can be totally bug free will be debated forever. See *industrial strength*.

rollback A database management system feature that reverses the current transaction out of the database, returning the database to its former state. This is done when some failure interrupts a half-completed transaction.

roll in/roll out A swapping technique for freeing up memory temporarily in order to perform another task. The current program or program segment is stored (rolled out) on disk, and another program is brought into (rolled in) that memory space.

ROM (Read Only Memory) A memory chip that permanently stores instructions and data. Its contents are created at the time of manufacture and cannot be altered. ROM chips are used to store control routines in personal computers (ROM BIOS), peripheral controllers and other electronic equipment. They are also often the sole component of a cartridge that plugs into printers, video games and other systems.

When computers are used in hand-held instruments, appliances, automobiles and any other such devices, the instructions for their routines are generally stored in ROM chips or some other non-volatile chip such as a PROM or EPROM. Instructions may also be stored in a ROM section within a general-purpose computer on a chip. See *PROM, EPROM* and *EEPROM*. Contrast with *RAM*.

ROMable Machine language capable of being programmed into a ROM chip. Being "read only" the chip cannot be updated and ROMable programs must use RAM or disk for holding changing data.

ROM BIOS (ROM Basic Input Output System) Instructions contained in a ROM chip that activate peripheral devices in a PC. It includes routines for the keyboard, screen, disk, parallel and serial port and for internal services such as time and date. It accepts requests from the device drivers in the operating system as well as from application programs.

It also contains an autostart routine that tests the system on startup and prepares the computer for operation. It searches for BIOS's on the plug-in boards and sets up pointers (interrupt vectors) in memory to access BIOS routines. It then loads the operating system and passes control to it.

▶ *The electronic and encyclopedic versions of this book provide more detail on this subject.*

ROM BIOS swapping Alternating areas in the UMA (640K-1M) between ROM BIOSs and applications as needed.

ROM card A credit-card-sized module that contains permanent software or data. See *memory card*.

ROM emulator A circuit that helps debug a ROM chip by simulating the ROM with RAM. The RAM circuit plugs into the ROM socket. Since RAM can be written over, whereas ROM cannot, programming changes can be made easily.

root directory In hierarchical file systems, the starting point in the hierarchy. When the computer is first started, the root directory is the current directory. Access to directories in the hierarchy requires naming the directories that are in its path.

In DOS, the command line symbol for the root directory is a backslash (\). In UNIX, it is a slash (/).

rotational delay The amount of time it takes for the disk to rotate until the required location on the disk reaches the read/write head.

RO terminal (Receive Only terminal) A printing device only (no keyboard).

round robin Continuously repeating sequence, such as the polling of a series of terminals, one after the other, over and over again.

routable protocol A communications protocol that contains a network address as well as a device address, allowing data to be routed from one network to another. Examples of routable protocols are SNA, OSI, TCP/IP, XNS, IPX, AppleTalk and DECnet. Contrast with *non-routable protocol*.

router A computer system in a network that stores and forwards data packets between LANs and WANs. Routers see the network as network addresses and all the possible paths between them. They read the network address in a transmitted message and can make a decision on how to send it based on the most expedient route (traffic load, line costs, speed, bad lines, etc.). Routers work at the network layer (layer 3 of the OSI model), whereas bridges work at the data link layer (layer 2). See *bridge, brouter, gateway, hub* and *intermediate node routing*.

router protocol A protocol used by routers to report their status to other routers in the network and keep their internal tables up-to-date. See *RIP* and *OSPF*.

routine A set of instructions that perform a task. Same as *subroutine, module, procedure* and *function*.

routing See *intermediate node routing* and *router*.

routing protocol A communications protocol used to update the routing table in a router.

row A horizontal set of data or components. In a graph, it is called the x-axis. Contrast with *column*.

RPC (Remote Procedure Call) A type of interface that allows one program to call another in a remote location. Using a standard RPC allows an application to be used in a variety of networks without change.

RPG (Report Program Generator) One of the first program generators designed for business reports, introduced in 1964 by IBM. In 1970, RPG II added enhancements that made it a mainstay programming language for business applications on IBM's System/3x midrange computers. RPG III, which added more programming structures, is widely used on the AS/400. RPG statements are written in columnar format.

rpm (Revolutions Per Minute) The measurement of the rotational speed of a disk drive. Floppy disks rotate at 300 rpm. Hard disks rotate at 3,600 rpm and more.

RPN See *reverse polish notation*.

RPQ (Request for Price Quotation) A document that requests a price for hardware, software or services to solve a specific problem. It is created by the customer and delivered to the vendor.

RS-170 An NTSC standard for composite video signals.

RS-232 (Recommended Standard-232) A TIA/EIA standard for serial transmission between computers and peripheral devices

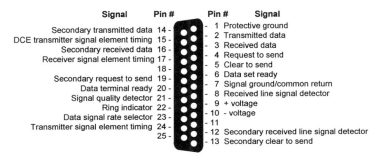

Signal	Pin #		Pin #	Signal
Secondary transmitted data	14		1	Protective ground
DCE transmitter signal element timing	15		2	Transmitted data
Secondary received data	16		3	Received data
Receiver signal element timing	17		4	Request to send
	18		5	Clear to send
Secondary request to send	19		6	Data set ready
Data terminal ready	20		7	Signal ground/common return
Signal quality detector	21		8	Received line signal detector
Ring indicator	22		9	+ voltage
Data signal rate selector	23		10	- voltage
Transmitter signal element timing	24		11	
	25		12	Secondary received line signal detector
			13	Secondary clear to send

RS-232 INTERFACE

(modem, mouse, etc.). It uses a 25-pin DB-25 or 9-pin DB-9 connector. Its normal cable limitation of 50 feet can be extended to several hundred feet with high-quality cable.

RS-232 defines the purpose and signal timing for each of the 25 lines; however, many applications use less than a dozen. RS-232 transmits positive voltage for a 0 bit, negative voltage for a 1.

In 1984, this interface was officially renamed TIA/EIA-232-E standard (E is the current revision, 1991), although most people still call it RS-232.

RS-422, 423 A TIA/EIA standards for serial interfaces that extend distances and speeds beyond RS-232. RS-422 is a balanced system requiring more wire pairs than RS-423 and is intended for use in multipoint lines. They use either a 37-pin connector defined by RS-449 or a 25-pin connector defined by RS-530.

RS-449 and RS-530 specify the pin definitions for RS-422 and RS-423. RS-422/423 specify electrical and timing characteristics.

RS-449 Defines a 37-pin connector for RS-422 and RS-423 circuits.

RS-485 A TIA/EIA standard for multipoint communications lines. It can be implemented with as little as a wire block with four screws or with DB-9 or DB-37 connectors. By using lower-impedance drivers and receivers, RS-485 allows more nodes per line than RS-422.

RS-530 Defines a 25-pin connector for RS-422 and RS-423 circuits. It allows for higher speed transmission up to 2Mbits/sec over the same DB-25 connector used in RS-232, but is not compatible with it.

RS/6000 (RISC System/6000) IBM family of RISC-based workstations introduced in 1990. It comes in workstation (POWERstation) and server (POWERserver) models and uses the Micro Channel bus. It introduced Version 3 of AIX and two graphical user interfaces: AIXwindows Environment/6000 (enhanced X Window system) and AIX NeXTStep Environment/6000 from NeXT Computer.

RSA (Rivest-Shamir-Adleman) A highly-secure encryption method by RSA Data Security, Inc., Redwood City, CA, that uses a two-part key. The private key is kept by the owner; the public key is published.

Data is encrypted by using the recipient's public key, which can only be decrypted by the recipient's private key. RSA is very computation intensive, thus it is often used to create an "RSA digital envelope," which holds an RSA-encrypted DES key and DES-encrypted data.

RSA is also used for authentication. You can verify who you are with a digital signature by encrypting with your private key and letting others decrypt your message with your public key. This requires the sender to compute a hash value of the message being sent, which is encrypted along with the message. The recipient decrypts the hash value and computes the hash value from the message using the same algorithm. If they match, the signature is authenticated.

The RSA algorithm is also implemented in hardware. As RSA chips get faster, RSA encoding and decoding add less overhead to the operation. For more on public keys, see *encryption*.

RSCS (Remote Spooling Communications Subsystem) Software that provides batch communications for IBM's VM operating system. It accepts data from remote batch terminals, executes them on a priority basis and transmits the results back to the terminals. The RSCS counterpart in MVS is called JES. Contrast with *CMS*, which provides interactive communications for VM.

RSI (Repetitive Strain Injury) Ailments of the hands, neck, back and eyes due to computer use. The remedy for RSI is frequent breaks which should include stretching or yoga postures. See *carpal tunnel syndrome*.

RSTS/E A PDP-11 operating system from Digital.

RSX-11 (Resource Sharing eXtension-PDP 11) A multiuser, multitasking operating system from Digital that runs on its PDP-11 series.

RT A RISC-based workstation from IBM introduced in 1986 that was superseded by the RS/6000 family.

RT-11 A single user, multitasking operating system from Digital that runs on its PDP-11 series.

RTF (Rich Text Format) A Microsoft standard for encoding formatted text and graphics. It was adapted from IBM's DCA format and supports ANSI, IBM PC and Macintosh character sets.

RTFM (Read The Flaming Manual) The last resort when having a hardware or software problem!

RTOS (RealTime Operating System) An operating system designed for use in a realtime computer system. See *realtime system, embedded system, process control* and *OS/9.*

RTS (Request To Send) An RS-232 signal sent from the transmitting station to the receiving station requesting permission to transmit. Contrast with *CTS.*

rubber banding In computer graphics, the moving of a line or object where one end stays fixed in position.

rubout key A keyboard key on a terminal that deletes the last character that was entered.

rule-based expert system An expert system based on a set of rules that a human expert would follow in diagnosing a problem. Contrast with *model-based expert system.*

ruler line A graphic representation of a ruler on screen that is used for laying out text and graphics.

rules (1) A set of conditions or standards which have been agreed upon.

(2) In printing, horizontal and vertical lines between columns or at the top and bottom of a page in order to enhance the appearance of the page.

RUMBA A PC-to-host connectivity software from Wall Data, Redmond, WA. It provides a Windows front end to IBM mainframes, AS/400s and VAXes and supports a variety of network configurations.

run (1) To execute a program.

(2) A single program or set of programs scheduled for execution.

run around In desktop publishing, the flowing of text around a graphic image.

run length encoding A simple data compression method that converts a run of identical symbols as a symbol followed by a count. A rough example might be []36* where [] is a code that signifies the compression and **36*** means 36 *'s follow.

run length limited See *RLL.*

run native To "run native" is to execute software written for the native mode of the computer. Contrast with running a program under some type of emulation or simulation.

Running native has traditionally been the fastest way to execute instructions on a computer. However, if as expected in the future, machines are so fast they can run emulated programs without any noticeable delay to the user, this will no longer be the important issue it is today.

run on top of To run as the control program to some other program, which is subordinate to it. Contrast with *run under.*

runtime Refers to the actual execution of a program.

runtime version Software that enables another program to execute on its own or with enhanced capabilities. For example, a DBMS often includes an interpreted programming language for developing applications. When running the programs, the DBMS must be used to execute each line of the program. A runtime version of a DBMS turns the programs into self-executing programs that will run on computers that do not have the DBMS installed.

run under To run within the control of a higher-level program. Contrast with *run on top of.*

RXD (Receiving Data) See *modem.*

S3 chip Refers to one of the graphics accelerator chips (86C911, 86C928, etc.) from S3, Inc., San Jose, CA, used in a variety of graphics accelerator boards.

S/3x See *System/3x.*

S-100 bus An IEEE 696, 100-pin bus standard used extensively in first-generation personal computers (8080, Z80, 6800, etc.). It is still used in various systems.

S/360 See *System/360.*

S/370 See *System/370.*

SAA (System Application Architecture) Introduced in 1987, SAA is a set of standards from IBM that provide consistency across all IBM platforms. It governs user interfaces, programming interfaces and communications protocols. Categories are Common User Access (CUA), Common Programming Interface for Communications (CPI-C) and Common Communications Support (CCS). See *CUA, CPI-C* and *CCS.*

sag A momentary drop in voltage from the power source. Contrast with *spike.*

SAM (1) (Symantec AntiVirus for Macintosh) A popular Macintosh antivirus program from Symantec Corporation, Cupertino, CA.

(2) See *sequential access method.*

Samna One of the first full-featured word processors for PCs (1983) from Samna Corporation, now part of Lotus.

sampling (1) In statistics, the analysis of a group by determining the characteristics of a significant percentage of its members chosen at random.

(2) In digitizing operations, the conversion of real-world signals or movements at regular intervals into digital code. See *sampling rate* and *oversampling.*

sampling rate In digitizing operations, the frequency with which samples are taken and converted into digital form. The sampling frequency must be at least twice that of the analog frequency being captured. For example, the sampling rate for hi-fi playback is 44.1KHz, slightly more than double the 20KHz frequency a person can hear. The higher the sampling rate, the closer real-world objects are represented in digital form.

Another attribute of sampling is quantizing, which creates a number for the sample. The larger the maximum number, also called resolution or precision, the more granularity of the scale and the more accurate the digital sampling. See *oversampling.*

sans-serif A typeface style without serifs, which are the short horizontal lines added at the tops and bottoms of the vertical member of the letter as in this sentence. This sentence is printed in an Arial font and is an example of sans-serif.

SAP (1) (Service Advertising Protocol) A NetWare protocol used to identify the services and addresses of servers attached to the network. The responses are used to update a table in the router known as the Server Information Table.

(2) (Secondary Audio Program) An NTSC audio channel used for auxiliary transmission, such as foreign language broadcasting or teletext.

SAS System Originally called the "Statistical Analysis System," SAS is an integrated set of data management tools from SAS Institute Inc., Cary, NC, that runs on PCs to mainframes. It includes a complete programming language as well as modules for spreadsheets, CBT, presentation graphics, project management, operations research, scheduling, linear programming, statistical quality control, econometric and time series analysis and mathematical, engineering and statistical applications.

SASI (Shugart Associates Systems Interface) A peripheral interface developed by Shugart and NCR in 1981 that evolved into the ANSI SCSI standard in 1986.

satellite See *communications satellite*

satellite channel A carrier frequency used for satellite transmission.

satellite computer A computer located remotely from the host computer or under the control of the host. It can function as a slave to the master computer or perform offline tasks.

satellite link A signal that travels from the earth to a communications satellite and back down again. Contrast with *terrestrial link*.

saturation (1) On magnetic media, a condition in which the magnetizable particles are completely aligned and a more powerful writing signal will not improve the reading back.

(2) In a bipolar transistor, a condition in which the current on the gate (the trigger) is equal to or greater than what is necessary to close the switch.

(3) In a diode, a condition in which the diode is fully conducting.

save To copy the document, record or image being worked on onto a storage medium. Saving updates the file by writing the data that currently resides in memory (RAM) onto disk or tape. Most applications prompt the user to save data upon exiting.
    All processing is done in memory (RAM). When the processing is completed, the data must be placed onto a permanent storage medium such as disk or tape.

save as To copy the document or image being worked on onto a storage medium as a new file. "Save as" provides an easy way to make multiple copies of a document or image. With your document or image on screen, select "Save as" from the File menu. You will be prompted for a new file name.

Sbus Originally a proprietary bus from Sun, the Sbus has been released into the public domain. The IEEE is standardizing on a 64-bit version in 1993.

SCAI (Switch-to-Computer Applications Interface) A standard for integrating computers to a PBX. See *switch-to-computer*.

scalability The ability to expand. Implies minimal change in current procedures in order to accomodate growth.

scalable Capable of being changed in size and configuration.

scalable font A font that is created in the required point size as needed to display or print a document. The dot patterns (bitmaps) are generated from a set of outline fonts, or base fonts, which contain a mathematical representation of the typeface. Although a bitmapped font designed from scratch for a particular font size will always look the best, scalable fonts eliminate storing dozens of different font sizes on disk. Contrast with *bitmapped font*.
    The two major scalable fonts are Adobe's Type 1 PostScript and Apple/Microsoft's TrueType. There are more Type 1 fonts available, although

TrueType fonts are rapidly becoming as abundant. Agfa's Intellifont and Bitstream's Speedo fonts are also used.

scalar A single item or value. Contrast with *vector* and *array*, which are made up of multiple values.

scalar processor A computer that performs arithmetic computations on one number at a time. Contrast with *vector processor*.

scalar variable In programming, a variable that contains only one value.

scale (1) To resize a device, object or system, making it larger or smaller.

(2) To change the representation of a quantity in order to bring it into prescribed limits of another range. For example, values such as 1249, 876, 523, -101 and -234 might need to be scaled into a range from -5 to +5.

(3) To designate the position of the decimal point in a fixed or floating point number.

scan (1) In optical technologies, to view a printed form a line at a time in order to convert images into bitmapped representations, or to convert characters into ASCII text or some other data code.

(2) In video, to move across a picture frame a line at a time, either to detect the image in an analog or digital camera, or to refresh a CRT display.

(3) To sequentially search a file.

scan head An optical sensing device in an scanner or fax machine that is moved across the image to be scanned.

ScanJet A family of popular desktop scanners from HP. Monochrome and color models are available.

scan line One of many horizontal lines in a graphics frame.

scanner A device that reads text, images and bar codes. Text and bar code scanners recognize printed fonts and bar codes and convert them into a digital code (ASCII or EBCDIC). Graphics scanners convert a printed image into a video image (raster graphics) without recognizing the actual content of the text or pictures.

scan rate The number of times per second a scanning device samples its field of vision. See *horizontal scan frequency*.

scatter diagram A graph plotted with dots or some other symbol at each data point. Also called a scatter plot or dot chart.

scatter plot Same as *scatter diagram*.

scatter read The capability that allows data to be input into two or more noncontiguous locations of memory with one read operation. See *gather write*.

SCbus See *SCSA*.

SC connector A fiber-optic cable connector that uses a push-pull latching mechanism. It is used in FDDI, Fiber Channel and B/ISDN applications. See *SMA connector* and *ST connector*.

SCERT II (Systems and Computers Evaluation and Review Technique) Pronounced "skirt." Software from Pinnacle Software Corporation, Washington, DC, that measures the performance of a system by modeling the computer environment and applications.

scheduler The part of the operating system that initiates and terminates jobs (programs) in the computer. Also called a dispatcher, it maintains a list of jobs to be run and allocates computer resources as required.

scheduling algorithm A method used to schedule jobs for execution. Priority, length of time in the job queue and available resources are examples of criteria used.

schema The definition of an entire database. See *subschema*.

Scheme A LISP dialect developed at MIT and Indiana University. TI has a personal computer version of Scheme called PC Scheme.

Schottky A category of bipolar transistor known for its fast switching speeds in the three-nanosecond range. Schottky II devices have switching speeds in the range of a single nanosecond.

scientific application An application that simulates real-world activities using mathematics. Real-world objects are turned into mathematical models and their actions are simulated by executing the formulas.

For example, some of an airplane's flight characteristics can be simulated in the computer. Rivers, lakes and mountains can be simulated. Virtually any objects with known characteristics can be modeled and simulated.

Simulations use enormous calculations and often require supercomputer speed. As personal computers become more powerful, more laboratory experiments will be converted into computer models that can be interactively examined by students without the risk and cost of the actual experiments.

scientific computer A computer specialized for high-speed mathematic processing. See *array processor* and *floating point processor*.

scientific language A programming language designed for mathematical formulas and matrices, such as ALGOL, FORTRAN and APL. Although all programming languages allow for this kind of processing, statements in a scientific language make it easier to express these actions.

scientific notation The display of numbers in floating point form. The number (mantissa) is always equal to or greater than one and less than 10, and the base is 10. For example, 2.345E6 is equivalent to 2,345,000. The number following E (exponent) represents the power to which the base should be raised (number of zeros following the decimal point).

scissoring In computer graphics, the deleting of any parts of an image which fall outside of a window that has been sized and laid over the original image. Also called clipping.

SCL (1) (Switch-to-Computer Link) Refers to applications that integrate the computer through the PBX. See *switch-to-computer*.

(2) A file extension used for ColoRIX raster graphics file format (640x400 256 colors).

SCO (The Santa Cruz Operation, Inc., Santa Cruz, CA) A system software company noted for its UNIX operating systems. Its first operating system was SCO XENIX in 1984 which ran on the Apple Lisa, IBM PC XT and the DEC Pro 350. Subsequently, all SCO products were developed for Intel's x86 machines. As of 1993, with nearly one million installed nodes and 10 years in the business, SCO is the leader in UNIX operating systems for the Intel platform.

SCO Open Desktop, Open Server SCO Open Desktop is a UNIX-based, single-user client operating system from SCO for 386s and up. It is based on SCO UNIX and includes the Motif and X Window user interfaces, standard UNIX networking (TCP/IP, NFS and NIS) as well as LAN Manager and NetBIOS support. It also includes SCO Merge, which adds DOS and Windows capability. SCO Open Server is the server version.

SCO UNIX A version of UNIX System V Release 3.2 for 386s and up from SCO. SCO UNIX has more security, networking and standards conformance than SCO XENIX and is the foundation of SCO's Open Desktop and Open Server products.

SCO UNIX is a character-based system that has been widely used on a single 386 in small offices with 10 to 20 dumb terminals attached.

SCO XENIX A version of UNIX System V for 286 PCs and up from SCO. Developed by Microsoft, it was the original UNIX system for personal computers. SCO XENIX is a fast multiuser operating system that takes less memory than SCO UNIX and is used in a variety of vertical market applications for small workgroups.

scope (1) A CRT screen, such as used on an oscilloscope or common display terminal.

(2) In programming, the visibility of variables within a program; for example, whether one function can use a variable created in another function.

(3) In dBASE, a range of records, such as the "next 50" or "current record to end of file."

scrambler A device or software program that encodes data for encryption. Scrambling data is encoding data to make it indecipherable. See *encryption*, *DES* and *RSA*.

Scrapbook A Macintosh disk file that holds frequently-used text and graphics objects, such as a company letterhead. Contrast with *Clipboard*, which holds data only for the current session.

scratch tape A magnetic tape that can be erased and reused.

scratchpad A register or reserved section of memory or disk used for temporary storage.

screen The display area of a video terminal or monitor. It is either a CRT or one of the flat panel technologies.

screen angle The angle at which a halftone screen is placed over an image, typically 45.

screen capture Transfering the current on-screen image to a text or graphics file.

screen dump Printing the current on-screen image. In PCs, pressing Shift-PrtSc prints the screen. If the screen contains graphics, the DOS Graphics utility must be loaded. Third party screen capture programs also dump graphic screens to the printer or to disk. In Windows, pressing PrintScreen places a copy of the current screen into the Clipboard, which can then be copied into a paint program for printing.

In the Macintosh, pressing Command-shift-3 creates a MacPaint file of the current screen.

screen font A font used for on-screen display. For true WYSIWYG systems, screen fonts must be matched as close as possible to the printer fonts. Contrast with *printer font*.

screen frequency The resolution of a halftone. It is the density of dots (how far they're spaced apart from each other) measured in lines per inch.

screen overlay (1) A clear, fine-mesh screen that reduces the glare on a video screen.

(2) A clear touch panel that allows the user to command the computer by touching displayed buttons on screen.

(3) A temporary data window displayed on screen. The part of the screen that was overlaid is saved and restored when the screen overlay is removed.

screen saver A utility that prevents a CRT from being etched by an unchanging image. After a specified duration without keyboard or mouse input, it blanks the screen or displays moving objects. Pressing a key or moving the mouse restores the screen.

It would actually take many hours to burn in an image on today's color monitors. However, the entertainment provided by these utilities (swimming fish, flying toasters, etc.) has made them very popular.

screen scraper See *frontware*.

script (1) A typeface that looks like handwriting or calligraphy.

(2) A program written in a special-purpose programming language such as used in a communications program or word processor. Same as *macro*.

ScriptX A multimedia technology from Kaleida Labs, Inc. that includes data formats, a scripting language and a runtime environment. It is designed for creating applications that can be played on a variety of personal computers and consumer electronic devices.

scroll To continuously move forward, backward or sideways through the images on screen or within a window. Scrolling implies continuous and smooth movement, a line, character or pixel at a time, as if the data were on a paper scroll being rolled behind the screen.

VERTICAL SCROLLING

scrollable See *scroll*.

scrollable field A short line on screen that can be scrolled to allow editing or display of larger amounts of data in a small display space.

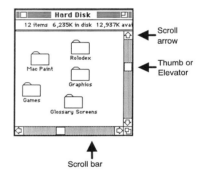

scroll arrow On-screen arrow that is clicked in order to scroll the screen in the corresponding direction. The screen moves one line, or increment, with each mouse click.

scroll back buffer Reserved memory that holds a block of transmitted data, allowing the user to browse back through it.

scroll bar A horizontal or vertical bar that contains a box that looks like an elevator in a shaft. The bar is clicked to scroll the screen in the corresponding direction, or the box (elevator, thumb) is clicked and then dragged to the desired direction.

Scroll Lock On PC keyboards, a key used to toggle between a scrolling and non-scrolling mode. When on, the arrow keys scroll the screen regardless of the current cursor location. This key is rarely used for its intended purpose and may be used for just about anything. Most applications do not use it a all.

SCSA (Signal Computing System Architecture) An open architecture from Dialogic Corporation for transmitting signals, voice and video. Its backbone is the SCbus, a 131Mbps data path that provides up to 2048 time slots, the equivalent of 1,024 two-way voice conversations at 64Kbps.

SCSI (Small Computer System Interface) Pronounced "scuzzy." SCSI is a hardware interface that allows for the connection of up to seven peripheral devices, such as a disk, tape or CD-ROM, to a single SCSI expansion board, called a *SCSI host adapter* (also called a *SCSI controller*), that plugs into the computer. The advantage of SCSI is that seven different devices use up only one expansion slot in the computer.

The original SCSI (SCSI-1) specification provides an 8-bit path with a maximum transfer rate of 5MB per second. SCSI-2 provides a variety of transfer rates and bus sizes: fast SCSI-2 is 8 bits wide with a 10MB transfer rate. Fast-wide SCSI-2 provides 16 bits at 20MB and 32 bits at 40MB transfer.

▶ *The electronic and encyclopedic versions of this book provide more detail on this subject.*

scuzzy See *SCSI*.

SDBN (Software-Defined Broadband Network) A future high-bandwidth service from AT&T for data, voice and video. It uses ATM cell relay technology with speeds up to 600 Mbits/sec.

SDF (Standard Data Format) A simple file format that uses fixed length fields. It is commonly used to transfer data between different programs.

SDF Format

```
Pat Smith      5 E. 12 St.      Rye        NY
Robert Jones   200 W. Main St.  Palo Alto  CA
```

Comma Delimited Format

```
"Pat Smith","5 E. 12 St.","Rye","NY"
"Robert Jones","200 W. Main St.","Palo Alto","CA"
```

SDH (Syncronous Digital Hierarchy) The European counterpart to SONET. Speeds supported include 155 and 622 Mbits/sec and 2.5 GBits/sec.

SDI (1) (Switched Digital International) An AT&T dial-up service providing 56 and 64 Kbits/sec digital transmission to international locations.

(2) (Single Document Interface) A Windows function that allows an application to display and lets the user work with only one document at a time. SDI applications require that the user load the application again for the second and each subsequent document to be worked on concurrently. Contrast with *MDI*.

(3) (Standard Drive Interface) A hard disk interface for VAXs.

(4) (Serial Data Interface) See *serial interface*.

(5) (Strategic Defense Initiative) A high-tech defense system for the U.S. proposed during the Reagan administration.

SDK (Software Developer's Kit) See *developer's toolkit* and *Windows SDK*.

SDLC (Synchronous Data Link Control) The primary data link protocol used in IBM's SNA networks. It is a bit-oriented synchronous protocol that is a subset of the HDLC protocol.

SDP (Streaming Data Procedure) A Micro Channel mode that increases data transfer from 20MB per second to 40MB per second.

SDRAM (Synchronous DRAM) A high-speed DRAM memory that can transfer bursts of non-contiguous data at 100MBytes/sec. JEDEC is also specifying SDRAM standard.

SE An earlier Macintosh model. Also see *systems engineer*.

seamless integration An addition of a new application, routine or device that works smoothly with the existing system. It implies that the new feature can be activated and used without problems. Contrast with *transparent*, which implies that there is no discernible change after installation.

search and replace To look for an occurrence of data or text and replace it with another set of data or text.

search key In a search routine, the data entered and used to match other data in the database.

SECAM (Systeme Electronique Couleur Avec Memoire) A French and Eastern Europe TV standard. Contrast with *NTSC*.

secondary channel In communications, a subchannel that is derived from the main channel. It is used for diagnostic or supervisory purposes, but does not carry data messages.

secondary index An index that is maintained for a data file, but not used to control the current processing order of the file. For example, a secondary index could be maintained for customer name, while the primary index is set up for customer account number. See *primary index*.

secondary storage External storage, such as disk and tape.

second-generation computer A computer made of discrete electronic components. In the early 1960s, the IBM 1401 and Honeywell 400 were examples.

second source An alternative supplier of an identical or compatible product. A second source manufacturer is one that holds a license to produce a copy of the original product from another manufacturer.

secret key See *encryption*.

sector The smallest unit of storage read or written on a hard or floppy disk. The disk's tracks (concentric circles) are divided into sectors. See *track*.

sector interleave Sector numbering on a hard disk. A one to one interleave (1:1) is sequential: 0,1,2,3, etc. A 2:1 interleave staggers sectors every other one: 0,4,1,5,2,6,3,7.

In 1:1, after data in sector 1 is read, the disk controller must be fast enough to read sector 2, otherwise the beginning of sector 2 will pass the read/write head and must rotate around to come under the head again. If it isn't fast enough, a 2:1 or 3:1 interleave gives it time to read all sectors in a single rotation, eliminating wasted rotations.

The best interleave depends on the disk and disk controller. It can be changed with a low-level format program.

sector map See *sector interleave*.

sector sparing Maintaining a spare sector per track to be used if another sector becomes defective.

security The protection of data against unauthorized access. Programs and data can be secured by issuing identification numbers and passwords to authorized users of a computer. However, systems programmers, or other technically competent individuals, will ultimately have access to these codes.

Passwords can be checked by the operating system to prevent users from logging onto the system in the first place, or they can be checked in software, such as DBMSs, where each user can be assigned an individual view (subschema) of the database. Any application program running in the computer can also be designed to check for passwords. See *NCSC*.

security kernel The part of the operating system that grants access to users of the computer system.

security levels See *NCSC*.

sed (Stream EDitor) A UNIX editing command that makes changes a line at a time and is used to edit large files that exceed buffer limitations of other editors.

seed (1) The starting value used by a random number generation routine to create random numbers.

(2) (SEED) (Self-Electro-optic-Effect Device) An optical transistor developed by David Miller at Bell Labs in 1986.

seek (1) To move the access arm to the requested track on a disk.

(2) An assembly language instruction that activates a seek operation on disk.

(3) A high-level programming language command used to select a record by key field.

seek time The time it takes to move the read/write head to a particular track on a disk.

segment (1) Any partition, reserved area, partial component or piece of a larger structure. See *overlay*.

(2) One of the bars that make up a single character in an LED or LCD display.

(3) For DOS segment addressing, see *paragraph*.

segmented address space Memory addressing in which each byte is referenced by a segment, or base, number and an offset that is added to it. Contrast with *flat address space*.

Sel (SELect) A toggle switch on a printer that takes the printer alternately between online and offline.

selection sort A search for specific data starting at the beginning of a file or list. It copies each matching item to a new file so that the selected items are in the same sequence as the original data.

selective calling In communications, the ability of the transmitting station to indicate which station in the network is to receive the message.

selector channel A high-speed computer channel that connects a peripheral device (disk, tape, etc.) to the computer's memory.

self-booting Refers to automatically loading the operating system upon startup.

self-checking digit See *check digit*.

self-clocking Recording of digital data on a magnetic medium such that the clock pulses are intrinsically part of the recorded signal. A separate timer clock is not required. Phase encoding is a commonly-used self-clocking recording technique.

self-documenting code Programming statements that can be easily understood by the author or another programmer. COBOL provides more self-documenting code than does C, for example.

self-extracting file One or more compressed files that have been converted into an executable program which decompresses its contents when run.

semantic error In programming, writing a valid programming structure with invalid logic.

semantic gap The difference between a data or language structure and the real world. For example, in order processing, a company can be both customer and supplier. Since there is no way to model this in a hierarchical database, the semantic gap is said to be large. A network database could handle this condition, resulting in a smaller semantic gap.

semantics The study of the meaning of words. Contrast with *syntax*, which governs the structure of a language.

semaphore (1) A hardware or software flag used to indicate the status of some activity.

(2) A shared space for interprocess communications (IPC) controlled by "wake up" and "sleep" commands. The source process fills a queue and goes to sleep until the destination process uses the data and tells the source process to wake up.

semiconductor A solid state substance that can be electrically altered. Certain elements in nature, such as silicon, perform like semiconductors when chemically combined with other elements. A semiconductor is halfway between a conductor and an insulator. When charged with electricity or light, semiconductors change their state from nonconductive to conductive or vice versa.

The most significant semiconductor is the transistor, which is simply an on/off switch.

semiconductor device An elementary component, such as a transistor, or a larger unit of electronic equipment comprised of chips.

sensor A device that measures or detects a real world condition, such as motion, heat or light and converts the condition into an analog or digital representation. An optical sensor detects the intensity or brightness of light, or the intensity of red, green and blue for color systems.

sequel See *SQL*.

sequence check Testing a list of items or file of records for correct ascending or descending sequence based on the item or key fields in the records.

Sequent (Sequent Computer Systems, Inc., Beaverton, OR)
A computer company founded by 17 ex-employees of Intel in 1983 that specializes in multiprocessing systems. It adapted UNIX to symmetric multiprocessing on x86 CPUs. Its WinServer series supports multiple 486 and Pentium CPUs and runs Windows NT.

sequential One after the other in some consecutive order such as by name or number.

sequential access method Organizing data in a prescribed ascending or descending sequence. Searching sequential data requires reading and comparing each record, starting from the top or bottom of file.

serial One after the other.

serial bus A type of bus that transmits data serially. Ethernet is an example of a serial bus on a network. Serial buses are also expected to become popular for attaching multiple peripherals to computers.

Although both use serial transmission, a serial bus differs from a serial port. The serial port connects the computer to one peripheral device. A serial bus allows for the connection of multiple devices.

serial computer A single-processor computer that executes one instruction after the other. Contrast with *parallel computer*.

serial interface A data channel that transfers digital data in a serial fashion: one bit after the other. Telephone lines use serial transmission for digital data, thus modems are connected to the computer via a serial port. So are mice and scanners. Serial interfaces have multiple lines, but only one is used for data. Contrast with *parallel interface*. See *RS-232*.

serialize To convert a parallel signal made up of one or more bytes into a serial signal that transmits one bit after the other.

serial mouse A mouse that plugs into the serial port on a PC. Serial mice are the most common. Contrast with *bus mouse*.

serial number A unique number assigned by the vendor to each unit of hardware or software. See *signature*.

serial port A socket on a computer used to connect a modem, mouse, scanner or other serial interface device to the computer. The Macintosh uses the serial port to attach a printer, whereas the PC uses the parallel port. Transferring files between two personal computers can be accomplished by cabling the serial ports of both machines together and using a file transfer program.

▶ *The electronic and encyclopedic versions of this book provide more detail on this subject.*

serial printer A type of printer that prints one character at a time, in contrast to a line or page at a time. In this context, serial has no relationship to a serial or parallel interface that is used to attach the printer to the computer. See *printer*.

serial transmission Transmitting data one bit at a time. Contrast with *parallel transmission*.

Series/1 An IBM minicomputer series introduced in 1976. It was used primarily as a communications processor and for data collection in process control.

serif Short horizontal lines added to the tops and bottoms of traditional typefaces, such as Times Roman. Contrast with *sans-serif*.

serpentine recording A tape recording format of parallel tracks in which the data "snakes" back and forth from the end of one track to the beginning of the next track.

server A computer in a network shared by multiple users. See *file server* and *print server*.

server application (1) An application designed to run in a server. See *client/server*.

(2) Any program that is run in the server, whether designed as a client/server application or not.

(3) See *OLE*.

service Functionality derived from a particular software program. For example, network services may refer to programs that transmit data or provide conversion of data in a network. Database services provides for the storage and retrieval of data in a database.

service bureau An organization that provides data processing and timesharing services. It may offer a variety of software packages, batch processing services (data entry, COM, etc.) as well as custom programming.

Customers pay for storage of data on the system and processing time used. Connection is made to a service bureau through dial-up terminals, private lines, or other networks, such as Telenet or Tymnet.

Service bureaus also exist that support desktop publishing and presentations and provide imagesetting, color proofing, slide creation and other related services on an hourly or per item basis.

servo An electromechanical device that uses feedback to provide precise starts and stops for such functions as the motors on a tape drive or the moving of an access arm on a disk.

session (1) In communications, the active connection between a user and a computer or between two computers.

(2) Using an application program (period between starting up and quitting).

set theory The branch of mathematics or logic that is concerned with sets of objects and rules for their manipulation. UNION, INTERSECT and COMPLEMENT are its three primary operations and they are used in relational databases as follows.

Given a file of Americans and a file of Barbers, UNION would create a file of all Americans and Barbers. INTERSECT would create a file of American Barbers, and

COMPLEMENT would create a file of Barbers who are not Americans, or of Americans who are not Barbers. See *fuzzy logic*.

set-top box The cable TV box that "sits on top" of the TV set. A variety of new set-top boxes are expected for emerging video-on-demand and other interactive cable services.

setup program Software that configures a system for a particular environment. It is used to install a new application and modify it when the hardware changes. When used with expansion boards, it may change the hardware by altering on-board memory chips (flash memory, EEPROMs, etc.). See *install program*.

setup string A group of commands that initialize a device, such as a printer. See *escape character*.

seven dwarfs IBM's early competitors in the mainframe business: Burroughs, CDC, GE, Honeywell, NCR, RCA and Univac.

seven-segment display A common display found on digital watches and readouts that looks like a series of 8s. Each digit or letter is formed by selective illumination of up to seven separately addressable bars.

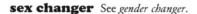

sex changer See *gender changer*.

SGI See *Silicon Graphics*.

SGML (Standard Generalized Markup Language) An ISO standard for defining the formatting in a text document. It is a comprehensive language that can even define hypertext links. In order to decipher format commands in an SGML document, SGML uses format definitions in a separately-created DTD (Document Type Definition) file. As a result, SGML is often called a metalanguage, because it describes another language; in this case, the actual formatting commands that are embedded in the text.

sh (SHell) A UNIX command that invokes a different shell. It can be used like a batch file to execute a series of commands saved as a shell.

shadow batch A data collection system that simulates a transaction processing environment. Instead of updating master files (customers, inventory, etc.) when orders or shipments are initiated, the transactions are stored in the computer. When a user makes a query, the master record from the previous update cycle is retrieved; but before it's displayed, it's updated in memory with any transactions that may affect it. The up-to-date master record is then displayed for the user. At the end of the day or period, the transactions are then actually batch processed against the master file.

shadow mask A thin screen full of holes that adheres to the back of a color CRT's viewing glass. The electron beam is aimed through the holes onto the phosphor dots.

shadow RAM A RAM copy of a PC's ROM BIOS. In order to improve performance, the BIOS, which is stored in a ROM chip, is copied to and executed from RAM. RAM chips are accessed faster than ROMs.

shared DASD A disk system accessed by two or more computers within a single datacenter. Disks shared in personal computer networks are called file servers or database servers.

shared logic Using a single computer to provide processing for two or more terminals. Contrast with *shared resource*.

shared media LAN A local area network that shares a common path (line, cable, etc.) between all nodes. The bandwidth of the line is the total transmission capacity of all transmitting stations at any given time. Contrast with a LAN that uses a *switching hub*, in which any two stations have the full bandwidth of the line.

shared resource Sharing a peripheral device (disk, printer, etc.) among several users. For example, a file server and laser printer in a LAN are shared resources. Contrast with *shared logic*.

shareware Software distributed on a trial basis through BBS's, online services, mail-order vendors and user groups. Shareware is software on the honor system. If you use it regularly, you're required to register and pay for it, for which you will receive technical support and perhaps additional documentation or the next upgrade. Paid licenses are required for commercial distribution.

sheet feeder A mechanical device that feeds stacks of cut forms (letterheads, legal paper, etc.) into a printer.

shelfware Products that remain unsold on a dealer's shelf or unused by the customer.

shell An outer layer of a program that provides the user interface, or way of commanding the computer. Shells are typically add-on programs created for command-driven operating systems, such as UNIX and DOS. It provides a menu-driven or graphical icon-oriented interface to the system in order to make it easier to use. Starting with DOS 4.0, DOS comes with its own optional shell called *DOSshell*.

shell out To temporarily exit an application, go back to the operating system, perform a function and then return to the application.

shell script A file of executable UNIX commands created by a text editor and made executable with the Chmod command. It is the UNIX counterpart to a DOS batch file.

shift register A high-speed circuit that holds some number of bits for the purpose of shifting them left or right. It is used internally within the processor for multiplication and division, serial/parallel conversion and various timing considerations.

short In programming, an integer variable. In C, a long is two bytes and can be signed (-32K to +32K) or unsigned (64K). Contrast with *long*.

short card In a PC, a plug-in printed circuit board that is half the length of a full-size board. Contrast with *long card*.

short-haul modem In communications, a device that transmits signals up to about a mile. Similar to a line driver that can transmit up to several miles.

shrink-wrapped software Refers to store-bought software, implying a standard platform that is widely supported.

SI See *systems integration*.

sideband In communications, the upper or lower half of a wave. Since both sidebands are normally mirror images of each other, one of the halves can be used for a second channel to increase the data-carrying capacity of the line or for diagnostic or control purposes.

SideBar A Windows shell from Quarterdeck Office Systems that streamlines the Windows desktop. It can replace Program Manager and File Manager or stay synchronized with them. SideBar was originally developed by Mike McCue of Paper Software.

Sidekick A PC desktop utility program from Borland. Introduced in 1984, it was the first popup (TSR) program for the PC. It includes a calculator, WordStar-compatible notepad, appointment calendar, phone dialer and ASCII table. Sidekick Plus (1988) adds more notepad commands, calendar alarms, scientific and programming calculators, limited file management and an outliner.

Sieve of Eratosthenes A benchmark program used to test the mathematical speed of a computer. The program calculates prime numbers based on Eratosthenes's algorithm.

SIG (Special Interest Group) A group of people that meets and shares information about a particular topic of interest. It is usally a part of a larger group or association.

SIGGRAPH A special interest group on computer graphics that is part of the ACM.

sign A symbol that identifies a positive or negative number. In digital code, it is either a separate character or part of the byte. In ASCII, the sign is kept in a separate character typically transmitted in front of the number it represents
(+ and - is 2B and 2D in hex).

signal Any electrical or light pulse or frequency.

signal converter A device that changes the electrical or light characteristics of a signal.

signal processing See *DSP*.

signal to noise ratio The ratio of the amplitude (power, volume) of a data signal to the amount of noise (interference) in the line. Usually measured in decibels, it measures the clarity or quality of a transmission channel or electronic device.

signaling in/out of band In communications, signaling "in band" refers to sending control signals within the same frequency range as the data signal. Signaling "out of band" refers to sending control signals outside of the frequency range of the data signal.

signature A unique number built into hardware or software for identification.

significant digits Those digits in a number that add value to the number. For example, in the number 00006508, 6508 are the significant digits.

silica Same as *silicon dioxide*.

silica gel A highly absorbent form of silicon dioxide often wrapped in small bags and packed with equipment to absorb moisture during shipping and storage.

silicon (Si) The base material used in chips. Next to oxygen, it is the most abundant element in nature and is found in a natural state in rocks and sand. Its atomic structure and abundance make it an ideal semiconductor material. In chip making, it is mined from rocks and put through a chemical process at high temperatures to purify it. To alter its electrical properties, it is mixed (doped) with other chemicals in a molten state.

silicon compiler Software that translates the electronic design of a chip into the actual layout of the components.

silicon dioxide (SiO^2) A hard, glassy mineral found in such materials as rock, quartz, sand and opal. In MOS chip fabrication, it is used to create the insulation layer between the metal gates of the top layer and the silicon elements below.

silicon disk A disk drive that is permanently simulated in memory. Typically used in laptops for weight reduction, it requires constant power from a battery to maintain its contents.

silicon foundry An organization that makes chips for other companies that have only design, but not manufacturing facilities. It is typically a large chip maker that uses excess manufacturing capacity in this manner.

Silicon Graphics (Silicon Graphics, Inc., Mountain View, CA) A manufacturer of very high-end graphics workstations, founded in 1982 by Jim Clark. Its UNIX-based operating systems are called IRIX. SGI had been using MIPS processors in its systems for a number of years and, in 1992, acquired MIPS

Computer Systems. SGI's current line of machines is based on the MIPS R4000 64-bit CPUs. MIPS chips continue to be sold to a large number of system manufacturers.

silicon nitride (Si^{3}N^4) A silicon compound capable of holding a static electric charge and used as a gate element on some MOS transistors.

silicon on sapphire See *SOS*.

Silicon Valley The area around San Jose (south of San Francisco) noted for its large number of high-tech companies.

SIM (Society for Information Management) An organization of MIS professionals founded as the Society for MIS in 1968. It is an exchange for technical information and offers educational and research programs, competitions and awards to its members. Address: 111 East Wacker Dr., Suite 600, Chicago, IL 60601.

SAN FRANCISCO

San Francisco Bay

Pacific Ocean

Menlo Park • • Palo Alto

Los Altos • • Mountain View • Sunnyvale

Santa Clara •

Cupertino San Jose

SILICON VALLEY

SIMD (Single Instruction stream Multiple Data stream) A computer architecture that performs one operation on multiple sets of data, for example, an array processor. One computer or processor is used for the control logic and the remaining processors are used as slaves, each executing the same instruction. Contrast with *MIMD*.

SIMM (Single In-line Memory Module) A narrow printed circuit board from three to four inches long that holds some number of memory chips. It plugs into a SIMM socket on the circuit board.

The first SIMM format that became popular on personal computer motherboards uses a 30-pin connector. A larger format that has 72-pins contains from one to 64 megabytes of RAM.

▶ *The electronic and encyclopedic versions of this book provide more detail on this subject.*

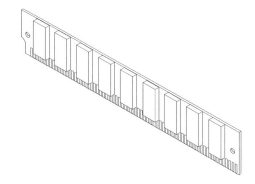

30-PIN SIMM MODULE

simplex One way transmission. Contrast with *half-duplex* and *full-duplex*.

SIMSCRIPT A programming language used for discrete simulations.

simulation (1) The mathematical representation of the interaction of real-world objects. See *scientific application*.

(2) The execution of a machine language program designed to run in a foreign computer.

sine wave A uniform wave that is generated by a single frequency.

single board computer A printed circuit board that contains a complete computer, including processor, memory, I/O and clock.

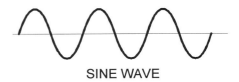

SINE WAVE

single density disk The first-generation floppy disk.

single-ended configuration Electrical signal paths that use a common ground, which are more susceptible to noise than *differential configuration*.

single-mode fiber An optical fiber with a core diameter of less than 10 microns, used for high-speed transmission and long distances. It provides greater bandwidth than multimode fiber, but its smaller core makes it more difficult to couple the light source. Contrast with *multimode fiber*.

single precision The use of one computer word to hold a numeric value for calculation. Contrast with *double precision*.

single sided disk A floppy disk that stores data on only one side.

single-system image An operational view of multiple networks, distributed databases or multiple computer systems as if they were one system.

single threading Processing one transaction to completion before starting the next.

sink A device or place that accepts something. See *heat sink* and *data sink*.

SIP (Single In-line Package) A type of chip module that is similar to a SIMM, but uses pins rather than edge connectors. SIPs are sometimes called SIPPs (Single In-Line Pin Package).

SIR (Serial InfraRed) An infrared (IR) technology from HP that allows wireless data transmission between two devices up to one meter apart. Both devices must be lined up to each other. Future enhancements will allow greater distances and wider angles. It is expected that SIR ports will be come standard on laptops by 1995.

SISD (Single Instruction stream Single Data stream) The architecture of a serial computer. Contrast with *SIMD* and *MIMD*.

site license A license to use software within a facility. It provides authorization to make copies and distribute them within a specific jurisdiction.

SIXEL A graphics language from Digital that supersedes ReGIS. ReGIS to SIXEL conversion programs are available.

skew (1) The misalignment of a document or punched card in the feed tray or hopper that prohibits it from being scanned or read properly.

(2) In facsimile, the difference in rectangularity between the received and transmitted page.

(3) In communications, a change of timing or phases in a transmission signal.

(4) See *cylinder skew* and *head skew*.

sky wave A radio signal transmitted into the sky and reflected back down to earth from the ionosphere.

SkyTel (SkyTel Corporation, Washington, DC) A paging service provider. In 1987, it was the first to provide nationwide paging. The SkyPager service transmits a 12-digit number. SkyTalk beeps the pager, and the user dials in to listen to voice messages. SkyWord transmits text to the recipient's paging device.

SL See *386SL* and *486SL*.

slave A computer or peripheral device controlled by another computer. For example, a terminal or printer in a remote location that only receives data is a slave. When two personal computers are hooked up via their serial or parallel ports for file exchange, the file transfer program may make one computer the master and the other the slave.

slave tube A display monitor connected to another monitor in order to provide an additional viewing station.

SLC See *386SLC*.

sleep (1) In programming, an inactive state due to an endless loop or programmed delay. A sleep statement in a programming language creates a delay for some specified amount of time.

(2) The inactive status of a terminal, device or program that is awakened by sending a code to it.

slew rate (1) How fast paper moves through a printer (ips).

(2) The speed of changing voltage.

sliding window (1) A communications protocol that transmits multiple packets before acknowledgement. Both ends keep track of packets sent and acknowledged (left of window), those which have been sent and not acknowledged (in window) and those not yet sent (right of window).

(2) A view of memory that can be instantly shifted to another location.

SLIP (Serial Line IP) A TCP/IP protocol that allows IP packets to be transmitted over a serial link, such as a dial-up or private telephone line. See *PPP*.

slipstream To fix a bug or add enhancements to software without identifying such inclusions by creating a new version number.

slot (1) A receptacle for additional printed circuit boards.

(2) A receptacle for inserting and removing a disk or tape cartridge.

(3) In communications, a narrow band of frequencies. See *time slot*.

(4) May refer to reserved space for temporary or permanent storage of instructions, data or codes.

slot mask The Sony Trinitron counterpart to the shadow mask. It uses vertical rectangular slots instead of holes.

slow scan TV The transmission of still video frames over telephone lines. Not realtime transmission, it takes several seconds to transmit one frame. Also called electronic still photography (ESP).

slug A metal bar containing the carved image of a letter or digit that is used in a printing mechanism.

SMA (1) (Software Maintenance Association) A non-profit professional organization founded in 1985 and dedicated to enhance understanding of software maintenance and to advance those concerned with it. Active chapters are in major cities worldwide. Annual conference is held in the spring. Address: Ms. Robin Gross, Box 12004, Vallejo, CA 94590, 707/643-4423.

(2) (Systems Management Architecture) An IBM network management repository.

(3) (Spectrum Manufacturers Association) A DBMS standard for application compatibility.

SMA connector A fiber-optic cable connector that uses a plug which is screwed into a threaded socket. It was the first connector for optical fibers to be standardized. See *ST connector* and *SC connector*.

Smalltalk An operating system and object-oriented programming language that was developed at Xerox Corporation's Palo Alto Research Center. As an integrated environment, it eliminates the distinction between programming language and operating system. It also allows the programmer to customize the user interface and behavior of the system.

Smalltalk was the first object-oriented programming language and was used on Xerox's Alto computer, which was designed for it. It was originally used to create prototypes of simpler programming languages and the graphical interfaces that are so popular today.

smart cable A cable with a built-in microprocessor used to connect two devices. It analyzes incoming signals and converts them from one protocol to another.

smart card A credit card with a built-in microprocessor and memory used for identification or financial transactions. When inserted into a reader, it transfers data to and from a central computer. It is more secure than a magnetic stripe card and can be programmed to self-destruct if the wrong password is entered too many times. As a financial transaction card, it can store transactions and maintain a bank balance.

smart hub See *intelligent hub*.

smart install program An install program that configures itself automatically based on the hardware environment.

smart terminal A video terminal with built-in display characteristics (blinking, reverse video, underlines, etc.). It may also contain a communications protocol. The term is often used synonymously with intelligent terminal. See *intelligent terminal* and *dumb terminal*.

Smartcom A family of communications programs for PCs and Macs from Hayes Microcomputer Products, Inc., Atlanta, GA. Versions emulate a several terminals and support a variety of protocols, including the Hayes V-series. Smartcom EZ is for the novice.

Smartdrive A disk cache program that comes with DOS and Windows. In DOS 4.0 and Windows 3.0, the name of the driver file is SMARTDRV.SYS. Starting with DOS 5 and Windows 3.1, the name of the driver is SMARTDRV.EXE.

SmartKey A PC keyboard macro processor from No Brainer Software, Midvale, UT. It was one of the first macro processors that let users eliminate repetitive typing by creating a macro for an occurrence of text or a series of commands.

SmartSuite A suite of Windows applications from Lotus that includes the 1-2-3 spreadsheet, Ami Pro word processor, Freelance Graphics, Approach database, Organizer PIM and Adobe Type Manager. Also included is a common toolbar for launching all the applications and selecting predefined macros that provide tighter integration between the applications.

SmartWare An integrated software package for PCs and various UNIX-based systems from Informix Software, Inc., Menlo Park, CA, that includes a programming language.

SMB (Server Message Block) A message format used in the Microsoft/3Com file sharing protocol for PC Network, MS-Net and LAN Manager. It is used to transfer file requests between workstations and servers as well as within the server for internal operations. For network transfer, SMBs are carried within the NetBIOS network control block (NCB) packet.

SMD (1) (Storage Module Device) A high-performance hard disk interface used with minis and mainframes that transfers data in the 1-4 MBytes/sec range (SMD-E provides highest rate). See *hard disk*.

(2) (Surface Mount Device) A surface mounted chip.

SMDS (Switched Multimegabit Data Services) A high-speed switched data communications service offered by the local telephone companies (LECs) to interconnect LANs. It uses the IEEE 802.6 DQDB MAN networking technology at rates up to 45 Mbps. SONET services at 155 Mbps are forthcoming.

SMF (1) (Standard Messaging Format) An electronic mail format for Novell's MHS messaging system. The application puts the data into this format in order to send an e-mail message. NGM (NetWare Global Messaging) is based on SMF-71, which supports long addresses and synchronized directories.

(2) (Standard MIDI file) The standard format for a MIDI file.

(3) See *single-mode fiber*.

SMI (1) (Simple Mail Interface) A subset of functions within the VIM messaging protocol used by applications to send e-mail and attachments. Future versions of VIM will use the CMC API rather than SMI.

(2) (Structure of Management Information) A definition for creating MIBs in the SNMP protocol.

(3) (System Management Interrupt) A hardware interrupt in Intel SL Enhanced 486 and Pentium CPUs used for power management. This interrupt is also used for virus checking.

SMM (System Management Mode) An energy conservation mode built into Intel SL Enhanced 486 and Pentium CPUs. During inactive periods, SMM initiates a sleep mode that turns off peripherals or the entire system. It retains the computer's status in a protected area of memory called the SMRAM (System Management RAM).

smoke test A test of new or repaired equipment by turning it on. If there's smoke, it doesn't work!

smoothed data Statistical data that has been averaged or otherwise manipulated so that the curves on its graph are smooth and free of irregularities.

smoothing circuit An electronic filtering circuit in a DC power supply that removes the ripples from AC power.

SMP See *symmetric multiprocessing*.

SMPTE (Society for Motion Picture and TV Engineers) An organization that prepares standards and documentation for TV production. SMPTE time code records hours, minutes, seconds and frames on audio or videotape for synchronization purposes. Address: 595 W. Hartsdale Ave., White Plains, NY 10607, 914/761-1100.

SMRAM See *SMM*.

SMT (1) See *surface mount*.

(2) (Station ManagemenT) An FDDI network management protocol that provides direct management. Only one node requires the software.

SMTP (Simple Mail Transfer Protocol) A messaging protocol used in TCP/IP networks.

SNA (Systems Network Architecture) IBM's mainframe network standards introduced in 1974. Originally a centralized architecture with a host computer controlling many terminals, enhancements, such as APPN and APPC (LU 6.2), have adapted SNA to today's peer-to-peer communications and distributed computing environment. The seven-layer SNA architecture is very similar to the OSI model, but the functions are not identical.

▶ *The electronic and encyclopedic versions of this book provide more detail on this subject.*

SNADS (SNA Distribution Services) An IBM messaging protocol used by IBM office automation products such as DISOSS and AS/400 Office. Various messaging gateways and messaging switches support SNADS.

snapshot The saved current state of memory including the contents of all memory bytes, hardware registers and status indicators. It is periodically taken in order to restore the system in the event of failure.

snapshot dump A memory dump of selected portions of memory.

snapshot program A trace program that provides selected dumps of memory when specific instructions are executed or when certain conditions are met.

snap to A feature in a drawing program that moves a text or graphic element to the closest grid line.

snd (SouND resource) A Macintosh resource fork that contains sound information, including compression ratios if used and sampling rate.

sneakernet Carrying floppy disks from one machine to another to exchange information, when you don't have a network.

sniffer Software and/or hardware that analyzes traffic and detects bottlenecks and problems in a network.

SNMP (Simple Network Management Protocol) A widely-used network monitoring and control protocol. Data is passed from SNMP agents, which are hardware and/or software processes reporting activity in each network device (hub, router, bridge, etc.) to the workstation console used to oversee the network. The agents return information contained in a MIB (Management Information Base), which is a data structure that defines what is obtainable from the device and what can be controlled (turned off, on, etc.).

snow The flickering snow-like spots on a video screen caused by display electronics that are too slow to respond to changing data.

SNR See *signal to noise ratio.*

socket See *UNIX socket.*

socket services Low-level software that manages a PCMCIA controller.

soft Flexible and changeable. Software can be reprogrammed for different results. The computer's soft nature is its greatest virtue; however, the reason it takes so long to get new systems developed has little to do with the concept. It is based on how systems are developed (file systems vs database management), the programming languages used (assembly vs high-level), combined with the skill level of the technical staff, compounded by the organization's bureaucracy.

soft boot Same as *warm boot.*

soft copy Refers to data displayed on a video screen. Contrast with *hard copy.*

soft error A recoverable error, such as a garbled message that can be retransmitted. Contrast with *hard error.*

soft font A set of characters for a particular typeface that is stored on the computer's hard disk, or in some cases the printer's hard disk, and downloaded to the printer before printing. Contrast with *internal font* and *font cartridge.*

soft hyphen A hyphen that prints if it winds up at the end of the line, but does not print otherwise. Contrast with *hard hyphen.* See *discretionary hyphen.*

soft key A keyboard key that is simulated by an icon on screen.

soft patch A quick fix to machine language currently in memory that only lasts for the current session.

SoftPC A family of PC emulation programs from Insignia Solutions, Inc., Andover, MA, that allow DOS and Windows programs to run on Macintosh, UNIX workstations and the PowerPC.

soft return A code inserted by the software into a text document to mark the end of the line. When the document is printed, the soft return is converted into the end-of-line code required by the printer. Soft returns are determined by the right margin and change when the margins are changed. Contrast with *hard return*.

soft sectored A common method of identifying sectors on a disk by initially recording sector information on every track with a format program. Contrast with *hard sectored*.

Soft-Switch E-mail switching software and hardware from Soft-Switch, Inc., Wayne, PA, that provides an e-mail backbone for organizations with diverse e-mail systems. It directly supports X.400, SNADS and SMTP and provides gateways to other e-mail systems. Soft-Switch Central is software for IBM MVS and VM mainframes. Its EMX 88000-based e-mail server connects to Token Ring, Ethernet, X.25 and SDLC.

software Instructions for the computer. A series of instructions that performs a particular task is called a program.

The two major categories are *system software* and *application software*. System software is made up of control programs, including the operating system, communications software and database manager. Application software is any program that processes data for the user (inventory, payroll, spreadsheet, word processor, etc.). A common misconception is that software is also data. It is not. Software tells the hardware how to process the data. Software is "run." Data is "processed."

software architecture The design of application or system software that incorporates protocols and interfaces for interacting with other programs and for future flexibility and expandability. A self-contained, stand-alone program would have program logic, but not a software architecture.

software bug A problem that causes a program to abend (crash) or produce invalid output. Problems that cause a program to abend are invalid data, such as trying to divide by zero, or invalid instructions, which are caused by bad logic that misdirects the computer to the wrong place in the program.

A program with erroneous logic may produce bad output without crashing, which is the reason extensive testing is required for new programs. For example, if the program is supposed to add an amount, but instead, it subtracts it, bad output results. As long as the program performs valid machine instructions on data it knows how to deal with, the computer will run.

software codec A compression/decompression routine that is implemented in software only without requiring specialized DSP hardware. See *codec*.

software engineering The design, development and documentation of software. See *CASE, systems analysis & design, programming, object-oriented programming, software metrics* and *Systemantics*.

software failure The inability of a program to continue processing due to erroneous logic. Same as *crash, bomb* and *abend*.

software house An organization that develops customized software for a customer. Contrast with *software publisher*, which develops and markets software packages.

software IC An object-oriented programming class packaged for sale. The term was coined by The Stepstone Corporation.

software interface Same as *API*.

software interrupt An interrupt caused by an instruction in the program. See *interrupt*.

software metrics Software measurements. Using numerical ratings to measure the complexity and reliability of source code, the length and quality of the development process and the performance of the application when completed.

software package An application program developed for sale to the general public.

software program A computer program (computer application). All computer programs are software. Usage of the two words together is redundant, but common.

software programmer Same as *systems programmer*.

software protection See *copy protection*.

software publisher An organization that develops and markets software. It does market research, production and distribution of software. It may develop its own software, contract for outside development or obtain software that has already been written.

software stack A stack that is implemented in memory. See *stack*.

software tool A program used to develop other software. Any program or utility that helps a programmer design, code, compile or debug sofware can be called a tool.

software vendors Although still not as big as hardware, software revenues are growing worldwide. Worldwide packaged software revenues exceeded 20 billion dollars in 1993.

▶ *The electronic and encyclopedic versions of this book provide a list of the top 100 software vendors in the U.S.*

SoftWindows Windows emulation software for the PowerPC and various UNIX platforms from Insignia Solutions.

SOG (Small Outline Gullwing) Same as *SOIC*.

SOHO (Small Office/Home Office) Refers to the small business or business-at-home user. This market segment demands as much or more than the large corporation. The small business entrepreneur generally wants the latest, greatest and fastest equipment, and this market has always benefited from high technology, allowing it to compete on a level playing ground with the bigger companies.

SOIC (Small Outline IC) A small-dimension, surface mount DIP that uses gullwing-shaped pins extending outward.

SOJ (Small Outline J lead) A small-dimension, surface mount DIP that uses J-shaped pins extending inward.

Solaris 2.0 A multitasking, multiprocessing distributed computing environment from SunSoft for SPARC computers, 386s and up and the PowerPC. Solaris is based on Sun's UNIX-based operating system and includes Sun's networking enhancements that provide an enterprise-wide environment that can manage up to 40,000 nodes from one central station.

solder mask An insulating pattern applied to a printed circuit board that exposes only the areas to be soldered.

solenoid A magnetic switch that closes a circuit, often used as a relay.

solid logic Same as *solid state*.

solid modeling A mathematical technique for representing solid objects. It is the least abstract form of CAD. Unlike wireframe and surface modeling, solid modeling systems ensure that all surfaces meet properly and that the object is geometrically correct. A solid model can also be sectioned (cut open) to reveal its internal features. Solids allow interference checking, which tests to see if two or more objects occupy the same space.

solid state An electronic component or circuit made of solid materials, such as transistors, chips and bubble memory. There is no mechanical action in a solid state device, although an unbelievable amount of electromagnetic action takes place within.

For data storage, solid state devices are much faster and more reliable than mechanical disks and tapes, but are more expensive. Although solid state costs continually drop, disks, tapes and optical disks also continue to improve their cost/performance ratio.

The first solid state device was the "cat's whisker" of the 1930s. A whisker-like wire was moved around on a solid crystal in order to detect a radio signal.

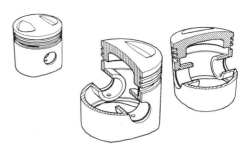

SOLID MODELING
(Courtesy Robo Systems Corporation)

solid state disk A disk drive made of memory chips used for high-speed data access or in hostile environments. Solid state disks are used in battery-powered, hand-held devices as well as in desktop units with hundreds of megabytes of storage that contain their own UPS systems.

Different types of storage chips are used for solid state disks, both volatile and non-volatile. However a solid state disk looks like a standard disk drive to the operating system, not a proprietary one that requires additional drivers. See *flash disk*.

solid state memory Any transistorized, semiconductor or thin film memory that contains no mechanical parts.

solid state relay A relay that contains no mechanical parts. All switching mechanisms are semiconductor or thin film components.

solver Mathematical mechanisms that allow spreadsheets to perform goal seeking.

SOM (1) (System Object Model) An object architecture from IBM that provides a full implementation of the CORBA standard. SOM is language independent and is supported by a variety of large compiler and application development vendors.

It is expected that IBM will promote SOM heavily because its future operating systems are built around objects. DSOM, for distributed SOM, allows objects to be used across the network.

(2) (Self Organizing Map) A two-dimensional map that shows relationships in a neural network.

SONET (Synchronous Optical NETwork) A fiber optic transmission system for high-speed digital traffic. Employed by telephone companies and common carriers, SONET speeds range from 51 megabits to multiple gigabits per second. SONET is an intelligent system that provides advanced network management, a standard optical interface and more flexibility than the T1 and T3 lines now in common use. Although it is expected to eventually obsolete T-carrier lines, SONET can be used to carry existing T-carrier traffic in the meantime. Following are the SONET services.

Service		Speed (Mbps)
STS-1	OC-1	51.84 (28 DS1s or 1 DS3)
STS-3	OC-3	155.52 (3 STS-1s)
STS-3c	OC-3c	155.52 (concatenated)
STS-12	OC-12	622.08 (12 STS-1s, 4 STS-3s)
STS-12c	OC-12c	622.08 (12 STS-1s, 4 STS-3c's)
STS-48	OC-48	2488.32 (48 STS-1s, 16 STS-3s)
STS-192	OC-192	9953.28 (192 STS-1s, 64 STS-3s)

sort To reorder data into a new sequence. The operating system can typically sort file names and text lists. Word processors typically allow lines of text to be reordered, and database programs sort records by one or more fields, often generating a new file.

sort algorithm A formula used to reorder data into a new sequence. Like all complicated problems, there are many solutions that can achieve the same results. One sort algorithm can resequence data faster than another. In the early 1960s, when tape was "the" storage medium, the sale of a computer system may have hinged on the sort algorithm, since without direct access capability, every transaction had to be sorted into the sequence of the master file.

sort field Same as *sort key*.

sort key A field or fields in a record that dictate the sequence of the file. For example, the sort keys STATE and NAME arrange the file alphabetically by name within state. STATE is the major sort key, and NAME is the minor key.

sorter (1) A sort program.

(2) A person who manually puts data into a specific sequence.

(3) An early tabulating machine that routed punched cards into separate stackers based on the content of a card column. The complete operation required passing the cards through the machine once for each column sorted.

SOS (1) (Silicon On Sapphire) An MOS chip-fabrication method that places a thin layer of silicon over a sapphire substrate (base).

(2) (Sophisticated Operating System) The operating system used on the Apple III.

sound bandwidth A range of sound frequencies. The human ear can perceive approximately from 20 to 20,000Hz, but human voice is confined to within 3,000Hz.

Sound Blaster A family of sound cards from Creative Labs, Inc., Milpitas, CA. The Sound Blaster protocol has become a de facto audio standard for PCs.

sound card Also called *sound board* and *audio adapter*, it is a personal computer expansion board that records and plays back sound, providing outputs directly to speakers or an external amplifier. Many sound cards also include MIDI capability.

The three major standards in the PC world for sound are SoundBlaster, Ad Lib and Windows. Some cards support all three, which is more desirable if you have a mix of DOS and Windows multimedia applications.
▶ *The electronic and encyclopedic versions of this book provide more detail on this subject.*

source (1) The source of current in a MOS transistor. Same as *emitter* in a bipolar transistor.

(2) (The Source) An online information service in McLean, VA, launched in 1979 and purchased by CompuServe in 1989.

source code A program in its original form as written by the programmer. It is not executable by the computer directly. It must be converted into machine language by compilers, assemblers and interpreters.

In some cases, source code can be converted into another dialect or a different language by a conversion program.

source code compatible Able to run a program on a different platform by recompiling its source code into that machine code.

source computer The computer in which a program is being assembled or compiled. Contrast with *object computer*.

source data The original data that is handwritten or printed on a source document or typed into the computer system from a keyboard or terminal.

source data acquisition Same as *source data capture*.

source data capture Capturing data electronically when a transaction occurs; for example, at the time of sale.

source directory The directory from which data is obtained.

source disk The disk from which data is obtained. Contrast with *target disk*.

source document The paper form onto which data is written. Order forms and employment applications are examples.

source drive The disk or tape drive from which data is obtained. Contrast with *target drive*.

source language The language used in a source program.

source program A program in its original form, as written by the programmer.

source routing A communications protocol in which stations are aware of bridges in the network and route messages via the bridges. Contrast with *transparent bridging*. See *SRT*.

source statement An instructional phrase in a programming language (source language).

SPA (Software Publishers Association) A trade organization of the personal computer software industry that supports legislation for copyright enforcement. It conducts raids on organizations suspected of illegal copying and files lawsuits against violators.

To blow the whistle on a company that has a policy of making illegal copies, call 800/388-PIR8. Address: 1730 M St., N.W., Washington, DC 20036, 202/452-1600.

space In digital electronics, a 0 bit. Contrast with *mark*.

space/time The following units of measure are used to define storage and transmission capacities.

Bits, bytes and cycles		Fractions of a second	
Kilo (K) Thousand	1,024	ms (millisecond) thousandth	1/1,000
Mega (M) Million	1,048,576	µs (microsecond) millionth	1/1,000,000
Giga (G) Billion	1,073,741,824	ns (nanosecond) billionth	1/1,000,000,000
Tera (T) Trillion	1,099,511,627,776	ps (picosecond) trillionth	1/1,000,000,000,000
Peta (P) Quadrillion	1,125,899,906,842,624	fs (femtosecond) quadrillionth	1/1,000,000,000,000,000

How Components Are Measured

Storage/channel capacity		Transmission speed	
CPU word size	Bits	CPU clock speed	MHz
Bus size	Bits	Bus speed	MHz
Disk, tape	Bytes	Network line/channel	bits per sec
MEMORY		Disk transfer rate	bits or bytes per sec
Overall capacity	Bytes	Disk acess time	ms
SIMM or SIP module	Bytes	Memory access time	ns
Individual chip	Bits	Machine cycle	µs and ns
		Instruction execution	µs and ns
		Transistor switching	ns, ps and fs

spaghetti code Program code written without a coherent structure. The logic moves from routine to routine without returning to a base point, making it hard to follow. It implies excessive use of the GOTO instruction, which directs the computer to branch to another part of the program without a guarantee of returning.

In structured programming, functions are used, which are subroutines that guarantee a return to the instruction following the one that called it.

SPARC (Scalable Performance ARChitecture) A 32-bit RISC CPU developed by Sun and licensed by SPARC International, Menlo Park, CA.

spatial data Data that is represented as 2-D or 3-D images.

spawn To launch another program from the current program. The DOS TSR version of this Glossary is called POPGLOSS.EXE. It resides in RAM and "spawns" GLOSS.EXE when the hotkey is pressed.

Spec 1170 See *X/Open*.

spec sheet A detail listing of the components of a system.

special character Non-alphabetic or non-numeric character, such as @, #, $, %, &, * and +.

special-purpose computer A computer designed from scratch to perform a specific function. Contrast with *general-purpose computer*.

special-purpose language A programming language designed to solve a specific problem or class of problems. For example, LISP and Prolog are designed for and used extensively in AI applications. Even more specific are languages such as COGO, for civil engineering problems, and APT for directing machine tools. Contrast with *general-purpose language*.

specification A definition (layout, blueprint, design) of hardware or software. See *specs* and *functional specification*.

SPECmark (Systems Performance Evaluation Cooperative MARK) A suite of 10 benchmarks that test integer (SPECint) and floating point (SPECfp) performance of a computer. SPEC reporting requires all 10 numbers as users may only need subsets. A VAX-11\780 is a one-SPECmark machine, and SPECmarks closely track VUPs ratings from Digital's internal benchmarks.

specs (SPECificationS) The details of the components built into a device. See *specification*.

spectral color In computer graphics, the color of a single wavelength of light, starting with violet at the low end and proceeding through indigo, blue, green, yellow and orange and ending with red.

spectral response The variable output of a light-sensitive device that is based on the color of the light it perceives.

spectrum A range of electromagnetic frequencies.

speech recognition Same as *voice recognition*.

speech synthesis Generating machine voice by arranging phonemes (k, ch, sh, etc.) into words. It is used to turn text input into spoken words for the blind. Speech

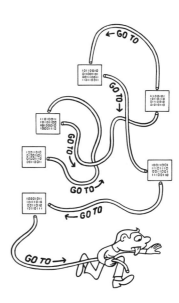

SPAGHETTI CODE

synthesis performs realtime conversion without a pre-defined vocabulary, but does not create human-sounding speech. Although individual spoken words can be digitized into the computer, digitized voice takes a lot of storage, and resulting phrases still lack inflection.

speed buffering A technique that compensates for speed differences between input and output. Data is accepted into the buffer at high speed and transferred out at low speed, or vice versa.

Speed Doubler The name of Intel's clock-doubled DX2 chips.

Speedo A scalable font technology from Bitstream Inc., Cambridge, MA. See *FaceLift*.

speed of electricity/light Electricity and light travel at approximately 186,000 miles per second, which is seven times around the equator per second. This inherent speed of Mother Nature is why computers are so fast. Within the tiny chip, electricity has to flow only a couple of millimeters, and, within an entire computer, only a few feet.

As fast as that is, it's never fast enough. There is resistance in the lines, and even though transistors switch in billionths of a second, CAD, image processing and scientific applications are always exhausting the fastest computers.

Speedware A development system from Speedware Corporation, Toronto, Ontario, that creates programs for the HP 3000, RS/6000 and AS/400. Applications can also be ported to run on DOS and Windows machines with runtime versions of Speedware for those platforms.

spelling checker A separate program or word processing function that tests for correctly-spelled words. It can test the spelling of a marked block, an entire document or group of documents. Advanced systems check for spelling as the user types and can correct common typos and misspellings on the fly.

Spelling checkers simply compare words to a dictionary of words, and the wrong use of a correctly-spelled word cannot be detected. See *grammar checker*.

spherization In computer graphics, turning an image into a sphere.

SPI (Service Provider Interface) The programming interface for developing Windows drivers under WOSA. In order to provide common access to services, the application (query, word processor, e-mail program, etc.) is written to a particular WOSA-supported interface, such as ODBC or MAPI, and the developer of the service software (database manager, document manager, print spooler, etc.) writes to the SPI for that class of service.

spike Also called a transient, a spike is a burst of extra voltage in a power line that lasts only a fraction of a second. Contrast with *sag*. See *power surge*.

spindle A rotating shaft in a disk drive. In a fixed disk, the platters are attached to the spindle. In a removable disk, the spindle remains in the drive.

SpinRite A popular low-level formatting program for PCs from Gibson Research, Aliso Viejo, CA, that reformats without erasing data. It rewrites only sector ID, which may have drifted over time. Version 3.0 can low-level format IDE drives, which have typically required proprietary format programs.

SPL (1) (Systems Programming Language) The assembly language for the HP 3000 series. See *assembly language* for an SPL program example.

(2) (Structured Programming Language) See *structured programming*.

spline In computer graphics, a smooth curve that runs through a series of given points. The term is often used to refer to any curve. See *Bezier* and *B-spline*.

split screen The display of two or more sets of data on screen at the same time. It implies that one set of data can be manipulated independently of the other. Split screens, or windows, are usually created by the operating system or application software, rather than the hardware.

spooler See *print spooler* and *spooling*.

spooling (Simultaneous Peripheral Operations OnLine) The overlapping of low-speed operations with normal processing. It originated with mainframes in order to optimize slow operations such as reading cards and printing. Card input was read onto disk and printer output was stored on disk. In that way, the actual business data processing was done at high speed, since all I/O was on disk.

Today, spooling is used to buffer data for the printer as well as remote batch terminals. See *print spooler*.

spot color A color that is printed from one printing plate which contains that particular ink. Contrast with *process color*.

spread spectrum A radio transmission that continuously changes carrier frequency according to a unique pattern in both sending and receiving devices. It is used for security as well as to allow multiple wireless transmissions in the same space.

spreadsheet Software that simulates a paper spreadsheet, or worksheet, in which columns of numbers are summed for budgets and plans. It appears on screen as a matrix of rows and columns, the intersections of which are identified as cells. Spreadsheets can have thousands of cells and can be scrolled horizontally and vertically in order to view them.

The heart of the spreadsheet is the formula, which is used to add, subtract, mulitply or divide the contents of any cell or group of cells. The formula automatically recalculates whenever any cell that is referenced is changed.

▶ *The electronic and encyclopedic versions of this book provide more detail on this subject.*

spreadsheet compiler Software that translates spreadsheets into stand-alone programs that can be run without the spreadsheet package that created them.

Spreadsheet Connector See *TM/1*.

sprite An independent graphic object controlled by its own bit plane (area of memory). Commonly used in video games, sprites move freely across the screen, passing by, through and colliding with each other with much less programming.

sprocket feed Same as *pin feed*.

SPS (Standby Power System) A UPS system that switches to battery backup upon detection of power failure.

SPS Association A nonprofit organization dedicated to an open PostScript standard. Address: 7 Stuart Road, Chelmsford, MA 01824.

SPSS A statistical package from SPSS, Inc., Chicago, that runs on PCs, most mainframes and minis and is used extensively in marketing research. It provides over 50 statistical processes, including regression analysis, correlation and analysis of variance. Originally named Statistical Package for the Social Sciences, it was written by Norman Nie, a professor at Stanford. In 1976, he formed SPSS, Inc.

spt (Sectors Per Track) The number of sectors in one track.

SPX (Sequenced Packet EXchange) The NetWare communications protocol used to control the transport of messages across a network. SPX ensures that an entire message arrives intact and uses NetWare's IPX protocol as its delivery mechanism. Application programs use SPX to provide client/server and peer-to-peer interaction between network nodes. SPX provides services at layer 4 of the OSI model.

SQL (Structured Query Language) Pronounced "SQL" or "see qwill," a language used to interrogate and process data in a relational database. Originally developed by IBM for its mainframes, there have been many implementations created for mini and micro database applications. SQL commands can be used to interactively work with a database or can be embedded within a programming language to interface to a database.

The following SQL query selects customers with credit limits of at least $5,000 and puts them into sequence from highest credit limit to lowest. The bold words are SQL verbs.

```
SELECT NAME, CITY, STATE, ZIPCODE
FROM CUSTOMER
WHERE CREDITLIMIT 4999
ORDER BY CREDITLIMIT DESC
```

SQL/DS (SQL/Data System) A full-featured relational DBMS from IBM for VSE and VM environments that has integrated query and report writing facilities.

SQL engine A program that accepts SQL commands and accesses the database to obtain the requested data. Users' requests in a query language or database language must be translated into an SQL request before the SQL engine can process it.

SQL Server A relational DBMS from Sybase, Inc., Emeryville, CA, that runs on OS/2 and Windows NT PCs, NetWare servers, VAXs and UNIX workstations. It is designed for client/server use and is accessed by applications using SQL or via Sybase's own QBE and decision support utilities. SQL Server is also available through Microsoft for Windows NT.

SQLWindows A high-level application development system for Windows from Gupta Corporation, Menlo Park, CA. It is used to write Windows applications that access SQL databases in a client/server environment.

square wave A graphic image of a digital pulse as visualized on an oscilloscope. It appears square because it rises quickly to a particular amplitude, stays constant for the duration of the pulse and drops fast at the end of it.

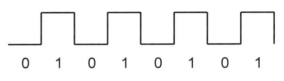

SQUARE WAVE

SQUID (Superconducting Quantum Interference Device) An electronic detection system that uses Josephson junctions circuits. It is capable of detecting extremely weak signals.

SRAM See *static RAM*.

SRPI (Server Requester Programming Interface) An IBM programming interface that allows a PC to interact with a mainframe. See *ECF*.

SRT (Source Routing Transparent) An IEEE-standard technology that allows bridging between Ethernet and token ring networks (Token Ring, FDDI). Existing token ring bridges are not compatible with SRT bridges, but Proteon's (Westborough, MA) Adaptive SRT bridges are compatibile with the installed base. See *source routing*.

SSA (Serial Storage Architecture) A peripheral interface from IBM that transfers data at 20MBytes/sec in one direction, but can operate full-duplex. SSA's ring configuration allows remaining devices to function if one fails. SCSI software can be mapped over SSA allowing existing SCSI devices to be used. SSA is expected to gain momentum in 1995.

SSCP (System Services Control Point) A controlling program in an SNA domain. It resides in the host and is a component within VTAM.

SS/DD (Single Sided/Double Density) Refers to earlier floppy disk formats that store data on only one side of the disk.

SSI (Small Scale Integration) Up to 100 transistors on a chip. See *MSI, LSI, VLSI* and *ULSI*.

SSP (System Support Program) A multiuser, multitasking operating system from IBM that is the primary control program for System/34 and System/36.

ST A personal computer series from Atari that uses a Motorola 68000 CPU and includes the GEM interface, ROM-based TOS operating system, a MIDI interface and a three-voice sound chip.

ST412 An enhancement to the ST506 standard that buffers track-to-track commands for a continuous seek to the required track. All new ST506 drives/controllers incorporate this, thus ST412, ST506/412 and current ST506 units are the same.

ST506 A hard disk interface commonly used in drives of 40MB and less. It transfers data at 625 KBytes/sec and uses the MFM encoding method. See *ST412* and *hard disk*.

ST506 RLL (ST506 Run-Length Limited) A hard disk interface (also called RLL interface) that increases capacity and speed by 50% over ST506 MFM drives and transfers data at 937 KBytes/sec. With MFM drives certified for increased capacity, the ST506 MFM controller can be replaced with an ST506 RLL controller and the drive can be reformatted. See *hard disk*.

stack (1) A set of hardware registers or a reserved amount of memory used for arithmetic calculations or to keep track of internal operations. Stacks keep track of the sequence of routines called in a program. For example, one routine calls another, which calls another and so on. As each routine is completed, the computer returns control to the calling routine all the way back to the first one that started the sequence.

An "internal stack failure" is a fatal error which means that the operating system has lost track of its next operation. Restarting the computer usually corrects this, otherwise the operating system may have to be re-installed.

(2) See *protocol stack* and *HyperCard*.

stack overflow An error condition that occurs when there is no room in the stack for a new item. This type of error occurs when the computer is not properly configured, or sometimes when a board isn't seated entirely in the slot. Contrast with *stack underflow*.
▶ *The electronic and encyclopedic versions of this book provide more detail on this subject.*

stack pointer An address that identifies the location of the most recent item placed on the stack.

stack underflow An error condition that occurs when an item is called for from the stack, but the stack is empty. Contrast with *stack overflow*.

stacker (1) An output bin in a document feeding or punched card machine. Contrast with *hopper*.

(2) (Stacker) A realtime compression program from Stac Electronics, Carlsbad, CA, that doubles (approximately) the disk capacity of a PC and is transparent to the user. A coprocessor board is optionally available.

stackware A HyperCard application that is made up of a HyperCard stack (data) and HyperTalk programming.

STAIRS (STorage And Information Retrieval System) An IBM text document management system for mainframes. It allows users to search for documents based on key words or word combinations.

standard A specification for hardware or software that is either widely used and accepted (de facto) or is sanctioned by a standards organization (de jure).

standard cell The finished design of an electronic function ready for chip fabrication. It can be as small as a clock circuit or as large as a microprocessor. It is used to make custom-designed chips.

standard deviation In statistics, the average amount a number varies from the average number in a series of numbers.

Standard Mode An operational mode in Windows 3.x that is used when running on a 286.

standards & compatibility Standards is the most important issue in the computer field. As an unregulated industry, we have wound up with thousands of data formats and languages. No matter how much the industry talks about compatibility, new formats, languages, plugs, sockets, modules and cartridges appear routinely. The standards makers are always trying to cast a standard in concrete, while the innovators are trying to create a new one. Even when standards are created, they are violated as soon as a new feature is added by the vendor.

If a format or language is used extensively and others copy it, it becomes a de facto standard and may become as widely used as official standards from ANSI and IEEE. When de facto standards are sanctioned by these organizations, they become stable, at least, for a while.

▶ *The electronic and encyclopedic versions of this book provide more detail on this subject, including an overview of all the major categories where standards are required and the common de facto and de jure standards that are in use.*

star network A communications network in which all terminals are connected to a central computer or central hub. PBXs are prime examples as well as IBM's Token Ring and AT&T's Starlan LANs.

Starlan A local area network from AT&T that uses twisted pair wire, the CSMA/CD access method, transmits at 1 Mbps and uses a star or bus topology. In 1988, Starlan was renamed Starlan 1, and Starlan 10 was introduced, a 10 Mbps Ethernet version that uses twisted pair or optical fibers.

start bit In asynchronous communications, the bit transmitted before each character.

start/stop transmission Same as *asynchronous transmission*.

startup routine A routine that is executed when the computer is booted or when an application is loaded. It is used to customize the environment for its associated software.

STARTUP.CMD (STARTUP.CoMmanD) An OS/2 file that is executed immediately upon startup. It contains instructions that can initialize operating system settings and call in a specific application program. The DOS counterpart is AUTOEXEC.BAT.

stat mux (STATistical MUltipleXor) See *statistical multiplexor*.

state-of-the-art The most advanced technique or method used.

statement In a high-level programming language, a descriptive phrase that generates one or more machine language instructions in the computer. In a low-level assembly language, programmers write instructions rather than statements, since each source language instruction is translated into one machine language instruction.

static binding Same as *early binding*.

static column memory A type of page mode memory that requires less electronic pulsing in order to access the memory bits.

static electricity A stationary electrical charge that is the result of intentional charging or of friction in low-humidity environments.

static RAM A memory chip that requires power to hold its content. Static RAM chips have access times in the 10 to 30-nanosecond range. Dynamic RAMs are usually above 30, and Bipolar and ECL memories are under 10.

A static RAM bit is made up of a pretzel-like flip-flop circuit that lets current flow through one side or the other based on which one of two transistors is activated. Static RAMs do not require refresh circuitry as do dynamic RAMs, but they take up more space and use more power.

static SQL See *embedded SQL*.

station A computer, workstation or terminal in a network. Same as *node*.

statistical multiplexor In communications, a device that combines several low-speed channels into a single high-speed channel and vice versa. A standard multiplexor is set to a fixed interleaving pattern, but the statistical multiplexor can analyze the traffic load and dynamically switch to different channel patterns to speed up transmission.

status line An information line displayed on screen that shows current activity.

ST connector A fiber-optic cable connector that uses a bayonet plug and socket. It was the first de facto standard connector for optical fibers for most commercial wiring. See *SMA connector* and *ST connector*.

STD bus A bus architecture used in medical and industrial equipment due to its small size and rugged design. Originally an 8-bit bus, extensions have increased it to 16 and 32 bits.

stealth virus A virus that is able to keep itself from being detected. See *polymorphic virus*.

step frame To capture video images one frame at a time. If a computer is not fast enough to capture analog video in realtime, the video can be forwarded and processed one frame at a time.

stepper motor A motor that rotates in small, fixed increments and is used to control the movement of the access arm on a disk drive. Contrast with *voice coil*.

stereophonic Sound reproduction that uses two or more channels. Contrast with *monophonic*.

stick font Same as *vector font*.

stick model A picture made of lines, or vectors. For example, in biomedical applications, the limbs of a person or animal are converted into lines so that the motion can be visually observed and graphically plotted and analyzed.

stiction (STatic frICTION) A type of hard disk failure in which the read/write heads stick to the platters. The lubricant used on certain drives heats up and liquifies. When the disk is turned off, it cools down and can become like a glue.

STN See *LCD*.

stop bit In asynchronous communications, a bit transmitted after each character.

storage device A hardware unit that holds data. In this Glossary, it refers only to peripheral equipment, such as disk and tape, in contrast with memory (RAM).

storage hierarchy The range of memory and storage devices within the computer system. The following list runs from lowest to highest speed.

Low	Punched cards
Speed	Punched paper tape
	Removable cartridge mass storage devices (non-disk)
	Magnetic tape
	Floppy disks
	CD-ROM and optical disks
	Magnetic disks (movable heads)
	Magnetic disks (fixed heads)
	Bubble memory
	Low-speed bulk memory
	Main memory
	Cache memory
High	Microcode
Speed	Registers

storage management Administration of a backup and archival program that moves less-timely information to more economical storage media; for example, from magnetic disk to optical disk to magnetic tape.

storage media Refers to disks, tapes and bubble memory cartridges.

store and forward The temporary storage of a message for transmission to its destination at a later time. Store and forward techniques allow for routing over networks that are not accessible at all times. For example, messages crossing time zones can be forwarded during daytime at the receiving side, or messages can be forwarded at night in order to obtain off-peak rates. See *messaging protocol*.

stored program concept The fundamental computer architecture in which the computer acts upon (executes) internally-stored instructions.

STP (Shielded Twisted Pair) Telephone wire that is wrapped in a metal sheath to eliminate external interference. See *twisted pair*.

Strand88 A parallel processing programming language developed by AI Ltd., England.

stream (1) A contiguous group of data.

(2) The I/O management in the C programming language. A stream is a channel through which data flows to/from a disk, keyboard, printer, etc.

streaming tape A high-speed magnetic tape drive that is frequently used to make a backup copy of an entire hard disk.

Streamline A Macintosh tracing program from Adobe Systems Inc., Mountain View, CA. It converts scanned or MacPaint images into PostScript files, which can be modified in Illustrator 88.

stream-oriented file A type of file, such as a text document or digital voice file, that is more openly structured than a data file. Text and voice are continuous streams of characters, whereas database records are repeating structures with a fixed or reasonably uniform format.

STREAMS A feature of UNIX System V that provides a standard way of dynamically building and passing messages up and down a protocol stack. STREAMS passes messages from the application "downstream" through the STREAMS modules to the network driver at the end of the stack. Messages are passed "upstream" from the driver to the application. A STREAMS module would be a transport layer protocol such as TCP and SPX or a network layer protocol such as IP and IPX.

Streettalk A directory service in the VINES network operating system.

string (1) In programming, a contiguous set of alphanumeric characters that does not contain numbers used for calculations. Names, addresses, words and sentences are strings. Contrast with *numeric* data.

(2) Any connected set of structures, such as a string of bits, fields or records.

string handling The abilty to manipulate alphanumeric data (names, addresses, text, etc.). Typical functions include the ability to handle arrays of strings, to left and right align and center strings and to search for an occurrence of text within a string.

striping Interleaving or multiplexing data to increase speed. See *disk striping*.

stroke (1) In printing, the weight, or thickness, of a character. For example, in the LaserJet, one of the specifications of the font description is the stroke weight from -3 to +3.

(2) In computer graphics, a pen or brush stroke or to a vector in a vector graphics image.

stroke font Same as *vector font*.

stroke weight The thickness of lines in a font character. The HP LaserJet III manual defines stroke weights from Ultra Thin (-7) to Ultra Black (+7), with Medium, or Text, as normal (0).

stroke writer Same as *vector display*.

structured analysis Techniques developed in the late 1970s by Yourdon, DeMarco, Gane and Sarson for applying a systematic approach to systems analysis. It included the use of data flow diagrams and data modeling and fostered the use of implementation-independent graphical notation for documentation.

structured design A systematic approach to program design developed in the mid 1970s by Constantine, Yourdon, et al, that included the use of graphical notation for effective documentation and communication, design guidelines and recipes to help programmers get started.

structured programming Techniques that impose a logical structure on the writing of a program. Large routines are broken down into smaller, modular routines. The use of the GOTO statement is discouraged (see *spaghetti code*).

Certain programming statements are indented in order to make loops and other program logic easier to follow. Structured walkthroughs, which invite criticism from peer programmers, are also used.

Structured languages, such as Pascal, Ada and dBASE, force the programmer to write a structured program. However, unstructured languages such as FORTRAN, COBOL and BASIC require discipline on the part of the programmer.

stub A small software routine placed into a program that provides a common function. Stubs are used for a variety of purposes. For example, a stub might be installed in a client machine, and a counterpart installed in a server, where both are required to resolve some protocol, remote procedure call (RPC) or other interoperability requirement.

style sheet In word processing and desktop publishing, a file that contains layout settings for a particular category of document. Style sheets include such settings as margins, tabs, headers and footers, columns and fonts.

stylus A pen-shaped instrument that is used to "draw" images or point to menus. See *light pen* and *digitizer tablet*.

subarea node In an SNA network, a system that contains network controlling functions. It refers to a host computer or a communications controller and its associated terminals.

subdirectory A disk directory that is subordinate to (below) another directory. In order to gain access to a subdirectory, the path must include all directories above it.

submarining The temporary visual loss of the moving cursor on a slow display screen such as found on a laptop computer. See *active matrix LCD*.

submenu An additional list of options within a menu selection. There can many levels of submenus.

subnet, subnetwork A division of a network into an interconnected, but independent, subgroup, or domain, in order to improve performance and security.

subnotebook A laptop computer that weighs less than four pounds. Subnotebooks may use an external floppy disk to reduce weight. If you need to exchange data via diskettes in remote locations, this may be inconvenient.

subroutine A group of instructions that perform a specific task. A large subroutine is usually called a module or procedure; a small one, a function or macro, but all terms are used interchangeably.

subschema Pronounced "sub-skeema." In database management, an individual user's partial view of the database. The schema is the entire database.

subscript (1) In word processing and mathematical notation, a digit or symbol that appears below the line. Contrast with *superscript*.

(2) In programming, a method for referencing data in a table. For example, in the table **PRICETABLE**, the statement to reference a specific price in the table might be `pricetable (item)`, ITEM being the subscript variable.

In a two-dimensional table that includes price and discount, the statement `pricetable (item,discount)` could reference a discounted price. The relative locations of the current ITEM and DISCOUNT are kept in two index registers.

subset A group of commands or functions that do not include all the capabilities of the original specification. Software designed to work with the subset will also work with the original. However, any component written to the full original specification will not operate with the subset. Contrast with *superset*.

substrate The base material upon which integrated circuits are built. Silicon is the most widely used substrate for chips.

substring A subset of an alphanumeric field or variable. The substring function in a programming language is used to extract the subset; for example, the programming expression `substr(prodcode,4,3)` extracts characters 4, 5 and 6 out of a product code field or variable.

subtract In relational database, an operation that generates a third file from all the records in one file that are not in a second file.

suite of applications See *application suite*.

SUM II (Symantec Utilities for Macintosh) A set of Macintosh utilities from Symantec Corporation, Cupertino, CA, that provides hard disk optimization, analysis and repair and security capabilities.

Sun (Sun Microsystems, Inc., Mountain View, CA) A manufacturer of network-based, high-performance workstations and servers founded in 1982. Sun's hardware is based on its SPARC architecture, and its Solaris operating system and networking enhancements are based on UNIX. Sun's Network File System (NFS) software, which allows data sharing across the network, has become an industry standard. SunSoft is the Sun division that provides system software.

SuperCalc A PC spreadsheet from Computer Associates. It was one of the first spreadsheets following in VisiCalc's footsteps in the early 1980s. SuperCalc5 (1988) provides 3-D capability, enhanced graphics and can link up to 256 spreadsheets.

supercomputer The fastest computer available. It is typically used for simulations in petroleum exploration and production, structural analysis, computational fluid dynamics, physics and chemistry, electronic design, nuclear energy research and meteorology. It is also used for realtime animated graphics.

superconductor A material that has little resistance to the flow of electricity. Traditional superconductors operate at -459 Fahrenheit (absolute zero).

Thus far, the major use for superconductors, made of alloys of niobium, is for high-powered magnets in medical imaging machines that use magnetic fields instead of x-rays.

Using experimental materials, such as copper oxides, barium, lanthanum and yttrium, IBM's Zurich research lab in 1986 and the University of Houston in 1987 raised the temperature of superconductivity to -59 degrees Fahrenheit. If superconductors can work at reasonable temperatures, they will have a dramatic impact on the future of computing. See *Josephson Junction*.

SuperDrive The floppy disk drive used in the Macintosh. It stores 1.44MB of data in its high-density format. It also reads and writes earlier Mac 400 and 800KB disks, as well as Apple II ProDOS, MS-DOS and OS/2 formats.

super floppy (1) A PC 3.5" floppy disk that holds 2.88MB and is compatible with the 1.44MB and 720KB formats.

(2) A very-high-capacity floppy disk in the 20MB range. See *Floptical*.

(3) (SuperFloppy) A Superdrive-compatible floppy disk for older Macintoshes from Peripheral Land, Inc., Fremont, CA.

superframe A T1 transmission format made up of 12 T1 frames (superframe) and 24 frames (extended superframe). See *D4*.

SuperKermit See *Kermit*.

SuperKey A PC keyboard macro processor from Borland that lets users create keyboard macros, rearrange the keyboard and encrypt data and programs.

supermini A large-scale minicomputer. Terminology is really a point of view. If you're a mini maker, your largest machine is "super." If you're a mainframe maker, your smallest machine isn't worth talking about! Note: Supermini is not the same as mini-supercomputer.

superscaler A CPU architecture that allows more than one instruction to be executed in one clock cycle.

superscript Any letter, digit or symbol that appears above the line. Contrast with *subscript*.

superserver A high-speed network server with very large RAM and disk capacity. Superservers typically support multiprocessing.

superset A group of commands or functions that exceed the capabilities of the original specification. Software designed for the original specification will also operate with the superset. However, software designed for the superset will not work with the original. Contrast with *subset*.

supertwist An LCD technology that twists liquid molecules greater than 90 in order to improve contrast and viewing angle. See *LCD*.

Super VGA See *VGA*.

supervisor Same as *operating system*.

supervisor call The instruction in an application program that switches the computer to supervisor state.

supervisor control program The part of the operation system that always resides in memory. Same as *kernel*.

supervisor state Typically associated with mainframes, it is a hardware mode in which the operating system executes instructions unavailable to an application program; for example, I/O instructions. Contrast with *program state*.

support (1) The assistance provided by a hardware or software vendor in installing and maintaining its product.

(2) Software or hardware designed to include or work with some other software or hardware product. For example, if a word processor "supports the LaserJet," it can activate special features of that printer. If a computer "supports multiprocessing," it can host more than one CPU internally.

SUPRA A relational DBMS from Cincom Systems, Inc., Cincinnati, OH, that runs on IBM mainframes and VAXs. It includes a query language and a program that automates the database design process.

surface In CAD, the external geometry of an object. Surfaces are generally required for NC (numerical control) modeling rather than wireframe or solids.

surface modeling In CAD, a mathematical technique for representing solid-appearing objects. Surface modeling is a more complex method for representing objects than wireframe modeling, but not as sophisticated as solid modeling.

Although surface and solid models can appear the same on screen, they are quite different. Surface models cannot be sliced open as can solid models. In addition, in surface modeling, the object can be geometrically incorrect; whereas, in solid modeling, it must be correct.

surface mount A circuit board packaging technique in which the leads (pins) on the chips and components are soldered on top of the board, not through it. Boards can be smaller and built faster.

surfing Scanning online material, such as databases, news clips and forums. The term originated from "channel surfing," the rapid changing of TV channels to find something of interest.

surge See *power surge*.

surge protector A device that protects a computer from excessive voltage (spikes and power surges) in the power line. See *voltage regulator* and *UPS*.

surge suppressor Same as *surge protector*.

suspend and resume To stop an operation and restart where you left off. In portable computers, the hard disk is turned off, and the CPU is made to idle at its slowest speed. All open applications are retained in memory.

SV (Scientific Visualization) See *visualization*.

SVC (Switched Virtual Circuit) A Network connection from sender to recipient that is established at the time the transmission is required. This is what occurs in a switched public network. Contrast with *PVC*.

SVGA (Super VGA) See *VGA*.

S-VHS (Super-VHS) A video recording and playback system that uses a higher-quality VHS cassette and the S-video technology. VCRs that support S-VHS can also record and play back normal VHS tapes.

SVID (System V Interface Definition) An AT&T specification for the UNIX System V operating system. SVID Release 3 specifies the interface for UNIX System V Release 4.

S-video (Super-video) A video technology, also called Y/C video, that records and maintains luminance (Y) and color information (C) separately. S-VHS and Hi-8 cameras and VCRs use this method, which provide a better color image than standard VHS and 8mm formats. S-video hookups use a special 5-pin connector rather than the common RCA phono plug.

SVR4 See *System V Release 4.0*.

swap file A disk file used to temporarily save a program or part of a program running in memory.

swapping Replacing one segment of a program in memory with another and restoring the original when required. In virtual memory systems, it is called paging.

switch (1) A mechanical or electronic device that directs the flow of electrical or optical signals from one side to the other. Switches with multiple input and output ports such as a PBX are able to route traffic." See *data switch* and *transistor*.

　　With regard to a simple on/off switch, remember!

　　　　Open is "off." Closed is "on."

(2) In programming, a bit or byte used to keep track of something. Sometimes refers to a branch in a program.

(3) A modifier of a command.

Switched 56 A digital service at 56Kbits/sec provided by the local telephone companies and long distance carriers. It works like the dial-up telephone system, only for digital data. You pay a monthly charge plus so much per minute of digital traffic. The rates are similar to voice calls on the analog network. For connection, a DSU/CSU is used instead of a modem.

switched Ethernet An Ethernet network that runs through a high-speed switch. Existing network adapters (NICs) are used, but they are all wired to the central switch rather than cabled together in a bus topology. The switch is capable of handling hundreds of megabits per second, and each user receives the full 10 Mpbs Ethernet bandwidth. See *FDSE*.

switched line In communications, a link that is established in a switched network, such as the international dial-up telephone system, a Switched 56 digital line or ISDN.

switched network (1) The international dial-up telephone system.

(2) A network in which a temporary connection is established from one point to another for either the duration of the session (circuit switching) or for the transmission of one or more packets of data (packet switching).

switching hub A device that acts as a central switch or PBX, connecting one line to another. In a local area network (LAN), a switching hub gives any two stations on the network the full bandwidth of the line. Contrast with *shared media LAN*, in which all stations share the bandwidth of a common transmission path. See *hub*.

switch-to-computer To integrate voice telephone and database access. For example, in customer service applications, using telephone services, such as automatic number identification (ANI) and automatic call distribution (ACD), an incoming call can retrieve and route the customer's file to the next available human agent.

SWITCHING IN THE EARLY DAYS
(Courtesy AT&T)
This was sophisticated switching technology circa 1915.

SX See *386SX* and *486SX*.

SYBASE System A family of SQL development tools from Sybase, Inc., that includes SQL Server, SQL Toolset (design, development and control) and Client/Services Interfaces (distributed database architecture). See *SQL Server*.

SYLK file (SYmbolic LinK file) A spreadsheet file format originating with Multiplan that is used by a number of spreadsheet programs.

symbol In data compression, a unit of data (byte, floating point number, spoken word, etc.) that is treated independently.

symbol set In printing, a group of symbols that are extensions to standard characters for use in a particular country or specific application. Symbol sets provide codes for the non-standard upper half of the ASCII character set.

symbolic language (1) A programming language that uses symbols, or mnemonics, for expressing operations and operands. All modern programming languages are symbolic languages.

(2) A language that manipulates symbols rather than numbers. See *list processing*.

symmetric multiprocessing A multiprocessing design in which any CPU can be assigned any application task. One CPU acts as a control processor, or scheduler, which boots the system, distributes work to the next available CPU and manages I/O requests. A copy of the operating system generally runs in each CPU. Contrast with *asymmetric multiprocessing*.

Symphony An Integrated software package for PCs from Lotus that includes word processing, database management, speadsheet, business graphics, communications and a macro language.

sync character In synchronous communications systems, a special character transmitted to synchronize timing.

sync generator A device that supplies synchronization signals to a series of cameras to keep them all in phase.

synchronous (1) A sequence of fixed or concurrent events. See *synchronous transmission*.

(2) Completing the current I/O operation before the next one is started.

(3) In SCSI, the transfer of data without immediate acknowledgment of each byte.

(4) Contrast with *asynchronous*.

synchronous protocol A communications protocol that controls a synchronous transmission, such as bisync, SDLC and HDLC. Contrast with *asynchronous protocol*.

synchronous transmission The transmission of data in which both stations are synchronized. Codes are sent from the transmitting station to the receiving station to establish the synchronization, and data is then transmitted in continuous streams.

Modems that transmit at 1200 bps and higher often convert the asynchronous signals from a computer's serial port into synchronous transmission over the transmission line. Contrast with *asynchronous transmission*.

syntax The rules governing the structure of a language statement. It specifies how words and symbols are put together to form a phrase.

syntax error An error that occurs when a program cannot understand the command that has been entered. See *parse*.

synthesize To create a whole or complete unit from parts or components.

synthesizer A device that generates sound by creating waveforms electronically (FM synthesis) or from stored samples of musical instruments (wave table synthesis). See *MIDI* and *speech synthesis*.

sysgen (SYStem GENeration) The installation of a new or revised operating system. It includes selecting the appropriate utilities and identifying the peripheral devices and storage capacities of the system the operating system will be controlling.

sysop (SYStem OPerator) Pronounced "siss-op." A person who runs an online communications system or bulletin board. The sysop may also act as mediator for system conferences.

Sysplex IBM System/390 multiprocessing. The Sysplex Timer external clock is used to synchronize time-of-day clocks in multiple processors. If failure occurs in a multiprocessor complex, precise transaction time stamps are required for accurate rollback and recovery.

SysReq key (SYStem REQuest key) A keyboard key on a terminal keyboard that is used to get the attention of the central computer. The key exists on PC keyboards, but is rarely used by applications.

system (1) A group of related components that interact to perform a task.

(2) A *computer system* is made up of the CPU, operating system and peripheral devices.

(3) An *information system* is made up of the database, all the data entry, update, query and report programs and manual and machine procedures.

(4) "The system" often refers to the operating system.

System/3 A batch-oriented minicomputer from IBM. Introduced in 1969, it introduced a new half-sized punched card. It could also handle interactive terminals.

System/3x Refers to IBM System/34, System/36 and System/38 midrange computers.

System 7 (1) A major upgrade of the Macintosh operating system (1991). It includes virtual memory, increased memory addressing, hot links (Publish & Subscribe), multitasking (MultiFinder no longer optional), TrueType fonts and a variety of enhancements to the user interface. System 7 Pro includes PowerTalk communications, the AppleScript scripting language and QuickTime for sound, movies and animation.

(2) (System/7) A sensor-based minicomputer from IBM introduced in 1970 and used for process control. It was superseded by the Series/1.

System/32 A batch-oriented minicomputer from IBM. Introduced in 1975, it provided a single terminal for operator use. It was superseded by the System/34, which could run System/32 applications in a special mode.

System/34 A multiuser, multitasking minicomputer from IBM, introduced in 1977. The typical system had from a handful to a dozen terminals and could run System/32 programs in a special mode. Most large System/34 users migrated to the System/38, while small users migrated to the System/36.

System/36 A multiuser, multitasking minicomputer from IBM that was introduced in 1983. It superseded the System/34 and is mostly compatible with it. System/34 programs run in the System/36 after recompilation. The typical system supports from a handful to a couple of dozen terminals. It has been superseded by the AS/400.

System/38 A minicomputer from IBM that includes an operating system with an integrated relational database management system. Introduced in 1978, it was an advanced departure from previous System/3x computers. The typical system handles from a dozen to several dozen terminals. It has been superseded by the AS/400.

System/88 A family of fault-tolerant midrange computers from IBM used for online transaction processing. It uses the System/88 virtual memory and System/88 FTX (Fault Tolerant UNIX) operating systems. Includes the 4579 and 4576 multiprocessor series and 4593 entry-level models.

System/360, System/370, System/390 In 1964, IBM introduced the System/360 family of computer systems. It was the first time in history that a complete line of computers was announced at one time. Much of the 360 architecture is still carried over in current-day IBM mainframes.

In 1970, the System/370 series was introduced, which added virtual memory and other enhancements. Subseqent series include the 303x, 43xx, 308x, 309x and 9370, all of which are based on the 370 architecture.

In 1990, IBM introduced the System/390 family that features the ESA/390 architecture and operating systems, ES/9000 hardware, ESCON fiber optic channels, Sysplex multiprocessing and SystemView.

System 2000 (1) A hierarchical, network and relational DBMS from the SAS Institute, Cary, NC, that runs on IBM, CDC and Unisys computers. It has been integrated into the SAS System. Also see *FTS 2000*.

system administrator A person who manages a multiuser computer system. Responsibilities are similar to that of a network administrator.

Systemantics An insightful book on the systems process by John Gall (1977). The following is copied with permission from Random House.

A Concise Summary of the Field of General Systemantics

Systems are seductive. They promise to do a hard job faster, better, and more easily than you could do it by yourself. But if you set up a system, you are likely to find your time and effort now being consumed in the care and feeding of the system itself. New problems are created by its very presence. Once set up, it won't go away, it grows and encroaches. It begins to do strange and wonderful things. Breaks down in ways you never thought possible. It kicks back, gets in the way, and opposes its own proper function. Your own perspective becomes distorted by being in the system. You become anxious and push on it to make it work. Eventually you come to believe that the misbegotten product it so grudgingly delivers is what you really wanted all the time. At that point encroachment has become complete...

you have become absorbed...

you are now a systems person!

system board A printed circuit board that contains the primary CPU. In a personal computer, it is also called the *motherboard*.

system development cycle The sequence of events in the development of an information system (application), which requires mutual effort on the part of user and technical staff.

1. SYSTEMS ANALYSIS & DESIGN
   feasibility study
   general design
   prototyping
   detail design
   functional specifications
2. USER SIGN OFF
3. PROGRAMMING
   design
   coding
   testing
4. IMPLEMENTATION
   training
   conversion
   installation
5. USER ACCEPTANCE

system development methodology The formal documentation for the phases of the system development cycle. It defines the precise objectives for each phase and the results required from a phase before the next one can begin. It may include specialized forms for preparing the documentation describing each phase.

system disk A hard or floppy disk that contains part or all of the operating system or other control program.

system failure A hardware or operating system malfunction.

system file A machine language file that is part of the operating system or other control program. It may also refer to a configuration file used by such programs.

system folder The operating system folder in the Macintosh that contains the System, Finder and MultiFinder, printer drivers, fonts, desk accessories, INITs and cdevs.

system font The primary font used by the operating system or other control program to display messages and menus unless otherwise directed.

system image The current contents of memory, which includes the operating system and running programs.

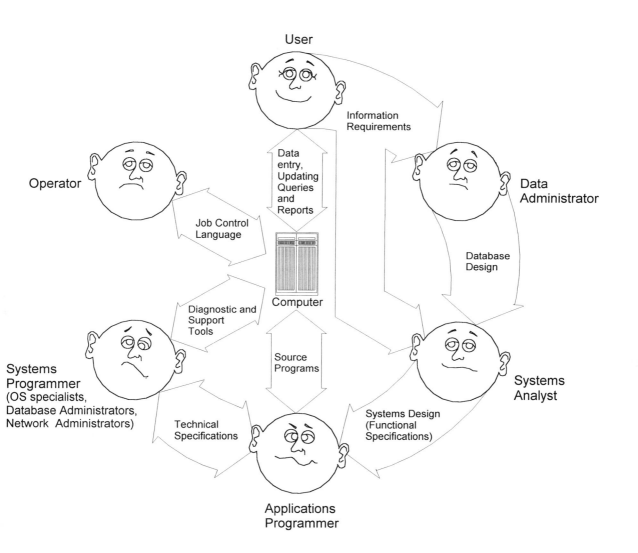

SYSTEM DEVELOPMENT CYCLE

SYSTEM.INI See *WIN.INI.*

system level An operation that is performed by the operating system or some other control program.

system life cycle The useful life of an information system. Its length depends on the nature and volatility of the business, as well as the software development tools used to generate the databases and applications. Eventually, an information system that is patched over and over no longer is structurally sound enough to be expanded.

Tools like DBMSs allow for changes more readily, but increased transaction volumes can negate the effectiveness of the original software later on.

system memory The memory used by the operating system.

system program A component of system software.

system prompt An on-screen symbol that indicates the operating system is ready for a command. See *DOS prompt.*

System Resources See *Windows memory limitations.*

system software Programs used to control the computer and develop and run application programs. It includes operating systems, TP monitors, network operating systems and database managers. Contrast with *application program.*
▶ *The electronic and encyclopedic versions of this book provide more detail on this subject.*

system test Running a complete system for testing purposes. See *unit test.*

system time/date The on-going time of day in the computer, which is maintained by a battery when the computer is turned off. It is used to time stamp all newly-created files and activate time-dependent processes.

System V Release 4.0 A unified version of UNIX released in 1989. See *UNIX.*

systems A general term for the department, people or work involved in systems analysis & design activities.

systems analysis & design The examination of a problem and the creation of its solution. Systems analysis is effective when all sides of the problem are reviewed. Systems design is most effective when more than one solution can be proposed. The plans for the care and feeding of a new system are as important as the problems they solve. See *system development cycle* and *Systemantics.*

systems analyst The person responsible for the development of an information system. They design and modify systems by turning user requirements into a set of functional specifications, which are the blueprint of the system. They design the database or help design it if data administrators are available. They develop the manual and machine procedures and the detailed processing specs for each data entry, update, query and report program in the system.

Systems analysts are the architects, as well as the project leaders, of an information system. It is their job to develop solutions to user's problems, determine the technical and operational feasibility of their solutions, as well as estimate the costs to develop and implement them.

They develop prototypes of the system along with the users, so that the final specifications are examples of screens and reports that have been carefully reviewed. Experienced analysts leave no doubt in users' minds as to what is being developed, and they insist that all responsible users review and sign off on every detail.

Systems analysts require a balanced mix of business and technical knowledge, interviewing and analytical skills, as well as a good understanding of human behavior. See *Systemantics.*

systems disk A disk pack or disk drive reserved only for system software, which includes the operating system, assemblers, compilers and other utility and control programs.

systems engineer Often a vendor title for persons involved in consulting and pre-sales activities related to computers. See *systems analyst, systems programmer, programmer analyst* and *application programmer.*

systems house An organization that develops customized software and/or turnkey systems for customers. Contrast with *software house*, which develops software packages for sale to the general public. Both terms are used synonymously.

systems integration Making diverse components work together. See *NASI.*

systems integrator An individual or organization that builds systems from a variety of diverse components. With increasing complexity of technology, more customers want complete solutions to information problems, requiring hardware, software and networking expertise in a multivendor environment. See *OEM, VAR* and *NASI.*

systems management (1) The management of systems development, which includes systems analysis & design, application development and implementation. See *system development cycle.*

(2) Software that manages computer systems in an enterprise, which may include any and all of the following functions: software distribution, version control, backup & recovery, printer spooling, job scheduling, virus protection and performance and capacity planning. Network management may be an integrated component of systems management.

systems program See *system program* and *system software.*

systems programmer (1) In the IS department of a large organization, a technical expert on some or all of the computer's system software (operating systems, networks, DBMSs, etc.). They are responsible for the efficient performance of the computer systems.

They usually don't write programs, but perform a lot of technical tasks that integrate vendors' software. They also act as technical advisors to systems analysts, application programmers and operations personnel. For example, they would know whether additional tasks could be added to the computer and would recommend conversion to a new operating or database system in order to optimize performance.

In mainframe environments, there is one systems programmer for about 10 or more application programmers, and systems programmers generally have considerably higher salaries than application programmers. In smaller environments, users rely on vendors or consultants for systems programming assistance. In fact, end users are actually performing systems programmer functions when they install new software or hardware on their own personal computers.

(2) In a computer hardware or software organization, a person who designs and writes system software. In this case, a systems programmer is a programmer in the traditional sense.

SystemView An IBM architecture for computer systems management introduced with System/390 that provides an enterprise-wide approach for controlling multiple systems and networks. It will be implemented in stages through the 1990s. NetView is a major component.

systolic array An array of processing elements (typically multiplier-accumulator chips) in a pipeline structure that is used for applications such as image and signal processing and fluid dynamics. The "systolic," coined by H. T. Kung of Carnegie-Mellon, refers to the rhythmic transfer of data through the pipeline like blood flowing through the vascular system.

SYZYGY Pronounced "SIZE-uh-gee." PC workgroup software from Information Research Corporation, Charlottesville, VA. Used for coordinating schedules, resources and budgets for group projects and includes e-mail and a calendar with to-do and activity blists.

T See *tera*.

T1 A 1.544 megabit T-carrier channel that can handle 24 voice or data channels at 64 Kbits/sec. The standard T1 frame is 193 bits long, which holds 24 8-bit voice samples and one synchronization bit. 8,000 frames are transmitted per second. See *DS, D4* and *ESF*.

T2 A 6.312 megabit T-carrier channel that can handle 96 voice or data channels at 64 Kbits/sec. See *DS*.

T3 A 44.736 megabit T-carrier channel that can handle 672 voice or data channels at 64 Kbits/sec. T3 requires fiber optic cable. See *DS*.

tabbing Moving the cursor on a video display screen or the print head on a printer to a specified column.

tab character A control character in a document that represents movement to the next tab stop. See *ASCII chart (9 and 11)*.

tab delimited A text format that uses tab characters as separators between fields. Unlike comma delimited files, alphanumeric data is not surrounded by quotes.

tab key A keyboard key that moves the cursor to the next tab stop.

table (1) In programming, a collection of adjacent fields. Also called an *array*, a table contains data that is either constant within the program or is called in when the program is run. See *decision table*.

(2) In a relational database, the same as a file; a collection of records.

table lookup Searching for data in a table, commonly used in data entry validation and any operation that must match an item of data with a known set of values.

tablet See *digitizer tablet*.

table view A screen display of several items or records in rows and columns. Contrast with *form view*.

tabular form Same as *table view* with respect to printed output.

tabulate (1) To arrange data into a columnar format.

(2) To sum and print totals.

tabulating equipment Punched card machines, including keypunches, sorters, collators, interpreters, reproducers, calculators and tabulators.

tabulator A punched card accounting machine that prints and calculates totals.

tag (1) A set of bits or characters that identifies various conditions about data in a file and is often found in the header records of such files.

(2) A name (label, mnemonic) assigned to a data structure, such as a field, file, paragraph or other object.

(3) The key field in a record.

(4) A brass pin on a terminal block that is connected to a wire by soldering or wire wrapping.

tag sort A sorting procedure in which the key fields are sorted first to create the correct order, and then the actual data records are placed into that order.

Taligent (Taligent, Inc., Cupertino, CA) A joint venture of IBM and Apple involved in developing a next-generation, object-oriented application development and operating system environment.

talk-off An unintentional command activation when a human voice generates the same tone as a control signal.

Tandem (Tandem Computers Inc., Cupertino, CA) A manufacturer of fault tolerant computers founded in 1974 by James Treybig to address the transaction processing market. Tandem introduced the first commercial computer based on a fault tolerant, multiprocessor architecture.

tandem processors Two processors hooked together in a multiprocessor environment.

Tandy (Tandy Corporation, Ft. Worth, TX) A manufacturer of PCs and electronics that started as a family leather business in 1919. In 1963, it acquired the nine Radio Shack stores in Boston. Today, it has over 7,000 company-owned stores and franchises.

tap In communications, a connection onto the main transmission medium of a local area network. See *transceiver*.

tape See *magnetic tape* and *paper tape*.

tape backup The use of magnetic tape for storing duplicate copies of hard disk files. QIC drives are the most widely used, but DAT and 8mm (Exabyte) formats are gaining ground. See *QIC, DDS (3), DATA/DAT, D/CAS and Exabyte*.

tape drive A physical unit that holds, reads and writes the magnetic tape. See *magnetic tape*.

tape dump A printout of tape contents without any report formatting.

tape mark A control code used to indicate the end of a tape file.

tape transport The mechanical part of a tape drive.

TAPI (Telephony API) A programming interface from Microsoft and Intel that is part of Microsoft's WOSA architecture. It allows Windows client applications to access voice services on a server. TAPI is designed to provide interoperability between PCs and telephone equipment, including phone systems and PBXs. See *WOSA*.

tar A UNIX utility for archiving files, often used in conjunction with "compress."

Targa A raster graphics file format developed by Truevision, Inc., Indianapolis, IN. It uses the .TGA file extension and handles 16-, 24- and 32-bit color. It is also the trade name of a line of video graphics boards used in high-resolution imaging.

target computer The computer into which a program is loaded and run. Contrast with *source computer*. See *cross assembler/compiler*.

target directory The directory into which data is being sent.

target disk The disk onto which data is recorded. Contrast with *source disk*.

target drive The drive containing the disk or tape onto which data is recorded. Contrast with *source drive*.

target language The language resulting from a translation process (assembler, compiler, etc.).

tariff A schedule of rates for common carrier services.

task An independent running program. See *multitasking*.

task management The part of the operating system that controls the running of one or more programs (tasks) within the computer at the same time.

task swapping Switching between two applications by copying the current running program to disk or other high-speed storage device (auxiliary memory, EMS, etc.) and loading another program into that program space.

task switching Switching between active applications. See *context switching*.

TB, Tb See *terabyte* and *terabit*.

Tbits/sec (TeraBITS per SECond) Trillion bits per second.

TBps, Tbps (TeraBytes Per Second, TeraBits Per Second) Trillion bytes per second. Trillion bits per second.

Tbytes/sec (TeraBYTES per SECond) Trillion bytes per second.

TC See *true color*.

TCAM (TeleCommunications Access Method) IBM communications software widely used to transfer data between mainframes and 3270 terminals.

T-carrier A digital transmission service from a common carrier. Introduced by AT&T in 1983 as a voice service, its use for data has grown steadily.

   T-carrier service requires multiplexors at both ends that merge the various signals together for transmission and split them at the destination. Multiplexors analyze the traffic load and vary channel speeds for optimum transmission. See *DS*.

TCM (1) (Trellis-Coded Modulation/Viterbi Decoding) A technique that adds forward error correction to a modulation scheme by adding an additional bit to each baud. TCM is used with QAM modulation, for example.

(2) (Thermal Conduction Module) An IBM circuit packaging technique that seals chips, boards and components into a module that serves as a heat sink. TCMs are mostly water cooled, although some are air cooled.

TCO Refers to the Swedish Confederation of Professional Employees, which has set stringent standards for devices that emit radiation. See *MPR II*.

TCP/IP (Transmission Control Protocol/Internet Protocol) A communications protocol developed under contract from the U.S. Department of Defense to internetwork dissimilar systems. It is a de facto UNIX standard, but is supported on almost all computer systems. TCP/IP is the protocol of the Internet.

   File Transfer Protocol (FTP) and Simple Mail Transfer Protocol (SMTP) provide file transfer and e-mail. The Telnet protocol provides terminal emulation for all types of computers in the network. TCP controls data transfer. IP provides the routing.

   The combination of TCP/IP, NFS and NIS comprise the primary networking components of UNIX.

   The following chart compares the TCP/IP layers with the Department of Defense and Open System Interconnection models.

TCP/IP stack An implementation of the TCP/IP protocol. Network architectures designed in layers, such as

TCP/IP	DOD	OSI
FTP SMTP Telnet	Process	Application
		Presentation
		Session
TCP	Host to host	Transport
IP	Internet	Network
IEEE 802 X.25, etc.	Network Access	Data Link
		Physical

TCP/IP, OSI and SNA, are referred to as *stacks*.

TCU (Transmission Control Unit) A communications control unit controlled by the computer that does not execute internally stored programs. Contrast with *front end processor*, which executes its own instructions.

TDM (Time Division Multiplexing) A technique that interleaves several low-speed signals into one high-speed transmission. For example, if A, B & C are three digital signals of 1,000 bps each, they can be mixed into one 3,000 bps as follows: AABBCCAABBCCAABBCC. The receiving end divides the single stream back into its original signals.

TDM is the technology used in T-carrier service (DS0, DS1, etc.), which are the leased lines common in wide area networks (WANs). Contrast with *FDM*. See *baseband*.

TDMA (Time Division Multiple Access) A cellular telephone technology that triples the capacity of the original analog method (FDMA). It divides each channel into three subchannels providing service to three users instead of one. See *FDMA, CDMA* and *CDPD*.

tear-off menu An on-screen menu or palette that can be moved off of its primary position and relocated to any part of the screen.

tech support Technical assistance from the hardware manufacturer or software publisher. Unless you have a simple, straightforward question, in order to get help from a tech support representative, place your telephone call while you are at your computer. Intermittent problems are very difficult to resolve. If you cannot recreate the problem on screen, there may be very little a tech support person can do to help you.

tech writer A person who is responsible for writing documentation for a hardware or software product.

telco (TELephone COmpany) A company that provides telephone services. It generally refers to the local telephone companies rather than the long-distance suppliers.

tele Operations performed remotely or by telephone.

telecom (TELECOMmunications) Telecom generally refers to the telephone industry. See *telecommunications*.

telecommunications Communicating information, including data, text, pictures, voice and video over long distance. See *communications*.

telecommunity A society in which information can be transmitted or received freely between all members without technical incompatibilities.

telecommuting Working at home and communicating with the office by electronic means.

teleconferencing (1) Video teleconferencing, or videoconferencing, is having a TV conference with several people at the same time. It is provided by inhouse cameras and monitors or in a public conferencing center.

Full-screen, full-motion video at 30 frames per second requires a high-bandwidth network. However, due to improving compression techniques, it is expected that a videoconferencing window will become commonplace on desktop computers within the next five years.

(2) Audio teleconferencing is having a telephone conversation with several people at the same time. It is provided by a conference function on a PBX or multiline telephone or by the telephone companies.

(3) Computer teleconferencing is having a simultaneous conference with several people at the same time at their computers. it is provided by software in a host computer or BBS.

telecopying (long distance copying) The formal term for fax.

telefax The european term for a fax machine.

telegraph A low-speed communications device that transmits up to approximately 150 bps. Telegraph grade lines, stemming from the days of Morse code, can't transmit a voice conversation.

telemanagement Management of an organization's telephone systems, which includes maintaining and ordering new equipment and monitoring the expenses for all telephone calls.

telemarketing Selling over the telephone.

telematics The convergence of telecommunications and information processing.

telemetry Transmitting data captured by instrumentation and measuring devices to a remote station where it is recorded and analyzed. For example, data from a weather satellite is telemetered to earth.

Telenet A value-added, packet switching network that enables many varieties of terminals and computers to exchange data. It is a subsidiary of US Sprint. See also *Telnet*.

telephone channel See *voice grade*.

telephone wiring See *twisted pair*.

telephony The science of converting sound into electrical signals, transmitting it within cables or via radio and reconverting it back into sound.

Telephony Server NLM A NetWare NLM that provides an interface between a NetWare server and a PBX. The physical connection is made by cabling the PBX to a card in the server. The NLM provides an open programming interface that allows PBX manufacturers to write drivers for their products.

The first implementation of this is AT&T's Definity PBX, which physically connects via an AT&T card in the NetWare server and allows all network users with AT&T phones to have access to the PBX through their PCs.

teleprinter A typewriter-like terminal with a keyboard and built-in printer, often a portable unit. Contrast with *video terminal*.

teleprocessing An early IBM term for data communications. It means "long distance" processing.

teleprocessing monitor See *TP monitor*.

Telescript A programming language and software for communications from General Magic. It embeds intelligence in e-mail and other applications allowing them to cooperate with one another and allows messages to move intelligently through diverse public and private networks.
Telescript can be added to existing and future operating systems. See *Magic Cap*.

TELEPRINTER

Teletex See *Telex*.

teletext A broadcasting service that transmits text to a TV set that has a teletext decoder. It uses the vertical blanking interval of the TV signal (black line between frames when vertical hold is not adjusted) to transmit about a hundred frames. See *videotex*.

Teletype The trade name of Teletype Corporation, which refers to a variety of teleprinters used for communications. The Teletype was one of the first communications terminals in the U.S.

teletype interface See *teletype mode*.

teletype mode Line-at-a-time output like a typewriter. Contrast with *full-screen mode*.

teletypewriter A low-speed teleprinter, often abbreviated "TTY."

televaulting Continuous transmitting of data to vaults for backup purposes. The term was coined by TeleVault Technology Inc.

Telex An international dial-up communications service that uses teleprinters and transmits Baudot code at 50 bps (66 words/minute). In the U.S., it is administered by Western Union, which in 1971 purchased the Bell System's TWX service and connected it to the Telex network.

In the early 1980s, a new service called Teletex was initiated that provides higher speeds and upper and lowercase text to subscribers using intelligent terminals and personal computers. Group 3 fax machines quickly supplanted Telex transmission.

TeLink An Xmodem protocol with batch file transfer designed for the Fido BBS. It sends file name, date and size in the first block.

Telnet A terminal emulation protocol commonly used on the Internet. It allows a user to log onto and run a program from a remote terminal or computer. Telnet was originally developed for ARPAnet and is part of the TCP/IP communications protocol.

Although most computers on the Internet require users to have an established account and password, there are many that allow public access to certain programs, typically, search utilities, such as Archie or WAIS. See also *Telenet*.

Telon See *CA-Telon*.

TEMPEST Security against external radiation from data processing equipment. Equipment and cables that meet TEMPEST requirements have extra shielding in order to prevent data signals from escaping and being picked up by unauthorized listeners.

template (1) A plastic or stiff paper form that is placed over the function keys on a keyboard to identify their use.

(2) The programmatic and descriptive part of a programmable application; for example, a spreadsheet that contains only descriptions and formulas or a HyperCard stack that contains only programming and backgrounds. When the template is filled with data, it becomes a working application.

temporary font A soft font that remains in the printer's memory until the printer is reset manually or by software. Contrast with *permanent font*.

ter Third version.

tera Trillion. Abbreviated "T." It often refers to the precise value 1,099,511,627,776 since computer specifications are usually binary numbers. See *space/time*.

terabit One trillion bits. Also Tb, Tbit and T-bit. See *tera* and *space/time*.

terabyte One trillion bytes. Also TB, Tbyte and T-byte. See *tera* and *space/time*.

teraflops (tera FLoating point OPerations per Second) One trillion floating point operations per second.

terminal (1) An I/O device for a computer that usually has a keyboard for input and a video screen or printer for output.

(2) An input device, such as a scanner, video camera or punched card reader.

(3) An output device in a network, such as a monitor, printer or card punch.

(4) A connector used to attach a wire.

terminal emulation Using a computer to simulate the type of terminal required to gain access to another computer. See *virtual terminal*.

terminal mode An operating mode that causes the computer to act like a terminal; ready to transmit typed-in keystrokes and ready to receive transmitted data.

terminal server A computer or controller used to connect multiple terminals to a network or host computer.

terminal session The time in which a user is working at a terminal.

terminal strip An insulated bar that contains a set of screws to which wires are attached.

terminate and stay resident See *TSR*.

terminator (1) A character that ends a string of alphanumeric characters.

(2) A hardware component that is connected to the last peripheral device in a series or the last node in a network.

terrestrial link A communications line that travels on, near or below ground. Contrast with *satellite link*.

test automation software Software used to test new revisions of software by automatically entering a predefined set of commands and inputs.

test data A set of data created for testing new or revised programs. It should be developed by the user as well as the programmer and must contain a sample of every category of valid data as well as many invalid conditions.

testing Running new or revised programs to determine if they process all data properly. See *test data*.

TeX A typesetting language used in a variety of typesetting environments. It uses embedded codes within the text of the document to initiate changes in layout including the ability to describe elaborate scientific formulas.

text Words, sentences and paragraphs. Contrast with *data*, which are defined units, such as name and amount due. Text may also refer to alphanumeric data, such as name and address, to distinguish it from numeric data, such as quantity and dollar amounts. A page of text takes about 2,000 to 4,000 bytes. See *text field*.

text based Also called character based, the display of text and graphics as a fixed set of predefined characters. For example, 25 rows of 80 columns. Contrast with *graphics based*.

text box An on-screen rectangular frame into which you type text. Text boxes are used to add text in a drawing or paint program. The flexibility of the text box is determined by the software. Sometimes you can keep on typing and the box expands to meet your input. Other times, you have to go into a different mode to widen the frame, then go back to typing in more text.

text editing The ability to change text by adding, deleting and rearranging letters, words, sentences and paragraphs.

text editor Software used to create and edit files that contain only text; for example, batch files, address lists and source language programs. Text editors produce raw ASCII or EBCDIC text files, and unlike word processors, do not usually provide word wrap or formatting (underline, boldface, fonts, etc.).

Editors designed for writing source code may provide automatic indention and multiple windows into the same file. They may also display the reserved words of a particular programming language in boldface or in a different font, but they do not embed format codes in the file.

text entry Entering alphanumeric text characters into the computer. It implies typing the characters on a keyboard. See *data entry*.

text field A data structure that holds alphanumeric data, such as name and address. If a text field holds large, or unlimited, amounts of text, it may be called a memo field. Contrast with *numeric field*.

text file A file that contains only text characters. See *ASCII file*. Contrast with *graphics file* and *binary file*.

text management The creation, storage and retrieval of text. It implies flexible retrieval capabilities that can search for text based on a variety of criteria. Although a word processor manages text, it usually has limited retrieval capabilities.

text mode (1) A screen display mode that displays only text and not graphics.

(2) A program mode that allows text to be entered and edited.

text-to-speech Converting text into voice output using speech synthesis techniques. Although initially used by the blind to listen to written material, it is now used extensively to convey financial data and other information via telephone for everyone.

texture mapping In computer graphics, the creation of a special surface. With algorithms, all kinds of textures can be produced: the rough skin of an orange, the metallic surface of a can and the irregularity of a brick. It can also be done by electronically wrapping a secondary image around an object.

TFT (Thin Film Transistor) See *thin film*.

TFT LCD (Thin Film Transistor LCD) See *LCD*.

TFTP (Trivial File Transfer Protocol) A version of the TCP/IP FTP protocol that has no directory or password capability.

TGA See *Targa*.

thermal dye transfer Also called *dye sublimation* and *thermal dye diffusion*, this is a printing process similar to thermal wax transfer except that dyes are used instead of ink. The printhead heats the ribbon causing the dye to turn from a solid to a gas and condense on special coated paper. The more heat, the denser the image. Unlike other printing techniques which simulate shades of colors by dithering, thermal dye transfer creates photographic quality color.

thermal printer A low-cost, low- to medium-resolution non-impact printer that uses heat-sensitive paper. Where the heated pins of the print head touch the paper, the paper darkens.

thermal wax transfer A printing process that transfers a waxlike ink onto paper. For example, in a color printer, a mylar ribbon is used that contains several hundred repeating sets of full pages of black, cyan, magenta and yellow ink. A sheet of paper is pressed against each color and passed by a line of heating elements that transfers the dots, or pixels, of ink onto the paper.

the Web See *Worldwide Web*.

thick film A layer of magnetic, semiconductor or metallic material that is thicker than the microscopic layers of the transistors on a chip. For example, metallic thick films are silk screened onto the ceramic base of hybrid microcircuits. Contrast with *thin film*.

thimble printer A letter quality printer similar to a daisy wheel printer. Instead of a wheel, characters are formed facing out and around the rim of a thimble-shaped cup. For example, the NEC Spinwriters are thimble printers.

thin Ethernet Also called *thinnet* and *cheapernet*, it is a type of Ethernet that uses a thinner coaxial cable than the standard Ethernet, which is also called *thicknet*.

thin film A microscopically thin layer of semiconductor or magnetic material that is deposited onto a metal, ceramic or semiconductor base. For example, the layers that make up a chip and the surface coating on high-density magnetic disks are called thin films.

thin film head A read/write head for high-density disks that is made from thin layers of a conducting film deposited onto a nickel-iron core.

ThinkPad A family of IBM notebook computers that include large screens and a built-in TrackPoint pointing device located between the G, H and B keys on the keyboard.

third-generation computer A computer that uses integrated circuits, disk storage and online terminals. The third generation started roughly in 1964 with the IBM System/360.

third-generation language A traditional high-level programming language such as FORTRAN, COBOL, BASIC, Pascal and C.

third normal form See *normalization*.

thrashing Excessive paging in a virtual memory computer. If programs are not written to run in a virtual memory environment, the operating system may spend excessive amounts of time swapping program pages in and out of the disk.

thread One transaction or message in a multithreaded system.

threading See *multithreading*.

three-state logic element An electronic component that provides three possible outputs: off, low voltage and high voltage.

throughput The speed with which a computer processes data. It is a combination of internal processing speed, peripheral speeds (I/O) and the efficiency of the operating system and other system software all working together.

thumb See *elevator*.

thumbnail A miniature representation of a page or image. A thumbnail program may be stand-alone or part of a desktop publishing or graphics program. Thumbnails take considerable time to generate, but provide a convenient way to browse through multiple images before retrieving the one you need. Programs often let you click on the thumbnail to retrieve it.

thunk In PCs, to execute the instructions required to switch between segmented addressing of memory and flat addressing.

THz (TeraHertZ) One trillion cycles per second.

TI (Texas Instruments, Inc., Dallas, TX) A leading semiconductor manufacturer founded in 1930 as Geophysical Service, Inc., to provide services to the petroleum industry. In 1951, GSI was renamed Texas Instruments and soon after entered the semiconductor business. TI was the first to commercialize the silicon transistor, pocket radio, integrated circuit, hand-held calculator, single-chip computer and the LISP chip.

TIA (Telecommunications Industry Association) A membership organization founded in 1988 that sets standards for physical level interfaces (RS-232, RS-422, etc.) as well as cellular radio. It was originally an EIA working group that was spun off and merged with the USTSA (U.S. Telecommunications Suppliers Association), sponsors of the annual Supercomm conference. TIA is involved with setting telecommunications standards worldwide. Address: 2001 Pennsylvania Ave., N.W., Washington, DC 20006, 202/457-4912.

TIA/EIA-232 See *RS-232*.

tickler A manual or automatic system for reminding users of scheduled events or tasks. It is used in PIMs, contact management systems and scheduling and calendar systems.

TIES (Time-Independent Escape Sequence) A modem escape sequence that uses three pluses like the Hayes sequence, but does not require a pause before and after them. If a valid AT command code and a return follows the +++, it is considered a legitimate command. See *Hayes Smartmodem*.

TIF A file extension used for TIFF files; for example, image1.tif. See *TIFF*.

TIFF (Tagged Image File Format) A widely-used raster graphics file format developed by Aldus and Microsoft that handles monochrome, gray scale, 8-and 24-bit color. Since 1986, there have been six versions of TIFF. It uses several compression methods: LZW provides ratios of about 1.5:1 to 2:1. Ratios of 10:1 to 20:1 are possible for documents with lots of white space using ITU-TSS Group III & IV compression methods (fax). See *JPEG*.

TIGA (Texas Instruments Graphics Architecture) A graphics standard from TI that provides a resolution-independent interface between a program and the graphics coprocessor. See *34010*.

Tiger Code name for Microsoft's multimedia video-on-demand software that runs on Windows NT. It is expected in late 1994 or early 1995.

tightly coupled Refers to two or more computers linked together and dependent on each other. One computer may control the other, or both computers may monitor each other. For example, a database machine is tightly coupled to the main processor. Two computers tied together for multiprocessing are tightly coupled. Contrast with *loosely coupled*, such as personal computers in a LAN.

tiled A display of objects side by side; for example, tiled windows cannot be overlapped on top of each other.

timbre A quality of sound that distinguishes one voice or musical instrument from another. For example, MIDI synthesizers are multi-timbral, meaning that they can play multiple instruments simultaneously.

time base generator An electronic clock that creates its own timing signals for synchronization and measurement purposes.

time-division multiplexing See *TDM*.

time slice A fixed interval of time allotted to each user or program in a multitasking or timesharing system.

time slot Continuously repeating interval of time or a time period in which two devices are able to interconnect.

timer interrupt An interrupt generated by an internal clock. See *interrupt*.

timesharing A multiuser computer environment that lets users initiate their own sessions and access selected databases as required, such as when using online services. A system that serves many users, but for only one application, is technically not timesharing.

timing clock See *clock*.

timing signals Electrical pulses generated in the processor or in external devices in order to synchronize computer operations. The main timing signal comes from the computer's clock, which provides a frequency that can be divided into many slower cycles. Other timing signals may come from a timesharing or realtime clock.

In disk drives, timing signals for reading and writing are generated by holes or marks on one of the platters, or by the way the digital data is actually recorded.

Tiny BASIC A subset of BASIC that has been used in first generation personal computers with limited memory.

TIRIS (Texas Instruments Registration and Identification System) An RF/ID system from TI that uses a 3.6x29mm cylindrical tag. Reading can be done from as far as 40 inches away.

TI-RPC (Transport-Independent-Remote Procedure Call) A functions from Sun for executing procedures on remote computers. It is operating system and network independent and allows the development of distributed applications in multivendor environments.

TLA (Three Letter Acronym) The epitome of acronyms!

TLI (Transport Level Interface) A common interface for transport services (layer 4 of the OSI model). It provides a common language to a transport protocol and allows client/server applications to be used in different networking environments.

Instead of directly calling NetWare's SPX for example, the application calls the TLI library. Thus, any transport protocol that is TLI compliant (SPX, TCP, etc.) can provide transport services to that application. TLI is part of UNIX System V. It is also supported by NetWare 3.x. See *STREAMS*.

TM/1 (Tables Manager/1) An analytical database engine for DOS and Windows from Sinper Corporation, Warren, NJ, that allows data to be viewed in up to eight dimensions. The data is kept in a database, and the formulas are kept in a spreadsheet, which is used as a viewer into the database. TM/1 makes it easy to display different slices of the data, and it is designed to import and cross tab large amounts of data.

TM/1 Pespectives is a spreadsheet add-in that lets Excel or 1-2-3 provide the user interface to a TM/1 database. Spreadsheet Connector is the server version.

TN (Twisted Nematic) The first LCD technology that twisted liquid crystal molecules 90 between polarizers. TN displays require bright ambient light and are still used for low-cost applications. See *LCD*.

TNT (1) (Transparent Network Transport) Services from the telephone companies and common carriers that provide Ethernet and Token Ring transmission over MANs and WANs.

(2) DOS extender from Phar Lap Software that allows DOS applications to use various Win32 features, including memory allocation, DLLs and threads.

TOF (Top Of Form) The beginning of a physical paper form. To position paper in many printers, the printer is turned offline, the forms are aligned properly and the TOF button is pressed.

toggle To alternate back and forth between two states.

token bus network A LAN access method that uses the token passing technology. Stations are logically connected in a ring but are physically connected by a common bus. All tokens are broadcast to every station in the network, but only the station with the destination address responds. After transmitting a maximum amount of data, the token is passed to the next logical station in the ring. The MAP factory automation protocol uses this method. See *token passing*.

token passing A communications network access method that uses a continuously repeating frame (the token) that is transmitted onto the network by the controlling computer. When a terminal or computer wants to send a message, it waits for an empty token. When it finds one, it fills it with the address of the destination station and some or all of its message.

Every computer and terminal on the network constantly monitors the passing tokens to determine if it is a recipient of a message, in which case it "grabs" the message and resets the token status to empty. Token passing uses bus and ring topologies (see *token bus network* and *token ring network*).

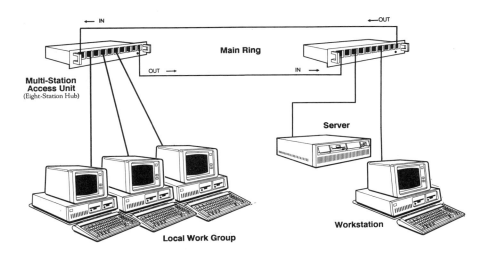

TOKEN RING NETWORK
(Courtesy Black Box Corporation)

token ring network (1) A LAN access method that uses the token passing technology in a physical ring. Each station in the network passes the token on to the station next to it. Token Ring and FDDI LANs use the token ring access method. See *token passing*.

(2) (Token Ring Network) A LAN access method from IBM that conforms to the IEEE 802.5 token ring standard. It connects up to 255 nodes in a star topology at 4 or 16 Mbits/sec. All stations connect to a central wiring hub called the Multi-station Access Unit, or MAU, using special twisted wire cable. The central hub makes it easier to troubleshoot failures.

Token Ring is a data link protocol and functions at the data link and physical levels of the OSI model (1 and 2).

TokenTalk Software for the Macintosh from Apple that accompanies its TokenTalk NB board and adapts the Mac to Token Ring Networks.

toner An electrically charged ink used in copy machines and laser printers. It adheres to an invisible image that has been charged with the opposite polarity onto a plate or drum or onto the paper itself.

tool (1) An on-screen function in an interactive program; for example, a line draw, circle draw or paintbrush option in a graphics program.

(2) A program used for software development or system maintenance. Utility programs, editors, debuggers and graphics routines are examples. A program that helps a user customize, adapt or work with a computer may be called a tool.

toolbar A row or column of on-screen buttons used to activate various functions of the application. The bar is typically movable so it can be placed close to the object being worked on in order to quickly switch modes and options. Toolbars can often be customized allowing buttons to be added and deleted as necessary for a user's own requirements.

ToolBook An application development system for Windows from Asymetrix Corporation, Bellevue, WA, that uses a "page and book" metaphor analogous to HyperCard's "card and stack." Its OpenScript language is similar to HyperTalk.

toolbox, toolkit A set of software routines that allow a program to be written for and work in a particular environment. The routines are called by the application program to perform various functions, for example, to display a menu or draw a graphic element.

TOP (Technical Office Protocol) A communications protocol for office systems from Boeing Computer Services. It uses the Ethernet access method and is often used in conjunction with *M*

tool palette A collection of on-screen functions, typically graphics related, that are grouped in a menu structure for interactive selection.AP, the factory automation protocol developed by GM. TOP is used in the front office, and MAP is used on the factory floor. TOP uses the CSMA/CD access method, while MAP uses token bus.

top of file The beginning of a file. In a word processing file, it is the first character in the document. In a data file, it is either the first record in the file or the first record in the index. For example, in a dBASE file that is indexed on name, **goto top** might go to physical record #608 if record #608 is AARDVARK.

topdown design A design technique that starts with the highest level of an idea and works its way down to the lowest level of detail.

topdown programming A programming design and documentation technique that imposes a hierarchical structure on the design of the program. See *structured programming*.

topology (1) In a communications network, the pattern of interconnection between nodes; for example, a bus, ring or star configuration.

(2) In a parallel processing architecture, the interconnection between processors; for example, a bus, grid, hypercube or Butterfly Switch configuration.

TOPS (1) A multiuser, multitasking, timesharing, virtual memory operating system from Digital that runs on its PDP-6, DECsystem 10 and DECsystem 20 series.

(2) (Transparent OPerating System) A peer-to-peer LAN from Sitka Corporation, Alameda, CA, that uses the LocalTalk access method and connects Apple computers, PCs and Sun workstations. Its Flashcard plugs LocalTalk capability into PCs.

TOPVIEW IBM's first PC windowing environment. It never caught on.

TOTAL An early network DBMS from Cincom Systems that ran on a variety of minis and mainframes.

total bypass Bypassing local and long distance telephone lines by using satellite communications.

touch screen A touch-sensitive display screen that uses a clear panel over on the screen surface. The panel is a matrix of cells that transmit pressure information to the software.

tower (1) A floor-standing cabinet taller than it is wide. Desktop computers can be made into towers by turning them on their side and inserting them into a floor-mounted base.

(2) (Tower) Series of UNIX-based single and multiprocessor computer systems from NCR that use the Motorola 68000 family of CPUs.

TP0-TP4 (Transport Protocol Class 0 to Class 4) The grades of OSI transport layers from least to most complete and specific. TP4 is a full connection-oriented transport protocol.

TP monitor (TeleProcessing monitor or Transaction Processing monitor) A control program that manages the transfer of data between multiple local and remote terminals and the application programs that serve them. It provides integrity in a distributed environment, ensuring that transactions do not get lost or damaged. It may also include programs that format the terminal screens and validate the data entered. Examples of TP monitors are CICS, a veteran TP monitor used on IBM mainframes and Novell's UNIX-based Tuxedo.

TP-PMD (Twisted Pair-Physical Medium Dependent) An ANSI standard for an FDDI network that uses UTP instead of optical fiber. See *CDDI*.

TPA (Transient Program Area) See *transient area*.

tpi (Tracks Per Inch) The measurement of the density of tracks recorded on a disk or drum.

TPS (1) (Transactions Per Second) The number of transactions processed within one second.

(2) (Transaction Processing System) Originally used as an acronym for such a system, it now refers to the measurement of the system (#1 above).

tpsA (TPS A-Benchmark) A transaction per second benchmark as specified by the Transaction Processing Council. Performance is rated as the number of TPS as well as the cost of the system per single TPS; for example, 100 tpsA and $8,100 per tpsA.

track A storage channel on disk or tape. On hard and floppy disks, tracks are concentric circles. On audio CDs and LaserDiscs, they are spirals. On tapes, they are parallel lines. Their format is determined by the specific drive they are used in. On magnetic devices, bits are recorded as reversals of polarity in the magnetic surface. On CDs, they are physical pits under a clear, protective layer.

trackball An input device used in video games and as a mouse alternative. It is a stationary unit that contains a movable ball rotated with the fingers or palm and, correspondingly, moves the cursor on screen.

tractor feed A mechanism that provides fast movement of paper forms through a printer. It contains pins on tractors that engage the paper through perforated holes in its left and right borders. Contrast with *sheet feeder*.

Tradacoms A European EDI standard developed by the Article Numbering Association. See *X12* and *EDIFACT*.

trailer In communications, a code or set of codes that make up the last part of a transmitted message. See *trailer label*.

trailer label The last record in a tape file. May contain number of records, hash totals and other ID.

training (1) Teaching the details of a subject. With regard to software, training provides instruction for each command and function in an application. Contrast with *education*.

(2) In communications, the process by which two modems determine the correct protocols and transmission speeds to use.

(3) In voice recognition systems, the recording of the user's voice in order to

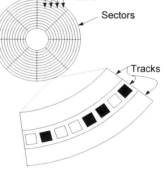

TRACKS ON DISK

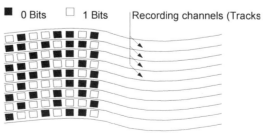

Recorded bits on magnetic tape

TRACKS ON TAPE

provide samples and patterns for recognizing that voice.

train printer

A line printer mechanism similar to a chain printer, but uses unconnected type slugs that ride in a track rather than a connected chain of type. The slugs are pushed around the track by engaging with a drive gear at one end. Slugs and track come as a replaceable cartridge.

transaction An activity or request. Orders, purchases, changes, additions and deletions are typical business transactions stored in the computer. Queries and other requests are also transactions, but are usually just acted upon and not saved. Transaction volume is a major factor in figuring computer system size and speed.

transaction file A collection of transaction records. The data in transaction files is used to update the master files, which contain the subjects of the organization. Transaction files also serve as audit trails and are usually transferred from online disks to the data library after some period of time.

As optical disks become more economical, transaction files will remain online in the computer so that an organization's history will be immediately available for ad hoc queries. See *information system* and *master file*.

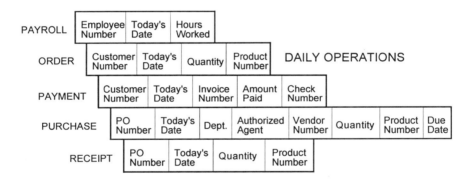

TYPICAL TRANSACTION RECORDS

transaction monitor See *TP monitor*.

transaction processing Processing transactions as they are received by the computer. Also called *online* or *realtime* systems, master files are updated as soon as transactions are entered at terminals or arrive over communications lines.

If you save receipts in a shoebox and add them up at the end of the year for taxes, that's batch processing. However, if you buy something and immediately add the amount to a running total, that's transaction processing.

transceiver A transmitter and receiver of analog or digital signals. It comes in many forms; for example, a transponder or network adapter.

transcribe To copy data from one medium to another; for example, from one source document to another, or from a source document to the computer. It often implies a change of format or codes.

transducer A device that converts one energy into another; for example, a read/write head converts magnetic energy into electrical energy and vice versa. In process control applications, it is used to convert pressure into an electrical reading.

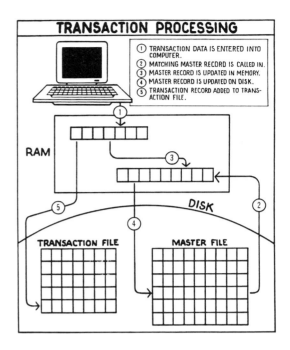

TRANSACTION PROCESSING

1. TRANSACTION DATA IS ENTERED INTO COMPUTER.
2. MATCHING MASTER RECORD IS CALLED IN.
3. MASTER RECORD IS UPDATED IN MEMORY.
4. MASTER RECORD IS UPDATED ON DISK.
5. TRANSACTION RECORD ADDED TO TRANSACTION FILE.

RAM

DISK

TRANSACTION FILE

MASTER FILE

transfer To send data over a computer channel or bus. "Transfer" generally applies to transmission within the computer system, and "transmit" refers to transmission outside the computer over a line or network.

Transfers are actually copies, since the data is in both locations at the end of the transfer. Input, output and move instructions activate data transfers in the computer.

transfer protocol See *file transfer protocol*.

transfer rate Also called data rate, the transmission speed of a communications or computer channel. Transfer rates are measured in bits or bytes per second.

transfer time The time it takes to transmit or move data from one place to another. It is the time interval between starting the transfer and the completion of the transfer.

transformer A device that changes AC voltage. Also called a *power adapter*. It is made of steel laminations wrapped with two coils of wire. The coil ratio derives the voltage change. For example, if the input coil has 1,000 windings, and the output has 100, 120 volts is changed to 12. In order to create direct current (DC), the output is passed through a rectifier.

transient A malfunction that occurs at random intervals; for example, a rapid fluctuation of voltage in a power line or a memory cell that intermittently fails.

transient area An area in memory used to hold application programs for processing. The bulk of a computer's main memory is used as a transient area.

transient state The exact point at which a device changes modes, for example, from transmit to receive or from 0 to 1.

transistor A semiconductor device used to amplify a signal or open and close a circuit. In a computer, it functions as an electronic switch. In its normal state, it is non-conductive. When voltage is applied at the gate, it becomes conductive and current flows from source to drain.

Transistors, resistors, capacitors and diodes, make up logic gates. Logic gates make up circuits, and circuits make up electronic systems.

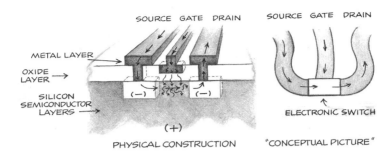

MOSFET TRANSISTOR

SOURCE GATE DRAIN SOURCE GATE DRAIN

METAL LAYER
OXIDE LAYER →
SILICON SEMICONDUCTOR LAYERS →

(−)   (−)

(+)

PHYSICAL CONSTRUCTION

ELECTRONIC SWITCH

"CONCEPTUAL PICTURE"

A PULSE ON THE GATE TEMPORARILY ALLOWS
CURRENT TO FLOW FROM ONE SIDE TO THE OTHER

translate (1) To change one language into another; for example, assemblers, compilers and interpreters translate source language into machine language.

(2) In computer graphics, to move an image on screen without rotating it.

(3) In telecommunictions, to change the frequencies of a band of signals.

TransLISP PLUS A version of LISP for PCs from Solution Systems, Inc., Wellesley, MA. It provides an interface to Microsoft C that allows a C routine to be added to the LISP library as a function.

transmission The transfer of data over a communications channel.

transmission channel A path between two nodes in a network. It may refer to the physical cable, the signal transmitted within the cable or to a subchannel within a carrier frequency. In radio and TV, it refers to the assigned carrier frequency.

transmission control unit See *TCU*.

transmit To send data over a communications line. See *transfer*.

transmitter A device that generates signals. Contrast with *receiver*.

transparent Refers to a change in hardware or software that, after installation, causes no noticeable change in operation.

transparent bridging A communications protocol in which the stations are unaware of bridges in the network. Ethernet uses this method. Contrast with *source routing*.

transponder A receiver/transmitter on a communications satellite. It receives a microwave signal from earth (uplink), amplifies it and retransmits it back to earth at a different frequency (downlink). A satellite has several transponders.

transport layer See *transport protocol*.

transport protocol A communications protocol responsible for establishing a connection and ensuring that all data has arrived safely. It is defined in layer 4 of the OSI model. Often, the term transport protocol implies transport services, which includes the lower level data link protocol that moves packets from one node to another. See *OSI model* and *transport services*.

transport services The collective functions of layers 1 through 4 of the OSI model.

transputer (TRANSistor comPUTER) A computer that contains a CPU, memory and communications capability on a single chip. Chips are strung together in hypercube or grid-like patterns to create large parallel processing machines, used in scientific, realtime control and AI applications.

trap To test for a particular condition in a running program; for example, to "trap an interrupt" means to wait for a particular interrupt to occur and then execute a corresponding routine. An error trap tests for an error condition and provides a recovery routine. A debugging trap waits for the execution of a particular instruction in order to stop the program and analyze the status of the system at that moment.

trapdoor A secret way of gaining access to a program or online service. Trapdoors are built into the software by the original programmer as a way of gaining special access to particular functions. For example, a trapdoor built into a BBS program would allow access to any BBS computer running that software.

trash can An icon of a garbage can used for deleting files. The icon of a file is dragged to the trash can and released. In the Mac, the trash can is also used to eject the floppy disk.

trashware Software that is so poorly designed that it winds up in the garbage can.

tree A hierarchical structure. See *directory tree*.

trichromatic In computer graphics, the use of red, green and blue to create all the colors in the spectrum.

trillion One thousand times one billion or 10^{12}. See *tera* and *picosecond*.

Trilogy A company founded in 1979 by Gene Amdahl to commercialize wafer scale integration and build supercomputers. It raised a quarter of a billion dollars, the largest startup funding in history, but could not create its 2.5" superchip. In 1984, it abandoned supercomputer development and later the superchip project.

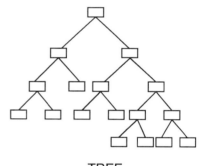

TREE

triple precision The use of three computer words to hold a number used for calculation, providing an enormous amount of arithmetic precision.

triple twist A supertwist variation that twists crystals to 260 for improved clarity. See *LCD*.

troff (Typesetting RunOFF) A UNIX utility that formats documents for typesetters and laser printers. Using a text editor, troff codes are embedded into the text and the troff command converts the document into the required output. See *nroff*.

Trojan horse A program routine that invades a computer system by being secretly attached to a valid program that will be downloaded into the computer. It may be used to locate password information, or it may alter an existing program to make it easier to gain access to it. A virus is a Trojan horse that continues to infect programs over and over.

TRON (The Realtime Operating System Nucleus) An advanced realtime computer architecture and operating system under development by Japanese universities and corporations. Its goal is a common architecture and user interface from the smallest consumer appliance to the largest supercomputer. TRON-based intelligent cars and houses are under research.

TRS (Tandy Radio Shack) An early Tandy trade name. In 1977, the TRS-80 was one of the three first personal computers. TRS-DOS was its operating system. Also see *TSR*.

True BASIC An ANSI-standard structured-programming version of BASIC for the PC, Mac and Amiga from True BASIC, Inc., West Lebanon, NH. Developed in 1984 by BASIC's creators, John Kemeny and Thomas Kurtz, it includes many enhancements over original BASIC. It comes in both interpreter and compiler form.

true color The ability to generate 16,777,216 colors (24-bit color). See *high color*.

TrueImage An enhanced PostScript interpreter from Microsoft that prints PostScript Type 1 and TrueType fonts.

TrueType A scalable font technology that renders fonts for both the printer and the screen. Originally developed by Apple, it was enhanced jointly by Apple and Microsoft. TrueType fonts are used in Windows, starting with Windows 3.1, as well as in the Mac System 7 operating system.

Unlike PostScript, in which the algorithms are maintained in the rasterizing engine, each TrueType font contains its own algorithms for converting the outline into bitmaps. The lower-level language embedded within the TrueType font allows unlimited flexibility in the design. See *TrueImage*.

truncate To cut off leading or trailing digits or characters from an item of data without regard to the accuracy of the remaining characters. Truncation occurs when data is converted into a new record with smaller field lengths than the original.

trunk A communications channel between two points. It often refers to large-bandwidth telephone channels between major switching centers, capable of transmitting many simultaneous voice and data signals.

truth table A chart of a logical operation's inputs and outputs. See *AND, OR & NOT*.

TSAPI (Telephony Services API) A telephony programming interface from Novell and AT&T. Based on the international CSTA standard, TSAPI is designed to interface a telephone PBX with a NetWare server to provide interoperability between PCs and telephone equipment.

TSAT See *VSAT*.

TSO (Time Sharing Option) Software that provides interactive communications for IBM's MVS operating system. It allows a user or programmer to launch an application from a terminal and interactively work with it. The TSO counterpart in VM is called CMS. Contrast with *JES*, which provides batch communications for MVS.

TSOP (Thin Small Outline Package) One-millimeter-thick package used to house dynamic RAM chips.

TSR (Terminate and Stay Resident) Refers to programs that remain in memory so they can be instantly popped up over the current application by pressing a hotkey. When the program is exited, previous screen contents are restored. TSRs are widely used in DOS-only environments. The term refers to loading a program, terminating its action but not removing it from memory.

TSS See *ITU-TSS*.

TTL (Transistor Transistor Logic) A digital circuit in which the output is derived from two transistors. Although TTL is a specific design method, it often refers generically to digital connections in contrast with analog connections. For example, a TTL input on a monitor requires digital output from the display board rather than analog output.

TTY (TeleTYpewriter) See *teletypewriter*.

TTY protocol A low-speed asynchronous communications protocol with limited or no error checking.

tube See *CRT* and *vacuum tube*.

tuner An electronic part of a radio or TV that locks on to a selected carrier frequency (station, channel) and filters out the audio and video signals for amplification and display.

tuple In relational database management, a record, or row. See *relational database*.

Turbo C A C compiler from Borland used to create a wide variety of commercial products. It is known for its well-designed debugger. Borland's object-oriented versions of C are Turbo C++ and Borland C++.

TURBOchannel A 32-bit data bus from Digital introduced in 1990. It has a peak transfer rate of 100 MBytes/sec.

Turbo Mouse A Macintosh trackball from Kensington Microware, Ltd., San Mateo, CA. If the ball is moved slowly, the cursor moves slowly, but if moved quickly, the same spatial ball movement moves the cursor a greater distance on the screen. Kensington popularized the trackball on the Apple II. Its model for the PC is the Expert Mouse.

Turbo Pascal A pascal compiler for DOS from Borland used in a wide variety of applications from accounting to complex commercial products. Turbo Pascal for Windows provides an object-oriented programming environment for Windows development. Borland is responsible for moving the Pascal language from the academic halls to the commercial world.

turnaround document A paper document or punched card prepared for re-entry into the computer system. Paper documents are printed with OCR fonts for scanning Invoices and inventory stock cards are examples.

turnaround time (1) In batch processing, the time it takes to receive finished reports after submission of documents or files for processing. In an online environment, turnaround time is the same as *response time*.

(2) In half-duplex transmission, the time it takes to change from transmit to receive and vice versa.

turnkey system A complete system of hardware and software delivered to the customer ready-to-run.

turnpike effect In communications, a lock up due to increased traffic conditions and bottlenecks in the system.

turtle graphics A method for creating graphic images in Logo. The turtle is an imaginary pen that is given drawing commands, such as go forward and turn right. On screen, the turtle is shaped like a triangle.

tutorial An instructional book or program that takes the user through a prescribed sequence of steps in order to learn a product. Contrast with *documentation*, which, although instructional, tends to group features and functions by category.

TUV (Technischer Überwachungs-Verein) Literally "Technical Watch-Over Association." A German certifying body involved with product safety for the European Community. The "TÜV Rheinland" mark is placed on tested and approved electrical and electronic devices like our UL (Underwriters Laboratory) seal.

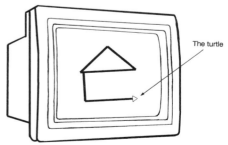

The turtle

TURTLE GRAPHICS
Go forward 100 units. Turn left 90 degrees.

Tuxedo A TP monitor from Novell that runs on a variety of UNIX-based computers. Originally developed by AT&T and sold as source code, Novell has enhanced the product and is offering it as shrink-wrapped software for various UNIX servers.

TWAIN A programming interface that lets a graphics application, such as a desktop publishing program, activate a scanner, frame grabber or other image-capturing device.

tweak To make minor adjustments in an electronic system or in a software program in order to improve performance.

tweening An animation technique that, based on starting and ending shapes, creates the necessary "in-between" frames. See *morphing*.

twinax See *twinaxial*.

twinax card An expansion board in a personal computer that emulates a 5250 terminal, the common terminal on an IBM midrange system (AS/400, System/3x).

TwinAxcess An IBM midrange terminal emulation system for the Macintosh from Andrew/KMW, Austin, TX. It includes a controller card and software that emulates the 5250 terminal used on System/3x and AS/400s. It allows the user to have seven concurrent sessions broadcast over LocalTalk, EtherTalk or TokenTalk networks.

twinaxial A type of cable similar to coax, but with two inner conductors instead of one. It is used in IBM midrange (AS/400, System/3x) communications environments.

TWIP (TWentIeth of a Point) Equal to 1/1440th of an inch.

twisted pair A thin-diameter wire (22 to 26 guage) commonly used for telephone wiring. The wires are twisted around each other to minimize interference from other twisted pairs in the cable. Twisted pairs have less bandwidth than coaxial cable or optical fiber.

The two major types are unshielded twisted pair (UTP) and shielded twisted pair (STP). UTP is popular because it is very pliable and doesn't take up as much room in ductwork as does shielded twisted pair and other cables.

Shielded twisted pair is wrapped in a metal sheath for added protection against external interference. See *cable categories*.

two-out-of-five code A numeric code that stores one decimal digit in five binary digits in which two of the bits are always 0 or 1 and the other three are always in the opposite state.

two-phase commit A technique for ensuring that a transaction successfully updates all appropriate files in a distributed database environment. All DBMSs involved in the transaction first confirm that the transaction has been received and is recoverable (stored on disk). Then each DBMS is told to commit the transaction (do the actual updating).

two-wire lines A transmission channel made up of only two wires, such as used in the common dial-up telephone network.

TWX (TeletypeWriter eXchange Service) A U.S. and Canadian dial-up communications service that uses teleprinters and transmits 5-bit Murray code or 7-bit ASCII code at up to 150 bps. Originally part of the Bell System, it

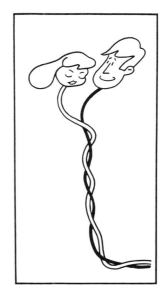

TWISTED PAIR

was sold to Western Union in 1971 and interconnected with Telex.

TXD (Transmitting Data) See *modem*.

TXT file A file that contains only text. See *ASCII file*.

Tymnet (BTC Tymnet) A value-added, packet switching network that enables many varieties of terminals and computers to exchange data. It is a subsidiary of British Telecom Corporation.

type (1) In data or text entry, to press the keys on the keyboard.

(2) In programming, a category of variable that is determined by the kind of data stored in it. For example, integer, floating point, string, logical, date and binary are common data types.

(3) (Type) In DOS and OS/2, a command that displays the contents of a text file.

Type 1 font, Type 3 font Type 1 fonts are the common type of PostScript fonts. Type 3 can be used to create more elaborate font designs, but are more complicated to program and not widely used.

typeahead buffer See *keyboard buffer*.

type ball A golf ball-sized element used in typewriters and low-speed teleprinters that contains all the print characters on its outside surface. It was introduced with IBM's Selectric typewriter.

typeface The design of a set of printed characters, such as Courier, Helvetica and Times Roman. The following chart shows common typeface measurements.

typeface family, type family A group of typefaces that include the normal, bold, italic and bold-italic variations of the same design.

type font A set of print characters of a particular design (typeface), size (point size) and weight (light, medium, heavy). See *font*.

type scaler See *font scaler*.

typematic A keyboard feature that contiues to repeat a key as long as it is held down. The speed of the repeating key as well as the time interval before the repeat begins can be set by the DOS Mode command and the Macintosh Control Panel.

typeover mode In word processing and data entry, a state in which each character typed on the keyboard replaces the character at the current cursor location. Contrast with *insert mode*.

typesetter See *phototypesetter* and *imagesetter*.

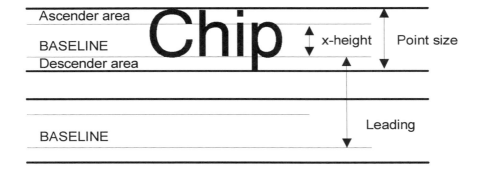

TYPEFACE MEASUREMENTS

UAE (Uninterruptible Application Error) An application program abend in Windows 3.0. See *GPF*.

UART (Universal Asynchronous Receiver Transmitter) An electronic circuit that transmits and receives data on the serial port. It converts bytes into serial bits for transmission, and vice versa, and generates and strips the start and stop bits appended to each character.

    The older 8250A and 16450 UART chips provide a one-byte buffer for storing data. The 16550 UART provides two 16-byte buffers for incoming data and is essential for receiving at 9,600 bps and higher rates, especially under Windows or when running the communications program in the background. See *UART overrun*.

UART overrun A condition in which a UART cannot process the byte that just came in fast enough before the next one arrives.

UCR (Under Color Removal) A method for reducing amount of printing ink used. It substitutes black for gray color (equal amounts of cyan, magenta and yellow). Thus black ink is used instead of the three CMY inks. See *GCR* and *dot gain*.

UCSD p-System (University of California at San Diego p-System) A software development system designed for portability. Source programs (BASIC, Pascal, etc.) are compiled into an interim "p-code," which is executed by an interpreter in the target machine.

UDP (User Datagram Protocol) A TCP/IP protocol that allows an application to send a message to one of several applications running in the destination machine. The application is responsible for reliable delivery.

UHF (Ultra High Frequency) The range of electromagnetic frequencies from 300MHz to 3GHz.

UI See *UNIX International* and *user interface*.

UIMX (User Interface Management System for X Window) Software from Visual Edge Software, Ltd., St. Laurent, Quebec, that allows a user to design and modify Open Look and Motif interfaces.

ULSI (Ultra Large Scale Integration) More than one million transistors on a chip. See *SSI, MSI, LSI* and *VLSI*.

ultrafiche Pronounced "ultra feesh." A microfiche that holds up to 1,000 document pages per 4x6" sheet of film. Normal microfiche stores around 270 pages.

ultraviolet An invisible band of radiation at the high-frequency end of the light spectrum. It takes about 10 minutes of ultraviolet light to erase an EPROM chip.

ULTRIX Digital's version of UNIX for its PDP-11 and VAX series.

UMA (Upper Memory Area) PC memory between 640K and 1024K. See *PC memory map*.

UMB (Upper Memory Block) Unused blocks in the UMA (640K-1M). A UMB provider, such as EMM386.EXE, is software that can load and manage drivers and TSRs in these unoccupied areas. See *PC memory map*.

unary Meaning one; a single entity or operation, or an expression that requires only one operand.

unbundle To sell components in a system separately. Contrast with *bundle*.

UNC (Universal Naming Service) A standard for identifying servers, printers and other resources in a network.

unconditional branch In programming, a GOTO, BRANCH or JUMP instruction that passes control to a different part of the program. Constrast with *conditional branch*.

undelete To restore the last delete operation that has taken place. There may be more than one level of undelete, allowing several or all previous deletions to be restored.

underflow (1) An error condition that occurs when the result of a computation is smaller than the smallest quantity the computer can store.

(2) An error condition that occurs when an item is called from an empty stack.

underscan Within the normal rectangular viewing area on a display screen. Contrast with *overscan*.

undo To restore the last editing operation that has taken place. For example, if a segment of text has been deleted or changed, performing an undo will restore the original text. Programs may have several levels of undo, including being able to reconstruct the original data for all edits performed in the current session.

Unibus A bus architecture from Digital that was introduced in 1970 with its PDP-11 series. Unibus peripherals can be connected to a VAX through Unibus attachments on the VAXs.

Unicode A superset of the ASCII character set that uses two bytes for each character rather than one. Able to handle 65,536 character combinations rather than just 256, it can house the alphabets of most of the world's languages. ISO defines a four-byte character set for world alphabets, but also uses Unicode as a subset.

unidirectional The transfer or transmission of data in a channel in one direction only.

uninstall To remove hardware or software from a computer system. In order to remove a software application from a PC, an uninstall program, also called an *uninstaller*, deletes all the files that were initially copied to the hard disk and restores the AUTOEXEC.BAT, CONFIG.SYS, WIN.INI and SYSTEM.INI files if they were modified.

   Many applications come with their own uninstall utility. Otherwise, a generic uninstall program can be used to uninstall any application. It must be used when the application is first installed, because it works by monitoring and recording all changes made to the computer system.

union In relational database, the joining of two files. See *set theory*.

UniSQL An object-oriented DBMS from UniSQL, Austin, TX. UniSQL/X is a relational and object-oriented DBMS for UNIX servers that provides SQL and object access to the database. UniSQL/M adds object-oriented capability to SQL Server, ORACLE, Ingres and other relational DBMSs.

Unisys (Unisys Corporation, Blue Bell, PA) A computer manufacturer formed in 1986 as a merger of Burroughs and Sperry corporations. This was the largest computer merger in history. Sperry started in 1933 in navigational guidance and control equipment and Burroughs started as a maker of calculating machines. Today, Unisys markets a full range of computer systems, including current versions of product lines originating from both companies. It also provides business consulting and integrated solutions for vertical markets.

UNIVAC I
(Courtesy Unisys)

unit record equipment See *tabulating equipment*.

unit test Running one component of a system for testing purposes. See *system test*.

UNIVAC I (UNIVersal Automatic Computer) The first commercially-successful computer, introduced in 1951 by Remington Rand. Over 40 systems were sold. Its memory was made of mercury-filled acoustic delay lines that held 1,000 12-digit numbers. It used magnetic tapes that stored 1MB of data at a density of 128 cpi. In 1952, it predicted Eisenhower's victory over Stevenson, and UNIVAC became synonymous with computer (for a while).

Univel A joint venture of Novell and USL, which created UnixWare. In 1993, Novell acquired USL and merged Univel and USL into Novell's Unix Systems Group.

UNIX A multiuser, multitasking operating system originally developed by AT&T. AT&T got out of the UNIX business in 1993, and its System V version of UNIX was acquired by Novell. UNIX is written in C, also developed by AT&T, which can be compiled into many different machine languages, causing UNIX to run in a wider variety of hardware than any other operating system. UNIX has thus become synonymous with "open systems."

The fact it runs on almost everything is its own Nemesis. There is at least one version, often several, for each hardware platform, making universal shrink-wrapped software an impossibility. Nevertheless, UNIX, with all its variants, continues to grow, because it provides an industrial-strength operating environment.

Its TCP/IP communications protocols are used in the Internet, the world's largest network of networks. SMTP provides e-mail, NFS allows files to be distributed across the network, NIS provides a "Yellow Pages" directory, Kerberos provides network security, and X Window allows a user to run applications on other machines in the network simultaneously. See *X/Open, OSF, POSIX, COSE* and *BSD UNIX*.

▶ *The electronic and encyclopedic versions of this book provide more detail on this subject.*

UNIX International A non-profit industry association that was founded to provide direction for UNIX System V. It was disbanded at the end of 1993 after Novell purchased UNIX from AT&T.

UNIX socket A UNIX communications interface that lets an application access a network protocol by "opening a socket" and declaring a destination. Sockets are very popular because they provide a simple way to direct an application onto the network (TCP/IP protocol). NetWare 3.x also supports sockets as one of the common transport interfaces.

UnixWare An operating system for 386s and up from Novell based on UNIX System V Release 4.2. UnixWare Personal Edition is a single-user version that provides client access to NetWare and runs UNIX, DOS and Windows applications. It also includes the Motif and Open Look graphical interfaces.

UnixWare Application Server provides a multiuser UNIX application server in a NetWare LAN. It supports TCP/IP and X Window.

unload To remove a program from memory or take a tape or disk out of its drive.

UNMA (Unified Network Management Archicture) A network strategy from AT&T for managing multi-vendor networks.

unmark (1) In word processing, to deselect a block of text, which usually removes its highlight.

(2) To deselect an item that has been tagged for a particular purpose.

unpack See *pack*.

unzip To decompress a file with PKUNZIP. See *PKzip, Pkunzip*.

up Refers to a device that is working.

UPC (Universal Product Code) The standard bar code printed on retail merchandise. It contains the vendor's identification number and the product number, which is read by passing the bar code over a scanner.

update To change data in a file or database. The terms update and edit are often used synonymously.

uplink A communications channel from an earth station to a satellite. Contrast with *downlink*.

upload See *download*.

upper CASE See *front-end CASE*.

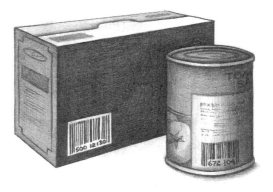

UNIVERSAL PRODUCT CODE

UPS (Uninterruptible Power Supply) Backup power used when the electrical power fails or drops to an unacceptable voltage level. Small UPS systems provide battery power for a few minutes; enough to power down the computer in an orderly manner. Sophisticated systems are tied to electrical generators that can provide power for days.

An online UPS provides a constant source of electrical power from the battery, while the batteries are being recharged from AC power. An offline UPS, also known as a standby power system (SPS), switches to battery within a few milliseconds after detecting a power failure.

uptime The time during which a system is working without failure. Contrast with *downtime*.

upward compatible Also called forward compatible. Refers to hardware or software that is compatible with succeeding versions. Contrast with *downward compatible*.

used computers There is so much computer equipment in the U.S. that a thriving used computer market has been created. There are at least four used computer exchanges in the country. See *computer exchange*.

▶ *The electronic versions of this book provide a current list of prices for popular computers and printers on the American Computer Exchange.*

USENET (USEr NETwork) A public access network on the Internet that provides user news and e-mail. It is a giant, dispersed bulletin board that is maintained by volunteers willing to provide news and mail feeds to other nodes. It began in 1979 as a bulletin board between two universities in North Carolina.

In 1993, the daily volume from all the USENET news groups and conferences was approximately 50MB of data. All the news that travels over the Internet is called NetNews.

user Any individual who interacts with the computer at an application level. Programmers, operators and other technical personnel are not considered users when working in a professional capacity on the computer.

user area A reserved part of a disk or memory for user data.

user defined Any format, layout, structure or language that is developed by the user.

user friendly A system that is easy to learn and easy to use. This term has been so abused that many vendors are reluctant to use it.

user group An organization of users of a particular hardware or software product. Members share experiences and ideas to improve their understanding and use of a particular product. User groups are often responsible for influencing vendors to change or enhance their products.

user interface The combination of menus, screen design, keyboard commands, command language and help screens, which create the way a user interacts with a computer. Mice, touch screens and other input hardware is also included. A well-designed user interface is vital to the success of a software package. In time, interactive video, voice recognition and natural language understanding will be included.

USL (UNIX System Laboratories, Inc.) An AT&T subsidiary formed in 1990, responsible for developing and marketing UNIX. In 1993, USL was acquired by Novell and merged into Novell's Unix Systems Group.

USO (UNIX Software Operation) AT&T's UNIX division before it turned into USL.

U.S. Robotics (U.S. Robotics, Inc., Skokie, IL) A modem manufacturer highly regarded for its quality modems. The company manufactures its own chipsets (data pumps) and often leads the industry with innovations. See *HST*.

USRT (Universal Synchronous Receiver Transmitter) An electronic circuit that transmits and receives data on the serial port. It converts bytes into serial bits for transmission, and vice versa, and generates the necessary signals for synchronous transmission.

utilities See *utility program*.

utility program A program that supports using the computer. Utility programs, or "utilities," provide file management capabilities, such as sorting, copying, comparing, listing and searching, as well as diagnostic and measurement routines that check the health and performance of the system.

UTP See *twisted pair*.

UTP Ethernet A type of Ethernet that uses twisted pair wires. All nodes connect in a star configuration using a hub as a central connector. This term may also refer to earlier pre-IEEE standards for Ethernet.

UTS (Universal Timesharing System) Amdahl's version of UNIX System V. Release 4.0 is POSIX compliant.

UUCP (UNIX to UNIX CoPy) A UNIX utility that copies a file from one computer to another. It is commonly used as a mail transfer. Unlike TCP/IP, which is a routable communications protocol, UUCP provides a point-to-point transmission where a user at one UNIX computer dials up and establishes a session with another UNIX computer.

UUNET (UNIX to UNIX NETwork) An information and communications network from UUNET Technologies, Inc., Falls Church, VA, that provides news, mail service and an extensive library of UNIX software. Custom networking for companies is available through its AlterNet service.

V.17 (1991) A fax standard that uses TCM modulation at 12000 and 14400 bps for Group 3. Modulation use is a half-duplex version of V.32bis.

V.21 (1964) Asynchronous 0-300 bps full-duplex modems for use on dial-up lines. It uses FSK modulation.

V.22 (1980) Asynchronous and synchronous 600 and 1200 bps full-duplex modems for use on dial-up lines. It uses DPSK modulation.

V.22bis (1984) Asynchronous and synchronous 2400 bps full-duplex modems for use on dial-up lines and two-wire leased lines, with fallback to V.22 1200 bps operation. It uses QAM modulation.

V.23 (1964) Asynchronous and synchronous 0-600 and 0-1200 bps half-duplex modems for use on dial-up lines. It uses FSK modulation.

V.24 (1964) Defines the functions of all circuits for the RS-232 interface.

V.25 1968) Automatic calling and/or answering equipment on dial-up lines.

V.25bis (1968) Second standard for automatic calling and/or answering equipment on dial-up lines.

V.26 (1968) Synchronous 2400 bps full-duplex modems for use on four-wire leased lines. It uses DPSK modulation and includes an optional 75 bps back channel.

V.26bis (1972) Synchronous 1200 and 2400 bps full-duplex modems for use on dial-up lines. It uses DPSK modulation and includes an optional 75 bps back channel.

V.26ter (1984) Asynchronous and synchronous 2400 bps full-duplex modems using DPSK modulation over dial-up and two-wire leased lines.

V.27 (1972) Synchronous 4800 bps full-duplex modems for use on four-wire leased lines. It uses DPSK modulation.

V.27bis (1976) Synchronous 2400 and 4800 bps full-duplex modems using DPSK modulation for use on four-wire leased lines. The primary difference between V.27 and V.27bis is the addition of an automatic adaptive equalizer.

V.27ter (1976) Synchronous 2400 and 4800 bps half-duplex modems using DPSK modulation on dial-up lines. It includes an optional 75 bps back channel. V.27ter is used in Group 3 fax transmission without the back channel.

V.28 (1972) Defines the functions of all circuits for the RS-232 interface. In the U.S., EIA-232 incorporates the electrical signal definitions of V.28, the control signals of V.25 and the connector and pin assignments defined in ISO 2110.

V.29 (1976) Synchronous 4800, 7200 and 9600 bps full-duplex modems using QAM modulation on four-wire leased lines. It has been adapted for Group 3 fax transmission over dial-up lines at 9600 and 7200 bps.

V.32 (1984) Asynchronous and synchronous 4800 and 9600 bps full-duplex modems using TCM modulation over dial-up or two-wire leased lines. TCM encoding may be optionally added. V.32 uses echo cancellation to achieve full-duplex transmission.

V.32bis (1991) Asynchronous and synchronous 4800, 7200, 9600, 12000 and 14400 bps full-duplex modems using TCM and echo cancellation. Supports rate renegotiation, which allows modems to change speeds as required.

V.32terbo This is an AT&T standard for 19200 bps modems adopted by some modem manufacturers. See *V.34*.

V.33 (1988) Synchronous 12000 and 14400 bps full-duplex modems for use on four-wire leased lines using QAM modulation. It includes an optional time-division multiplexor for sharing the transmission line among multiple terminals.

V.34 (1994) A standard for 28800 bps modems. AT&T's V.32terbo and Rockwell International's V.FC are competing technologies that are faster than the V.32bis 14400 bps standard.

V.35 (1968) Group band modems that combine the bandwidth of several telephone circuits to achieve high data rates.

V.42 (1989) Modem error checking that uses LAP-M as the primary protocol and provides MNP Classes 2 through 4 as an alternative protocol for compatibility.

V.42bis (1989) Modem data compression. It uses the British Telecom Lempel Ziv technique to achieve up to a 4:1 ratio. V.42bis implies the V.42 error checking protocol.

V.54 (1976) Various loopback tests that can be incorporated into modems for testing the telephone circuit and isolating transmission problems.

V.56 (1972) Method of testing modems to compare their performance. Newer procedures are currently under study.

V.110 (1984) Specifies how data terminal equipment (DTE) with asynchronous or synchronous serial interfaces can be supported on an ISDN network.

V.120 (1988) Specifies how DTEs with asynchronous or synchronous serial interfaces can be supported on an ISDN network using a protocol (similar to LAP-D) to encapsulate the data to be transmitted.

The V.Dot Standards
The V.Dot standards are transmission standards that were originally developed by the CCITT, now known as the Telecommunications Standards Section of the International Telecommunications Union (ITU-TSS).
▶ *The electronic and encyclopedic versions of this book provide more detail on this subject.*

VAC (Volts Alternating Current) See *volt* and *AC*.

vacuum tube An electronic device that controls the flow of electrons in a vacuum, used as a switch, amplifier or display screen. Used as on/off switches, they allowed the first computers to perform digital computations. Today, it is primarily the CRT in monitors and TVs.

VAD (Value Added Dealer) Same as *VAR*.

validity checking Routines in a data entry program that tests the input for correct and reasonable conditions, such as numbers falling within a range and correct

CRT   AMPLIFIER OR SWITCH

VACUUM TUBES

spelling, if possible. See *check digit.*

value (1) The content of a field or variable. It can refer to alphabetic as well as numeric data. For example, in the expression, `state = "PA"`, PA is a value.

(2) In spreadsheets, the numeric data within the cell.

value-added network A communications network that provides services beyond normal transmission, such as automatic error detection and correction, protocol conversion and message storing and forwarding. Telenet and Tymnet are examples of value-added networks.

VAN See *value-added network.*

VAP (Value Added Process) Software that enhances or provides additional server functions in a NetWare 286 server. Support for different kinds of workstations, database engines, fax and print servers are examples. The NetWare 386 counterpart is the NLM.

vaporware Software that has been advertised but not delivered.

VAR (Value Added Reseller) An organization that adds value to a system and resells it. For example, it could purchase a CPU and peripherals from different vendors and graphics software from another and package it together as a specialized CAD system. See *OEM.*

variable A programming structure that holds data. It can contain numbers or alphanumeric characters and is given a unique named by the programmer. It holds the data until a new value is stored in it or the program is finished.

variable length field A record structure that holds fields of varying lengths. For example, PAT SMITH would take nine bytes and GEORGINA WILSON BARTHOLOMEW would take 27 plus a couple of bytes that would define the length of the field. If fixed length fields were used, at least 27 bytes would have to be reserved for both names.

variable length record A data record that contains one or more variable length fields.

varname
(VARiable NAME)
An abbreviation for
specifying the name of
a variable.

Each data field is preceded by an identification field that indicates its length

| ID | Williams, James T. | ID | 5 Main St. | ID | Harrisburg | ID | PA |
| ID | Maloney, Pat | ID | 75 Arbor Lane | ID | Rye | ID | NY |

VARIABLE LENGTH FIELDS/RECORDS

VAX (Virtual Address eXtension) A family of 32-bit computers from Digital introduced in 1977 with the VAX-11/780 model. VAXes range from desktop personal computers to mainframes all running the same VMS operating system. Software compatibility between models caused the VAX family to achieve outstanding success during the 1980s.

VAXmate A partially IBM-compatible PC from Digital introduced in 1986, which has been superseded by the DECstation 200 and 300 series in 1989.

VAXstation A single-user VAX computer that runs under VMS introduced in 1988.

VB See *Visual Basic.*

VBA (Visual Basic for Applications) A subset of Visual Basic that provides a common macro language for Microsoft applications. VBA lets power users and programmers extend the functionality of programs such as Word, Excel and Access.

VBE (VESA BIOS Extension) A VESA VGA standard for interrogating the capabilities of a graphics adapter. It allows the software developer to write a universal driver for all VBE-compliant VGA cards. See *PC display modes* for VBE specs.

Vbox (Video box) A hardware interface from Sony that attaches up to seven VCRs, videodiscs and camcorders to the serial port. Devices must have the Control-L (LANC) connector.

VBX A dynamic link library file that contains user-developed controls for Visual Basic applications.

VCPI (Virtual Control Program Interface) A DOS extender specification for 386s and up that allows DOS extended programs to run with Real Mode programs. VCPI allows for example, Paradox 386, a DOS-extended program, to run cooperatively with DESQview, which runs multiple Real Mode programs in Virtual 8086 mode. Developed by Quarterdeck, Phar Lap Software, et al, it was the first DOS extender standard. See *DPMI*.

XMS Versus VCPI/DPMI

XMS, VCPI and DPMI all deal with extended memory. However, XMS allows data and programs to be stored in and retrieved from extended memory, whereas the VCPI and DPMI interfaces allow programs to "run" in extended memory.

VCR (Video Cassette Recorder) A videotape recording and playback machine. The most common format is VHS.

VDE (1) (Video Display Editor) A WordStar and WordPerfect-compatible shareware word processor written by Eric Meyer.

(2) (Verband Deutscher Elektrotechniker) The German counterpart of the U.S. Underwriters Lab.

Vdeck (video deck) A frame-accurate, Super 8mm tape drive from Sony for serial-port connection to a personal computer. It contains an internal Vbox, is controlled by the ViSCA language and has no external play buttons.

VDI (Video Device Interface) An Intel standard for speeding up full-motion video performance. It has been incorporated into DCI.

VDM (Virtual DOS Machine) A DOS session created by OS/2 and Windows NT in order to run an individual DOS or 16-bit Windows applications.

VDT (Video Display Terminal) A terminal with a keyboard and display screen.

VDT radiation The electromagnetic radiation emitted from a computer display screen. Exhaustive testing so far seems inconclusive, but vendors recommend keeping the face at least 18 to 20 inches from the screen.

VDU (Video Display Unit) Same as *VDT*.

vector (1) In computer graphics, a line designated by its end points (x-y or x-y-z coordinates). When a circle is drawn, it is made up of many small vectors. See *vector graphics* and *graphics*.

(2) In matrix algebra, a one-row or one-column matrix.

vector display A display terminal that draws vectors on the screen. Contrast with *raster display*.

vector font A scalable font made of vectors (point-to-point line segments). It is easily scaled as are all vector-based images, but lacks the hints and mathematically-defined curves of outline fonts, such as Adobe Type 1 and TrueType.

vector graphics In computer graphics, a technique for representing a picture as points, lines and other geometric entities. This format is used in CAD and drawing programs. Contrast with *raster graphics*.

vector processor A computer with built-in instructions that perform multiple calculations on vectors (one-dimensional arrays) simultaneously. It is used to solve the same or similar problems as an array processor; however, a vector processor passes a vector to a functional unit, whereas an array processor passes each element of a vector to a different arithmetic unit. See *pipeline processing* and *array processor*.

vector to raster See *rasterize*.

Vectra A family of PCs from HP. Vectras are noted for their ruggedness and reliability.

veesa See *VESA*.

Venn diagram A graphic technique for visualizing set theory concepts using overlapping circles and shading to indicate intersection, union and complement.

Ventura Publisher See Corel VENTURA.

verify In data entry operations, to compare the keystrokes of a second operator with the files created by the first operator.

Veronica A program that searches the Internet for specific resources. Using Boolean searches (this AND this, this OR this, etc.), users can search Gopher servers to retrieve a selected group of menus. See *Gopher*.

VersaCAD A family of CAD systems for PCs and the Macintosh from Computervision, Bedford, MA, that features 2-D geometric and construction drafting and 3-D modeling with 16 viewports. It features complete programmability and universal CAD communications. The Mac version includes CAD-oriented HyperCard stacks.

version control The management of source code in a large software project. Version-control software provides a database that keeps track of the revisions made to a program by all the programmers involved in it.

version number The identification of a release of software. The difference between Version 2.2 and 2.3 can be night and day, since new releases not only add features, but often correct bugs. What's been driving you crazy may have been fixed!

Numbers, such as 3.1a or 3.11, often indicate a follow-up release only to fix a bug in the previous version, whereas 3.1 and 3.2 usually mean routine enhancements. Version "1.0" drives terror into the hearts of experienced users. The program has just been released, and bugs are still to be uncovered.

vertical bandwidth See *vertical scan frequency*.

vertical recording A magnetic recording method that records the bits vertically instead of horizontally, taking up less space and providing greater storage capacity. The vertical recording method uses a specialized material for the construction of the disk.

vertical redundancy checking See *VRC*.

vertical refresh See *vertical scan frequency*.

vertical resolution Number of lines (rows in a matrix). Contrast with *horizontal resolution*.

vertical scan frequency The number of times an entire display screen is refreshed, or redrawn, per second. Measured in Hertz, display systems range from 45 to over 100Hz. For example, VGA in the U.S. is generally 56 to 60Hz; in Europe, 70Hz and above. TV is refreshed 60 half-frames/sec (interlaced) resulting in 30 full frames/sec. Contrast with *horizontal scan frequency*.

VESA (Video Electronics Standards Association) An organization of major PC vendors dedicated to improving video and multimedia standards. VESA has defined standards for the VL-bus local bus as well as VGA and Super VGA standards (see *VL-bus*). Address: 2150 N. 1st St., Suite 360, San Jose, CA 95131, 408/435-0333.

VESA BIOS A BIOS chip that conforms to a VESA standard. It typically refers to the BIOS on a VGA display adapter that is VESA compliant.

VESA/EISA Refers to an EISA-bus motherboard or system that contains from one to three VL-bus slots.

VESA/ISA Refers to an ISA-bus motherboard or system that contains from one to three VL-bus slots.

VESA local bus See *VL-bus*.

vesicular film A film used to make copies of microforms. It contains its own developer and creates a pink negative or positive copy when exposed to a negative master through ultraviolet light.

V.FC, V.Fast Class A modem technology for 28800 bps from Rockwell International endorsed by many modem vendors including Hayes Microcomputer Products. The upcoming V.34 standard for 28800 bps modems may be very close to or almost identical to V.FC.

VFAT (Virtual File Allocation Table) A file system used in Windows for Workgroups and Windows 95. It provides higher-speed, 32-bit Protected Mode access for file manipulation. It also supports file names up to 255 characters in length compared to DOS' 8.3 file names (name-8, extension-3).

VFW See *Video for Windows*.

VGA (Video Graphics Array) An IBM video display standard that originated with its PS/2 models. VGA has become the minimum standard for PC display. VGA supports previous CGA and EGA modes and requires an analog monitor. Its highest-resolution mode is 640x480 with 16 colors, but VESA and third parties have boosted colors and resolution to so-called Super VGA standards. Most VGA adapters provide 640x480, 800x600 and 1024x768 resolutions with at least 256 colors.

VGA feature connector A port on a VGA board that is used to pass clock signals and palette information to another board in the computer that processes video in some manner. For example, a board that displays TV on screen requires synchronization from the VGA adapter. The feature connector uses a 26-pin male connector or a 26-pin (13 each side) edge connector at the top of the VGA board.

VGA HC (VGA HiColor) A VGA board that provides 32K or 64K colors using Tseng Labs' ET4000 chip or equivalent.

VGA pass through A feature of a high-resolution display adapter that does not contain a standard VGA display. It couples internally to another VGA card inside the machine.

VHD (Very High Density) Floppy disk technologies that place 20MB and more of data on a 3.5" disk. See *Floptical*.

VHF (Very High Frequency) The range of electromagnetic frequencies from 30MHz to 300MHz.

VHS A VCR format introduced by JVC in 1976 to compete with Sony's Beta format. VHS has become the standard for home and industry, and Beta is now obsolete. SVHS (Super VHS) is a subsequent format that improves resolution.

VHSIC (Very High Speed Integrated Circuit) Pronounced "vizik." Ultra-high-speed chips employing LSI and VLSI technologies.

vi (Visual Interface) A UNIX full-screen text editor that can be run from a terminal or the system console. It is a fast, programmer-oriented utility.

video An audio/visual playback and recording technology used in TV. It also refers to computer screens and terminals. However, there is only one TV/video standard in the U.S., but there are dozens of computer/video display standards.

video adapter Same as *video display board*.

video bandwidth The maximum display resolution of a video screen, measured in MHz, and calculated by horizontal x vertical resolution x refreshes/sec. For example, 800x600x60 = 28.8MHz. Traditional TV studio recording is limited to 5MHz, and TV broadcasting is limited to 3.58Mhz.

video board Now that full-motion digital video is deployed on personal computers, the term "video board" can refer to either (1) a video display board, also called a graphics adapter or video card (VGA, Super VGA, etc.), or (2) a video capture board that digitizes full-motion video into the computer.

video camera A camera that takes continuous pictures and generates a signal for display or recording. It captures images by breaking down the image into a series of lines. The U.S. and Canadian standard (NTSC) is 525 scan lines. Each line is scanned one at a time, and the continuously varying intensities of red, green and blue light across the line are filtered out and converted into a variable signal. Most video cameras are analog, but digital video cameras are also available. See *digital camera*.

video capture board An expansion board that digitizes full-motion video from a VCR, camera or other NTSC video source. The board may also provide digital to analog conversion for recording onto a VCR.

video card Same as *video display board*.

Video CD Video playback on a CD. Developed by Matsushita, Philips, Sony and JVC, Video CD holds 74 minutes of VHS-quality video, including CD-quality sound. Video CD movies are compressed using the MPEG I method and require an MPEG decoder.

video codec A circuit that converts NTSC video into digital code and vice versa. It incorporates a compression technique to reduce the data and may or may not provide full-motion video.

video conferencing See *teleconferencing*.

video controller (1) A device that controls some kind of video function.

(2) Same as *video display board*.

video digitizer Same as *frame grabber*.

videodisc See *LaserDisc* and *Video CD*.

video display board An expansion board that plugs into a desktop computer that converts the images created in the computer to the electronic signals required by the monitor. It determines the maximum resolution, maximum refresh rate and the number of colors that can be sent to the monitor. The monitor must be equally capable of handling its highest resolution and refresh. The VGA card is the common video display board for the PC.

video display card Same as *video display board*.

video display terminal/unit Same as *video terminal*.

video editing See *nonlinear video editing*.

video editor A dedicated computer that controls two or more videotape machines. It keeps track of frame numbers in its own database and switches the recording machine from playback to record. The video editor reads SMPTE time codes provided on professional tape formats.

Video for Windows A video driver and utilities from Microsoft for Windows 3.1 and higher. It supports the AVI movie file format and three video compression methods (Microsoft Video 1, Microsoft RLE and Intel's Indeo).

videographer A person involved in the production of video material.

video graphics board A video display board that generates text and graphics and accepts video from a camera or VCR. Truevision's Targa board and Vision Technologies Vision board are examples.

The terms video graphics board and video display board sound alike, but video display boards (display adapters) do not handle NTSC video.

video overlay card A graphics controller that allows NTSC video and computer images to be mixed.

video port A socket on a computer used to connect a monitor. On a PC, the standard video port is a 15-pin VGA connector. See *VGA*.

video RAM Also called *VRAM*, it is a type of memory in a video display board that holds the image that appears on the video screen. It uses dual-ported memory, which allows simultaneous reads and writes and is faster than dynamic RAM (DRAM).

videotape A magnetic tape used for recording full-animation video images. The most widely used videotape format is the 1/2" wide VHS cassette. VHS has all but obsoleted earlier videotape formats for home and commercial use.

videotex An interactive information technology for home shopping, banking, news, weather and e-mail. It is delivered by telephone line to a subscriber's TV through a decoder box and attached keyboard. Information is broadcast and stored in the decoder as predefined frames that are retrieved by menu. Videotex delivers simple graphics and limited animation. Used in several countries worldwide, it has yet to catch on in the U.S.

video teleconferencing See *videoconferencing*.

video terminal A data entry device that uses a keyboard for input and a display screen for output. Although the display screen resembles a TV, it usually does not accept TV/video signals.

Video Toaster A popular video production system for the Amiga computer from NewTek, Inc., Topeka, KS. The Toaster includes hardware and software that provides digital effects, character generation and 3-D animation.

video window The display of full-motion video (TV) in an independent window on a computer screen.

view (1) To display and look at data on screen.

(2) In relational database management, a special display of data, created as needed. A view temporarily ties two or more files together so that the combined files can be displayed, printed or queried; for example, customers and orders or vendors and purchases. Fields to be included are specified by the user. The original files are not permanently linked or altered; however, if the system allows editing, the data in the original files will be changed.

Viewdata The British term for videotex.

viewer See *file viewer*.

viewport (1) In the Macintosh, the entire scrollable region of data that is viewed through a window.

(2) Same as *window*.

VIM (Vendor Independent Messaging Interface) A programming interface developed by Lotus, Novell, IBM, Apple, Borland, MCI, WordPerfect and Oracle. In order to enable an application to send and receive mail over a VIM-compliant messaging system such as cc:Mail, programmers write to the VIM interface.

VINES (VIrtual NEtworking System) A UNIX System V-based network operating system from Banyan Systems Inc., that runs on DOS and OS/2-based servers. It provides internetworking of PCs, minis, mainframes and other computer resources providing information sharing across organizations of unlimited size.

Incorporating mainframe-like security with a global directory service called Streettalk, VINES allows access to all network users and resources. Options include printer sharing, e-mail, remote PC dial-in, bridges and gateways.

virtual An adjective applied to almost anything today that that expresses a condition without boundaries or constraints.

Virtual 8086 Mode An operational mode in Intel 386s and up that allows it to perform as multiple 8086 CPUs. Under direction of a control program, each virtual machine runs as a stand-alone 8086 running its own operating system and applications, thus DOS, UNIX and other operating systems can be running simultaneously. All virtual machines are multitasked together.

This mode divides up the computer into multiple address spaces and maintains virtual registers for each virtual machine. This is not the same as the 386's virtual memory mode, which extends main memory to disk.

virtual circuit The resulting pathway created between two devices communicating with each other in a switched communications system. A message from New York to Los Angeles may actually start in New York and go through Atlanta, St. Louis, Denver and Phoenix before it winds up in Los Angeles.

It can also be confined to smaller geography, say within a building or campus, in which case the virtual circuit traverses some number of switches, hubs and other network devices. See *PVC* and *SVC*.

virtual desktop An infinitely-large desktop, which is provided either by a virtual screen capability or a shell program that enhances the user interface.

virtual device See *virtual peripheral* and *VxD*.

virtual device driver See *VxD*.

virtual disk Same as *RAM disk*.

virtual image In graphics, the complete graphic image stored in memory, not just the part of it that is displayed at the current time.

virtualize (1) To activate a program in virtual memory.

(2) To create a virtual screen.

virtual machine (1) A computer that runs an operating system that can host other operating systems or multiple copies of itself. Each operating system runs its own set of applications timeshared equally or in some priority with all the other operating systems. Computers can be built with hardware circuits that support a virtual machine environment; for example, the Virtual 8086 Mode in the 386. See *VM*.

(2) A computer that has built-in virtual memory capability.

virtual memory Simulating more memory than actually exists, allowing the computer to run larger programs or more programs concurrently. It breaks up the program into small segments, called *pages*, and brings as many pages into memory that fit into a reserved area for that program. When additional pages are required, it makes room for them by swapping them to disk. It keeps track of pages that have been modified, so that they can be retrieved when needed again.

virtual monitor In the Macintosh, the ability to dynamically configure to any monitor type and to use multiple monitors of different types including displaying the same object across two or more screens.

virtual network An interconnected group of networks (an internet) that appear as one large network to the user. Optionally, or perhaps ideally, a virtual network can be centrally managed and controlled.

Banyan Systems, creator of VINES, which stands for VIrtual NEtworking System, defines virtual networking as "the ability for users to transparently communicate locally and remotely across similar and dissimilar networks through a simple and consistent user interface."

virtual operating system An operating system that can host other operating systems. See *virtual machine*.

virtual peripheral A peripheral device simulated by the operating system.

virtual printer A simulated printer. If a program is ready to print, but all printers are busy, the operating system will transfer the printer output to disk and keep it there until a printer becomes available.

virtual private network See *VPN*. **Remember... use acronyms!**

virtual processing A parallel processing technique that simulates a processor for applications that require a processor for each data element. It creates processors for data elements above and beyond the number of processors available.

virtual processor A simulated processor in a virtual processing system.

virtual reality An artificial reality that projects the user into a 3-D space generated by computer. Implementations by AutoDesk and others include the use of a data glove and head-mounted stereoscopic display, which allow users to point to and manipulate illusory objects in their view. See *cyberspace*.

virtual route Same as *virtual circuit*.

virtual screen An infinetly-large viewing area. The screen on the monitor serves as a scrollable window into a much larger viewing area. Scrolling is accomplished by pushing the mouse pointer beyond the edge of the screen in the direction you want to go. Video display boards may offer this capability; for example, you could browse a 2048x2048 viewing area with an 800x600 screen resolution. See *virtual desktop*.

virtual storage Same as *virtual memory*.

virtual terminal Terminal emulation that allows access to a foreign system. Often refers to a personal computer gaining access to a mini or mainframe.

virtual toolkit Development software that creates programs for several computer environments. Its output may require additional conversions or translations to produce executable programs.

virus Software used to infect a computer. After the virus code is written, it is buried within an existing program. Once that program is executed, the virus code is activated and attaches copies of itself to other programs in the system. Infected programs copy the virus to other programs.

The effect of the virus may be a simple prank that pops up a message on screen out of the blue or the actual destruction of programs and data.

A virus cannot be attached to data. It must be attached to a runnable program that is downloaded into or installed in the computer. The virus-attached program must be executed in order to activate the virus. See *polymorphic virus, stealth virus* and *worm*.

Be Careful Out There!
Before you run a shareware, public domain or freeware program, check it with a virus detection program first!

virus signature The binary pattern of the machine code of a particular virus. Antivirus programs use virus signatures for fast detection of known viruses.

VIS (Voice Information Service) A variety of voice processing service applications.

visa See *VESA*.

ViSCA (VIdeo System Control Architecture) A Sony protocol for synchronized control of multiple video peripherals. ViSCA is the software interface. Control-L is the hardware interface. A ViSCA-compatible VCR can be controlled directly by video capture software.

VisiCalc The first electronic spreadsheet, introduced in 1978 for the Apple II. It was a command-driven program followed by SuperCalc, MultiPlan, Lotus 1-2-3 and others, each improving the user interface. Spreadsheets have also been implemented on minis and mainframes. It all started with VisiCalc.

Visual Basic A version of BASIC from Microsoft specialized for developing Windows applications that has become popular. It is similar to Microsoft's QuickBASIC, but is not 100% compatible with it. User interfaces are developed by dragging objects from the Visual Basic Toolbox onto the application form.

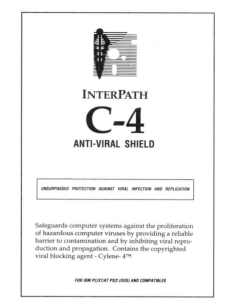

PROCESSOR MEDICINE
(Courtesy InterPath)
You'd think this was on the shelf with the cough medicine at your local drug store.

Visual C++ A C and C++ development system for DOS and Windows applications from Microsoft. Introduced in 1993, the Standard Edition of Visual C++ replaces QuickC for Windows and the Professional Edition includes the Windows SDK and replaces Microsoft C/C++ 7.0.

visual programming Developing programs with tools that allow menus, buttons and other graphics elements to be selected from a palette and drawn and built on screen. It may include developing source code by creating and/or interacting with flow charts that graphically display the logic paths and associated code.

visualization In computer graphics, the converting of numeric data into picture form to allow humans to recognize patterns that are difficult to identify in numeric form. It is used especially in research situations, both theoretical and practical.

VLB See *VL-bus*.

VL-bus (VESA Local-BUS) A local bus for PCs standardized by VESA that provides a high-speed data path between the CPU and peripherals (video, disk, network, etc.). Up to three VL-bus slots can be placed onto the motherboard. See *local bus*.

The VL-bus runs at speeds up to 40MHz or up to 66MHz for controllers built directly on the motherboard. It is currently a 32-bit bus with 64-bit capability forthcoming to handle the Pentium CPU. The VL-bus expansion slot uses one 32-bit Micro Channel slot placed adjacent to the standard ISA, EISA or Micro Channel slot, allowing vendors to design boards that use only the local bus or both buses at the same time. VL-bus also supports bus mastering.

VLF (Very Low Frequency) See *low radiation*.

VLSI (1) (Very Large Scale Integration) Between 100,000 and one million transistors on a chip. See *SSI, MSI, LSI* and *ULSI*.

(2) (VLSI Technology, Inc., Tempe, AZ) A designer and manufacturer of custom chips.

VM (Virtual Machine) An IBM mainframe operating system, originally developed by its customers and eventually adopted as an IBM system product (VM/SP). It can run multiple operating systems within the computer at the same time, each one running its own programs. CMS (Conversational Monitor System) provides VM's interactive capability.

v-mail (Video mail) The ability to send video clips along with e-mail messages. This is not the same as video conferencing, which requires realtime capabilities between sender and receiver, but it does require high-speed computers and networks.

VMEbus (VersaModule Eurocard bus) A 32-bit bus developed by Motorola, Signetics, Mostek and Thompson CSF. It is widely used in industrial, commercial and military applications with over 300 manufacturers of VMEbus products worldwide. VME64 is an expanded version that provides 64-bit data transfer and addressing.

VMS (1) (Virtual Memory System) A multiuser, multitasking, virtual memory operating system for the VAX series from Digital. VMS applications will run on any VAX from the MicroVAX to the largest VAX.

(2) (Voice Messaging System) See *voice mail*.

VMTP (Virtual Message Transaction Protocol) A datagram communications protocol that provides efficient and reliable transmission across networks.

voice See *MIDI voices*.

voice channel A transmission channel or subchannel that carries human voice.

voice coil A type of motor used to move the access arm of a disk drive in very small increments. Like the voice coil of a speaker, the amount of current determines the amount of movement. Contrast with *stepper motor*, which works in fixed increments.

voice grade Refers to the bandwidth required to transmit human voice, which is usually about 4,000Hz.

voice mail A computerized telephone answering system that digitizes incoming voice messages and stores them on disk. It usually provides auto attendant capability, which uses prerecorded messages to route the caller to the appropriate person, department or mail box.

voice messaging Using voice mail as an alternative to electronic mail, in which voice messages are intentionally recorded, not because the recipient was not available.

voice processing The computerized handling of voice, which includes voice store and forward, voice response, voice recognition and text to speech technologies.

voice recognition The conversion of spoken words into computer text. Speech is first digitized and then matched against a dictionary of coded waveforms. The matches are converted into text as if the words were typed on the keyboard.

voice response The generation of voice output by computer. It provides pre-recorded information either with or without selection by the caller. Interactive voice response allows interactive manipulation of a database. See *audiotex*.

voice store and forward The technology behind voice mail and messaging systems. Human voice is digitized, stored in the computer, routed to the recipient's mailbox and retrieved by the user when required.

volatile memory A memory that does not hold its contents without power. A computer's main memory, made up of dynamic RAM or static RAM chips, loses its content immediately upon loss of power.

volt A unit of measurement of force, or pressure, in an electrical circuit. The common voltage of an AC power line is 120 volts of alternating current (alternating directions). Common voltages within a computer are from 5 to 12 volts of direct current (one direction only).

volt-amps The measurement of electrical usage that is computed by multiplying volts times amps. See *watt*.

voltage regulator A device used to maintain a level amount of voltage in the electrical line. Contrast with *surge suppressor*, which filters out excessive amounts of current, and contrast with *UPS*, which provides backup power in the event of a power failure.

volume (1) A physical storage unit, such as a hard disk, floppy disk, disk cartridge or reel of tape.

(2) A logical storage unit, which is a part of one physical drive or one that spans several physical drives.

volume label (1) A name assigned to a disk (usually optional).

(2) An identifying stick-on label attached to the outside of a tape reel or disk cartridge.

(3) See *header label*.

voxel (VOlume piXEL) A three-dimensional pixel. A voxel represents a quantity of 3-D data just as a pixel represents a point or cluster of points in 2-D data.

VPN (Virtual Private Network) A wide area communications network provided by a common carrier that provides what seems like dedicated lines when used, but backbone trunks are shared among all customers as in a public network. It allows a private network to be configured within a public network. See *PVC*.

VPS (Vectors Per Second) The measurement of the speed of a vector or array processor.

VR See *virtual reality*.

VRAM See *video RAM*.

VRC (Vertical Redundancy Check) An error checking method that generates and tests a parity bit for each byte of data that is moved or transmitted.

VS (1) (Virtual Storage) Same as *virtual memory*.

(2) (Virtual Storage) A family of minicomputers from Wang introduced in 1977, which use virtual memory techniques.

VSAM (Virtual Storage Access Method) An IBM access method for storing data, widely used in IBM mainframes. It uses the B+tree method for organizing data.

VSAT (Very Small Aperture satellite Terminal) A small earth station for satellite transmission that handles up to 56 Kbits/sec of digital transmission. VSATs that handle the T1 data rate (up to 1.544 Mbits/sec) are called *TSATs*.

VSE (Disk Operating System/Virtual Storage Extended) An IBM multiuser, multitasking operating system that typically runs on IBM's 43xx series. It used to be called DOS, but due to the abundance of DOS PCs, it is now referred to as VSE.

VSX (Verification Suite for X/Open) A testing procedure from X/Open that verifies compliance with their endorsed standards. VSX3 has over 5,500 tests for compliance with XPG3.

VT100, 200, 300 A series of asynchronous display terminals from Digital for its PDP and VAX computers. Available in text and graphics models in both monochrome and color.

VTAM (Virtual Telecommunications Access Method) Also called ACF/VTAM (Advanced Communications Function/VTAM), software that controls communications in an IBM SNA environment. It usually resides in the mainframe under MVS or VM, but may be offloaded into a front end processor that is tightly coupled to the mainframe. It supports a wide variety of network protocols, including SDLC and Token Ring. VTAM can be thought of as the network operating system of SNA.

VTOC (Volume Table Of Contents) A list of files on a disk. The VTOC is the mainframe counterpart to the FAT table on a PC.

VTR (VideoTape Recorder) A video recording and playback machine that uses reels of magnetic tape. Contrast with *VCR*, which uses tape cassettes.

VUE See *HP-VUE*.

VUP (VAX Unit of Performance) A unit of measurement equal to the performance of the VAX 11/780, the first VAX machine.

VxD (Virtual Device Driver) A special type of Windows driver for 386 Enhanced Mode. VxDs run at the most priviledged CPU mode (ring 0) and allow low-level interaction with the hardware and internal Windows functions, such as memory management. WIN386.EXE, the 386 Enhanced Mode kernel of Windows, is itself made up of VxDs.

Wabi (Windows ABI) Software from SunSoft that emulates Windows applications under UNIX by converting the calls made by Windows applications into X Window calls. It executes native code and thus runs Windows applications with good performance. Wabi is an option for Sun's Solaris environment as well as for OEM products.

wafer (1) The base material in chip making. It is a slice, approx. 1/30" thick, from a salami-like silicon crystal from 3 to 6" in diameter. The wafer goes through a series of photomasking, etching and implantation steps.

(2) A small, continuous-loop magnetic tape cartridge that is used for the storage of data.

TAPE WAFER

SILICON WAFER

wafer scale integration A semiconductor technology that builds a complete computer on an entire wafer. It has been tried, but not yet successful.

WAIS (Wide Area Information Server) A database on the Internet that contains indexes to documents that reside on the Internet. Using the Z39.50 query language, text files can be searched based on key words. Information resources on the Internet are called "sources." A directory of WAIS servers and sources is avalable from Thinking Machines Corporation, Cambridge, MA, at address **quake.think.com**. See *Archie* and *Gopher*.

wait state The time spent waiting for an operation to take place. It may refer to a variable length of time a program has to wait before it can be processed, or to a fixed duration of time, such as a machine cycle.

When memory is too slow to respond to the CPU's request for it, wait states are introduced until the memory can catch up.

wallpaper A pattern or picture used to represent the desktop surface (screen background) in a graphical user interface. GUIs comes with several wallpaper choices, and third-party wallpaper files are available. You can also scan in your favorite picture and make it wallpaper.

If you wonder why you cover a desktop with wallpaper, don't. Very little makes sense in this industry, why should this?

WAN (Wide Area Network) A communications network that covers a wide geographic area, such as state or country. It requires the network facilities of common carriers.

WAN analyzer See *network analyzer*.

wand A hand-held optical reader used to read typewritten fonts, printed fonts, OCR fonts and bar codes. The wand is waved over each line of characters or codes in a single pass.

Wang Labs (Wang Laboratories, Inc., Lowell, MA) A computer manufacturer and applications developer. Founded in 1951 by Dr. An Wang, the company's desktop calculator became a standard in the late 1960s. Its future plans are to continue enhancing its VS computer line while specializing in software and services for the client/server market.

WANG CALCULATOR (1965)
(Courtesy Wang Labs)

warm boot Restarting the computer by performing a reset operation (pressing reset, Ctrl-Alt-Del, etc.). See *boot, cold boot* and *clean boot*.

Warnier-Orr diagram A graphic charting technique used in software engineering for system analysis and design.

WARP A parallel processor developed at Carnegie-Mellon University that was the predecessor of iWARP.

watt The measurement of electrical power. One watt is one ampere of current flowing at one volt. Watts are typically rated as AMPS x VOLTS; however, AMPS x VOLTS, or VOLT-AMP (V-A) ratings and watts are only equivalent when powering devices that absorb all the energy such as electric heating coils or incandescent light bulbs. With computer power supplies, the actual watt rating is only 60 to 70% of the VOLT-AMP rating.

WAV A Windows sound file, which uses the .WAV extension. Wave files take up a lot of disk space. Depending on sampling frequency and rate, one minute of audio, without compression, can take from 644KB to 5MB.

wave The shape of radiated energy. All radio signals, light rays, x-rays, and cosmic rays radiate an energy that looks likes rippling waves. To visualize waves, take a piece of paper and start drawing an up and down line very fast while pulling the paper perpendicular to the line.

wave table synthesis A MIDI technique for creating musical sounds by storing digitized samples of the actual instruments. It provides more realistic sound than the FM synthesis method, which generates the sound waves entirely via electronic circuits. The more notes sampled in the wave table method, the better the resulting sound recreation.

waveform The pattern of a particular sound wave or other electronic signal in analog form.

waveform synthesis Same as *wave table synthesis*.

waveguide A rectangular, circular or elliptical tube through which radio waves are transmitted.

wavelength The distance between crests of a wave, computed by speed divided by frequency (speed / Hz). Wavelength in meters of electromagnetic waves equals 300,000,000 / Hz. Wavelength in meters for sound travelling through the air equals 335 / Hz.

WDM (Wavelength-Division Multiplexing) A high-speed optical fiber transmission technique that carries multiple signals, each within its own wavelength (color) of light.

weak typing Programming languages that allow different types of data to be moved freely among data structures, as is found in Smalltalk and other earlier object-oriented languages.

Web See *Worldwide Web*.

Weitek coprocessor A high-performance math coprocessor from Weitek Corporation. Since 1981, Weitek has been making coprocessors for CAD and graphics workstations. In order to use a coprocessor, the software must be written to activate it.

well behaved Refers to programs that do not deviate from a standard.

well mannered Same as *well behaved*.

wetware A biological system. It typically refers to the human brain and nervous system.

WFW See *Windows for Workgroups*.

Whetstones A benchmark program that tests floating point operations. Results are expressed in Whetstones per second. Whetstone I tests 32-bit, and Whetstone II tests 64-bit operations. See *Dhrystones*.

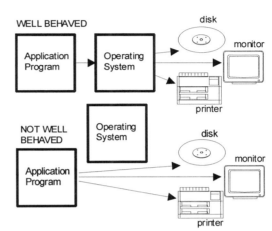

WELL BEHAVED

whiteboard The electronic equivalent of chalk and blackboard. Whiteboards allow participants across a network to simultaneously view one or more users drawing on the computer.

White Book The documentation for the technical specification of Video CDs.

white noise Same as *Gaussian noise*.

wide area network See *WAN*.

widget set A group of screen structures (menu, button, scroll bar, etc.) provided in a graphical interface.

widow & orphan A *widow* is the last line of a paragraph that appears alone at the top of the next page, and an *orphan* is the first line of a paragraph that appears alone at the bottom of a page. Widow and orphan settings are usually set for a minimum of two lines.

width table A list of horizontal measurements for each character in a font, used by word processing and desktop publishing programs.

wild cards Symbols used to represent any value when naming files. In DOS and UNIX, the asterisk (*) represents any name, and the question mark (?) represents any single character. For example, the DOS directory command **dir *.exe** would display all .EXE files regardless of name. The command **dir ?.exe** would display .EXE files that contain only one letter in their name, such A.EXE, B.EXE, etc.

wimp interface (Windows, Icons, Menus and a Pointing device) Same as *GUI*.

Win32 A programming interface (API) for the 386's 32-bit mode fully supported in Windows NT. Many functions are also supported in Windows 3.1, and applications can be written to the Win32 subset (Win32s) to gain improved performance on a 386 or up running Windows 3.1 or higher.

Winbench A series of tests that analyze computer performance from Ziff-Davis' PC Labs. See *Winmark*.

Winchester disk An early removable disk from IBM that put the heads and platters in a sealed unit for greater speed. Its dual 30MB modules, or 30-30 design, caught the "Winchester rifle" nickname. The term later referred to any fixed hard disk.

window (1) A scrollable viewing area on screen. Windows are generally rectangular, although round and polygonal windows are used in specialized applications. A window may refer to a part of the application, such as the scrollable index or text in the electronic versions of this Glossary, or it may refer to the entire application in a window. See *GUI*.

(2) A reserved area of memory.

(3) A time period.

window manager Software incorporated into all popular GUIs, which displays a window with accompanying menus, buttons and scroll bars. It allows the windows to be relocated, overlapped, resized, minimized and maximized. See *desktop manager*.

windowing software Same as *windows program*.

Windows A graphics-based operating system from Microsoft that provides a desktop environment similar to the Macintosh, in which applications are displayed in re-sizable, movable windows on screen. Windows 3.0 and Windows 3.1 are actually add-ons to DOS and can run in 286s on up. Starting with Windows 95, Windows is a self-contained, 32-bit operating system that requires a 386 minimum.

   In order to use all the features of Windows, applications must be written for it. However, Windows also runs DOS applications and is increasingly being used as the primary operating environment from which all programs are launched.
▶ *The electronic and encyclopedic versions of this book provide more detail on Windows, including tips, techniques and "how to's."*

Windows accelerator A graphics accelerator with a driver for Windows. See *graphics accelerator*.

windows environment Any operating system, operating system extension or application program that provides multiple windows on screen. DESQview, Windows, Macintosh and X Window are examples.

Windows for Workgroups A version of Windows 3.1 that includes built-in peer-to-peer networking and e-mail.

Windows Metafile A Windows file format that is primarily used for vector graphics, but also holds bitmaps and text. The Aldus Placeable Metafile is a PageMaker variation that contains a header indicating into what size rectangle the object will be rendered.

Windows NT (Windows New Technology) An advanced 32-bit network operating system from Microsoft that runs DOS and Windows applications. Introduced in 1993, it runs on 386s and up, MIPS, Alpha and PowerPC platforms. Features include peer-to-peer networking, preemptive multitasking, multithreading, multiprocessing, fault tolerance and support for the Unicode character set. NT provides extensive security features and includes NetWare, TCP/IP and NetBEUI communications protocols.

windows program (1) Software that adds a windows capability to an existing operating system.

(2) An application program written to run under Windows.

Windows requirements Windows places far more demands of a PC than does DOS. The recommended minimum system requirements are a 486/66, 8MB RAM, 500MB hard disk and a graphics accelerator card. A DX4 or Pentium is better. If you keep a lot of applications open, 16MB or 32MB of RAM is recommended.

Windows Resource Kit Windows technical documentation from Microsoft written for support personnel. It is a comprehensive document with over 500 pages of technical details that includes flow charts and a chapter on troubleshooting. The text has been compiled by WUGNET into a Windows help system program with hypertext links.

Windows SDK A set of development utilities for writing Windows applications in Microsoft C. It provides tools for creating custom cursors, fonts and icons, bitmaps, menus and online help.

Windows shell An add-on user interface for Windows. There are many Windows shells available that streamline the Windows interface by providing such features as foldering, customized toolbars and quick access to the DOS command line. Windows shells can replace Program Manager and File Manager or coexist with them side by side. They often come with a variety of utility programs.

Popular shells are Norton Desktop for Windows, PC Tools for Windows and HP's Dashboard.

Windows swap file A disk file used for virtual memory in Windows. The file SPART.PAR and hidden file 386SPART.PAR make up the permanent swap file. If these files are not present, or if Windows is in Standard Mode, Windows creates temporary swap files as needed.

Windows Telephony See *TAPI.*

WIN.INI (WINdows INItialization) The file read by Windows on startup that contains data about the current environment (desktop, fonts, sounds, etc.) and individual applications. It is often updated by an install program to provide information for the application when it runs. SYSTEM.INI, another startup file, contains data about the hardware (drivers, 386 Enhanced Mode settings, etc.).

Winmark A unit of performance based on Ziff-Davis' PC Labs Winbench tests. Graphics Winmarks rate Windows video performance as a weighted average of 12 benchmarks.

Winsock API (WINdows SOCKets API) A Windows programming interface for TCP/IP software. Since most TCP/IP software for Windows supports the Winsock API, writing a client/server application to this specification allows it to be used on different TCP/IP stacks across the network.

WinWord See *Microsoft Word.*

wire wrap An early method of wiring circuit boards. A tool strips the end of the wire and coils it. The coil is pressed onto a metal prong on the board.

wireframe modeling In CAD, a technique for representing 3-D objects, in which all surfaces are visibly outlined in lines, including the opposite sides and all internal components that are normally

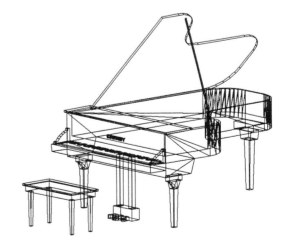

WIREFRAME MODELING
(Courtesy CADKEY, Inc.)

hidden from view. Compared to surface and solid modeling, wireframe modeling is the least complex method for representing 3-D images.

wireless Radio transmission via the airwaves. Various communications techniques are used to provide wireless transmission including infrared line of sight, cellular, microwave, satellite. packet radio and spread spectrum. See *TDMA, CDMA* and *CDPD*.

wiring closet The central distribution or servicing point for cables in a network.

wizard Instructional help that guides the user through a series of steps to accomplish a task.

wizzy wig See *WYSIWYG*.

WK1 Lotus 1-2-3 Version 2.0 file extension.

WKS Lotus 1-2-3, Version 1A file extension.

WMF See *Windows Metafile*.

word (1) The computer's internal storage unit. Refers to the amount of data it can hold in its registers and process at one time. A word is often 16 bits, in which case 32 bits is called a double word. Given the same clock rate, a 32-bit computer processes four bytes in the same time it takes a 16-bit machine to process two.

(2) The primary text element, identified by a word separator (blank space, comma, etc.) before and after a group of contiguous characters.

(3) See *Microsoft Word*.

word addressable A computer that can address memory only on word boundaries. Contrast with *byte addressable*.

WordBASIC A subset of Microsoft QuickBASIC with added word processing functions used to customize Microsoft Word word processors.

Word for Windows See *Microsoft Word*.

WordPerfect A full-featured word processing program from WordPerfect Corporation. Introduced in 1980 for the Data General mini, WordPerfect is the most widely used word processor in the world, with versions for all major personal computer and workstation environments.
   The WordPerfect Corporation in Orem, UT, was acquired by Novell in 1994.

word processing The creation of text documents. Except for labels and envelopes, it has replaced the electric typewriter in most offices, because of the ease in which documents can be edited, searched and reprinted.
   Advanced word processors function as elementary desktop publishing systems. Although there are still machines dedicated only to word processing, most word processing is performed on general-purpose computers using word processing software.
   ▶ *The electronic and encyclopedic versions of this book provide more detail on this subject.*

word processing machine A computer that is specialized for only word processing functions.

word processor (1) Software that provides word processing functions on a computer.

(2) A computer specialized for word processing. Until the late 1970s, word processors were always dedicated machines. Today, personal computers have replaced almost all dedicated word processors.

word separator A character that separates a word, such as a blank space, comma, period, -, ? and !.

WordStar A full-featured word processing program for DOS and Windows from Softkey International, Inc., Cambridge, MA. Introduced in 1978 for CP/M machines, it was the first program to give full word processing capabilities to personal computer users at far less cost than the dedicated word processors of the time. Many WordStar keyboard commands have become de facto standards.

word wheel A lookup method in which each character that is typed in moves the on-screen index to the closest match. By watching the index move character by character, you can easily tell if you have made a typo.

word wrap A word processing feature that moves words to the next line automatically as you type based on the current right margin setting. Some word processing programs allow word wrap to be turned off for writing source code.

workflow automation Automatically routing data and documents over the network to the users responsible for working with them. A workflow automation system keeps track of the processes a document goes through and alerts users when operations are overdue.

workgroup Two or more individuals who share files and databases. LANs designed around workgroups provide electronic sharing of required data. See *groupware* and *workflow automation*.

working directory See *current directory*.

Workplace A set of strategies and system software technologies from IBM that will guide its desktop products into the next century. Based on Carnegie-Mellon's Mach operating system, it includes object-oriented technologies, multimedia, handwriting and voice recognition.

Workplace Shell The primary component of the OS/2 2.x user interface, which provides the equivalent functionality of Window's Program Manager and File Manager.

worksheet Same as *spreadsheet*.

worksheet compiler Same as *spreadsheet compiler*.

workstation (1) A high-performance, single-user microcomputer or minicomputer that is used for graphics, CAD, CAE, simulation and scientific applications. It is typically a RISC-based computer that runs under some variation of UNIX.

(2) A personal computer in a network. In this context, a workstation is the same as a client. Contrast with *server* and *host*.

(3) In the telecom industry, a combined telephone and computer.

(4) Any terminal or personal computer.

Worldwide Web An Internet service that links documents by providing hypertext links from server to server. It allows a user to jump from document to related document no matter where it is stored on the Internet. Worldwide Web client programs, such as Mosaic and Cello, allow users to browse "the Web."

The Web differs from Gopher systems. The Web links everything via hypertext, whereas Gopher provides hierarchical menus of items and services.

worm (1) A destructive program that replicates itself throughout disk and memory, using up the computers resources and eventually putting the system down. See *virus* and *logic bomb*.

(2) A program that moves through a network and deposits information at each node for diagnostic purposes or causes idle computers to share some of the processing workload.

(3) (WORM) (Write Once Read Many) An optical disk that can be recorded only once. Updating requires destroying the existing data (all 0s made 1s), and writing new data to an unused part of the disk.

WOSA (Windows Open System Architecture) Umbrella term from Microsoft for a variety of programming interfaces, such as ODBC and MAPI, that are designed to provide application interoperability across the Windows environment. It provides standards between Windows clients and servers, allowing Windows applications to access services on the network from any software provider (database manager, document manager, network services, etc.) that supports the WOSA interface.

WP See *word processing* and *WordPerfect*.

WPcom See *write precompensation*.

wrist rest A platform used to raise the wrist to keyboard level for typing.

wrist support A product that prevents and provides a therapy for carpal tunnel syndrome by keeping the hands in a neutral wrist position.

write To store data in memory or record data onto a storage medium, such as disk and tape. Read and write is analogous to play and record on an audio tape recorder.

write back cache A disk or memory cache that handles writing. Data written into the high-speed cache memory from the CPU is written onto disk or into real memory during idle machine cycles.

Computers write funny!

write cycle The operation of writing data into a memory or storage device.

write error The inability to store into memory or record onto disk or tape. Malfunctioning memory cells or damaged portions of the disk or tape's surface will cause those areas to be unusable.

write precompensation Using a stronger magnetic field to write data in sectors that are closer to the center of the disk. In CAV recording, in which the disk spins at a constant speed, the sectors closest to the spindle are packed tighter than the outer sectors.

One of the hard disk parameters stored in a PC's CMOS RAM is the WPcom number, which is the track where precompensation begins.

write protect A mode that restricts erasing or editing a disk file. See *file protection*.

write protect notch A small, square cutout on the side of a floppy disk used to prevent it from being written and erased. On 5.25" floppies, the notch must be covered for protection. To protect a 3.5" diskette, press the slide lever toward the edge of the disk uncovering a hole (upper left side viewed from the back).

WSI See *wafer scale integration*.

WUGNET (Windows Users Group NETwork) An organization of Windows users and developers founded in 1988. It provides technical information, software resources and tools, CompuServe forums and newsletters. Address: 126 E. State St., Media, PA 19063, 215/565-1861.

WWW See *Worldwide Web*.

WXmodem (Window Xmodem) A faster version of the Xmodem protocol that allows the sending system to transmit data without waiting for the receiving system to acknowledge the transfer.

WYSIWYG (What You See Is What You Get) Pronounced "wizzy-wig." Refers to text and graphics appearing on screen the same as they print. To have WYSIWYG text, a screen font must be installed that matches each printer font. Otherwise, a 24-point font may display in correct size relationship to a 10-point font, but it won't look like the printed typeface.

It is almost impossible to get 100% identical representation, because screen and printer resolutions rarely match. Even a 300 dpi printer has a higher resolution than almost every monitor.

WYSIWYG

x (1) In programming, symbol used to identify a hexadecimal number. For example, 0x0A and \x0A specify the hex number 0A.

(2) See *X Window*.

X.3 An ITU-TSS standard (1977) for a PAD (packet assembler/disassembler), which divides a data message into packets for transmission over a packet-switched network and reassembles them at the receiving side.

X11 The current version of the X Window System. X11R5 (Version 11, Release 5, Sept. 1991) provides a stable and feature-rich environment.

X12 An ANSI standard protocol for EDI. See *Tradacoms* and *EDIFACT*.

X.21 An ITU-TSS standard protocol for a circuit switching network.

X.25 An ITU-TSS standard (1976) for protocols and message formats that define the interface between a terminal and a packet switching network. See *packet switching*.

X.28 An ITU-TSS standard (1977) for exchange of information between a DTE and a PAD; commonly known as PAD commands.

X.29 An ITU-TSS standard (1977) for exchange of information between a local PAD and a remote PAD; procedures for interworking between PADs.

X.32 An ITU-TSS standard (1984) for connecting to an X.25 network by dial up. It defines how the network identifies the terminal for billing and security purposes and how default parameters are negotiated for the connection.

X.75 An ITU-TSS standard for connecting X.25 networks.

x86 Refers to the Intel 8086 CPU family (8086, 8088, 80186, 80286, 386, 486, Pentium). Starting with the 386, Intel has dropped the "80" prefix in its reference manuals. Same as *80x86*.

CPU# (word size)	Clock Speed (MHz)	MIPS	Bus size	Maximum RAM (Bytes)	Floppy Disk (Bytes)	Typical Hard Disk (MB)
8088 (16)	5	.33	8	1M	5.25" 360K	10-20
8086 (16)	5-10	.33-.66	16	1M		10-40
286 (16)	6-12	1.2-2.4	16	16M	5.25" 1.2M	20-80
386DX (32)	16-40	6-15	32	4G	5.25" 1.2M	80-200
386SX (32)	16-33	2.5-5	16	16M	3.5" 1.44M	60-100
386SL (32)	20-25	3.2-4	16	32M		60-100
486DX (32)	25-100	20-80	32	4G		100-2000
486SX (32)	20-25	16-20	32	4G		80-500
Pentium	60-100	100-168	64	4G		500-5000

X.400 An OSI and ITU-TSS standard messaging protocol. It is an application layer protocol (layer 7 in the OSI model). X.400 has been defined to run over various network transports including Ethernet, X.25, TCP/IP and dial-up lines. See *messaging protocol* and *CMC*.

X.500 An OSI protocol for maintaining online directories of users and resources. It is primarily designed to return information rather than update it. X.500 can be used to support X.400 and other messaging systems, but is not restricted to e-mail usage. It provides a hierarchical structure that fits the world's classification system: countries, states, cities, streets, houses, families, etc. The goal is to have a directory that can be used globally.

XA See *CD-ROM XA* and *370/XA*.

XAPIA (X.400 API Association) A consortium dedicated to standardizing X.400 and other specifications, such as the CMC messaging API. For information, contact Leslie Schroeder Press Relations, 10151 Western Drive, Cupertino, CA 95014, 408/446-9158.

x-axis See *x-y matrix*.

Xbase A dBASE-like languages such as Clipper and FoxPro. Originally almost identical to dBASE, new commands and features over the years have made them only partially dBASE compatible.

X-based See *X Window* and *Xbase*.

XCMD (eXternal CoMmanD) A user-developed HyperCard command written in a language such as C or Pascal. See *XFCN*.

Xcopy A DOS and OS/2 utility that copies files and subdirectories.

XDR (EXternal Data Representation) A data format developed by Sun that is part of its networking standards. It deals with integer size, byte ordering, data representation, etc. and is used as an interchange format. Different systems convert to XDR for sending and from XDR upon receipt.

xe file See *EXE file*.

XENIX See *SCO XENIX*.

xerography See *electrophotographic*.

XFCN (eXternal FunCtioN) A user-developed HyperCard function that is written in a language, such as C or Pascal. XFCNs usually return a value. See *XCMD*.

xfr Often used as an abbreviation for "transfer" in may electronic and communications terms and phrases.

XGA (EXtended Graphics Array) An IBM video display standard (1990) optimized for graphical user interfaces. It adds 132 column text to VGA, plus additional resolutions up to 1024x768 with 256 colors interlaced. XGA-2 (1992) provides non-interlaced 1024x768x64K.

XGML A family of text manipulation software for PCs, Macs, IBM mainframes, UNIX and others from Software Exoterica Corporation, Ottawa, Ontario. With strong support for SGML, it includes XTRAN, a language that translates, matches and links text.

x-height In typography, the height of the letter x in lower case. Point size includes the x-height, the height of the ascender and the height of the descender. See *typeface*.

XIP (Execute In Place) The ability to execute a program directly from a memory card.

XL See *Excel*.

Xlib (X LIBrary) Functions in the X Window System. See *X toolkit*.

XLISP A microcomputer version of the LISP programming language that has been in the public domain for a number of years.

XMI A high-speed bus from Digital used in large VAX machines.

Xmodem The first widely-used file transfer protocol for personal computers, developed by Ward Christensen for CP/M machines. Early versions used a checksum to detect errors. Later versions use the more effective CRC method. Programs typically include both methods and drop back to checksum if CRC is not present at the other end.

XMP (X/Open Management Protocol) A high-level network management protocol governed by X/Open. Network management software written to the XMP interface is shielded from the details of the underlying SNMP or CMIP protocols.

XMS (eXtended Memory Specification) A programming interface that allows DOS programs to use extended memory in 286s and up. It provides a set of functions for reserving, releasing and transferring data to and from extended memory without conflict, including the high memory area (HMA). See *HIMEM.SYS* and *DOS extender*.

XMS Versus VCPI/DPMI

XMS, VCPI and DPMI all deal with extended memory. However, XMS allows data and programs to be stored in and retrieved from extended memory, whereas the VCPI and DPMI interfaces allow programs to "run" in extended memory.

XMT In communications, an abbreviation for transmit.

XNS (Xerox Network Services) An early networking protocol suite developed at Xerox's Palo Alto Research Center (PARC). XNS has been the basis for many popular network architectures including Novell's NetWare, Banyan's VINES and 3Com's 3+.

xon-xoff In communications, a simple asynchronous protocol that keeps the receiving device in synchronization with the sender. When the buffer in the receiving device is full, it sends an *x-off* signal (transmit off) to the sending device, telling it to stop transmitting. When the receiving device is ready to accept more, it sends the sending device an *x-on* signal (transmit on) to start again.

X/Open A consortium of international computer vendors founded in 1984 to resolve standards issues. Incorporated in 1987 and based in London, North American offices are in San Francisco. Its purpose is to integrate evolving de facto and international standards in order to achieve an open environment, or CAE (Common Application Environent). XPG defines X/Open's specification, and VSX defines its testing and verification procedure.

In late 1993, Spec 1170 was announced, a specification that contains over 1,100 APIs. Spec 1170 is designed to provide a unified programming interface for the UNIX operating system and will be available in 1994. Telephones: U.S. 415/323-7992, U.K. 44-734-508311.

XPG (X/Open Portability Guide) Standards that specify compliance with X/Open's Common Application Environment (CAE). XPG3 (Release 3), introduced in early 1989, specifies standards for UNIX System V Release 4.0.

X protocol The message format of the X Window System.

X server The receiving computer in an X Window system. The X server displays the application that is running on a remote machine, which is the X client. See *X Window*.

X standard See *X Window* and *X.400*.

XT (1) (EXtended Technology) The first IBM PC with a hard disk, introduced in 1983. See *PC*.

(2) (Xt) See *X toolkit*.

XT bus See *PC bus*.

XT class Refers to first-generation PCs, which includes the first floppy-disk PC, the actual "XT" PC with a hard disk and all compatibles that use the 8088 or 8086 or compatible CPU and an 8-bit bus.

X terminal A terminal with built-in X server capability.

XT interface See *XT bus*.

XTP (Xpress Transfer Protocol) A research transport protocol designed by Greg Chesson of Silicon Graphics. It is a type of lightweight protocol designed for high-speed networks and provides services at layers 3 and 4 of the OSI model.

XTree A PC disk management program and DOS shell from XTree Co., San Luis Obispo, CA. Introduced in 1985, it was the first program to help users manage hard disks by providing a hierarchical display of directories.

Xtrieve A menu-driven query language and report writer from Novell that accesses Btrieve files.

X toolkit Development software for building X Window applications. Typically includes a widget set, X Toolkit Intrinsics (Xt) libraries for managing the widget set and the X Library (Xlib).

XVT (EXtensible Virtual Toolkit) A developers toolkit for creating user interfaces across multiple environments from XVT Software, Inc., Boulder, CO. Programmers create the XVT functions, which are translated to DOS, Windows, OS/2, PM or the Mac.

X Window Formally "X Window System," also called "X Windows" and "X," it is a windowing system developed at MIT, which runs under UNIX and all major operating systems. X lets users run applications on other computers in the network and view the output on their own screen.

X client software resides in the computer that performs the processing and X server software resides in the computer that displays it. Both components can also be in the same machine. This seems opposite to today's client/server terminology, but the concept is that the server is "serving up" the image.

x-y matrix A group of rows and columns. The x-axis is the horizontal row, and the y-axis is the vertical column. An x-y matrix is the reference framework for two-dimensional structures, such as mathematical tables, display screens, digitizer tablets, dot matrix printers and 2-D graphics images.

x-y monitor In graphics, the display screen of a vector display terminal. The entire vector display comprises the monitor and vector graphics controller.

x-y plotter Same as *plotter*.

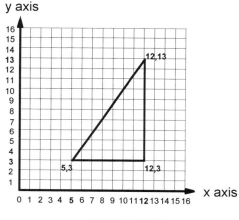

X-Y MATRIX

XyWrite Pronounced "zy-write." A word processing program for DOS and Windows from the XYQUEST division of The Technology Group, Baltimore, MD. XyWrite word processors, including XyWrite III and XyWrite III Plus, have been used extensively by major newspapers and magazines throughout the country. XyWrite was noted for its typesetting orientation long before it was common to have the variety of fonts found in today's software. XyWrite differs from most word processors in that it generates a pure ASCII file like a text editor.

x-y-z matrix A three-dimensional structure. The x and y axes represent the first two dimensions; the z axis, the third dimension. In a graphic image, the x and y denote width and height; the z denotes depth.

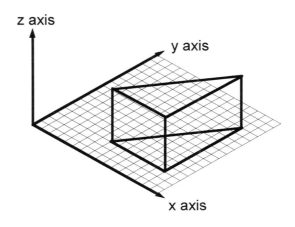

X-Y-Z MATRIX

y-axis See *x-y matrix*.

Yellow Book The standard for the physical format of a CD-ROM disk. The ISO 9660 standard defines the logical format for the disk. See *CD*.

Yellow Pages See *NIS* and *naming service*.

YIQ The color model used for color TV. The Y stands for luminosity or lightness, which was the original black and white TV signal. The I and Q were added to make color TV backward compatible with the black and white standard. Known as chromacity, the I and Q signals are the color differences that are derived from the difference between red, blue and the luminosity (I=red-Y, Q=blue-Y).

Ymodem A file transfer protocol identical to Xmodem-1K plus batch file transfer (also called Ymodem Batch). It is faster than standard Xmodem and sends the file name before sending the data. Ymodem-G transmits without acknowledgment for error-free channels or when modems are self correcting, but transmission is cancelled upon any error.

Z A mathematical language used for developing the functional specification of a software program. Developed in the late 1970s at Oxford University, IBM's CICS software is specified in Z.

Z39.50 An ANSI standard query language that is a simplified version of SQL. It is used on the Internet to search for documents. See *WAIS*.

Z80 An 8-bit microprocessor from Zilog Corporation that was the successor to the Intel 8080. The Z80 was widely used in first-generation personal computers that used the CP/M operating system.

Z8000 A 16-bit microprocessor from Zilog Corporation that is the successor to the Z80.

zap A command that typically deletes the data within a file but leaves the file structure intact so that new data can be entered.

z-axis The third dimension in a graphics image. The width is the x-axis and the height is the y-axis.

ZBR (Zone Bit Recording) A technique that records more bits on a disk. The tracks on a disk become longer the farther they are from the center. However, on regular disks, the clock rate that records the bits doesn't change, which results in the outer tracks being less densely packed than the inner tracks. With ZBR, the clock rate is changed based on which track is being written, and each track is filled to capacity.

zenix See *SCO XENIX*.

zero-slot LAN Refers to transmitting between computers over a serial or parallel port, thus freeing up an expansion slot normally used by LAN cards (NICs).

zero wait state Refers to a high-speed memory that transfers its data immediately upon being accessed without waiting one or more machine cycles to respond.

ZIF socket (Zero Insertion Force socket) A chip socket that is easy to plug a chip into. Intel has popularized this type of socket with its OverDrive upgrades. The chip is dropped into the socket's holes and a small lever is turned to lock them in.

ZiffNet An online information service for PC users from Ziff-Davis Interactive, a division of Ziff-Davis Publishing Company. It provides a wide of variety of shareware and public domain software as well as technical forums and information. ZiffNet can be accessed via PRODIGY and CompuServe. Address: 25 First St., Cambridge, MA 02141, 617/252-5000. See *online services*.

zinc air A rechargeable battery technology that provides more charge per pound than nickel cadmium or nickel hydride and does not suffer from the memory effect. It uses a carbon membrane that absorbs oxygen, a zinc plate and potassium hydroxide as the electrolyte. AER Energy Systems, Smyrna, GA, is the pioneer in this emerging battery technology.

zip (1) To compress a file with PKZIP. See *PKZIP*.

(2) (ZIP) (Zig-Zag Inline Package) Similar to a DIP, but smaller and tilted on its side for mounting on boards with limited space.

IP) A proprietary messaging protocol from IBM. PROFS uses ZIP for its e-mail transport.

Zmodem A file transfer protocol that has become very popular because it handles noisy and changing line conditions very well, including satellite transmission. It sends file name, date and size first, uses variable length blocks and CRC error correction. If a download is interrupted using Zmodem or Ymodem, Zmodem will transmit only the remainder of the file on the next try. This is great insurance when sending extremely long files.

zone bit recording See *ZBR*. Remember... use acronyms!

Zoo A freeware compression program, including source code, used in UNIX, DOS and other environments.

zoom To change from a distant view to a more close-up view (zoom in) and vice versa (zoom out). An application may provide fixed or variable levels of zoom. A video display board (graphics adapter) may also have built-in zoom, which provides zoom capability for everything that is displayed independent of and in addition to the application's zoom levels.

zywrite See *XyWrite*.

0-9

0x In programming, the symbol for a hexadecimal number. See *x*.

10BaseT An Ethernet configuration that uses twisted pair wires. 10BaseT uses a multiport repeater (hub) that provides a central connecting point for broadcasting Ethernet packets to all nodes.

100BaseT, 100BaseVG, 100VG-AnyLAN See *Fast Ethernet*.

1-2-3 See *Lotus 1-2-3*.

1284 See *IEEE 1284*.

16450, 16550 See *UART*.

286 The successor to the 8088 CPU used in the first PC (XT-class). Refers to the Intel 80286 CPU chip or to a PC (AT class) that uses it. It is more responsive than an XT and isn't limited to its infamous one-megabyte barrier, but is still sluggish for Windows and graphics-intensive applications. In a designation such as 286/12, the second number is the clock rate: 286/12 means 12MHz.

2780, 3780 Standard communications protocols for transmitting batch data. The numbers originated with early IBM remote job entry (RJE) terminals that included a card reader and a printer.

3 C's (Calculate, Compare and Copy) The basic functions a computer performs to process data. It calculates by adding, subtracting, multiplying and dividing. It makes decisions by comparing one set of data with another and determining whether one set is equal to or higher or lower in ASCII sequence to the other. It is capable of reordering data by copying one set in front of or behind the other.

3Com 3+ A network operating systems from 3Com Corporation, Santa Clara, CA. 3+Share is a DOS-based system that supports PC and Mac clients. 3+Open is OS/2 based and supports DOS, OS/2 and Mac clients.

   In 1993, 3Com discontinued its network operating systems business to remain in hardware, offering a wide variety of network adapters, hubs and related products. 3Com was founded in 1979.

3GL See *third-generation language*.

32-bit processing In a PC with a 386 or higher CPU, this refers to programs written for the 386's 32-bit mode, which is its fastest mode of operation. Starting with the 386, Intel CPUs have a split personality in order to maintain backward compatibility with previous CPUs. They can process 16-bits, or two bytes at a time, or process 32-bits, or four bytes at a time.
▶ *The electronic and encyclopedic versions of this book provide more detail on this subject.*

360 See *System/360*.

370 See *System/370*.

370 architecture Refers to a computer that will run IBM mainframe applications. See *System/370*.

370/XA (370 EXtended Architecture) A major enhancement (1981) to System/370 architecture which improved multiprocessing, introduced a new I/O system and increased addressing from 24 to 31 bits (16MB to 2GB).

386 The successor to the 286. Also known as the 386DX, it refers to the Intel 386 CPU chip or to a PC that uses it. The 386 is faster than the 286 and provides a more sophisticated method for running multiple DOS programs. It is more responsive than the 286, but is still slow for Windows and graphics-based applications. The 386 architecture has been followed in all of Intel's subsequent CPUs (486, Pentium, etc.).

The 386 is a 32-bit CPU that addresses 4GB of memory, supports a 32-bit data bus and provides enhanced memory management by allowing both extended and expanded (EMS) memory to be allocated on demand. In a designation such as 386/25, the second number is the clock rate: the 25 means 25MHz. See *x86*.

▶ *The electronic and encyclopedic versions of this book provide more detail on this subject.*

386 Enhanced Mode An operational mode in Windows that requires a 386 or higher CPU. It is the common mode for running Windows 3.1. Contrast with *Standard Mode*.

386MAX A DOS memory manager for 386s and up from Qualitas, Inc., Bethesda, MD, noted for its advanced capabilities. BlueMAX is a version for PS/2 models.

386SL A version of the 386SX designed for laptops. It has built in power management, and its variable clock rate allows it to idle for long suspend and resume periods.

386SLC An IBM version of the 386SX that includes an internal 8KB memory cache. It includes power management capabilities and runs as fast as a 386DX.

386SX A version of the 386 from Intel that runs at slower speeds than the 386DX, addresses only 16MB of memory (not 4GB) and supports only a 16-bit data bus (not 32). It uses less power and dispells less heat than the 386DX.

387 The math coprocessor for the 386.

390 See *System/390*.

303x A series of medium to large-scale IBM mainframes introduced in 1977, which includes the 3031, 3032 and 3033.

308x A series of large-scale IBM mainframes introduced in 1980, which includes the 3081, 3083 and 3084.

3090 A series of large-scale IBM mainframes introduced in 1986. Before the ES/9000 models (System/390), 3090s were the largest mainframes in the System/370 line. Models 120, 150 and 180 are single CPUs. Models 200 through 600 are multiprocessor systems (first digit indicates the number of CPUs). The E, S and J models represent increased speed respectively.

3270 A family of IBM mainframe terminals and related protocols (includes 3278 mono and 3279 color terminal). See *3270 emulator*.

3270 emulator A plug-in board that converts a personal computer or workstation into an interactive IBM mainframe terminal. The first 3270 emulator in widespread use was the IRMAboard.

3770 The standard communications protocol for batch transmission in an IBM SNA environment.

3780 See *2780, 3780*.

37xx IBM communications controllers that includes the 3704, 3705, 3720, 3725 and 3745 models. The 3704 and 3705 are early units, and the 3745 models are newer and more versatile. The 3745 includes a cluster controller that can connect 512 terminals, eight token ring networks and 16 T1 lines.

4GL See *fourth-generation language*.

4mm tape See *DAT*.

486 Also known as the 486DX, it refers to the Intel 486 CPU chip or to a PC that uses it. It is currently the entry-level machine in the Intel x86 line. It is the successor to and uses the base architecture of the 386, but runs from two to five times as fast, depending on clock rates. 486s provide the minimum speed necessary for Windows, CAD and other graphics-intensive applications. Its built-in math coprocessor is often required by CAD applications. In a designation such as 486/33, the second number is the clock speed: 33 means 33MHz.

Intel has improved the performance of the 486 by offering versions with double and triple the internal speed while maintaining the same external speeds and connections (see *DX2* and *DX4*). See *OverDrive chip* and *x86*.

▶ *The electronic and encyclopedic versions of this book provide more detail on this subject.*

486DLC A 486SX-compatible CPU from Cyrix Corporation that is pin compatible with the 386DX. Designed for upgrading 386s, it comes in a variety of speeds including clock doubling versions.

486DX, 486DX2 See *486*.

486SL A version of the 486 from Intel designed for laptops. It runs on 3.3 volts (instead of 5) and includes power management features like the 386SL.

486SLC (1) A 486SX-compatible CPU from Cyrix Corporation that is pin compatible with the 386SX, has a 1K cache and uses a 16-bit bus. It provides an upgrade path for 386SXs.

(2) The IBM version of the 486SX.

486SX A version of the 486 from Intel that runs at slower clock speeds than the 486DX and does not include the math coprocessor. 486SXs can be upgraded to 486DX2s with Intel's OverDrive chip, which includes the coprocessor. The DX2 chip is plugged into the empty coprocessor socket, disabling the original CPU. See *486*.

487 The math coprocessor for the 486.

4004 The first microprocessor. Designed by Marcian E. "Ted" Hoff at Intel, it was a 4-bit, general-purpose CPU initially developed for the Japanese Busicom calculator.

43xx A series of medium-scale IBM mainframes initially introduced in 1979, which include the 4300, 4321, 4331, 4341, 4361 and 4381.

586 See *Pentium*.

5250 A family of terminals and related protocols for IBM midrange computers (System 3x, AS/400).

640K (640 Kilobytes) Typically refers to the first 640 kilobytes of memory in a PC, known as conventional memory. See *PC memory* and *PC memory map*.

686 See *P6*.

6502 An 8-bit microprocessor from Rockwell International Corporation used in the Apple II and earlier Atari and Commodore computers.

6800 An 8-bit microprocessor from Motorola. The 6801 is a computer-on-a-chip version.

68000, 680x0 A family of 32-bit microprocessors from Motorola that are the CPUs in Macintoshes and a variety of workstations.

68000	Addresses up to 16MB of memory and uses a 16-bit data bus.
68020	Addresses up to 4GB of memory and uses a 32-bit data bus.
68030	Runs at higher clock speeds and has a built-in cache memory.
68040	Runs up to three times as fast as the 68030.

68K Refers to the Motorola 68000 family of CPU chips or to applications that are written for that chip. See *68000*.

7-bit ASCII Refers to transferring ASCII text in which an 8-bit byte holds the ASCII character plus a parity bit. Some PBXs allow only 7-bit transmission.

7-track Refers to older magnetic tape formats that record 6-bit characters plus a parity bit.

750 See *i750*.

786 See *P7*.

8mm tape A tape format used in high-capacity tape drives for backup. See *Exabyte*.

802.1, 802.2, etc. See *IEEE 802*.

860 See *i860*.

8080 An Intel 8-bit CPU chip introduced in 1974. It was the successor to the first commercial 8-bit microprocessor (8008) and precursor to the x86 family. It contained 4,500 transistors and other electronic components.

8086 Introduced in 1978, the CPU chip that defines the base architecture of Intel's x86 family (XT, AT, 386, 486, Pentium, etc.). 8086s are used in some XT-class machines. See *x86*.

80x86 See *x86*.

8087 The math coprocessor for the 8086/8088.

8088 The Intel CPU chip used in first-generation PCs (XT class). It is a slower version of the 8086, chosen for migration from CP/M programs, the predominate business applications of the early 1980s. See *x86*.

8250A See *UART*.

8514 The IBM monitor used with its 8514/A display adapter.

8514/A An IBM high-resolution display adapter that provides an interlaced display of 1024x768 with 256 colors or 64 shades of gray. It contains an on-board coprocessor for performing 2-D graphics and it is designed to coexist with VGA for dual monitor capability. Introduced on Micro Channel machines, third-party vendors provide non-interlaced versions for the ISA bus.

80286, 80386, 80486 See *286, 386, 486*.

80860 See *860*.

88000 A family of 32-bit RISC microprocessors from Motorola. The 88100 is the first processor in the 88000 family. Introduced in 1988, it incorporates four built-in execution units that allow up to five operations to be performed in parallel.

9-track Refers to magnetic tape that records 8-bit bytes plus parity, or nine parallel tracks. This is the common format for 1/2" tape reels.

9370 A series of IBM entry-level mainframes introduced in 1986 that use the 370 architecture. In 1990, the Enterprise System models (ES/9370) were introduced, which use the Micro Channel bus and a 386 for I/O processing. The ES/9370 Model 14 biprocessor system adds a second 386 that can run DOS and OS/2 applications. A high-speed link is available between the 386 and 370 processors.

9660 See *ISO 9660*.

Use Acronyms...

Most of the terms in this book are defined by their acronymns, not their formal names. If you cannot find a multi-word term in the book, TRY ITS ACRONYM!

Even more on Disk and in Print...

More...
in-depth definitions!

More...
charts, diagrams and specs!

More...
DOS and Windows help, tips
and techniques!

More...
"how to's", more of everything!

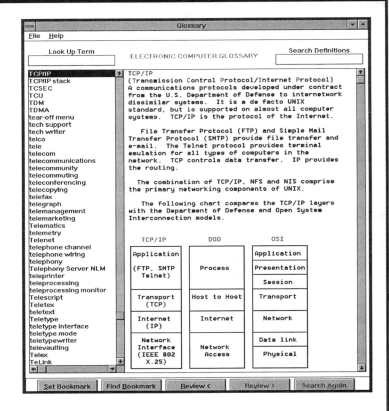

The electronic versions
are a snap to use.
Just type in your term...
Every definition is linked
to every other!
Click on a term anywhere
to retrieve it!

ELECTRONIC COMPUTER GLOSSARY (Both DOS & Windows versions included.)
Takes 2.5MB hard disk space. Minimum requirements: DOS 3.0, Windows 3.1.

ISBN #	Format	Price	AMA members
0-8144-0128-7	3.5" Floppy disk	$29.95	$26.95

COMPUTER DESKTOP ENCYCLOPEDIA 800 Illustrations. Available June 1995.

ISBN #	Format	Price	AMA members
0-8144-0010-8	Paperback book, 900 pages	$39.95	$35.95
0-8144-0011-6	CD-ROM** for Windows (Windows 3.1 or higher)	$39.95	$35.95
0-8144-0012-4	Book and CD-ROM**	$65.00	$58.50

**The text of the CD-ROM can be copied to the hard disk for quick every-day use.

Call, fax or write
AMACOM
P. O. Box 1026
Saranac Lake, NY 12983-9986
Phone (518) 891-5510   *FAX (518) 891-3653*

For multiple copy site licenses, call the
Director of Special Sales at (212) 903-8420